Photoshop CC

2015 release

ELAINE WEINMANN

PETER LOUREKAS

 Peachpit Press

For Alicia and Simona

Visual QuickStart Guide
Photoshop CC (2015 release)
Elaine Weinmann and Peter Lourekas

Peachpit Press
www.peachpit.com

To report errors, please send a note to errata@peachpit.com
Peachpit Press is a division of Pearson Education

Cover Design: RHDG/Riezebos Holzbaur Design Group, Peachpit Press
Logo Design: MINE™ www.minesf.com
Interior Design: Elaine Weinmann
Production: Elaine Weinmann and Peter Lourekas
Illustrations: Elaine Weinmann and Peter Lourekas, except as noted

ISBN-13: 978-0-134-30889-0

ISBN-10: 0-134-30889-1

4   17

Printed and bound in the United States of America

Acknowledgments

First and foremost, we owe an abundance of gratitude to the dynamic, intelligent leadership of Nancy Aldrich-Ruenzel, the former publisher of Peachpit Press. For nearly two decades, she steered Peachpit through a changing publishing landscape with steady, yet flexible, hands, while continuing to cultivate original and creative content. She accomplished these feats with boundless energy, sustained passion, and steadfast integrity. Not easy.

Paul Boger, the new publisher of Peachpit Press, is gracefully following in Nancy Ruenzel's footsteps.

Nancy Davis, editor-in-chief of Peachpit Press and consummate multitasker, has helped guide various facets of the company for nearly two decades.

Victor Gavenda, executive editor at Peachpit Press, has been instrumental to our work in more ways than we can recount, for as long as we have been writing books. Victor is exceedingly knowledgeable about computer book publishing and all things techie.

Susan Rimerman and Cliff Colby, our former editors at Peachpit Press, assisted us with everything from furnishing resources to noodging whoever needed to be noodged to keep the project on track.

It's one thing to produce good InDesign files and what looks like a handsome design onscreen; it's another thing to see our work come to fruition in print as we envision. Lisa Brazieal, senior production editor at Peachpit Press, worked her prepress magic on our InDesign files before sending them to RR Donnelley, who does a first-rate print job.

Sara Todd, marketing manager; Alison Serafini, contracts manager; and many other capable, hard-working people at Peachpit contribute their respective talents to making every step of the publishing process run smoothly, from contracts to distribution and promotion. It all matters.

Elaine Soares, photo research manager, and Lee Scher, photo research coordinator, of the Image Resource Center at Pearson Education (the parent company of Peachpit Press), procured the stock photos from Shutterstock.com that we feature in this book.

codeMantra converted our pages to ebook format. One book, two ways.

Adobe Systems, Inc. produces innovative software that is a pleasure to use and write about. For continuing to push the envelope of graphics software, and for helping product testers like ourselves untangle the mysteries and complexities of prerelease versions of Photoshop CC by way of the online forum, we thank the entire Photoshop team, especially Zorana Gee and Stephen Nielson, senior product managers; Vishal Rana, project lead, prerelease programs; and Steve Guilhamet, quality engineer (the oracle who replied to a slew of user questions on the prerelease forums).

In addition to writing and testing the instructional material in this book, we designed, illustrated, and composed (packaged) it in Adobe InDesign, which is as time consuming as it sounds. To help us clean, finish, and polish sections of this edition, we engaged the services of the following people.

A special shout-out to Rebecca Pepper, who has copy edited so many editions of this book she probably recalls some passages by heart. She did her usual meticulous job on portions of this iteration.

Over the years, we have also been blessed by the comprehensive (not to mention customized) indexing work of Steve Rath. When we need an industrial-grade index, we know who we're gonna call.

We were also assisted by Lisa Fridsma, Adobe software expert, who keystroked the new material, and by Liz Welch, proofreader, who scoured our final-final pages for errors.

Hey, and thanks to the college bookstores, online retailers, and other outlets that order and sell our titles, and to the drivers who transport buckets of our print books cross country. And to the people who build the trucks — okay, enough.

Speaking of country, after a long sojourn in the Northeast, we are now snugly nestled in Asheville, North Carolina. We can't express enough gratitude for the continued presence and love of our old friends and family (you know who you are — we got a lotta history), as well as to our newfound friends in Asheville who, with graciousness and warmth, have made us feel right at home.

— Elaine Weinmann and Peter Lourekas

In this table of contents and throughout this book, sections that cover new or improved features of Photoshop CC (2015 release) are identified by red stars. ★

Contents

REGISTER THIS BOOK, THEN DOWNLOAD PHOTOS FOR FREE!

Purchasing this book entitles you to more than just a couple of pounds of paper. If you register the book with Peachpit Press, you will also be entitled to download copies of many of the images that are used throughout the book, which you can use to practice with as you follow our step-by-step tutorials. Also available for download is a bonus chapter (Presentation).

To register your book and access the bonus images and chapter, go to www.peachpit.com/register. Sign in to your account or create one (it's free). On the Register a Product page, enter the ISBN number for this book: 0134308891, then click Submit. You'll be taken to your My Registered Products page. Finally, locate the title of this book and click the **Access Bonus Content** link.

Note: The downloadable images that we have made available are low resolution (not suitable for printing), and they are copyrighted by their owners, who have watermarked them to discourage unauthorized reproduction. They are for your personal use only—not for distribution or publication.

A NOTE REGARDING THE CONTENT OF THIS BOOK

Before going to press with this book, we tested (and retested) our text to ensure that it accurately describes the options and features we viewed in the prerelease version of Photoshop. Due to the nature of Creative Cloud subscriptions, however, some features may change or be updated at a later date.

KEEPING YOUR COPY OF PHOTOSHOP UP-TO-DATE

As a subscriber to Creative Cloud, you will be able to access updates to Photoshop (and any other Adobe Creative Cloud programs you have installed) as soon as they are released by Adobe. To access updates, and to manage your assets (files and fonts) stored in the Cloud, click the Creative Cloud icon in the taskbar (in Windows) or on the menu bar (in the Mac OS) to open the application. Click Apps, then click Update for Photoshop (or any other program). It's that simple.

Welcome to Photoshop! We know you want to dive into the editing features of Camera Raw or Photoshop right away, but achieving successful results will depend on your establishing proper color management settings first.

In this chapter, you will launch Photoshop and familiarize yourself with the Photoshop color basics. Key color management tasks that you will learn about include calibrating your display, choosing and saving color settings in Photoshop, and downloading and installing the correct printer profiles. (In Chapter 24, color management will come into play once more, when you prepare your final files for output.)

Launching Photoshop

To launch Photoshop in Windows:

In Windows 8 or later, do one of the following:

Display the Start screen, then click the tile for Adobe Photoshop CC 2015.

Double-click a Photoshop file icon.

➤ To enable Photoshop to be launched from the Start screen or Desktop, in Apps view, right-click its app icon and choose either Pin to Start or Pin to Taskbar.

To launch Photoshop in the Mac OS:

On a Mac running OS X 10.9.5 or later, do one of the following:

Click the Adobe Photoshop CC 2015 icon in the Dock. (To put the icon in your Dock, open the Adobe Photoshop CC 2015 folder in the Applications folder, then drag the Adobe Photoshop CC 2015 application icon into the Dock.)

Open the Adobe Photoshop CC 2015 folder in the Applications folder, then double-click the Adobe Photoshop CC 2015 application icon.

Double-click a Photoshop file icon.

To launch Photoshop via the Creative Cloud desktop app: ★

On your taskbar or menu bar, click the Creative Cloud icon. Click Apps, locate Photoshop CC (2015) on the list, then click **Open** (or click **Update**, if necessary).

FINDING THE NEW STUFF IN THIS BOOK

This symbol ★ identifies Photoshop features that are new or improved.

(COLOR MANAGEMENT)

1

WANT TO SEE AN IMAGE ONSCREEN?

If you want to make the screen more "live" as you read through this chapter, open one of the photos that we have made available for our readers to download (see **page viii**).

Photoshop color

The building blocks of a Photoshop image

Onscreen, your Photoshop image is a bitmap — a geometric arrangement, or mapping, of dots on a rectangular grid. Each dot (pixel) represents a different color or shade. If you drag with a painting tool, such as the Brush tool, across an area of an image, pixels below the pointer are recolored. If you display your document at a high zoom level, you will be able to see the individual pixels (and also edit them individually).**A** Bitmap programs like Photoshop are best suited for editing photographic or painterly images that contain subtle gradations of color, called "continuous tones." The images you work with in Photoshop can originate from a digital camera, from a photo print that was input via a scanner, from a file that was saved in another application, or even from scratch using Photoshop features, such as painting tools and filters.

To enable color images to be viewed onscreen, your computer display projects red, green, and blue (RGB) light. Combined in their purest form, these additive primaries produce white light. If you were to send your Photoshop file to a commercial print shop for four-color process printing, it would be rendered using cyan (C), magenta (M), yellow (Y), and black (K) inks. Because your display uses the RGB model, it can only simulate the CMYK inks used in commercial printing.

The successful translation of a digital image to a printed one is more complex than you might expect. For one, the same document may look surprisingly dissimilar on different displays, due to such variables as the temperature of the display, the lighting in the room, and even the paint color on the office wall. Second, many colors that you see in the natural world or that can be displayed onscreen can't be printed (have no ink equivalents), and conversely, some colors that can be printed cannot be displayed the same way onscreen. And third, the same image will produce different results depending on the output device and paper type. The color management techniques that we outline in this chapter are designed to help smooth out the color discrepancies that can arise when an image is transferred from digital input to display onscreen, then finally to print.

Photoshop channels

Every Photoshop image contains one, three, or four channels, each of which stores the intensity of a particular color component (e.g., red, green, or blue) as one of 256 levels of gray. Because the 256 gray levels are represented by 8 bits (short for "binary digits") of computer data, the bit depth of such an image is said to be 8 bits per channel. Files that have a higher bit depth of 16 or 32 bits per channel contain more color information than those containing 8 bits per channel (to learn about 16-bit images, see page 17).

➤ Open an RGB Color image and display the Channels panel ▣ (Window > Channels) (**A**, next page). Click Red, Green, or Blue on the panel to display only that channel in your document, then click the topmost channel name on the panel to restore the composite display. Although you can make adjustments to individual channels, normally you will edit all the channels simultaneously while viewing the composite image.

In addition to the core channels (e.g., RGB or CMYK), you can add two other kinds of channels to a Photoshop document. You can save a selection as a mask in a grayscale (alpha) channel, and you can add channels for individual spot colors (colors that are output by a commercial print shop using pre-mixed inks).

A In this extreme close-up of a photo in Photoshop, you can see the individual pixels that make up the image.

Photoshop document color modes

In Photoshop, a document can be converted to, displayed in, and edited in any of the following color modes: Bitmap, Grayscale, Duotone, Indexed Color, RGB Color, CMYK Color, Lab Color, or Multichannel. The availability of some Photoshop commands and options varies depending on the color mode of the current document, so one reason to make a color mode conversion is to take advantage of specific editing or output options.

To convert a document to a different mode, make a selection from the Image > **Mode** submenu.**B** If a mode is dimmed on the menu and you want to make it available, you need to convert the file to a different mode as a transitional step. For example, to convert a file to Duotone mode, you need to put it into Grayscale mode first. The mode that Photoshop users most commonly work in is RGB Color.

Some mode conversions can cause noticeable color shifts. For example, if you convert a file from RGB Color mode (the mode used by computer displays) to CMYK Color mode (which contains fewer colors than RGB but is necessary for commercial printing), printable colors in the image will be substituted for any RGB colors that are outside the printable range, or gamut. The fewer times you convert a file, the better, as the color data is altered with each conversion. Some conversions cause layers to be flattened, such as a conversion to Indexed Color, Multichannel, or Bitmap mode. Other conversions (such as from RGB to CMYK) give you the option to preserve layers via a Don't Flatten button in an alert dialog that pops up.

Digital cameras and medium- to low-end scanners produce images in RGB color mode. We recommend keeping your files in that mode for faster editing, and to preserve your access to all the Photoshop filters. In fact, most desktop color inkjet printers, especially those that use six or more ink colors, are designed to accept RGB files.

➤ To "soft-proof" your RGB document onscreen (make it look as if it was converted to CMYK Color mode without performing an actual mode change), see pages 474–475.

Continued on the following page

The main image channels

A spot color channel

An alpha channel

A *The number of main image channels is determined by the document color mode (alpha and spot color channels are optional additions).*

B *Use the Mode submenu to change the color mode of your document.*

CHANNELS AND THE DOCUMENT COLOR MODE

The number of channels in a document has a major impact on its file size. For instance, if you convert a document from Grayscale mode (one channel) to RGB mode (three channels), it will become three times larger.

DEFAULT NUMBER OF CHANNELS	DOCUMENT COLOR MODE
1	Bitmap, Grayscale, Duotone, Indexed Color
3	RGB, Lab, Multichannel
4	CMYK, Multichannel

The following is a brief summary of the document color modes that are available in Photoshop:

In **Bitmap** mode, pixels are either 100% black or 100% white, and no layers, filters, or adjustment commands are available. To convert a file to this mode, you must convert it to Grayscale mode first.

In **Grayscale** mode, pixels are black, white, or up to 254 shades of gray (a total of 256). If you convert a file from a color mode to Grayscale mode and then save and close it, its luminosity (light and dark) values are preserved, but its color information is deleted permanently. (In Chapter 12, we show you how to change the colors in a layer to grayscale without actually changing the document color mode.)

To produce a **duotone**, a grayscale image is printed using two or more extra plates, which add tonal richness and depth. Producing a duotone requires special preparatory steps in Photoshop, and in the case of commercial printing, expertise on the part of the print shop.

A file in **Indexed Color** mode contains just one channel, no layers, and a maximum of 256 colors or shades in an 8-bit color table. Options for the color table are set in a dialog (Image > Mode > Color Table).

RGB Color is the most versatile and widely used of all the Photoshop modes. It's the mode in which digital cameras save your photos; the only mode in which all the Photoshop tool options and filters are accessible; and the mode of choice for export to the Web, mobile devices, video, multimedia programs, and most inkjet printers.

In Photoshop, although you can display and edit a document in **CMYK Color** mode, a better approach is to perform all your image edits in RGB Color mode first, then convert a copy of your file to CMYK Color mode only when required for commercial printing or for export to a page-layout application. Images that are saved by high-end scanners in CMYK Color mode are exceptions; you should keep those files in CMYK to preserve their original color data.

Lab Color, a three-channel mode, was developed for the purpose of achieving consistency among various devices, such as between printers and displays. Lab Color files are device independent, meaning their color definitions stay the same regardless of how each output device defines color. The channels represent lightness (the image details), the colors green to red, and the colors blue to yellow. The lightness and color values can be edited independently

of one another. Although Photoshop uses Lab Color to produce conversions between RGB and CMYK Color modes internally, Photoshop users like us rarely, if ever, need to convert files to this mode.

Multichannel images contain multiple 256-level grayscale channels. If you convert an image from RGB Color to Multichannel mode, its Red, Green, and Blue channels are converted to Cyan, Magenta, and Yellow (as a result, the image may become lighter and its contrast is reduced). Some Photoshop pros assemble individual channels from several images into a single composite image by using this mode.

A *The mode of this document is RGB Color, so it contains three channels.*

B *We converted the document to CMYK Color mode, which upped the number of channels to four.*

THE COLOR MODELS IN PHOTOSHOP

In Photoshop, you can choose colors using the Grayscale, RGB, HSB, CMYK, or Lab Color model, or choose predefined colors from a color matching system, such as PANTONE. See Chapter 11.

Introduction to color management

Problems with color inconsistency can arise due to the fact that hardware devices and software packages read or output color differently. If you were to compare an image onscreen in an assortment of imaging programs and Web browsers, the colors might look completely different in each case, and worse still, might look different from the picture you originally shot with your digital camera. Print the image, and you'd probably find the results were different yet again. In some cases, these differences might be slight and unobjectionable, but in other cases such color shifts could wreak havoc with your design or even turn a project into a disaster!

A color management system can prevent most color discrepancies from arising by acting as a color interpreter. The system knows how each particular device and program interprets color, and if necessary, adjusts the colors accordingly. The result is that the colors in your files will display and output more consistently as you shuttle them among various programs and devices. Applications in the Adobe Creative Cloud adhere to standard ICC (International Color Consortium) profiles, which tell your color management system how each specific device defines color.

Each particular device can capture and reproduce only a limited gamut of colors. In the jargon of color management, this gamut is known as the color space. The mathematical description of the color space of each device, in turn, is known as a color profile. Furthermore, each input device, such as a camera, attaches its own profile to the files it produces. Photoshop uses that profile in order to display and edit the colors in your document; or if a document doesn't contain a profile, Photoshop will use the current working space (a color space that you choose for the program) instead. Color management is important for both print and online output, and when outputting the same document in different media.

On the following pages, we give instructions for choosing color management options, and we strongly recommend that you follow them before editing your images in Photoshop. The steps are centered on using Adobe RGB as the color space for your image-editing work in order to maintain color consistency throughout your workflow. We'll show you how to set the color space of your digital camera to Adobe RGB, give guidelines on calibrating a display, specify Adobe RGB as the color space for Photoshop, acquire the proper profiles for your inkjet printer and paper type, and assign the Adobe RGB profile to files that you have opened in Photoshop.

You'll need to focus on color management later in the production cycle if and when you prepare your file for printing. In Chapter 24, we'll show you how to create a soft-proof setting for your particular inkjet printer and paper using the profiles you have acquired, and then use that setting to soft-proof your document onscreen. The same profile will also be used to output files on a color inkjet printer. Finally, we'll show you how to obtain and install the proper profiles for outputting either to the Web or to a commercial press.

Continued on the following page

SETTING ADOBE RGB AS THE COLOR SPACE FOR YOUR CAMERA

Before shooting photos (and before choosing color settings in Photoshop), you should establish Adobe RGB as the color space your camera will use to process your photos. You can do this via the onscreen menu on most high-end, advanced amateur cameras and digital SLRs. This is especially important if you shoot photos in JPEG format. If you shoot raw files, setting the color space in your camera makes for the most efficient workflow, but if you forget to do it, you can assign Adobe RGB as the color space to your photos later in Camera Raw (see page 56).

Calibrating your display

Why calibrate a display?

In an LCD (liquid crystal, or flat panel) display, a grid of fixed-sized liquid crystals filters color from a light source in the back. Although the color profile that is provided with a typical LCD display (and that is installed in your system automatically) describes the display characteristics accurately, over time — a period of weeks or months — the colors you view onscreen will gradually become less accurate and the device will need adjustment.

Although you can adjust the brightness setting on an LCD monitor, it's best to leave that setting alone and give your display a periodic tune-up using an external calibration device instead. This device, or calibrator, will produce a profile containing the proper settings (white point, black point, and gamma) for your particular display. The Adobe color management system, in turn, will interpret the colors in your Photoshop document and display them more accurately, based on that profile.

Calibrators range widely in cost, from a $100 to $300 colorimeter to a much more expensive (but more precise) high-end professional gadget, such as a spectrophotometer. Even with a basic colorimeter and its simple step-by-step wizard, you will be able to calibrate your display more precisely than by using subjective "eyeball" judgments. Among moderately priced calibrators, some currently popular and reliable models include Spyder5PRO and Spyder5ELITE by Datacolor and i1 Display Pro by X-Rite.

Note: Don't be tempted to calibrate your display using the utility that's built into your computer system — it's not going to yield accurate results. If you want to achieve good output from Photoshop, you owe it to yourself to invest in a hardware calibrator. Even the least expensive external device is superior to the internal controls.

The basic calibration settings

An external calibrator will evaluate and then adjust three basic characteristics of your display: It will set the white (brightest) point to a consistent working standard; it will set the black (darkest) point to the maximum value; and it will establish a gamma (neutral gray) by equalizing the values of R, G, and B.

➤ The **white point** data sets the brightest white for the display to the industry-standard color temperature. Photographers favor using D65/6500K as the temperature setting for the white point; it is the standard white point setting in LCD displays.

➤ The **black point** is the darkest black a display can project. In other words, all the other shades that a monitor displays are lighter than this black. With the black point set correctly, you will be better able to view the shadow details in your photos.

➤ The **gamma** controls the display of midtones (the tones between the black and white points), for improved contrast. A gamma setting of 1.0 reproduces the linear brightness scale that is found in nature. However, a setting of 1.0 would make your photos look washed out because human vision responds to brightness in a nonlinear fashion. Instead, photography experts recommend using a gamma setting of 2.2 for both Windows and Macintosh displays. This higher setting redistributes more of the midtones into the dark range, which our eyes are more sensitive to, and enables your photos to look closer to the way you expect them to.

CALIBRATE, AND STAY CALIBRATED

➤ Computer displays become uncalibrated gradually, and you may not notice the change until the colors are way off. To maintain the color consistency of your display, stick to a regular monthly calibration schedule. Our calibration software reminds us to recalibrate via a monthly onscreen alert. If yours offers this option, you should take advantage of it.

➤ Also, be sure to recalibrate your display if you adjust its brightness and contrast settings (intentionally or not), change the temperature or amount of lighting in your office — or repaint the walls in your office!

Choosing a color space for Photoshop

Next, you will establish the color space for Photoshop (the gamut of colors that Photoshop works with and displays). This is an essential step in color management. If you produce images primarily for print output and you want to get up and running quickly, you can choose a preset, as in these steps.

To choose a color settings preset for Photoshop:

1. Choose Edit > **Color Settings** (Ctrl-Shift-K/ Cmd-Shift-K). The Color Settings dialog opens.

2. Choose Settings: **North America Prepress 2 A** (readers residing outside North America, choose an equivalent for your geographic location). This preset changes the RGB working space to Adobe RGB (1998), and sets all the color management policies to the safe choice of Preserve Embedded Profiles, enabling each file you open in Photoshop to keep its own profile.

3. Click OK.

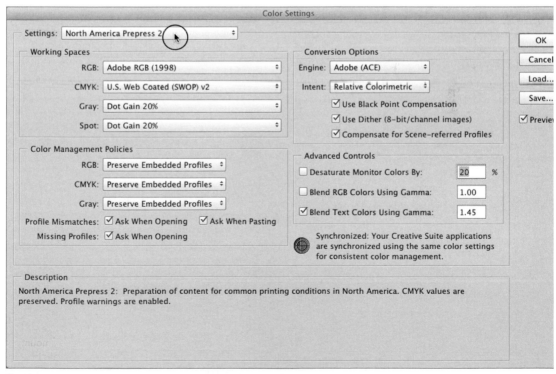

A From the Settings menu in the Color Settings dialog, we chose North America Prepress 2.

Here you can delve further into the Color Settings dialog. Be sure to choose options that are suitable for your output requirements.

To choose color settings options for Photoshop:

1. Choose Edit > **Color Settings** (Ctrl-Shift-K/ Cmd-Shift-K). The Color Settings dialog opens.

2. From the **Settings** menu, choose one of the following presets, depending on your output needs:

   Monitor Color sets the RGB working space to your display profile. This preset is a good choice for video output, but not for print output.

   North America General Purpose 2 meets general requirements for screen and print output in North America, but we don't recommend it for print output because it uses the sRGB IEC61966-2.1 color space (see step 3, at right). All profile warnings are shut off.

   North America Newspaper manages color for output on newsprint paper stock.

   North America Prepress 2 manages color to conform to common press conditions in North America using the Adobe RGB (1998) color space. We recommend this preset for print documents. When CMYK documents are opened into Photoshop, their values are preserved.

   North America Web/Internet is designed for online output. All RGB images are converted to the sRGB IEC61966-2.1 color space.

3. The **Working Spaces** settings govern how colors are treated in documents that lack an embedded profile. You can either leave these menu settings as they are or choose one of these recommended **RGB** color spaces, depending on your output needs:

   Adobe RGB (1998) contains a wide range of colors and is useful when converting RGB images to CMYK. This option is recommended for print output but not for Web output.

   ProPhoto RGB contains a very wide range of colors and is useful for output to high-end inkjet and dye-sublimation printers.

   sRGB IEC61966-2.1 is a good choice for Web output, as it reflects the settings of the average computer display. Although this setting isn't a good choice for print output (because it contains fewer colors in the printable CMYK gamut than Adobe RGB), many online Web printing sites accept or require files to be in this color space.

4. Click OK.

➤ We recommend that you avoid the Working Spaces settings of Apple RGB and ColorMatch RGB, which were designed for displays that are no longer standard. Also avoid the Monitor RGB [current display profile] and ColorSync RGB profiles, both of which rely on the viewer's display and system settings — variables that can undermine color consistency.

Synchronizing color settings among Adobe applications

If the color settings differ among the Adobe programs that you have installed on your system (such as between Photoshop and Illustrator or InDesign), the word "Unsynchronized" will display in the Color Settings dialog in those programs. If you have a Creative Cloud subscription or have installed multiple Adobe programs (including Adobe Bridge), you can use the Color Settings dialog in Bridge to quickly synchronize the color settings for all of your color-managed Adobe programs.

   Note: Before using Bridge to synchronize the color settings among your Adobe programs, you should establish the correct settings in Photoshop (see the preceding page).

To synchronize the color settings among your Adobe Creative Cloud applications:

1. If you're in Photoshop, choose File > **Browse in Bridge** (Ctrl-Alt-O/Cmd-Option-O).

2. In Bridge, choose Edit > **Color Settings** (Ctrl-Shift-K/Cmd-Shift-K). The Color Settings dialog opens.**A**

3. Click the same settings preset that you chose in the Color Settings dialog in Photoshop (e.g., North America Prepress 2), then click **Apply**. Bridge will change (synchronize) the color settings of the other Adobe applications to conform to those in the preset you have selected.

➤ The preset choices in the Color Settings dialog in Bridge match the presets on the Settings menu in the Color Settings dialog in Photoshop (see the preceding page). In the Color Settings dialog in Bridge, keep Show Expanded List of Color Settings Files unchecked to limit the display to just the five basic presets.

A *Use the Color Settings dialog to synchronize the color settings of all your color-managed Adobe applications.*

Customizing the color policies for Photoshop

Photoshop supports document-specific color, meaning that the profile that is embedded in a document controls how colors in that file are previewed onscreen, edited, and converted upon output. The current color management policies govern whether Photoshop honors or overrides a document's settings if the color profile in the file, when opened or imported, doesn't conform to the current color settings in Photoshop. If you chose the North America Prepress 2 setting in the Color Settings dialog (see page 7), the Ask When Opening policy (the safest option, in our opinion) is already chosen for you, and you can skip these steps.

To customize the color management policies for Photoshop:

1. Choose Edit > **Color Settings** (Ctrl-Shift-K/Cmd-Shift-K). The Color Settings dialog opens. **A**

2. From each of the **Color Management Policies** menus, choose an option for files that you open or import into Photoshop:

   Off to prevent Photoshop from color-managing the files.

   Preserve Embedded Profiles if you expect to work with both color-managed and non-color-managed files, and you want each document to keep its own profile.

   Convert to Working RGB, **Convert to Working Gray**, or **Convert to Working CMYK** to have all files that you open or import into Photoshop adopt the program's current color working space.

3. *Optional:* For Profile Mismatches, check Ask When Opening to have Photoshop display an alert when the color profile in a file you're opening doesn't match the current working space. Via the alert, you will be able to either convert the document colors to the current working space or keep the embedded profile in the document.

   Check Ask When Pasting to have Photoshop display an alert if it encounters a color profile mismatch when you paste or drag and drop imagery into a document. Via the alert, you will be able to accept or override the current color management policy.

4. *Optional:* For Missing Profiles, check Ask When Opening to have Photoshop display an alert when opening a file that lacks a profile, giving you the opportunity to assign one.

5. Click OK.

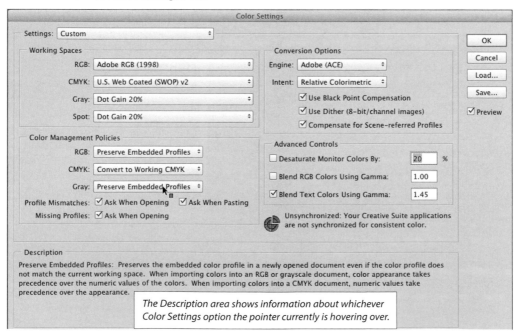

A *Choose Color Management Policies in the Color Settings dialog.*

Installing and saving custom color settings

For desktop color printing, we recommended choosing North America Prepress 2 as the color setting for Photoshop (see page 7). For commercial printing, you can let the pros supply the proper color settings: Ask your print shop for a .csf (custom settings) file, which should contain all the correct Working Spaces and Color Management Policies settings for the particular press they will be using for your project. Once you receive the .csf file, all you need to do is install it in the proper location, as described below, and when needed, choose it from the Settings menu in the Color Settings dialog.

To install a .csf file in your system:

In Windows, place the .csf file in a folder of your choice. Choose Edit > Color Settings, click Load, locate and click the .csf file, then click Open.

In the Mac OS, put the file in Users/[user name]/Library/Application Support/Adobe/Color/Settings.

The .csf is now available as a choice on the Settings menu in the Color Settings dialog.

➤ To access the hidden Library folder in the Mac OS X or later, in the Finder, hold down Option and choose Library from the Go menu.

If your print shop gives you a list of recommended settings for the Color Settings dialog instead of a .csf file, you can create your own .csf file that contains the recommended settings, as in these steps.

To save custom color settings as a .csf file:

1. Choose Edit > **Color Settings** (Ctrl-Shift-K/Cmd-Shift-K). The Color Settings dialog opens.

2. Choose and check the settings that your print shop has recommended.

3. Click Save. In the dialog, enter a file name (we suggest including the printer type in the name). Keep the .csf extension (make sure Hide Extension is unchecked), and keep the default location. Click Save.

4. Click OK to exit the Color Settings dialog.

Acquiring printer profiles

Here we summarize how to acquire the proper printer profile(s) so you can incorporate color management into your specific printing scenario. Most printer manufacturers have a website from which you can download either an ICC profile for a specific printer/paper combination or a printer driver that contains a collection of specific ICC printer/paper profiles. Be sure to choose a profile that conforms to the particular printer/paper combination you are planning to use.

Note: If you're using Windows 8 or later or Mac OS X 10.9.5 or later and a Canon inkjet printer, the latest Canon drivers (which include profiles) are already installed in your system and you don't need to follow these steps. If you're running an older operating system, download the needed driver from usa.canon.com.

To download the printer profile for your inkjet printer:

1. Do either of the following:

Download the correct profile from the website for your printer. For example, for an Epson Stylus Photo Inkjet device, visit epson.com, locate your printer model, then locate either the driver or the ICC profile for your paper type.

Download an ICC profile for a specific printer/paper combo from the website of a paper manufacturer, such as ilford.com or museofineart.com.

2. After visiting the website, install the profile you have downloaded by following the instructions that accompany it.

On pages 474–475, we'll show you how to use the profile you have downloaded to soft-proof your document onscreen.

Changing a document's color profile

When the profile that is embedded in a document doesn't conform to the current working space for Photoshop (which in our case is Adobe RGB), or the document lacks a profile altogether, you can use the Assign Profile command to assign the correct one. You may notice visible color shifts if the color data of the file is reinterpreted to conform to the new profile, but rest assured, the color data in the actual image is preserved. Do keep Preview checked, though, so you can see what you're getting into.

To change or remove a file's color profile:

1. With a file open in Photoshop, choose Edit > **Assign Profile**. If the file contains layers, an alert may appear, warning you that the appearance of the layers may change; click OK.

2. The Assign Profile dialog opens.**A** Check Preview, then click one of the following:

   To remove the color profile, click **Don't Color Manage This Document**.

   To assign the current working space, as established in the Color Settings dialog, click **Working** [the document color mode and the name of your chosen working space]. If you followed our steps on page 7, the menu should already be set to the option of Adobe RGB (1998).

   To assign a different profile, click **Profile**, then choose a profile that differs from your current working space.

3. Click OK. Using the File > Save As dialog, save your file in the Photoshop (.psd) format (see page 20). In that dialog, be sure to check ICC Profile (in Windows) or Embed Color Profile (in the Mac OS) to embed the assigned profile into the file.

The Convert to Profile command lets you preview the conversion of a document to a different output profile and intent, then it converts the color data to the chosen profile. Use this command to convert a file to sRGB, if that color space is required (e.g., for online Web printing). Note: This command performs a mode conversion and changes the actual color data in your file, so you should apply it to a copy of your file, not to the original (see page 20).

To convert a file's color profile:

1. Choose Edit > **Convert to Profile**. In the Convert to Profile dialog, check Preview.**B**

2. Under Destination Space, from the **Profile** menu, choose the profile to which you want to convert the file (it doesn't necessarily have to be the current working space).

3. Under Conversion Options, choose an **Intent** (for the intents, see the sidebar on page 475).

4. Leave the default Engine as **Adobe (ACE)**, keep the **Use Black Point Compensation** and **Use Dither** options checked and, if it's available, check **Flatten Image to Preserve Appearance** to allow Photoshop to merge all layers and adjustment layers into the Background.

5. Click OK.

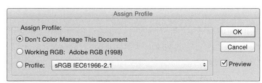

A Use the Assign Profile dialog to either remove a color profile from a file or assign a different one.

B Use the Convert to Profile dialog to convert your document to a different color profile. Here we switched our file from the Adobe RGB profile to the Working CMYK – U.S. Web Coated (SWOP) v2 profile (for commercial printing).

In Photoshop, you can edit a single photo to your heart's content, create a complex montage of imagery that you gather from multiple files, or paint an image entirely from scratch. Photoshop generously accepts and reads files in a wide assortment of file formats, so your imagery can be gathered from a variety of sources, such as from a digital camera, scanner, or drawing application.

In this chapter, you will learn how to create a new, blank document, create document presets for your favorite settings, understand the characteristics of 16-bits-per-channel files, save and generate new versions of a file, use the Status bar, and close up shop.

Just to give you an idea of where you're headed, in the next chapter, you will learn how to download photos from a camera and use Bridge to open and manage files, and, in Chapter 4, you will learn how to correct photos in Camera Raw, and open them into Photoshop.

Calculating the correct file resolution

Resolution and dimensions for Web output

Choosing the correct resolution for Web output is a no-brainer: Set the resolution for your file to 72 ppi.

Choosing the correct dimensions for Web output requires a little more forethought, because you need to calculate how your Photoshop document is going to be used in the Web page layout. The easiest way to create a document with the proper dimensions and resolution for Web output is by choosing a preset, as described in step 3 on page 15.

To determine a maximum custom size for a Photoshop image that is going to be displayed on a Web page, you need to estimate how large the average user's browser window is likely to be, then calculate how much of that window the image is going to fill. On a desktop computer, viewers commonly have their browser window open to a width of approximately 1024 pixels. Subtract the space that is occupied by the menu bar, scroll bars, and other controls in the browser interface, and you're left with an area around 975 pixels wide by 600 pixels high; you can use those dimensions as a guideline. In the more likely event that your Photoshop file is going to be used as a small element within a Web page layout, you can choose smaller dimensions.

CREATING FILES

2

IN THIS CHAPTER

Resolution for print output

Most digital cameras provide a choice: You can let the camera capture and save all the pixels as raw files (recommended) or you can let the camera process, compress, and save the data into small, medium, or large JPEG files. We prefer raw files, for reasons that we explain in Chapter 4. When using a scanner to acquire images for Photoshop, you can set the input resolution in the scanner software to control how many pixels the device captures.

Your image files should contain the minimum resolution needed to obtain quality output from your target output device, at the desired output size. High-resolution photos contain more pixels, and therefore finer details, than low-resolution photos, but they also have a larger file size, take longer to render onscreen, require more processing time to edit, and are slower to print. Low-resolution images, however, look coarse and jagged and lack detail, most noticeably when printed. Your goal is to set an appropriate resolution — one that is neither too high nor too low.**A–C**

There are three ways to set the resolution value for a digital file:

► If you use Camera Raw to process a raw or JPEG photo, as we recommend, you can specify an image resolution in its Workflow Options dialog (see page 56).

► When scanning a photo, you should set the image resolution using the scanning software for that device.

► After opening a file into Photoshop, you can change the image resolution via the Image Size dialog (see pages 138–141).

The print resolution for digital images is measured in pixels per inch, or ppi for short. For output to a desktop inkjet printer, an appropriate file resolution is between 240 and 300 ppi. For commercial printing, the first step is to ask your print shop what resolution you should set your document to for their press. If you are told only the halftone screen frequency (lines per inch, or lpi) setting, you can use that number to quickly calculate the correct resolution for your files. For a grayscale image, set the resolution to approximately one-and-a-half times the lpi setting of the output device (usually a resolution of around 200 ppi); for a color image, set the resolution to approximately twice the lpi (usually a resolution of around 250–350 ppi).

A *72 ppi*

B *150 ppi*

C *300 ppi*

Creating a new, blank document

Although in most cases you are going to open existing photos into Photoshop, you still need to know how to create a new, blank document, as we show you in these steps. To create image content, you can drag and drop or copy and paste imagery into the document from other files, draw or paint imagery by hand using brushes, create vector shapes, or enter type.

To create a new, blank document:

1. Do either of the following:

   Choose File > **New** (Ctrl-N/Cmd-N).

   Right-click the tab of an existing open document and choose **New Document**.

2. The New dialog opens.**A** Type a name in the **Name** field.

3. Do either of the following:

   From the **Document Type** menu, depending on your output medium, choose Default Photoshop Size, a paper type, a Web or screen type (including Mobile App Design or Iconography ★), or Artboard.★ Next, from the **Size** (or **Artboard Size**) menu, choose a specific preset size for the output type (the latest devices for Web, mobile, and mobile icons are listed as presets★).

   Choose a unit of measure from the menu next to the Width field; the same unit will be chosen automatically for the Height (or to change the unit for just one dimension, hold down Shift while choosing it). Enter custom **Width** and **Height** values.

4. Enter the **Resolution** required for your target output device, or keep the preset value. For print output, see the preceding page.

5. Choose a document **Color Mode** (we recommend working in RGB Color mode and converting to other modes for output), then from the adjacent menu, choose **8 bit** or **16 bit** as the color depth (see page 17).

6. Note the current **Image Size** on the right side of the dialog. If you need to reduce that size, you can choose smaller dimensions, a lower resolution, or a lower bit depth.

7. From the **Background Contents** menu, choose **White** (the option we recommend if you're a new Photoshop user), or choose **Transparent** if you want the bottommost tier of the document to be a transparent layer (see Chapter 8). If you are familiar with Photoshop's color controls, you can click the color square and choose a custom color.

8. Under Advanced, choose a **Color Profile**. The list of available profiles will vary depending on the document Color Mode. If you chose RGB Color in step 5, we recommend choosing Adobe RGB (1998) for print output. (Note: You can assign or change the

Continued on the following page

New		
Name: film poster		OK
Document Type: Custom		Cancel
Size:		Save Preset...
Width: 7	Inches	Delete Preset...
Height: 12	Inches	
Resolution: 300	Pixels/Inch	
Color Mode: RGB Color	8 bit	
Background Contents: White		Image Size: 21.6M
Advanced		
Color Profile: Working RGB: Adobe RGB (1998)		
Pixel Aspect Ratio: Square Pixels		

A *In the New dialog, enter a file Name; either choose a Document Type option and Size option or enter custom Width, Height, and Resolution values; also choose the Color Mode option of RGB Color, a Background Contents option, and a Color Profile option.*

profile at a later time via the Edit > Assign Profile dialog. To learn more about color profiles, see pages 10–12.)

For Web or print output, leave the **Pixel Aspect Ratio** on the default setting of Square Pixels. For video output, choose an applicable option (see Photoshop Help).

9. Click OK. A new, blank document window appears onscreen. To save the file, see page 18.

➤ To force the New dialog settings to display the specs of an existing open document, from the bottom of the Preset menu, choose the name of the document that has the desired dimensions.

➤ If the Clipboard contains image data (artwork that you copied from Adobe Photoshop or Illustrator), the New dialog will automatically display the dimensions of that content. Those dimensions will also display if you choose Clipboard from the Preset menu in the New dialog. If you want to prevent the Clipboard dimensions from displaying (and have the dialog show the last-used file dimensions instead), hold down Alt/Option as you choose File > New.

SETTING DEFAULT RESOLUTION VALUES

In Edit/Photoshop CC > Preferences > Units & Rulers, under New Document Preset Resolutions, you can enter Print Resolution and Screen Resolution values. Thereafter, one or the other of those values will appear in the Resolution field in the File > New dialog when you choose a preset from the Preset menu. The Print Resolution value is used for the Paper and Photo presets (the default value is 300 ppi); the Screen Resolution value is used for the Web, Mobile App Design, ★ Film & Video, and Iconography ★ presets (the default value is 72 ppi).

Creating document presets

If you tend to choose the same custom document size, color mode, and other settings over and over in the New dialog, here's a way to streamline your workflow and save yourself some startup time. Create a preset for each "group" of settings. Then, as you create a new document, choose one of your presets from the menu in the New dialog.

To create a document preset:

1. Choose File > **New** or press Ctrl-N/Cmd-N. The New dialog opens.

2. Choose settings, including the width, height, resolution, color mode, bit depth, background contents, color profile, and pixel aspect ratio. Ignore any setting that you don't want to include in the preset; you'll exclude it from the preset in step 4.

3. Click **Save Preset**. The New Document Preset dialog opens.**A**

4. Enter a **Preset Name**. Under **Include in Saved Preset**, uncheck any New dialog settings that you don't want to save in the preset. Click OK. Your new preset is now listed on the Document Type menu in the New dialog.

➤ To delete a user-created preset, choose it from the Document Type menu, click Delete Preset, then click Yes (this cannot be undone).

A Use the New Document Preset dialog to name your new preset and to control which of the current settings in the New dialog it will contain.

Editing 16-bit files in Photoshop

The 16-bit advantage

To get high-quality output from Photoshop, a wide range of tonal values must be captured by the input device (e.g., your camera or a scanner). The wider the dynamic range of your chosen input device, the finer the subtleties of color and shade in the resulting images.

Most advanced amateur and professional digital SLR cameras capture 12 bits or more of accurate data per channel. Like cameras, scanners range widely in quality: Low-end models capture approximately 10 bits of accurate data per channel, whereas high-end models capture up to 16 bits of accurate data per channel. If your camera can capture 12 to 16 bits per channel, or you work with high-resolution scans, your images will be higher quality, because they will contain an abundance of pixels in all levels of the tonal spectrum. Details (or a lack thereof) will be more noticeable in the shadow areas, because those are the hardest areas for a device to capture well.

The editing and resampling commands in Photoshop (and in particular, tonal adjustment commands, such as Levels and Curves), remove pixel data from a photo and alter the distribution of pixels across the tonal spectrum. Signs of pixel loss from these destructive edits are more visible, for example, in a high-end print of an 8-bit image than in one of a 16-bit image. **A–B** Because 16-bit images contain more pixels in all parts of the tonal spectrum at the outset, more tonal values are preserved, even after editing (it's like extra "padding").

Working with 16-bit files

Photoshop can open files that contain 8, 16, or 32 bits per channel. All the Photoshop commands, modes, and tools are available for 8-bit files, whereas most but not all commands, modes, and tools are available for 16-bit files. 16-bit files are higher quality, so we recommend downgrading them only when necessary. When editing a 16-bit file, you can access all the filters in the top part of the Filter menu (e.g., Camera Raw, Lens Correction), but not the Filter Gallery. On the submenus, you can access all filters except Blur > Smart Blur; Render > Lighting Effects; and Stylize > Extrude, Tiles, and Wind. 32-bit files can be edited using only a limited number of Photoshop commands, so they are not a practical choice.

If system or storage limitations prevent you from working with 16-bit images in Photoshop, try this two-stage approach: Perform your initial tonal corrections on the 16-bits-per-channel image, then via the Image > Mode menu, convert the file to 8 Bits/Channel mode for further editing.

If your output service provider requests that you submit an 8-bit file instead of a 16-bit one, and your computer setup allows you to work with 16-bit files, do all your editing on the higher-quality file, then save a copy of it in the lower bit depth for output.

16-bit files can be saved in many formats, such as Photoshop (.psd), Large Document (.psb), Photoshop PDF (.pdf), PNG (.png), TIFF (.tif), and JPEG 2000 (.jpf).

Finally, 16-bit files can be printed as 16-bit from Photoshop, provided the target output device supports 16-bit printing.

A A Levels adjustment that we applied to this 8-bit image caused some image data to be discarded, as shown by the spikes and gaps in the histogram.

B Here we applied the same Levels adjustment to a 16-bit version of the same image. Due to the higher bit depth, the smooth tonal transitions were preserved.

Saving your document

Although Photoshop lets you create, open, edit, and save files in over a dozen different formats, you'll probably encounter or use just a few of them, such as Photoshop (the native Photoshop file format, or PSD for short), Photoshop PDF, JPEG, and TIFF. If you're not sure what format to use, stick with the Photoshop format (we use it for most of our work).

To save an unsaved document:

1. If your document contains any content, you can choose File > **Save** (Ctrl-S/Cmd-S); if it's completely blank, choose File > **Save As** (Ctrl-Shift-S/Cmd-Shift-S). The Save As dialog opens.

2. Type a name in the **File Name** field (Windows) or the **Save As** field (Mac OS).

3. Choose a location for the file.

   In Windows, if you need to navigate to a different folder or drive, use the Navigation pane on the left side of the dialog.

   In the Mac OS, click a drive or folder in the Sidebar panel on the left side of the window, then click a subfolder in one of the columns, if necessary. To locate a recently used folder, use the menu below the Save As field.

4. From the **Save as Type/Format** menu, choose a file format (**A–B**, next page). The Photoshop (PSD), Large Document Format (PSB), Photoshop PDF, and TIFF formats support layers, a feature that you will be using extensively in Photoshop (learn about flattening layers on page 168).

5. If you're not yet familiar with the features listed in the **Save** area, leave the settings as they are. For the As a Copy option, see step 5 on page 20.

6. If the file contains an embedded color profile and the format you have chosen supports profiles, in the **Color** area, you can check **ICC Profile** [profile name] (in Windows) or **Embed Color Profile** [profile name] (in the Mac OS) to save the profile with the file. (To learn about embedded profiles, see pages 7–8, 10, and 12.)

7. Click Save.

➤ In the Mac OS, to have Photoshop append a three-character extension (e.g., .tif, .psd) to the file name automatically when a file is saved for the first time, in Edit/Photoshop CC > Preferences > File Handling, choose Append File Extension: Always. Extensions are required when exporting Macintosh files to the Windows platform and when posting files to a Web server.

➤ To learn about the Maximize PSD and PSB File Compatibility option in the File Handling panel of the Preferences dialog, see page 462.

Once a file has been saved for the first time, each subsequent use of the Save command overwrites (saves over) the previous version.

To save a previously saved document:

Choose File > **Save** (Ctrl-S/Cmd-S).

➤ An asterisk on a document tab or title bar indicates that the document contains unsaved changes.

➤ To learn about the automatic save recovery feature in Photoshop, see page 462.

The simple Revert command restores your document to the last-saved version.

Note: We know you can't learn everything at once, but keep in mind for the near future that the History panel, which is covered in Chapter 10, serves as a full-service multiple undo feature. In fact, each use of the Revert command is listed as a separate state on the History panel, so you can undo any revert by clicking an earlier history state.

To revert a document to the last saved version:

Choose File > **Revert**.

➤ To undo the last edit, choose Edit > Undo [name of edit] (Ctrl-Z/Cmd-Z). Not all edits can be undone by this command.

➤ For more undo and redo commands, see the sidebar on page 111.

A *This is the Save As dialog in Windows.*

B *This is the Save As dialog in the Mac OS.*

FORMATS THAT PRESERVE PHOTOSHOP FEATURES

Choose the Photoshop (PSD), Large Document (PSB), TIFF, or Photoshop PDF format to preserve the following Photoshop features in a document: multiple layers; layer transparency; adjustment, editable type, Smart Object, and shape layers; layer effects; alpha channels; and grids and guides. ICC color management profiles are also preserved by the above-mentioned formats, and by the JPEG format.

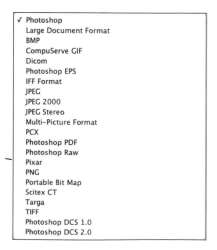

Using the Save As command, you can save a copy of a file under a new name (say, to create a design or tonal adjustment variation), save it with different options chosen (e.g., with or without alpha channels or layers), or save a flattened copy of it in a different format for export to another application (a necessity when exporting to most non-Adobe applications, which can't import Photoshop PSD files or read Photoshop layers).

To save a new version of a file:

1. Choose File > **Save As** (Ctrl-Shift-S/Cmd-Shift-S). The Save As dialog opens.

2. Change the name in the **File Name/Save As** field (if you're planning to change only the file format, this step is unnecessary).

3. Choose a location for the new version of the file from the Navigation pane in Windows or by using the Sidebar panel and columns in the Mac OS.

4. *Optional:* From the Save as Type/Format menu, choose a different file format. Only formats that are available for a file's current color mode and bit depth are listed. Note: If you try to save a 16-bit file in the JPEG (.jpg) format, Photoshop will produce a flattened, 8-bit copy of the file automatically.

   Beware! If you choose a format that doesn't support layers, the Layers option is dimmed automatically, a yellow alert icon displays, and layers in the new version will be flattened.

5. Check any available options in the **Save** area that you deem necessary. For example, you could check **As a Copy** to have the copy of the file remain closed and the original file stay open onscreen, or uncheck this option to have the original file close and the copy stay open.

   In Edit/Photoshop CC > Preferences > File Handling, under File Saving Options, we choose the setting of Image Previews: Always Save to have Photoshop include file previews automatically. If you choose Ask When Saving as the preference, this preview option will display in the Save As dialog instead; see page 462. For the Append File Extension option (Mac OS only), we also choose the setting of Always.

6. In the **Color** area, check **ICC Profile/Embed Color Profile**: [profile name], if available, to include the current profile, for good color management (see pages 7–8, 10, and 12).

7. Click Save. Depending on the file format you have chosen, another dialog may appear. For the PDF format, see page 483; for the TIFF format, see page 486; for other formats, see Photoshop Help.

➤ If you fail (or forget) to change the file name or format in the Save As dialog, but you do proceed to click Save, an alert will appear.**A** Click Yes/Replace to replace the original file, or click No/Cancel to return to the Save As dialog, where you should change the file name or format.

➤ To have the location in the Save As dialog always default to the location of the current file, go to Edit/Photoshop CC > Preferences > File Handling, and check Save As to Original Folder.

➤ For Web output, learn how to create GIF, JPEG, PNG, and SVG image assets from Photoshop layers on pages 487–489.

A *If you try to save a file via the Save As command without changing the file name or format, you will get this friendly warning.*

PHOTOSHOP GIGANTIC

In Photoshop, you can create and save a file as large as 300,000 x 300,000 pixels — over 2 gigabytes (GB) — and each Photoshop file can contain up to 56 user-created channels. The **Large Document (PSB)** format (nicknamed "Photoshop Big") is designed specifically for saving such huge files.

What can you do with PSB files? If you have enough disk space to store and work with them and have access to a wide-format printer that can output extra-large images (up to 32,000 x 32,000 pixels), awesome. If not, you will need to drastically lower the resolution of a copy of your PSB file in order to output it to an ordinary printer.

Using the Status bar

Using the Status bar and menu at the bottom of the document window, you can read data pertaining to the current document or find out how Photoshop is currently using available memory. Note: To view more detailed data about a file, use the Metadata panel in Bridge; see page 26.

To use the Status bar:

Open a document, then from the menu adjacent to the Status bar at the bottom of the Application frame, choose the type of data you want Photoshop to display on the bar:

Document Sizes to list the approximate file storage size of a flattened version of the file if it were to be saved in the PSD format (the value on the left) and the storage size of the file including all its current layers and any alpha channels (the value on the right). Note: For the most accurate file size value, view the file listing in Explorer/Finder.

Document Profile to list the color profile that is embedded in the current file and the number of bits per channel.**A** If the document doesn't have an embedded profile, it will be listed as untagged.

Document Dimensions to list the image dimensions (width and height) and resolution.

Measurement Scale to list the current pixel scale ratio for the document, as set via the Measurement Log panel.

Scratch Sizes to list the amount of RAM that Photoshop is using to process all the currently open files (the value on the left) and the amount of RAM that is currently available to Photoshop (the value on the right). When Photoshop is utilizing virtual memory on the scratch disk, the first value is greater than the second one.

Efficiency to list the percentage of program operations that are being done in RAM as opposed to on the scratch disk (see page 465). When the scratch disk is being used, this value is below 100.

Timing to list the duration of the last operation.

Current Tool to list the name of the current tool.

32-Bit Exposure to display a slider that you can drag to adjust the preview of an HDR image that has 32 bits per channel.

Save Progress to have a dynamic percentage value display as a file is being saved (e.g., "Saving 88%").

Smart Objects to list the number of Missing and Changed (modified) linked Smart Objects in the document.

GETTING DOCUMENT INFO FAST

Regardless of which info category is selected on the Status bar menu, at any time you can click and hold on the Status bar to learn the dimensions, number of channels, color mode, bit depth, and resolution of the current document.

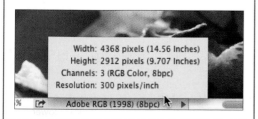

Width: 4368 pixels (14.56 Inches)
Height: 2912 pixels (9.707 Inches)
Channels: 3 (RGB Color, 8bpc)
Resolution: 300 pixels/inch

Status bar

A *From the menu for the Status bar, choose the type of data you want Photoshop to display on the bar.*

Adobe Drive
Document Sizes
✓ Document Profile
Document Dimensions
Measurement Scale
Scratch Sizes
Efficiency
Timing
Current Tool
32-bit Exposure
Save Progress
Smart Objects

Ending a work session

To close a document:

1. Do one of the following:

   Click the X in a document tab.**A**

   Choose File > **Close** (Ctrl-W/Cmd-W).

   Click the Close (X) button in the upper-right corner of a floating document window in Windows,**B** or click the Close button in upper-left corner of a floating document window in the Mac OS.**C**

2. If you try to close a file that was modified since it was last saved (as indicated by an asterisk in the document tab), an alert dialog will appear.**D** Click No (N)/Don't Save (D) to close the file without saving it, or click Yes (Y)/Save (S) to save the file before closing it (or click Cancel or press Esc to dismiss the Close command).

➤ To quickly close all (multiple) open documents, press Ctrl-Alt-W/Cmd-Option-W. If an alert dialog appears, you can check Apply to All, if desired, to have just one response apply to all the open documents, then click No/Don't Save or Yes/Save.

➤ In Photoshop, to close a file and launch or go to Bridge, choose File > Close and Go to Bridge or press Ctrl-Shift-W/Cmd-Shift-W.

To exit/quit Photoshop and close all open files:

1. In Windows, choose File > **Exit** (Ctrl-Q) or click the Close button for the application frame.

   In the Mac OS, choose Photoshop > **Quit Photoshop** (Cmd-Q).

2. If any open files contain unsaved changes, an alert dialog will appear for each one. Click No (N)/Don't Save (D) to close the file without saving it, or click Yes (Y)/Save (S) to save it before exiting/quitting Photoshop (or click Cancel or press Esc to dismiss the Exit/Quit command).

A *To close a document that is docked as a tab, click the X on the tab in the Mac OS or in Windows.*

B *To close a floating document window in Windows, click the Close button.*

C *To close a floating document window in the Mac OS, click the Close (red) button.*

D *If you try to close a file that contains unsaved changes, this alert prompt will appear. A similar prompt will appear if you exit/quit Photoshop and any of your open files contain unsaved changes.*

The Adobe Bridge application is aptly named because it serves as a link to the programs in Adobe Creative Cloud. You will initially find that Bridge is useful for viewing both thumbnails and large previews of your images before you open them into Camera Raw or Photoshop. Dig a little deeper, and you will find it offers a wealth of other useful features as well. In Chapter 1, you used Bridge to synchronize the color settings for your Creative Cloud programs. Here we show you first how to use Bridge to download photos from a digital camera. Then you will learn how to preview and examine thumbnails in the Bridge window; open files into Photoshop; customize the Bridge workspace; assign keywords to thumbnails; label, rate, sort, and filter image thumbnails in the Bridge window; move and copy files; export the Bridge cache; search for files; and organize thumbnails into collections.

Note: Adobe Bridge must be downloaded and installed separately from Photoshop.

Launching Adobe Bridge

When you launch Adobe Bridge, the Bridge window opens.

To launch Adobe Bridge:

Do one of the following:

In Windows 8, display the Start screen, then click the tile for **Adobe Bridge CC**.

➤ To enable Bridge CC to be launched from the Start screen or Desktop, in Apps view, right-click its app icon and choose either Pin to Start or Pin to Taskbar.

In the Mac OS, click the **Adobe Bridge CC** icon ▓ in the Dock. Or in the Applications > Adobe Bridge CC folder, double-click the **Adobe Bridge CC** application icon. ▓

In Photoshop, press Ctrl-Alt-O/Cmd-Option-O.

On your taskbar or menu bar, click the Creative Cloud icon. Click Apps, locate **Bridge CC** on the list, then click **Open** (or click **Update**, if necessary). ★

➤ If you want to have Bridge launch automatically at startup, but without the Bridge window opening, go to Edit/Adobe Bridge CC > Preferences (Ctrl-K/Cmd-K), display the Advanced panel, and check Start Bridge at Login. This is called "stealth mode."

Downloading photos from a camera

When you use a digital camera, your photos are stored on a removable memory card — most likely a CompactFlash (CF) or Secure Digital (SD) card. Rather than having to tether your camera directly to a computer, you can remove the memory card and insert it into a card reader device, then download your photos from the card reader to your computer via a USB or other cable, depending on which connection your camera supports.

When you start downloading images from a camera, the default application or dialog for acquiring images in your system may launch automatically. Instead of using that application, we recommend using the Photo Downloader application that is included with Bridge, the instructions for which we provide here.

To download photos from a card reader via Photo Downloader:

1. Take the card out of your camera and insert it into the appropriate slot in the card reader.

2. Plug the card reader into your computer. If the default system application for acquiring photos launches, exit/quit it.

3. Launch **Bridge**, then click the **Get Photos from Camera** button at the top of the Bridge window. The Photo Downloader dialog opens.**A** If an alert dialog appears and you want to make Photo Downloader the default capture application, click Yes (as we do); if not, click No.

4. From the **Get Photos From** menu in the Source area, select your card reader.

5. In the **Import Settings** area, do the following:

   To change the save location, click **Browse/Choose**, then navigate to the desired folder. Click OK/Open to assign that folder and return to the Photo Downloader dialog.

   To create a new subfolder within the currently selected folder, choose a naming convention from the **Create Subfolder(s)** menu, or choose Custom Name and enter a folder name (or choose None for no new subfolder).

To assign recognizable names and shorter sequential numbers to your digital images instead of the long default number, choose a Custom Name option from the Rename Files menu, then enter a name and a starting number. A sample of your entry displays below the field.

Keep **Preserve Current Filename in XMP** unchecked.

Check **Open Adobe Bridge** to have the photos display in Bridge when the downloading process is complete.

Also keep **Convert to DNG** and **Delete Original Files** unchecked.

To send copies of your photos to a designated folder on an external hard drive (as a backup), check **Save Copies To**, click **Browse/Choose**, choose a location, then click OK/Open. This will be your first backup copy.

A This is the Standard dialog of the Photo Downloader.

6. If you want to download select photos (instead of the whole batch) from your memory card, click **Advanced Dialog** to expand the dialog.**A** Below the thumbnail window, click **UnCheck All**, then check the box below each photo you want to download. Or hold down Ctrl/Cmd and click multiple photo thumbnails, then check the box for one of them; a check mark will appear below each of the selected photos.

Optional: In the Apply Metadata area, enter Creator and Copyright info to be added to the metadata of all the downloaded photos. (This metadata will display in Bridge.)

► To switch back to the smaller Standard dialog at any time, click Standard Dialog.

7. Click Get Media to begin the downloading process. When it's completed, the Photo Downloader dialog is dismissed automatically. Since you checked the Open Adobe Bridge option, your photos will display in a new window in Bridge. Don't worry about previewing or opening them just yet. We'll step you through that process later.

8. Unmount your card reader.

9. We recommend that you copy your photos to a removable hard drive.

A *The Advanced dialog of the Photo Downloader contains the same options as the Standard dialog, plus metadata features and an area for selecting specific photos to be downloaded.*

Features of the Bridge window

We'll identify the main components of the Bridge window first, starting from the top (**A**, next page). The two rows of buttons and menus running across the top of the window are referred to jointly as the toolbar. The second row of the toolbar is also called the Path bar. If the Path bar is hidden, choose Window > Path Bar.

The large sections of the Bridge window are called panes. Each pane contains one or more panels, each of which is accessed via its own tab: Favorites, Folders, Filter, Collections, Content, Preview, Metadata, and Keywords. In the default workspace, Essentials, the panels in the two side panes let you manage files, preview image thumbnails, filter the display of thumbnails, and display file data; the Content panel in the middle displays file and folder thumbnails. At the bottom of the Bridge window are controls for changing the thumbnail size and layout. (To customize the Bridge window, see pages 28 and 36–37.)

Next, we'll briefly describe the Bridge panels that you will learn about in this chapter.

The **Favorites** panel displays a list of folders that you've designated as favorites, for quick and easy access. See page 29.

The **Folders** panel contains a scrolling window with a hierarchical listing of all the top-level and nested folders on your hard drive(s). See page 29.

The **Filter** panel lists criteria pertaining to the images in the currently selected folder, such as how many have a specific label, star rating, file type, creation date, or modification date. By clicking various criteria in the Filter panel on or off, you can control which images in the current folder display in the Content panel. To expand or collapse a category, click its arrowhead. See page 41.

The **Collections** panel displays the names and icons of collections, which are thumbnail groups that you create to organize your images. See pages 45–46.

The **Content** panel displays thumbnails for images within the currently selected folder (and optionally, thumbnails for nested folders). In the lower-right corner of the Bridge window, you can click a View Content As button to control whether, and in what

format, metadata pertaining to the current files displays for each thumbnail in the Content panel (see page 37). For any view type, you can change the thumbnail size (see page 36). The Content panel is used and illustrated in many tasks throughout this chapter.

The **Preview** panel displays a large preview of the image (or folder) thumbnail that is currently selected in the Content panel. Or if the thumbnail for a video or PDF file is selected, controls for playing the video or for viewing the pages display in this panel. Two or more selected image thumbnails can be previewed in this panel, for comparison, and it has a loupe mechanism that you can use to inspect small details. See pages 29–31.

The **Metadata** panel has two main sections, both of which display data pertaining to the currently selected thumbnail. The placard at the top contains a quick summary (see the sidebar on page 29), and the main part of the panel lists more detailed data, in collapsible categories. In the File Properties category, for example, you can view the current file name, file size, etc. Via the IPTC Core category, you can attach a copyright notice and other data to a file (see page 39). When the thumbnail for a digital photo is selected, the Camera Data (Exif) category lists the camera settings with which the photo was captured. If the photo was edited in Camera Raw, the panel will also show a Camera Raw category in which the Basic tab settings that are applied to the current photo are listed (to add more Camera Raw data to this category, go to Edit/Adobe Bridge CC > Preferences, Metadata pane, and check the desired boxes under Camera Raw).

Use the **Keywords** panel to assign one or more descriptive subkeywords to your images, such as an event, subject, client, or location, so they can be located quickly using other Bridge features (see pages 38–39). You can run a search to find image thumbnails based on keyword criteria, or narrow the display of thumbnails in the Content panel to subcategories of images by checking specific keywords in the Filter panel.

Note: The Inspector panel isn't covered in this book.

Browse Quickly
by Preferring
Embedded Images

Options for
Thumbnail Quality
and Preview
Generation menu

Filter Items
by Rating
menu

Sort
menu

Open
Recent
File menu

Create
New
Folder

Delete
Item

Display thumbnails in
Descending Order or
Ascending Order

Get Photos
from Camera

Open in
Camera Raw

For the navigation controls
on the toolbar, see page 29.

Return to last
Adobe application

Refine menu
(Review Mode,
Batch Rename,
File Info)

Rotate selected
thumbnails 90°
counterclockwise
or clockwise

Name of
currently
displayed folder

Workspace
switcher

Workspace
menu

Path bar

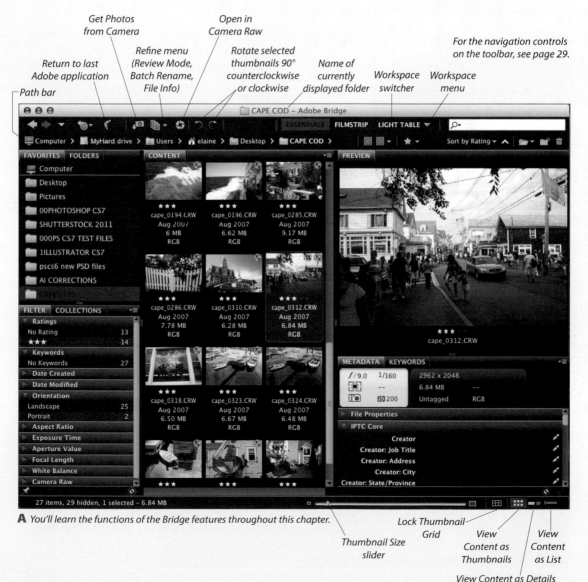

Lock Thumbnail
Grid

View
Content as
Thumbnails

View
Content
as List

View Content as Details

Thumbnail Size
slider

A You'll learn the functions of the Bridge features throughout this chapter.

Choosing a workspace for Bridge

To reconfigure the Bridge window quickly, choose one of the predefined workspaces. (To create and save custom workspaces, see pages 36–38.)

To choose a workspace for Bridge:

Do one of the following:

On the upper toolbar, click **Essentials**, **Filmstrip**, **Light Table**, **Metadata** (List View for the thumbnails), **Keywords**, **Preview**, **Folders**, or a saved custom workspace.**A** (If there's room on the toolbar and you want to display more workspace names, pull the gripper bar to the left.)

From the **Workspace** menu on the toolbar, choose a workspace.**B–C**

Press the shortcut for one of the first six workspaces on the switcher (as listed on the Workspace menu): Ctrl-F1/Cmd-F1 through Ctrl-F6/Cmd-F6.

The shortcuts are assigned automatically to the first six workspaces on the switcher, according to their current order from left to right. (Not working? These shortcuts may already be used by your operating system, in which case they won't work in Bridge.)

➤ To change the order of workspaces on the switcher, drag a name to the left or right.

➤ To learn how to resize the thumbnails in the Content panel, see page 36.

➤ To create a second Bridge window, choose File > New Window (Ctrl-N/Cmd-N). You can display a different workspace and folder in each window.

To reveal more workspace names, drag the gripper bar to the left.

A To change workspaces, click a workspace name from the workspace switcher …

B … or choose a workspace name from the Workspace menu.

C The Filmstrip workspace features a large preview of the currently selected thumbnail(s).

Previewing images in Bridge

To add a folder to the Favorites panel:

Do either of the following:

Drag a folder icon from the Content panel or the Explorer/Finder into the Favorites panel (the pointer will be a + symbol).

Right-click a folder in the Folders or Content panel and choose **Add to Favorites**.

➤ Via check boxes in the Favorite Items area of Edit/ Adobe Bridge CC > Preferences > General, you can control which system folders are listed in the Favorites panel.

➤ To remove a folder from the list of Favorites, right-click it and choose Remove from Favorites.

To display and select images in Bridge:

1. Do any of the following:

   In the **Folders** panel, navigate to a folder. To expand or collapse a folder, click its arrowhead.

   Display the contents of a folder by clicking its icon in the **Folders** panel or by double-clicking its thumbnail in the **Content** panel. Note: For folder thumbnails to display in the Content panel, Show Folders must be checked on the View menu.

   Click the **Go Back** button 🔳 on the toolbar **A** to step back through the last folders viewed, or the **Go Forward** button 🔳 to reverse your steps.

   Click a folder name in the **Favorites** panel.

   From the **Go to Parent or Favorites** menu 🔳 on the toolbar, choose a parent or Favorites folder.

   Click a folder name on the **Path** bar (if the bar is hidden, choose Window > Path Bar).

   From one of the menus 🔳 on the Path bar, choose a folder. If another submenu displays, click yet

another folder; repeat until you reach the desired folder.

   ➤ To display thumbnails for images in all nested subfolders within the current folder, choose Show Items from Subfolders from the folder menu.🔳 To restore the normal view, click the Cancel button 🔳 on the Path bar.

2. In the **Content** panel, do one of the following:

   Click an image thumbnail. A colored border appears around it, and data about the file is listed in the Metadata panel. An enlarged preview of the image also displays in the **Preview** panel, if that panel is showing.

   To select multiple, nonconsecutive thumbnails, Ctrl-click/Cmd-click them.

   To select a series of consecutive thumbnails, click the first thumbnail in the series, then Shift-click the last one.

   ➤ A number in the upper-left corner of an image thumbnail signifies that it's part of a stack (group) of thumbnails. To display or hide the contents of a stack, click the stack number.

   ➤ To cycle through thumbnails in the currently displayed folder, press an arrow key on the keyboard.

   ➤ To quickly locate and select a particular thumbnail, start typing the file name without clicking anywhere first.

Go Back   Go Forward   Go to Parent or Favorites   Reveal Recent File or Go to Recent Folder

Path bar   **A** These are the navigation controls in Bridge.

THE METADATA PLACARD

To show the Metadata placard, check **Show Metadata Placard** on the Metadata panel menu. The left side of the placard lists settings that were used to shoot the currently selected photo (the icons and data vary depending on the camera settings and model). The right side of the placard lists the pixel dimensions, size, resolution, color profile, and color mode of the current file.

Shutter speed

Aperture
Metering mode
White balance

Exposure compensation (bias)

You can control whether thumbnails and the preview render quickly at low resolution, or more slowly and color-managed at high resolution.

To choose a quality option for the Bridge thumbnails and previews:

From the **Options for Thumbnail Quality and Preview Generation** menu ▓ on the Bridge toolbar, choose a preference for the preview quality of image thumbnails:

Prefer Embedded (Faster) displays low-resolution thumbnails and is useful for displaying a high volume of images quickly.

High Quality on Demand displays high-resolution, color-managed thumbnails and previews (generated from the source files) for selected thumbnails and low-resolution previews for unselected thumbnails. This is a good compromise between the two other options.

Always High Quality, the default setting, displays high-resolution thumbnails and previews, whether the thumbnails are selected or not. Rendering is the slowest with this option.

➤ To quickly access lower-quality, faster previewing, click the Browse Quickly by Preferring Embedded Images button ▓ on the Path bar; this enables the Prefer Embedded (Faster) option. Click the button again to return to the current setting on the Options for Thumbnail Quality and Preview Generation menu.

➤ The Generate 100% Previews option on the Options for Thumbnail Quality and Preview Generation menu saves actual-size JPEG versions of thumbnails, which in turn enables Bridge to generate higher-quality previews when the loupe is used or when images are displayed at 100% size in Full Screen Preview or Slideshow view. This option uses a lot of disk space and can make browsing slower, so we recommend keeping it unchecked.

To compare two or more image previews:

1. In Bridge, display the Filmstrip or Preview workspace.

2. In the Content panel, Ctrl-click/Cmd-click up to nine thumbnails (the maximum number that can be previewed at a time) (**A**, next page). Large versions of the thumbnails will display in the Preview panel.

3. *Optional:* Ctrl-click/Cmd-click an unselected thumbnail in the Content panel to add it to the Preview panel, or do the same for a selected thumbnail to remove it from the Preview panel.

To display a full-screen preview of an image thumbnail:

1. Press the Spacebar to display a full-screen preview of the currently selected thumbnail and hide the Bridge window temporarily.

2. To zoom in or out, press + or – or use the scroll wheel on your mouse (you can drag the magnified preview). If desired, press the left or right arrow key to cycle through other thumbnails in the same folder.

3. To redisplay the Bridge window, press the Spacebar or Esc.

To inspect image details via an onscreen loupe:

1. To make the loupe appear, click an image in the Preview panel;**B** or if Bridge is in Review mode, click the frontmost image (see the next page).

   Note: If the loupe doesn't appear, it's because the Ctrl-Click/Cmd-Click Opens the Loupe When Previewing or Reviewing option is checked in Edit/Adobe Bridge CC > Preferences > General. To make the loupe appear (or disappear), Ctrl-click/Cmd-click the preview.

2. Click the area to be examined. To zoom in on the loupe display (up to 800%), press +, or to zoom out, press –.

3. To examine a different area, click that area or drag the loupe to it.

4. *Optional:* If you're previewing two images using two loupes, you can Ctrl-drag/Cmd-drag either loupe to move them both simultaneously.

5. To remove the loupe, click inside it.

B *Use the loupe to inspect small details in the preview.*

A *We Ctrl/Cmd-clicked two image thumbnails to display them in the Preview panel, then clicked one preview to display the loupe.*

When you put selected thumbnails into Review mode, they display as large previews on a black background (the Bridge window is hidden), and you can cycle through them as if they're on a carousel. You can also rate thumbnails in this mode.

To preview images in Review mode:

1. Do one of the following:

   Open a folder of images.

   Hold down Alt/Option and click a thumbnail stack.

   Select five or more image thumbnails (Ctrl/Cmd or Shift-click them).

2. Press Ctrl-B/Cmd-B, or from the **Refine** menu at the top of the Bridge window, choose Review Mode. The Bridge window is hidden temporarily, and the images display on a black background.

3. To rotate the carousel, do any of the following:

   Drag any image preview to the left or right.

   Click one of the smaller previews to bring it to the forefront.

   Press the left or right arrow key.

Click (and keep clicking) the Go Forward or Go Backward button in the lower-left corner.

4. To examine the frontmost (enlarged) image with a loupe, click it. Drag the loupe to move it. Click the loupe again to remove it.

5. To rate or label the frontmost thumbnail, right-click it and choose a star rating or a label from the context menu **A** or press Ctrl/Cmd plus a numeral between 1 and 9. (To view a list of shortcuts, press H.)

6. To take the frontmost image out of the carousel, click the down-pointing arrow in the lower-left corner, or drag the image to the bottom of your screen. (This won't delete the actual file.)

   ➤ You can use this method to pare down a selection of images before grouping them as a stack or putting them in a collection (see pages 45–46).

7. To exit Review mode, press Esc or click the in the lower-right corner.

8. Click any image thumbnail to deselect the rest.

A *We held down Ctrl/Cmd and clicked six image thumbnails, pressed Ctrl-B/Cmd-B to view them in Review mode, then right-clicked the frontmost thumbnail and are choosing a label from the context menu.*

Opening files from Bridge into Photoshop

You can open as many files into Photoshop as the currently available RAM and scratch disk space on your computer will allow.

Note: To open a raw, JPEG, or TIFF digital photo into Camera Raw (so you can apply corrections to it before opening it into Photoshop), see pages 50–51.

To open files from Bridge into Photoshop:

1. In the Content panel, display the thumbnail for the image(s) to be opened.

2. Do either of the following:

   Double-click an image thumbnail.

   Click an image thumbnail or select multiple thumbnails, then double-click one of them or press Ctrl-O/Cmd-O.

3. Photoshop will launch, if it isn't already running, and the image(s) will appear onscreen. If any alert dialogs appear, see the next page.

➤ If a photo has been opened and edited in Camera Raw, it will have this icon ⬇ in the top-right corner of its thumbnail. If you want to open such a file (or a raw photo) directly into Photoshop — without opening it into Camera Raw first — double-click the thumbnail with Shift held down.

➤ To locate an "actual" file in Explorer/Finder, right-click its thumbnail in Bridge and choose Reveal in Explorer/Reveal in Finder from the context menu. The folder that the file resides in will open in a window in Explorer/Finder and the file icon will be selected.

➤ By default, the Bridge window stays open after you use it to open a file. To minimize the Bridge window as you open a file, hold down Alt/Option while double-clicking the file thumbnail.

➤ To open an image from Review mode in Bridge into Photoshop, right-click it and choose Open from the context menu.

To reopen a recently opened file:

To reopen a file that was recently opened and then closed, choose the file name in one of these locations:

In Bridge, choose from the **Open Recent File** menu ▰▱ on the right side of the Path bar.

In Bridge or Photoshop, choose from the File > **Open Recent** submenu.

In Bridge, from the **Reveal Recent File or Go to Recent Folder** menu, ◉ choose **Adobe Photoshop** > **Recent Adobe Photoshop Files**. Thumbnails for the recently opened files will display in the Content panel. Double-click a thumbnail to open that file. To redisplay the last displayed folder when you return to Bridge, click the Go Back arrow.◄

GETTING TO PHOTOSHOP QUICKLY

If Photoshop was the last Adobe application you were using, you can return to it quickly from Bridge by clicking the Return to Adobe Photoshop (boomerang) button ◼ on the toolbar. Photoshop will launch, if it isn't already running.

ALAS, THE POOR OPEN COMMAND

With Bridge serving as the best vehicle for opening files, the Open command is relegated to this sidebar. To use the Open command in Photoshop, choose File > Open (Ctrl-O/Cmd-O). In Windows, from the file type menu, choose All Formats; in the Mac OS, choose Enable: All Readable Documents. Locate and click the desired file name, then click Open.

When you open a Photoshop file that is using missing fonts (the fonts are either unavailable or not installed in your system), a Creative Cloud dialog opens. For each missing font, you can let Typekit substitute a matching font from its collection, choose a default font, or open the document into Photoshop without resolving the issue. (To learn more about Adobe Typekit, see pages 388–389.)

Note: To verify that Typekit is turned on for the following task, see the sidebar on this page.

To respond to an alert regarding missing fonts:

1. If you open a Photoshop file in which one or more missing fonts are being used, the Missing Fonts dialog will appear. **A** (The first time this feature is activated, an intro screen will display. Click Next.)

2. From the menu next to the name of each missing font, choose one of these options:

   If Typekit finds a **matching font** from its collection, you can leave that font as the choice on the menu. Note the Typekit icon.

   If Typekit cannot locate a matching font, you can choose the **default substitution font**.

   If you want to leave a missing font as unresolved, choose **Don't Resolve** from the menu.

   If other **fonts that are being used** in the file are available, you can choose from that list on the lower part of the menu.

(If you want to dismiss the dialog immediately and open the file into Photoshop, click Cancel.)

3. Click **Resolve Fonts** to close the Missing Fonts dialog and open the document into Photoshop. All matching Typekit fonts that were chosen on the menus in that dialog will be synced to your computer. Note: If you chose Don't Resolve from the menu(s) for all the missing fonts, click **Don't Resolve** instead (same button, different name).

4. If you chose Don't Resolve from any menu (or you clicked Cancel) in the Missing Fonts dialog, when the file opens into Photoshop, a Font Missing on System alert icon ▲ will display on the Layers panel for every layer that is using missing fonts. If you try to edit one of those layers, another alert dialog will appear, indicating that font substitution will occur. You can either click OK to allow the missing font(s) to be replaced by the default font, or click Cancel, make the required fonts available, then close/reopen the document.

➤ In Photoshop, if you would like to reopen the Missing Fonts dialog to resolve missing fonts, choose Type > Resolve All Missing Fonts. Or if you want to replace all missing fonts with the default substitution font, choose Type > Replace All Missing Fonts.

TURNING ON TYPEKIT

Typekit will search for and sync fonts between the Creative Cloud and Photoshop only if the feature is turned on. You can verify this in either of two ways:

➤ Open the Creative Cloud desktop app, ◉ click Assets, then click Fonts. If Typekit is off, a Turn Typekit On button displays; click the button.

➤ Open the Creative Cloud desktop app, ◉ click the gear icon, ▦ then click Preferences. In the Preferences panel, click Creative Cloud, click Fonts, then under Typekit On/Off, make sure the On button is clicked. Click the back arrow at the top. ★

A The Missing Fonts dialog will appear if any fonts used in the document that you're opening are missing. If Typekit finds a matching font, you can leave that choice on the menu or choose other menu options.

To respond to an alert regarding a missing color profile:

If the color profile of the document you're opening doesn't match the current working space for Photoshop, the Embedded Profile Mismatch alert dialog will appear.**A** Click **Use the Embedded Profile (Instead of the Working Space)** if you must keep the current profile. Or for consistency with the color management workflow that we have recommended, click **Convert Document's Colors to the Working Space** to convert the profile to the current working space. Click OK. See pages 7, 8, 10, and 12.

If the Missing Profile alert dialog appears,**B** click **Assign Working RGB: Adobe RGB (1998)** to assign the profile that you chose as the working space for Photoshop. Click OK. See pages 7 and 12.

To respond to an alert regarding missing linked Smart Objects:

1. If the Photoshop document that you're opening contains Smart Objects that are linked to external files, and if those files were renamed or moved, Photoshop may not be able to locate and update the link(s) to them automatically. In this case, an alert dialog will appear.**C** Click the **Relink** ★ button for a missing link. In the Locate Missing File dialog, locate the file, then click Place. A check mark should appear before the file name, and before the names of any other missing linked files that were found in the same folder.

2. Repeat the preceding step for any other missing links, then click OK.

➤ To learn about linked Smart Objects, see pages 280–283.

A *If this Embedded Profile Mismatch alert dialog appears, indicate whether you want to continue to use the embedded profile or convert the file to the current working space.*

B *If this Missing Profile alert dialog appears, click Assign Working RGB: Adobe RGB (1998) to convert the file to the default working space for Photoshop.*

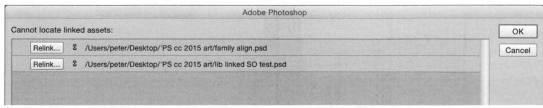

C *This alert dialog will appear if Photoshop can't locate the external files for one or more linked Smart Objects in your document. For each missing link, click Relink, locate the file, then click Place.*

Customizing the Bridge window

To display or hide individual panels:

On the **Window** menu, check the panels you want to show and uncheck the ones you want to hide.

➤ To quickly hide (and then show) the side panes, press Tab or double-click the dark vertical bar between a side pane and the middle pane.

To configure the Bridge panes and panels manually:

Do any of the following:

To make a panel or panel group taller or shorter, drag its horizontal gripper bar upward or downward.**A**

To make a whole pane wider or narrower, drag its vertical gripper bar horizontally;**B** the adjacent pane resizes accordingly.

To minimize a panel or panel group to just a tab (or to restore its former size), double-click its tab.

To move a panel into a different group, drag the panel tab and release the mouse when the blue drop zone border appears around the desired group.

To display a panel as a separate group, drag its tab upward or downward between two panels and release the mouse when the horizontal blue drop zone line appears.

To resize the image thumbnails:

At the bottom of the Bridge window, drag the **Thumbnail Size** slider.**C** You could also click the Smaller Thumbnail Size or Larger Thumbnail Size button, located to the left and right of the slider.

➤ To display only full thumbnails, with grid lines between them, click the Lock Thumbnail Grid button ▦ at the bottom of the Bridge window. With this option on, no shuffling of thumbnails will occur if you resize the Content panel.

A *We're dragging the horizontal bar upward to shorten the Favorites/Folders panel group and lengthen the Filter/Collections panel group.*

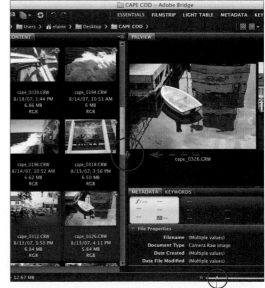

B *Here we're dragging the vertical bar (for the right pane) to the left to widen the Preview, Metadata, and Keywords panels.*

C *To resize your image thumbnails, use this slider.*

To control how metadata is displayed in the Content panel:

1. In the lower-right corner of the Bridge window, click one of these View Content buttons: **A**

   View Content as Thumbnails (minimal file data), **View Content as Details** (more file data),**B** or **View Content as List** (small icons with columns of data).

2. To control which categories of metadata display below or next to the image thumbnails when the View Content as Thumbnails option is chosen, go to Edit/Adobe Bridge CC > Preferences > Thumbnails, then select from any or all of the **Details: Show** menus. For example, to display exposure settings, you would choose Exposure.

➤ With the View Content as List option chosen, you can change the column order by dragging any column header to the left or right. You can also right-click any column header to access options for changing the column data, inserting and closing columns, and changing the column width.

➤ When the View Content as Thumbnails option is chosen for Bridge, you can toggle the display of metadata on and off by pressing Ctrl-T/Cmd-T. When viewing thumbnails in the Light Table workspace, we prefer to keep the metadata hidden.

View Content as Thumbnails | View Content as Details | View Content as List

A *These buttons control the display of metadata in the Content panel.*

METADATA IN THE TOOL TIPS

If Show Tooltips is checked in Edit/Adobe Bridge CC > Preferences > Thumbnails and you rest the pointer on an image thumbnail, the Tool Tip will list the metadata for that image. (Turn this feature off if you find it annoying.)

B *With the View Content as Details button clicked, metadata displays next to the file thumbnails.*

Saving custom workspaces

If you save your customized workspaces, you'll be able to access them again quickly at any time and will avoid having to reconfigure the Bridge window at the beginning of each work session.

To save a custom workspace for Bridge:

1. Do all of the following:

   Choose a size and location for the overall Bridge window.

   Arrange the panel sizes and groups as desired.

   Set the thumbnail size for the Content panel.

   Choose a sorting order for thumbnails from the Sort menu at the top of the Bridge window (see page 41).

   Click a View Content button (see the previous page).

2. From the **Workspace** menu on the workspace switcher, choose **New Workspace**.

3. In the New Workspace dialog, **A** enter a Name for the workspace. If desired, check Save Window Location as Part of Workspace and/or Save Sort Order as Part of Workspace, then click Save.

   Note: Your new workspace will be listed first on the switcher and will be assigned the first short-cut (Ctrl-F1/Cmd-F1). To change the order of workspaces on the switcher, drag any workspace name horizontally to a different slot. When you do this, the shortcuts will be reassigned based on the new order.

➤ To delete a user-saved workspace, from the Workspace menu, choose Delete Workspace. From the menu in the dialog, choose the workspace to be deleted, then click Delete.

➤ To choose colors for the Bridge interface (including the background shade behind the panels and image previews, and the highlight border around selected thumbnails), see page 470.

A Use the New Workspace dialog to name your custom workspace and choose options for it.

Resetting the Bridge workspaces

If you make a manual change to a saved workspace, the change will stick with the workspace even if you switch to a different one (or exit/quit and relaunch Bridge). For instance, if you were to change the thumbnail size for the Filmstrip workspace, switch to the Essentials workspace, then switch back to Filmstrip, you would see your chosen thumbnail size again. On the occasion that you want a fresh start, however, there are commands for restoring the default settings to any individual predefined (standard Adobe) or user-saved workspace, or to all the predefined workspaces at once.

To reset the Bridge workspace:

Do either of the following:

To restore the default settings to one workspace, right-click the workspace name on the switcher and choose **Reset**.

To restore the default settings to all the Adobe predefined workspaces, choose **Reset Standard Workspaces** from the Workspace menu.

Assigning keywords to files

Keywords (words that are assigned to files) are used by operating system search utilities to locate files and by file management programs to organize them. In Bridge, you can create parent keyword categories (for events, places, themes, clients, etc.), and nested subkeywords within those categories, and then assign them to your files. You can locate files by entering keywords as search criteria in the Find dialog, build a Smart Collection based on a search for keywords (see page 45), and display files by checking Keywords criteria in the Filter panel (see page 41).

To create keywords and subkeywords in the Keywords panel:

1. Display the Keywords panel. To create a new parent keyword category, click the **New Keyword** button, type a keyword, then press Enter/Return.

2. To create a nested subkeyword, click a parent keyword, click the **New Sub Keyword** button, type a word, then press Enter/Return (**A**, next page). Each time you want to add a subkeyword, click the parent keyword first. You can also create nested sub-subkeywords.

➤ You can move (drag) any subkeyword from one parent keyword category into another.

To assign keywords to files via the Keywords panel:

1. Select one or more image thumbnails in the Content panel. If keywords are already assigned to any of those files, they will be listed at the top of the Keywords panel (you can assign more).

2. Check the box for one or more subkeywords.**B** To remove a keyword from a file, uncheck the box.

➤ Read about the Keywords preferences on page 472.

➤ If you select the thumbnail for a file to which keywords were assigned outside of Bridge (e.g., in Photoshop via File > File Info), those keywords will display temporarily in the Keywords panel, under Other Keywords. To convert a temporary subkeyword to a permanent one, right-click it and choose Make Persistent from the context menu.

To assign keywords to files via the Metadata panel:

1. Select one or more image thumbnails in the Content panel.

2. Display the Metadata panel, and expand the **IPTC Core** category.

3. Click the **Keywords** listing, then enter keywords, separated by semicolons or commas. Be on the alert for typing errors!

4. Click the **Apply** button ![icon] in the lower-right corner of the panel.**C**

➤ You can also use the IPTC Core category in the Metadata panel to assign other data to a file, such as a copyright notice. Use the same method as in the steps above (you can press Tab to proceed from one field to the next).

C We're assigning keywords to a file via the Metadata panel.

A We created a new parent keyword "Desserts," then added some subkeywords to it via the New Sub Keyword button.

B We clicked four image thumbnails, then assigned the subkeyword "Baked desserts" to them by checking the box.

USING THE KEYWORDS PANEL

Rename a parent keyword or subkeyword	Right-click the word, choose Rename from the context menu, then type a name (this won't alter data that is already embedded).
Delete a parent keyword or subkeyword	Click the word, then click the Delete Keyword button.🗑 If that keyword is assigned to any files, it will now be listed in italics. (To reinstate an italicized keyword, choose Make Persistent from the context menu.)
Find a keyword or subkeyword	Type the word in the field at the bottom of the panel. Choose a search parameter from the menu.🔍▾

Rating and labeling thumbnails

If you assign each thumbnail a star rating and/or a color label, you'll be able to use those criteria to sort thumbnails in the Content panel, filter them via the Filter panel, and locate them via the Find command. In addition, you can apply a Reject rating to any image thumbnails that you want to hide from the Content panel but aren't ready to delete from your hard drive.

To rate and label thumbnails:

1. Select either View Content as Thumbnails or View Content as Details as the view option for thumbnails (see page 37). Select one or more image thumbnails in the Content panel.

2. When you do any of the following, either a specific number of stars, a "Reject" label, or a colored label appears below the image thumbnail:

   From the Label menu, choose a **Rating** and/or a **Label.A**

   Click a thumbnail, then click any one of the five dots below it; stars will appear.**B** To remove one star, click the star to its left. To remove all the stars

from a thumbnail, click to the left of the first one.**C** (If you don't see the dots or stars, enlarge the thumbnails via the Thumbnail Size slider.)

Press one of the keyboard shortcuts that are listed on the Label menu, such as Ctrl/Cmd plus a number (e.g., Ctrl-2/Cmd-2 for two stars, or Ctrl-8/Cmd-8 for Approved).

Right-click a thumbnail in the Content panel, then choose a category from the **Label** submenu on the context menu.

Right-click in the Preview panel and choose a star rating and/or label from the context menu.

To label the losers with a red "Reject" label, choose Label > **Reject** or press Alt-Del/Option-Delete.**D** Via the Show Reject Files option on the View menu, you can show or hide all rejected thumbnails.

➤ You can assign custom names to the labels in Edit/Adobe Bridge CC > Preferences > Labels.

To remove ratings or labels from thumbnails:

1. Select one or more image thumbnails.

2. To remove stars, choose **No Rating** from the Label menu or press Ctrl-0/Cmd-0 (zero). To remove a label, choose **No Label** from the Label menu or press the shortcut for the currently assigned label. (If the selected thumbnails have different labels, you'll need to press the shortcut twice.)

honeycomb.tif

A *We gave this thumbnail an Approved (green) rating.*

pasta and wine.tif

B *We clicked the third dot on this thumbnail to give it a three-star rating…*

pasta and wine.tif

C *…but then we changed our minds, so we clicked to the left of the stars to remove them.*

CRW_6550.CRW

D *We gave this poor fellow a Reject rating (Alt-Del/Option-Delete).*

RATING THUMBNAILS IN REVIEW MODE

To rate or label images in Review mode, right-click the large, frontmost image and choose from the context menu or use one of the assigned shortcuts (as listed on the Label menu.)

Rearranging and sorting thumbnails

To rearrange thumbnails manually:

Drag a thumbnail to a new location; or Ctrl-click/Cmd-click multiple thumbnails, then drag one of the selected thumbnails. The listing on the Sort menu on the Path bar changes to "Sort Manually."

The current criterion on the Sort menu controls the order in which thumbnails display in the Content panel. After applying ratings to our thumbnails, we choose By Rating from the Sort menu to display them by rating, in ascending order. The sorting order also affects the batch and automate commands in Bridge, because those commands process files based on the current sequence of thumbnails.

To choose a sorting order for thumbnails:

From the **Sort** menu on the Path bar, choose a sorting criterion (such as By Rating).**A** All thumbnails that are currently displaying in the Content panel will be re-sorted. Sorting doesn't change the order of thumbnails within stacks. Note: If you display a different folder, the current sorting order will apply.

➤ To restore the last sequence of thumbnails that was created by dragging them manually, choose Manually from the Sort menu.

➤ To reverse the current order, click the Ascending Order ◢ or Descending Order ◣ arrowhead.

Filtering thumbnails

The categories and listings on the Filter panel (e.g., Ratings, Keywords, Date Created) change dynamically depending on the data contained in the currently displayed folder of thumbnails, and also on the categories checked on the panel menu. When you check the boxes for specific criteria in the panel, only the thumbnails that meet those criteria will display in the Content panel. Note: Filtering doesn't affect the thumbnails in stacks.

To filter the display of thumbnails:

Do either of the following:

On the **Filter** panel, click the arrowhead to expand any category, such as Labels, Ratings, or Keywords, then check one or more criteria.**B** For example, to display only files that have an Approved label and a rating of three stars, check Approved under Labels and check the three-star listing under Ratings. To remove a criterion, click the listing again.

From the **Filter Items by Rating** menu ★▾ on the Bridge toolbar,**C** check the desired criteria.

➤ To prevent the current filters (those with check marks) from clearing when you display other folders, activate the Keep Filter When Browsing button on the panel; when activated, the button displays in color.

➤ To remove all check marks from the Filter panel, click the Clear Filter ⊘ button at the bottom of the panel or press Ctrl-Alt-A/Cmd-Option-A.

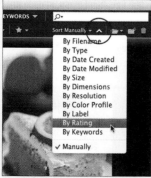

A *From the Sort menu on the Path bar, we're choosing a sorting order for our thumbnails.*

B *Because we checked the three-star rating in the Filter panel (Ratings category), only thumbnails that have three stars will display in the Content panel.*

C *Via the Filter Items by Rating menu, you can filter thumbnails based on their ratings.*

Managing files using Bridge

To create a new folder:

1. Via the Folders panel or the Path bar, navigate to the folder to which you want to add a folder.

2. Click the **New Folder** button 📁 at the right end of the Bridge toolbar (Ctrl-Shift-N/Cmd-Shift-N). Type a name to replace the highlighted one, then press Enter/Return.

You can move files to a different folder on your hard disk either by dragging them manually or by using a command.

To move or copy files between folders:

Method 1 (by dragging)

1. Select one or more thumbnails (Content panel).

2. In the Folders panel, navigate to (but don't click) the folder or subfolder into which you want to move the selected files.

3. To move the selected files, drag them over the folder name in the Folders panel (then release), or to copy them, do the same except hold down Ctrl/ Option while dragging (a + symbol displays in the pointer). Note: If you want to move (not copy) files to another hard disk, hold down Shift/Cmd while dragging.

➤ You can also move or copy files to a folder in the Favorites panel.

Method 2 (via the context menu)

1. Select one or more thumbnails in the Content panel.

2. Right-click one of the selected thumbnails, then from the **Move To** or **Copy To** submenu on the context menu, do either of the following:

   Select a folder name under **Recent Folders** or **Favorites**.

   Select **Choose Folder**. Locate a folder in the Open dialog, then click Open.

➤ To copy files via the Clipboard, select one or more thumbnails, press Ctrl-C/Cmd-C to copy them, click the desired folder, then press Ctrl-V/Cmd-V to paste.

To delete a file or folder:

1. Click an image or folder thumbnail or Ctrl-click/ Cmd-click multiple thumbnails, or Shift-click a series of them.

2. Do either of the following:

   Press Ctrl-Backspace/Cmd-Delete. If an alert dialog appears, click OK.

   Press Del/Delete on your extended keyboard. If an alert dialog appears, click Delete.

➤ Oops! Change your mind? To retrieve a deleted file or folder, choose Edit > Undo immediately. Or to dig it out of the trash, double-click the Recycle Bin/Trash icon for your operating system, then drag the item into the Content panel in Bridge.

To rename a file or folder:

1. Click a thumbnail, then click the file or folder name. The name becomes highlighted. **A**

2. Type a new name **B** (leave the extension), then press Enter/Return or click outside the name field.

Exporting the Bridge cache

Bridge uses a cache to display program features, such as ratings, labels, and high-quality thumbnails. Thumbnails in a given folder redisplay more quickly once the cache has been created.

You can set a preference to ensure that Bridge will include cache data with any files that you copy.

To have Bridge export the cache automatically:

1. In Bridge, choose Edit/Adobe Bridge CC > Preferences (Ctrl-K/Cmd-K), then click **Cache**.

2. Under Options, check **Automatically Export Cache to Folders When Possible**, then click OK.

➤ To display the cache file icons for the current folder, choose View > **Show Hidden Files**.

To purge cache files from a folder:

To purge all the cache files from the current folder, choose Tools > Cache > **Purge Cache for Folder** "[current folder name]." New (hidden) cache files will be generated.

A *To rename a file, click the existing name…*   **B** *…then type a new name.*

Batch-renaming files

When you download digital photos from your camera to your computer, they keep the sequential numerical labels (e.g., "CRW_3816") that your camera assigned to them. Via the Batch Rename command in Bridge, you can assign more recognizable names to your photos, to make them easier to identify.

To batch-rename files:

1. Display the contents of the folder that contains the files to be renamed, then select the thumbnails for the files to be renamed.

2. Do either of the following:

   Choose Tools > **Batch Rename** (Ctrl-Shift-R/ Cmd-Shift-R).

   From the Refine menu at the top of the Bridge toolbar, choose **Batch Rename**. The Batch Rename dialog opens.**A**

3. From the **Preset** menu, choose **Default**.

4. Under Destination Folder, click one of the following:

   Rename in Same Folder to have Bridge rename the files and leave them in their current location.

   Move to Other Folder to have Bridge rename the files and move them to a new location.

   Copy to Other Folder to leave the original files unchanged but rename the copies and move them to a new location (this is a quick way to duplicate a batch of photos). We recommend using this option, especially if you didn't elect to copy your photos when you downloaded them.

   For the Move or Copy option, also click **Browse**, choose or create a new folder, then click Open.

5. In the New Filenames area, specify data to be included in the names: **Text** (enter the desired name); **Date Time** (choose an option from both menus in the row); and **Sequence Number** to include an incremental number in the names (enter a starting number and choose a digit option).

   To add another row of criteria fields, click the ⊕ button, or to remove a row of fields, click the ⊖ button.

   Click **Preview** to view a listing of the new file names, then click OK to exit that dialog.

6. Under Options, leave Preserve Current Filename in XMP Metadata unchecked (unless you need to preserve the old names), but for **Compatibility**, check any other operating system(s) in which you want your renamed files to be readable.

7. *Optional:* To save the current New Filenames and Options settings as a preset for future use, click Save, enter a name, then click OK. Your custom preset will appear on the Preset menu.

8. To apply your naming choices to the selected thumbnails, click Rename.

A *Via the Batch Rename dialog, you can quickly rename an entire folder full of photos.*

Searching for files

To find files via Bridge:

1. In Bridge, choose Edit > **Find** (Ctrl-F/Cmd-F). The Find dialog opens.**A**

2. From the **Look In** menu in the Source area, choose the folder to be searched (by default, the current folder is listed). To select a folder that isn't listed on the menu, choose Browse, locate the desired folder, then click Open.

3. From the menus in the **Criteria** area, choose search criteria (e.g., Filename, Date Created, Keywords, Label, Rating, or a category of camera settings), choose a parameter from the adjoining menu, and enter data in the field. To add another criterion to the search, click the ⊕ button, or to remove a row of fields, click ⊖.

4. From the **Match** menu, choose "If any criteria are met" to find files based on one or more of the criteria you have specified, or choose "If all criteria are met" to narrow the selection to just the files that meet all your criteria.

5. Check **Include All Subfolders** to include, in the search, any of the subfolders that are inside the folder you chose in step 2.

6. *Optional:* Check Include Non-Indexed Files to search through files that Bridge hasn't yet indexed (any folder Bridge has yet to display). As indicated, this could slow down the search.

7. Click Find. The results of the search will be placed in a temporary folder called Search Results: [name of source folder] and will display in the Content panel.**B** The folder will be listed on the Path bar and on the Reveal Recent File or Go to Recent Folder menu 📷 on the Bridge toolbar.

8. To create a collection from the results of the search, follow the steps on the next page.

➤ To discard the current search results and start a new search, click New Search, or to cancel the results, click the Cancel button.❌

QUICK SEARCH FOR A FILE

In the Favorites panel, click Computer, then double-click the thumbnail for your hard drive; or navigate to a particular folder. In the search field 🔍▾ on the Bridge toolbar, type the name of the file you're looking for or type a keyword, then press Enter/Return.

A *We entered three criteria in the Find dialog (then we clicked Find).*

B *The results from our search appeared in the Content panel. The parameters used for the search and the folder that was searched are listed next to "Find Criteria."*

Creating and using collections

Using the collection features in Bridge, you can catalog your file thumbnails without having to relocate the actual files. There are two kinds of collections: a Smart Collection that you create from the results of a Find search, and a standard collection, which you create by dragging thumbnails manually.

To create a Smart Collection:

1. Click the tab for the Collections panel. (If it's hidden, choose Window > Collections Panel.)

2. Perform a search via the Edit > Find command (see the preceding page). When the search is completed, click the **Save as Smart Collection** button ![icon] at the top of the Content panel. **A**

3. A new Smart Collection icon ![icon] appears in the Collections panel. Type a name in the highlighted field, then press Enter/Return. **B**

➤ To add a collection to the Favorites panel, right-click the icon and choose Add to Favorites.

➤ To delete a collection, click it, click the Delete Collection button, ![icon] then click Yes if an alert dialog appears (this won't delete the actual files).

To display the contents of a collection:

In the Collections panel, click the icon or name of a Smart Collection. ![icon]

If you run a new search for an existing Smart Collection using different criteria, the contents of the collection will update automatically (this is what makes it "smart").

To edit a Smart Collection:

1. In the Collections panel, click the icon for an existing Smart Collection. ![icon]

2. At the top of the Content panel or in the lower-left corner of the Collections panel, click the **Edit Smart Collection** button. ![icon] **C**

3. The Edit Smart Collection dialog opens. It looks just like the Find dialog, which is shown on the preceding page. To add another criterion, click the next ⊕ button, choose and enter data, and choose "If any criteria are met" from the Match menu. You can also change the source folder and/or change or eliminate the original criteria.

4. Click Save. The results of the new search will display in the Content panel.

Note: If you move a thumbnail from a Smart Collection (or move the actual file) into a folder that wasn't used in the search, it will be removed from the collection, but not from your hard disk. If you delete a thumbnail from a Smart Collection, on the other hand — *watch out!* — the actual file will be deleted from your hard disk!

A *To create a Smart Collection, use the Find command, then click the Save as Smart Collection button in the Content panel.*

B *A new Smart Collection icon appears in the Collections panel. Type a name for it in the field.*

C *To edit a Smart Collection, click its icon in the Collections panel, then click the Edit Smart Collection button.*

You can also create a standard, "nonsmart" collection without running a search first.

To create a standard collection:

1. Do either of the following:

   On the Content panel, select the image thumbnails to be put into a collection. In the **Collections** panel, click the **New Collection** button, then click Yes in the alert dialog.

   While viewing some thumbnails in **Review mode** (Ctrl-B/Cmd-B), drag any files you don't want to include in the collection out of the carousel, then click the **New Collection** button.

2. Type a name in the highlighted field in the Collection panel. **A** The number of thumbnails the collection contains is listed next to the name.

To add thumbnails to a standard collection:

1. Display the Collections panel.

2. Drag one or more thumbnails from the Content panel over a standard collection icon. **B**

➤ You can copy and paste, or drag, thumbnails from a Smart Collection into a standard one, or from one standard collection into another. You can't drag thumbnails into a Smart Collection.

To remove thumbnails from a standard collection:

1. On the Collections panel, click the icon for a standard collection to display its contents.

2. Select the thumbnails to be removed, then click **Remove from Collection** at the top of the Content panel. **C**

If you rename a file in Explorer/Finder or move a file from its original location on disk, it may be listed as missing from any standard collections it is a part of, and Bridge will try to relink it to those collections. If Bridge is unsuccessful, do as follows.

To relink a missing file to a standard collection:

1. On the Collections panel, click the collection to which you need to relink one or more files.

2. At the top of the Content panel, click **Fix.D**

3. In the Find Missing Files dialog, click Browse, click the missing file (the name is listed at the top of the dialog), click Open, then click OK.

A *To create a standard collection, click the New Collection button, then type a name.*

B *Drag thumbnails to a standard collection listing.*

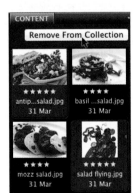

C *To remove one or more selected thumbnails from the currently displayed collection, click Remove from Collection.*

D *To relink a file that's missing from a collection, click Fix.*

Using the powerful and wide-ranging controls in the Adobe Camera Raw plug-in, you can apply corrections to your photos before opening them into Photoshop. In this comprehensive chapter, you'll learn about the Camera Raw tools and tabs; choose workflow options for Camera Raw; apply cropping and straightening; and correct photos for defects, such as poor contrast, under- or overexposure, color casts, blurriness, geometric distortion, and noise. You will also learn how to enhance your photos with special effects, such as a vignette, grain texture, or tint; retouch blemishes; access Camera Raw controls from Photoshop; save and synchronize Camera Raw settings among related photos; then finally, open your corrected photos into Photoshop.

Note: The Camera Raw plug-in, which we refer to simply as "Camera Raw," is included with Photoshop. Some users also refer to the plug-in as "ACR," short for Adobe Camera Raw.

Why use Camera Raw?

Amateur-level digital cameras store images in the JPEG or TIFF format, whereas advanced amateur and pro models offer the option to save images as raw data files, which offers substantial advantages. Cameras apply internal processing to photos that are captured as JPEG or TIFF, such as sharpening, automatic color adjustments, and a white balance setting. With raw files, you get only the original raw information that the lens captured onto the camera's digital sensor, leaving you with full control over subsequent image processing and correction.

These are some basic facts about Camera Raw:

➤ Camera Raw can process raw, TIFF, and JPEG photos from most digital camera models.

➤ Camera Raw offers powerful controls for correcting problems in your photos, such as over- and underexposure and color casts, and for applying enhancements, such as a vignette or a grain texture.

➤ Camera Raw saves edits to TIFF and JPEG files in the file itself, whereas edits to raw files are saved as instructions (in a separate "sidecar" file or in the Camera Raw database). When you open a photo from Camera Raw into Photoshop, the instructions are applied to a copy of the file, and the original raw file is preserved.

➤ To any image layer in Photoshop, you can apply some Camera Raw features via the Filter > Camera Raw Filter command.

IN THIS CHAPTER

More reasons to use Camera Raw

In case you're not fully sold on the benefits of correcting your digital photos in Camera Raw before opening them into Photoshop, consider these points:

Ability to preview raw files: The only way to preview a raw photo is in Camera Raw (or other software that converts raw files). Note: The photo that you view on the LCD screen of your digital camera is merely a JPEG preview of the raw capture, not the "actual" raw capture.

Great correction features: Camera Raw offers many unique adjustment controls that you simply won't find in Photoshop.

Less destructive edits: When applying corrections to a photo, the goal is to preserve as much of the image quality as possible. Adjustments that you make to a photo in Camera Raw (and that are applied automatically when the photo is opened in Photoshop) cause less data loss than similar adjustment commands in Photoshop.

Preserves 16 bits per channel: To preserve more of the original pixel data in a raw photo, Camera Raw keeps the bit depth as 16 bits per channel. This helps offset the data loss from subsequent image edits in Photoshop, and results in a better-quality photo.

Tonal redistribution: The sensor in a digital camera captures and records the existing range of tonal values in a scene as is, in a linear fashion, without skewing the data toward a particular tonal range.**A** That sounds fine on paper, but the reality is that the human eye is more sensitive to lower light levels than to higher light levels. In other words, we're more likely to notice if shadow areas lack detail and less likely to notice extra details in highlight areas. The result is that digital photos typically contain more data than necessary for the highlight values in a scene and insufficient data for the lower midtone and shadow values. In a Camera Raw conversion, data is shifted more into the midtone and shadow ranges of your photo. This not only helps compensate for the peculiarities of human vision, but also helps prepare your photos for subsequent image edits in Photoshop.**B** If you apply tonal adjustments in Photoshop to a photo that contains insufficient shadow data, the result is posterization and a noticeable loss of detail; if you apply the same edits to a good-quality photo that has been converted in Camera Raw, the destructive edits will be far less noticeable.

Superior noise reduction and **sharpening:** Not to knock Photoshop, but the noise reduction and sharpening features in Camera Raw cause less data loss than similar features in Photoshop.

Learning the Camera Raw features will give you a head start: The tonal and color controls in Camera Raw are similar to many of the adjustment controls in Photoshop (e.g., Levels, Curves, and Hue/Saturation) that are discussed in later chapters. As you proceed through the lessons in this book, you will apply and build on the skills you have mastered in this chapter.

CAPTURING TONAL VALUES: YOUR CAMERA VERSUS THE HUMAN EYE

50% light value

50% light value

A *The digital sensor in a camera captures tonal values in a linear fashion, from light to dark, without altering the incoming data. A light value of 50% is located at the midpoint of the tonal range.*

B *Camera Raw redistributes some of the captured tonal values to the shadows and midtones, shifting the 50% light value past the midpoint. As a result, the lower tonal values — the range the human eye tends to be more sensitive to — contain more data.*

Raw, JPEG, or TIFF?

Unfortunately, Camera Raw can't correct deficiencies in digital JPEG and TIFF photos as fully as it can in raw photos, for several reasons. First, cameras reduce digital JPEG and TIFF photos to a bit depth of 8 bits per channel, and in so doing discard some of the captured pixels. Cameras save raw photos at a bit depth of 16 bits per channel, and preserve all the captured pixels.

Second, cameras apply color and tonal corrections to JPEGs and TIFFs (called "in-camera" processing). Camera Raw must reinterpret this processed data, with less successful results than when it has access to the raw, unprocessed data.

All of the above notwithstanding, if your camera doesn't shoot raw photos or you acquire JPEG or TIFF photos from other sources, you can still use practically all of the outstanding correction and adjustment features in Camera Raw to process them.

Note: In this chapter, we focus only on processing raw and JPEG files in Camera Raw — not TIFF files. The JPEG format is mentioned only when a particular feature treats a JPEG differently than a raw file.

➤ Factoid: Each digital camera manufacturer creates its own version of a raw file and attaches a different extension to the names of its raw files, such as .nef for Nikon and .crw or .cr2 for Canon.

KEEPING CAMERA RAW UP TO DATE ★

The easiest way to ensure that you are using the latest version of Camera Raw is to click the Creative Cloud icon 🔲 on your taskbar/menu bar, click Apps, then click any Update that is posted for Photoshop CC (2015) or Bridge CC.

JPEG …

JPEG advantages
➤ JPEG files have a smaller storage size than raw files, so your digital camera can store more of them.

➤ In sports, nature, and other fast-action photography, speed is a necessity. Photo sequences can be captured more rapidly as JPEG files (due to their smaller storage size) than as raw files.

➤ Most software programs can read JPEG files, but only a few programs can read raw files.

JPEG drawbacks
➤ The JPEG format discards some captured pixels due to its lower bit depth of 8 bits per channel.

➤ The JPEG compression methods destroy some image data and can produce defects, such as artifacts, banding, and loss of detail.

➤ The pixel data in JPEG photos is processed internally by the camera. Although Camera Raw can be used to improve your JPEG photos, it won't have access to the original pixel data (nor will you).

… COMPARED TO RAW

Raw advantages
➤ The raw compression methods are nondestructive.

➤ Raw files have a higher bit depth of 16 bits per channel.

➤ Raw files contain the original, unprocessed pixel data and full range of tonal levels that were captured by the camera. Camera Raw is given all that image data to work with, and the result is a higher-quality image — even after adjustments.

➤ Because the white point setting isn't applied to your raw photo (it's merely stored in the metadata of the file), you can adjust that setting at any time in Camera Raw.

➤ Camera Raw does a better job of redistributing tonal values in raw files than in JPEG files, making raw files better candidates for Photoshop edits.

Raw drawbacks
➤ Raw files have larger storage sizes than JPEG files.

➤ Digital cameras create and store raw files more slowly than JPEG files, a potential drawback in fast-action photography (although as camera technology improves, this may become less of an issue).

The bottom line
Despite the faster speed and smaller storage sizes of JPEG files, raw files have more advantages.

Opening photos into Camera Raw

For a smooth workflow, we recommend setting the proper preferences so your raw photos (and JPEG or TIFF photos, if any) will open directly into Camera Raw.

To set a preference so your raw photos open directly into Camera Raw:

1. In Photoshop, go to Edit/Photoshop CC > Preferences (Ctrl-K/Cmd-K) > **File Handling**.

2. Under File Compatibility, check **Prefer Adobe Camera Raw for Supported Raw Files**, then click OK. When you double-click a raw file, it will open into Camera Raw (as opposed to other software that can be used to convert raw files).

To set a preference so your JPEG or TIFF photos open directly into Camera Raw:

1. In Bridge, choose Edit/Adobe Bridge CC > **Camera Raw Preferences**.

2. At the bottom of the dialog, from the JPEG menu, choose **Automatically Open JPEGs with Settings**.

3. If you shoot digital TIFF photos, from the TIFF menu, choose **Automatically Open TIFFs with Settings**; or if you shoot only raw or JPEG photos (not TIFF photos), choose **Disable TIFF Support**.

4. Click OK.

   When you want to open a JPEG or TIFF photo into Camera Raw that has *not* yet been edited (doesn't have Camera Raw settings), click the thumbnail in Bridge, then click the **Open in Camera Raw** button ⬛ or press Ctrl-R/Cmd-R.

   To open a JPEG or TIFF photo that *has* been edited previously in Camera Raw (that is "with Settings"), double-click its thumbnail or press Ctrl-R/Cmd-R.

➤ If you enable both "Automatically Open" options (steps 2–3, above), but there is an occasion when you want to open a JPEG or TIFF photo directly into Photoshop instead of Camera Raw, click the thumbnail, then press Ctrl-O/Cmd-O. This shortcut will work only if the file hasn't yet been edited in Camera Raw.

➤ If the Open in Camera Raw button ⬛ is available when you click a thumbnail in Bridge, it's a sign that the file can be opened into Camera Raw.

You can set a preference to have either Bridge or Photoshop host the Camera Raw plug-in when you open a raw or JPEG photo. In the case of Photoshop, the program will launch, if it's not already running. Also, when Bridge is the host for Camera Raw, the default (highlighted) button for exiting that dialog is labeled Done, whereas when Photoshop is the host for Camera Raw, the default exit button is Open Image or Open Object, depending on a setting in the Workflow Options dialog (see step 10 on page 56).

To choose a host for Camera Raw:

1. In Bridge, choose Edit/Adobe Bridge CC > Preferences (Ctrl-K/Cmd-K), then show the **General** pane.

2. Check **Double-Click Edits Camera Raw Settings in Bridge** if you want Camera Raw to be hosted by Bridge when you double-click a thumbnail in Bridge (a raw photo or a JPEG that was previously edited in Camera Raw), or uncheck this option to have the file open into Camera Raw hosted by Photoshop. Click OK.

RECOGNIZING THE BADGE

In Bridge, the thumbnail for a file that has been opened and edited previously in Camera Raw will display this badge ⬛ in the upper-right corner, and the thumbnail and preview will reflect the current settings. Another clue: If the currently selected file has been edited in Camera Raw, you will see a Camera Raw category in the Metadata panel.

After setting the necessary preferences, and before learning the particulars of Camera Raw, you should familiarize yourself with this basic workflow.

To open a raw or JPEG digital photo into Camera Raw:

1. Launch Bridge, display the thumbnail for a raw or JPEG photo, then do either of the following:

   For a raw photo, double-click the thumbnail.

   For a raw or JPEG photo, click the thumbnail, then press Ctrl-R/Cmd-R or click the **Open in Camera Raw** button on the Bridge toolbar 🔘 (or right-click the photo and choose Open in Camera Raw).

2. The Camera Raw dialog opens.**A** An alert symbol 🔺 may display in the upper-right corner of the preview while Camera Raw reads in the image data, and will disappear when it's done.

   Information about your photo (taken from the metadata that was embedded into it by the camera) is listed in several locations: the camera model in the title bar at the top of the dialog; the file name below the preview; and the camera settings used to take the photo (aperture, shutter speed, ISO, and focal length) below the histogram.

The adjustment features are located in 10 tabs: Basic, Tone Curve, Detail, HSL/Grayscale, Split Toning, Lens Corrections, Effects, Camera Calibration, Presets, and Snapshots. Switch among the tabs to correct your photo (we cover most of the tabs in depth in this chapter).

3. When you're done correcting the photo, you can either click Open Image to open the photo into Photoshop or click Done to close Camera Raw without opening the photo. In either case, the Camera Raw settings will stick to the photo, and the original data will be preserved. (Note: If you want to open the photo into Photoshop as a Smart Object, see the Note on page 95.)

➤ The Camera Raw preview and interface supports high-DPI displays.★

A *The Camera Raw dialog*   *Toolbox*   *Toggle Full Screen Mode/previous dialog size (F)*

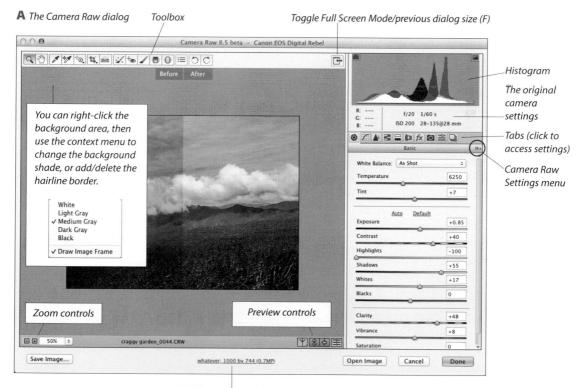

Histogram

The original camera settings

Tabs (click to access settings)

Camera Raw Settings menu

You can right-click the background area, then use the context menu to change the background shade, or add/delete the hairline border.

Zoom controls

Preview controls

Link to the Workflow Options dialog (see pages 56–58)

A file that you open from Camera Raw into Photoshop as a Smart Object can be reedited using the full array of features in Camera Raw at any time. A standard image layer in a Photoshop document can also be edited using most — but not all — of the Camera Raw features by way of the Camera Raw Filter, as described in the task below. If you convert the image layer to a Smart Object first (an optional step), you will be able to edit the filter settings at any time. Note: To learn about layers, which are used in this task, see Chapter 8. To learn more about Smart Objects, see pages 272–283. See also the first Note on page 95.

Among the Camera Raw features that aren't available via the Camera Raw Filter are the Crop and Straighten tools, the rotate buttons, the Workflow Options dialog, the Snapshots tab, and some options on the Camera Raw Settings menu. Don't be dissuaded by this list of "nos," however — the filter gives you access to the essential Camera Raw features.

To open and edit a Photoshop image layer in Camera Raw:

1. In an RGB document in Photoshop, display the Layers panel. Click the image layer (or the Background) that you want to edit in Camera Raw, then press Ctrl-J/Cmd-J to duplicate it. Keep the duplicate layer selected. **A**

2. *Optional (but recommended):* To keep your Camera Raw settings editable, choose Filter > Convert for Smart Filters, or right-click the duplicate image layer and choose Convert to Smart Object. **B** If an alert dialog appears, click OK.

3. With the image layer or Smart Object selected, choose Filter > **Camera Raw Filter** (Ctrl-Shift-A/ Cmd-Shift-A).

4. The image layer opens in Camera Raw. Apply the needed corrections.

5. Click OK (a progress bar may display while the filter is processing).

6. If you applied the filter to a Smart Object, on the Layers panel, you will see a Camera Raw Filter listing below a Smart Filters listing. **C** To edit the Camera Raw settings at any time, double-click the Camera Raw Filter listing. To learn more about Smart Filters, see pages 374–378.

➤ To create a document via the Merge to HDR Pro command, and adjust the new document via the Camera Raw Filter, see pages 254–258.

CAMERA RAW FILTER OR PHOTOSHOP?

Although we sing the praises of Camera Raw in the first two pages of this chapter and strongly recommend using it as a first step before opening a photo into Photoshop, Photoshop is no slouch when it comes to adjustment options. In fact, Photoshop has some commands and features that you won't find in Camera Raw, such as adjustment layers. You can easily hide, show, clip, or restack any adjustment layer; edit its layer mask; and change its opacity or blending mode (see Chapter 12). Fortunately, you don't have to decide between Camera Raw and Photoshop — you can use both!

A *We duplicated an image layer.*

B *We converted the duplicate layer to a Smart Object.*

C *We applied the Camera Raw Filter to the Smart Object. A Smart Filters listing appeared below the Smart Object.*

The Camera Raw tools A

In the upper-left corner of the dialog, click the **Zoom** tool, then click the image preview to zoom in or Alt-click/Option-click it to zoom out. Or right-click with the Zoom tool on the preview, check **Scrubby Zoom** on the context menu, then drag to the right to zoom in or to the left to zoom out. ★

Use the **Hand** tool to move a magnified preview image in the window (if another tool is selected, hold down the Spacebar for a temporary Hand tool).

For the **White Balance** tool, see the sidebar on page 60.

Choose the **Color Sampler** tool, then click in the image preview to place up to nine samplers. A breakdown of the RGB components below each sampler in the photo displays in a readout below the toolbox; the readouts will update as you make color and tonal adjustments. To reposition a sampler, drag it with the Color Sampler tool. To remove a sampler, hold down Alt/Option and click it. To remove all samplers, click Clear Samplers.

For the **Targeted Adjustment** tool (or TAT for short), see pages 66–67 and 71.

For the **Crop** tool, see page 54.

For the **Straighten** tool, see page 55.

For the **Spot Removal** tool, see pages 90–91.

The **Red Eye Removal** tool works like the Red Eye tool in Photoshop (see page 317).

For the **Adjustment Brush** tool, see pages 72–76.

For the **Graduated Filter** tool, see pages 86–87.

For the **Radial Filter** tool, see pages 88–89.

Note: If tool settings are displaying on the right side of the Camera Raw dialog (if, say, you were using the Adjustment Brush tool) and you want to redisplay the row of tab icons, click one of the first seven tools.

➤ The tools in Camera Raw are "memory-loaded," meaning that you can toggle them. Press a tool shortcut to select a different tool, then press the same key again to return to the original tool.

Other buttons at the top of the dialog:

➤ The **Open Preferences Dialog** button (or press Ctrl-K/Cmd-K) opens the Camera Raw Preferences dialog.

➤ The **Rotate 90° Counterclockwise** button and the **Rotate 90° Clockwise** button rotate the image. The results preview in the dialog.

MORE WAYS TO ZOOM IN THE PREVIEW

➤ Hold down Alt/Option-Spacebar and click to zoom out, or hold down Ctrl/Cmd-Spacebar and click to zoom in.

➤ Press Ctrl –/Cmd – (hyphen) to zoom out or Ctrl-+/Cmd-+ to zoom in.

➤ Use the zoom buttons (– or +) or the Zoom Level menu, located below the image preview.

➤ Double-click the Zoom tool to set the zoom level to 100%.

➤ Double-click the Hand tool to fit the image in the preview window.

H *Hand: Moves a magnified preview in the window*

S *Color Sampler: Places up to nine RGB color sampler points in the preview*

A *Straighten: Straightens the photo along a line you drag*

E *Red Eye Removal: Corrects red-eye in a portrait photo*

Graduated Filter **G** *and Radial Filter* **J** *tools: Apply edits gradually across an area that you designate*

L *Rotates the image 90° counterclockwise*

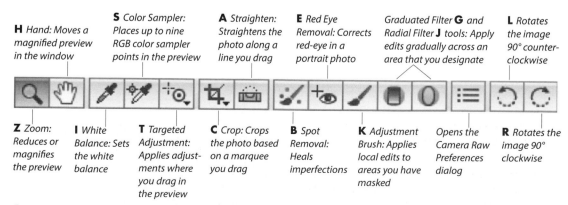

Z *Zoom: Reduces or magnifies the preview*

I *White Balance: Sets the white balance*

T *Targeted Adjustment: Applies adjustments where you drag in the preview*

C *Crop: Crops the photo based on a marquee you drag*

B *Spot Removal: Heals imperfections*

K *Adjustment Brush: Applies local edits to areas you have masked*

Opens the Camera Raw Preferences dialog

R *Rotates the image 90° clockwise*

A *The shortcuts for the Camera Raw tools are listed in boldface above.*

Cropping and straightening photos

With the Crop and Straighten tools, you can control which portion of a photo opens into Photoshop. You can readjust the crop box at any time without losing any image data, and the outlying areas will remain available even after you click Save, Done, or Open.

To crop a photo:

1. Open a photo into Camera Raw **A** (see step 1 on page 51).

2. Choose the **Crop** tool (C).

3. Drag in the preview to make a crop box appear.**B**

4. *Optional:* To move the crop box, drag inside it. To resize the box, drag a handle.

5. To preview the results of the Crop tool, press Enter/Return or click any tool except the Crop or Straighten tool.**C**

➤ To redisplay the current crop box after exiting crop mode, click the Crop tool. If you want to remove the box and redisplay the whole image, press Esc.

A *This is the original photo, in Camera Raw.*

B *With the Crop tool, we drew a crop box in the preview window. Here, we are resizing the box.*

C *We pressed Enter/Return to preview the results.*

To straighten a crooked photo automatically:

1. Open a photo into Camera Raw, then double-click the **Straighten** tool (A); or choose the Straighten tool, then double-click anywhere in the image.

2. Press Enter/Return.

➤ To turn the Crop tool into a temporary Straighten tool, hold down Ctrl/Cmd.

To straighten a crooked photo manually:

1. Open a photo into Camera Raw, then choose the **Straighten** tool (A).

2. Drag along an edge in the photo that you want to align to the horizontal or vertical axis.**A** A crop box will display, aligned to the angle you drew.**B**

3. To preview the straighten results, press Enter/Return.**C**

➤ To change the straighten results after exiting crop mode, choose the Straighten tool (A), then drag again.

➤ If you want to remove the crop box, choose the Crop tool (C), then press Esc.

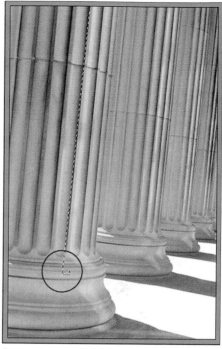

A With the Straighten tool, we are dragging along an edge that we want to align to the vertical axis.

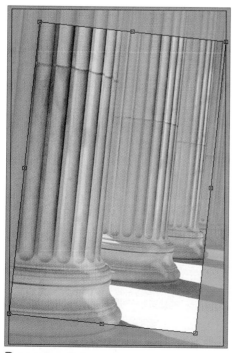

B A crop box displays.

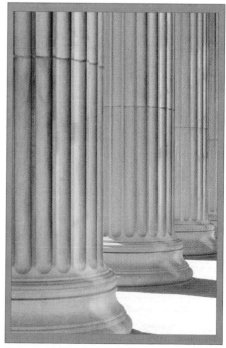

C We pressed Enter/Return to preview the results.

Choosing default workflow options

Via the Workflow Options dialog, you can resize or sharpen a photo, or change its color space or bit depth, before opening it into Photoshop — the original raw or JPEG file isn't altered. Note that the choices that you make in this dialog become the new default settings, so they apply not only to the current photo, but also to subsequent photos that you open into Camera Raw. The dialog contains new Color Space and Preset options (see this page and the next), as well as Image Sizing options (see page 58).

To choose settings in the Workflow Options dialog:

1. Open a photo into Camera Raw, then below the large image preview, click the underlined link. The **Workflow Options** dialog opens (**A**, next page).

2. If you want to apply a user-saved preset, choose it from the **Preset** menu (**B**, next page). Next, either click OK to exit the dialog, or choose custom options, as in the remaining steps.

3. From the **Space** menu, choose a color profile to be used for converting the raw file to RGB: Adobe RGB (1998), ColorMatch RGB, ProPhoto RGB, or sRGB IEC61966-2.1 (or "sRGB," for short). The menu also lists preset RGB and CMYK output profiles for printers and displays, as well as any other profiles that you have installed in your system. In Chapter 1, you assigned Adobe RGB (1998) as the default color space for color management, so for optimal color consistency, we recommend also choosing that option here.

4. The **Intent** options control how colors will change in a photo when it is converted to the chosen profile. If you chose any profile from the Space menu except one of the first five, from the Intent menu, choose Perceptual or Relative. If your photos tend to contain many colors that are outside the gamut of the chosen color space, Perceptual is the best choice because it attempts to preserve the appearance of colors as it shifts them into gamut. If your photos contain few colors that are out of gamut, Relative is the best choice, as it preserves more of the original colors. Your photo will display as a soft proof (a simulation of print output from your target device).

5. To control the amount of color and tonal information in your photos, from the **Depth** menu, choose 8 Bits/Channel or 16 Bits/Channel. If you choose 16 Bits/Channel, more of the original capture information will be preserved in your photos as you edit them in Photoshop, but they will also have a larger file size and will require a large hard disk and a fast system with a lot of RAM for processing (see page 17).

6. If you chose a printer profile, check **Simulate Paper & Ink** to preview the photo using the range of black values that can be produced by that printer, on a simulation of white printing paper.

7. In a standard workflow, you can keep Resize to Fit unchecked. If, on the other hand, you need to resize the current photo and other photos that you open into Camera Raw, keep the dialog open after step 12, and follow the task on page 58.

8. Camera Raw applies a **Resolution** of 300 ppi to all photos as they are opened into Photoshop. If needed, you can choose a different value here.

9. *Optional:* Use options under Output Sharpening to apply predefined sharpening. Check Sharpen For, then from the Sharpen For menu, choose an output medium of Screen, Glossy Paper, or Matte Paper; and from the Amount menu, choose the desired level of sharpening (Standard is a good all-purpose choice).

   ➤ The sharpening values that Camera Raw applies via this dialog aren't listed anywhere. If you want to control specific values when sharpening, uncheck Sharpen For and use the sliders in the Detail tab (see pages 68–69).

10. The **Open in Photoshop as Smart Objects** option converts the Open Image button in the main Camera Raw dialog to an Open Object button, which opens your photo into Photoshop as a Smart Object.

    ➤ If you leave this workflow option unchecked, you can convert the Open Image button to Open Object in the main Camera Raw dialog (for any photo) by holding down Shift. Learn about Smart Objects on pages 272–283.

11. *Optional:* To save your current, custom Workflow Options settings as a preset that can be applied to any photo, from the Preset menu, choose New Workflow Preset. Enter a descriptive name for the preset, then click OK.

12. *Optional:* If you chose a preset and then changed any of the settings in the dialog, the word "(edited)" is now listed in the preset name. If you want to permanently update the current preset with your new custom settings, from the Preset menu, choose Update [preset name].

13. Click OK. Your chosen workflow settings will be applied to the current photo and to all photos that you subsequently open into Camera Raw.

➤ To rename a user-saved Workflow Options preset, from the Preset menu in the dialog, choose the preset to be renamed, choose Rename [preset name], type the desired name, then click OK.

A *Via the Workflow Options dialog, you can choose Preset, Color Space, Image Sizing, and Output Sharpening settings for the current and future photos.*

USING THE GAMUT WARNING BUTTON IN THE CAMERA RAW HISTOGRAM

If you choose a printer profile from the Space menu in the Workflow Options dialog, instead of two clipping warning buttons on the histogram in the main Camera Raw dialog, you will see just one **Gamut Warning** button ▣ (O). When this button is activated, areas of the photo that are outside the gamut of the chosen output device will display as red in the preview. If you need to bring those errant colors back into gamut, you can use either the Vibrance slider in the Basic tab or the Saturation sliders in the HSL/Grayscale tab.

QUICK AND EASY WAY TO APPLY A WORKFLOW OPTIONS PRESET

To apply a Workflow Options preset to a photo, instead of opening the Workflow Options dialog, right-click the link below the preview in the main Camera Raw dialog and choose a preset name from the context menu.

B *From the Preset menu in the Workflow Options dialog, you can choose a user-saved workflow preset.*

If you need to resize multiple photos according to a specific criterion, such as the dimension of a long or short side of one of the photos, use the Resize to Fit feature in the Workflow Options dialog. If you don't require the original high-megapixel count of your photos for image editing or output, shrinking them is an acceptable option. Enlarging photos, on the other hand, should be done only when necessary, as it diminishes their quality (preferably, don't enlarge your photos by more than 25% or 30%).

Note: To resize or change the resolution of an individual photo for a particular output medium, instead of using the options dialog in Camera Raw, we recommend using the Image Size dialog in Photoshop after you exit Camera Raw (see pages 138–141). The latter offers many image resizing options, including choices for resampling, with a document preview.

To resize images via the Workflow Options dialog:

1. Open one or more photos into Camera Raw, then click the Workflow Options link. Under Image Sizing, check **Resize to Fit**.

2. *Optional:* Check Don't Enlarge if you want to prevent your photos from being enlarged.

3. Under Image Sizing, from the **Resize to Fit** menu, **A** do one of the following (Camera Raw will resize all your photos proportionately, whether or not you enter proportionate values):

   Choose **Width & Height**, then enter the desired maximum W and H values within which the current and future photos will be resized. For resizing to occur, both of these values must be either larger or smaller than the original dimensions of the current photo.

   Choose **Dimensions**, **B** then enter the desired maximum values in the two fields within which Camera Raw will resize your photos. Camera Raw will fit the longer dimension of each photo to the larger of the two values (regardless of the orientation of the photo). You could use this option to resize a series of horizontal or vertical photos to the same long dimension.

   ➤ If the Width & Height or Dimensions option produces unexpected resizing results in your photos, try entering the same value in both fields, thereby providing a larger resizing area, or use the Long Side or Short Side option instead (see the next option).

Choose **Long Side** or **Short Side**, then enter the desired value for that dimension.

Choose **Megapixels**, then enter the desired total pixel count value. All photos will be resized to that value.

Choose **Percentage**, then enter a percentage by which you want your photos to be resized (preferably, less than 130%, and not more).

➤ When you use the Resize to Fit option, the new dimensions and megapixel (MP) count are listed in the right side of the Image Sizing area. If you want to learn the original dimensions of the current photo, uncheck Resize to Fit; the original dimensions will display in the dimmed W and H fields; now recheck the box.

4. Click OK. Note: Because the current settings in the Workflow Options dialog are applied to all photos that you open into Camera Raw, after using the dialog to resize the desired photos, exit Camera Raw. Upon reopening Camera Raw, be sure to open the Workflow Options dialog and uncheck Resize to Fit.

A *From the Resize to Fit menu in the Workflow Options dialog, choose a criterion for resizing your photos.*

B *If you choose Dimensions as the Resize to Fit option, you must then enter pixel values in the two fields below the menu.*

Using the Camera Raw tabs

Tone Curve · HSL/Grayscale · Lens Corrections · Presets · Snapshots

Basic · Detail · Split Toning · Effects · Camera Calibration

The Camera Raw tabs

To access a panel of related settings in Camera Raw, click one of the tab icons (shown above). We perform most of our work in the first four tabs, and recommend that you do the same. Use the other tabs for specialty corrections or enhancements, as needed.

Basic: Adjust the white balance and exposure (see pages 61–65).

Tone Curve: Fine-tune a specific tonal range, such as the upper or lower midtones (see pages 66–67).

Detail: Apply capture sharpening and reduce unwanted noise (see pages 68–69).

HSL/Grayscale: Adjust the hue, saturation, and luminance of individual colors (see pages 70–71).

Split Toning: Apply one color tint to the highlight areas of a photo and a second tint to the shadow areas (see page 77).

Lens Corrections: Correct a photo for the effects of lens distortion, such as geometric distortion (e.g., a building that is tilted backward or isn't level), under- or overexposure at the edges (an unwanted vignette), chromatic aberration, and color fringes.

Effects: As a special effect, apply a grain texture, a vignette, or a dehaze correction (see pages 82–85).

Camera Calibration: The Process menu in this tab lets you update a file to the latest Camera Raw processing (see the sidebar on the next page). If the profile that Camera Raw provides for your camera model doesn't produce satisfactory color results, use the sliders in this tab to tweak the settings manually.

Presets: Create a custom preset of the current Camera Raw settings for future application to any other photos (see page 92).

Snapshots: For flexibility in editing, save interim versions of a photo as you make corrections. When necessary, you can restore the photo to any snapshot version (see the sidebar on page 92).

If you find a need to undo or reset your slider settings as you work in Camera Raw, you can use any of the methods below. (To learn about related options on the Camera Raw Settings menu, see the next page.)

To restore default settings to sliders in the Camera Raw tabs:

Do any of the following:

Double-click a slider to reset it to its default value (usually 0).

Shift-double-click a slider in the Basic tab to reset it to the **Auto** value.

Click **Default** in the Basic or HSL/Grayscale tab to reset all the sliders in just that tab to 0.

Hold down Alt/Option and click **Reset** at the bottom of the dialog (Cancel becomes Reset) to restore the settings, in all tabs, that were in effect when you opened the dialog.

When you open a photo into Camera Raw, by default, it's adjusted according to the built-in profile for your camera model, and all the sliders in the Basic tab are set to 0. At any time, you can assign a different collection of settings to your file, or restore the original settings.

To restore settings via the Camera Raw Settings menu:

From the Camera Raw Settings menu, ▤ ▦ choose one of these options: **A**

Image Settings to restore the settings that were attached to the file during the initial photo shoot or, if the photo was previously edited in Camera Raw, from the last Camera Raw session. When a photo is opened for the first time into Camera Raw, these settings will match the Camera Raw Defaults settings.

Camera Raw Defaults to remove all custom settings and reapply the default settings for your camera model, your specific camera, or the ISO setting that was used to take the photo.

Previous Conversion to apply the settings from the prior image that was adjusted in Camera Raw.

Custom Settings to reapply the custom settings that you have chosen since opening the photo into Camera Raw.

If a **user-saved preset** is applied to the current photo, that preset will also be listed as an option on this menu (see page 92).

TOGGLING THE DEFAULT SETTINGS FOR A TAB

To quickly toggle between any **custom** settings made via the current tab only and the **Camera Raw Default** settings for that tab, click the rightmost button below the preview ▤ (Ctrl-Alt-P/Cmd-Option-P). If the photo is displayed in a divided preview, the default settings will display in just the "After" section.

A Use options on the Camera Raw Settings menu to restore default settings to your photo or to reapply the prior settings.

UPDATING LEGACY PHOTOS AND THE CAMERA RAW SLIDERS

When you bring an unprocessed photo into Camera Raw 9.x, the dialog uses its most up-to-date profiles for noise reduction, de-mosaicing, sharpening, color calibration, and other processing. If you want to update a raw photo that was already processed in Camera Raw 6 or earlier using the new profiles, and also update the sliders in the Basic and other tabs to the newest versions (as described in this chapter), before applying any custom adjustments, click the Update to Current Process (2012) ⚠ icon at the bottom right of the preview window. The Process menu in the **Camera Calibration tab** ⬛ changes to the setting of 2012 (**Current**). Note: If you want to preserve access to the older rendering of the photo, take a snapshot of it before you update it (see the sidebar on page 92).

SETTING THE WHITE BALANCE

The color temperature of the lighting in which a photo is shot, whether natural or artificial, influences the relative amounts of red, green, and blue that are recorded by the camera. A digital camera attempts to balance the three colors to produce an accurate white, which in turn makes other colors in the photo more accurate; this is called the "white balance."

There are a few ways to adjust the white balance of a photo in Camera Raw. Note: Before adjusting the white balance, make sure your display is properly calibrated.

▶ Our recommended method is to drag the **Temperature** and **Tint** sliders in the Basic tab, choosing settings based on how the photo looks to your eye (see the next page).

▶ For photos that are shot in controlled lighting, such as in a studio, another method is to use the **White Balance tool** ✐ (I). Drag (don't click) to define a rectangle on a medium to light gray area of the photo—if you can find one. Camera Raw will set the White Balance based on pixel values in the sampled area. Note that although the White Balance tool is improved, sampling a larger area of "nearly gray" pixels than before, the resulting color temperature and tint correction may still not be adequate, and may need further adjustment.

▶ Here's an iffy, but quick, method: Shift-double-click the Temperature slider, and Shift-double-click the Tint slider. Camera Raw will apply auto settings for those controls.

Using the Basic tab

As its name implies, the Basic tab contains the most essential correction features of Camera Raw — and it displays first, by default, when you open the dialog. We have divided the use of this tab into several tasks, beginning with setting the White Balance, on this page, then proceeding through exposure, contrast, and saturation adjustments, on pages 62–65.

To apply white balance adjustments via the Basic tab:

1. With a photo open in Camera Raw, click the **Basic** tab. 🔄 **A** If the whole photo isn't visible in the preview, double-click the Hand tool 🖑 in the toolbox.

2. Do either of the following:

   From the **White Balance** menu, choose a preset that best describes the lighting conditions in which the photo was taken, such as Daylight or Shade. (Choose As Shot, if needed, to restore the original camera settings. Note that only As Shot and Custom are available for JPEG and TIFF files.)

   Lower the **Temperature** value to add blue and make the image look cooler, **B** or raise it to add yellow and make the image look warmer. **C** To fine-tune the temperature correction, move the **Tint** slider slightly to the left to add a bit of green or to the right to add magenta. (The White Balance menu setting changes to Custom, to indicate that you have chosen manual settings.)

A When a photo is opened for the first time into Camera Raw, the White Balance menu in the Basic tab is set to As Shot. This photo has a high Temperature value and looks too warm (yellowish).

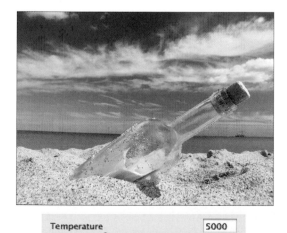

B We lowered the Temperature value too much. Now the photo looks too cool (has a bluish cast).

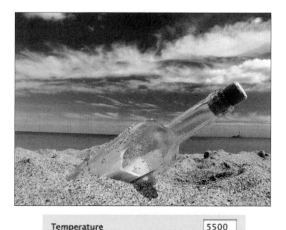

C A Temperature value of 5500 strikes a good balance between warm and cool.

On the histogram in the Camera Raw dialog, the red, green, and blue areas represent the three color channels in a photo, and the white areas represent the areas where those three colors overlap. Clipping, the shifting of tonal values to absolute black or white in a photo, occurs if the tonal range of a scene is wider than the range that can be captured by the camera. You can tell that pixels are clipped in a photo if the vertical bars are primarily clustered in taller peaks at one or both ends of the histogram (shadow pixels on the left, highlight pixels on the right). You can also drag in the histogram to apply tonal adjustments.

As you make slider adjustments in Camera Raw, your goal is to bring the pixels into the range of your chosen RGB color space and minimize clipping. When tonal values are redistributed, the histogram updates accordingly. Note: Remember, we recommended that you choose Adobe RGB as the color space both for your camera (see page 5) and for photos that you open into Camera Raw (see page 56).

To turn on the histogram clipping warnings for the preview:

In the top-left corner of the histogram, click the **Shadow Clipping Warning** button (U); **A** clipped shadows display in the preview as blue. In the top-right corner, click the **Highlight Clipping Warning** button (O); clipped highlights display in the preview as red. (When a button is activated, it has a white border.)

In the two tasks that follow this one, we show you how to use a number of sliders in the Basic tab. Once you learn the function of the sliders, remember that you can also make adjustments by dragging in the histogram, as described here.

To make tonal edits via the histogram:

1. In Camera Raw, display the Basic tab,⑤ then roll over the histogram. **A** As you move the pointer, one of five vertical gray drag zones will appear. The drag zone, as well as the data in the info area below the histogram, corresponds to one of these five sliders: **Blacks**, **Shadows**, **Exposure**, **Highlights**, or **Whites**.

2. Drag horizontally in a drag zone to adjust that tonal range; the corresponding slider will shift accordingly. **B**

Use the middle batch of sliders in the Basic tab to apply tonal corrections to your photo, preferably in the order listed in the dialog (there's a logic to their sequence). At first, all the sliders are set to 0 and the underlined word "Default" is dimmed.

To apply exposure and contrast adjustments via the Basic tab:

1. Turn on the Clipping Warning buttons.

2. Use the **Exposure** slider to lighten or darken the entire photo, as needed.

3. Use the **Contrast** slider to increase or reduce the color intensity and tonal contrast (**A–B**, next page).

Instructions continue on page 64

A *When we rolled over an area of the histogram, a drag zone appeared, and the corresponding Basic slider name and setting appeared in the info area.*

B *When we positioned our pointer within the drag zone for the Shadows range in the histogram, then dragged horizontally, the corresponding Shadows slider in the Basic tab shifted accordingly.*

A This original photo was underexposed (too dark), causing the colors to look dull. The blue warning color in the preview indicates the shadow areas in the photo that are clipped.

B Our first goal is to lighten the overall photo and recover details in the midtones and shadows without washing out the highlights. In the Basic tab, we increased the Exposure value,* then increased the Contrast value to intensify the highlights, shadows, and color saturation. We're not concerned that the photo is still too dark, as it can be lightened with further adjustments.

	Auto	Default	
Exposure			+0.60
Contrast			+25
Highlights			0
Shadows			0
Whites			0
Blacks			0
Clarity			0
Vibrance			0
Saturation			0

*We chose an Exposure value of +0.60 for the raw version of this photo. If you are working with the JPEG version that we have supplied for downloading, use an Exposure value of +0.80 instead.

4. If you increased the contrast, the highlights and shadows probably now need to be adjusted:

To restore details in the highlights, move the **Highlights** slider to the left until only a smidgen remains of the red highlight warning color.

To restore details in the shadows, move the **Shadows** slider to the right until only a smidgen remains of the blue shadow warning color.**A** Or if you need to darken the shadows, move this slider to the left.

5. Now that details have been restored to the midtones and highlights, you're ready to adjust the whites and blacks:

Increase the **Whites** value to brighten the white areas in the photo. This slider also has the effect of lightening the upper midtones and brightening the colors.

Use the **Blacks** slider to lighten or darken the black areas (**A**, next page). This slider may also affect the color brightness.

➤ If the colors are now washed out as a result of your increasing the Whites or Blacks value, you could try increasing the Contrast value.

➤ To further adjust the tonal values in the midtones, see pages 66–67.

➤ To have Camera Raw set the Whites or Blacks value automatically, hold down Shift while double-clicking one of those sliders.

REMOVE CLIPPING IN THRESHOLD PREVIEW

To remove shadow clipping a different way, Alt-drag/ Option-drag the Shadows or Blacks slider. A **Threshold preview** displays (as shown below). Release the mouse when small amounts of color or black display in the white preview.

You can also Alt-drag/Option-drag the Exposure, Highlights, or Whites slider to display a Threshold preview for that adjustment. Release the mouse when only a smidgen of white displays in the black preview.

	Auto	Default	
Exposure			+0.60
Contrast			+25
Highlights			−100
Shadows			+50
Whites			0
Blacks			0

A We reduced the Highlights value to recover details in the sky and increased the Shadows value to recover details in the shadows and lower midtones. The colors and detail in the midtones, and the overall balance of lights and darks, are improved. However, reducing the Highlights value caused the white areas to look dull.

	Auto	Default	
Exposure			+0.60
Contrast			+25
Highlights			−100
Shadows			+50
Whites			+33
Blacks			+53

A *We increased the Whites value to lighten the upper midtones and brighten the whites, and increased the Blacks value to recover more details in the shadows. Overall, the brightness, as well as the colors, are much improved.*

To apply edge contrast and color saturation adjustments using the Basic tab:

1. To add depth by intensifying the edge contrast in the midtones, increase the **Clarity** value; or for a deliberate soft-focus effect (such as in a portrait or landscape), reduce the Clarity value.

2. Change the **Vibrance** value to adjust the color saturation.**B**

3. Turn off both clipping warnings by pressing U, then O.

➤ We recommend using the Vibrance slider instead of the Saturation slider to adjust color saturation because the former is less likely to cause oversaturation (and it protects skin tones), whereas the latter is more likely to cause oversaturation and highlight clipping. To view the effect of this, drag the Saturation slider to the far right.

Clarity	+22
Vibrance	+22
Saturation	0

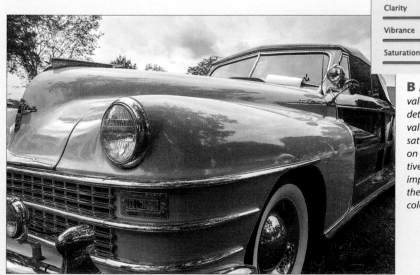

B *Finally, we increased the Clarity value slightly to sharpen the details and increased the Vibrance value slightly to boost the color saturation (note the change on the car body). Our cumulative adjustments to this photo improved the contrast, clarified the details, and produced richer color. Vroom, vroom!*

Using the Tone Curve tab

After using the Basic tab, a next logical step is to make a more refined adjustment of the upper and lower midtones, which we recommend doing individually via the Parametric sliders in the Tone Curve tab.

Note: We avoid manipulating the curve in the nested Point tab, because a misshapen curve can cause a photo to look posterized. The sliders in the Parametric tab don't cause this problem.

To apply tonal adjustments using the Parametric sliders in the Tone Curve tab:

1. With a photo open in Camera Raw, **A** click the **Tone Curve** tab, then the nested **Parametric** tab. Behind the curve you'll see a static display of the current histogram.

2. Do either of the following:

   If you have already adjusted the Highlights and Shadows sliders in the Basic tab, leave the Highlights or Shadows sliders in this tab alone and just tweak the upper and lower midtones using the **Lights** and **Darks** sliders. If you didn't adjust the Highlights and Shadows sliders in the Basic tab, you can use the sliders here to lighten or darken any individual tonal range: **Highlights**, **Lights** (upper midtones), **Darks** (lower midtones), or **Shadows**. As you move a slider, the

corresponding portion of the curve will be raised above or lowered below the diagonal line (**A–B**, next page).

Click the **Targeted Adjustment** tool (T). Drag within a tonal range of the photo that needs adjustment (**C**, next page). As you do this, the slider and curve that correspond to the tonal range under the pointer will move accordingly.

➤ To boost the contrast in a photo, try moving the Lights slider to the right and the Darks slider to the left.

3. To control the range of tonal values that are affected by the slider adjustments you made in the preceding step, move any of the region controls (located below the graph). The left region control affects the Shadows slider, the right region control affects the Highlights slider, and the middle region control affects both the Lights and Darks sliders (**D–E**, next page). Move a control to the left to raise the curve and lighten adjacent tonal ranges, or move a control to the right to lower the curve and darken adjacent tonal ranges.

➤ To use one shortcut to get to the nested Parametric tab in the Tone Curve tab and select the Targeted Adjustment tool, press Ctrl-Alt-Shift-T/Cmd-Option-Shift-T.

A In this photo, the midtones are too dark — few details are visible in those areas.

B *More details are now visible in the lightened midtones, such as on the sides of the buildings and on the side and surface of the canal. However, the sky looks a bit dull.*

A *To lighten the lower midtones, we increased the Darks value. This adjustment raised the middle of the curve.*

C *To lighten the upper midtones (and thereby brighten the clouds, sky, and trees), we dragged upward over a light midtone area with the Targeted Adjustment tool; the Lights value increased automatically.*

D *Finally, we moved the middle region control slightly to the right, which had the effect of increasing the contrast and lightening the sky.*

E *Now the tonal values in the image look just right.*

Using the Detail tab

Via the Sharpening sliders in the Detail tab, you can adjust the sharpness of your photo (a process called "capture" sharpening), and via the Noise Reduction sliders, you can reduce any unwanted color noise.

To sharpen a photo using the Detail tab:

1. Click the **Detail** tab **A** and choose a zoom level of 100%. In the preview, drag to reveal an area of the photo that has some detail (hold down the Spacebar for a temporary Hand tool).

   Note: If the words "Sharpening (Preview Only)" display at the top of the Detail tab, click the Open Preferences Dialog button ▤ in the toolbox. In the Camera Raw Preferences dialog, choose Apply Sharpening To: All Images, then click OK.

2. Under **Sharpening**, adjust the **Amount** value for the degree of edge definition. For subject matter that needs a lot of sharpening, such as hard-edged objects or buildings, try a value of 100; if less sharpening is needed, try a value of 50–60. (For a raw photo, the default Amount value is 25; for a JPEG photo, the default value is 0.)

   ➤ To better evaluate the Amount value via a grayscale preview, Alt-drag/Option-drag the slider.

3. Use the **Radius** slider to control how many pixels surrounding each sharpened edge are modified. We keep this value between 1 and 1.3.

4. Alt-drag/Option-drag the **Detail** slider slightly to the right to emphasize edge details and textures.

5. Alt-drag/Option-drag the **Masking** slider to around 50 to protect low-contrast areas with a black mask, and thereby sharpen only high-contrast areas.

All digital cameras produce some luminance (gray-scale) noise and color artifacts (randomly colored pixels). Although budget cameras tend to produce the most noise, it can also be produced by a high-end camera if it's used with a high ISO (light sensitivity) setting in a poorly lit scene. It's a good practice to remove as much noise from your photos as possible in Camera Raw, because it can become accentuated by image editing in Photoshop.

As you follow these steps, you'll discover that after you shift one slider, another slider will need adjusting.

To reduce luminance and color noise using the Detail tab:

1. With a photo open in Camera Raw (**A**, next page), click the **Detail** tab and choose a zoom level of 200–300% for the preview.

2. To reduce grayscale noise (graininess), increase the **Luminance** value (**B**, next page). Try a value between 20 and 70.

3. Increasing the Luminance can cause high-contrast edges in a photo to lose definition. To resharpen edges, raise the **Luminance Detail** value—but not so much that you reintroduce noise (**C**, next page).

   ➤ To move a different area of the photo into view, hold down the Spacebar and drag.

4. Raise the **Luminance Contrast** value to restore some edge contrast. The effect of this slider is most noticeable in photos that contain a lot of noise.

5. Color artifacts and random speckling tend to be most noticeable in solid-color areas of a photo (e.g., flat surfaces), especially in shadow areas. To reduce these defects in a raw photo, increase the **Color** value to around 40–50, depending on the subject matter (for a JPEG photo, which has a default Color value of 0, use a lower Color value).

6. Raising the Color value may lower the intensity of colors in areas of the photo that were poorly lit. To restore some saturation and intensity to those areas, increase the **Color Detail** value from the default value of 50 to around 75, or just until the color saturation looks good (**D**, next page).

7. To help reduce color mottling and artifacts in dark, low-contrast (low-frequency) areas of the photo, use the **Color Smoothness** slider.

8. Lower the zoom level for the preview to judge the overall effect of the Detail settings.

A These are the Sharpening controls in the Detail tab.

A *This is a close-up of a photo of a shop window (viewed at a zoom level of 300%), with the Noise Reduction: Luminance and Color sliders in the Detail tab set to 0 (no noise reduction applied). Grayscale noise is evident in the signage, and color artifacts are evident on the poorly lit interior surfaces behind the letters.*

B *To remove noise from the letters, we increased the Luminance value to 69, but this also diminished the edge definition.*

ANOTHER WAY TO REDUCE NOISE

To reduce noise in select areas via the **Adjustment Brush** tool and a mask, see pages 72–76.

C *To resharpen the edges of the letters, we increased the Luminance Detail value to 65.*

D *To remove color artifacts from the dark areas, we increased the Color value to 40; this also had the effect of desaturating the colors. To revive the colors and produce the final version of the image (shown at left), we increased the Color Detail value to 60.*

Using the HSL/Grayscale tab

Using the powerful sliders in the HSL/Grayscale tab, you can adjust the hue, saturation, and luminance of each color component of a photo individually.

To adjust individual colors via the HSL sliders:

1. Click the **HSL/Grayscale** tab, ▦ and double-click the Hand tool 🖑 to fit the image in the preview.**A**

2. Click the nested **Hue** tab. Move any slider to shift that color into adjacent hues, as shown in the bar. For example, you could shift the Greens slider toward yellow to make a landscape look warmer, or toward aqua to make it look cooler.

3. Click the **Saturation** tab. Move any slider to the left to desaturate that color (add gray to it) or to the right to make it more vivid (pure).**B–C** Avoid oversaturating the photo, to keep it looking realistic and so it stays printable.

➤ To make a bluish sky more vivid, increase the saturation of the Blues and Aquas. To make a sunset look warmer, increase the saturation of the Oranges or Yellows.

A In the original photo, the sky lacks contrast and the reds on the car body are slightly undersaturated.

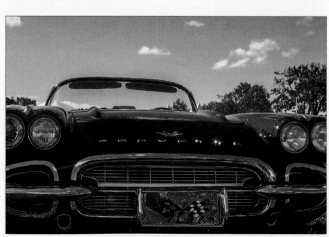

C The Saturation adjustments intensified the reds in the car (particularly in the upper midtones) and intensified the blues in the sky.

B In the nested Saturation tab of the HSL/Grayscale tab, we reduced the saturation of the Yellows and increased the saturation of the Reds and Blues.

4. Click the **Luminance** tab. **A–B** Move a slider to the left to darken that color (add black) or to the right to lighten it (add white). Avoid lightening any of the colors too much, to prevent the highlights from being clipped.

➤ For a more accurate rendering of your adjusted pixels, choose a zoom level of 66% or 100% for the Camera Raw preview.

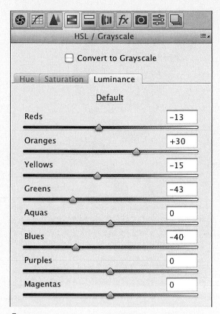

A *In the nested Luminance tab, we lightened the Oranges and darkened the Reds, Yellows, Greens, and Blues. (Tip: Reducing the Blues value can make a photo look as if it was shot with a polarizing filter on the camera.)*

B *Decreasing the luminance of the Blues darkened the colors in the sky, while decreasing the luminance of the Reds and increasing the luminance of the Oranges produced a brighter, richer red on the car body. Now the colors are equally intense in the upper and lower areas of the photo.*

USING THE TARGETED ADJUSTMENT TOOL

To apply local color adjustments to a photo, hold down Ctrl-Alt-Shift/Cmd-Option-Shift and press H, S, or L. The nested Hue, Saturation, or Luminance tab in the HSL/Grayscale tab displays and the Targeted Adjustment tool becomes selected. Drag upward or to the right over a color area to increase the slider values specifically for that area, or downward or to the left to decrease those values. The sliders that correspond to the color under the pointer will shift automatically.

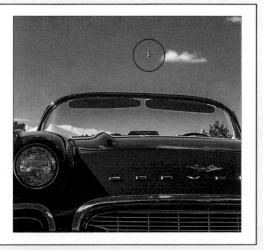

Using the Adjustment Brush tool

Unlike corrections that are made in the Camera Raw tabs, which apply to the overall photo, corrections made with the Adjustment Brush tool are "local" (affect specific areas of the photo). You apply a mask in the preview to define which areas are going to be affected by the adjustment, then you apply the correction via the sliders, including the Whites and Blacks sliders. ★ Use this tool after you have finished your broad, overall corrections, to fix a few specific areas or to accentuate some details. **A** Awesome feature!

To apply local edits with the Adjustment Brush tool:

1. After making adjustments in the Basic and Tone Curve tabs, click the **Adjustment Brush** tool 🖌 (K). The sliders for the tool display (some are like the sliders in the Basic tab).

2. Click the + or − button for any slider to "zero out" all the sliders except the one you click.

3. For the brush settings (the last four sliders), try a **Feather** value of 50–95 (to allow the edits to fade into surrounding areas), a **Flow** value of 60 (for the amount of adjustment produced by each stroke), and a **Density** value of 60 (for the level of transparency in the stroke).

4. Check **Mask** (Y) (scroll down in the settings area if you don't see this option), adjust the brush size by pressing [or], then draw strokes over areas of the photo that need the same adjustment. A tint covers the areas where you apply strokes, and a pin appears where you started dragging. **B**

   ➤ The brush size is represented by the solid circle in the pointer; the feather value is represented by the black-and-white dashed circle.

5. Uncheck Mask, then use the sliders to apply adjustments to the masked areas (**A**, next page).

   ➤ To show or hide all the pins, press V or check or uncheck Overlay.

   ➤ To display the mask for an existing pin temporarily, with your mouse or stylus, roll over the pin.

A We studied this photo and decided what improvements to make: Smooth the skin, sharpen the eyelashes, darken the eyebrows, and minimize the under-eye circles.

B We clicked the Adjustment Brush tool, zeroed out the sliders, checked Mask, then drew strokes on the broad areas of the face in the preview, being careful to avoid the key facial features.

A *We hid the mask, then chose a higher Tint value to add magenta to the skin tones, higher Exposure and Shadows values to lighten the skin tones, and lower Clarity and Sharpness values to smooth the skin texture. The results are shown at right.*

B *To sharpen the eyelashes, we clicked New, showed the mask, then covered the lashes using a small brush.*

6. To apply different adjustment settings to another area of the photo, click New, then repeat steps 2–5 **B–C** (and **A–E**, next page).

   If you want to duplicate a pin and its mask, hold down Ctrl-Alt/Cmd-Option and drag the pin (you don't have to click it first). Or click a pin, right-click it and choose **Duplicate** from the context menu, then drag the new pin.

7. To redisplay the main Camera Raw tabs, press H (Hand tool).

C *We hid the mask, then chose higher Contrast, Clarity, and Sharpness values to accentuate the masked areas, and a lower Exposure value to darken them.*

A *To darken the eyebrows, we clicked New, checked Mask, then masked those areas.*

C *To minimize the dark circles under the eyes, we clicked New, checked Mask, then applied a mask to those areas.*

D *We hid the mask again, then reduced the Temperature value to cool the redness of the skin tones; increased the Exposure, Highlights, Shadows, Whites, and Blacks values to lighten the skin; and reduced the Clarity and Sharpness values to soften the skin texture.*

B *We hid the mask, then chose a higher Contrast value to define the hairs more crisply against the skin, and lowered Highlights, Whites, and Blacks values for a darkening effect.*

E *This final image shows the cumulative results of all the local corrections that we applied via the Adjustment Brush tool.*

To edit an Adjustment Brush tool correction:

1. Choose the **Adjustment Brush** tool ✏ (K).

2. Check **Mask** (Y) and **Overlay** (V).

3. Click a pin. A black dot appears in the center of the pin.

4. Do any of the following:

   To **add** areas to the mask, drag with the brush in the image preview.**A–B**

   To **move** the mask to a different area of the photo, drag its pin.

   To **adjust** the correction for the current pin, uncheck Mask (Y), then move the sliders.

USING THE AUTO MASK OPTION WITH THE ADJUSTMENT BRUSH TOOL

To mask an area according to color, zoom into that area. Check Auto Mask (M), position the Adjustment Brush tool over the color, scale the brush tip to cover just the width of the area, and start drawing a stroke. The mask will cover only the areas that match the first color area the brush touches.

► If you want to change the mask overlay color, click the Mask Overlay Color swatch, then choose a color in the Color Picker.

A *After using the Adjustment Brush tool in this photo, we clicked an existing pin, and checked Mask to display the mask associated with that pin (we changed our mask color to yellow).*

B *We dragged with the Adjustment Brush tool to add an area to the mask for the currently selected pin (note the brush cursor on the right side of the photo).*

To remove Adjustment Brush tool edits:

1. Choose the **Adjustment Brush** tool ✎ (K).

2. Check **Mask** (Y) and **Overlay** (V).

3. Do either of the following:

   To remove adjustments locally, click a pin, click the **Erase** button (or hold down Alt/Option), then apply strokes where you want to erase the mask.**A**

   To remove a pin and its adjustments, click the pin, then press Backspace/Delete; or right-click a selected pin, then choose **Delete** from the context menu;**B** or hold down Alt/Option and click a selected or unselected pin (note the scissors pointer).

➤ To remove all Adjustment Brush tool edits from the current photo and reset the tool mode to New, click the Clear All button.

A We clicked an existing Adjustment Brush pin, and checked Mask to display the mask associated with that pin. Next, we clicked the Erase button, then dragged with the brush to remove an area from the selected mask.

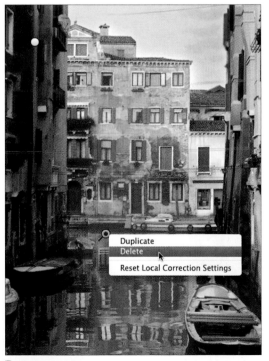

B To remove a selected Adjustment Brush pin, we right-clicked it and chose Delete from the context menu.

Using the Split Toning tab

Using the Split Toning controls, you can apply one color tint, or tone, to the highlight areas of a photo and a different tint to the shadow areas. For the best results with this technique (and to mimic its traditional origins), convert the colors in your photo to grayscale first. We've gotten good results on photos of metallic objects, such as the antique car shown here.**A**

To apply a color tint to a grayscale version of a photo:

1. Click the **HSL/Grayscale** tab, ▤ then check **Convert to Grayscale**.

2. Click the **Basic** tab, and adjust the exposure and contrast.

3. Click the **Split Toning** tab. ▤

4. Move both of the **Saturation** sliders approximately halfway across the bar to make it easier to judge the colors you will apply in the next step (don't worry that the photo looks awful).

5. Move the **Highlights Hue** slider to tint the high-lights **B** and the **Shadows Hue** slider to tint the shadows.

6. Readjust the **Saturation** value for each hue.

7. Reduce the **Balance** setting to apply more of the Shadows tint to the entire photo, or increase it to apply more of the Highlights tint to the entire photo.**C–D**

A This is the original, full-color photo.

B After converting the colors in the photo to grayscale, we used the Split Toning tab to tint the highlights with a brownish yellow hue.

C Next, we tinted the shadows with blue, then moved the Balance slider to the right to favor the highlight color more.

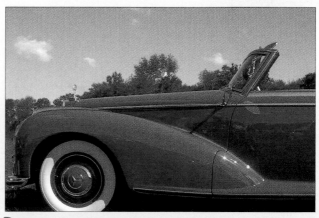

D This is the final result of our Split Toning adjustments. Applying separate tints to the highlights and shadows accentuated the lines and graceful curves of this sleek antique.

Using the Lens Corrections tab

Via the Lens Corrections tab in Camera Raw, you can correct a photo for various adverse effects of lens distortion. You can straighten out an architectural feature, such as a building or fence, that looks as if it's leaning toward or away from the viewer, or that is tilted horizontally (isn't level); and you can correct for under- or overexposure at the edges of a photo (vignetting). The corrections can be applied using a preset profile (this page) or manually (next page).

To correct geometric distortion and vignetting via Profile settings:

1. Click the **Lens Corrections** tab. 📷 Double-click the Hand tool 🖑 to fit the image in the preview.

2. To access predefined lens profiles, click the **Profile** tab, then check **Enable Lens Profile Corrections**.

3. From the **Setup** menu, **A** do the following:

   Choose **Auto** to have Camera Raw read the EXIF metadata in the photo and attempt to select the proper lens make, model, and predefined profile.

   If an error message indicates that the Auto option was unable to locate a profile, choose your lens manufacturer from the **Make** menu. **B** Camera Raw will locate a matching lens model and list it on the Model menu, and will locate a predefined profile and list it on the Profile menu. If the Model menu

lists more than one model, choose the one with which the photo was shot.

4. Under Correction Amount, do the following:

   Set the **Distortion** value to control the amount of correction.

   Set the **Vignetting** value to correct for under- or overexposure at the edges of the photo.

5. *Optional:* If Camera Raw managed to locate your lens profile (step 3), you can save that profile and any custom Correction Amount settings as your new default profile by choosing Save New Lens Profile Defaults from the Setup menu. In future Camera Raw editing sessions, if you choose Default from the Setup menu, and the current photo was taken with this lens, the saved profile and settings will be applied. (To restore the Adobe predefined settings for your chosen lens, from the Setup menu, choose Reset Lens Profile Defaults.)

6. *Optional:* If you want to further correct any lens distortion manually, see the next task.

➤ When applying lens corrections to a Smart Object in Photoshop, we use the Lens Corrections tab in Camera Raw (accessed via Filter > Camera Raw Filter) because it has more extensive manual controls than the Lens Correction filter in Photoshop.

A *Check Enable Lens Profile Corrections, then choose Auto from the Setup menu …*

B *… or choose your lens maker from the Make menu. Regardless of the Setup option, if necessary, adjust the Distortion value.*

To correct geometric distortion or vignetting via the Manual tab:

1. Click the **Lens Corrections** tab, and double-click the Hand tool ✍ to fit the image in the preview. **A**

2. Click the **Manual** tab. **B**

3. In the **Upright** area, click a button to apply a preset correction:

   Auto A to apply level correction and fix horizontal and vertical convergence, balanced with as little distortion as possible. **C**

   Level ⊟ to apply only level correction (not fix horizontal or vertical convergence).

   Vertical ⊞ to apply level correction and fix vertical convergence (but not horizontal convergence).

   Full ⊞ for a stronger correction of horizontal and vertical convergence, in addition to level correction (**A**, next page).

4. If further manual correction is needed, do any of the following:

   To spread the image out (fix pincushion distortion), lower the **Distortion** value; or to pinch the image inward (fix barrel distortion), increase the Distortion value.

   ➤ To display a grid over the image so you can check the alignment, check Show

   Continued on the following page

A *The original photo (above) shows signs of lens distortion: The house looks as if it's tilting away from the camera, and it's not level.*

B *We clicked the Manual tab (under Lens Corrections) to access these menu options and sliders.*

C *Under Upright, we clicked the Auto button for a balanced correction. This partially corrected the vertical lines and vertical tilt, but the left side of the house still looks as if it's farther away from the viewer than the right side.*

Grid or press V. Adjust the grid size via the slider.**B**

To widen the top of the image, (correct keystoning) reduce the **Vertical** value; to widen the bottom of the image, increase the Vertical value. Readjust the Distortion value, if needed.

To widen the left edge of the image, reduce the **Horizontal** value; to widen the right edge of the image, increase the Horizontal value.

To rotate the image, change the **Rotate** value.

To enlarge or shrink the photo, change the **Scale** value. Note: You could crop the photo instead.

To stretch the image horizontally or vertically, change the **Aspect** value. This option is useful for correcting strong perspective distortion in photos taken with a wide-angle lens (**A–B**, next page).

➤ If you moved the Distortion slider, you can click Reanalyze (below the buttons) to force a recalculation of the Upright correction based on the Distortion value. If you want to turn off (but preserve) all your Upright corrections, click the Off button.⊘ If you click a different Upright button, as an alert will inform you, all the Transform sliders (except Distortion) will be reset to 0.

5. To correct or apply Lens Vignetting (lighten or darken the outer areas of the photo), set the **Amount** value for the strength of the correction, then set the **Midpoint** value to expand the vignette inward or outward. Readjust the Amount value, if needed.

A We clicked the Full button instead, which successfully made the house level and upright. To lighten the outer areas of the photo, we increased the Amount value (under Lens Vignetting).

B We made some minor Vertical and Rotate adjustments, with Show Grid checked to help us gauge the effect.

A *We tried increasing the Aspect value, but this setting exaggerated and distorted the verticals of the house too much.*

B *Instead, we set the Aspect value to –5, which exaggerated the horizontal proportion only slightly. The final settings we chose for the image are shown at right.*

SYNCING LENS CORRECTIONS TO MULTIPLE PHOTOS ★

To apply Lens Corrections edits to multiple photos opened in Camera Raw:

► If the photos *don't* require exactly the same corrections, click one photo and choose settings in the Manual tab of Lens Corrections. On the left side of the dialog, right-click a thumbnail and choose Select All; right-click again and choose Sync Settings. In the dialog, choose Lens Corrections from the menu, check only Transform and Lens Vignetting, then click OK. Camera Raw will analyze and correct each photo separately (see also page 94).

► If the photos *do* require exactly the same correction (e.g., bracketed shots of the same subject), click one photo, then click an Upright button in Lens Corrections. On the left side of the dialog, right-click a thumbnail and choose Select All, then click Sync Results in Lens Corrections. The first photo will be analyzed according to the chosen Upright mode, then the same correction will be applied to all the other photos.

Using the Effects tab

In traditional photography, the faster the film speed, the larger and more apparent the grain. As an intentional effect, you can simulate this grainy texture via the Grain controls in Camera Raw. Choose a photo that won't suffer aesthetically when its details lose definition.

To add a grain texture to a photo:

1. Click the **Effects** tab, *fx* and double-click the Hand tool to fit the image in the preview.**A**

2. To create a noticeable grain, under Grain, choose an **Amount** value of around 50.

3. To emulate the fine grain of slow film or the coarse grain of fast film, do as follows:

   Set the **Size** value for the size of the grain particles.**B** When this value is greater than 25, a small degree of blurring is also applied, to help blend the grain with the imagery.

   Reduce the **Roughness** value below the default value of 50 for a more uniform grain, or increase it for an uneven, coarse grain.**C** Zoom in to examine the grain, then readjust the Amount value, if needed.

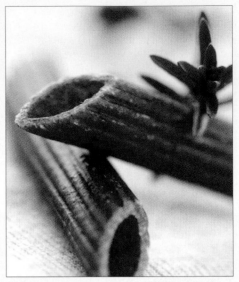

A *This photo is a good candidate for the Grain effect because we won't mind if the details are softened and it contains muted colors.*

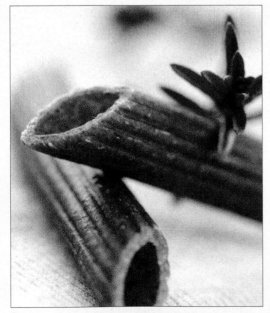

B *The first settings we chose were Grain Amount 50 and Size 80 (we left the Roughness control at the default value of 50). The food textures are beginning to blend with the soft background.*

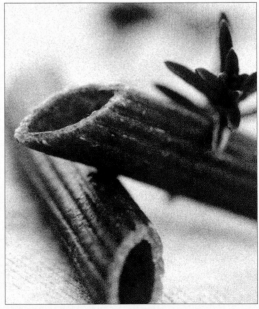

C *We increased the Amount to 75, the Size to 60, and the Roughness to 65. The coarser grain unifies the highlights and background with the food textures even more. Please pass the Parmesan…*

Using the Post Crop Vignetting controls, you can apply a light or dark vignette to a photo (lighten or darken the outer areas). If you crop the photo subsequently in Camera Raw, the vignette will reconform to the new dimensions.

To apply a vignette to a photo:

1. Click the **Effects** tab, *fx* and double-click the Hand tool ✋ to fit the image in the preview. **A**

2. Under **Post Crop Vignetting**, do all of the following: **B–D**

   Choose Style: **Highlight Priority**.

   Choose a negative **Amount** value for a dark vignette or a positive value for a light vignette.

   Adjust the **Midpoint** value to expand the vignette inward or outward.

   Adjust the **Roundness** value to make the vignette shape more oval or more like a rounded rectangle.

   Adjust the **Feather** setting to control the softness of the transition to the nonvignetted areas.

   Adjust the **Highlights** setting to control the brightness of the highlights within the vignette area.

A *This is the original image.*

B *In the Effects tab, under Post Crop Vignetting, we chose the values above.*

C *We lowered the Midpoint value and raised the Feather and Highlights values.*

D *When we cropped the image, the vignette readjusted automatically.*

Outdoor photos capture not only objects in the scene, but also the atmospheric conditions — namely haze. The Dehaze slider can be used to control how much haze is either removed from or added to the photo.

To decrease or increase haze in a photo: ★

1. Click the **Basic** tab, and double-click the Hand tool 🖐 to fit the image in the preview. Do the following:

   Adjust the White Balance; increase the Exposure value; increase the Shadows value to lighten the shadows; increase the Whites value; increase the Clarity value to sharpen edge contrast; and adjust the other slider values as needed. **A–B**

2. Click the **Effects** tab. *fx* Do either of the following:

   Enter a positive **Dehaze** value to decrease the amount of haze. This will increase both the tonal and color contrast and intensify color in the photo (**A**, next page).

   Enter a negative **Dehaze** value to increase the amount of haze (or fog). This will add a soft white tint that reduces tonal and color contrast and softens the detail in the photo (**B**, next page).

3. Go back to the Basic tab and readjust those sliders, if desired. We recommend you experiment with different Shadows, Blacks, and Clarity values (**C**, next page).

A In the Basic tab, we used the settings shown above…

B … to initially adjust our photo. This photo is a good candidate for the Dehaze effect because it contains adequate overall contrast, a substantial amount of whites, dark contrasts in the midground, and very few areas of green.

A *We set the Dehaze value to +48. The photo now has substantial tonal contrast and greater color saturation and intensity. An amazing result from one slider adjustment!*

B *Next, we changed the Dehaze value to −73. In the Basic tab, we lowered the Clarity value to +28 and the Blacks value to −44. The Dehaze effect has transformed the scene into a gray, foggy day, with a soft white tint enveloping the scene from the foreground to the background.*

C *Finally, in the Basic tab, we reduced the Clarity value to −44 and the Blacks value to −53. This adjustment softened the entire image and removed some of the haze from the closest foreground elements.*

By experimenting in the Basic tab, we found that the Shadows and Blacks sliders can control the amount of haze in the foreground, while the Contrast and Highlights sliders can control the amount of definition in background.

Using the Graduated Filter tool

When shooting landscapes, you may have run into this common predicament: You set the proper exposure for the foreground, and the sky winds up being overexposed. To solve this problem on site, you can reduce the light on the upper part of the lens with a graduated neutral-density filter. To darken a sky in a photo that is shot without such a filter (Plan B!), you can use the Graduated Filter tool in Camera Raw.

With this tool, you create an overlay to define the area to be edited, then you apply the adjustment via any of a dozen sliders. The slider options are the same as for the Adjustment Brush tool.

To adjust an area of a photo using the Graduated Filter tool:

1. After adjusting your photo via the Basic and Tone Curve tabs, **A** choose the **Graduated Filter tool** 🔲 (G). The sliders for the tool display in the right panel.

2. Click the + or – button for any slider to "zero out" all the sliders except the one you click.

3. To define where the filter edits will be applied, Shift-drag over an area in the photo, beginning from the location where you want the adjustment to be strongest. The filter will be applied fully at the green dashed border of the overlay, gradually diminishing to nil at the red dashed border. Note: If you want to draw the overlay on a diagonal, don't hold down Shift while dragging.

4. Do either or both of the following:

   Use the Temperature and/or Tint slider to make the filtered area warmer or cooler.

A *Despite our applying Basic and Tone Curve adjustments, the sky in this photo looks overexposed (washed out).*

Use other sliders to adjust such characteristics as the exposure, sharpness, whites or blacks, ★ or noise in the filtered area (**A–C**, next page).

5. To redisplay the main tabs, press H (for the Hand tool).

➤ At any time, you can lengthen or shorten the filter overlay by dragging or Shift-dragging the green or red dot. To reposition the whole overlay, drag the line that connects the two dots.

➤ To apply a separate overlay to another area of the photo, click New, then repeat steps 2–4. If you want to clone an overlay, hold down Ctrl-Alt/Cmd-Option and drag the dashed line that connects the two pins; or right-click a selected overlay and choose Duplicate from the context menu, then move the duplicate overlay.

➤ To hide the filter overlay, uncheck Overlay or press V.

➤ To remove a filter overlay, right-click a selected pin then choose Delete from the context menu; or hold down Alt/Option and click the overlay (note the scissors pointer); or click the overlay, then press Backspace/Delete.

EDITING A GRADUATED OR RADIAL FILTER MASK WITH A BRUSH

➤ Create or select a filter overlay. Click the Brush button at the top of the panel (Shift-K) to display brush options, then click the Brush + (add to) or Brush – (erase from) button. Press [or] to size the brush, then apply strokes in the preview. (You can also toggle the plus and minus buttons for the brush by holding down Alt/Option.) If you want to choose different sizes for the plus and minus functions of the brush, check Separate Eraser Size on the panel menu.

➤ In the panel, you can set the Feather value to control how much the brush edits fade into surrounding areas, and the Flow value to control the amount of adjustment. Check Auto Mask (M) to mask only the areas that match the first color area the brush touches (see also the sidebar on page 75).

➤ To remove all manual brush strokes from the currently selected overlay, click Clear.

A *After zeroing out the sliders for the Graduated Filter tool, we Shift-dragged downward in the photo (as shown by the arrow above), then chose slider settings to darken the exposure within the overlay area.*

B *To add more blue to the upper area of sky, we lowered the Temperature value.*

C *In the final image, the adjustment is strongest in the sky, fading to nil in the upper part of the ground.*

Using the Radial Filter tool

With the Radial Filter tool, you define an elliptical area with an overlay, then apply adjustments via sliders to the area either inside or outside the overlay.

To darken an area of a photo via the Radial Filter tool:

1. After adjusting your photo via the Basic and Tone Curve tabs, **A** click the **Radial Filter** tool ⓤ (J). The sliders for the tool display.

2. Click the + or – button for any slider to "zero out" all the sliders except the one you click. At the bottom of the panel, click Effect: **Outside** or **Inside** to control where the filter effect will occur relative to the overlay you will draw in the next step.

3. Drag over an area in the photo to produce an overlay. **B** If you want to reposition the overlay as you create it, drag with the Spacebar held down.

4. Use any of the sliders, including the Whites and Blacks sliders, ★ to adjust the filtered area (**A–C**, next page). If the Effect setting is Outside, the adjustment will be at full strength outside the overlay, then diminish gradually to no adjustment at the dashed border. If the Effect setting is Inside, the adjustment will be at full strength at the center of the overlay and diminish gradually to no adjustment at the dashed border.

A Although the exposure in this photo is well balanced, we want to spotlight the spa products more.

B We zeroed out the sliders for the Radial Filter tool, then dragged in the preview to create an overlay.

5. To control how gradual the adjustment is at the edge of the overlay, use the **Feather** slider.

6. To hide the overlay(s) to gauge the adjustment, uncheck **Overlay** or press V. Redisplay the overlay for the next step.

7. To edit the overlay, do any of the following (all optional):

   To **reposition** the overlay, drag inside it.

   To **reshape** the overlay, drag one of its handles.

   To **resize** the overlay, Shift-drag a handle.

   To **swap** the adjustment from Outside to Inside the overlay, or vice versa, click the unselected Effect button or press X.

8. *Optional:* To add another overlay, click New, then follow steps 2–7. To clone an overlay, hold down Ctrl-Alt/Cmd-Option and drag its center pin; or right-click the pin and choose Duplicate from the context menu, then drag the new pin. Note: Adjustments are cumulative where overlays overlap; to edit adjustment settings, click a pin first.

9. To redisplay the main tabs, press H (Hand tool).

➤ To delete an overlay, select its center pin, then right-click the pin and choose Delete from the context menu; or hold down Alt/Option and click the pin (scissors pointer); or click the pin, then press Backspace/Delete.

➤ To expand an overlay to the edges of a photo, double-click inside it; or to do this when creating a new overlay, double-click in the preview.

A *We used the first four sliders to darken the filtered area and the Clarity and Sharpness sliders to soften the image details.*

EDIT THE MASK WITH A BRUSH

To edit a Radial Filter mask with a brush, follow the steps in the sidebar on page 86.

B *To make the lighting in the darkened areas cooler, we reduced the Temperature value (added blue).*

C *The tonal, temperature, and sharpness adjustments helped to accentuate the candle, soap, and white bottle.*

Using the Spot Removal tool

Use the Spot Removal tool to remove imperfections from a photo, such as spots caused by dust on the camera lens, blemishes in a portrait, or insects on flowers. You can let Camera Raw locate a source area for the repair automatically, or you can choose a source area.

The Spot Removal tool does an improved job of locating a source area automatically, especially when used to heal nonsmooth textures (Adobe mentions bark, rocks, and foliage as examples of textures in which healing results are improved). Also, if you use this tool on a photo that you cropped in Camera Raw, the tool will look for source areas within the crop boundary first.

To remove blemishes or spots:

1. Choose the **Spot Removal** tool ✋ (B).

2. Zoom in on an area to be repaired.

3. Press [or] to size the brush cursor, then do one of the following:

   Ctrl-Alt-drag/Cmd-Option-drag outward from the center of a blemish to create and scale a target circle **A**; or click a blemish; or if you want to control which area Camera Raw uses as the source, Ctrl-drag/Cmd-drag from the target area to the desired source area. When you release the mouse, a red dashed circle surrounds the target region and a green dashed circle surrounds the source area.**B**

   Drag across a blemish to create a target region. When you release the mouse, a border with a red pin surrounds the target region and a border with a green pin surrounds a source region.**C–E**

A *With the Spot Removal tool, we held down Ctrl-Alt/Cmd-Option and dragged to create a target circle around a blemish.*

B *The tool created a linked source circle in a similar area and repaired the blemish.*

C *To remove an imperfection from a leaf, we're dragging to create a target region.*

D *The tool created a source region and two pins.*

E *The line is eliminated from the leaf.*

➤ To display a black-and-white version of the photo to help you pinpoint dust spots or other irregularities, check Visualize Spots (Y). Adjust the black-to-white threshold via the slider. Press Y to return to the normal display.

4. *Optional:* To soften the transition between the current target area and surrounding areas, adjust the Feather value. **A–C** Or to adjust the Feather value interactively (within the current size of the brush cursor), with Shift and right-click held down, drag horizontally in the preview. The new Feather value will display within the selected target area. The Feather value is sticky, meaning the current value will persist for future editing sessions until you change it.

5. From the **Type** menu, choose **Heal** to blend source pixels into the texture and luminosity values of the target pixels (often the best choice), or **Clone** to copy the source pixels exactly without any healing.

   Optional: To cycle through alternative source locations that Camera Raw detects, press (and keeping pressing) /.

6. To hide all regions and circles at any time in order to judge the Spot Removal results, uncheck **Overlay** (V). Recheck it for the remaining steps.

7. Select a target or source region by clicking its pin, or select a circle by clicking inside it, then do any of the following optional steps:

   To **reposition** a region or circle, drag inside it.

   To control the opacity of the repair, change the **Opacity** value in the panel.

   To **resize** a pair of target and source circles (not irregular-shaped regions), drag the dashed border.

   To **add** to an existing region (or to convert a circle to a region), position the pointer just outside it, then hold down Shift and click or drag.

8. *Optional:* Create more regions or circles to correct other blemishes.

   To remove a pair of circles or regions, hold down Alt/Option and click in the target or source area; or to delete multiple circles and/or regions, Alt/Option drag a marquee across them; or to remove all Spot Removal circles and regions, click Clear All.

9. To redisplay the main tabs, press H (Hand tool).

➤ To redisplay the current Spot Removal overlays at any time, choose the tool again (press B).

A *The shed in this photo is a distracting element.*

B *Using the Spot Removal tool, we dragged outward from the center of the shed. With the Feather value for the tool set to 100%, the healing is fading around the rim of the circle, and sections of the original background aren't replaced.*

C *We changed the Feather slider for the tool to 10%. Now the shed is more fully replaced with tree pixels, with minimal fading along the rim of the target region.*

Saving and applying Camera Raw settings

After carefully choosing custom settings for a photo in Camera Raw, you'll be glad to know that you can save those settings as a preset and then apply the preset to other photos that need the same or similar corrections.

To save Camera Raw settings as a preset:

Method 1 (Camera Raw Settings menu)

1. With your corrected photo open in Camera Raw, choose **Save Settings** from the Camera Raw Settings menu.

2. The Save Settings dialog opens.**A**

3. Choose **Subset:** All Settings, then check the categories of settings you want saved in the preset. If you want to filter which boxes are checked for a subset, choose a tab name from the Subset menu, then check/uncheck boxes. For any menu choice, you can also click Check All or Check None; or to select one box exclusively, hold down Alt/Option and click it.

4. Click Save. A "navigation" Save Settings dialog opens. Enter a name (preferably one that describes the function of the preset), keep the location as the Settings folder, then click Save.

5. The saved settings preset is now available in the Presets tab ▦ for any open photo.

Method 2 (Presets tab)

1. With your corrected photo open in Camera Raw, click the **Presets** tab, ▦ then click the **New Preset** button. ▣

2. In the New Preset dialog, enter a name for the preset. Follow step 3, above.

3. Click OK. Your new preset is now available in the Presets tab for any open photo.

➤ To delete a user-saved preset, click the preset name, then click the Delete button. 🗑

You can apply a user-defined preset (saved collection of settings) to a single photo via Camera Raw (see below), to multiple photos via Bridge (see the following page), or to multiple thumbnails via the Synchronize option in Camera Raw (see page 94).

To apply a Camera Raw preset to a photo:

With a photo open in Camera Raw, click the **Presets** tab, ▦ then click a preset name.

➤ You can also apply a preset via the Apply Preset submenu on the Camera Raw Settings menu.

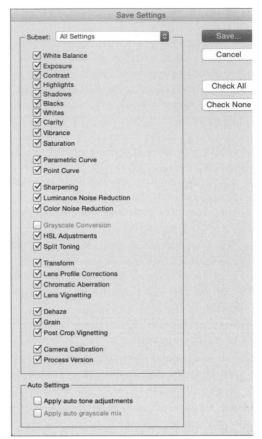

A In the Save Settings dialog, check which categories of custom Camera Raw settings are to be saved in a preset.

TAKING SNAPSHOTS OF YOUR CR SETTINGS

A snapshot is a record of the current Camera Raw settings that you have chosen for a photo. By saving snapshots of your photo periodically while editing it, you preserve the option to restore the photo to those earlier settings. Unlike snapshots on the History panel in Photoshop, snapshots save with the Camera Raw file. Click the Snapshots tab, 🖻 then click the New Snapshot button. ▣ In the New Snapshot dialog, enter a name, then click OK. To restore the photo to a snapshot at any time, click a snapshot name in the Snapshots tab. (For other ways to restore Camera Raw settings, see pages 59–60.)

➤ To update an existing snapshot with the current settings, right-click the snapshot listing and choose Update with Current Settings from the context menu.

The settings presets that you save in the Presets tab of the Camera Raw dialog can also be applied to multiple photos via the Develop Settings submenu in Bridge. In fact, as a strategy, you could save separate presets for settings in individual Camera Raw tabs and then assign them to multiple photos in succession (e.g., a preset for the Basic tab first, then a preset for the Tone Curve tab, and so on). If you haven't saved the needed settings as presets, a quick alternative method is to copy and paste all the current settings from one photo into one or more other photos.

To apply Camera Raw settings to multiple photos via Bridge:

Method 1 (apply a preset)

1. In Bridge, Ctrl-click/Cmd-click multiple photo thumbnails (or Shift, then Shift-click a consecutive series of thumbnails).

2. To apply settings, from the Edit > **Develop Settings** submenu, choose a preset; or right-click a selected thumbnail and choose a preset from the Develop Settings submenu on the context menu.**A** Choose additional presets, if needed.

Method 2 (copy and paste settings from a photo)

1. Click the thumbnail for a photo that has the desired settings, then choose Edit > Develop Settings > **Copy Camera Raw Settings** (Ctrl-Alt-C/ Cmd-Option-C), or right-click the selected thumbnail and choose Develop Settings > Copy Settings from the context menu.

2. Click another thumbnail (or Ctrl-click/Cmd-click multiple thumbnails), then choose Edit > Develop Settings > **Paste Camera Raw Settings** (Ctrl-Alt-V/ Cmd-Option-V), or right-click the selected thumbnail and choose Develop Settings > Paste Settings from the context menu.

3. The Paste Camera Raw Settings dialog opens. Uncheck any settings you don't want to paste; or choose a tab name from the Subset menu, then remove or add any check marks; or to select one box exclusively, hold down Alt/Option and click it. Click OK.

➤ To remove *all* Camera Raw settings from a selected photo thumbnail in Bridge, choose Edit > Develop Settings > Clear Settings or right-click the thumbnail and choose Develop Settings > Clear Settings from the context menu.

A *Using commands on the Develop Settings submenu in Bridge, you can apply one or more saved settings presets to multiple selected thumbnails, or copy and paste the current settings from one thumbnail to other thumbnails.*

Synchronizing Camera Raw settings

When you open multiple photos into Camera Raw, they are represented by thumbnails in a panel on the left side of the dialog. After adjusting one photo, you can use Sync Settings to apply those settings to one or more of the other photos. Because it's unlikely that every single adjustment needed for one photo will be perfectly suited to all the others (even photos taken during the same shoot), a more practical approach is to adjust subsets of the grouping. For instance, you could apply a settings preset or some Basic tab adjustments to one photo (say, to correct the white balance and exposure), apply those settings to most or all of the other photos, then select specific photos and apply more targeted or specialty adjustments.

To synchronize the Camera Raw settings among multiple photos:

1. In Bridge, select two or more photo thumbnails, preferably ones that were shot under the same lighting conditions and that require the same kind of correction (for the most accurate and consistent corrections, select all raw files or all JPEG files). Double-click one of the selected thumbnails.

2. On the filmstrip panel on the left side of the Camera Raw dialog, click one of the thumbnails. **A**

3. Make the needed adjustments to the selected image (including cropping, if you want to crop all the images in exactly the same way). You can apply adjustments via the tabs or tools or by clicking a preset in the Presets tab.

4. Right-click a thumbnail. From the context menu choose **Select All**; right-click again and choose **Sync Settings**. Or Ctrl-click/Cmd-click specific thumbnails, then right-click a selected thumbnail and choose **Sync Settings**. ★

5. The Synchronize dialog opens (it looks like the Save Settings dialog, which is shown on page 92). Check only the settings you want to apply to all the selected thumbnails; or choose a category from the Synchronize menu, then remove or add any check marks. Click OK.

➤ To cycle through the photos on the filmstrip panel, click the left or right arrowhead below the preview (in the lower right). If more than one thumbnail is selected, Camera Raw will cycle among only the selected photos.

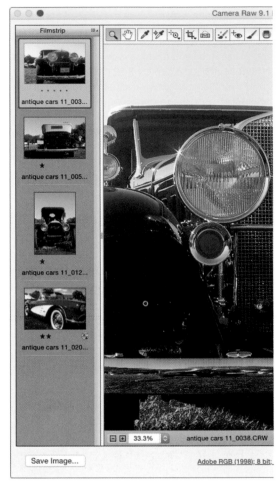

A *We opened four photos into Camera Raw. The thumbnails for the images display on the filmstrip panel on the left side of the dialog.*

NEW MERGE COMMANDS IN CAMERA RAW ★

Camera Raw enables you to apply the Merge to HDR and the Merge to Panorama commands to photos via the filmstrip panel menu or via the panel context menu. See pages 258–259 and 292–293 for steps for using these commands.

WHERE CR IMAGE SETTINGS ARE SAVED

Depending on the current setting on the Save Image Settings In menu in the Camera Raw Preferences dialog (Ctrl-K/Cmd-K), settings for raw photos (not JPEGs) are saved either in the internal Camera Raw Database on your system or as hidden Sidecar .xmp Files in the same folder as the raw files.

Converting, opening, and saving Camera Raw files

Still with us? At long last, you get to open your Camera Raw file into Photoshop.

To open a photo from Camera Raw into Photoshop:

1. After applying adjustments to your photo in Camera Raw, click **Open Image**; or if you opened and corrected multiple files, select them on the left side of the dialog, then click **Open Images**.

2. The photo appears as the Background in a new Photoshop document (or documents). Save the file(s) in the Photoshop (PSD) format.

   Note: If Open in Photoshop as Smart Objects is checked in the Workflow Options dialog (see step 10 on page 56), the Open Image button is labeled Open Object and a photo opens as a Smart Object in a new Photoshop document. To learn about Smart Objects, see pages 272–283 (to edit the Camera Raw settings of a Smart Object, see page 276). If the workflow option is off, you can convert the Open Image button to Open Object by holding down Shift.

➤ To close the Camera Raw dialog without opening your file, but save your settings to the file as instructions, click Done. The settings will redisplay if you reopen the file in Camera Raw.

ARCHIVING PHOTOS AS DNG FILES

Photographs capture unrepeatable moments, and archiving them is both a priority and a concern for photographers. Ideally, there would be one standard file format for digital photos that photographers could depend on with confidence, knowing their photos will be stable and accessible for the foreseeable future. At the present time, each camera maker uses a unique, proprietary format for their raw files. Should a maker discontinue its format, raw photos from their cameras might become unreadable by Photoshop or other image-editing applications.

Luckily, DNG (short for Digital Negative), a format developed by Adobe, preserves all the raw, unprocessed pixel information that is captured by the camera. The coding for the DNG format is nonproprietary (open standard), meaning that it is accessible to all interested companies. DNG may be the long-term solution that photographers will eventually come to rely on — provided it is adopted as the standard by a majority of camera and software manufacturers.

If desired, you can open a copy of a Camera Raw file with its current (custom) settings into Photoshop without changing the settings in the original raw or JPEG file.

To open a copy of a Camera Raw file:

In the Camera Raw dialog, hold down Alt/Option and click **Open Copy** (Open Image or Open Object becomes Open Copy).

Settings in the Workflow Options dialog are assigned automatically to all photos that you open into Camera Raw (see pages 56–58). If you want to convert and save a copy of an individual photo in the Digital Negative (DNG), JPEG, TIFF, or Photoshop (PSD) format using custom file naming, format, color space, sizing, or sharpening settings instead, use the Save Options dialog, as described below. New Color Space, Image Sizing, and Preset features, found in the Workflow Options dialog, are also available in the Save Options dialog.

When you save a copy of a photo in the Digital Negative format via Save Options, the Camera Raw settings it inherits from the original file remain accessible and editable in Camera Raw. See also the sidebar on this page.

When you save a photo in the JPEG, TIFF, or PSD format via Save Options, the Camera Raw settings are applied to the copy of the photo permanently. Although you can open and edit the resulting JPEG or TIFF file in Camera Raw, you will see that the sliders are reset to their default values. PSD files can't be opened into Camera Raw.

Note: Settings that you choose in the Save Options dialog are independent of — and have no effect on — the settings in the Workflow Options dialog.

To save a copy of a Camera Raw file in the DNG, JPEG, TIFF, or PSD format:

1. Open and adjust a photo in Camera Raw, then in the lower-left corner of the dialog, click **Save Image**.

2. The Save Options dialog opens (**A**, next page). For the **Destination**, choose Save in Same Location or Save in New Location. For the latter, choose a location in the Select Destination Folder dialog, then click Select.

Continued on the following page

3. Under **File Naming**, choose a naming or numbering convention from the menu or enter a file name. If desired, you can also choose an additional naming or numbering convention from the adjacent menu.

4. Choose a **Format** of Digital Negative, JPEG, TIFF, or Photoshop, then choose related options. For instance, if you cropped the photo in Camera Raw and then choose the Photoshop format here, you will need to decide whether to check Preserve Cropped Pixels.

5. For a photo in the JPEG, TIFF, or Photoshop format, choose an option from the **Metadata** menu to control what metadata will be saved with the file. And via the Remove Location Info check box, control whether you want location information for the file to be preserved.

6. For a photo in the JPEG, TIFF, or Photoshop format, you can choose options under Color Space, Image Sizing, and Output Sharpening. For Color Space, see step 3 on page 56; for Image Sizing, see page 58; and for Output Sharpening, see step 9 on page 56.

7. *Optional:* To save the current dialog settings as a preset for future use on any photo, from the Preset menu, choose New Save Options Preset. In the dialog, enter a name, then click OK.

8. Click Save. A copy of the file appears in the designated location. The original file, with its current settings, remains open in Camera Raw.

➤ User-created presets are available on the Preset menu. Once you choose a preset, the menu also provides Delete [preset name] and Rename [preset name] commands.

➤ When you assign a color space and an intent to a photo via the Workflow Options dialog, those settings display as a soft proof in the main Camera Raw dialog, whereas when you choose color space and an intent options in the Save Options dialog, no soft proof displays.

A *In the Save Options dialog, choose Destination, File Naming, Format, Color Space, Image Sizing, and Output Sharpening settings.*

Now that you know how to create and open documents, you're ready to customize the Photoshop workspace for your needs. In this chapter, you'll learn how to use the main features of the Photoshop interface, such as the Application frame and document tabs. You'll change the zoom level and screen mode, rotate the canvas view, configure the panels, choose a workspace, save custom workspaces, and use the Options bar. Note: The individual panels (including the Tools panel) are described and illustrated in the next chapter.

ENABLE OPENGL FOR THIS CHAPTER

To use the OpenGL features in Photoshop, such as Animated and Scrubby Zoom (see page 101), flick panning (see page 102), and the Rotate View tool (see page 103), your system must contain a video driver or card that provides OpenGL acceleration, and in Photoshop, Use Graphics Processor must be enabled in Edit/Photoshop CC > Preferences > Performance. If the preference option isn't checked, check it, then close and reopen your document.

Using the Application frame

In Windows, all the Photoshop features are housed in an Application window. It contains a menu bar and Options bar along the top; panels (including the Tools panel); and any open documents, which by default are docked as tabs.**A**

Continued on the following page

5

IN THIS CHAPTER

Menu bar   Options bar

A *This is the onscreen environment for Photoshop in Windows.*

The Application frame in the Mac OS serves the same purpose as the Application window in Windows: It holds the Options bar (see page 110), panels, and open documents (which are docked as tabs).**A** Although the Application frame is an optional feature in the Mac OS, there are good reasons for using it. It keeps all the Photoshop features neatly organized and readily accessible (and hides Desktop clutter!). If the frame is hidden, choose Window > Application Frame. We use and refer to it throughout this book.

Note: For the sake of simplicity, we also refer to the Windows application window generically as the "Application frame."

➤ To resize the Application frame, drag an edge or a corner.

➤ To minimize the Application frame and any tabbed documents in the Mac OS, click the Minimize button in the upper-left corner; in Windows, click the Minimize button in the upper-right corner.

DESIGN SPACE PREVIEW ★

Adobe has added an alternative interface for Photoshop called Design Space. The dark-theme, modern interface is intended for Web and mobile app designers. See pages 499–500 for more on this technology preview option.

The document tab lists the file name, file format, current zoom level, current layer if the file contains layers, color mode, and bit depth. An asterisk indicates that the file contains unsaved changes. To close a document, click the X.

Use the Options bar to choose settings for the current tool.

Store open panels in one or more docks. To save space, you can collapse any dock to icons (see page 106).

A *This is the Application frame in the Mac OS.*

We recommend docking all open document windows as tabs (the default setting for Photoshop) rather than floating them as separate windows outside the frame (the only option in early versions of Photoshop). With documents docked as tabs, you will be able to keep the documents you're not working on out of view but readily accessible. To display a document that is docked as a tab, simply click the tab.

If documents aren't docking as tabs automatically, we recommend resetting the preference so that they do.

To set a preference to have documents open as tabs:

1. Choose Edit/Photoshop CC > Preferences, then click Workspace ★ on the left to display that pane.

2. Check **Open Documents as Tabs**, then click OK.

If you inadvertently (or out of curiosity) drag a document out of the tab area, and thereby turn a tabbed document into a floating one, follow these instructions to bring it home.

To dock floating document windows as tabs:

Do either of the following:

To dock one floating document window manually, drag its title bar to the tab area (just below the Options bar) of the Application frame, and release when the blue drop zone border appears.**A–B**

To dock all floating documents as tabs via a command, choose Window > Arrange > **Consolidate All to Tabs**; or if at least one document is docked as a tab, right-click a tab and choose **Consolidate All to Here** from the context menu.

➤ To cycle among all currently open documents, press Ctrl-Tab/Control-Tab or Ctrl-~ (tilde)/Cmd-~.

➤ One of the drawbacks to floating document windows when using the Application frame is that if you click in the frame, your floating documents will be hidden behind it. If you insist on floating your documents, consider at least docking them together by dragging the title bar of one window just below the title bar of another.

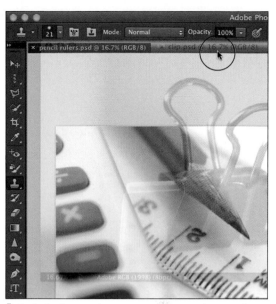

A *To dock a floating document window as a tab manually, drag its title bar to the tab area of the Application frame and release the mouse when the blue drop zone border appears.*

B *Our document is now docked within the Application frame.*

Tiling multiple documents

If you need to view or edit multiple documents simultaneously, you can arrange them in a preset layout, such as two documents side by side or in a vertical format, or four or six documents in a grid.

To tile multiple documents:

1. From the Window > **Arrange** submenu, choose a tiling command, such as 2-Up Vertical or 4-Up.**A** The availability of commands will vary depending on how many documents are open.

   ➤ To resize a window, drag either the bar between two windows or the lower-right corner. To reduce the number of visible windows by one, drag the tab of a document to the tab of another document, and release when the blue drop zone border appears.

2. When you're ready to view just one document at a time, do either of the following:

   Choose Window > Arrange > **Consolidate All to Tabs.**

Right-click a tab and choose **Consolidate All to Here** from the context menu.

➤ If any open documents are floating when you choose a tiling command, they will be docked as tabs automatically.

ONE IMAGE, TWO WINDOWS

To display the current document in a duplicate (tabbed) window, we recommend closing any other open documents first, then choose Window > Arrange > **New Window for [document name].** To show both windows, choose a Tile All or 2-Up option from the Window > Arrange submenu. In this setup, you could choose an option on the View > Proof Colors submenu for one of the documents and not the other, or display the documents at different zoom levels.

A To arrange these tabbed documents in quadrants, we chose 4-Up on the Window > Arrange submenu.

Changing the zoom level

You can easily switch between displaying the entire live canvas area of an image in the document window and magnifying just part of the image to concentrate on a small detail. The current zoom level percentage is listed in three locations: on the document tab, in the lower-left corner of the document window, and on the Navigator panel (if showing).

Note: For smoother and more continuous zooming, in Edit/Photoshop CC > Preferences > Tools, ★ check Animated Zoom. Also, to use both the Animated Zoom and Scrubby Zoom features, Use Graphics Processor must be checked in Preferences > Performance. For more Zoom preferences, see page 459.

To change the zoom level with the Zoom tool:

1. Choose the **Zoom** tool, 🔍 or to spring-load the Zoom tool (select it temporarily) if another tool is selected, hold down Z.

2. Do one of the following:

   Check **Scrubby Zoom** on the Options bar, then in the image, drag to the right to zoom in **A** or to the left to zoom out.

   Click and hold (don't drag) in the image to zoom in, or hold down Alt/Option and click and hold to zoom out. This is the **Animated Zoom** feature, also known as bird's-eye zooming.

   Click in the image to zoom in, or hold down Alt/Option and click to zoom out.

   Right-click in the image and choose a zoom option from the context menu, or click one of these buttons on the Options bar: **100%**; **Fit**

Screen to display the entire image at the largest size that can fit in the window; or **Fill Screen** to have the image completely fill the window (only part of the image may be visible).

➤ The View menu lists 100% and 200% commands (Actual Pixels has been removed).

A VIEW FOR USERS OF RETINA DISPLAYS

For more accurate rendering on a retina display, Photoshop draws interface elements at twice their normal size (this is because a retina display has double the pixel density of a nonretina display). To view "actual pixels" in your image on a retina display, choose View > 200% (double the zoom level of 100%).

SHORTCUTS FOR ZOOMING IN AND OUT

	Windows	Mac OS
Zoom in via the keyboard	Ctrl-+ (plus)	Cmd-+ (plus)
Zoom out via the keyboard	Ctrl-− (minus)	Cmd-− (minus)
Zoom in manually	Ctrl-Spacebar click or drag	Cmd-Spacebar click or drag
Zoom out manually	Alt-Spacebar click or drag	Option-Spacebar click or drag
Fit on Screen	Ctrl-0 (zero)	Cmd-0 (zero)
100% view	Ctrl-1	Cmd-1

Note: The zoom shortcuts also can be used when some Photoshop dialogs are open.

A *With the Zoom tool, and with Scrubby Zoom checked on the Options bar, we're dragging to the right to zoom in.*

The Navigator panel has two functions. You can use it to change the zoom level of an image or to reposition the image in the document window (to bring an area you want to edit or examine into view).

To change the zoom level or reposition the image in the window via the Navigator panel:

1. Display the Navigator panel.✷ A

2. To change the zoom level, in the Navigator panel, do any of the following:

   Ctrl-drag/Cmd-drag across part of the image thumbnail to target that area for magnification.

   Double-click the existing value in the zoom field, type the desired percentage, then press Enter/Return. Or to zoom to a value and rehighlight the field, enter the desired value, then press Shift-Enter/Shift-Return.

   Drag the Zoom slider.

   Click the Zoom Out or Zoom In button.

3. If the image is magnified to the degree that areas are hidden outside the document window, you can reposition it by dragging the view box on the panel.

➤ You can also change the zoom level by entering a percentage in the Zoom field in the lower-left corner of the document window.

A magnified image can also be moved in the document window by using the Hand tool.

To reposition a magnified image with the Hand tool:

Do one of the following:

Choose the **Hand** tool 🖑 (H) or hold down the Spacebar for a temporary Hand tool, then drag in the document window.

Choose the **Hand** tool 🖑 (H) or hold down the Spacebar for a temporary Hand tool, do a quick little drag in the document, then release. The magnified image will float across the screen (this is called "flick panning"); click again to stop the motion. Note: For this to work, Use Graphics Processor must be checked in Edit/Photoshop CC > Preferences > Performance before you open your document, and Enable Flick Panning must be checked in Preferences > Tools. ★

➤ If a document is in a tabbed window in the Application frame and is magnified, you can drag it far off to the side to reveal the edges of the canvas against the background of the Application frame.

➤ If you check Overscroll ★ in Preferences > Tools, you can also move a non-magnified image in the document window either by "flick panning" it with the Hand tool or by dragging a scroll bar at the right and/or bottom edge of the window.

| Zoom field | Zoom Out button | Zoom slider | View box | Zoom In button |

A *You can use the Navigator panel to change the zoom level of your document and, if the image is magnified, to move it in the document window.*

MATCHING THE ZOOM LEVEL, LOCATION, OR ROTATION AMONG MULTIPLE DOCUMENTS

If you have multiple documents open in Photoshop, from the Window > Arrange submenu, you can choose Match Zoom to match the zoom level of all open images to that of the currently active image, Match Location to match the relative positions of all open and magnified images within the document window to that of the current one, Match Rotation to match the canvas angle of all open images to that of the current one (the angle is produced by the Rotate View tool; see the next page), or Match All to do all of the above.

If you have multiple documents open (say, in a 2-Up or 3-Up layout), you can save time by scrolling or zooming all of them simultaneously.

To scroll or zoom in multiple document windows:

1. Open two or more documents, then on the Window > Arrange submenu, choose a Tile command or a 2-Up, 3-Up, 4-Up, 5-Up, or 6-Up command.

2. When using the **Hand** tool 🖐 (H), check Scroll All Windows on the Options bar; or when using the **Zoom** tool, 🔍 check Zoom All Windows on the Options bar. Alternatively, when using either tool, you can leave the above-mentioned options unchecked and enable them temporarily by holding down Shift.

Rotating the canvas view

Unlike the Image > Image Rotation commands, which rotate an image permanently, the Rotate View tool tilts the canvas temporarily so you can draw, paint, or perform other edits at a more comfortable angle.

Note: To use the Rotate View tool, Use Graphics Processor must be checked in Edit/Photoshop CC > Preferences > Performance. If the preference is off, check it, then reopen the document.

To rotate the canvas view:

1. Change the zoom level, if necessary, so the entire image is showing in the document window.

2. Choose the **Rotate View** tool 🔄 (R) (in the Hand tool fly-out menu) or hold down R to spring-load the tool, then drag in the image (a compass displays temporarily).**A**

➤ When the Rotate View tool is selected, you can also change the rotation angle on the Options bar (use the scrubby slider, or enter a value, or move the dial.

To reset the canvas view to the default angle:

1. Choose the **Rotate View** tool 🔄 (R) or hold down R to spring-load the tool.

2. On the Options bar, click **Reset View**.

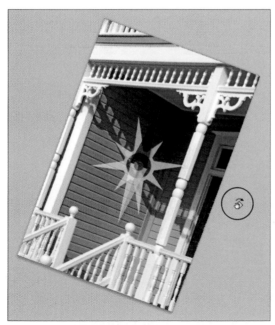

A *With the Rotate View tool, we're dragging to tilt the canvas to the desired angle.*

TOUCH GESTURE SUPPORT ★

Photoshop CC supports and recognizes touch gestures that are used with multi-touch devices connected to a Macintosh computer or with the Microsoft Surface Pro touch device running under Windows 8.1 or newer.

You can use two-finger touch gestures to adjust the x/y location, rotation, and zoom level of the image view in the document window. You can switch between using touch view controls and using mouse or stylus features to manipulate your image view. (You just can't use both simultaneously.)

For more information on using touch controls, see Photoshop Help > Touch Gestures.

Changing the screen mode

The three screen modes control which Photoshop interface features display onscreen.

To change the screen mode:

Press F to cycle through the screen modes, or choose a mode from the **Screen Mode** menu 🖵, at the bottom of the Tools panel: **A**

Standard Screen Mode (the default mode) to display the full Photoshop interface, including the Application frame, Photoshop menu bar, Options bar, current document, document tabs, and panels — with the Desktop (and any other open application windows) visible outside it.

Full Screen Mode with Menu Bar to display the current document on a full-screen background with all of the above-mentioned interface features showing, but with the Application frame, document tabs, Desktop, and other windows hidden. **B**

Full Screen Mode to display only the current document on a full-screen background with all the Photoshop interface features hidden and the panels visible only upon rollover (see "To make hidden panel docks reappear" on the next page).

A *Choose an option from the Screen Mode menu on the Tools panel.*

Standard Screen Mode	F
Full Screen Mode With Menu Bar	F
Full Screen Mode	F

Choosing a workspace

To change your panel setup quickly, choose one of the predefined workspaces, which are designed for different kinds of tasks, or choose a user-defined workspace (see pages 108–109).

To choose a workspace:

From the **Workspace** menu on the right side of the Options bar **C** or from the Window > **Workspace** submenu, choose a predefined workspace, such as Essentials (Default), What's New, Painting, Photography, or Typography, or a user-defined workspace.

CUSTOMIZING THE BACKGROUND

▶ To quickly change the background shade around the canvas area for the current screen mode, right-click the background, then on the context menu, choose default, Black, or a shade of gray. Although you could choose Select Custom Color (then choose a custom color via the Color Picker), we recommend sticking with neutral gray or black because it provides the best setting for judging color and tonal adjustments.

▶ In the Interface panel of the Edit/Photoshop CC > Preferences dialog, for the canvas area in each of the three screen modes, you can choose a background color or shade and a border style of Line, Drop Shadow, or None (see page 457).

B *When performing color correction work, we use the screen mode option of Full Screen Mode with Menu Bar.*

C *We're choosing a workspace from the Workspace menu on the Options bar.*

Configuring the panels

If you have chosen Standard Screen Mode or Full Screen Mode with Menu Bar and you want to fully maximize your screen space, you can hide all your open panels (see the shortcuts below) and make them reappear only when needed (see the next task). If you put your document into Full Screen mode, in which panels are hidden by default, you can also use these shortcuts to show the panels and keep them visible.

To hide (or show) the panels:

Do either of the following:

Press Tab to hide (or show) all the currently open panels, including the Tools panel.

Press Shift-Tab to hide (or show) all the currently open panels except the Tools panel.

➤ To open an individual panel when the panels are hidden, choose the panel name from the Window menu.

To make hidden panel docks reappear:

1. Hide the panels as described above, or choose Full Screen Mode from the Screen Mode menu 🖵 on the Tools panel.

2. If your document is in Standard Screen mode, let the pointer hover over the dark gray vertical bar at the left or right edge of the Application frame. If your document is in either one of the Full Screen modes, let the pointer hover at the edge of your monitor; the dark gray vertical bar appears, then the docks appear.**A**

   The panel docks will redisplay temporarily (free-standing panels will remain hidden).**B** Move the pointer away from the panels, and they'll disappear again.

   Note: If this mechanism doesn't appear to be working, right-click any panel tab or icon and check Auto-Show Hidden Panels on the context menu. That should do the trick.

➤ If you prefer to keep your panels visible onscreen, but you want to minimize how much space they occupy, shrink them to icons (see the last paragraph on the next page).

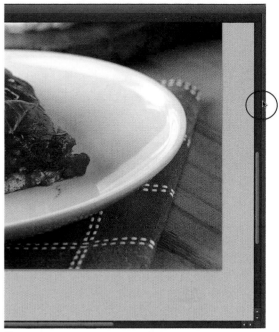

A *If the panels are hidden, let the pointer pause just inside the right edge of the monitor or Application frame …*

B *… to make the panel docks appear temporarily. (Move the pointer away from the panels, and away they go.)*

Most of the edits that you make in Photoshop will require the use of at least one of the panels — and more likely several. Fortunately, the panels are easy to hide, collapse, and expand so they don't intrude on your document space when you're not using them.

In the predefined workspaces, panels are arranged in docks on the right side of your screen, except for the Tools panel, which is on the left side. Each dock can hold one or more panels or panel groups, and you can customize how they're configured. (To save your custom workspaces, see pages 108–109.)

To reconfigure the panel groups and docks:

Show or hide a panel: Show a panel by choosing its name from the Window menu. The panel will display either in its default group and dock or in its last open location. To bring a panel to the front within its group, click its tab (panel name).

Expand a panel that's collapsed to an icon: Click the icon or panel name. If Auto-Collapse Iconic Panels is checked in Edit/Photoshop CC > Preferences > Workspace ★ and you open a panel from an icon, it collapses to an icon when you click outside it. With this preference off, the panel stays expanded; to collapse it back to an icon, click the Collapse to Icons button on the panel bar (the horizontal gray bar to the right of the panel tab) or click the panel icon in the dock.

➤ To quickly access the Auto-Collapse Iconic Panels option via a context menu, right-click any panel tab, bar, or icon.

Maximize or minimize an expanded panel or group vertically (to toggle the full panel to just a panel tab, or vice versa): Double-click the panel tab or bar.

Use a panel menu: Click the 🔳 icon to access the menu for the panel that is currently in front in its group.

Close a panel or group: To close a panel, right-click the panel tab and choose Close from the context menu. To close a whole panel group, choose Close Tab Group from the same context menu. To close a floating panel, you can click the close button in the upper-left corner.

Collapse a whole dock to icons, or to icons with names: Click the Collapse to Icons button 🔳 at the top of the dock; or double-click the topmost bar; **A–B** or right-click a panel tab, bar, or icon and choose Collapse to Icons from the context menu. To expand icons to icons with names, or to reduce icons with names to just icons, drag the vertical edge of the dock horizontally. **C**

A In this workspace, panels in the left dock are collapsed to icons, whereas the panels in the right dock are expanded. The Histogram panel is minimized vertically. We are double-clicking the bar for the rightmost dock …

B … to shrink that dock to icons. Note that the panel groups were preserved.

C Here we're dragging the edge of the rightmost dock to shrink that dock to just icons.

Widen or narrow a dock (and panels): Position the pointer over the vertical edge of the dock (✛◂▸ cursor), then drag horizontally.

Move a panel into a different group: Drag the panel tab over the panel bar of the desired group, and release when the blue drop zone border appears.**A**

Move a panel to a different slot in the same group: Drag the panel tab (name) to the left or right.

Move a panel group upward or downward in a dock: Drag the panel bar, then release it when the horizontal blue drop zone bar appears in the desired location.**B**

Create a new dock: Drag a panel tab or bar sideways to the vertical edge of the dock,**C** and release the mouse when the blue vertical drop zone bar appears.

Reconfigure a dock that's collapsed to icons: Use methods like those you would use for an expanded group. Drag the double dotted line ▦▦▦▦▦ to the edge of a dock to create a new dock, or drag it vertically between groups to restack the group (release when the horizontal drop zone line appears), or drag it into another group to move it to that group (release when the blue drop zone border appears).

Float a docked panel or group: Drag the panel tab, icon, or bar out of the dock. To stack floating panels or groups together, drag the bar of one to the bottom of another (release when the horizontal blue drop zone line appears). To resize a floating panel, drag an edge or the resize box ▦ ; not all panels are resizable.

To redock floating panels into the Application frame: If there is no existing dock, create one by dragging the topmost panel bar of a floating group or stack to the right edge of the Application frame, and release the mouse when the pointer is over the edge of the frame and a vertical blue drop zone line appears. If there is an existing dock, follow the instruction in "Create a new dock," above, or drag the panel bar of a floating panel, group, or stack into an existing dock (release when the horizontal blue drop zone line appears).

➤ To prevent a floating panel from docking as you move it, drag it with Ctrl/Cmd held down.

➤ When using a tool that uses brushes, you can show the Brush panel by clicking the Toggle Brush Panel button 🖾 on the Options bar or on the Brush Presets panel. Similarly, when using a type tool, you can show the Character/Paragraph panel group by clicking this toggle button 🈁 on the Options bar.

A *A blue drop zone border appears as we drag a panel into a different group.*

B *A blue horizontal drop zone bar appears as we move our Layers/Channels panel group upward within the same dock.*

C *A blue vertical drop zone bar appears as we create a new dock for the History panel.*

Saving custom workspaces

Now that you have learned how to personalize your workspace for Photoshop, the next step is to save some custom workspaces for various kinds of editing work you do in Photoshop. Your custom workspaces should reflect your normal work habits (and by this we don't mean working late and sleeping late!). For example, to set up a type-related workspace, you could open the Character, Paragraph, Paragraph Styles, and Character Styles panels, hide the panels you don't normally use when you work with type, and assign color labels to your favorite commands on the Type menu.

The current panel locations are included automatically when you save a custom workspace. Optionally, you can also include custom keyboard shortcuts and/or menu sets (menu sets control the color label and visibility settings for menu commands).

To save a custom workspace:

1. Do any or all of the following:

    Open and position all the desired panels in groups and docks.**A**

    Collapse the panels you use occasionally to icons, and close the ones you rarely use. Or if you prefer to keep all your panels collapsed to icons or icons with names, set them up that way.

    Resize any of the panels, as well as any of the pickers that open from the Options bar.

    Choose Edit > Menus (Ctrl-Alt-Shift-M/Cmd-Option-Shift-M) and use the dialog to assign visibility settings and/or color labels to menu commands (for quick identification). Save your changes in a new menu set. (To learn about customizing the Photoshop keyboard shortcuts, see Photoshop Help.)

2. From the Workspace menu on the Options bar, choose **New Workspace**.

3. In the New Workspace dialog, enter a **Name** for the workspace (include your name, if desired).**B**

4. Under **Capture**, if you customized the Keyboard Shortcuts or the Menus, check those options.

5. Click Save. Your workspace will appear at the top of the Workspace menu on the Options bar (**A**, next page) and on the Window > Workspace submenu.

➤ To edit a saved workspace, display the workspace to be edited, make the desired changes to the

A This is the panel setup in one of our custom workspaces.

B In the New Workspace dialog, enter a Name for your workspace and check either or both of the Capture options.

Photoshop interface, choose the New Workspace command, retype the same name, click Save, then click Yes in the alert dialog.

➤ If you have dual displays, you can distribute free-standing panel groups or stacks between them and save that arrangement as a new workspace.

➤ All the panels that are open when you exit/quit Photoshop will display in the same location upon relaunch.

To delete a workspace:

1. From the Workspace menu on the Options bar, choose any workspace *except* the one you want to delete.

2. From the same menu, choose **Delete Workspace**.

3. In the Delete Workspace dialog, choose the name of the workspace to be deleted,**B** click Delete, then click Yes in the alert dialog.

➤ To restore all the default workspaces, see the last task on this page.

Resetting workspaces

Say you chose a workspace and then rearranged some panels manually. If you were to switch to another workspace and then back to your original one, your manual changes would redisplay (in other words, the manual changes are "sticky"). Perform the first task below to restore the original settings to an individual workspace, or the second task to restore the factory-default settings to all the predefined (non-user-defined) workspaces.

To reset the current workspace:

From the Workspace menu on the Options bar, choose **Reset** [workspace name].

To reset all non-user-defined workspaces: ★

1. Choose Edit/Photoshop CC > Preferences > **Workspace** to display the Preferences dialog.

2. In the center of the Workspace panel, click **Restore Default Workspaces**. If an alert dialog appears, click OK, then click OK to exit the Preferences dialog.

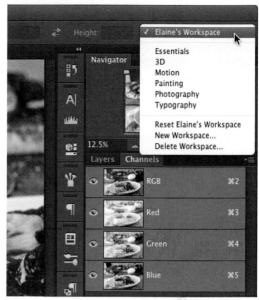

A *Our new workspace (named "Elaine's Workspace") appeared on the Workspace menu on the Options bar.*

B *In the Delete Workspace dialog, choose the user-saved workspace you want to get rid of.*

Using the Options bar

If the Options bar is hidden and you want to show it, choose Window > Options. You will use this bar primarily to choose settings for the current tool. For instance, for the Clone Stamp tool, you can choose a brush; a blending mode; opacity, flow, alignment, and sampling settings; and settings for a stylus, if you're using one. For a type tool, you can choose a font family, style, and size; anti-aliasing and alignment settings; and a color. The current Options bar settings remain in effect for each individual tool until you change them.

To open a picker, which displays one or more libraries of presets (e.g., brushes or gradients), click the picker icon or arrowhead.**A** To close a preset picker or other pop-up panel, either click outside it or click the arrowhead on the Options bar.

To cancel a value you have entered on the Options bar and exit the bar, press Esc (this also works for some pickers).

Features on the Options bar change depending on what tool is selected and the way it is being used in the document. For instance, if you begin to apply a transformation with the Move tool, Cancel Transform ⊘ and Commit Transform ✔ buttons will appear on the Options bar. If you click either button to exit transformation mode, those buttons will disappear.

The Workspace menu (not shown below) is located on the right side of the Options bar; see pages 104 and 108–109.

Note that some tool settings can also — or only — be chosen in a panel or dialog. For instance, for the type tools, you will find additional options on the Character and Paragraph panels; for the Brush or Pencil tool, you will need to choose a Foreground color via the Color panel, Swatches panel, or Color Picker.

Click here to open the Tool Preset picker.

A *Click an icon or arrowhead to open a preset picker (the Brush Preset picker is shown here).*

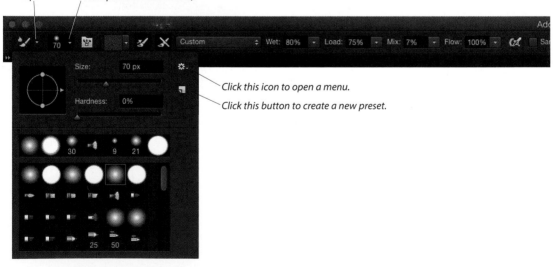

Click this icon to open a menu.

Click this button to create a new preset.

Here the Options bar is displaying settings for the Mixer Brush tool.

You will accomplish most of your editing work in Photoshop using the panels, which are the focus of this chapter, as well as via the Options bar and various editing tools. To open a panel, choose the panel name from the Window menu. To become a Photoshop speed demon, avoid using the menu bar except to choose commands that aren't available elsewhere in the interface.

In the preceding chapter, you learned how to arrange the panels onscreen (see pages 106–107). Here you will learn more about their specific functions. After a quick view of the panel icons and instructions for using the Tools panel, you will find illustrations and a brief summary (in alphabetical order) of all the panels that are used in this book. You can browse through our descriptions with or without viewing or fiddling with the panels onscreen. Later, as you become more acquainted with Photoshop, you can revisit this chapter and use it as a reference guide. (This chapter is just an introduction to the panels. In other chapters, you will find detailed instructions for using specific panels, and you will put them to lots of practical use.)

Also included in this chapter is a primer on choosing basic brush settings — steps that apply to many tools in Photoshop, not just the Brush tool. The final section of this chapter includes steps for managing and saving presets (predefined settings), which are stored and accessed via the many Photoshop panels and pickers. Some examples of presets are solid colors on the Swatches panel, styles on the Styles panel, and shapes on the Custom Shape picker.

PANELS AND PRESETS

IN THIS CHAPTER

USING THE UNDO SHORTCUTS

	Windows	Mac OS
Undo the last Photoshop edit (some edits can't be undone)	Ctrl-Z or Edit > Undo [name of edit]	Cmd-Z or Edit > Undo [name of edit]
Undo multiple editing steps in reverse order (Step Backward)	Ctrl-Alt-Z	Cmd-Option-Z
Step Forward through your editing steps (reinstate what you have undone)	Ctrl-Shift-Z	Cmd-Shift-Z

The Photoshop panel icons

Each panel in Photoshop has a unique icon that displays when the panel is either fully or partially collapsed. Until you learn to identify collapsed panels by their icons, you may want to keep your panel docks only partially collapsed (so the names display) rather than fully collapsed to just icons.**A** You can also identify the panels via Tool Tips (see the sidebar at right).

A Eventually, you will be able to quickly identify the panels by their icons.

USING CONTEXT MENUS

When you right-click in the document window—depending on where you click and which tool is selected—a menu of context-sensitive commands pops up onscreen temporarily. Context menus are also available for some features of the Photoshop interface, such as the Layers panel. If a command is available on a context menu (or can be executed quickly via a keyboard shortcut), we let you know in our instructions—to spare you from a trek to the main menu bar.

Note: If your mouse doesn't have a right-click button, hold down Control and click to open the context menu. If you're using a Trackpad on a Mac, you can tap with two fingers.

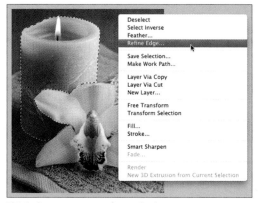

This is the context menu for a selection.

USING TOOL TIPS

If you need to identify a panel, button, icon, or menu in the Photoshop interface, you can find the information you need via the Tool Tip: Let the pointer hover over a feature without clicking the mouse button, and the item name pops up onscreen. Not happening? Go to Edit/Photoshop CC > Preferences > Interface, and check Show Tool Tips.

This Tool Tip is listing a tool name and shortcut.

This Tool Tip is identifying a panel.

The Photoshop panels that are used in this book*

Using the Tools panel

To display the Tools panel if it's hidden, choose Window > **Tools** (the panel is illustrated on the next three pages). To select a tool, do one of the following:

➤ If the desired tool is visible on the Tools panel, just click it.

➤ To cycle through related tools in the same slot, hold down Alt/Option and click the visible one.

➤ To choose a hidden tool, click and hold on the visible tool, then click a tool on the menu.

➤ To select a tool quickly, press its designated letter shortcut (don't do this if your cursor is inserted in type). The shortcuts are shown on the next three pages, as well as in the Tool Tips. If the Use Shift Key for Tool Switch option is unchecked in Edit/Photoshop CC > Preferences > Tools, ★ you can simply press the designated letter to cycle through related tools in the same slot (e.g., press L to cycle through the three lasso tools). If the Preferences option is checked, you have to press Shift plus the designated letter (e.g., Shift-L).

➤ To spring-load (access) a tool temporarily while another tool is selected, press and hold down its assigned letter key. See the sidebar on this page.

To see information pertaining to the current tool (called a tool hint), look at the bottom of the Info panel. If you don't see the tool hint, choose Panel Options from the Info panel menu (upper-right corner of the panel), then check Show Tool Hints (see page 124).

Before using a tool that you've selected, you need to choose settings for it on the Options bar. For example, for the Brush tool, you would choose a brush preset, as well as size, hardness, blending mode, and opacity settings. If the Options bar is hidden, show it by choosing Window > Options (see page 110).

The current Options bar settings for a specific tool remain in effect until you change them, reset that tool, or reset all tools. To restore the default settings to the current tool, right-click the thumbnail for the Tool Preset picker (located at the left end of the Options bar) and choose Reset Tool from the context

menu.**A** To restore the default settings to all tools (including their default order on the fly-out menus in the Tools panel), choose Reset All Tools from the same menu, then click OK in the alert dialog.

In Edit/Photoshop CC > Preferences > Cursors, you can control whether the pointer displays as a crosshair, as the icon of the current tool or, for some tools, as a circle either the size or half the size of the current brush diameter, with or without a crosshair inside it (see page 466).

For editing tools — such as the Brush, Pencil, Clone Stamp, Pattern Stamp, History Brush, Art History Brush, Blur, Sharpen, Smudge, Dodge, and Burn tools — you can choose from hundreds of brush tips, and you can also change many brush characteristics, such as size, hardness, and opacity (see pages 130–131).

A *To access these two commands, right-click the Tool Preset picker thumbnail, which is located at the left end of the Options bar.*

SPRING-LOADING A TOOL

➤ To quickly access a tool and its current Options bar settings temporarily without having to actually click the tool on the Tools panel, hold down its letter shortcut key. For example, say the Brush tool is selected but you want to reposition the contents of a layer, which requires using the Move tool. You would hold down the V key, drag in the document window, then release the V; the Brush tool will be reselected automatically. To access the Zoom tool temporarily, you would hold down the Z key.

➤ Spring-loading is slightly less efficient if you need to access a tool that shares a slot with other tools (as most tools do). In this case, the letter shortcut selects whichever tool happens to be visible on the Tools panel. To make this work, you need to plan ahead and select the tools that you want to switch back and forth between before using them.

The 3D tools, and the 3D, Measurement Log, and Notes panels aren't covered in this book, so they are not discussed in this chapter.

Tools panel

Click this collapse/expand button to toggle the panel's double-column and single-column formats.

Move Tool V — *Moves a layer, selection, guide, etc.; also functions as a transform tool*
Artboard Tool V — *Creates, moves, resizes artboards ★*

Rectangular Marquee Tool M — *Creates rectangular selections*
Elliptical Marquee Tool M — *Creates oval and circular selections*
Single Row Marquee Tool — *Creates horizontal selections, 1 pixel wide*
Single Column Marquee Tool — *Creates vertical selections, 1 pixel wide*

Lasso Tool L — *Creates freehand selections*
Polygonal Lasso Tool L — *Creates straight-edged polygonal selections*
Magnetic Lasso Tool L — *Creates freehand selections that snap to high-contrast edges in an image*

Quick Selection Tool W — *Selects shapes that it detects in the image*
Magic Wand Tool W — *Selects pixels that are similar in color to the one that's clicked*

Crop Tool C — *Crops the image (unconstrained or fixed ratio)*
Perspective Crop Tool C — *Crops the image within a perspective grid*
Slice Tool C — *Slices images for optimization (for Web output)*
Slice Select Tool C — *Selects slices by clicking*

Eyedropper Tool I — *Samples colors from an image*
3D Material Eyedropper Tool I — *Samples attributes of 3D objects*
Color Sampler Tool I — *Places readout points in an image (for the Info panel)*
Ruler Tool I — *Measures a distance or angle, or straightens the image*
Note Tool I — *Creates Acrobat-compatible annotations*
Count Tool I — *Counts objects in an image by clicking*

Spot Healing Brush Tool J — *Corrects flaws without sampling*
Healing Brush Tool J — *Corrects flaws based on a sampled area*
Patch Tool J — *Corrects flaws based on a selected area*
Content-Aware Move Tool J — *Repositions or extends an area of an image*
Red Eye Tool J — *Corrects red-eye in a portrait photo*

Brush Tool B — *Applies brush strokes*
Pencil Tool B — *Draws freehand lines*
Color Replacement Tool B — *Recolors an area while preserving the existing texture*
Mixer Brush Tool B — *Simulates traditional paint strokes; allows colors to mix and smudge*

Clone Stamp Tool S — *Clones imagery within or between documents*
Pattern Stamp Tool S — *Stamps patterns*

The upper part of the Tools panel

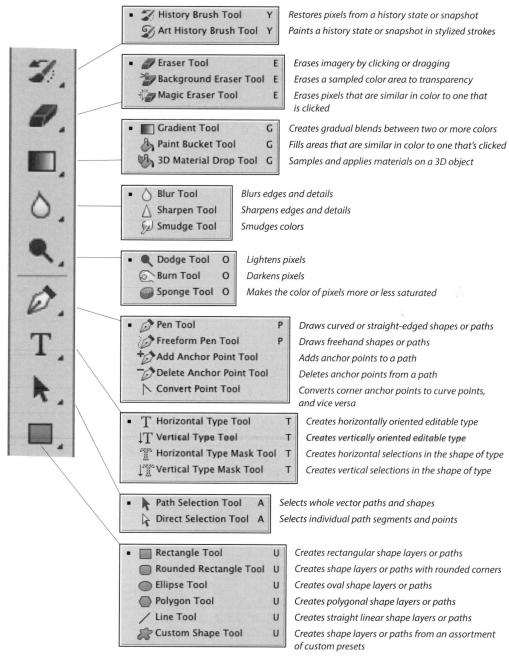

History Brush Tool — Y — *Restores pixels from a history state or snapshot*

Art History Brush Tool — Y — *Paints a history state or snapshot in stylized strokes*

Eraser Tool — E — *Erases imagery by clicking or dragging*

Background Eraser Tool — E — *Erases a sampled color area to transparency*

Magic Eraser Tool — E — *Erases pixels that are similar in color to one that is clicked*

Gradient Tool — G — *Creates gradual blends between two or more colors*

Paint Bucket Tool — G — *Fills areas that are similar in color to one that's clicked*

3D Material Drop Tool — G — *Samples and applies materials on a 3D object*

Blur Tool — *Blurs edges and details*

Sharpen Tool — *Sharpens edges and details*

Smudge Tool — *Smudges colors*

Dodge Tool — O — *Lightens pixels*

Burn Tool — O — *Darkens pixels*

Sponge Tool — O — *Makes the color of pixels more or less saturated*

Pen Tool — P — *Draws curved or straight-edged shapes or paths*

Freeform Pen Tool — P — *Draws freehand shapes or paths*

Add Anchor Point Tool — *Adds anchor points to a path*

Delete Anchor Point Tool — *Deletes anchor points from a path*

Convert Point Tool — *Converts corner anchor points to curve points, and vice versa*

Horizontal Type Tool — T — *Creates horizontally oriented editable type*

Vertical Type Tool — T — *Creates vertically oriented editable type*

Horizontal Type Mask Tool — T — *Creates horizontal selections in the shape of type*

Vertical Type Mask Tool — T — *Creates vertical selections in the shape of type*

Path Selection Tool — A — *Selects whole vector paths and shapes*

Direct Selection Tool — A — *Selects individual path segments and points*

Rectangle Tool — U — *Creates rectangular shape layers or paths*

Rounded Rectangle Tool — U — *Creates shape layers or paths with rounded corners*

Ellipse Tool — U — *Creates oval shape layers or paths*

Polygon Tool — U — *Creates polygonal shape layers or paths*

Line Tool — U — *Creates straight linear shape layers or paths*

Custom Shape Tool — U — *Creates shape layers or paths from an assortment of custom presets*

The midsection of the Tools panel

Continued on the following page

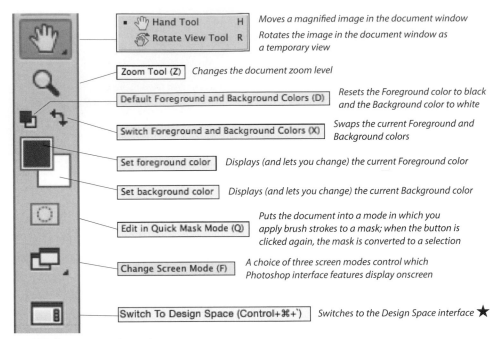

The lower part of the Tools panel

Note: If one of the panels listed on the next 14 pages is not displayed in your current workspace dock, choose its name from the Window menu to display it.

Actions panel

An action is a recorded sequence of commands that can be replayed on one image or on a batch of images. For instance, you could use an action to save a copy of a document (or multiple documents) in a different format or color mode, or to apply filters for a special effect, such as to add a texture or a frame. Using the Actions panel, you can record, store, edit, play, delete, save, and load actions. See Chapter 22.

Adjustments panel

Each button on the Adjustments panel produces a different kind of adjustment layer, which you can use to apply flexible color and tonal edits and corrections to an image (the buttons are identified on page 228). Adjustment layers are listed on the Layers panel, but you choose and edit settings for them on the Properties panel. See Chapter 12.

Adjustment buttons

Create pane for editing

Adobe Color Themes panel ★

You can use the Adobe Color Themes panel to create and save a color theme (a collection of five color swatches), view and edit your own saved themes, or explore themes created by other designers who used the Adobe Color CC web service (formerly Adobe Kuler) to create and post their themes.

The panel consists of three panes. Click Create to move sliders or markers on a color wheel to generate the five colors in a theme. Click Explore to view themes created by the Adobe Color CC design community. Click My Themes to view your own saved color themes.

Launching any Creative Cloud application (like Photoshop) requires you to be signed in to your Creative Cloud account. Your account automatically syncs your assets between the different Creative Cloud applications. Color themes (a type of asset) created in Photoshop CC or created via the Adobe Color CC web service will be available automatically in any other Creative Cloud application that works with color themes. See pages 210–212.

My Themes pane for displaying your themes

Actions menu of options

Show the Brush
Presets panel

Activate an options
set and display
its current settings

Brush panel

You will use the Brush panel to choose brush tips and custom brush settings for editing tools, such as the Art History Brush, Blur, Brush, Burn, Clone Stamp, Dodge, Eraser, History Brush, Mixer Brush, Pattern Stamp, Pencil, Sharpen, and Smudge tools. If you use a graphics tablet and stylus, you will have access to additional options on this panel.

If you click an option set name on the left side of the panel, the current settings for that set display on the right side. At the bottom of the panel, an example of a brush stroke made with the currently selected tip and settings displays in a preview. See Chapter 14.

Note: You can open this panel in several different ways: by choosing the panel name from the Window menu; by clicking the Toggle Brush Panel button on the Brush Presets panel; or if a tool that uses brushes is selected, by clicking the Toggle Brush Panel button on the Options bar.

Brush stroke preview

Live Tip Brush Preview

Open Preset Manager

New Brush

Brush Presets panel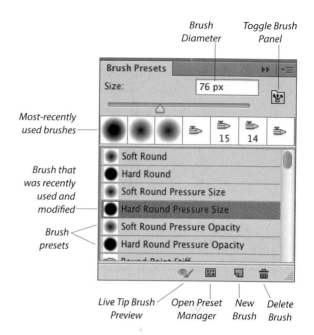

Use the Brush Presets panel to store, display, and choose from an assortment of predefined and user-created brush presets (tips and settings), for use with various editing tools. You can also use this panel to change the size of any brush preset temporarily, and to save any brush that you have customized as a new preset.

Via buttons at the bottom of the panel, you can show or hide the Live Tip Brush Preview, and also access the Preset Manager dialog. This panel can be opened from the Window menu or by clicking the Brush Presets button on the Brush panel. See page 303.

Channels panel

The Channels panel lists and displays thumbnails for all the color channels in the current document. To show a single channel in your document, click the channel name or press the keystroke that is listed on the panel. To redisplay the composite image (all the channels combined, such as RGB or CMYK), click the topmost channel on the panel or press Ctrl-2/Cmd-2. See pages 2–4.

You can also use this panel to save and load alpha channels, which are saved selections (see page 184). And you can use it to create and store spot color channels, which are printed from separate plates by a commercial shop using mixed ink colors (such as PANTONE PLUS colors).

Character panel

To choose attributes for a type tool, or to change the attributes of existing type, you can use the Character panel, which is shown here, or the Options bar (see page 384). Open this panel (or the Paragraph panel) from the Type or Window menu, or when a type tool is selected, by clicking the Toggle Character and Paragraph Panels button on the Options bar. See Chapter 19.

Font family — Myriad Pro | Bold — Font style
Font size — 220 pt | 72 pt — Leading
Kerning — Metrics | -10 — Tracking
Vertical scaling — 100% | 100% — Horizontal scaling
Baseline shift — 0 pt | Color: — Text color
Type styles — T T TT Tr T¹ T₁ T T̶
OpenType glyphs — fi ℰ st 𝒜 aⱥ T 1ˢᵗ ½
Language for hyphenation and spelling — English: USA | Sharp — Anti-aliasing method

Character Styles panel

With type styles, you can format and style your text more efficiently than by choosing individual type attributes, as well as ensure that your type has a consistent look throughout a document and among related documents. When you edit a style, all the type in which the style is being used updates automatically.

Use character styles to apply unique attributes (e.g., a boldface font style, larger size, or different color) in order to accentuate key characters or phrases. Using the Character Styles panel, you can create and edit character styles and apply them to your text. See pages 395–397. Note: We recommend styling paragraphs via the Paragraph Styles panel before applying character styles.

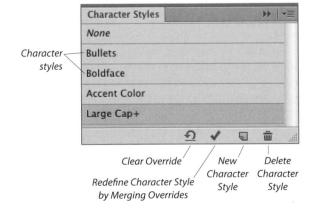

Character styles — None, Bullets, Boldface, Accent Color, Large Cap+

Clear Override
Redefine Character Style by Merging Overrides
New Character Style
Delete Character Style

Clone Source panel

The Clone Source panel lets you keep track of up to five different source documents when cloning image pixels with the Clone Stamp tool. The sources are represented by a row of buttons at the top of the panel. You can also use this panel to hide, show, and control the opacity and mode of the clone overlay, and flip, scale, rotate, invert, or reposition the source pixels before or as you clone them. See pages 290–291.

Clone sources

Flip Horizontal and Flip Vertical

Horizontal offset

Vertical offset

Clone relative to original source frame (for video)

Display the clone source as an overlay

Opacity of overlay

Blending mode for the overlay

Horizontal and Vertical Scale

Maintain Aspect Ratio

Rotate the clone source

Reset transform

Lock original frame as source (for video)

Display the overlay only within the brush cursor

Hide the overlay while cloning

Invert the overlay

Color panel

There are several ways to choose colors in Photoshop, including via the Color panel. After selecting a color model from the panel menu, you can mix a color via the sliders or quick-select a color by clicking in the ramp at the bottom of the panel (other methods are described on page 208). Colors are applied to an image by various tools (e.g., the Brush or Pencil tool) and commands (e.g., Image > Canvas Size).

To open the Color Picker (or interchangeably, the Color Libraries dialog), in which you can also choose a color, click once on the Foreground Color or Background Color square on the Color panel if it's already selected (has an outer white border), or double-click the square if it's not selected. See also pages 205–208.

Set Foreground Color

Set Background Color

Warning that the current color isn't printable

Resizable color ramp

Glyphs panel 𝒜 ★

Using the Glyphs panel, you can find out which character variations (alternate glyphs) are available for any given character in a specific OpenType or non-OpenType font, and insert specific glyphs from that font into your document (including glyphs that can't be entered via the keyboard.) See page 393.

Font family

Menu for choosing which categories of glyphs display on the panel

Font style

Pop-up showing alternate glyphs for a selected character

Zoom Out   Zoom In   Scale Down   Scale Up
                       (glyph)   (glyph)

Histogram panel

On the Histogram panel, you can view a graph of the distribution of tonal (light and dark) values in the current image, and compare them with modified tonal values as you apply color and tonal adjustments.

Via the Channel menu, you can opt to have the panel display data for the composite channel (all the channels combined, as shown at right) or for just a single channel. Via the panel menu, you can also expand the panel to display a separate histogram for each channel. See pages 234–235.

Source channel for the graph

Click to display uncached data

Uncached Refresh

Source of the pixel data (all layers or just the currently selected layer)

CHOOSING VALUES IN PHOTOSHOP

► For a quick way to change numerical values on the Options bar, on some panels (such as the Layers and Character panels), and in some dialogs, use the scrubby slider: Drag slightly to the left or right across the option name or icon.

► To access a pop-up slider (e.g., to choose an Opacity percentage on the Layers panel), click the arrowhead. To close a slider, click anywhere outside it or press Enter/Return. Tip: If you click an arrowhead to open a slider, you can press Esc to close it and restore its last setting.

► To change a value incrementally, click in a field in a dialog or panel (such as on the Character panel), then press the up or down arrow key on the keyboard.

► After typing a value in a field, you can press Tab to accept your edit (and highlight the value in the next field, if any) without exiting the dialog or panel.

History panel

Each edit that you make to a document during the current work session (e.g., the use of a filter, tool, or command; the creation of a shape, type, or image layer; the application of a layer or layer comp) is listed as a separate state on the History panel, from the "Open" unedited state of the document at the top to the most recent state at the bottom. The most recent (last) edit keeps changing as you edit your document. If you click a prior state, the document is restored to that stage of editing. See Chapter 10.

The oldest history states are deleted from the panel as new edits are made — that is, when the maximum number of history states is reached (as specified in the History States field in Edit/Photoshop CC > Preferences > Performance). All states are deleted when you close your document.

The New Snapshot command creates states that remain on the panel until you close your document, regardless of the current History States preference setting or the number of edits you apply.

You can use the History Brush tool to restore areas of an image by hand, after designating a state or snapshot as a source in the History panel (see pages 309–310).

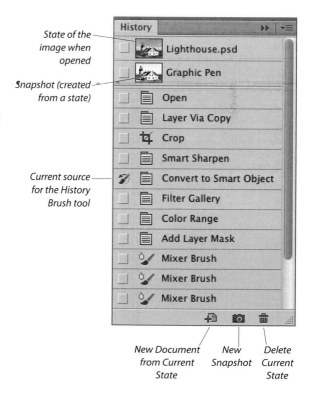

State of the image when opened

Snapshot (created from a state)

Current source for the History Brush tool

New Document from Current State

New Snapshot

Delete Current State

Info panel ⓘ

The Info panel provides up-to-the-minute data about your document. For example, it displays a color breakdown of the pixel under the pointer at its current location. As you apply color corrections, the panel displays the post-edit percentages, too. If you need yet more color data, you can place up to four color samplers in your document, and the Info panel will display readouts for those locations. The panel also lists the current coordinates of the pointer on the *x/y* axes.

Additional data may display on the Info panel depending on which tool is being used, such as the angle (A) and distance (L) between points as you use the Ruler tool; the dimensions (W and H) of a rectangular or elliptical selection or of a crop box; or the width (W), height (H), angle (A), and horizontal skew (H) or vertical skew (V) values of a layer or selection as you apply a transform edit.

Press a mini arrowhead for a color readout on the panel to choose a color model (it can differ from the current document color mode). If you prefer to do this via a dialog, choose Panel Options from the panel menu, then select a Mode for the First Color Readout and the Second Color Readout (see the dialog below).

In the Info Panel Options dialog, you can also choose Ruler Units for Photoshop (including the rulers in the document window), check which categories of Status Information you want Photoshop to display in the lower part of the panel, and check Show Tool Hints to have the panel display helpful tips about the current tool. Alternatively, you can choose a unit of measurement for Photoshop via the menu in the X and Y area on the Info panel.

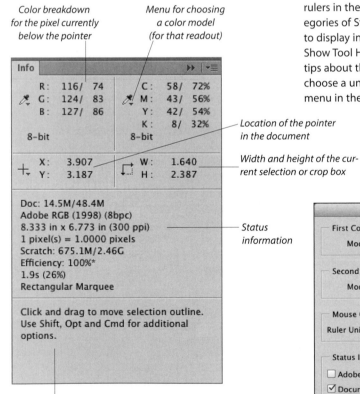

Color breakdown for the pixel currently below the pointer

Menu for choosing a color model (for that readout)

Location of the pointer in the document

Width and height of the current selection or crop box

Status information

Tool hint (tips pertaining to the current tool)

Use the Info Panel Options dialog to control which features display on the panel.

Libraries panel ★

Creative Cloud Libraries are used to gather and organize common design assets or elements into one panel, then use them across various projects and applications to preserve design consistency.

By simply copying colors, color themes, character styles, layer styles, and layer content (graphics) into the Libraries panel, you can then use those assets to place graphic content or apply a color or style to any open Photoshop CC or Illustrator CC file. All CC Library assets are stored in the Creative Cloud (and synced to a storage cache on your local machine). See pages 270–272.

Four separate categories are listed on the panel.

Roll over an asset to display information about it in a Tool Tip.

Graphic · Character Style · Layer Style · Fill Color · Stroke Color · Foreground Color

Add buttons

Layer Comps panel

When you create a layer comp (short for "composition"), it includes, collectively, any of the following document characteristics: the current layer Visibility settings (which layers are showing and which are not), the Position of imagery on each layer, and the layer Appearance (layer styles, including the layer blending mode and opacity settings, and any layer effects). You can decide which document attributes will be included in a comp, as well as add explanatory comments for the viewer. Layer comps save with the document in which they're created.

Layer comps are useful if you're weighing the pros and cons of multiple versions of a document or if you need to present versions to a client for review. For example, say you've created a few designs for a book cover. You could create a layer comp of each one (e.g., the image with and without type, or with type in two different colors). When presenting your concepts, instead of having to open and close each separate file, you could simply display each version of the same file by clicking an individual Layer Comp icon. See the bonus chapter (Presentation).

Enable/Disable the Visibility, Position, or Appearance Settings of Layer Comp

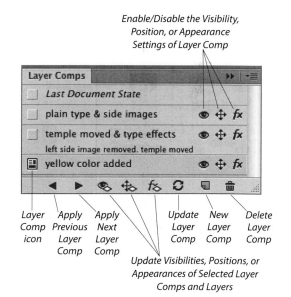

Layer Comp icon · Apply Previous Layer Comp · Apply Next Layer Comp · Update Layer Comp · New Layer Comp · Delete Layer Comp

Update Visibilities, Positions, or Appearances of Selected Layer Comps and Layers

Layers panel

At minimum, every document in Photoshop contains either a solid-color Background or a transparent layer. Above that, you can add various kinds of layers:

➤ **Image** layers contain pixel imagery, such as a digital photo or paint strokes. See Chapter 8.

➤ **Adjustment** layers apply editable and removable adjustments to underlying layers. See Chapter 12.

➤ **Fill** layers apply an editable color, gradient, or pattern to underlying layers. See pages 216–218.

➤ A **Smart Object** can be created by converting an existing Photoshop layer, or by placing an Illustrator or PDF file, another Photoshop file, or a Camera Raw file into a Photoshop document. See pages 272–283.

➤ **Editable type** layers are created by the Horizontal Type or Vertical Type tool. See pages 384–385.

➤ **Shape** layers are produced by a shape tool, and contain vector shapes. See Chapter 21.

Using the Layers panel, you can create, hide, show, duplicate, restack, group, link, lock, merge, flatten, and delete layers. You can also use this panel to change the blending mode, opacity, or fill opacity of a layer; attach a mask to a layer; and apply layer effects. Via the Filter Type menu and buttons at the top of the panel, you can control which layers are listed.

You'll be using this panel in every work session!

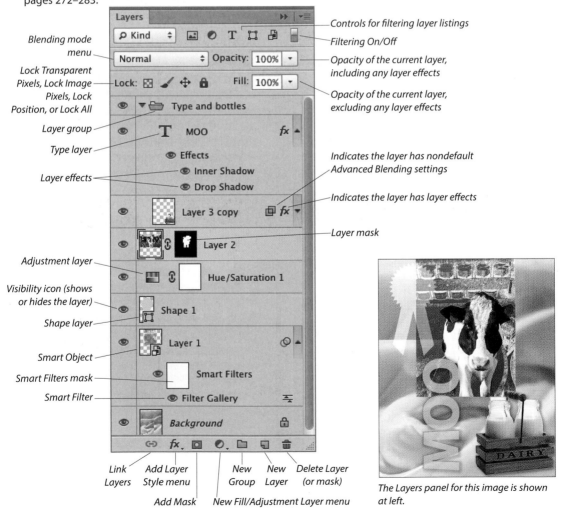

Blending mode menu
Lock Transparent Pixels, Lock Image Pixels, Lock Position, or Lock All
Layer group
Type layer
Layer effects
Adjustment layer
Visibility icon (shows or hides the layer)
Shape layer
Smart Object
Smart Filters mask
Smart Filter

Controls for filtering layer listings
Filtering On/Off
Opacity of the current layer, including any layer effects
Opacity of the current layer, excluding any layer effects
Indicates the layer has nondefault Advanced Blending settings
Indicates the layer has layer effects
Layer mask

Link Layers
Add Layer Style menu
Add Mask
New Group
New Layer
Delete Layer (or mask)
New Fill/Adjustment Layer menu

The Layers panel for this image is shown at left.

Navigator panel ✳

Using the Navigator panel, you can change the document zoom level, magnify a specific area of your document, or move a magnified document in the window. See page 102. (For other ways to zoom or move an image in the window, see pages 101–103.)

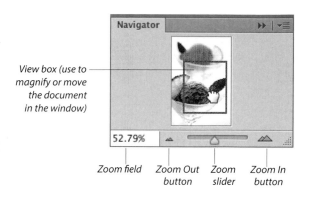

View box (use to magnify or move the document in the window)

Zoom field — *Zoom Out button* — *Zoom slider* — *Zoom In button*

Paragraph panel ¶

For paragraph type, you can use the Paragraph panel to apply paragraph-level settings, including alignment, indentation, spacing before, spacing after, and automatic hyphenation. Via the panel menu, you can access other type formatting commands (such as hanging punctuation and line-composer options), and open the Justification and Hyphenation dialogs. See page 394.

Paragraph Styles panel 🔲

Using paragraph styles, you can format and style whole paragraphs of text more efficiently than if you were to choose individual settings, and also ensure that your type styling is consistent. When you edit a style, all the type in which the style is being used updates automatically. Use the Paragraph Styles panel to create, edit, and apply paragraph-level styles. See pages 395–397.

Indent Right Margin

Alignment
Indent Left Margin
Indent First Line
Add Space Before Paragraph
Automatic Hyphenation
Add Space After Paragraph

Paths panel 🝰

The Paths panel is used for storing and accessing paths — vector shapes that are drawn with the Pen tool, Freeform Pen tool, or a shape tool. Also use this panel to apply a fill or stroke to a path, create a path from a selection, load a path as a selection, or access the path of a shape layer. See pages 434–435 and 439–442.

Clear Override
Redefine Paragraph Style by Merging Overrides
New Paragraph Style
Delete Paragraph Style

Fill Path with Foreground Color

Stroke Path with Brush — *Load Path as Selection* — *Make Work Path from Selection* — *Add a Mask* — *Create New Path* — *Delete Current Path*

Properties panel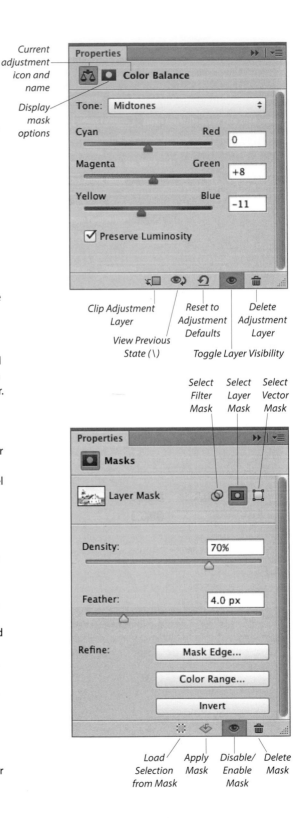

Adjustment layer options

Tonal and color corrections that you apply directly to a layer via any of the Image > Adjustments submenu commands are permanent, whereas corrections that you apply to underlying layers via an adjustment layer remain editable and reversible.

To create an adjustment layer, you can use either the Adjustments panel or the New Fill/Adjustment menu on the Layers panel. To choose and edit adjustment settings, you use the sliders and fields on the Properties panel (the options are different for each kind of adjustment layer). Via buttons on the Properties panel, you can clip (limit) the adjustment effect to just the underlying layer, view the previous state of the adjustment, restore the default settings, hide and show the current adjustment effect, or delete the current adjustment layer. See Chapter 12.

Mask options

In Photoshop, the black areas in a mask hide areas of a layer. A mask is created for every adjustment layer, fill layer, and Smart Filter automatically, but you can add a mask to other kinds of layers, such as to an image layer.

When you click a layer that contains a mask and then click the Select Filter Mask, Select Layer Mask, or Select Vector Mask button on the Properties panel, or click a mask thumbnail on the Layers panel, options for editing the mask appear on the Properties panel.

The nondestructive controls on the Properties panel include a Density slider for setting the overall opacity of a layer mask and a Feather slider for softening the edges of the mask. The Mask Edge button opens the Refine Mask dialog, which provides controls for refining a mask (the controls are the same as for the Refine Edge dialog; see pages 184–185). The Color Range button opens the Color Range dialog, which you can use to redefine the black and white areas in the mask. The Invert button swaps the black and white areas in the mask. Via other buttons on this panel, you can load a mask as a selection, apply a mask to a layer permanently, disable or enable the mask, or delete the mask.

For layer and vector masks, see pages 192–196; for vector masks, see also pages 430–433; for filter masks, see pages 376–378.

Other uses for the Properties panel

You can also use the Properties panel to access commands and info for a linked Smart Object (see pages 280–283), or to change the properties of a shape layer (see pages 423–425).

Styles panel

In Photoshop, a style is a collection of specific layer settings. A style may include the settings for layer effects (e.g., Drop Shadow, Outer Glow) and/or the settings for blending options (e.g., layer opacity and blending mode). In addition to using the Styles panel to apply a style to a layer, you can also use it to create custom styles, to be applied in any document. Via commands on the panel menu, you can save, load, and replace style libraries, which are collections of styles. See pages 416–417.

Swatches panel

The Swatches panel stores predefined and user-defined solid-color swatches, which are applied by various tools, filters, and commands. Via commands on the panel menu, you can save, load, and replace libraries of swatches. See page 209.

Timeline panel

Using the Timeline panel, you can compose a sequence of audio clips and video files (including files from a DSLR camera that captures digital video). Imported clips display as tracks on the Timeline. Using the panel, you can alter the duration of a clip, apply a filter or adjustment effect to all or part of a clip, apply transition effects, and finally, render a group of tracks into a choice of video file formats. See the bonus chapter (Presentation).

Tool Presets panel

A tool preset is a collection of settings for a particular tool that has been saved to, and can be accessed from, the Tool Presets panel. By using this panel (or the Tool Preset picker, which opens from the Options bar), you can create, save, load, sort, rename, reset, and delete presets for any Photoshop tool. See page 136.

Choosing basic brush settings

Brush settings (e.g., size, hardness, and opacity), apply to many Photoshop tools, such as the Brush, Pencil, Mixer Brush, Clone Stamp, History Brush, Sharpen, Dodge, Burn, and Eraser. The image-editing tool we use most often is the Brush — but not necessarily in the way that you might expect. We use it to edit the pixels in a layer mask, and sometimes to apply paint.

When you're using a tool for any purpose besides painting, the only values that you typically need to set are the brush size, hardness, and opacity. The current brush settings for a tool remain in effect until you choose a different preset for that tool. (In Chapter 14, you will learn many other ways to customize a brush. To learn how to manage brush presets via the Brush Presets panel, see page 303.)

Below are the steps for choosing a Soft Round or Hard Round brush tip and basic settings — steps that you will be requested to do in many tasks in this book.

To choose basic brush settings:

1. Choose an editing tool from the second grouping of tools on the Tools panel. Tools that use brush presets include the Brush, Pencil, Mixer Brush, Clone Stamp, Pattern Stamp, History Brush, Art History Brush, Eraser, Sharpen, and Smudge tools.

2. Right-click in the image to display the Brush Preset picker. You can also access the picker by clicking the Brush Preset arrowhead or thumbnail ⬚ on the Options bar, which is located at the top of the Application frame (Window > Options). Note: You must use the bar to choose a preset for some tools, such as the Spot Healing Brush, Healing Brush, Color Replacement, and Background Eraser.

3. Do the following:

   Click a brush tip that is labeled Soft Round ● or Hard Round ● (if those tips are available). (To load another library of brush tips onto the Brush Presets panel, see pages 133 and 135.)

   Set the **Size** value. **A**

   Optional: Change the Hardness (or Spacing) value.

   Optional: Change the Roundness value by dragging the small dot on the circle **B** and/or adjust the Angle value by dragging the arrowhead.

   Press Enter/Return to exit the picker.

➤ To choose other settings for a tool, such as an opacity value, use the Options bar. To choose a color for a tool (if applicable), see Chapter 11.

A *We right-clicked in the image to display the Brush Preset picker, clicked a Soft Round preset in the scrolling window, and are setting the brush size via the scrubby slider.*

B *Here we're changing the brush roundness.*

IDENTIFYING THE TYPES OF BRUSH PRESETS

Below are the basic icons (or examples of them) that you will see on the Brush Preset picker. They are also found on the Brush and Brush Presets panels.

You can also change the brush size, hardness, or opacity by dragging in the image.

Note: For the tasks below, to have the current brush values (e.g., Diameter, Hardness, Opacity) display in a label as you adjust a brush interactively, go to Edit/ Photoshop CC > Preferences > Interface, then from the Show Transformation Values menu, choose a location option for the readout.

To change the brush size interactively:

1. Choose a tool that uses brush presets (see step 1 on the preceding page).

2. Choose a brush tip.

3. Press [or] or hold down Alt-right-click/Control-Option and drag horizontally in the image.**A**

➤ To choose preferences for cursors, such as whether the tool icon or a crosshair displays in the pointer and whether the brush diameter displays as a full or half-size black circle, see page 466.

➤ You can also change the Size value for a tool on the Brush panel 🖌 or the Brush Presets panel.🖌

To change the brush hardness or opacity interactively:

1. Go to Edit/Photoshop CC > Preferences > General, and check **Vary Round Brush Hardness Based on HUD Vertical Movement** to allow the shortcut to be used in step 3, below, change the hardness of a round brush tip, or uncheck this option to have the shortcut change the opacity of any tip.

   In the Interface panel of the same dialog, make sure the **Show Transformation Values** menu is set to any option except Never.

   And finally, to display the hardness or opacity value within the cursor as a tint (for round brush tips only), show the Performance panel of the Preferences dialog and make sure **Use Graphics Processor** is checked (if it's not, check it, then close and reopen your document after clicking OK).

   Click OK.

2. Choose the Brush, Pencil, Color Replacement, Clone Stamp, Pattern Stamp, History Brush, Art History Brush, Background Eraser, Blur, Sharpen, Smudge, Dodge, or Burn tool.

3. Hold down Alt-right-click/Control-Option and drag vertically in the image. Note: For the Eraser tool, you can change only the hardness value.

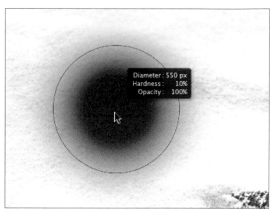

A *With Alt-right-click/Control-Option held down, we're dragging horizontally in the image to change the brush size (to change the brush hardness or opacity, depending on the current preference setting, drag vertically instead).*

BRUSH DIAMETER, OPACITY, AND HARDNESS

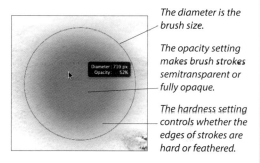

The diameter is the brush size.

The opacity setting makes brush strokes semitransparent or fully opaque.

The hardness setting controls whether the edges of strokes are hard or feathered.

SHORTCUTS FOR CHANGING TOOL SETTINGS

One or both of the shortcuts listed below apply to image-editing tools, such as the Healing Brush, Brush, Pencil, Clone Stamp, History Brush, Sharpen, Dodge, and Burn tools.

Cycle through **blending modes** for the tool	Shift- + (plus) or Shift- – (minus)
Change the **opacity, exposure,** or **strength** percentage (or Shift-press a number to change the Flow level)*	Press a digit between 0 and 9 (e.g., 2 = 20%) or quickly type a percentage (e.g., "38"; 0 = 100%

*If the Airbrush button is activated on the Options bar, press a number to change the Flow percentage or Shift-press a number to change the opacity.

Managing presets via the pickers and panels

Photoshop presets are predefined items that you choose from a picker, such as brushes on the Brush Presets panel or picker and swatches on the Swatches panel. Other presets are found in less obvious locations, such as on the Contour pickers in some panels of the Layer Style dialog and on the Gradient picker in the Gradient Fill dialog. The preset categories include brushes, swatches, gradients, styles, patterns, contours, custom shapes, and tools. A collection of saved presets that can be loaded onto a picker is called a library.

New presets are created in various ways, such as when you define a pattern via the Define Pattern command, add a swatch to the Swatches panel, add a style to the Styles panel, create a gradient in the Gradient Editor dialog, or create a tool preset or brush (see the sidebar on this page).

Unsaved presets are stored in the Adobe Photoshop CC 2015 Prefs.psp file temporarily. They stay on the picker when you relaunch Photoshop, but will be discarded if you replace them with another library or restore the default library to the picker. Thankfully, you can save your custom presets as a library, either via an individual picker (see the steps on the next page) or via the Preset Manager dialog (see page 135). You can load a saved library of presets onto its related picker at any time, and you can share preset libraries with other Photoshop users.

Note: To sync your Photoshop preference settings and presets between computers via Adobe Creative Cloud, see pages 495–496.

When you use the Preset Manager to create a library, you can pick and choose which presets are included. When you create a library from a panel or a preset picker, all the presets currently on the picker are included — you can't choose only some of them. In the latter case, you should delete the presets that you want to exclude from the library first, as in the steps below.

Note: When you delete a preset from a picker or panel, no documents are altered and no existing presets are deleted from any libraries.

To delete presets from a panel or picker:

1. Display the picker or panel from which you want to delete presets, such as the Brush Presets panel or picker, the Custom Shape picker, or the Styles, Swatches, or Tool Presets panel.

2. Do either of the following:

   Alt-click/Option-click a preset (scissors pointer). **A**

   Right-click a preset and choose **Delete** [preset type]. If an alert dialog appears, click OK.

HOW ARE PRESETS CREATED?

All of the following methods will produce a preset:

► Customize a brush using the Brush panel, then click the New Brush button on the Brush or Brush Presets panel, or on the Brush Preset picker, which opens from the Options bar.

► Add the current Foreground color as a swatch by clicking the New Swatch of Foreground Color button on the Swatches panel.

► Create a tool preset by clicking the New Tool Preset button on the Tool Presets panel or the Tool Preset picker (see page 136).

► Create a gradient by clicking New in the Gradient Editor, which opens if you select the Gradient tool, then click the Gradient thumbnail on the Options bar, in the Gradient Fill dialog, or in the Layer Style dialog (for a Gradient Overlay effect).

► Create a style by clicking the New Style button on the Styles panel or by clicking New Style in the Layer Style dialog.

► Create a pattern via Edit > Define Pattern.

► Create a custom shape by drawing a path or shape, then choosing Edit > Define Custom Shape.

A Alt-click/Option-click a swatch to delete it.

To save the presets currently on a picker as a library:

1. Make sure the preset picker or panel contains only the presets to be saved in a library (see the preceding page).

2. Do one of the following:

   From the Brush Presets, Swatches, Styles, or Tool Presets panel menu, ▼≡ or from the Brush Preset, Tool Preset, or Custom Shape picker menu, ✿▾ choose **Save** [preset type].**A**

   For a gradient, in the Gradient Editor, click **Save**; or choose **Save Gradients** from the Gradient picker menu ✿▾ in the Gradient Fill dialog (for a Gradient fill layer) or in the Gradient picker (Options bar, with the Gradient tool chosen).

   For a pattern, choose **Save Patterns** from the Pattern picker menu ✿▾ in the Layer Style dialog for the Pattern Overlay effect, in the Edit > Fill dialog (with Pattern chosen on the Use menu), or in the Pattern Fill dialog (for a Pattern fill layer).

3. In the Save dialog, enter a name, keep the default extension and location, then click Save.

4. Relaunch Photoshop to make your new library appear on the panel and/or preset picker menu and on the menu in the Preset Manager.

➤ To overwrite an existing library, in step 3 above, locate and click the library name, click Save, then click Replace in the alert dialog.

A *To save the brushes that are currently on the Brush Presets panel as a library, we're choosing Save Brushes from the panel menu.*

To load a library of presets onto a panel or picker via an individual panel or picker, follow the steps below; to load presets via the Preset Manager, see page 135.

To load a library of presets:

1. Choose a preset library name in one of these locations:

   The menu on the Brush Presets, Styles, Swatches, or Tool Presets panel. ▼≡

   The menu ✿▾ in the Custom Shape picker on the Options bar (the Custom Shape tool must be selected first); see page 422.

   The Gradient picker menu ✿▾ in the Gradient Editor dialog (the Gradient tool must be selected first, then the Gradient thumbnail clicked on the Options bar); see pages 219–220.

   The Gradient picker menu ✿▾ in the Gradient Fill dialog for a Gradient fill layer; see pages 217–218.

   The Custom Pattern picker menu ✿▾ in the Edit > Fill dialog (choose Pattern from the Use menu); see page 222.

   The Pattern picker menu ✿▾ in the Pattern Fill dialog for a Pattern fill layer.

   The Styles, Contour, Gradient Overlay, or Pattern Overlay picker menu ✿▾ in the Layer Style dialog (see pages 403–404, 410–413, and 416).

   The menu ✿▾ in the Tool Preset picker (see page 136) or Brush Preset picker (see page 131) on the Options bar.

2. In the alert dialog, click **Append** to add the chosen library of presets to the currents ones on the panel or picker, or click **OK** to replace the current presets with those in the library.

   Note: If the panel or picker contains unsaved presets, another alert dialog will appear, giving you the option to save the existing presets as a library. Click Don't Save or Save.

➤ If the library you want to load isn't in the default location (and therefore isn't listed on its related panel or picker menu), choose Load [preset name] from the menu, locate the library, then click Open.

You can restore the default library to any panel or picker.

To restore the default presets to a panel or picker:

1. From a panel or picker menu, choose **Reset** [preset name].

2. When the alert dialog appears, click OK to replace the existing presets on the panel or picker with the default ones.

   Note: If you made changes to the current presets, another alert dialog will appear. Click Don't Save; or click Save, then use the Save dialog to save the current presets as a library.

Exporting and importing presets

Using the Export/Import Presets dialog, it's easy to export and import preset libraries and share them among Photoshop users on your network.

To export preset libraries:

1. Choose Edit > Presets > **Export/Import Presets**.

2. Click the **Export Presets** tab, then double-click each preset library you want to export **A** (or click a library, then click the right arrowhead ➤). Repeat

for any other libraries you want to export. (To remove a preset from the Presets to Export list, double-click it. To remove or add all the presets on the list, click Remove All or Add All.)

3. Click **Export Presets**.

4. In the Choose a Folder dialog, choose a location, then click Open.

To import preset libraries:

1. Choose Edit > Presets > **Export/Import Presets**.

2. Click the **Import Presets** tab, click **Select Import Folder**, locate and click the folder containing the desired preset library or libraries, then click Open.

3. Double-click each preset library you want to import. (To remove a preset from the Presets to Import list, double-click it. To remove or add all the presets on the list, click Remove All or Add All.)

4. Click **Import Presets**. If an alert dialog appears, click Yes.

➤ To import *all* earlier Photoshop presets into Photoshop CC (from both the user library and the Presets folder in the program folder), choose Edit > Presets > Migrate Presets, then click Yes in the alert dialog. You don't need to restart your system.

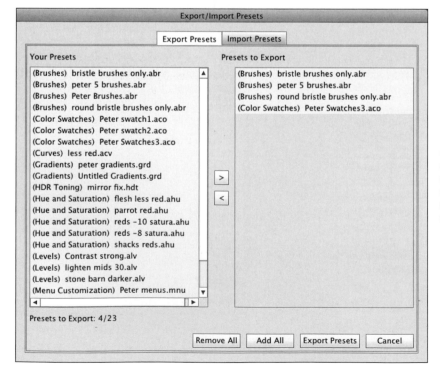

A *In the Export/Import Presets dialog, we double-clicked each selected library we wanted to export. (Our next step will be to click Export Presets.)*

Using the Preset Manager

Using the all-inclusive Preset Manager dialog, you can save and load Photoshop presets of any variety.

To save presets as a library via the Preset Manager:

1. To open the Preset Manager, do one of the following:

   Choose Edit > Presets > **Preset Manager**.

   Choose **Preset Manager** from the menu of any picker or panel (e.g., the Custom Shape picker or the Swatches or Styles panel).

   On the Brush or Brush Presets panel, click the **Open Preset Manager** button.

2. From the **Preset Type** menu, choose the category of presets for which you want to create a library, or press the shortcut that is listed on the menu.

3. From the menu in the dialog, ✿▾ choose a view option for the scrolling window (such as Small Thumbnail or Small List). For Brushes, you can choose Stroke Thumbnail view to display a sample of the brush stroke alongside each thumbnail.

4. Shift-click or Ctrl-click/Cmd-click the presets to be saved in a library, then click **Save Set**.A

5. In the Save dialog, enter a name for the new library, keep the default extension and location, then click Save.

6. Click Done to exit the Preset Manager.

7. Relaunch Photoshop.

➤ To rename a preset when the Preset Manager is in a thumbnail view, double-click the thumbnail, then change the name in the dialog. If the Preset Manager is in a text-only or list view, double-click the preset name. You can also select multiple presets and then click Rename, in which case each naming dialog will open in succession.

You can reset any category of presets to the factory defaults, append (add) more presets to the current ones on the picker or panel, or replace the current presets with those in a library. Presets on the pickers and panels remain there when you relaunch Photoshop. Changes made in the Preset Manager appear in the corresponding picker, and vice versa.

To load presets via the Preset Manager:

1. Open the Preset Manager by following step 1 in the instructions at left.

2. From the **Preset Type** menu, choose a category of presets.

3. Any unsaved presets on the chosen picker will be deleted in the next step, unless you select the Append option in that step. To save the current presets as a library before proceeding, follow steps 4–5 at left.

4. From the menu in the dialog, ✿▾ choose a library name; or to reload the default library, choose **Reset** [preset type]. In the alert dialog, click **Append** to add the new library to the current ones on the picker, or click OK to replace the current presets with the newly loaded ones.

   If the picker contains any unsaved presets (you didn't save them in a library), another alert will appear. Click Don't Save or Save.

5. *Optional:* To delete presets from the picker (but not from the library), click a preset to be deleted or Shift-click or Ctrl-click/Cmd-click multiple presets, then click Delete. This can't be undone (but of course you can reload any library).

6. Click Done to exit the Preset Manager.

A *In the Preset Manager dialog, choose a category from the Preset Type menu, select all the presets to be saved in a library, then click Save Set.*

Creating tool presets

For any tool, you can choose a preset (such as a brush), Options bar settings, and a Foreground color (if applicable), then save that collection of settings as a tool preset. Thereafter, upon selecting that tool, you can simply choose your preset from the Tool Preset picker on the Options bar or from the Tool Presets panel; it contains all your saved settings. Although tool presets take some time to set up initially, it's time well spent.

To acquaint yourself with the Tool Presets panel, show it, then uncheck Current Tool Only. The tool presets for all tools display. Click a tool preset; the tool with which that preset is used becomes selected automatically. Check Current Tool Only; only presets for the current tool display. Via the panel or picker menu, you can load additional presets (see page 133).

To create a tool preset:

1. Select a tool and choose Options bar settings for it.

   For some tools, such as the brush and shape tools, the current Foreground color can be included in the preset; for the Gradient tool, you can include the currently selected gradient. If you opt to do this, choose that color or gradient now.

2. Do either of the following:

   At the far left end of the Options bar, click the Tool Preset picker thumbnail or arrowhead. **A**

   Show the Tool Presets panel. **B**

3. Click the **New Tool Preset** button on the picker or panel. The New Tool Preset dialog opens.

4. *Optional:* Rename the preset, if desired.

5. *Optional:* Check Include Color or Include Gradient (if that option is present).

6. Click OK. The new preset appears on the Tool Preset picker and the Tool Presets panel.

7. The presets that are on the Tool Presets panel (for all tools) will still be there when you relaunch Photoshop, but will disappear if you replace them with a library. To preserve your custom presets for future use, see the first task on page 133.

➤ To restore the default tool presets, follow the steps on page 134. Don't confuse the Reset All Tools command with the Reset Tool Presets command.

➤ To create a variation of an existing tool preset, click a preset, choose custom settings for it, then follow steps 3–6, above, making sure to rename it in step 4.

A *To open the Tool Preset picker, click the thumbnail or arrowhead on the Options bar.*

B *Tool presets can also be created via the Tool Presets panel.*

SOME SUGGESTIONS FOR TOOL PRESETS

Take note of which tools you use most often, and which settings you normally choose for them. Here are a few ideas for custom presets:

➤ Brush panel settings, Options bar settings, and a Foreground color for the Brush tool or Mixer Brush tool (for the latter tool, remember to choose a combination of Wet, Load, and Mix settings)

➤ Options bar settings for the Crop tool

➤ Character panel and Options bar settings for the Horizontal Type or Vertical Type tool, including a type color

➤ Oft-used Options bar settings for healing tools, such as the Healing Brush and Spot Healing Brush tools, or for the Clone Stamp or Sharpen tool

➤ Oft-used settings for the selection tools (e.g., Fixed Ratio values for the Rectangular Marquee tool)

➤ Options bar settings for the Gradient tool, with the "Black, White" gradient preset chosen

Before applying adjustment commands or other edits to an image in Photoshop, you need to make sure it has the proper resolution and dimensions. At any point, you can also **crop or rotate it.** In this chapter, you will learn how to change the resolution, dimensions, and canvas size of a file, and how to crop, straighten, flip, and rotate it.

Changing the document resolution and/or dimensions

In this chapter, you will encounter three related terms:

➤ The pixel count (pixel dimensions) of a file is arrived at by multiplying its pixel height and width values (as in 3000 x 2000 pixels equals 6 megapixels).

➤ The resolution (or "res," for short) of a file — the fineness of detail — is measured in pixels per inch, or ppi (as in 250 or 300 ppi).

➤ The process of changing a file's pixel count (adding or deleting pixels) is called "resampling." More specifically, the process of adding pixels is called "upscaling," and the process of deleting pixels is called "downsampling."

Some input devices (e.g., digital cameras that capture 10 megapixels of data or more, as well as high-end scanners) produce files with a higher pixel count than is necessary for most standard printing devices. If your Photoshop file falls into that category, you will be able to resize it via the Image Size dialog without having to resample it. Because its pixel count remains the same, its image quality is preserved.

If your file contains too low a pixel count for your target output device, you will need to resize it with resampling via the Image Size dialog. As you increase its resolution or dimensions, its pixel count and storage size will also increase. Although resampling is sometimes necessary, it reduces the image sharpness. For print output, this is a concern, but it can be compensated for somewhat by applying a sharpening filter afterward (see pages 344–348). Resampling is not a concern for Web output.

Using the Image Size dialog (and its large preview), we'll show you how to resize a file for print output without resampling, how to upscale a file for print output, and how to downsample a file for print or Web output.

7

IN THIS CHAPTER

PIXELS

Pixels, short for "picture elements," are the building blocks that make up a digital image — the tiny individual dots that a digital camera uses to capture a scene or that a computer uses to display images onscreen. When working in Photoshop and for Web output, you'll need to be aware of the pixel dimensions, or pixel count, of an image. For print output, you'll need to be aware of its resolution.

When setting the proper resolution of an image for print output, you need to decide whether to permit resampling. For a digital photo that is shot with a digital SLR camera, the ideal scenario of no resampling is possible because it contains a sufficient number of pixels for high-quality output. However, such a photo will initially have a low resolution (usually 72 to 180 ppi) and very large width and height dimensions, so you will need to increase its resolution to the required value, as in these steps. Photos from a 16-megapixel camera can be output as high-quality prints up to 16 x 11 , and photos from a 12-megapixel camera can be output as high-quality prints up to 14 x 9 .

To change the resolution of an image for print output (no resampling):

1. With your photo open in Photoshop, choose Image > **Image Size** (Ctrl-Alt-I/Cmd-Option-I). The Image Size dialog opens.

2. *Optional:* To enlarge the dialog and preview, drag any side or corner. You can Ctrl-click/Cmd-click in the preview to zoom in, or Alt-click/Option-click it to zoom out, or roll over the preview and click the – or + button. To bring a different area of a magnified image into view, either drag in the preview or click in the document.

3. From the menu next to the **Width** field, choose Inches (or a unit that is suitable for your output device); the same unit will be chosen automatically for the Height. Note: In this new dialog interface, there is only one set of Width and Height fields.

4. Uncheck **Resample** because the image contains a sufficient number of pixels for you to increase its resolution without resampling.**A**

5. Enter a **Resolution** of 300. The Width and Height values will change, but the document proportions and pixel count will stay the same (**A**, next page).

6. Click OK. No pixels were eliminated from the image, so you don't need to resharpen it.

PRESERVING IMAGE SIZE SETTINGS

➤ The current Resample and units menu settings (and dialog size) that you choose in the Image Size dialog stick for the application until you change them.

➤ The Fit To menu lists preset image sizes (width, height, and resolution) in three categories: display sizes, paper sizes, and photo print sizes. To add the current dialog values as a new preset, choose Save Preset from the Fit To menu, enter a name, then click Save; the preset appears on the menu.

A *In the Image Size dialog, we unchecked Resample to make the Width, Height, and Resolution values interdependent (note the lines linking the Resolution to the Width and Height).*

A *When we increased the resolution value to 300, the Width and Height values changed automatically, but the Dimensions remained the same. We noted in the preview that the image quality was preserved.*

If a file lacks a sufficient number of pixels to produce a medium-size, good-quality print, such as an 8 x 10 (e.g., the file has both small dimensions and a resolution of 200 ppi or below), you will need to upscale it so it has the necessary pixel count, as in the steps below. (For a smaller print, see the first task on page 141 instead.)

To upscale an image for print output:

1. Use File > Save As to copy your file.

2. Choose Image > **Image Size** (Ctrl-Alt-I/Cmd-Option-I). The Image Size dialog opens. Follow steps 2–3 on the preceding page.

3. Check **Resample**, and from the **Dimensions** menu, ⬇ choose Pixels. To preserve the width-to-height ratio of the image (prevent distortion), click the **Constrain Aspect Ratio** button 🔗 to activate it.

4. In the **Resolution** field, enter 300.

5. In the **Width** or **Height** field, enter the dimension needed for the print.

6. From the Resample menu, choose the method you want Photoshop to use to reassign color values to added pixels based on the values of existing pixels:

Automatic to let Photoshop choose and apply the best method.

Preserve Details (Enlargement) to improve the sharpness and detail in the enlarged image. Also increase the Reduce Noise value until any artifacts that were produced by the detail enhancement are reduced (**A–C**, next page).

Bicubic Smoother (Enlargement).

➤ In the preview, zoom to 100%, and compare the results of choosing different Resample methods. Also use this zoom level to gauge the Noise setting (if you chose the Preserve Details option).

7. Click OK. Because the image was resampled, the next step is to resharpen it (see pages 344–348).

➤ To restore all the original settings that were in effect when you opened the Image Size dialog, either choose Original Size from the Fit To menu or hold down Alt/Option and click Reset (Cancel becomes Reset).

A *As indicated by the original values shown in this Image Size dialog, this photo doesn't contain enough pixels, nor a high enough resolution, to produce a large, high-quality print.*

USING AUTO RESOLUTION

To let Photoshop set the resolution of a document for commercial print output, from the Fit To menu in the Image Size dialog, choose Auto Resolution. The Auto Resolution dialog opens. Enter a Screen value as the lines per inch setting (such as 133 for a typical commercial press), then click a print Quality option. When you click OK to return to the Image Size dialog, you will see that Photoshop set the Resolution value.

SCALING STYLES

If your document contains layer styles and you want to permit them to be scaled as you change the Image Size, on the menu in that dialog, ⚙️ make sure Scale Styles is checked (see Chapter 20).

B *We checked Resample, increased the Width value (the Height changed automatically), increased the Resolution value, chose the Resample method of Preserve Details (Enlargement), and set the Reduce Noise value to 60. In the preview (set to 100% view), we noted that the edges and lines were softened, such as on the ruler and graph paper.*

C *To resharpen the edge details, we reset the Reduce Noise value to 0.*

Say your photo was shot with a high-megapixel camera (and therefore has a high pixel count), but you want to print it at a smaller size, such as 5" x 8". If you downsample (a copy of) it first, its data will transfer more efficiently to your printer.

To downsample a photo for a smaller print size:

1. Use File > Save As to copy your file, then choose Image > **Image Size** (Ctrl-Alt-I/Cmd-Option-I). The Image Size dialog opens.**A** If you want to enlarge the dialog and preview, drag any side or corner.

2. Check **Resample**, and click the **Constrain Aspect Ratio** button 🔒 to activate it.

3. If the **Resolution** value isn't 300 ppi, enter that value now.

4. From the **Resample** menu, choose Automatic (this tells Photoshop to use the best method).

5. From the menu next to the Width field, choose Inches, then enter the **Width** or **Height** value needed for your print.**B**

6. Click OK. Because the image was resampled, you should resharpen it (see pages 344–348).

To produce a GIF, JPEG, PNG, or SVG file from a Photoshop layer for output to the Web or a mobile device, we use the Export As command; ★ see pages 487–489. It's an easy process. If you want to use the Image Size dialog to specify lower resolution, width, and height values for a file in order to downsample the image (that is, lower its pixel count to enable it to download efficiently), follow the steps below.

To downsample an image for Web output:

1. Follow step 1 in the preceding task.

2. Check **Resample**, and to preserve the width-to-height ratio of the image (prevent it from becoming distorted), click the **Constrain Aspect Ratio** button 🔒 to activate it.

3. From the **Resample** menu, choose Automatic (this enables Photoshop to use the best method).**C**

4. Enter a **Resolution** of 72 ppi.

5. From the menu next to the Width field, choose **Pixels**, then enter the desired **Width** or **Height** value.**D**

6. Click OK.

A These are the original settings for our high-resolution photo (note the Image Size and Dimensions values).

B We checked Resample and activated the Constrain Aspect Ratio button, then changed the Width value to 8 inches. The Image Size and Dimensions shrank accordingly.

C These are typical Image Size values of a digital photo that has not been resized or resampled.

D We checked Resample, then set the Resolution to 72 and the Width to 600 pixels. The result was a much smaller image size.

Changing the canvas size

The canvas area is the live, editable part of a document. By using the Canvas Size command, you can add or delete pixels from one, two, three, or all four sides of the canvas. Adding pixels would be useful, say, if you want to make room for some type, as in the example shown here, or to accommodate imagery from other documents in a multilayer collage (see Chapter 13).

To change the canvas size of a document:

1. Choose Image > **Canvas Size** (Ctrl-Alt-C/Cmd-Option-C). The Canvas Size dialog opens.

2. From the **Width** menu, choose a unit of measure.

3. Do either of the following:

   Enter new **Width** and/or **Height** values. The dimensions work independently; changing one won't affect the other. **A–B**

   Check **Relative**, then increase or reduce the **Width** and/or **Height** values to alter the ratio between those dimensions.

4. *Optional:* The black dot in the center of the Anchor arrows represents the existing image area. Click a square to reposition the image relative to the canvas. The arrows point to where canvas area will be added or deleted.

5. If you're adding to the canvas, from the **Canvas Extension Color** menu, choose a color option for the new area. Or to choose a custom color, choose Other or click the color square next to the menu, then choose a color in the Color Picker (see pages 206–207) or by clicking in the document window. Note: If the image doesn't have a Background (take a peek at the Layers panel), this menu won't be available, and the added canvas area will be filled with transparency.

6. Click OK. **C** If your settings made the canvas smaller, an alert dialog may appear. Click Proceed.

➤ To enlarge the canvas area manually with the Crop tool, see page 148. To enlarge the canvas to include all layer content, including any content that is hidden outside it, choose Image > Reveal All.

A *This is the original image.*

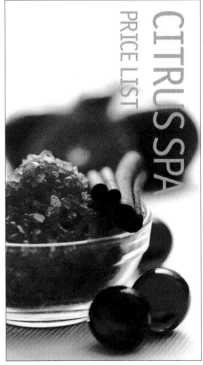

B *To add canvas area to the top of this image, in the Canvas Size dialog, we increased the Height value, then clicked the bottom middle Anchor square to shift the black dot downward.*

C *After adding pixels to the top of the canvas, we created an editable type layer.*

Cropping an image

To crop an image manually:

1. Choose the **Crop** tool ⬚ (C or Shift-C).

2. Choose one of the following options, either from the **Aspect Ratio** (first) menu on the Options bar or from the context menu (right-click in the image):

   To crop the image without constraints, on the Options bar, choose **Ratio**, then click **Clear**; or choose **Clear Ratio** from the context menu.

   To preserve the original proportions of the document while cropping it, choose **Original Ratio**.

   Choose a ratio preset, such as 5:7 (or enter custom width and height ratio values on the Options bar).

3. To preserve the cropped areas, uncheck **Delete Cropped Pixels** on the Options bar.

4. Define which part of the image you want to keep by dragging a handle or an edge of the crop box.**A–B** Areas outside the crop box will be covered with a tinted shield (see the next page).

   ➤ To resize the crop box from the center, drag a handle with Alt/Option held down.

   ➤ To preserve the current ratio (even if the ratio fields on the Options bar are blank), Shift-drag a corner handle.

5. Do any of the following optional steps:

   To **reposition** the part of the image that is going to be preserved, drag inside the box.

   To **rotate** the image in the crop box, position the cursor just outside the box, then drag in a circular direction. (To change the locus from which the image rotates, drag the reference point away from the center of the box before rotating.)

   To **hide**, then **show**, the areas outside the crop box, press H.

   To switch the orientation of the crop box, click the **Swap Width and Height** button ⇄ on the Options bar.

6. To accept the crop edits, double-click inside the crop box or press Enter/Return. You should resharpen the image, as you have just changed its pixel count.

   Note: Because you used the Crop tool with the Delete Cropped Pixels option off (step 3), the Background was converted to a layer; see the next chapter. You can drag the hidden cropped areas into view with the Move tool ⬥ (see page 263).

A *We're dragging a handle on the crop box with the Ratio option chosen on the Aspect Ratio menu.*

B *Here we're dragging a handle on the crop box with the Original Ratio option chosen on the Aspect Ratio menu.*

CLEAR, RESET, AND ORIGINAL RATIO

To clear the Width, Height (and Resolution) fields on the Options bar at any time and release the Crop tool from any ratio constraints, click the **Clear** button. The crop box won't change.

To restore the crop box to the edges of the canvas, reset the image rotation to the x/y axis (if it was rotated), and release the Crop tool from any ratio constraints, either click the **Reset** button ↻ on the Options bar or right-click in the image and choose **Reset Crop**.

To restore the crop box to the original aspect ratio of the image at any time (and also clear the fields, if displaying), without restoring the box to the edges of the canvas, choose **Original Ratio** from the Aspect Ratio menu on the Options bar or from the context menu.

To choose preview and shield options for the Crop tool:

Choose the **Crop tool** 🔲 (C or Shift-C), click to open the **Crop Options** menu ⚙️ on the Options bar,**A** then check any or all of these options:

Show Cropped Area (H) to display the image areas outside the crop box.

Auto Center Preview to allow the image to shift in the opposite direction as you drag a handle on the crop box.

Enable Crop Shield to display a tint over the cropped areas. From the Color menu, choose Match Canvas (the least obtrusive option); set the Opacity value for the tint; and check Auto Adjust Opacity to let the tint display in a reduced opacity while you drag to edit the crop box.

➤ To use the updated crop features of Photoshop, as described here, keep Use Classic Mode unchecked.

➤ If you crop an image nondestructively (with Delete Cropped Pixels unchecked), then reselect the Crop tool and click in the image (Show Cropped Area option checked), the cropped areas will redisplay.

The preset geometric guide lines that you can use with the Crop tool are based on timeless design principles.

To use guide lines with the Crop tool:

1. Choose the **Crop tool** 🔲 (C or Shift-C).

2. From the **Overlay** menu 🔲 **B** on the Options bar, do the following:

   Choose an overlay icon/option. Your choice will display as the current menu icon.

   Choose **Auto Show Overlay** to display the overlay only while the mouse button is pressed or **Always Show Overlay** to have the overlay stay visible after you click in the image with the Crop tool.

3. As you drag a handle of the crop box or reposition the image within it, let one or more key elements or shapes in your photo fall below a guide line (or areas within the guide lines) **C–D** (and **A–D**, next page). (When you're done using the overlay, you can hide it by choosing Auto Show Overlay or Never Show Overlay from the Overlay menu.)

➤ To cycle through the six guide options, choose the Crop tool, choose Always Show Overlay from the Overlay menu, click in the image, then keep pressing the letter O. To swap the orientation of the Triangle or Golden Spiral guide lines, press Shift-O.

A *From the Crop Options menu, choose preview and shield options for the Crop tool.*

B *On the Overlay menu, click an icon and a display option.*

GOLDEN RATIO

C *Using the Golden Ratio option, we're positioning the horizontal guide lines at natural divisions in the landscape, and at an intersection over the red buildings. (The Rule of Thirds, a simplified form of the Golden Ratio, has equal divisions.)*

D *This is the result.*

TRIANGLE

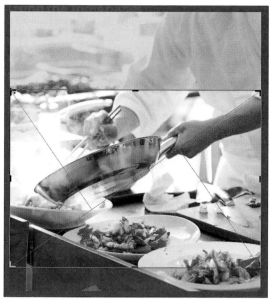

A *Here we're using the Overlay option of Triangle (on the Options bar, the Aspect Ratio menu is set to Ratio). Note where key features of the photo are located within the overlay: the chef's hands and skillet in one triangle and the plates in another triangle.*

B *This is the result.*

OVERRIDING THE SNAP

Normally, if you resize a crop box near the edge of the canvas area and the View > Snap To > Document Bounds option is on (has a check mark), the box will snap to the edge of the canvas area. If you want to position the crop box ever so slightly inside or outside the edge of the canvas, you will need to override the Snap to Document Bounds function temporarily: Start dragging one of the handles of the box, then hold down Ctrl/Control and continue to drag.

GOLDEN SPIRAL

C *Using the Overlay option of Golden Spiral, we're positioning the center of the spiral over what we consider to be the key element of the photo.*

D *This is the result.*

Cropping multiple images

Because the Crop tool keeps its current settings until you change them, you can easily apply the same aspect (width-to-height) ratio, size, or resolution values to multiple images, such as photos taken during the same shoot. In the first task below, we'll show you how to crop documents using the same aspect ratio. The dimensions of the images can vary.

To crop one or more images according to an aspect ratio:

1. Open one or more images, then click in one of them. Choose the **Crop tool** 🖼 (C or Shift-C).

2. Do one of the following:

   Right-click in the image and choose **Use Front Image Aspect Ratio** from the context menu.

   Choose a ratio preset (e.g., 5 : 7) from the **Aspect Ratio** menu on the Options bar, or enter width and height ratio values in the fields.

   Resize the crop box, then right-click in the image and choose **Use Crop Box Aspect Ratio** from the context menu.

3. Values for the current document will be listed on the Options bar and will stick with the Crop tool until you change them. Size the crop box, if desired, then double-click inside the box or press Enter/Return to accept it.

4. Click the tab of another open document. Resize the crop box, then accept the crop edits; or to accept the crop without resizing it, press Enter/Return twice. Repeat this entire step for any other open images.

Here you will crop multiple documents to specific resolution and dimensions values.

To crop multiple images to a specified size and resolution:

1. Open two or more images, then click in one of them. Choose the **Crop tool** 🖼 (C or Shift-C).

2. On the Options bar, do either of the following:

   From the Aspect Ratio menu, choose **W x H x Resolution**, then enter the desired width, height, and resolution values.

   From the Aspect Ratio menu, choose a W x H x Resolution preset (e.g., 4 x 5 in 300 ppi).

3. *Optional:* Resize the crop box (the specified dimensions and resolution will still apply to the crop box, regardless of its size).

4. To accept the crop edits, either double-click inside the box or press Enter/Return.

5. Click the tab of another open document. Resize the crop box, then accept the crop; or to accept the crop without resizing it, press Enter/Return twice. Repeat this entire step for any other open documents.

➤ To correct perspective problems in a photo resulting from camera lens distortion, we recommend using the Lens Corrections tab in Camera Raw (see pages 78–81). Using those controls, you can preview the results, whereas with the Perspective Crop tool, you cannot.

You can also crop multiple images to the dimensions and resolution of an existing document (this task), or to a crop box and resolution (next task).

To crop multiple images to the size and resolution of a document:

1. Open two or more images, and click in the one that has the desired dimensions and resolution.

2. Choose the **Crop tool** 🖼 (C or Shift-C).

3. From the Aspect Ratio menu, choose **Front Image**; or right-click in the image and choose **Use Front Image Size & Resolution** from the context menu (**A**, next page). The document's width, height, and resolution display on the Options bar.

4. Click the tab of another open image (**B**, next page). Resize the crop box, if desired, then accept the crop edits; or to accept the crop without editing it, press Enter/Return twice. Repeat this entire step for any other documents.

To crop multiple images to a crop box in, and resolution of, a document:

1. Open two or more images, including one that has the desired resolution.

2. Choose the **Crop tool** 🖼 (C or Shift-C).

3. In the document that has the desired resolution, resize the crop box to the desired proportions, then right-click in the image and choose **Use Crop Box Size & Resolution** from the context menu.

4. To accept the crop edits, either double-click inside the box or press Enter/Return.

5. Click the tab of another open document. Resize the crop box, if desired, then accept the crop edits; or to accept the crop without editing it, press Enter/Return twice. Repeat this entire step for any other documents.

To save the current settings of the Crop tool as a preset:

1. Choose the **Crop** tool 🏛 (C or Shift-C) and the desired values and settings, then from the Aspect Ratio menu, choose **New Crop Preset**.

2. In the New Crop Preset dialog, keep the name or change it, then click OK. Your new preset will appear on the menu.

APPLYING STICKY SETTINGS QUICKLY

The current Ratio and W x H x Resolution values for the Crop tool remain in effect until you change them, even after you exit/quit and relaunch Photoshop. To apply either set of those "sticky" values to a document, click the Crop tool, choose W x H x Resolution from the Aspect Ratio menu on the Options bar, press Enter/Return to activate the crop box, then press Enter/Return once more to accept the crop edit.

USING A SELECTION TO DEFINE A CROP BOX

If you create a rectangular selection before choosing the Crop tool, the crop box will match the selection boundary. If you want to force the crop box to ignore the selection, press Esc.

A *With the Crop tool, we right-clicked in the "tomatoes" image (which has the desired width, height, and resolution values) and chose Use Front Image Size & Resolution from the context menu.*

B *We clicked another document tab. The width, height, and resolution of the front image are still displaying in the fields on the Options bar. If we were to accept the crop, this "pizza" image would adopt the values of the "tomatoes" image.*

Another use of the Crop tool is to increase the canvas size, say, to add a blank area or to reveal imagery that is hidden outside the canvas. This is similar to the Canvas Size command, except here you use manual controls. All the layers in a document are affected.

To enlarge the canvas area with the Crop tool:

1. To display more of the work canvas (gray area) around the image, enlarge the Application frame or lower the zoom level of your document.

2. Choose the **Crop** tool 🔳 (C or Shift-C).

3. On the Options bar, click **Clear**.

4. Drag a handle of the box outside the canvas area.**A**

5. On the Options bar, check whether you want Photoshop to **Delete Cropped Pixels** or preserve them. On all layers, regardless of this setting, any added areas that don't contain content will be filled with transparency. If the document has a Background and you check Delete Cropped Pixels, you should choose a Background color for the added canvas area now (see Chapter 11) . With Delete Cropped Pixels off, the Background will convert to a layer and the added area will fill with transparency (for layers, see the next chapter).

6. To accept the crop edits, either press Enter/Return or double-click inside the crop box.**B**

The Trim command trims away any excess transparent or solid-color areas from the perimeter of all the layers in a document, while preserving existing imagery, type, and shapes. Of course, the document remains rectangular.

To trim areas from around an image:

1. If you want to trim transparent areas from a document that contains layers, on the Layers panel,🔖 hide the Background by clicking its visibility icon.👁

2. Choose Image > **Trim**.

3. In the Trim dialog, click a **Based On** option:

   Transparent Pixels trims transparent pixels from the edges of the image. If Photoshop doesn't detect any such areas in the image, this option won't be available.

   Top Left Pixel Color removes any border areas that match the color of the left uppermost pixel in the image.

   Bottom Right Pixel Color removes any border areas that match the color of the bottommost right pixel in the image.

4. Check which edges of the image you want Photoshop to **Trim Away: Top**, **Bottom**, **Left**, and/or **Right**.

5. Click OK.

A With the Crop tool, we're dragging the right midpoint handle outside the canvas, to add more canvas area to that side of the image.

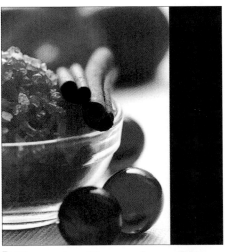

B When we released the mouse, because Delete Cropped Pixels was checked for the tool, the added canvas area filled automatically with the current Background color (brown). We accepted the crop edit.

Straightening a crooked image

When you straighten a crooked image with the Crop tool, all the layers in the document are affected.

To straighten a crooked image with the Crop tool:

1. Choose the **Crop** tool 🔲 (C or Shift-C). The crop box displays.

2. Read step 5 of the first task on the preceding page, and either check **Delete Cropped Pixels** on the Options bar or not.

3. Do either of the following:

   On the Options bar, click **Straighten** or the Straighten icon.🔲

   Hold down Ctrl/Cmd.

4. Drag along a shape in the image that you want Photoshop to align to the horizontal or vertical axis, then release.**A**

5. *Optional:* To tweak the rotation angle, drag outside the crop box. You can also edit the crop box via the usual controls.

6. Press Enter/Return, or double-click inside the box.**B**

➤ To cancel the straighten and crop edits while the Crop tool is still selected, click the Reset button 🔄 on the Options bar.

When you straighten a crooked image with the Ruler tool, only the current layer is affected, and any pixels that lie outside the live canvas area on that layer are preserved.

To straighten a crooked layer with the Ruler tool:

1. Click the Background or a layer. If you select the Background, the Straighten Layer command will convert it to a layer.

2. Choose the **Ruler** tool 🔲 (I or Shift-I).

3. Drag along a shape in the image that you want Photoshop to align to the horizontal or vertical axis. The angle will be listed as the **A** value on the Options bar.

4. *Optional:* To change the angle of the line, move either one of its endpoints.

5. On the Options bar, click **Straighten Layer**.

6. *Optional:* Reposition the layer with the Move tool.

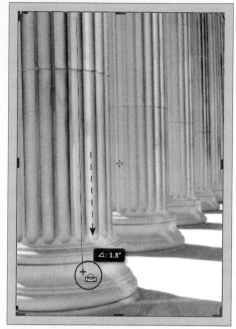

A *This image is slightly askew. We chose the Crop tool, clicked Straighten on the Options bar, then dragged downward along one of the columns.*

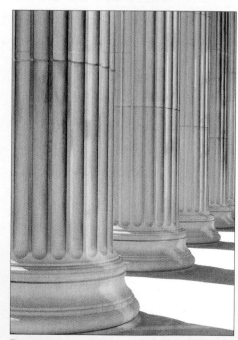

B *When we accepted the crop, the image was reoriented along the angle we defined.*

Flipping or rotating an image

You can flip or rotate all the layers in an image, or just one layer at a time. (To learn about layers, see the next chapter.)

To flip all the layers in an image:

Choose Image > Image Rotation > **Flip Canvas Horizontal A–B** or **Flip Canvas Vertical**.

► If you flipped a whole image that contains type, and the letters are now reading backwards, don't flip out! Just "unflip" the type layer using the Flip Horizontal command (see the next task). We've noticed photos in magazines and catalogs that were obviously flipped, because the lettering (e.g., in a stack of books) was unreadable.

To flip one layer:

1. Click a layer on the Layers panel.

2. Choose Edit > Transform > **Flip Horizontal** or **Flip Vertical**. Note: Any layers that are linked to the selected layer or layers will also flip.

To rotate all the layers in an image:

Do either of the following:

Choose Image > Image Rotation > **180°**, **90° CW** (clockwise), or **90° CCW** (counterclockwise).

Choose Image > Image Rotation > **Arbitrary**. Enter an **Angle** value, click **°CW** (clockwise) or **°CCW** (counterclockwise), then click OK. Any exposed areas on the Background will be filled with the current Background color (see Chapter 11).

► If you want any areas that are exposed by a rotation command to be filled with transparency instead of a solid color, click the lock icon 🔒 in the Background listing to convert it to a layer before applying the command.

To rotate one layer:

1. On the Layers panel, 🔽 click a layer.

2. Choose Edit > Transform > **Rotate 180°**, **Rotate 90° CW**, or **Rotate 90° CCW**.

A *This is the original image.*

B *This is the same image after we chose the Flip Canvas Horizontal command.*

In a standard Photoshop document, the image is listed as the Background on the Layers panel. By adding layers of various kinds on top of the Background, you can build complexity and flexibility into your documents.A

For example, above the Background, you could add some editable text on one layer and perhaps a shape or some imagery surrounded by transparency on another layer. Layers can be added, deleted, or hidden when needed, and they can be edited individually.

Unlike the Background, which stays fully opaque and is stacked at the bottom of the Layers panel, ⬎ a layer can contain partially or fully transparent areas and can be moved upward or downward in the stack. Within the transparent areas in a layer, you can see through to underlying layers. Photoshop uses a checkerboard pattern to represent transparent areas.

Because the Layers panel is so essential to image editing in Photoshop, we have devoted this whole chapter to helping you master its features. By the end of this chapter, you will know how to create, duplicate, select, restack, group, delete, hide, show, move, lock, filter, merge, and flatten layers, as well as change their opacity. Those techniques, along with the selection and masking techniques in the next chapter, will give you the necessary foundation for future tasks in this book.

LAYER ESSENTIALS

IN THIS CHAPTER

A *This document contains a type layer and five image layers, all of which are stacked above the Background.*

PRACTICE ON AN IMAGE

You can download the file shown at left (see page viii). When you open it, click next to a layer name, then hide that layer by clicking the visibility icon. 👁 Click again to redisplay the icon and layer.

Creating layers

If you open a digital photo from Camera Raw into Photoshop using the Open Image button, the image will appear on the Background. If you create a document via the File > New dialog and choose the option of Background Contents: White or Background Color, your new document will have a Background; or if you choose Background Contents: Transparent instead, the document will contain a layer and no Background. Note: In this book, we identify the Background in a Photoshop document with an initial cap "B," to distinguish it from the general background (versus foreground) area of an image.

In these steps, you will learn how to create a new, blank image layer. To that layer, you can add pixels by applying brush strokes, cloning imagery, pasting into a selection, or performing other edits. You may add as many layers to a file as you like, but remember that a large image containing many image layers will utilize a fair amount of storage space and system memory.

Note: In other chapters, you will create adjustment, type, Smart Object, and shape layers.

To add a new, blank layer to a document:

1. Display the Layers panel.

2. Click a layer or the Background. The new layer is going to appear above this selected one.

3. Click the **New Layer** button at the bottom of the panel. **A** The new layer will have the default blending mode of Normal and the default setting for both Opacity and Fill of 100%. **B**

➤ To choose options for a layer as you create it, Alt-click/Option-click the New Layer button or press Ctrl-Shift-N/Cmd-Shift-N. In the New Layer dialog, you can enter a layer Name and choose a nonprinting Color for the area on the Layers panel behind the visibility icon (see "To color-code a layer" on page 161).

➤ To rename a layer right on the panel, see the sidebar on page 154.

A We clicked the Background, then clicked the New Layer button.

B A new blank layer (Layer 1) appeared above the Background.

Another way to create a layer is by copying or cutting imagery from an existing layer or the Background and transferring it to a new layer. This can be done easily via a simple command.

To turn a selection of pixels into a layer:

1. On the Layers panel, click an image layer or the Background, then create a selection in the document (if you're new to Photoshop, see the steps on page 170).**A**

2. Do either of the following:

   To put a copy of the selected pixels onto a new layer while leaving the original layer unchanged, right-click in the document and choose **Layer via Copy**, or press Ctrl-J/Cmd-J.**B**

   To put the selected pixels on a new layer and remove them from the original layer, right-click in the document and choose **Layer via Cut**, or press Ctrl-Shift-J/Cmd-Shift-J. If you cut pixels from a layer, Photoshop will fill the exposed area on the original layer with transparency; if you cut pixels from the Background, the exposed area will be filled with the current Background color (see pages 205 and 261).

Follow these steps to duplicate a layer or layer group, or to turn a copy of the Background into a layer. (To learn about layer groups, see pages 156–157.)

To duplicate a layer or layer group:

On the Layers panel, do one of the following:

Click a layer or a layer group, or Ctrl-click/Cmd-click multiple layers, then press Ctrl-J/Cmd-J.

Drag a layer, a layer group, or the Background over the **New Layer** button. The duplicate will appear above the one you dragged.

To name the new layer as you create it, right-click a layer, a layer group, or the Background and choose **Duplicate Layer** or **Duplicate Group**. In the dialog, change the name in the "As" field (ignore the Destination field), then click OK.

➤ To control whether Photoshop adds the word "copy" to duplicate layer names automatically, choose Panel Options from the Layers panel menu, then check or uncheck Add "Copy" to Copied Layers and Groups.

➤ When you duplicate a layer, any masks and/or effects on that layer are also duplicated.

A *We selected an area of the Background in this document.*

B *When we pressed Ctrl-J/Cmd-J, a copy of the selected pixels appeared on a new layer (Layer 1).*

There are many things that can be done to a layer that can't be done to the Background. For example, you can't move the Background upward in the layer stack; change its blending mode, Opacity, or Fill setting; attach a mask to it; or embellish it with layer effects. You can, however, convert the Background to a layer, at which time it will adopt all the functions of a normal layer.

To convert the Background to a layer:

On the Layers panel, do either of the following:

To convert the Background to a layer without choosing options, click the **Lock** icon 🔒 in the Background listing.

Double-click the Background **A** to open the New Layer dialog, **B** then do any of the following: Change the Name, choose a Color for the area behind the visibility icon, or change the blending Mode or Opacity setting. Click OK. **C**

You can also do the reverse of the preceding instructions, which is to convert any layer to the Background. This will come in handy, say, if you use the Crop tool with the Delete Cropped Pixels option off (which converts the Background to a layer), then decide you want to make the bottommost layer into the Background again.

To convert a layer to the Background:

1. Click the layer to be converted.

2. Choose Layer > New > **Background from Layer**. The new Background will appear as the bottom listing (its standard stacking position) on the panel.

A We double-clicked the Background in this image.

B We typed a name for the layer in the New Layer dialog.

C The former Background is now a full-fledged layer.

RENAMING LAYERS AND LAYER GROUPS

► To rename a layer or layer group, double-click the layer or layer group name, type a new name, then press Enter/Return or click outside the field.

► After double-clicking a layer name, you can press Tab to highlight the name of the next listing below it, or press Shift-Tab to highlight the listing above it (don't include the Background in the cycle).

Tip: To identify a layer name that isn't fully displayed (e.g., if the panel shape is narrow), use the Tool Tip.

Selecting layers

There are good habits and bad habits. Here's a good one: Before applying a filter, brush stroke, or other image edit to your document, select the listing for the layer that you want Photoshop to alter. Easy to do, easy to forget! When a layer or layer group listing is selected, it has a blue highlight and the layer or group name appears in the document tab.

To select layers via the Layers panel:

Do one of the following:

To select a layer or layer group, click either the layer thumbnail or the blank area to the right of the layer or group name.**A**

To select multiple layers, click a layer, then Shift-click the last in a series of consecutively listed layers, or Ctrl-click/Cmd-click individual layers (not their thumbnails). If you need to deselect an individual layer, Ctrl-click/Cmd-click it.

To select all the layers in your document (but not the Background), choose Select > All Layers or press Ctrl-Alt-A/Cmd-Option-A.

To select a layer or layer group with the Move tool:

1. Choose the **Move** tool ⯈⊹ or hold down V.

2. Do either of the following:

To select a layer that contains nontransparent pixels below the pointer, right-click in the document window and choose a layer or layer group name from the context menu.**B** (Adjustment layers may also be listed on the menu; see Chapter 12.)

On the Options bar, check **Auto-Select** and choose **Group** or **Layer** from the adjacent menu. Next, click a visible pixel area in the document. The Background can't be selected via this method.

➤ When Auto-Select is checked (Options bar), click the canvas or the area beyond the canvas to quickly deselect all layers.

➤ When the Move tool is selected and Show Transform Controls is checked on the Options bar, a bounding box surrounds the nontransparent content of the currently selected layer. If you find the box to be distracting, uncheck the option. To transform a layer via its bounding box (e.g., scale or skew it), see pages 358–359.

A *To select a layer, just click it.*

B *From the context menu, choose the name of the layer you want to select.*

Restacking layers

When you restack a layer listing, the layer contents shift forward or backward in the document.

To restack layers:

Drag a layer or group name upward or downward on the Layers panel, and release the mouse when a double horizontal line appears in the desired stacking position. **A–B**

➤ To move the Background upward on the list, you must convert it to a layer first (see page 154). Layers can't be stacked below the Background.

➤ You can also restack a selected layer via commands on the Layer > Arrange submenu (or via the shortcuts that are listed on that submenu).

A We're moving the "bottles" layer upward in the stack.

B Now the "bottles" layer is above the "cows" layer.

Creating layer groups

Putting layers in groups is more than just a convenient way to streamline and organize the listings on your Layers panel. You can also move, transform, duplicate, restack, hide, show, lock, or change the blending mode, Opacity, or Fill setting of all the layers in a group simultaneously. When you add a layer mask to a layer group, the mask applies to all the layers in the group (see page 192). You can also nest groups inside other groups.

To create a layer group:

Method 1 (from existing layers)

1. Click a layer, then Shift-click or Ctrl-click/Cmd-click one or more additional layers. **C** The layers can be nonconsecutive or hidden, and they can be different kinds.

2. Do either of the following:

   Press Ctrl-G/Cmd-G.

   Right-click one of the selected layers in the panel and choose **Group from Layers** from the context menu (or choose New Group from Layers from the panel menu). In the dialog, type a Name for the group, then click OK. **D**

3. *Optional:* To add more layers to the group, follow step 2 on the next page.

➤ To learn about artboards — a different type of layer group — see pages 362–365. ★

C We selected three layers.

D We used the New Group from Layers command to put those layers in a group.

Method 2 (create a group, then add layers)

1. On the Layers panel, do either of the following:

To create a group without choosing settings for it, click the layer above which you want the group to appear, then click the **New Group** button.

To name the group as you create it, Alt-click/Option-click the New Group button or choose **New Group** from the panel menu. In the dialog, enter a name in the Name field, then click OK.

2. Do either of the following:

Drag layers into the new group listing, releasing the mouse when the drop zone border appears around it.

Click the arrowhead to expand the group list, then drag layers into the group, releasing the mouse when the double lines appear in the desired stacking position.**A**

➤ To expand or collapse a group, including any and all subgroup, effect, and Smart Filter listings within it, Alt-click/Option-click the arrowhead.

➤ To collapse all layer groups, choose Collapse All Groups from the Layers panel menu.★

MOVING LAYERS OUT OF A GROUP

➤ To move a layer **out of a group**, expand the group listing, then drag a layer above or below the group.

➤ To move a layer from **one group to another**, expand the source group, then drag a layer over the target group (a border appears around it); or if the target listing is expanded, you can release the layer in the desired stacking position.

A We're moving a layer upward into an existing group.

USING CONTEXT MENUS ON THE LAYERS PANEL

Options on the context menu change depending on where on the Layers panel you right-click.

Deleting layers and groups

To delete a layer:

1. If there is an active selection in your document, deselect (press Ctrl-D/Cmd-D).

2. Click the layer to be deleted, then press Backspace/Delete.

➤ Change your mind? Choose Edit > Undo immediately, or click the prior state on the History panel.

➤ To delete a selected layer another way, click the Delete Layer button, 🗑 then click Yes in the alert dialog; or to bypass the alert, Alt-click/Option-click the Delete Layer button.

You can delete a layer group and its layers or merely disband the group while preserving the layers.

To delete or ungroup a layer group:

On the Layers panel, do one of the following:

To delete a group and its contents, click the group, then press Backspace/Delete.

Right-click a group and choose **Delete Group** from the context menu (or click a group, then click the Delete Layer button 🗑). In the alert dialog, click **Group Only** or **Group and Contents**.

To ungroup a layer group without deleting its layers, click the group, then press Ctrl-Shift-G/Cmd-Shift-G. The group icon disappears from the panel and the layer listings are no longer indented.

Hiding and showing layers

You can hide any layer you're not currently working on, either because it's getting in the way of your editing or to eliminate it as a visual distraction. Hidden layers don't print. The instructions below apply to both layers and the Background.

To hide or show layers:

On the Layers panel, do one of the following:

To hide or show one layer or layer group, click in the visibility column 👁 **A–B** (or select a layer or layer group, then press Ctrl-, /Cmd-,). ★

To hide or show multiple layers, drag upward or downward in the visibility column.

To hide all layers and layer groups except one, Alt-click/Option-click the visibility column for the layer or layer group that you want to keep visible. Repeat to redisplay all the layers (except for layers that were hidden before you used the command).

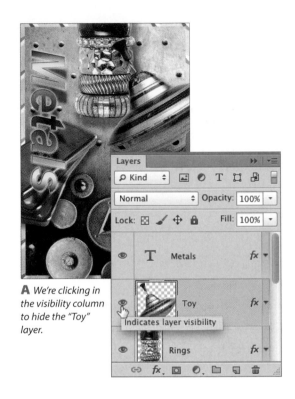

A *We're clicking in the visibility column to hide the "Toy" layer.*

B *The visibility icon disappears and the "Toy" layer is hidden.*

Repositioning layer content

You can reposition a selected layer or group of layers in your document.

To reposition layers manually:

Do either of the following:

On the Layers panel, click a layer or layer group, or Shift-click or Ctrl-click/Cmd-click multiple layers, hold down V to spring-load the Move tool, then drag in the document.**A–B**

Hold down V to spring-load the Move tool. On the Options bar, check Auto-Select, choose Group or Layer from the adjacent menu, then drag a non-transparent area in the document.

➤ If you move part of the layer or layers outside the canvas area, not to worry—those pixels will save with the document and can be moved back into view at any time. See "Working with pixels outside the canvas area" on page 263.

➤ To nudge a selected layer by one pixel at a time, choose the Move tool, then press an arrow key. Or press Shift-arrow to move a layer by 10 screen pixels at a time. (Don't press Alt-arrow/Option-arrow—unless you want to duplicate the layer.)

➤ For a more precise way to reposition layers, use the align buttons on the Options bar. See page 289.

ALIGNING LAYER CONTENT USING SMART GUIDES

As you drag a layer, you can align its edge with the edge or center of content of another layer by using Smart Guides. Verify that View > Show > Smart Guides has a check mark, then with the Move tool (V), start moving a layer or layer group. Temporary magnetic guide lines will appear onscreen when the edge of the layer imagery you're moving encounters the edge or center of nontransparent pixels, type, or a shape on another layer. To learn more about this feature, see page 294.

A We're dragging the "Toy" layer with the Move tool.

B Now the "Toy" layer is on the right side of the image.

Changing the layer opacity

The Opacity setting on the Layers panel controls whether a layer is semitransparent or opaque.

To change the opacity of a layer or layer group:

1. Select one or more layers or a layer group.

2. Change the **Opacity** percentage on the Layers panel (we like to use the scrubby slider).**A–B**

➤ To learn about the Fill slider, see page 415.

➤ In the Transparency Settings area of Edit/ Photoshop CC > Preferences > Transparency & Gamut, you can change the size or color of the gray and white checkerboard pattern that Photoshop uses to represent transparent pixels (or to hide the pattern, choose None from the Grid Size menu).

➤ To change the Opacity setting of the currently selected layer or layer group via the keyboard (standard or extended), choose a nonediting tool (such as the Move or Eyedropper tool or a selection tool), then press a digit between 0 and 9 (e.g., 2 = 20%) or quickly type a percentage (such as "38" for 38%). Press 0 to set the opacity to 100% or 00 to set it to 0%.

Using the lock options

The Lock Transparent Pixels button on the Layers panel prevents or allows the editing of transparent pixels by any command or tool. In these steps, you will use this feature with the Brush tool, just to learn how it works in practice.

To limit edits by locking transparent pixels:

1. Click an image layer (not an editable type layer) that contains some transparent pixels.

2. Choose the **Brush** tool ![brush icon] (B or Shift-B). To change the brush diameter, press [or].

3. Show the Swatches panel, ![swatches icon] then click a color.

4. On the Layers panel, click the **Lock Transparent Pixels** button, ![lock icon] then draw a few brush strokes in the document.**C** Only nontransparent pixels will be recolored.

5. Deactivate the Lock Transparent Pixels button by clicking it again or by pressing /.

6. Apply a few more brush strokes to the layer. Note that both transparent and opaque parts of the layer can be recolored.**D**

A *In this image, all the layers have an opacity of 100%.*

B *We reduced the opacity of the tomatoes layer to 49%.*

C *With the Lock Transparent Pixels option on, our brush strokes can recolor only nontransparent pixels.*

D *With Lock Transparent Pixels off, our brush strokes can recolor transparent and opaque pixels.*

To prevent layer characteristics from being edited, there are three other lock options on the Layers panel, in addition to the Lock Transparent Pixels button.

To lock one or more layers or a layer group:

1. Select one or more layers or a layer group.

2. Click any of the following:

    The **Lock Image Pixels** button ![brush icon] prevents image layer pixels from being edited, such as by filters or brush strokes. Note: You can still move or restack the layer or change its layer style settings (blending mode, opacity, and effects).

    The **Lock Position** button ![move icon] locks only the location of the layer. The layer content (e.g., pixels, type characters) can be edited as usual.

    The **Lock All** button ![lock icon] prevents the layer from being moved and edited.**A** Unlike the other lock options, this button is also available for layer groups. (You can also press Ctrl-"/"/Cmd-"/" to lock a selected layer or layer group.) ★

    When any lock button is activated for a layer, a padlock icon displays next to the layer name.

Choosing Layers panel options

To choose thumbnail options for the Layers panel:

Right-click any layer thumbnail and choose any of the following:

Small Thumbnails, **Medium Thumbnails**, or **Large Thumbnails**. Note: Turning off thumbnails by choosing No Thumbnails can help boost Photoshop's performance, but frankly, it's pretty darn hard to work productively without them.

Clip Thumbnails to Layer Bounds to preview, in the panel thumbnails, only the layer content,**B** or **Clip Thumbnails to Document Bounds** to preview the layer content relative to the full canvas size.

You can assign a color to the area behind the visibility icons to categorize your layers or make them easier to identify (or just to make the panel look pretty).

To color-code a layer:

Click a layer (or Ctrl-click/Cmd-click multiple layers), then right-click the visibility column (or the layer thumbnail or listing) and choose a color label from the context menu.**C**

A When the Lock All button option is activated for a layer, the padlock icon is black.

B For our Layers panel display options, we chose Large Thumbnails and Clip Thumbnails to Layer Bounds.

C Click a layer, then from the context menu, choose a color.

Filtering listings on the Layers panel

When you first start working in Photoshop, your Layers panel may look relatively spare, but before you know it, you will be adding image, adjustment, and type layers, Smart Objects, Smart Filters, and layer styles, and the number of listings will grow considerably. Finding the layers you need will require you to either scroll in the panel (a pain in the butt) or enlarge the panel to display all the listings (uses too much screen space).**A** Via the filtering features, you can reduce the listings that display on the panel at a given time to just the categories of layers you need to work on.

To filter the listings on the Layers panel:

At the top of the Layers panel, do one of the following:

Set the Filter Type menu to the default option of **Kind,** then click the **Filter for Pixel Layers,** Filter for Adjustment Layers (**A–B,** next page), **Filter for Type Layers,** Filter for Shape Layers, or **Filter for Smart Objects** button. Only listings in that chosen category will display. *Optional:* Click another of those buttons to display more listings.

From the Filter Type menu, choose **Name, Effect, Mode, Attribute, Color,** or **Smart Object.** Next, choose a criterion from the adjacent menu (**C–F,** next page); or for the Name option, start typing a word that appears in one or more layer names; or for the Smart Object option, click the Up-to-Date Library Linked Smart Objects, ★ Up-to-Date Locally Linked Smart Objects, Out-of-Date Linked Smart Objects, Missing Linked Smart Objects, or Embedded Smart Objects button. For example, to display only layers that contain a layer mask, choose Attribute from the Filter Type menu and Layer Mask from the second menu. See also the sidebar on the next page.

For the **Selected** option on the Filter Type menu, see pages 164–165.

To deactivate layer filtering:

To deactivate layer filtering, in the upper-right corner of the Layers panel, click the **Layer Filtering On/Off** button. (If you click the button again, the last settings will be restored.)

➤ Layer filtering settings remain in effect only while a file is open, and while the Layer Filtering On/Off button is activated on the Layers panel.

Filter Type menu

Layer Filtering On/Off button

A *This is the Layers panel for the image shown above, with all the listings showing (unfiltered).*

A *We clicked the Filter for Pixel Layers button: Only image layers are displaying.*

B *We also clicked the Filter for Adjustment Layers button: Now both image and adjustment layers are displaying.*

C *We chose Attribute from the Filter Type menu and Visible from the second menu: Only layers that have a visibility icon are displaying.*

THE LAYER FILTERING CRITERIA

FIRST MENU	BUTTON OR MENUS
Kind	Click the button to display only pixel, adjustment, type, or shape layers, or Smart Objects
Name	Enter a layer name (or partial name) to be searched
Effect	Drop Shadow, Inner Glow, and other effects (from the Layer Style dialog)
Mode	Blending mode (e.g., Normal, Multiply, Screen)
Attribute	Visible, Locked, Empty, Linked, Clipped, Layer Mask, Vector Mask, Layer Effects, Advanced Blending (or the "Not" version of the above)
Color	Red, Orange, Yellow, etc. (the color that is assigned to the visibility column)

For Smart Objects, see the preceding page.

D *We assigned colors to the visibility column of most of the layers.*

E *We chose Color from the Filter Type menu and Yellow from the second menu.*

F *We chose Effect from the Filter Type menu and Drop Shadow from the adjacent menu.*

Unlike the filtering controls that are discussed on the prior two pages, the Isolate Layers feature lets you pick and choose which layers remain accessible (and they can be a mixture of different types). It's easier to select, then isolate, the layers you want to edit than it is to hide the layers you want to ignore. Like the other layer filtering controls, this feature is especially useful if you're working on a complex document that contains many layers.

Isolated layers can be edited as usual. For example, you can click any individual listing to edit just that layer; or select multiple layers of the same type and apply related edits (e.g., a fill or stroke color to multiple shape layers, or a font family to multiple type layers); or select multiple layers of the same or different types, and apply other edits, such as transformations.

While the Isolate Layers option is on, all the Layers panel features (except for a few buttons) are fully functional, such as the blending mode menu, the Opacity and Fill sliders, and the ability to restack, group, copy, and delete layers (among the ones that are isolated).

To isolate selected layers:

1. On the Layers panel, hold down Ctrl/Cmd and click the layers you want to keep editable.**A** The layers can be of any kind.

2. Do either of the following:

   From the Filter Type menu at the top of the Layers panel, choose **Selected**.**B**

   If you're using the Move, Path Selection, or Direct Selection tool or a pen tool, right-click in the document and choose **Isolate Layers** from the context menu.

3. As you edit the isolated layers, the nonisolated ones will remain visible in the document but will be uneditable (**A–B**, next page).

4. *Optional:* To release an individual layer from isolation, click the listing for the layer to be released, then right-click it and choose Release from Isolation from the context menu.

5. *Optional:* To change which layers are isolated, on the Layers panel, click the Layer Filtering On/Off button ▮ (to deactivate layer filtering). All the document layers will redisplay on the Layers panel. Change the selection of layers (e.g., Ctrl/Cmd click a layer to add it to the selection, or click any selected layer to deselect it), then click the Layer Filtering On/Off button again to reactivate it.

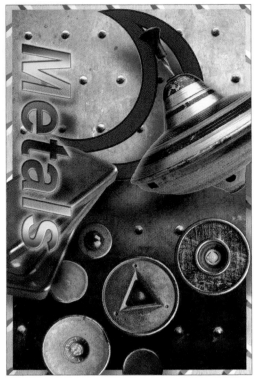

A *This image contains multiple layers.*

B *We selected three layers, then chose Selected from the Filter Type menu.*

If you want to add an existing layer to the ones that are isolated (without having to use the Layers panel), choose the Move tool ▸✛ (V). Right-click in the document, then from the context menu, choose the name of the additional layer you want to isolate.

➤ If you add a layer to your document while the Isolate Layers feature is on, the new layer will also be isolated. This includes fill and adjustment layers.

➤ Layer filtering settings, including isolation mode, remain in effect only while a document is open (and while the Layer Filtering On/Off button is activated on the Layers panel). When you close and then reopen your document, layer filtering is reset to the default setting of no filtering.

➤ To learn about isolating shape layers, see page 428.

➤ In Photoshop, nonisolated layers display at their full opacity, whereas in Isolation Mode in Adobe Illustrator, nonisolated objects are dimmed.

When you exit isolation mode, you can either make all the layers in the document accessible again, or revert to a prior layer filtering setting.

To exit isolation mode:

Do either of the following:

To exit isolation mode and also clear any other layer filtering, choose the Move, Path Selection, Direct Selection tool, or a pen tool, then right-click in the document and uncheck **Isolate Layers** on the context menu. This command works regardless of the current state of the Layer Filtering On/Off button.◫ (You can also exit isolation mode by unchecking Isolate Layers on the Select menu.)

To exit isolation mode by switching to a different filtering mode, make sure the Layer Filtering On/Off button is activated,◫ then from the **Filter Type** menu at the top of the Layers panel, choose any filtering option except Selected.

A Only the listings for the layers that we isolated displayed on the panel.

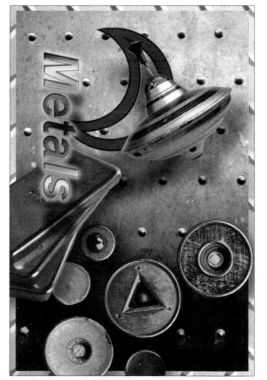

B Using the Free Transform command, we scaled down the three isolated layers simultaneously, while the nonisolated layers remained visible but uneditable.

Merging layers

The Merge Down command merges the current layer into the layer directly below it. The other merge commands — Merge Layers and Merge Visible — merge two or more selected layers into the bottommost of the selected layers. You can apply any of these commands periodically during the editing process to reduce the file size of your document or to declutter your Layers panel — just remember that you can't unmerge layers after you merge them except by using the History panel.

Note: Compare the merge commands with the Flatten Image command (see page 168), which is typically applied to a copy of a file as a final step before output.

To merge select layers:

1. Do one of the following:

   Click the upper layer of two layers to be merged. **A** The bottom one must be an image layer or the Background; it can't be fully locked (the Lock All button can't be activated) and it can't be a group.

   Ctrl-click/Cmd-click multiple layers. The layers can be solo, within a group, or a combination thereof.

   Click a group. (All the layers in the group will be merged — but just with one another.)

   Note: You can merge an adjustment layer into an image layer, but you can't merge adjustment layers into one another. If you merge a shape layer, an editable type layer, or a Smart Object, it will be rasterized into the underlying image layer.

2. Do either of the following:

   Right-click the selected layer or group, or one of the selected layers, and choose **Merge Down**, **Merge Layers**, or **Merge Group** from the context menu.

   Press Ctrl-E/Cmd-E (this is the only method that works for a type layer). **B**

   Note: If only one layer is selected and you merge it downward into an underlying layer that contains a layer mask, an alert dialog will appear. Click Preserve to keep the mask editable, or click Apply to apply the mask effect but discard the mask.

➤ If you merge a group, the group icon will disappear from the panel.

➤ To merge an editable type layer into a shape layer, or vice versa, select both, then press Ctrl-E/Cmd-E.

A *We clicked the "violin" layer.*

B *We chose the Merge Down command, which merged the "violin" layer into the "trumpet" layer.*

SMART OBJECT IN LIEU OF MERGE OR FLATTEN

Instead of merging or flattening layers, consider grouping them into a **Smart Object** (see page 272). You'll achieve the same reduction of layers, plus you'll gain the ability to access and edit the original layers individually by double-clicking the Smart Object thumbnail (see page 276).

The Merge Visible command merges all the currently visible layers into the bottommost visible layer while preserving any hidden layers. By hiding the layers you don't want to merge before choosing this command, you can control which ones will be merged.

To merge all visible layers:

1. Make sure the layers that you want to merge are visible (have eye icons), and the layers that you don't want to merge are hidden.**A**

2. Right-click one of the visible layers (not a type layer) and choose **Merge Visible** (Ctrl-Shift-E/ Cmd-Shift-E).**B**

   Note: This sort of goes without saying, but if you merge down an editable type layer, shape, or adjustment layer, the specific features of that kind of layer (such as the font and other character settings for a type layer, or the settings for an adjustment layer) will no longer be editable.

Both of the commands in this task will copy and merge ("stamp") two or more selected layers into a new layer in one step, while preserving the original, separate layers. This might come in handy, say, if you want to test some edits (such as filters or transformations) on multiple layers simultaneously; use one of these commands first, then apply your edits to the newly merged layer. The Note above also applies to these commands.

To copy and merge layers:

Do either of the following:

Ctrl-click/Cmd-click the layers (not the Background) to be copied or merged into a new layer, then press Ctrl-Alt-E/Cmd-Option-E.

To copy and merge all the currently visible layers into a new layer, including the Background (if visible), click any visible layer, then press Ctrl-Alt-Shift-E/Cmd-Option-Shift-E.

➤ If any layers and the Background are selected when you use the first shortcut listed above, content from the selected layers will be stamped into the Background, and no new layer will be created.

➤ For an alternative to the merge commands, see the sidebar on the preceding page.

➤ To create a document from one or more selected layers, from the Layers panel menu, choose Duplicate Layers. From the Document menu in the dialog, choose New, enter a document Name, then click OK. Save the new file.

A In this document, we hid the Background because we didn't want our layers to merge into it.

B The Merge Visible command merged all the layers except the Background, which was preserved and stayed hidden.

Flattening layers

When you flatten all the layers in a document, you reduce its file storage size and free up space on your hard disk (see the sidebar at right). Flattening layers may also be a necessary step when preparing a file for output or export. Although multiple layers are preserved by several formats (Photoshop PDF, Photoshop, Large Document, Dicom, and TIFF), if the application into which you're planning to import your file doesn't read or accept layers, you will have to produce a flattened copy of it, as in these steps. Any transparency in the bottommost layer will be converted to fully opaque white.

To save a flattened copy of a document:

1. Choose File > **Save As** (Ctrl-Shift-S/Cmd-Shift-S). The Save As dialog opens.

2. Do all of the following:

   Change the file name.

   Choose a location.

   Uncheck Layers (the As a Copy option becomes checked automatically; keep it that way).

   Choose a file format from the Format menu.

   Click Save.

   Note: The layered version will remain open; the flattened version will be saved to disk.

If you're confident that your image is totally complete, *finis,* you can use the Flatten Image command instead of saving a flattened copy. This command merges all currently visible layers (including type, Smart Object, and adjustment layers) into the bottommost visible layer, rasterizes all type and shape layers, and applies the effect of all masks and layer styles to the document. Note: This command discards all hidden layers!

To flatten all the layers in a document:

1. Make sure all the layers and layer groups you want to flatten are visible (have eye icons).**A** It doesn't matter which layer is selected.

2. Right-click any layer name (not a type layer) and choose **Flatten Image**.

3. If the file contains any hidden layers, an alert dialog will appear; click OK. Any formerly transparent areas in the bottommost layer are now opaque white.**B**

LAYERS INCREASE THE FILE SIZE

From the Status bar menu at the bottom of the document window, choose Document Sizes, then note the value on the left (the file size without layers) versus the value on the right (the approximate file size with layers and alpha channels). The file for this status bar contains three image layers and a Background:

A *In this document, the "Bottles" layer is hidden.*

B *The Flatten Image command flattened all the visible layers into the Background and discarded the hidden layer.*

In this chapter, you will learn how to create and refine selections and layer masks. These techniques are put to practical use in many other chapters, and you will discover that they are essential to your work in Photoshop.

When you select an area of an image layer, only that area can be edited, and the rest of the layer is protected. If you apply a filter, for example, only pixels within the selection area on the currently active layer are affected. The function of a layer mask is to hide parts of a layer. Moreover, a selection can be converted to a layer mask, and a layer mask can be loaded as a selection.

Creating layer-based selections

To select the entire canvas area of a layer:

On the Layers panel, ☞ click a layer or the Background, then choose Select > **All** or press Ctrl-A/Cmd-A. A border of "marching ants" surrounds the entire layer.

To select just the nontransparent areas of a layer:

On the Layers panel, ☞ Ctrl-click/Cmd-click a layer thumbnail. **A–B**

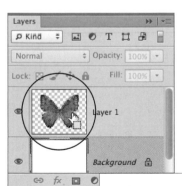

A To select only the nontransparent pixels on a layer, Ctrl-click/Cmd-click the layer thumbnail.

B Just the butterfly is selected.

SELECTIONS & MASKS

Using the Rectangular and Elliptical Marquee tools

To create a rectangular or elliptical selection:

1. Click the layer you want to edit.

2. Choose the **Rectangular Marquee** ▢ or **Elliptical Marquee** ◯ tool (M or Shift-M).

3. *Optional:* For a smoother edge on an elliptical selection, check Anti-alias on the Options bar (see the sidebar on page 177) and set the Feather value to 0 px.

4. Drag diagonally. Hold down Shift while dragging to create a perfect square or circle; hold down Alt/ Option while dragging to draw the selection from the center.**A** As you draw a selection, width and height dimensions display in a readout next to the selection and on the Info panel. When you release the mouse, a selection border appears.

5. *Optional:* To add to the selection, Shift-drag; to subtract from it, Alt-drag/Option-drag.

➤ To move the selection while drawing it, keep the mouse button down, then drag with the Spacebar held down. To move the selection after releasing the mouse, drag inside it with any selection tool.

➤ To create the thinnest possible selection, choose the Single Row Marquee or Single Column Marquee tool, then click in the image.

To create a selection that has a fixed ratio or specific dimensions:

1. Click a layer.

2. Choose the **Rectangular Marquee** ▢ or **Elliptical Marquee** ◯ tool (M or Shift-M).

3. On the Options bar, set the Feather value to 0, then do either of the following:

From the Style menu, choose **Fixed Ratio**, enter a **Width** and **Height** for the ratio of the selection (e.g., 5 to 7),**B** then drag in the image diagonally to create a selection.**C**

From the Style menu, choose **Fixed Size**, enter exact **Width** and **Height** values in any unit that can be used in Photoshop (see page 467), then click in the image.**D**

➤ To swap the current Fixed Ratio or Fixed Size values, click the Swap Height and Width ⇄ button on the Options bar.

A *With the Elliptical Marquee tool, we're holding down Alt/Option while dragging to draw a selection from the center.*

B *For the Rectangular Marquee tool, we chose Fixed Ratio and entered a width-to-height ratio of 5 to 7…*

C *… so any size selection we draw with the tool will have that fixed ratio.*

D *We chose Fixed Size, entered exact Width and Height values, then clicked in the image to make the border appear (here, we're repositioning it).*

Using two of the lasso tools

We use the Lasso tool to select an area loosely, say, to limit subtle color adjustments to a general area. We also use this tool to clean up selections made with other tools, such as the Magic Wand or Quick Selection tool.

To create a free-form selection:

1. Click the layer you want to edit.

2. Choose the **Lasso** tool 🔾 (L or Shift-L).

3. *Optional:* For a smoother edge on a curved selection, check Anti-alias on the Options bar and set the Feather value to 0 px.

4. Drag around an area on the layer.**A** Your initial selection doesn't have to be perfect; you will have a chance to refine it in the next step. When you release the mouse, the open ends of the selection will join automatically.

5. To add to the same selection area, position the pointer inside it, then Shift-drag around the area to be added.**B** To subtract from the selection area, position the pointer outside it, then Alt-drag/ Option-drag around the area to be removed.**C–D**

➤ To feather an existing selection, see page 265.

➤ To create a straight side with the Lasso tool, with the mouse button still down, hold down Alt/ Option and click to create corners. To resume creating free-form edges, press the mouse button, release Alt/Option, then drag.

To create a straight-sided selection:

1. Click the layer you want to edit.

2. Choose the **Polygonal Lasso** tool 🔾 (L or Shift-L).

3. Click to create corners.**E** To create a selection edge at a multiple of 45°, hold down Shift while clicking.

4. To **join** the open ends of the selection, do either of the following:

   Click the starting point (a small circle appears in the pointer).

   Ctrl-click/Cmd-click or double-click anywhere in the document. Photoshop will complete the selection with a straight side.

➤ To draw a free-form segment while creating a polygonal selection, Alt-drag/Option-drag. Release Alt/Option and click to create more straight sides.

➤ To delete the last corner while using the Polygonal Lasso tool, press Backspace/Delete.

A *With the Lasso tool, we are selecting the left part of the ice cream.*

B *Using Shift, we are adding to the selection, to complete the shape.*

C *To eliminate the pistachio nut from the selection …*

D *… we are holding down Alt/Option and dragging around it with the Lasso tool.*

E *The Polygonal Lasso tool produces straight-edged selections.*

CREATING A SELECTION WITH A VECTOR TOOL

To create a smooth, custom-shaped selection, draw a path with a shape tool or the Pen tool, then convert the path to a selection. See Chapter 21.

Deselecting and reselecting selections

If you don't like having to retrace your steps (we sure don't), deselect a selection only when you're sure you're done using it. Although selections register as states on the History panel, states disappear when the panel listings reach their maximum number or when you close your document. To preserve a selection for future access and use, save it in an alpha channel (see page 184) or convert it to a layer mask (see page 192).

To deselect a selection:

Do one of the following:

Press Ctrl-D/Cmd-D (Select > Deselect). Memorize this shortcut!

Choose any selection tool, then right-click anywhere in the document and choose **Deselect**.

Hold down M or L to spring-load a marquee or lasso tool, then click inside or outside the selection.**A** (If this doesn't work, click the New Selection button ▢ on the Options bar and try again.)

To reselect the last selection:

Do one of the following:

Press Ctrl-Shift-D/Cmd-Shift-D (Select > Reselect).

With any selection tool except the Magic Wand, right-click in the document and choose **Reselect**.

On the History panel, 🖫 click the state that is labeled with the name of the tool or command that you used to create the selection.

Deleting or filling a selection

When you delete a selection of image pixels from a layer, Photoshop fills that area automatically with transparent pixels. When you delete a selection of pixels from the Background, Photoshop fills the exposed area with a solid color.

To delete or fill a selection:

1. On the Layers panel, 🖾 click a layer or the Background. For the Background, also choose a Foreground or Background color (see Chapter 11).

2. Do one of the following:

   If a layer is active, press Backspace/Delete.**B–C**

   If the Background is active, press Alt-Backspace/Option-Delete to fill the selection with the Foreground color or Ctrl-Backspace/Cmd-Delete to fill the selection with the Background color.**D**

   To delete the selection and put it on the Clipboard, choose Edit > Cut (Ctrl-X/Cmd-X). (To learn about the Clipboard, see pages 261–264.)

➤ To put a selection onto a new layer, see page 153.

B *We selected the blue sky on an image layer, then pressed Backspace/Delete.*

C *Photoshop replaced the deleted area with transparent pixels.*

D *Here, with the Background selected, we pressed Ctrl-Backspace/Cmd-Delete, so the selection filled with the current Background color (in this case, the color red).*

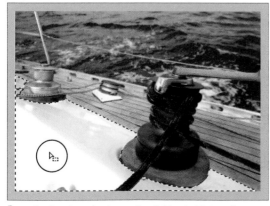

A *To deselect this selection, we're clicking inside it with a selection tool.*

Moving a selection border

You can move a selection border to a different area of an image without moving its contents.

To move a selection border:

1. Choose any selection tool except the Quick Selection tool or hold down M or L to spring-load a marquee or lasso tool, and activate the **New Selection** button ▢ on the Options bar.

2. Do either of the following:

   Drag inside an existing selection.**A** To constrain the movement to a multiple of 45°, start dragging, then hold down Shift and continue to drag. The horizontal and vertical distance the selection border is being moved displays in a dynamic read-out onscreen.

   Press any arrow key to nudge the selection border by one pixel at a time, or press Shift-arrow to nudge the border by 10 pixels at a time.

➤ To transform a selection border (but not its contents), choose any selection tool except the Magic Wand. Right-click the image and choose Transform Selection. Use the handles on the transform box to scale, rotate, skew, distort, or apply perspective to the selection, as described on pages 358–359.

➤ To copy a selection border between documents, drag it to the tab of another open document with a selection tool, pause to let the second document display, then drag into the active window.

Moving selection contents

In these steps, you will move a selection with its contents.

To move the contents of a selection:

1. Create a selection.

2. *Optional:* For help in positioning the selection precisely at a specific location in the document, display the rulers (Ctrl-R/Cmd-R), drag a guide from the horizontal or vertical ruler, and turn on View > Snap To > Guides.

3. Do either of the following:

   On the Layers panel, click the Background, then choose a Background color (see Chapter 11). The area that is exposed when you move the selection will be filled with this color.

   Click a layer. The area you expose when you move the selection will be filled with transparent pixels.

4. Choose the **Move** tool ▸⊕ or hold down V to spring-load the Move tool.

5. Drag from within the selection.**B** You can let the edge of the selection snap to a ruler guide, if you created one. The distance you move the selection displays in a dynamic readout onscreen.

6. Deselect (Ctrl-D/Cmd-D).

➤ In Chapter 13 you will learn how to copy the contents of a selection and how to use other alignment aids, such as Smart Guides.

➤ With the Move tool chosen, you can press an arrow key to nudge a selection (and its contents) by one pixel at a time, or press Shift-arrow to nudge it by 10 pixels at a time.

A *A selection border is moved with a selection tool.*

B *Selection contents are moved on a layer with the Move tool.*

Using the Quick Selection tool

The Photoshop features we're going to discuss next — the Quick Selection tool, Magic Wand tool, and Color Range command — create selections in a more automatic way than the marquee and lasso tools. With these tools, Photoshop does the work of detecting color boundaries for you.

If the area you want to select has fairly well-defined borders, try using the Quick Selection tool instead of a lasso tool. Rather than tediously tracing a precise contour, with this tool, you merely drag within a shape and pause to let it detect and select the shape's edge. You can push the resulting selection outward to include an adjacent color boundary or inward to make it smaller. This tool is awesome!

To use the Quick Selection tool:

1. Click the layer you want to edit.

2. Choose the **Quick Selection** tool 🖌 (W or Shift-W).

3. On the Options bar, do all of the following:

   Click the **New Selection** button 🖌 to replace any existing selections with the one you're about to create (or press Ctrl-D/Cmd-D to deselect).

   Check **Sample All Layers** to let the tool detect color boundaries on all layers, or uncheck this option to allow it to detect color boundaries on just the current layer.

   Check **Auto-Enhance** for a smoother, more refined selection edge.

4. To choose a brush diameter, press] or [, then drag within the area to be selected.**A** The selection will expand to the first significant color or shade boundary that the tool detects. The selection will preview as you drag, and will become more precise when you release the mouse.

5. Do either of the following (optional):

   To **enlarge** the selection, click or drag in an adjoining area; the selection will expand to include it.**B–C**

   To **shrink** the selection, Alt-drag/Option-drag along the edge of the area to be subtracted (the modifier key is equivalent to clicking the Subtract From button on the Options bar) (**A–B**, next page).

➤ You can change the tool diameter between clicks.

➤ To block an adjacent area from being included as you enlarge an existing selection, hold down

A *We selected the kumquat in the center of this layer by dragging inside it with the Quick Selection tool.*

B *After enlarging the brush diameter slightly, we clicked the kumquat on the right to add it to the selection.*

C *Next, we dragged across the green leaf above the kumquats. The selection spread beyond the edge of the leaf to include some of the background area, which wasn't our intention.*

Alt/Option and click or drag in that area, release Alt/Option and the mouse, then drag to enlarge the selection area, while avoiding the blocked area. The area will remain blocked until you click it again with the Quick Selection tool.**C–E**

➤ To undo the last click or drag of the Quick Selection tool, press Ctrl-Z/Cmd-Z.

➤ To save a selection, see page 184.

➤ To clean up a Quick Selection, you can use another selection tool, such as the Lasso. To refine the selection, see pages 184–185.

A *We Alt-dragged/Option-dragged below the leaf to subtract the background area from the selection…*

B *…and did the same thing to subtract the area below the kumquats.*

C *We zoomed in, reduced the brush diameter, then Alt-clicked/Option-clicked areas around the stems to prevent them from becoming selected.*

D *We dragged along the stems to select them, then held down Alt/Option and clicked the background areas between the stems to remove them from the selection.*

E *Finally, we cleaned up the selection of the stems. (At this point, we could copy the selection to a new layer; it would be surrounded by transparent pixels.)*

Using the Magic Wand tool

With the Magic Wand tool, you simply click a color in the image and the tool selects all adjacent pixels of the same (or a similar) shade or color. Like the Color Range command (see pages 178–180), the Magic Wand lets you control the range of pixels the tool selects, but unlike Color Range, this tool also lets you add nonsimilar colors to the selection.

To use the Magic Wand tool:

1. Click a layer or the Background.

2. Choose the **Magic Wand** tool ![wand icon] (W or Shift-W).

3. On the Options bar, do all of the following:

   Choose a **Tolerance** value to control the range of colors the tool selects. The higher the value, the wider the range.

   Check **Anti-alias** to let the tool add semitransparent pixels along the edges of the color areas it detects. This will produce smoother edge transitions for your image edits.

   Check **Contiguous** to limit the selection to areas that are connected to the first pixel you click, or uncheck this option to allow the tool to select similarly colored, noncontiguous (unconnected) areas throughout the image with each click.

   To select occurrences of a similar color on all visible layers, check **Sample All Layers**, or uncheck this option to select colors on just the current layer.

4. Click a color in the image.

5. Do either of the following (optional):

   To **add** to the selection, Shift-click any unselected areas.**A**

   To **subtract** areas from the selection, hold down Alt/Option and click them. Or choose the Quick Selection tool, then with the Alt/Option key held down, drag short strokes across the areas to be subtracted.**B**

   See also the options in "To expand or add to a selection via a command," on the next page.

6. *Optional:* If you selected an area of the image that you want to remove and you clicked a layer in step 1, press Backspace/Delete;**C** or if you clicked the Background in step 1, choose a Background color, then press Ctrl-Backspace/Cmd-Delete. Deselect (Ctrl-D/Cmd-D).

A *To select the sky in this image layer, we clicked on the right side with the Magic Wand tool (Tolerance 38; Contiguous checked), then Shift-clicked more sky areas to add them to the selection (as shown above).*

B *Some parts of the keys became selected, so we are using the Quick Selection tool with Alt/Option held down to subtract them from the selection.*

C *Finally, we pressed Backspace/Delete to get rid of the selected pixels, to isolate the hand and keys (in this document, the Background is hidden).*

➤ To select just one color or shade with the Magic Wand tool, choose a Tolerance value of 0 or 1. You can also lower the Tolerance value incrementally between clicks. For instance, you could use a Tolerance of 30–40 for the first click, lower the value to 15–20 and Shift-click, then to add unselected areas along the edges of the selection, lower the value to 5–10 and Shift-click once more.

The Grow command expands a selection only into contiguous areas, whereas the Similar command can add both contiguous and noncontiguous areas to a selection. Both commands select a range of pixels up to the current Tolerance setting of the Magic Wand tool.

To expand or add to a selection via a command:

Create a selection, then choose Select > **Grow** or **Similar**;**A–B** or if the Magic Wand tool is selected, right-click in the image and choose either command from the context menu. You can repeat either command to enlarge the selection further.

➤ To undo the results of the last click made with the Magic Wand tool or the last use of the Grow or Similar command, press Ctrl-Z/Cmd-Z.

Inverting a selection

If one area of a layer is easier to select than another, select the easy part first (such as the sky in a landscape photo), then invert the selection.

To invert a selection:

Do either of the following:

With any tool chosen, press Ctrl-Shift-I/Cmd-Shift-I (Select > Inverse).**C–D**

With any selection tool chosen, right-click in the document and choose **Select Inverse**.

A *We clicked the blue sky area with the Magic Wand tool (Tolerance of 35), Shift-clicked once on the clouds…*

B *…then chose Select > Similar. The Tolerance setting controlled which pixel range was added to the selection.*

TO ANTI-ALIAS OR NOT?

Before using a selection tool that you have chosen, check **Anti-alias** (if available) on the Options bar to have the edge of the selection fade to transparency, or uncheck this option to produce a crisp, hard-edged selection. The effect of anti-aliasing won't be visible until you copy and paste, move, or edit the selected pixels.

C *This is the original selection.*

D *And this is the inverse of the same selection.*

Using the Color Range command

Using the Color Range dialog, you can select areas of an image based on color or tonal values, such as a sampled color, a range of specific hues, a luminosity range, or skin tones.

To use the Color Range command to create a selection:

1. In an RGB document, click a layer. Note: The command samples colors from all the currently visible layers, regardless of which layer is active. *Optional:* Create a selection to restrict the area in which the command may select colors.**A**

2. Choose Select > **Color Range**.

3. In the Color Range dialog, choose from the **Select** menu to limit the selection to Sampled Colors (shades or colors you'll click with the Color Range eyedropper); to a specific preset color range (e.g., Reds or Blues); to a luminosity range (Highlights, Midtones, or Shadows); or to Skin Tones.

4. If you chose the Select menu option of Sampled Colors, with the **Eyedropper** tool *🖉* chosen in the dialog, click to sample a color in the preview or in the image.**B**

5. *Optional:* Check Localized Color Clusters to limit the selection to colors near the one you clicked.

6. To add colors or shades to the selection, Shift-click or Shift-drag in the document or preview; or to subtract colors or shades from the selection, hold down Alt/Option and click or drag.

7. If you chose the Select menu option of Sampled Colors, you can select a wider or narrower range of similar colors by adjusting the **Range** value.

   Similarly, for the Select menu option of Highlights or Shadows, you can use the Range slider to include or exclude adjacent tonal levels from the selection.

   Or if you chose Midtones as the Select menu option, you can use the black Range slider to include or exclude adjacent tonal levels from lower midtone areas, or use the white Range slider to include or exclude adjacent tonal levels from the upper midtones.

8. For any Select menu option except a specific hue, you can use the **Fuzziness** slider to expand or narrow the number of partially selected pixels along the edges of the selection.**C**

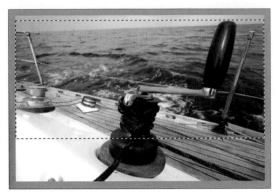

A *We created a rough rectangular selection of the water area in this image.*

B *We opened the Color Range dialog, then with the eyedropper, clicked the water in the preview. (White represents fully selected pixels; gray represents partially selected pixels.)*

C *To add to the selection, we Shift-clicked a couple more areas of water, then reduced the Fuzziness value to 48.*

A *With the Color Range selection still active, we created a Hue/Saturation adjustment layer. The selection converted to white areas in the layer mask.*

B *Although the ocean area wasn't selected completely, enough of it was selected for the Hue/Saturation adjustment to be successful. Now the ocean looks darker and more blue.*

9. If you chose Skin Tones in step 3, you can check **Detect Faces** to improve the accuracy of the selection (**A–D**, page 180).

10. For the document preview, choose an option from the **Selection Preview** menu: None for no preview, Grayscale to see an enlarged version of the dialog preview, Black Matte to view the selection against a black background, or White Matte (our favorite) to view the selection against a white background.

   ➤ To toggle the Selection and Image previews in the dialog, press Ctrl/Cmd, then release.

11. *Optional:* To save the current dialog settings as a preset, click Save, enter a name, keep the default location and extension, and click Save. The settings file saves to the same location as other presets.

12. Click OK.

13. *Optional:* With the selection still active, create an adjustment layer (see Chapter 12). The selection will be converted to white areas in the adjustment layer mask.**A–B**

➤ To load a Color Range preset into the dialog, click Load, locate the desired preset, then click Open.

➤ Color Range settings are sticky, meaning that the last-used settings — including the last color that was sampled with the eyedropper in the dialog — will be in effect the next time you open the dialog. If you want to use the current Foreground color as the sampled color instead, hold down the Spacebar as you open the dialog.

A *This is the original image.*

B *In the Color Range dialog, we chose Select: Skin Tones, checked Detect Faces, then adjusted the Fuzziness value.*

C *The Color Range command produced the selection shown to the left above. With the Lasso tool, we removed some extraneous areas from the selection.*

D *Finally, we used a Hue/Saturation adjustment layer to correct the hue, saturation, and lightness of the selected skin areas (to learn about Hue/Saturation, see pages 242–243).*

Hiding and showing the selection border

You can hide the blinking selection border without having to deselect the selection (say, to preview the results of an edit). If you do hide the border, remember that the selection remains in effect!

To hide or show the selection border:

Press Ctrl-H/Cmd-H or chose View > **Extras**.

Note: A one-time alert dialog may appear, offering you the option to assign the Ctrl-H/Cmd-H shortcut to the Extras command in Photoshop (our preference) or to the Hide Photoshop command.

➤ If the Ctrl-H/Cmd-H shortcut doesn't hide the selection border, it's because the Selection Edges option is unchecked in the Show Extra Options dialog. To make it available, choose View > Show > Show Extra Options, and in the dialog, check Selection Edges. (We like to keep all the options in that dialog checked so they can all be enabled or disabled quickly via the Ctrl-H/Cmd-H shortcut.)

A *We drew an inner selection with the Rectangular Marquee tool on this 300 ppi image, applied a Feather value of 25 px via Refine Edge, then chose Select > Inverse. Next, we used a Levels adjustment to lighten the area within the selection (see pages 236–237).*

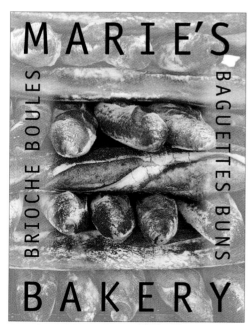

B *Finally, we added four separate editable type layers. The type is easy to read on the lightened background.*

Creating a frame-shaped selection

With the Rectangular Marquee or Elliptical Marquee tool, you can create a selection in the shape of a frame, either at the edge of the canvas area or floating within it. Image edits that you apply to the frame-shaped selection (e.g., filters or adjustments) will be visible only within that area.

To create a selection in the shape of a frame:

Method 1 (at the edge of the canvas area)

1. Click a layer.

2. Choose the **Rectangular Marquee** tool (M or Shift-M).

3. In the document window, drag a border to define the inner edge of the frame selection.

4. *Optional:* To soften the edges of the selection, click Refine Edge on the Options bar. In the dialog, choose On White (W) from the View menu, set the sliders to 0, adjust the Feather value to achieve the desired level of softness, then click OK.

5. Press Ctrl-Shift-I/Cmd-Shift-I (or right-click in the document and choose Select Inverse).**A–B**

Method 2 (within the image)

1. Click a layer.

2. Choose the **Rectangular Marquee** or **Elliptical Marquee** tool (M or Shift-M), then drag to define the outer edge of the frame selection.

3. Alt/Option drag inside the first selection to create the inner edge of the "frame."**C** Before releasing the mouse, you can release Alt/Option then hold down the Spacebar and drag the inner selection. After releasing the mouse, you can drag between the selection borders to reposition the entire "frame."

C *We are holding down Alt/Option and dragging to subtract one rectangular selection from the other.*

Selecting in-focus areas of a photo

The Focus Area command selects the areas of a photo that are most in focus automatically, and lets you modify the selection via sliders and brushes. For the best results, use this command on a photo in which foreground shapes are in sharp focus against a blurry background. You can further improve the selection afterward by using the Refine Edge dialog.

To use the Focus Area command:

1. Open a photo in which one area is more in focus than other areas. **A**

2. Choose Select > **Focus Area**. The dialog opens. Check Preview.

3. To control how the selection previews in the document, from the **View** menu, choose Overlay, On Black, On White, or On Layers (these options are described in step 4 on pages 184–185). Pause while the command selects the in-focus areas.

4. Under Parameters, do the following:

   For the **In-Focus Range**, keep Auto checked to let Photoshop determine the focus range for the selection; or increase the In-Focus Range value to enlarge the selection area, **B** or decrease the value to reduce the selection area.

   For the **Image Noise Level** (Advanced area), with Auto checked, Photoshop will try to remove noise (extraneous pixels) it detects from the area around the selection. If the Auto results aren't satisfactory, increase the Image Noise Level slightly.

5. To enlarge or reduce the selection manually, do the following:

   Click the **Focus Area Add** tool (E), then either press X (to view the original image) or V (for the View: Overlay option). Press [or] to set the brush to a small to medium size, then drag over the shape you want to add to the selection (**A–B**, next page). The tool will try to detect the edges of the shape automatically.

   To remove an area from the selection, set the brush size, then hold down Alt/Option and drag over the area to be removed. This is a temporary **Focus Area Subtract** tool.

6. To output the selection, do either of the following:

   Choose an option from the Output To: menu. Choose **Selection** or **Layer Mask** to output the selection without putting the contents on a new

A *In the original image, the violinist in the foreground is as prominent as the violinist in the background.*

B *We chose Select > Focus Area, chose On White from the View menu, then increased the In-Focus Range value to select more of the in-focus area. Most of the violin and arm became selected.*

layer (the Layer Mask option adds a mask to the current layer). Or to copy the selection contents to a new layer, choose **New Layer** (no mask) or **New Layer with Layer Mask** (the selection will be converted to white areas in a layer mask). Click OK.**C–D**

➤ To soften the edge of the selection, check Soften Edge.

Click **Refine Edge** to open the Refine Edge dialog, then use the dialog to clean up the edges of the selection; see pages 184–185. Refine Edge has the same output options as described in the preceding paragraph.

A *To fine-tune the selection (pun intended), we chose the Focus Area Add tool, then dragged the tool over the neck and pegs of the violin; those areas are now fully selected.*

B *Continuing with the Focus Area Add tool, we dragged over the lower hand and bow to select those areas. Next, with the Focus Area Subtract tool, we removed the dark triangle from the lower-left corner of the selection (shown in **B** on the preceding page).*

C *From the Output To: menu, we chose New Layer with Layer Mask. To accentuate the imagery on the new layer, we lightened it via a Brightness/Contrast adjustment, then clipped the adjustment layer to the new layer. Finally, we added another Brightness/Contrast adjustment to darken the entire Background.*

D *In the final image, the foreground figure stands out clearly from the other elements.*

Saving and loading selections

Creating a selection can be a laborious process, but fortunately, you can preserve your selection either as an alpha channel (this page) or as a layer mask (see page 192). The channel or mask can be loaded as a selection at any time (see this page and page 196) and can also be edited.

To save a selection to an alpha channel:

1. Create a selection. **A**

2. Do either of the following:

   On the Channels panel, 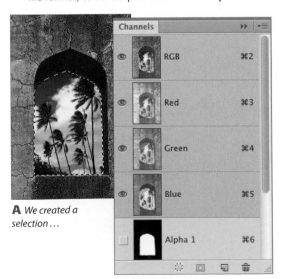 click the **Save Selection as Channel** button.

   Choose Select > **Save Selection**. The Save Selection dialog opens. Enter a Name, then click OK.

3. An alpha channel listing appears on the Channels panel. **B** Press Ctrl-D/Cmd-D to deselect.

➤ To reverse the masked and unmasked areas in an alpha channel, click the alpha channel listing on the Channels panel, then press Ctrl-I/Cmd-I.

➤ To rename an alpha channel, double-click the name, type a new one, then press Enter/Return.

➤ To delete an alpha channel, right-click the listing and choose Delete Channel.

➤ When using the File > Save As dialog, you can check Alpha Channels (if available for the current file format) to save alpha channels with your file.

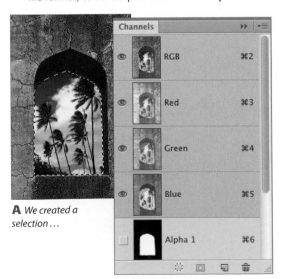

A We created a selection…

B … then clicked the Save Selection as Channel button on the Channels panel. The Alpha 1 listing appeared.

To edit an alpha channel:

1. On the Channels panel, click an alpha channel.

2. Choose the Brush tool (B or Shift-B), set the brush opacity, then paint with white to expand the selection area or with black to remove areas from it (press X to swap the two colors).

3. Click the topmost channel on the Channels panel.

➤ If you prefer to display and edit an alpha channel as a rubylith (red tint) over the image, click the alpha channel, then click the visibility icon for the topmost channel. To restore the normal display, Shift-click the alpha channel.

To load an alpha channel as a selection:

On the Channels panel, do either of the following:

Ctrl-click/Cmd-click the alpha channel thumbnail or listing.

Drag the channel listing to the **Load Channel as Selection** button.

Refining selection edges

The Refine Edge dialog provides many useful options for refining (e.g., smoothing, contracting) the edges of a selection, as well as options for outputting the selection (e.g., to a new layer or as a layer mask).

To refine the edges of a selection:

1. Create a selection and keep the selection tool chosen. Click a layer or the Background. Note: If you're going to output the selection as a layer mask (step 7), you must click a layer.

2. Click **Refine Edge** on the Options bar or press Ctrl-Alt-R/Cmd-Option-R. The dialog opens (**A**, next page).

3. If the sliders aren't set to 0, reset them all to that value. Zoom in on the selection in the document by pressing Ctrl-+/Cmd-+.

4. To control how the selection previews in the document, choose an option from the **View** menu; or use the assigned letter shortcut, as listed on the menu; or cycle through the options by pressing F. We find these options to be the most useful:

   Overlay (V) to view the selection as a Quick Mask (to judge the selection relative to the areas outside it) (**B**, next page).

   On Black (B) to view the selection on a black background (useful if you're going to copy the selection to a dark background).

On White (W) to view the selection on a white background (useful if you're going to copy the selection to a light background).**C**

On Layers (L) to view the selection on top of the layer directly below it, if any (to judge how the selection looks on top of that layer).

5. Under Edge Detection, check **Smart Radius** to allow the Radius to adapt to hard and soft edges that Photoshop detects in the image.

   If you want to enlarge the refinement area to include pixels just outside the selection edge, increase the **Radius** value.

   To view just the current refinement area, check **Show Radius** (J); uncheck it before proceeding.

   ➤ Press P to toggle the refinement off, then on.

6. Under Adjust Edge, adjust any of these sliders:

   To smooth out small bumps or jaggedness along the edges, raise the **Smooth** value slightly.

   To feather the edge, increase the **Feather** value. Note: If you're going to output your selection as a mask, keep this slider at 0 and use the nondestructive Feather slider on the Masks panel instead (see page 194).

   To produce a crisp selection edge, increase the **Contrast** value. This option counters the effect of an increased Radius, Smooth, or Feather value.

   To contract the selection inward to eliminate background pixels, or to expand it outward to include more, adjust the **Shift Edge** value.

7. Under Output:

   If you want to replace a fringe of background pixels along the selection edge with colors from within the selection, check **Decontaminate Colors**, then adjust the **Amount** value.

   Choose **Output To: Selection** or **Layer Mask** to output the refined selection without putting the contents on a new layer. Or to copy the selection contents to a new layer, choose **New Layer** (no mask) or **New Layer with Layer Mask** (the selection is converted to white areas in a layer mask). If Decontaminate Colors is checked, only the "New" layer options will be available.

8. *Optional:* Check Remember Settings to have the current settings become the new default values for the dialog (we keep this option off).

9. Click OK. (See also the task on the next four pages.)

A *The Refine Edge dialog provides many options for refining and outputting a selection.*

B *With Overlay chosen on the View menu in the Refine Edge dialog, the selection displays on a red-tinted Quick Mask.*

C *With the On White option chosen on the View menu, the selection displays on a white background.*

Using the Refine Radius tool in the Refine Edge dialog, along with the sliders, you can fine-tune the edge of a selection manually. Here we'll show you how to use these controls to refine a selection of hair (the bane of any Photoshopper's existence!), so you will be able to stack just the figure — surrounded by transparent pixels — above a different background.

To improve a selection of hair via the Refine Edge dialog:

1. Open an RGB portrait in which the figure has flyaway hair, and duplicate the Background.

2. Click the Background, and create a new Solid Color fill layer (see page 216); via the Color Picker, choose a color to appear behind the figure. **A** Note: You won't see the color in the image until step 5.

3. Click the duplicate image layer, then with the Quick Selection tool, 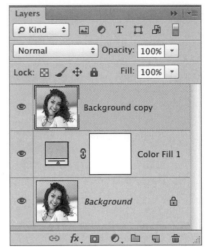 loosely select the face and hair. **B** Don't try to select the fine strands.

4. On the Options bar, click **Refine Edge** (Ctrl-Alt-R/ Cmd-Option-R). Make sure all the sliders are set to 0 and Decontaminate Colors is unchecked.

A *We duplicated the Background in this 300 ppi photo, then created a Solid Color fill layer directly above the Background.*

B *With the Quick Selection tool, we made a rough selection of the figure, including just the main part of her hair, not the fine outer strands.*

A *In the Refine Edge dialog, we checked Smart Radius and increased the Radius value to 120 px.*

B *In On Layers view, the underlying layer is visible below the unselected areas. Now the selection includes most of her hair, but we will refine it further to add the fine strands.*

5. From the View menu, choose On Layers (L). Under Edge Detection, check **Smart Radius** and set the **Radius** value to 80–120 px.**A–B** The higher the Radius value, the wider the area of edge pixels the command analyzes.

   To display just the refinement area in the image so you can see how it is affected by the two radius options, check **Show Radius** or press J.**C** The Smart Radius feature analyzes the content of the refinement area, narrowing that area where the edges are well defined while keeping it wide where the edges are complex or more finely detailed. Press J again to turn off the Show Radius option.

   Continued on the following page

C *We pressed J (Show Radius) to view the refinement area, noting where it was wide versus narrow. Afterward, we pressed J to return to On Layers view.*

6. Choose the **Refine Radius tool** ✏ (E), then press **X** to view the original image layer. Press] or [to set the brush to a medium to large size, then drag over the fine hair strands. Your brush work will display temporarily as green strokes.**A–B**

7. Press X to return to On Layers view.

   To better define the hard edges, if needed, adjust the Radius value, but keep the Contrast, Smooth, and Feather values at 0 so they don't impede the effect of the Refine Radius strokes.

8. Check **Decontaminate Colors**, then raise the Amount value until all colors from the background are removed. If you need to include yet more fine strands in the selection, increase the Shift Edge value slightly.

9. Choose Output To: **New Layer with Layer Mask**, then click OK (**A–B**, next page).

➤ To make the fine hair strands in dark hair more visible, duplicate the new layer and its layer mask after the last step above (**C**, next page).

A *We clicked the Refine Radius tool,* ✏ *pressed X to view the original image, then applied strokes over the fine hair strands to include them in the radius. (We didn't apply strokes to the edge of the sweater because the original selection of that area didn't need more refinement.)*

B *Because we widened the refinement area, Refine Edge added the fine hair strands to the selection.*

A *We checked Decontaminate Colors, set the Amount value to 70%, and increased the Shift Edge value just enough to include more hair strands but none of the original background. From the Output To menu, we chose New Layer with Layer Mask (then clicked OK).*

➤ *If you find that the Decontaminate Colors option produces unwanted colors along the selection edge, narrow the refinement area in those areas with the Erase Refinements tool.*

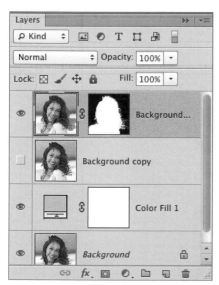

B *A new layer and layer mask appeared on the Layers panel (Photoshop hid the original duplicate layer automatically).*

C *We duplicated the new layer with its mask (panel not shown) to make the hair strands look darker, then finally to soften the results, we lowered the Opacity of the newest layer to 70%.*

Using Quick Masks

In these steps, you will create a selection, then put your document into Quick Mask mode; the selection displays temporarily as a semitransparent red tint over the image (like a traditional rubylith). You will add or subtract areas from the mask using brush strokes, then put the document back into Standard mode; the mask converts back to a (newly reshaped) selection. You can also use this mode to create a selection from scratch, as described on the next page.

To reshape a selection in Quick Mask mode:

1. Select an area of a layer.**A**

2. Click the **Edit in Quick Mask Mode** button 🔲 on the Tools panel or press Q. A red-tinted mask should cover the unselected areas of the image.**B** (If the mask is covering the selected area, double-click the same button, click Color Indicates: Masked Areas, click OK, then press Q to reenter Quick Mask mode.)

3. Choose the **Brush** tool ✏️ (B or Shift-B).

4. On the Options bar, click the Brush Preset picker arrowhead, then click a Hard or Soft Round brush (Soft if you want the selection edge to be slightly feathered); choose Mode: Normal; and set both the Opacity and Flow to 100%.

5. Zoom in on the mask, size the brush cursor by pressing [or], then do either of the following:

    To enlarge the masked (protected) area, press D for the default colors (black becomes the Foreground color), then apply brush strokes.

    To enlarge the unmasked area, press X to swap the Foreground and Background colors (make the Foreground color white), then apply strokes.**C**

    ➤ To create a partial mask, lower the brush opacity before applying strokes. When you edit pixels within the selection, that area will be only partially affected by your edits.

6. To restore the normal document mode, click the **Edit in Standard Mode** button 🔘 on the Tools panel or press Q. The unmasked areas will turn into a selection.

7. *Optional:* To preserve the selection, store it as an alpha channel (see page 184) or as a layer mask (see page 192). There is no way to save the Quick Mask as a mask or selection while your document is in Quick Mask mode.

A *We selected an area of a layer.*

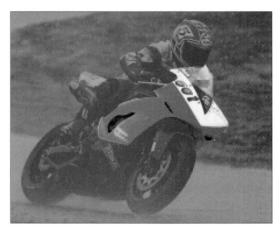

B *When we put the document into Quick Mask mode, Photoshop covered the unselected area with a red mask.*

C *Here, we're unmasking the helmet by applying strokes with the Brush tool.*

In these steps, you will paint a mask directly in a document without creating a selection first. As with any Quick Mask, when you restore the document to Standard mode, it is converted to a selection. One practical use for this technique is to select areas for retouching, such as the eyes or teeth areas in a portrait.

To create a selection via a Quick Mask:

1. Choose the **Brush** tool, and choose tool options as described in step 4 on the preceding page.

2. Double-click the **Edit in Quick Mask Mode** button on the Tools panel.

3. In the Quick Mask Options dialog,**A** click Color Indicates: **Selected Areas**. This will enable the areas that you cover with your red-tinted brush strokes (not the masked areas) to convert to a selection when you exit Quick Mask mode. Click OK.

4. Zoom in, size the brush cursor by pressing [or], then using black as the Foreground color, apply brush strokes to create a mask.**B**

   ➤ You can start by painting with a medium-sized brush, then refine the mask with a smaller one.

   If you need to remove any areas from the mask, press X to switch the Foreground color to white.

5. Press Q to put the document back into Standard mode.**C** The mask converts to a selection.

6. *Optional:* To feather all the edges of the selection, use the Feather slider in the Refine Edge dialog (see page 185).

7. *Optional:* To store the selection as a mask on the current layer, see the next page. Or to save it as an alpha channel, see page 184.**D**

A *We clicked Selected Areas in the Quick Mask Options dialog, and also changed the mask color from the default of red to blue to have it contrast better with the image.*

B *We're painting a Quick Mask on teeth.*

C *When we restored the document to Standard mode, the mask converted to a selection. (To use a selection like this one to whiten teeth, see page 316.)*

D *We saved the selection as an alpha channel.*

Creating layer masks

A layer mask is an editable (and removable) 8-bit grayscale channel that hides all or some of the pixels, type, or vector shapes on a layer. White areas in a layer mask reveal parts of the layer, black areas hide, and gray areas hide partially. Memorizing this simple phrase will help: White reveals, black conceals.

When a layer mask thumbnail is selected, you can edit the mask or move or copy it to other layers. At any time, you can disable a mask temporarily, apply it to make its effect permanent, or discard it altogether.

A *The original image contains a photo of tile on a layer above a photo of an archway on the Background. We selected the archway, then clicked the tile layer.*

B *To add a black mask to the tile layer, we held down Alt/Option and clicked the Add Layer Mask button on the Layers panel. To blend the tile with the stone wall, we chose Pin Light blending mode and lowered the layer opacity.*

To add a layer mask via the Layers panel:

1. *Optional:* Create a selection, which is to become a shape in the mask.
2. On the Layers panel, click an image, type, or shape layer, a layer group, or a Smart Object.**A**
3. Do either of the following:

   To create a white mask that hides none of the layer or that hides only the areas outside an active selection, at the bottom of the Layers panel, click the **Add Layer Mask** button.

   To create a black mask that hides the whole layer or that hides only the areas inside an active selection, Alt-click/Option-click the **Add Layer Mask button** on the Layers panel.**B–C**

➤ To create a selection from type, Ctrl-click/Cmd-click the thumbnail for an editable type layer. You can then hide the type layer by clicking its visibility icon, and use the selection to produce a mask on another layer.

To output a selection as a layer mask via the Refine Edge dialog:

1. Create a selection to become a shape in the mask.
2. On the Layers panel, click a layer, layer group, or Smart Object.
3. Click **Refine Edge** on the Options bar, and use the dialog to refine the selection edges (see pages 184–185). From the Output To menu, choose **Layer Mask**, then click OK.

C *The center of the tile layer is hidden by the arch-shaped mask.*

Editing masks

In this task, you'll edit a layer mask by applying strokes in the image with the Brush tool. In the steps on the next two pages, you will edit a mask via the Properties panel. Throughout this book, you will have many opportunities to practice these essential skills.

To reshape an existing layer mask:

1. Choose the **Brush** tool ![brush icon] (B or Shift-B).

2. On the Options bar, click a brush on the Brush Preset picker; choose Mode: Normal; and choose an Opacity of 100% to mask or unmask areas fully or a lower Opacity to mask or unmask them partially.

3. Do either of the following:

   To display a mask as a colored overlay on the image, Alt-Shift-click/Option-Shift-click a layer mask thumbnail on the Layers panel.**A–B**

   To display a mask in black and white with the image hidden, Alt-click/Option-click a layer mask thumbnail on the Layers panel.

4. Size the brush cursor by pressing [or], then do either or both of the following (to change the brush hardness or opacity, see pages 130–131):

   If the Foreground Color square on the Tools panel isn't white, press D. Apply brush strokes to remove areas of the mask and reveal more of the layer.**C**

   Press X (to switch the Foreground color to black), then apply brush strokes to enlarge the mask and hide more of the layer.**D–E**

5. Click the layer (not the mask) thumbnail.

➤ In lieu of step 3, you can double-click the layer mask thumbnail, then hold down Alt-Shift/Option-Shift or Alt/Option and click the Layer Mask thumbnail on the Properties panel.![icon]

➤ To open a dialog in which you can change the color or opacity that is used to display layer masks in your document, right-click a layer mask thumbnail on the Layers panel and choose Mask Options.

To swap the black and white areas in a layer mask:

Do either of the following:

Click a layer mask thumbnail on the Layers panel, then press Ctrl-I/Cmd-I.

Double-click a layer mask thumbnail on the Layers panel to display the Properties panel, then click the **Invert** button.

A *We're painting out areas of the mask, which we chose to display as a red overlay.*

B *This is the result.*

C *Here we're subtracting areas from the mask (painting with white) with just the mask showing in the document.*

D *We're adding to the mask by painting with black.*

E *Here we're partially hiding an area of the archway layer by painting on the mask with our brush set to 60% Opacity.*

A *In this document, a black, hard-edged layer mask is hiding everything on the image layer except the car.*

In the Masks pane of the Properties panel, you can use the Density slider to change the overall opacity of a layer or vector mask and/or the Feather slider to adjust the softness of the edge of the mask. These sliders are nondestructive, meaning they don't alter the mask permanently and can be readjusted at any time. (To learn about vector masks, see pages 430–433.)

To adjust the density or feather value of a layer or vector mask:

1. Double-click a layer or vector mask thumbnail on the Layers panel **A** to show the Properties panel.

2. Do either or both of the following:

   Reduce the **Density** value to lighten the black part of the mask and partially reveal areas of the layer (make the mask more transparent).**B**

   Increase the **Feather** value to soften the edge of the mask, for a more gradual transition between the masked and unmasked areas.**C**

B *To lighten the black part of the mask, we reduced the Density value on the Properties panel.*

C *Next, we increased the Feather value on the Properties panel to soften the edges of the mask. (Note that the layer Opacity is still 100%.) The car is the star of the show, while the faded background plays a supporting role.*

To refine the edges of a layer mask:

1. Double-click a layer mask thumbnail on the Layers panel to show the Properties panel.

2. Click **Mask Edge** to open the Refine Mask dialog. Note: If you don't see the Mask Edge button, either scroll downward in the panel or enlarge the panel by dragging the gripper bar downward.

3. Use the Refine Mask controls to adjust the softness or sharpness of the edge of the mask. For an illustration of this feature, see page 267. The Refine Mask controls work like the controls in the Refine Edge dialog, which is discussed on pages 184–189.

➤ When we need to feather the edge of a mask, we use the Feather slider on the Properties panel because it's nondestructive, and keep the Feather slider in the Refine Mask dialog at 0 because it's destructive.

➤ If you create a mask by applying brush strokes or by converting an imprecise selection, some unwanted image pixels may still be visible along the edges. To expand or contract the mask to include or exclude more pixels, in the Refine Mask dialog, try setting the Radius to around 1 or 2, and fiddle with the Shift Edge slider.

➤ If you click Color Range on the Properties panel for a selected mask, you can edit the mask using the same dialog controls as you would use to create a selection via the Select > Color Range command (see pages 178–179).

Working with masks

By default, every layer mask that you create is linked to its layer thumbnail, and when moved, the two travel together as a unit. If you want to move either component separately, you have to unlink them first. Note: This task applies only to layer masks, not to vector masks.

To reposition layer content or a mask independently:

1. On the Layers panel, click the **Link** icon 🔗 between a layer thumbnail and layer mask thumbnail. The icon disappears.

2. Click either the layer thumbnail or the layer mask thumbnail, depending on which component you want to move.**A–B**

3. Choose the **Move** tool ➤⊕ (or hold down V to spring-load the tool), then drag in the document window.**C**

4. Click between the layer and layer mask thumbnails to restore the Link icon.

A A layer mask is hiding the center of the tile layer and revealing part of the underlying Background.

B We clicked the Link icon to disengage the layer image from the mask, then clicked the layer mask thumbnail.

C With the Move tool, we dragged the mask in the document to reveal a different part of the Background.

Note: All the tasks on this page apply to both layer and vector masks.

You can move or copy a layer or vector mask to a different layer (but not to the Background).

To move a mask to a different layer:

Drag a layer or vector mask thumbnail to another layer. The mask disappears from the original layer and appears on the destination layer.

To copy a mask to another layer:

Alt-drag/Option-drag a layer or vector mask thumbnail to another layer.

When you load a layer or vector mask as a selection, it displays in your document as a border of "marching ants."

To load a mask as a selection:

Do either of the following:

On the Layers panel, Ctrl-click/Cmd-click a mask thumbnail.

On the Layers panel, double-click a mask thumbnail, then on the Properties panel, click the **Load Selection from Mask** button.

When you disable a layer or vector mask, a red X appears in the thumbnail on both the Layers and Properties panels, and the entire layer becomes visible.

To disable or enable a mask:

Method 1 (Layers panel)

To disable a mask, on the Layers panel, Shift-click the mask thumbnail **A** (this doesn't select the thumbnail). To re-enable a layer mask, just click the mask thumbnail; to re-enable a vector mask, Shift-click the thumbnail.

➤ You can also right-click the mask thumbnail and choose Disable Layer Mask or Disable Vector Mask from the context menu (or choose the "Enable" version of either command).

Method 2 (Properties panel)

To disable or re-enable a mask, on the Layers panel, double-click a mask thumbnail, then on the Properties panel, click the Disable/Enable Mask button.

You can discard any masks you don't need. Deleting a layer mask will reduce the file size slightly; deleting a vector mask will have little impact on the file size.

To delete a mask:

1. *Optional:* Copy the file via File > Save As.

2. Do one of the following:

On the Layers panel, right-click a mask thumbnail and choose **Delete Layer Mask** or **Delete Vector Mask**.

On the Layers panel, click a mask thumbnail, click the **Delete Layer** button, then if an alert dialog appears, click OK (or Alt-click/Option-click the button to bypass the prompt).

On the Layers panel, double-click a mask thumbnail to display the Properties panel, then click the **Delete Mask** button.

On an image layer (no other kind of layer), you can apply the effect of a layer or vector mask and delete the hidden pixels permanently. The mask thumbnail disappears from the Layers panel.

To apply a mask to its layer:

1. *Optional:* Applying a mask is a permanent change, so you may want to either duplicate its layer or copy the file via File > Save As.

2. Do either of the following:

On the Layers panel, right-click a layer mask thumbnail and choose **Apply Layer Mask**.

On the Layers panel, double-click a layer or vector mask thumbnail to display the Properties panel, then click the **Apply Mask** button.

A *To disable a layer mask, Shift-click the mask thumbnail.*

Using the History panel, you can selectively restore your document to one of its previous states (in the current work session). The panel provides many more options and much more flexibility than the simple Undo command. In this chapter, you will learn how to set options for the History panel; restore your document to a previous history state; delete, purge, and clear history states; preserve states of the current work session via snapshots; and generate a new document from a state or snapshot.

Choosing History panel options

The History panel keeps a running list of the states, or edits, that you have made to the currently open document, from the "Open" unedited state of the document at the top of the list to the most recent state at the bottom. (This happens even if you don't have the panel open.)

When you click an earlier state, the document is restored to that stage of the editing process. Recent states may become dimmed and unavailable when you do this, depending on whether the panel is in linear or nonlinear mode.**A** Before using the panel, you need to understand this difference between the two modes.

Source for the History Brush tool —

Current history state —

Create New Document from Current State

Create New Snapshot

Delete Current State

A With our History panel in linear mode, we clicked an earlier state, which caused subsequent states to become dimmed.

A BRUSH WITH HISTORY

In Chapter 14, we provide generic instructions on the use of brushes. On pages 309–310 in that chapter, we provide specific instructions for using the History Brush tool, which you can use to restore a history state within brush strokes.

Choosing a mode for the History panel

To choose a mode for the History panel, choose History Options from the panel menu, then in the History Options dialog, check or uncheck **Allow Non-Linear History.A** We recommend keeping the History panel in **linear mode** (unchecking Allow Non-Linear History), particularly if you're a newcomer to Photoshop. With the panel in this mode, if you click an earlier state and either resume image editing from or delete that state, all the subsequent (dimmed) states are discarded. Although this mode offers less flexibility, it enables you to restore your document to an earlier state with a simple, clean break.

In **nonlinear mode**, if you click or delete an earlier state, subsequent states aren't deleted or dimmed.**B** If you resume image editing while an earlier state is selected, your next edit will show up as the latest state on the panel, and all the states in between will be preserved. That is, the latest state will incorporate the earlier stage of the image plus your newest edit. If you change your mind, you can click any intermediate state whenever you like and resume editing from there. Nonlinear is the more flexible of the two modes, but it can also be confusing.

Choosing other settings for the History panel

The last option in the History Options dialog, **Make Layer Visibility Changes Undoable**, controls whether the panel creates a "Layer Visibility" state each time you click the visibility icon for a layer on the Layers panel. We keep this option off in order to reserve space on the panel for other states. (For the snapshot options in this dialog, see page 201.)

To specify the number of states that can be listed on the History panel, go to Edit/Photoshop CC > Preferences (Ctrl-K/Cmd-K) > Performance and, under History & Cache, choose a **History States** value (the default value is 50). If the maximum number of history states is exceeded during an editing session, the oldest states are removed to make room for new ones. The maximum number of states may also be limited by other factors, including the image size, the kind of edits made to the image, and currently available system memory. Each open document has its own separate list of states.

Beware! Regardless of the current preference setting, when you close a document, all of its history states and snapshots are deleted from the panel.

A *In the History Options dialog, uncheck Allow Non-Linear History to put the panel in linear mode, or check it for nonlinear mode.*

B *With our History panel in nonlinear mode, we clicked an earlier state. All the states remained available, including the recent states below the one we clicked.*

Changing history states

Before changing history states, let us remind you of the difference between the two modes for the History panel. If the panel is in linear mode (the Allow Non-Linear History option is off) and you click an earlier state, all the states below the one you click will become dimmed. If you then delete the state you clicked or continue editing the image while that earlier state remains selected, all the dimmed states will be deleted (if you change your mind, you can choose Undo immediately to restore the deleted states).

If the panel is in nonlinear mode and you click an earlier state, then proceed to edit your document, the newest edit will become the latest state, but Photoshop won't delete the prior states.

To change history states:

1. Perform some edits on an image.

2. Do any of the following:

   On the History panel, click a state. **A–B**

   To **Step Forward** one state, press Ctrl-Shift-Z/Cmd-Shift-Z.

   To **Step Backward** one state, press Ctrl-Alt-Z/Cmd-Option-Z.

➤ When you choose File > Revert, it is listed as a state on the History panel. You can restore the image to a state prior to or after the Revert state.

➤ When you choose File > Save, the term "(Save)" is added to the current state on the History panel. ★

➤ Each time you click and change the settings for an existing adjustment layer, the panel lists those edits collectively as one new state (e.g., "Modify Levels Layer" or "Modify Curves Layer").

➤ You can't restack (change the order of) history states on the panel.

A With our History panel in linear mode, we're clicking a prior state.

B All the states listed below the one we clicked became dimmed.

Deleting, purging, and clearing history states

This task presumes that your History panel is in linear mode (you unchecked the Allow Non-Linear History option). With the panel in this mode, if you delete a state and then resume editing your document, that state and all the subsequent ones will be discarded from the panel.

To delete a history state:

On the History panel, do one of the following:

Right-click a state, choose **Delete** from the context menu,**A** then click Yes in the alert dialog. That state and all the subsequent ones will be deleted.**B**

To bypass the alert, drag the state to be deleted to the **Delete Current State** button.

To delete previous states in reverse order without an alert appearing, click a state, then Alt-click/Option-click the **Delete Current State** button as many times as needed.

Note: The Undo command restores only the last deleted state.

When you purge or clear states from the History panel, the most recent state is left as the only state remaining. All snapshots are preserved (see the next page).

To purge or clear the History panel:

To clear all states from your History panel for all of the currently open documents in order to free up memory for Photoshop, choose Edit > Purge > **Histories**, then click OK if an alert appears. (To prevent the alert from reappearing, check Don't Show Again.) As the alert warns you, this command cannot be undone!

To clear all states from the History panel for just the current document, right-click any state and choose **Clear History**. This command doesn't free up memory for Photoshop, but it can be undone.

A *Right-click a state and choose Delete from the context menu, then click Yes in the alert dialog.*

B *Because our History panel was in linear mode when we deleted a state, Photoshop also deleted all the subsequent states.*

Using snapshots

Photoshop deletes states from the History panel if any of the following events occur: the specified maximum number of history states is exceeded, you clear or purge the panel, or you click an earlier state when the panel is in linear mode and then resume editing the document. Snapshots, which are created from a history state, remain on the panel even if any of the above-mentioned events occur. When you click a snapshot, the document is restored to the state from which it was created.

Snapshots are represented by thumbnails at the top of the panel, for easy identification.**A** Note that like states, all snapshots are deleted when you close your document.

On this page, you will choose default settings for snapshots that apply to all Photoshop files. On the next page, you will create snapshots for a specific document.

To choose snapshot options:

1. From the History panel menu, choose **History Options**. The History Options dialog opens.**B**

2. Check or uncheck any of the following options, all of which pertain to snapshots:

   Automatically Create First Snapshot to have Photoshop create a snapshot each time a file is opened (this option is checked by default and we keep it that way).

   Automatically Create New Snapshot When Saving to have Photoshop create a snapshot every time a file is saved. Each snapshot is labeled with the time of day it was created.

   Show New Snapshot Dialog by Default to have the New Snapshot dialog appear whenever you click the New Snapshot button, enabling you to enter a name and choose a "From" option (see the next page).

3. Click OK.

A *Because the Automatically Create First Snapshot option was enabled when we opened this document, Photoshop created a snapshot of the document's opening state (the top snapshot). During the course of editing, we added three more snapshots.*

B *The History Options dialog has three snapshot options. We usually keep just the first two checked.*

If the Automatically Create New Snapshot When Saving option is turned off for your History panel, you should get in the habit of creating snapshots periodically as you work and before running any actions on your document. If you follow Method 2 (right), you can choose whether the snapshot is made from all the layers in the document, from all the layers present at a particular state, or from just the current layer.

To create a snapshot of a state:

Method 1 (without choosing options)

1. Edit your document so it contains the changes that you want to capture as a snapshot.

2. If the Show New Snapshot Dialog by Default option is off in the History Options dialog, click the **New Snapshot** button on the History panel; or if that option is on, Alt-click/Option-click the New Snapshot button. A new snapshot thumbnail appears below the last one, in the upper section of the panel.

Method 2 (choosing options)

1. Edit your document so it contains the changes that you want to capture as a snapshot.

2. On the History panel, right-click the state to be captured as a snapshot and choose **New Snapshot** from the context menu.**A** The layer that was being edited at that state becomes selected, and the New Snapshot dialog opens.**B**

3. Type a name for the snapshot, then choose an option from the **From** menu:

   Full Document to preserve all the layers that were in the document at the designated state.

   Merged Layers to merge all the layers in the document at the designated state into one layer.

   Current Layer to create a snapshot of just the layer that was selected at the designated state.

4. Click OK.**C**

5. If you didn't create the snapshot from the latest state, click the state from which you want to resume editing your document.

➤ To rename a snapshot, double-click the name.

A *After applying some edits to this image, we right-clicked the latest state and are choosing New Snapshot from the context menu.*

B *In the New Snapshot dialog, we entered a name for the snapshot and chose From: Full Document.*

C *A thumbnail for the new snapshot appeared on the History panel.*

Creating snapshots of promising or key document states periodically while editing is a good habit to get into. With their thumbnails, snapshots are easier to identify than states, and unlike states (which Photoshop may delete to make room for new states), snapshots stay on the panel until you close your document. Compare the two different options below, noting the different effect they have on the History panel.

To make a snapshot become the newest state:

After applying some edits to your document and creating one or more snapshots, do either of the following: **A–B**

Click a snapshot name or thumbnail.**C–D** If the History panel is in linear mode, the document will revert to the snapshot stage of editing, and all the states will be dimmed. If you now resume editing, all those dimmed states will be discarded.

Alt-click/Option-click a snapshot name or thumbnail. Earlier states will remain available and the snapshot you clicked will become the most recent state. Use this method if you want to preserve access to prior edits.

➤ To delete a snapshot, drag it to the Delete Current State button 🗑 or right-click the snapshot name and choose Delete from the context menu.

A *This is the original image.*

B *During the course of editing the image (applying some filters), we created a few snapshots of different states.*

C *We clicked a snapshot.*

D *Now the image matches the state of the snapshot.*

Creating documents from history states

By using the New Document command, you can spin off versions of your current document (and the current state of the Layers panel) from any state or snapshot.

To create a new document from a history state or snapshot:

1. On the History panel, do either of the following:

   Right-click a snapshot or a state and choose **New Document** from the context menu.**A**

   Click a snapshot or a state, then click the **New Document from Current State** button.

2. Save the new document that appears onscreen.**B** The starting state for the document will be listed as "Duplicate State."

3. In the original document, click the history state from which you want to continue editing.

A *We right-clicked a snapshot and are choosing New Document from the context menu.*

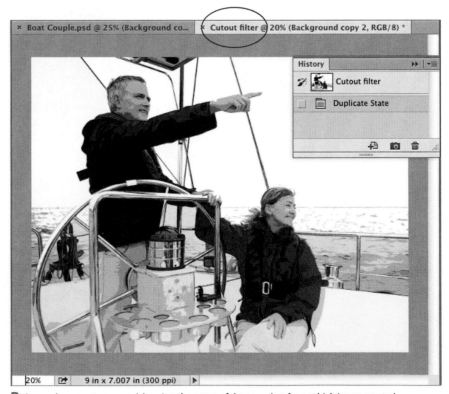

B *A new document appeared, bearing the name of the snapshot from which it was created.*

In this chapter, you'll learn ways to choose the colors that are applied by various Photoshop tools and commands. You will also learn how to work with color themes, choose a blending mode for a layer or tool, apply a tint via a Solid Color fill layer, work with gradients, and create and apply patterns.

Choosing colors in Photoshop
The Foreground and Background colors

The current Foreground color is applied by some tools, such as the Brush, Pencil, and Mixer Brush, and by some commands. The current Background color is applied by other procedures, such as when you enlarge the canvas area with the Crop tool (Delete Cropped Pixels option enabled) or cut an area from, or use the Eraser tool on, the Background. One or both of these colors are also used by some of the Photoshop filters.

The Foreground and Background colors are displayed in color squares on the Tools panel **A** and on the Color panel. **B** Note: In this book, Foreground color and Background color are written with an uppercase "F" and "B" to differentiate them from the general foreground and background areas of a picture.

On the following pages, you will learn how to choose Foreground and Background colors via these methods:

➤ Use the controls in the **Color Picker** dialog or via an on-image color picker.

➤ Choose a predefined color from a matching system via the **Color Libraries** dialog.

➤ Use the sliders on the **Color** panel.

➤ Click a solid-color swatch on the **Swatches** panel.

➤ Sample a color in an image with the **Eyedropper** tool.

USING COLOR

11

The Default Foreground and Background Colors button (D) makes the Foreground color black and the Background color white.

The Switch Foreground and Background Colors button (X) swaps the two current colors.

The currently selected square has an extra outer border.

Foreground color square

Background color square

Foreground color square

Background color square

A *These are the color controls on the Tools panel.*

Color ramp

B *The two color squares also appear on the Color panel.*

The color models

Colors in Photoshop can be chosen from four models and a wide assortment of matching systems. When output on a commercial press, your Photoshop image will be printed using different percentages of cyan (C), magenta (M), yellow (Y), and black (K) inks, which together create the impression of smooth, continuous tones. In the printing industry, colors are standardized by number, with each company providing its own system and printed fan guide or chip book (similar to the way you might pick colors of house paint). Spot colors, which are premixed inks based on set formulas (e.g., PANTONE PLUS), are sometimes used in addition to CMYK inks where color accuracy is critical, such as for a company logo.

For commercial printing, the only way to get dependable results is by referring to a printed guide. If you pick colors based on whether they look appealing onscreen (even on a well-calibrated display), you may be in for an unpleasant—and potentially costly—surprise when you see them in print.

RGB colors (based on the components of red, green, and blue light in a computer display) are used solely for screen output; for these colors, you don't need to refer to a printed guide. For Web output, some designers also use hexadecimal colors. For the HSB color model, see the sidebar on page 208.

Using the Color Picker

To choose a color via the Color Picker:

1. Do either of the following:

   On the Tools panel, click the Foreground or Background color square.

   On the Color panel, click the Foreground or Background color square if it's already selected (has an extra outer border), or double-click the square if it's not selected.

   Note: If the square you click contains a custom color from a matching system (such as PANTONE PLUS), the Color Libraries dialog will open instead of the picker. Click the Picker button to get to the Color Picker dialog.

2. Do one of the following:

   Click a color on the vertical color ramp or drag the slider to choose a hue, then click a brightness and saturation value of that hue in the large square.**A** (You can also click or drag in the image to sample a color while the Color Picker dialog is open.)

A *To pick a color, click a hue on this color ramp or drag the slider, then click a saturation and brightness variation in the large square.*

Alternatively, enter a hex # or enter values in a set of fields.

USING THE HUD COLOR PICKER

To access Color Picker controls quickly without opening the dialog, choose a tool that uses colors, Alt-Shift-right-click/Cmd-Option-Control-click in the image to display the on-image picker, drag to choose a hue on the hue (spectrum) bar or wheel, then drag to choose a brightness and saturation value in the square. If you want to change the hue without changing the current brightness and saturation values, when the picker displays, release the keys but keep the mouse button down, hold down the Spacebar and drag the pointer to the hue bar or wheel, release the Spacebar, then drag to the desired hue (practice, practice).

Note: For this feature to work, Use Graphics Processor must be checked in Edit/Photoshop CC > Preferences > Performance. From the HUD Color Picker menu in General Preferences, choose a strip or wheel design and size for the HUD Color Picker.

To choose a hexadecimal color (for Web output), enter the desired number in the # field. This field is highlighted by default.

To choose a process color for print output, enter C, M, Y, and K percentages from a printed formula guide for a process color matching system.

For onscreen output, enter R, G, and B values (0 to 255).

3. Click OK. The color will appear in the designated color square on the Tools and Color panels.

➤ To change the interface of the Color Picker, in Edit/Photoshop CC > Preferences > General, from the Color Picker menu, select either Windows/Apple (the picker for your system) or Adobe (the default Photoshop picker).

➤ You don't need to restrict yourself to Web-safe colors for Web graphics, because most computers display millions of colors. Ignore the non-Web-safe icon 🎲 if it appears in the Color Picker, and keep Only Web Colors unchecked. For the out-of-gamut icon, ⚠ see the sidebar on the next page.

Choosing colors from a library

Before choosing spot colors for print output, ask your commercial print shop which brand of ink they're going to use, then choose colors from a printed guide for that system (each manufacturer makes its own guide). Note: By default, Photoshop color-separates both the process and spot colors in a file into C, M, Y, and K process colors. To output a spot color to a separate plate, you must create a separate channel for it (this is done with type as an example on page 402).

To choose a color from a library:

1. Do either of the following:

   On the Tools panel, click the Foreground or Background color square.

   On the Color panel, 🎨 click the Foreground or Background color square if it's already selected (has an extra outer border), or double-click the square if it's not selected.

2. If the color square you clicked isn't a custom color, the Color Picker dialog will open. Click **Color Libraries** to show the Color Libraries dialog.

3. From the **Book** menu, choose a matching system. For commercial printing, choose the system that your print shop has recommended, and find the desired color in a formula guide.

4. Do either of the following:

   Without clicking anywhere, type the number of the desired color; that swatch will become selected. **A**

   Click a color on the vertical color ramp (or set the slider) to display a family of hues, then click a swatch on the left side of the dialog. **B**

5. Click OK. To add the chosen color to the Swatches panel, see page 209.

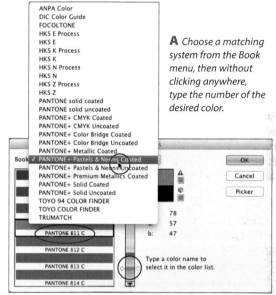

A Choose a matching system from the Book menu, then without clicking anywhere, type the number of the desired color.

B Another option is to click a color on the vertical color ramp (or move the slider), then click a swatch on the left side.

COLOR LIBRARIES FOR PRINT OUTPUT

➤ ANPA colors are used in the newspaper industry.

➤ DIC Color Guide and TOYO Color Finder colors are used in Japan.

➤ FOCOLTONE is a process color system that was developed to help prevent registration problems. It can be used in North America.

➤ HKS process colors and HKS spot colors (without "Process" in the name) are used primarily in Europe.

➤ PANTONE PLUS (+) process and spot colors are widely used in North America.

➤ TRUMATCH is a process color system, organized in a different way from PANTONE. It is used worldwide.

Using the Color panel

Another way to select RGB or HSB colors for Web output, or for output to an inkjet printer, is via the Color panel.

To choose an RGB or HSB color using the Color panel:

1. Click the Foreground or Background color square on the Color panel, ⬛ if the desired square isn't already selected.**A**

2. From the top portion of the panel menu, choose one of these color models for the sliders: Hue Cube, Brightness Cube, RGB Sliders, or HSB Sliders.**B** (See also the sidebar at right.)

3. For any model except a Cube, move any of the sliders; or click or drag in the color ramp; or enter values in the fields.**C**

   ➤ To enlarge the ramp, drag the bottom of the panel downward.

   For the Hue Cube model, drag in the hue bar on the right, then drag in the large square to select a brightness and saturation value.**D** Or for the Brightness Cube model, move the brightness slider and/or drag in the large square to select a hue and saturation value.

4. *Optional:* To add your new color to the Swatches panel, see the instructions on the next page.

➤ Alt-click/Option-click the color ramp to choose a color for whichever color square (Foreground or Background) isn't currently selected.

➤ If Dynamic Color Sliders is checked in Preferences (Ctrl-K/Cmd-K) > Interface, ★ colors in the bars above the sliders will update instantly as you mix or choose a color.

HSB AND RGB DEMYSTIFIED

➤ In the HSB model, the hue (H) is the wavelength of light for which a color is named (such as "red" or "blue"); brightness (B) is the lightness of a color; and saturation (S) is the purity of a color (how much gray it contains versus pure color).

➤ In the RGB model, which is used by your computer display, white (the presence of all colors) is produced when all the sliders are at the far right (at 255) on the Color panel, black (the absence of all colors) is produced when all the sliders are at the far left (0), and gray is produced when all the sliders are aligned vertically with one another at any other location.

THE OUT-OF-GAMUT ALERT

An out-of-gamut alert icon ⚠ on the Color Picker or Color panel indicates that the current color isn't printable (has no ink equivalent). If you click the icon, Photoshop will substitute the closest printable color, as shown in the swatch next to or below the icon.

Similarly, if the color currently under the pointer is outside the printable gamut, exclamation points will display next to the CMYK color values on the Info panel.

The out-of-gamut range is defined by the current CMYK output profile, which is chosen on the Working Spaces: CMYK menu in Edit > Color Settings. When your image is converted to CMYK mode for commercial printing, all the image colors are brought into the printable gamut automatically. You need to pay attention to the alerts only if you want to convert specific colors manually.

A *Click the Foreground or Background color square.*

B *Choose a model for the sliders.*

To learn about these options, see page 213.

Choose a display option for the color ramp (or right-click the ramp and choose from the context menu).

C *Click in the color ramp or move any of the sliders.*

D *If you chose the Hue Cube model, drag in the bar to choose a hue, then drag in the large square to choose a brightness and saturation value of that hue.*

Using the Swatches panel

Note: For easy access, detach the Swatches panel from the Color panel group by dragging its tab.

To choose a color via the Swatches panel:

1. Display the Swatches panel.

2. Do either of the following:

    To choose a Foreground or Background color for the color square that is currently selected on the Tools and Color panels, click a swatch.

    To choose a Foreground or Background color for the color square that isn't selected on the Tools and Color panels, Ctrl-click/Cmd-click a swatch.

    Note: In addition to the swatches in the main part of the panel, you can also click any recently used swatch in the top row of the panel.

➤ To access other libraries of swatches, see page 135.

LOADING SWATCHES FROM AN HTML, CSS, OR SVG FILE

To load color swatches from an HTML, CSS, or SVG file, use the Load Swatches or Replace Swatches command on the Swatches panel menu. To prevent duplication, Photoshop will load each unique color only once.

A To add a color to the Swatches panel, we clicked the blank area below the swatches.

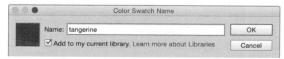

B We entered a name for the swatch.

Colors that you add to the Swatches panel will remain there until the swatches are deleted, replaced, or reset, and are available for use in all documents. (To save swatches as a permanent library, see "To save the presets currently on a picker as a library," on page 133.)

To add a color to the Swatches panel:

1. Choose a Foreground color via the Color panel or Color Picker, or select a color in the image with the Eyedropper tool (see the next page).

2. On the Swatches panel, do one of the following:

    Click the **New Swatch of Foreground Color** button.

    Click the blank area below the swatches.**A**

    Right-click any existing swatch and choose **New Swatch** from the context menu.

3. In the Color Swatch Name dialog, enter a name for the swatch.**B** *Optional:* Check **Add to My Current Library** to add the swatch as a color asset to the Libraries panel.★ (See pages 270–272.) Click OK. The new swatch will be displayed last on the Swatches panel.**C**

➤ To create a new swatch without opening the Color Swatch Name dialog, hold down Alt/Option and click the blank area in the Swatches panel.

➤ To rename an existing swatch, double-click it, then change the name in the dialog. To learn a swatch name, either use the Tool Tip or list the swatches by name (choose Small List or Large List from the panel menu).

➤ To restore the default swatches to the Swatches panel, see page 134.

➤ If you want to use the current swatches on the panel in another Adobe Creative Cloud application, save them via the Save Swatches for Exchange command on the panel menu.

C Our new swatch appeared on the panel.

Working with Adobe color themes

Use the Adobe Color Themes panel to create color themes, explore themes from other designers, or view and edit your own saved themes.

Color themes are saved to one of your Creative Cloud Libraries (see pages 270–272) for use in any Adobe program that supports CC Libraries; themes are also displayed on the Adobe Color CC web service.

To create a color theme via the panel: ★

1. Display the Adobe Color Themes panel 🎨 by choosing that command from the Window > Extensions submenu.

2. On the panel, click **Create.A** To edit the current colors based on a rule, click an option from the color rule **menu** at the top of the pane.**B**

3. Near the bottom of the pane, click the **color model** you wish to edit in. (If only one color model is listed, click it to display the other models.)

4. To edit the **non-base colors** (no white triangle icon), do the following:

   Click a color square below the wheel or a marker on the wheel, then drag any of the color component sliders.**C** All the colors (except the base color) will be modified. Drag the **Brightness** (bottommost) slider to modify the selected color only.

   Drag a color marker around the wheel to reposition all the markers (and shift their hues) except the base color marker. Drag a marker toward or away from the center to modify the **saturation** for that color only.

   Note: Colors and markers will be modified independently of one another if Custom was chosen from the color rule menu.

5. To edit the **base color**, click the color square or color marker on the wheel that displays a white triangle icon, then drag the color sliders, including the **Brightness** (bottommost) slider, to modify all the colors in unison. Drag the base color marker toward or away from the wheel center to modify the saturation of all the colors, or drag it around the wheel to shift all the hues.**D** Note: To make another color into the base color, click near the bottom of its color square.

6. To name your new theme, replace the default name in the field at the bottom of the pane, then click **Save**. In the Save to Library widget, choose a library, then click **Save** again.

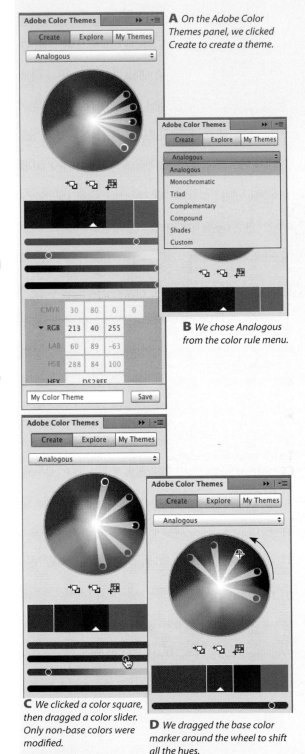

A *On the Adobe Color Themes panel, we clicked Create to create a theme.*

B *We chose Analogous from the color rule menu.*

C *We clicked a color square, then dragged a color slider. Only non-base colors were modified.*

D *We dragged the base color marker around the wheel to shift all the hues.*

- ➤ To make the selected color square the Foreground color, click the Click to Set Active Color button.

- ➤ To apply the Foreground color to the selected color square, click the Set Color from Active Color button.

- ➤ To add the color theme to the Swatches panel, click the Add to Swatches Panel button.

To view your color themes: ★

1. Display the Adobe Color Themes panel, then click **My Themes**.

2. From the menu below the search field, choose All Libraries or a specific CC Library to **filter** which themes display.

3. From the **Actions** menu below any theme, **A** do any of the following:

   Choose **Edit This Theme** to load the theme into the Create pane for editing. You can choose to save any edits to the existing theme or to a copy.

   Choose **Add to Swatches Panel** to add the theme to the Swatches panel.

   Choose **View Online** to open the Adobe Color CC web service in your browser and view all your themes.

4. Click any **color square** in a theme to make it the Foreground color.

- ➤ To delete a theme, display its library in the Libraries panel, then right-click and choose Delete.

To view color themes from the Adobe Color CC community: ★

1. Display the Adobe Color Themes panel, then click **Explore.B**

2. See step 3 in the task above to learn about the Actions menu options for each color theme.

3. Click any **color square** in a theme to make it the Foreground color.

4. To **filter** which themes will display, do either of the following:

   Choose one of the six **categories** from the menu at the top of the pane, then choose a **time period** from the adjacent menu (if available).

   In the **Search** field, enter a descriptive word, general topic, or tag name, then press Enter/Return.

- ➤ To mark a theme from the Explore pane as a favorite for viewing in the My Appreciations category, choose Add to My Favorites from its Actions menu.

Choose a CC Library name from this menu to filter which themes display.

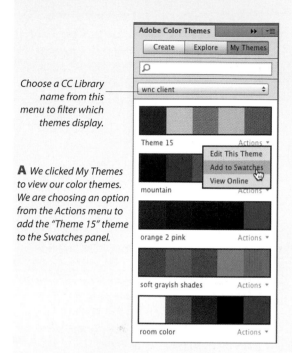

A *We clicked My Themes to view our color themes. We are choosing an option from the Actions menu to add the "Theme 15" theme to the Swatches panel.*

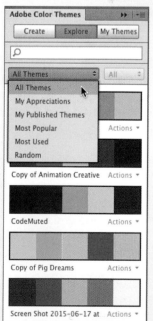

B *We clicked Explore to view themes from the Adobe Color CC community of designers. From the menu at top, we could choose one of six categories to filter which themes will display.*

The Adobe Color CC web service (formerly Kuler) provides all the features found on the Adobe Color Themes panel and more. Use the steps and screen shots below to become familiar with this feature.

To use the Adobe Color CC web service: ★

1. In Photoshop, display the Adobe Color Themes panel. Click **My Themes**, then from any Actions menu, choose **View Online**.

2. The **Adobe Color CC** web service (color.adobe. com) displays in your browser. The three tabs along the menu bar on the top match the tabs on the Adobe Color Themes panel.

3. Click **Create A** and follow the task on the previous two pages to create a theme.

4. Click **My Themes** to view your themes. Choose a library from the **Library** menu to display themes from one or all of your CC Libraries.

5. Roll over a theme **B** to display its option icons, then do any of the following:

   Click **Edit Copy** to edit the theme on the Create page. You can save your changes to the existing theme or to a copy of the theme.

   Click **Copy Link** to copy the URL for the theme, which you can paste into an email or text message.

   Click **Delete,** then click Delete again, to delete a theme from the service and from the Photoshop panel (which is synced to the service).

6. Click the **Info** button to access Actions and Info options (in addition to the Delete and Edit buttons) for a theme, such as Publish (for viewing by the CC community in the Explore tab) and a window for entering search tags.

➤ In the Explore tab, the symbols and numbers below each theme indicate how many times the theme has been viewed, appreciated, and commented upon.

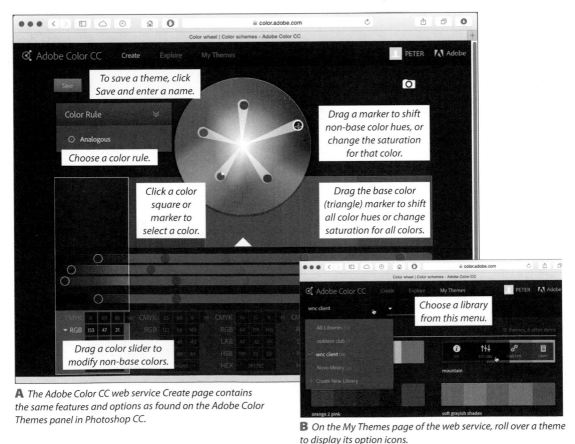

A The Adobe Color CC web service Create page contains the same features and options as found on the Adobe Color Themes panel in Photoshop CC.

B On the My Themes page of the web service, roll over a theme to display its option icons.

Using the Eyedropper tool

To sample a color from an image using the Eyedropper:

1. Choose the **Eyedropper** tool ![eyedropper icon] (or hold down I to spring-load the tool) and click the Foreground or Background color square on the Color panel.

2. On the Options bar, do the following:

   Choose a **Sample Size** (see the sidebar below, right).

   To control the layer(s) from which the tool can sample a color, choose an option from the **Sample** menu. Notes: If you choose a "Current" option, also click a layer. Choose a "No Adjustments" option to sample color values minus the effect of any adjustment layers.

   Optional: Check Show Sampling Ring. Note: To access the sampling ring, Use Graphics Processor must be checked in Edit/Photoshop CC > Preferences > Performance.

3. Do either of the following:

   Click a color in any open document. **A**

   Drag in any document, and release the mouse when the pointer is over the desired color.

   If you checked Show Sampling Ring, the sampled color will preview at the top of a ring in the image and the former color will display on the bottom.

➤ Alt-click/Option-click or drag in an image with the Eyedropper tool to choose a Background color when the Foreground color square is selected on the Color panel, or vice versa.

A *With Show Sampling Ring checked for the Eyedropper tool on the Options bar, we are clicking a color in the image.*

Copying colors as hexadecimals

For Web output, you can copy a color as a hexadecimal value from a document in Photoshop and then paste it into an HTML file or Web page layout program.

To copy a color as a hexadecimal value:

1. To copy a color to the Clipboard as a hexadecimal value, do either of the following:

   Choose the **Eyedropper** tool ![eyedropper icon] (I or Shift-I) and choose settings for the tool from the Options bar (see step 2 at left). Right-click a color in the document and choose **Copy Color as HTML** (HTML color tag) or **Copy Color's Hex Code** (hex number) from the context menu.

   Choose a Foreground color via the Color panel, Color Picker, or Swatches panel. From the Color panel menu, choose **Copy Color as HTML** or **Copy Color's Hex Code**.

2. To paste the color into an HTML file, display the HTML file in your HTML-editing application, then choose Edit > Paste (Ctrl-V/Cmd-V).

SAMPLE SIZE FOR THE EYEDROPPER TOOL

➤ To specify a size for the area from which the Eyedropper tool takes a sample, from the Options bar, choose Sample Size: Point Sample (to sample only the exact pixel you click) or one of the Average options to sample an average value from the area (e.g., from a 5 x 5-pixel square area). The 3 by 3 Average and 5 by 5 Average options are useful for sampling continuous tones, such as skin tones in a portrait photo or the background area in a landscape (we usually use 3 by 3 Average). The 11 by 11 Average through 101 by 101 Average options are better choices for very high-resolution files.

➤ You can also right-click in the document with the Eyedropper tool and choose a sample size from the context menu.

Choosing a blending mode

The blending mode that you choose for a tool or layer affects how that tool or layer interacts with underlying pixels. To produce a blending mode effect, Photoshop compares colors in one of the following ways: It compares the colors of two layers on a channel-by-channel basis, it compares each color in a layer to a corresponding color in the underlying layer (the base color), or it compares the paint color being applied by a tool to the existing color in the layer.

You can choose from a menu of blending modes **A** in many locations in Photoshop, such as the Options bar (for most painting and editing tools), the Layers panel, the Layer Style and Fill dialogs, and the Blending Options dialog for a Smart Filter. In order for you to see the results of a blending mode choice for a layer, its contents must overlap some contents of the underlying layer. **B–C**

➤ When choosing an Opacity percentage for a tool (via the Options bar), keep in mind that the tool results will also be affected by the opacity of the layer that you edit. For example, strokes applied with the Brush tool at an Opacity setting of 50% on a layer that has an Opacity setting of 50% will appear lighter than the same strokes if applied to a layer that has an Opacity setting of 100%.

Menu	Description
✓ Normal Dissolve	*The Basic blending modes replace the base colors.*
Darken Multiply Color Burn Linear Burn Darker Color	*The Darken blending modes darken the base colors.*
Lighten Screen Color Dodge Linear Dodge (Add) Lighter Color	*The Lighten blending modes lighten the base colors.*
Overlay Soft Light Hard Light Vivid Light Linear Light Pin Light Hard Mix	*The Contrast blending modes change the amount of contrast.*
Difference Exclusion Subtract Divide	*The Comparative blending modes invert the base colors.*
Hue Saturation Color Luminosity	*The Component blending modes apply a specific color component.*

A *Blending modes are grouped in categories on the menu, based on their function and effect.*

B *We applied light blue strokes to a blank layer above the image layer. The layer containing the brush strokes has a blending mode of Darker Color.*

C *This is the same image, except we chose the blending mode of Lighter Color for the layer that contains the brush strokes.*

Here you will choose a blending mode for a layer to change how its color values blend with values in the underlying layer. Some blending modes, such as Soft Light, produce subtle changes, whereas others, such as Difference, produce marked color shifts. You can't choose a blending mode for the Background. (To learn about the advanced blending controls in the Layer Style dialog, including an alternative way to access the blending modes, see pages 356–357.)

To choose a blending mode for a layer:

1. Click any kind of layer (not the Background), such as a duplicate image layer **A** or a type, adjustment, fill, shape, or Smart Object layer. You could also select multiple layers or a group.

2. From the menu in the upper-left corner of the Layers panel, choose a **blending mode.B** (No blending occurs in the default mode of Normal.)

3. *Optional:* Adjust the Opacity setting.**C**

A *This is the original image.*

B *We duplicated the Background, chose Color Dodge mode for the duplicate layer, and lowered the layer Opacity to 57%.*

CYCLING THROUGH THE BLENDING MODES

To cycle through the blending modes for the current painting or editing tool, or for the currently selected layer when using a nonediting tool (such as the Move tool or a selection tool), press Shift - + (plus) or Shift - – (minus).

C *The final image is a combination of the two layers.*

Creating a Solid Color fill layer

When we need to add a solid background below type or below an image layer that contains transparent areas, we use a Solid Color fill layer. The advantages to using this method are that we can preview the results, change the color quickly at any time, and edit the fill layer mask. There are other methods of applying a solid color, but although the settings for a Color Overlay layer effect are editable, the effect can't be masked, and if you use Edit > Fill, the only way to change the color is by reapplying the command.

To create a Solid Color fill layer:

1. Click the layer above which you want the fill layer to appear. It can be below a type layer, or below an image layer that contains some transparent pixels.

2. From the Layers panel menu, choose Panel Options. In the dialog, check **Use Default Masks on Fill Layers**, then click OK.

3. *Optional:* To make the solid color visible in only part of the layer, create a selection.

4. From the **New Fill/Adjustment Layer** menu ⬤. on the Layers panel, choose **Solid Color**.

5. In the Color Picker dialog, choose a color for the tint. Don't sweat over your color choice; you can easily change it later. Click OK.**A–B**

➤ To change the color of the fill layer, double-click the layer thumbnail; the Color Picker reopens.**C–D** You can also change the opacity of the fill layer.

➤ Whether you created a selection in step 3 or not, you can edit the mask on the fill layer by applying brush strokes (black to reveal, white to conceal).

A *We clicked the Background in this document, then created a Solid Color fill layer (we chose a tan color).*

B *The color from the fill layer is visible below the transparent areas in the "BOOKS" layer.*

C *We double-clicked the fill layer thumbnail on the Layers panel, then, via the Color Picker, changed the tan color to teal.*

D *This is the image after we changed the color in the fill layer.*

Creating a Gradient fill layer

A gradient is a soft blend between two or more opaque or semitransparent colors. It can be used to enhance the visible area behind a type or shape layer, or behind an image layer that contains transparent pixels. We will show you how to apply a gradient via a Gradient fill layer and the Gradient tool, and how to create and modify a gradient via the Gradient Editor.

A gradient that you apply via a Gradient fill layer appears in its own layer, complete with an editable mask. Like adjustment layers (and unlike gradients that are applied directly to a layer), Gradient fill layers are editable and don't increase the file size.

To apply a gradient via a fill layer:

1. Click a layer on the Layers panel. If you want the gradient fill to display below type or an image layer that contains some transparency, click the layer directly below that image or type layer. **A**

2. From the Layers panel menu, choose Panel Options. In the dialog, check **Use Default Masks on Fill Layers**, then click OK.

3. *Optional:* To make the gradient visible in only part of the layer, create a selection.

4. From the **New Fill/Adjustment Layer** menu ⬤. on the Layers panel, choose **Gradient**. The Gradient Fill dialog opens.

5. Click the Gradient picker arrowhead at the top of the dialog, click a gradient preset on the picker, **B** then click back in the dialog and keep it open.

   ➤ To load more gradients, open the preset picker menu, ⚙ - choose a library name from the assortment at the bottom, then click Append or OK in the alert dialog (see page 133).

6. Choose a gradient **Style** of Linear (a good choice if this is your first try), Radial, Angle, Reflected, or Diamond.

7. Do any of the following optional steps:

   To change the angle of the gradient, move the **Angle** dial or enter a value. **C**

   To control how gradually the gradient colors transition across the layer, choose a **Scale** percentage via the slider or scrubby slider.

   To **reposition** the gradient, drag in the document window (with the dialog still open). To reset the

Continued on the following page

A *The original image consists of an image layer (that contains transparent pixels) above a white Background. We clicked the Background on the Layers panel...*

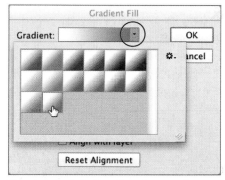

B *... then chose Gradient from the New Fill/Adjustment Layer menu. In the Gradient Fill dialog, we clicked the Gradient picker arrowhead, then loaded the Simple library via the picker menu. Here, we are clicking a preset in the picker.*

C *Finally, we chose the settings shown above, including changing the Angle to align the gradient with the saucepan in the image.*

gradient to its default position at any time, click **Reset Alignment**.

To swap the order of colors in the gradient, check **Reverse**.

To minimize banding (stripes) in the gradient on print output, check **Dither**.

If you created a selection in step 3, check **Align with Layer** to fit the complete gradient within the selection area. Uncheck this option to have the gradient stretch across the whole layer (with only part of the gradient displaying within the selection).

8. Click OK. A

9. If the Gradient fill layer is completely obscuring all the layers below it, do any of the following: Lower the opacity of the fill layer; **B** restack it below the layers you want to reveal; lower the opacity of some of the color stops within the gradient (see the next page); or click the fill layer mask thumbnail, then apply black strokes in the desired brush opacity to hide areas of the gradient manually.

To edit the settings for the Gradient fill layer at any time, double-click the layer thumbnail; the Gradient Fill dialog reopens.

➤ To apply a gradient by matching its luminosity values to the values in an image layer, see pages 252–253.

➤ Via the Properties panel, you can adjust the density of the black areas in a mask, or feather its edge.

A *This is the image with the Gradient fill layer.*

B *As a variation, we created a new, blank layer below the Gradient fill layer and filled it with a scripted pattern (Stucco 2 in the Texture Fill 2 library, Script: Spiral), and lowered the Opacity of the Gradient fill layer to 77%.*

Creating and editing a gradient preset

You can create a variation of any existing gradient preset or create new, custom presets. When you edit a preset, Photoshop forces you to work on a copy of it automatically in order to preserve the original one in the library. We'll show you how to add and change the colors in a gradient, adjust the color transitions, and make parts of the gradient semi- or fully transparent.

To create or edit a gradient preset:

1. Open the Swatches and/or Color panels, which you will be using to pick colors for the gradient (you can collapse the panels to icons).

2. To open the Gradient Editor, do either of the following:

   Choose the **Gradient** tool �" (G or Shift-G), then click the Gradient thumbnail on the Options bar. **A**

   Double-click the thumbnail for an existing Gradient fill layer, then click the gradient thumbnail at the top of the Gradient Fill dialog.

3. In the Gradient Editor, click a preset swatch from which you want to create a variation (when you begin to edit the gradient, the Name will change to Custom). Keep the Gradient Type as Solid and the Smoothness setting at 100%.

   If you want to create a gradient that uses the Foreground and Background colors that are in effect when the gradient is applied, click the Foreground to Background preset. (Foreground to Background is the first preset in the default gradient library. If you need to reload that library, choose Reset Gradients from the Gradient picker menu, then click Append or OK.)

4. For any preset except Foreground to Background, click the starting (left) or ending (right) color stop under the gradient bar (**A**, next page), then do either of the following:

   Click a color in the gradient bar; or outside the Gradient Editor, you can click in the Swatches panel, in the color ramp at the bottom of the Color panel, or in any open document window (the pointer becomes a temporary Eyedropper tool).

   Click the Color swatch at the bottom of the Gradient Editor (or you can simply double-click the color stop). Choose a color in the Color Picker, then click OK.

5. For any kind of gradient preset, do any of these optional steps:

   To add an **intermediate** color to the gradient, click below the gradient bar to produce a stop, then choose a color for that stop, as described in the preceding step (**B**, next page).

   To add an **opacity** stop, click above the gradient bar, then change the Opacity percentage via the scrubby slider (**C**, next page). You can also click any existing opacity stop and change its Opacity percentage. In the gradient bar, transparency is represented by a checkerboard pattern.

   To change the **location** of a color or opacity stop in the gradient, drag the stop to the left or right.

   To control the abruptness of a transition between color or opacity stops, click a stop, then drag a **midpoint diamond** (found on either side of the stop) to the left or right (**D**, next page). The diamond marks the point at which two adjacent colors or opacity values are evenly mixed.

   To **delete** an opacity or color stop, drag it upward or downward off the bar.

   ➤ Use Ctrl-Z/Cmd-Z if you need to undo the last edit (some edits can't be undone).

6. Don't click OK yet! To create a preset of your custom gradient, type a name in the **Name** field, then click **New**.

   Note: Your custom presets will be deleted from the picker if you allow them to be replaced by another gradient library or if the Photoshop Preferences file is deleted or damaged. To save the presets on the picker as a permanent library, click Save, enter a name, keep the default location, then click Save again. (See page 133 or 135.)

7. Click OK to exit the Gradient Editor, and again, if necessary, to exit the Gradient Fill dialog (**E**, next page). Your new gradient preset is the last one on the Gradient picker. If you chose and want to use the Gradient tool, see the next task.

➤ To delete a gradient preset from the picker, Alt-click/Option-click the preset thumbnail.

A We are opening the Gradient Editor by clicking the Gradient thumbnail on the Options bar.

A *In the Gradient Editor dialog, we clicked a preset (in the Simple library), double-clicked one of the original color stops, and changed the Color.*

B *We clicked below the gradient bar to add three more color stops, and chose a color for each one.*

C *We clicked above the bar to add an intermediate opacity stop, and lowered the Opacity setting for that stop. (We also lowered the Opacity of the leftmost opacity stop to 80%.)*

D *We dragged the right midpoint diamond for the middle opacity stop. (We named our custom gradient, clicked New, then exited both dialogs.)*

CREATING A MORE COMPLEX — OR SIMPLER — GRADIENT EFFECT

► For a complex effect, apply gradients that contain some transparency to multiple layers, either via Gradient fill layers (vary the gradient angle or style), or via the Gradient tool (drag in different directions).

► To create a gradient that contains just one color that transitions to transparency, delete the starting or ending stop, and lower the opacity for that end of the bar.

E *We applied our custom gradient via a Gradient fill layer (above an image layer). The dialog settings we chose are shown above. Note that we chose the Reflected style.*

Using the Gradient tool

With the Gradient tool, you apply a gradient by dragging in the image. Although you can't edit the results in the same way that you would edit a Gradient fill layer, if you use the tool on a separate layer, at least you will be able to change the layer blending mode or opacity.

To apply a gradient via the Gradient tool:

1. Create a new, blank layer to contain the gradient.

2. *Optional:* To confine the gradient to an area of the layer, create a selection.

3. Choose the **Gradient** tool ▦ (G or Shift-G).

4. On the Options bar, do all of the following:

   Click the Gradient picker arrowhead, then click a preset on the picker.

   Click a Style button: Linear, Radial, Angle, Reflected, or Diamond.

   Choose Mode: Normal and Opacity 100%.

5. On the Options bar, check any of the following optional features:

   Reverse to swap the order of colors in the gradient.

   Dither to minimize banding (stripes) in the gradient on print output.

   Transparency to enable any transparency that was edited into the gradient, or turn this feature off to apply a fully opaque gradient.

6. Drag in the document in any direction. For a Linear or Reflected gradient, try dragging from one side or corner of the image or selection to the other, or for any other gradient style, try dragging from the center of the layer outward. Shift-drag to constrain the angle to a multiple of 45°.**A–C**

   ➤ To produce subtle transitions between colors in the gradient, drag a long distance, or for abrupt transitions, drag a short distance. This has the same effect as changing the Scale value in the Gradient Fill dialog.

7. *Optional:* Change the gradient layer mode or opacity.

➤ To delete the Gradient tool results, click the prior state on the History panel.

➤ You can use a gradient to create a gradual transition in the mask on an image, editable type, adjustment, fill, Smart Filter, or shape layer. See pages 287–288.

A *With the Gradient tool (Diamond style chosen), we dragged diagonally from the middle to the lower right on a new, blank layer.*

B *This is the Layers panel for the image shown below.*

C *This is the final image.*

Creating custom and scripted patterns

To create a custom pattern:

1. In a document, do either of the following:

   Click an image layer.

   Create a shape layer using the Custom Shape tool (see page 422).

2. *Optional:* If you want the pattern tile to be an irregular shape surrounded by transparency, select a nonrectangular area of the layer (see Chapter 9), then press Ctrl-J/Cmd-J to copy the selection to a new layer.

3. Hide the layers that you don't want to include in the pattern tile.

4. Choose the **Rectangular Marquee** tool,⬚ then drag to select the area to become the pattern tile.**A**

5. Choose Edit > **Define Pattern**. In the Pattern Name dialog, type a name, then click OK.**B** Your new pattern is now available on the Custom Pattern preset picker in the Edit > Fill dialog, in the Layer Style dialog for the Pattern Overlay effect (see page 411), as a Texture option for the Bevel & Emboss effect (see pages 406–407), and for a pattern fill layer (choose Pattern from the New Fill/Adjustment Layer menu ⬤. on the Layers panel).**C–D**

A *We selected an area of an image layer to become the pattern tile.*

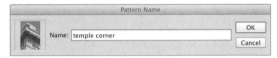

B *We chose Edit > Define Pattern to create a custom pattern tile. In the Pattern Name dialog, we entered a name, then clicked OK.*

C *From the New Fill/Adjustment Layer menu on the Layers panel, we chose Pattern. When the Pattern Fill dialog opened, we clicked OK.*

D *The Pattern Fill command repeated the tiles to produce a pattern fill.*

The Filter > Render submenu contains three new filters (Flame, Picture Frame, and Tree) that can create patterns on a blank layer or image layer without altering or stylizing existing layer pixels as most filters do (see Chapter 18). We will explore these "pattern" filters in conjunction with scripted patterns. Note: These three filters require a minimum of 512 MB of Video RAM (VRAM) on the graphics card in your system.

To fill a layer with a Render filter: ★

1. Create a new, blank layer for the Render filter.

2. For the Picture Frame filter, you can let Photoshop apply the frame to the dimensions of the canvas, or if you prefer to define a rectangle for the frame, choose the **Rectangular Marquee** tool (M or Shift-M), then draw a rectangle.

   Note: For the Flame filter, ★ you will need to first draw a path with the **Pen** tool (see page 436) or the **Freeform Pen** tool (see page 434), and keep the path selected. For the Tree filter, no path is needed.

3. Choose Filter > Render > **Picture Frame.** ★ A dialog opens automatically, which you will use to customize the filter pattern. **A**

   The options are too numerous for us to discuss individually here — we recommend that you just experiment with various settings until you get a result you like (that's how we use the dialog).

4. *Optional:* To save the current custom filter settings for future use, from the preset menu, choose Save Preset. In the Save As dialog, enter a name (keep the default location), then click Save.

5. Click OK (**A**, next page). (To add to the design, continue with the next task.)

➤ To load a saved preset into the filter dialog, use the Load Preset command on the preset menu.

Using the scripted patterns feature in the Fill dialog, you can choose from an assortment of presets (e.g., Brick Fill, Spiral) that control how pattern tiles are colored and positioned. When you exit that dialog, an additional dialog opens automatically, which lets you customize the pattern. You can get some great effects by applying scripted patterns to different layers.

To fill a layer with a scripted pattern: ★

1. *Optional:* Create a custom pattern (**B**, next page) via the task on the previous page.

2. Create a new layer to contain the scripted pattern.

3. The Place Along Path scripted pattern option requires that a path be selected first. Draw a path with the **Pen** tool (see pages 436–438) or the

Continued on the following page

A *In the [Picture] Frame filter dialog, we chose settings in the Basic tab (shown above) and settings in the Advanced tab (insert).*

Freeform Pen tool (see page 434), and keep the path selected (**A**, next page).

4. Choose Edit > **Fill** (Shift-Backspace/Shift-Delete). The Fill dialog opens (**B**, next page).

5. From the Contents menu, choose **Pattern**. Check **Script**, then choose a script option from the menu to the right. Keep the Opacity setting at 100%, and uncheck Preserve Transparency to permit transparent areas in the layer to be filled.

    For any script option, click the **Custom Pattern** thumbnail, then click a pattern preset (if you created a custom pattern in step 1, choose it now) or load additional pattern libraries from the lower part of the picker menu. Click OK.

6. Another dialog opens automatically, which you will use to customize the pattern (**C**, next page). Options in the dialog will vary depending on the chosen script. Again, the options are too numerous for us to discuss individually here.

    ➤ To produce more variety or naturalism in your pattern, take advantage of dialog options that allow for randomness, such as scale, spacing (either between the tiles or from the path), color, and brightness.

7. *Optional:* To save the current custom pattern settings for future use, from the preset menu, choose Save Preset. In the Save As dialog, enter a name (keep the default location), then click Save.

8. Click OK (**D**, next page, and **A–C**, page 226).

    ➤ To load a saved preset into one of the custom scripted pattern dialogs, use the Load Preset command on the preset menu.

    ➤ If you use a custom pattern when applying a script, then discover that, after exiting the options dialog, the tiles look too large on the layer, undo. Then redo steps 4–6 above, using the scale control to reduce the pattern size.

    ➤ For added richness, try choosing different blending modes for the pattern layers.

    ➤ To hide areas of a filter or pattern on a layer, add a layer mask, then paint with black (see pages 192–196). For a partial mask, lower the brush opacity.

A *We duplicated the frame filter layer, scaled the duplicate layer to make it smaller (see pages 358–359), then lowered its opacity.*

B *In the file containing the frame layer, we created a custom shape layer using a leaf preset from the Nature library (see page 422). We applied a 50% gray fill and a stroke of None, hid the other layers, selected the leaf with the Rectangular Marquee tool, then chose Edit > Define Pattern to create a custom pattern. We deleted the new shape layer and redisplayed the Background.*

A *With the two frame filter layers still hidden, we created a new, blank layer. We drew a path using the Freeform Pen tool and kept the path selected on the Paths panel.*

B *We opened the Fill dialog, chose Contents: Pattern, checked Script, then chose the Place Along Path script; we clicked our new leaf pattern in the Custom Pattern preset picker, then clicked OK.*

C *In the Place Along Path dialog, we chose the settings shown above. We used the Color Randomness and Brightness Randomness options to colorize the gray tiles in the pattern.*

D *This is a view of the layer, showing the leaf pattern that the script placed along our hand-drawn path.*

A *To add the next element to our design, we created a new layer, opened the Fill dialog, chose Contents: Pattern, kept the leaf as the custom pattern, checked Script, and chose Random Fill. In the Random Fill dialog, we chose the settings shown above.*

B *We redisplayed the two frame filter layers. We created a Solid Color fill layer, then restacked that fill layer below the pattern layers. We placed a photo of a landscape into our document and stacked the new image layer above the Solid Color fill layer.*

C *Finally, to reduce the image layer to flat color areas, and to let some of the solid color from the underlying fill layer show through, we set the blending mode of the image layer to Darker Color, and lowered the image layer Opacity to 40%. The Layers panel for the final image is shown at left.*

When you open a photo into Photoshop, take a few minutes to study it. Is it overexposed (too light) or underexposed (too dark)? Could it use a boost in contrast (brighter highlights, richer shadows)? Are the colors too bright or too dull (over- or undersaturated)? Does it have a color cast? Would you like to transform the photo in some way, say by tinting it with colors from a gradient, or give it a vintage look by converting the colors to grayscale? Enter the digital darkroom!

If you normally capture your photos as raw files or in the JPEG format, you can rectify most or all of their tonal and color flaws in Camera Raw. If for some reason you didn't use Camera Raw to correct your photos, Photoshop offers its own impressive array of adjustment commands, along with the Camera Raw filter (for applying most of the Camera Raw correction options).

Most of the tonal and color corrections that are available in Photoshop can be applied via adjustment layers, a method that offers the greatest flexibility in editing. At the beginning of this chapter, you will find generic instructions for creating and editing an adjustment layer and its mask. You will also learn how to read the graph on the Histogram panel to monitor changes in the tonal levels of your document as you apply corrections. From page 236 onward, you will find specific instructions for a splendid array of adjustment features. You will also learn two methods for merging HDR photos. By the end of this chapter, you will have mastered most of the key Photoshop adjustment commands!

ADJUSTMENTS

12

IN THIS CHAPTER

A FEW BASIC RECOMMENDATIONS

➤ Before performing any tonal or color adjustments in Photoshop, make sure your display is **calibrated** properly (see page 6).

➤ Keep your documents in **RGB Color mode** for your work in Photoshop, including the adjustments in this chapter (remember, digital photos are captured as RGB).

➤ If you need to make final corrections to an image for CMYK output (such as for commercial printing), copy the file, **soft-proof** the copy onscreen to make sure there are no color problems (see pages 474–475), apply any needed adjustments, then convert the image to CMYK (see page 482).

Creating adjustment layers

The effects of a command that you apply via the Image > Adjustments submenu are permanent, whereas the effects of an adjustment layer become permanent only when you merge it downward into the underlying layer or flatten your document. The advantages of using an adjustment layer are that its settings stay editable and you can hide its effect in areas of the image by editing its mask—plus you can restack, hide, or delete it, and drag-copy it between files.

You create an adjustment layer via either the Adjustments or Layers panel, then choose and edit the settings for it via the Properties panel. Each adjustment type has unique options, and each adjustment layer keeps its own settings. Some controls are easy to get the hang of, whereas others take some effort to master but enable you to apply more targeted corrections. For some adjustment types, you can choose from a menu of presets. The Properties panel also has controls for hiding, clipping, and restoring adjustment settings.

To create an adjustment layer:

1. On the Layers panel, ▼ click an image layer or the Background. **A** The adjustment layer is going to appear above the layer you select.

2. *Optional:* Create a selection, to become the white area in the editable adjustment layer mask, and therefore the only area in which the adjustment effect is visible.

3. Do either of the following:

   On the **Adjustments** panel, ⊘ click the button for the desired adjustment type. **B**

   From the **New Fill/Adjustment Layer** menu ⊘. on the Layers panel, choose an adjustment type (**A**, next page).

4. Controls for the chosen command appear on the Properties panel. Choose settings to correct your document (**B**, next page). For a Levels, Curves, Exposure, Hue/Saturation, Black & White, Channel Mixer, or Selective Color adjustment, another option is to choose a preset from the menu at the top of the panel (you can also customize the settings from the preset).

   A new adjustment layer with a layer mask appears on the Layers panel (**C–D**, next page).

A *The original image lacks contrast.*

B *On the Adjustments panel, we clicked the Levels button.*

BUTTONS ON THE ADJUSTMENTS PANEL

Brightness/Contrast Levels Curves Exposure Vibrance

Hue/Saturation Color Balance Black & White Photo Filter Channel Mixer Color Lookup

Invert Posterize Threshold Selective Color Gradient Map

A *Adjustment layers can also be created via the New Fill/Adjustment Layer menu on the Layers panel (the results are the same as if you used the Adjustments panel).*

B *To darken the midtones, we dragged the top middle slider to the right.*

C *You can identify each adjustment layer type by its unique icon in the layer thumbnail.*

D *One simple (editable) step corrected the contrast.*

USING AUTO-SELECT PARAMETER

The **Auto-Select Parameter** option on the Properties panel menu (and Adjustments panel menu) affects adjustment types that have entry fields. When this option is checked and you create an adjustment layer or click an existing adjustment layer on the Layers panel, the first field on the Properties panel becomes highlighted automatically. Although this option may be appreciated by some power Photoshop users, for others it can be an annoyance because it prevents some shortcuts from working (e.g., you won't be able to select a tool via its letter shortcut or delete a layer by pressing Backspace/Delete). We keep it unchecked.

Editing adjustment layer settings

Note: For the steps in this section, we recommend showing the Properties panel (it can be in a dock). If your Properties panel is closed, you will need to double-click the adjustment layer to display the Properties panel (instead of just a single click, as in our instructions).

To change the settings for an adjustment layer:

1. On the Layers panel, click an adjustment layer. The layer becomes selected and the current settings display on the Properties panel.**A**

2. Edit the settings.**B**

➤ To undo the last individual Properties panel edit, press Ctrl-Z/Cmd-Z.

➤ To lessen the overall impact of an adjustment layer, lower its opacity via the Layers panel.

The View Previous State button gives you a temporary view of the image without the current edits you are making to the adjustment layer settings.

To view the image without the newest adjustment layer edits:

1. On the Layers panel, click an adjustment layer, then edit the settings on the Properties panel. Keep the layer selected and stay on the panel.

2. To toggle your latest edits off (and then on again), press and hold down the **View Previous State** button or the \ key, then release.

To restore settings to an adjustment layer:

1. On the Layers panel, click an adjustment layer.

2. After editing any of the settings on the Properties panel, click the **Reset to Adjustment Defaults** button; the last chosen settings will be restored. To restore the default settings for that adjustment type, click the button again.

To hide the effect of an adjustment layer:

To hide the effect of an adjustment layer, click the visibility icon on the Properties panel or Layers panel (clicking the icon in one location also deactivates it or makes it disappear in the other location). To show the effect, click the icon (or in the icon column) again.

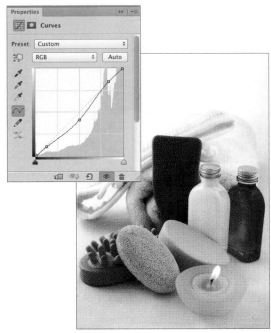

A We used a Curves adjustment to darken the midtones in this photo.

B Later, we double-clicked the Curves layer thumbnail to display the current settings, and tweaked the adjustment by reshaping the curve for the midtones and highlights.

Normally, an adjustment layer affects all the layers below it, but you can clip (restrict) its effect to just the layer directly below it.

To clip an adjustment layer to the layer directly below it:

1. On the Layers panel, click an adjustment layer.**A–B** Make sure it is stacked directly above the layer that you want to clip it to.

2. Do either of the following:

   On the Properties panel,⬚ click the **Clip to Layer** button.⬚ **C–D**

   On the Layers panel, hold down Alt/Option and click the line between the adjustment layer and the layer below it (⬚ icon).

   Note: The adjustment layer listing is now indented and the underlying layer name has an underline. To unclip it at any time, repeat either method in step 2.

ADJUSTMENTS AS SMART FILTERS ★

Adjustments can now become part of a Smart Object (see pages 272–283). Use the Image > Adjustments submenu to select an adjustment command, then enter settings in the dialog that displays. The adjustment will be listed on the Layers panel as a Smart Filter (see pages 374–376).

The advantages to this method of creating an adjustment are: The adjustment is part of the Smart Object and moves with it; the adjustment is automatically clipped to the Smart Object. (You can achieve these same advantages by placing an adjustment layer and image layer into a layer group and clipping the adjustment layer to the image layer.)

The disadvantages are: You can't use the Properties panel (with its view previous state, reset, and save settings options) to edit the Smart Filter; you can't create a layer mask for each adjustment; if you rasterize the Smart Object, any adjustments are permanently applied to the resulting image layer.

A *This image contains an image layer, a type layer, and a Background image (the texture).*

B *We applied a Hue/Saturation adjustment to boost the saturation of the Tomatoes layer, but the edit gave the Background texture a pinkish cast.*

C *We clipped the adjustment layer so it is affecting just the Tomatoes layer.*

D *This is the result of our clipping the adjustment.*

Saving adjustment presets

You can save your custom adjustment settings for future use in any document. For instance, say you have a group of photos that were shot under the same lighting conditions, have the same color profile, and require the same corrections. You could save your settings as a preset, then apply it to each file.

To save custom adjustment layer settings as a preset:

1. Create and choose settings for an adjustment layer. Presets can be saved only for a Levels, Curves, Exposure, Hue/Saturation, Black & White, Channel Mixer, or Selective Color adjustment.

2. From the Properties panel menu, choose **Save** [adjustment type] **Preset**. In the Save dialog, enter a name, keep the default location and extension, then click Save. Your user preset is now available on the menu at the top of the Properties panel when the controls for that adjustment type are displaying.

➤ To delete a user preset, choose that preset, choose Delete Current Preset from the panel menu, then click Yes in the alert dialog.

➤ If you create an adjustment that you want to copy to another document — and it can't be saved as a preset — open the source and target documents, make sure they have the same document color mode, and tile them via the Window > Arrange submenu. Click in the source document, then drag and drop the adjustment layer from the Layers panel into the target document window.

Merging and deleting adjustment layers

When you merge an adjustment layer downward, the adjustments are applied permanently to the underlying image layer. If you change your mind, click the prior state on the History panel.

To merge an adjustment layer:

On the Layers panel, ☷ do either of the following:

Click the adjustment layer to be merged downward (or Shift-click multiple adjustment layers and the layer into which you want to merge them),**A** then press Ctrl-E/Cmd-E.**B**

Right-click on or near the adjustment layer name and choose **Merge Down** or **Merge Layers** from the context menu.

Note: Adjustment layers can't be merged with one another. If you use the Merge Visible command (see page 167) or the Flatten Image command (see page 168), the effect of any adjustment layers in the file will be applied to the resulting merged layer (and will disappear from the Layers panel).

To delete an adjustment layer:

Do either of the following:

Click the icon for an adjustment layer on the Layers panel, then click the **Delete Layer** button 🗑 on the same panel or the **Delete Adjustment Layer** button 🗑 on the Properties panel. If an alert dialog, appears, click Yes. (Click Don't Show Again if you want to prevent the alert from reappearing.)

Click the adjustment layer on the Layers panel, then press Backspace/Delete.

A We clicked the adjustment layer to be merged downward.

B The Merge Down command applied the Levels values from the adjustment layer to the underlying image layer, which in this case was a copy of the Background.

Editing an adjustment layer mask

Photoshop creates a mask for every adjustment layer. If you create a selection before creating an adjustment layer, the selection will appear as the white area in the mask. If you didn't create a selection first, or you want to edit the mask at any time, follow these steps.

To edit the adjustment layer mask:

1. Click the mask thumbnail on an adjustment layer.

2. Press D to choose the default colors, then press X to switch to black as the Foreground color.

3. To hide the adjustment in some areas of the image, do either or both of the following:

   Create a selection with any selection tool (e.g., Rectangular Marquee or Lasso); refine it via the Refine Edge dialog, if desired; choose Edit > **Fill** (Shift-Backspace/Shift-Delete); choose Use: Foreground Color; then click OK. Deselect.

   Choose the **Brush** tool ✦ (B or Shift-B). On the Options bar, choose a Soft Round brush, Mode: Normal, and an Opacity of 100% (or a lower opacity to apply a partial mask), press [or] to set the brush diameter, then apply strokes in the image.**A–C**

4. *Optional:* To remove black areas of the mask, press X to swap colors (make the Foreground color white), then apply brush strokes.

➤ To remove all black areas from the mask, deselect, click the adjustment layer mask, choose Edit > Fill, then choose Use: White in the dialog.

➤ To confine the effect of an adjustment layer to a small area, start with a fully black mask (click Invert on the Properties panel or apply Edit > Fill, Use: Black), then apply strokes with white.

➤ To create a gradual mask by applying a gradient, see pages 287–288. To adjust the density or edges of a mask, see pages 194–195.

C Our brush strokes are represented by black areas in the adjustment layer mask thumbnail.

A The bottom area of this photo looks too pink.

B We corrected the color via Curves, clicked the mask thumbnail on the adjustment layer, then applied brush strokes to hide the adjustment in the top part of the image. The adjustment is visible in only the bottom half of the photo.

SHORTCUTS FOR LAYER MASKS

View just the mask in the document window	Alt/Option click the layer mask thumbnail; repeat to restore the normal view
View the mask in the image as a Quick Mask	Alt-Shift/Option-Shift click the layer mask thumbnail; repeat for normal view
Deactivate or activate the mask	Shift-click the layer mask thumbnail (Layers panel) or click the Disable/Enable button 👁 (Properties panel)
Load the unmasked area as a selection	Ctrl/Cmd click the layer mask thumbnail (Layers panel) or click the Load Selection from Mask button ▦ (Properties panel)

Using the Histogram panel

The **Histogram** panel displays a graph of the distribution of tonal (light and dark) values in the current image. The horizontal axis on the graph represents the grayscale or color levels between 0 and 255, the vertical bars represent the number of pixels at specific color or tonal levels, and the contour of the graph shows the overall tonal range. Before you begin editing your document, study the histogram to evaluate the existing distribution of tonal values. Then as you edit your document, note how the graph updates to reflect changes to the tonal values. The panel remains accessible even while the Properties panel is being used or an adjustment dialog is open.

A *This Histogram panel is in Compact View.*

To choose a view for the Histogram panel:

1. From the Histogram panel menu, choose one of the following: **Compact View** (just the histogram), **A Expanded View** (the histogram plus a menu providing access to individual channels), **B** or **All Channels View** (all the features of Expanded View, plus a separate histogram for each channel). When the panel is in either of the latter two views, you can check Show Statistics on the panel menu to display file data on the panel.

2. For Expanded or All Channels view, choose an option from the **Channel** menu: RGB (all the channels combined), **C** a specific channel, Luminosity, or Colors. To display the individual channels in color when the panel is in All Channels view, check Show Channels in Color on the panel menu.

3. For Compact View, click a layer or the Background; for Expanded View or All Channels View, from the Source menu, choose **Entire Image**.

While a large file is being edited, Photoshop maintains the redraw speed of the Histogram panel by reading the data from the histogram cache — not from the actual image. When this is occurring, a Cached Data Warning icon ![warning] displays on the panel. Remember to keep updating the panel, as described below (even while editing the settings for an adjustment layer), so it reflects the current tonal values of the image.

To update the Histogram panel:

Do one of the following:

Double-click anywhere on the histogram.

Click the **Cached Data Warning** icon. ![warning]

Click the **Uncached Refresh** button. ![refresh]

B *Here the panel is in Expanded View. By default, the Channel menu is set to Colors.*

C *With RGB chosen on the Channel menu, the current tonal values in the image are represented by black areas in the graph.*

SETTING THE CACHE

To specify a Cache Levels value for screen redraw in Photoshop (including this panel), see page 464.

Interpreting the histogram

If you want to focus on monitoring tonal values when using the Histogram panel, choose Expanded View from the panel menu, RGB from the Channel menu, and Entire Image from the Source menu.

In the graph, pixels are represented by vertical bars: shadows on the left, midtones in the middle, and highlights on the right. In a dark, low-key image, the tallest peaks will be clustered on the left side of the graph; in a medium-key image in which the lights and darks are relatively balanced, the tallest peaks will be clustered at one or more spots in the middle of the graph; and in a very light, high-key image that contains few or no shadow areas, the tallest peaks will be clustered on the right side of the graph.

If an image has a wide tonal range, the bars will stretch fully from one side of the histogram to the other, and the overall contour of the graph will be relatively solid and smooth. **A** If an image lacks detail in a tonal range, the graph will contain gaps and spikes, like teeth on a comb.

The following are some typical graph profiles:

➤ In an average-key but underexposed image that lacks details in the highlights, the bars will rise sharply on the left side of the histogram. **B**

➤ In an overexposed image that lacks details in the shadows, the tallest peaks will rise sharply on the right side of the histogram. **C**

➤ In an image in which pixels were clipped (details discarded) in the extreme shadows or highlights, the bars will rise sharply in a very tall cluster at the left or right edge, respectively, of the histogram. **D**

➤ If an image has lost detail as a result of editing (such as from Photoshop filters or adjustments), the histogram will contain many gaps and spikes. **E** The gaps indicate a loss of specific tonal or color levels, and the spikes indicate that pixels from different levels have been averaged together and been given the same value (the bar will be taller at that level). A few gaps and spikes are an acceptable result of editing, whereas large gaps signify that posterization has occurred and too many continuous tonal values have been discarded. On the other hand, an imperfect histogram doesn't always signify failure; the graph can be thrown off by a simple edit, such as adding a white border to the image. If you like the way the image looks, go with that!

A *The tonal ranges in this image are well balanced.*

B *This image is underexposed.*

C *This image is overexposed.*

D *Shadow pixels are clipped in this image.*

E *This image has lost some detail.*

Applying a Levels adjustment

You can use either Levels or Curves to apply essential tonal corrections to a photo, both prior to image editing and at any time thereafter. One of the bonus features of Levels is that it displays a histogram of the tonal values of your image. (Levels is also used on page 260. For Curves, which also has unique correction features, see pages 246–249.)

To correct tonal values using Levels:

1. Click an image layer that needs tonal correction.**A**

2. On the Adjustments panel,⬤ click the **Levels** button.▥▥ The Levels controls display on the Properties panel.

3. Do either of the following:

   To intensify the contrast, brighten the highlights by moving the white input highlights slider to the left and darken the shadows by moving the black input shadows slider to the right.**B** Any pixels located to the left of the black slider will become black; any pixels located to the right of the white slider will become white. (This shifting of tonal values to black or white is called "clipping.")

   To control when clipping starts to occur in a temporary high-contrast display called Threshold mode, hold down Alt/Option and drag the highlights slider, then release when only a few areas of color or white display (**A**, next page); those pixels will be given the lightest tonal value. Next, hold down Alt/Option and drag the shadows slider, then release when only a few areas of color or black appear (**B**, next page); those pixels will be given the darkest tonal value.

4. With the shadows and highlights sliders now in their proper positions, move the middle (midtones) input slider to lighten or darken just the midtones.

5. To compare the original and adjusted images, press and hold \, then release (**C–D**, next page).

➤ If the "Calculate More Accurate Histogram" alert button ▥⚠ appears on the Properties panel as you're applying a Levels adjustment, you can click the button to refresh the histogram in the panel.

➤ To apply the current Levels settings to other images — such as to a group of photos that were taken under similar lighting conditions and need the same adjustments — save and apply them as a preset (see page 232). There are also some ready-made Levels presets.

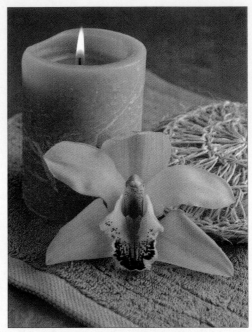

A *This image lacks contrast (looks flat and dull).*

B *The histogram in this Levels panel doesn't extend all the way to the edges, an indication that the tonal range of the photo is narrow. To expand the range, we moved the shadows and highlights input sliders inward to align with the outer edges of the histogram, and moved the middle slider to the right to darken the midtones.*

A *We held down Alt/Option and dragged the white highlights slider.*

B *Next, we held down Alt/Option and dragged the black shadows slider.*

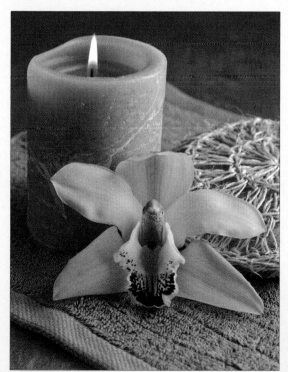

C *Our Levels adjustments improved the contrast (the shadows are darker and the highlights are brighter).*

D *The Histogram shows that the adjustment expanded the tonal range of the image; the bars now extend from one end of the graph to the other.*

The Enhance Brightness and Contrast algorithm is a good option for an image that needs substantial tonal correction. The algorithm uses content-aware technology to evaluate data in the entire image, then corrects tonal values for the composite RGB channel (instead of for each channel).

To apply the Enhance Brightness and Contrast algorithm:

1. Create a **Levels** or **Curves** adjustment layer. On the Properties panel, hold down Alt/Option and click **Auto.**

2. The Auto Color Correction Options dialog opens. Click **Enhance Brightness and Contrast**, then click OK.

3. If further refinement is needed, modify the adjustment layer settings.

Applying a Brightness/Contrast adjustment

The Brightness and Contrast controls are ultra simple to use, but can have a big impact.

To apply Brightness/Contrast adjustments:

1. Click a layer or the Background.**A**

2. On the Adjustments panel, click the **Brightness/Contrast** button. The Brightness/Contrast controls display on the Properties panel.

3. Do either of the following:

   Move the **Brightness** and/or **Contrast** sliders.**B**

   Click **Auto** to let Photoshop set the sliders; you can tweak the settings afterward.

➤ The Use Legacy option for Brightness/Contrast causes tonal levels to be eliminated from the shadows or highlights (after adjustment, the histogram will show clipped areas on the left or right edge of the graph). Keep this option off to preserve pixel data (in which case, after you move the sliders, the histogram will show only a minor redistribution of tonal values).

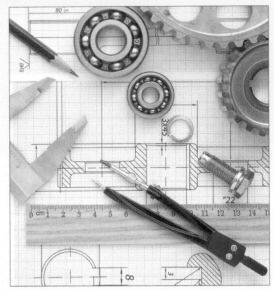

A *The original image is too light and lacks contrast.*

B *We reduced the Brightness to darken the image and increased the Contrast to intensify the shadows and highlights (settings shown at left).*

Applying a Photo Filter adjustment

To change the color temperature of a scene (make it look warmer or cooler) during a shoot, photographers use colored lens filters. You can simulate the effect of these filters in Photoshop via a Photo Filter adjustment layer, either to neutralize an unwanted color cast or to apply a tint (as a special effect). Choose from among the 20 preset tints that are offered, or choose a custom color.

When you use this feature, we recommend aiming for subtle (sophisticated) or extreme (so it looks deliberate), but not in between. If you go for in between, you will simply give the image an ugly color cast.

A *This is the original image.*

To apply a Photo Filter adjustment:

1. Click a layer or the Background.**A**

2. On the Adjustments panel,◐ click the **Photo Filter** button.🔘 The Photo Filter controls display on the Properties panel.

3. Do either of the following:

    Click **Filter**, then from the menu, choose a preset warming or cooling filter, or a filter color. The current filter color displays in the swatch.

    Click the **Color** swatch, choose a color for the filter via the Color Picker, noting the change in the image, then click OK.

    ➤ For a subtle change, pick a color that is similar to colors in the image. Or for a more striking change, pick a color that is complementary to the predominant colors in the image (one that is on the opposite side of the color wheel — as in red/green, blue/orange, purple/yellow).

4. Using the **Density** slider or scrubby slider, choose an opacity percentage for the tint. Try a modest value between 10% and 25% first.**B–C**

    ➤ You can also lessen the Photo Filter effect after using the Properties panel by lowering the opacity of the adjustment layer.

5. Check **Preserve Luminosity** to preserve the overall brightness and contrast values of the image. With this option unchecked, the highlights may be softened, but the resulting colorization effect may be too pronounced.

6. To compare the original and adjusted images, press and hold \, then release.

B *For our Photo Filter adjustment layer, we chose Cooling Filter (82) from the Filter menu and a Density value of 20%.*

C *The Photo Filter adjustment made the image look cooler.*

Applying a Color Balance adjustment

You can use a Color Balance adjustment layer to apply a warm or cool cast to an image or, conversely, to neutralize an unwanted cast. You choose a tonal range to adjust first (Shadows, Midtones, or Highlights), then move any of the sliders toward a warmer or cooler hue. Note: If you need to restrict color adjustments to an even smaller tonal range, use Curves or Hue/Saturation.

To apply a Color Balance adjustment:

1. Click a layer or the Background.**A**

2. On the Adjustments panel,⬤ click the **Color Balance** button.⚖

3. The Color Balance settings display on the Properties panel. From the **Tone** menu, choose the range you want to adjust: **Shadows**, **Midtones**, or **Highlights**.

   Optional: Keep Preserve Luminosity checked to preserve the tonal values of the layer as you make color corrections, or uncheck this option to allow the adjustment to change both the luminosity and color values.

4. Each slider pairs a cool hue with a warm one. Move a slider toward any color you want to add more of or away from any color you want to reduce **B–C** (and **A–B**, next page). For instance, you could move a slider toward green to reduce magenta, or toward yellow to reduce blue.

   ➤ Try moving two or more sliders toward similar hues. For example, to add a cool cast, you could move the first slider toward Cyan and the third one toward Blue. Or to make an image warmer, move the first slider toward Red and the third one toward Yellow.

5. Choose any other range from the Tone menu, then adjust the color sliders for that range. To compare the original and adjusted images, press and hold \, then release.

A *This image has a blue cast.*

B *For a Color Balance adjustment layer, we chose Tone: Shadows, then moved the sliders toward Red, Green, and Yellow to neutralize the colors in that tonal range.*

C *The shadow areas look more neutral than they did before, but further corrections are needed.*

A *To neutralize the blue cast in the mid-tones, we chose Tone: Midtones, then moved the sliders toward Red and Yellow. Only the highlight adjustment remains.*

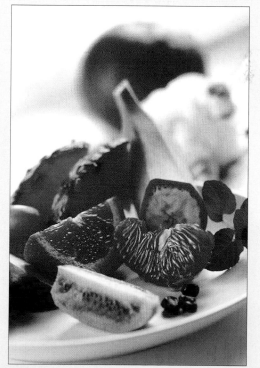

B *To warm the highlights and neutralize the remaining traces of the blue color cast, we chose Tone: Highlights, then moved the sliders toward Red and Yellow (and very slightly toward Magenta). Now the food and the plate look warmer (and more appetizing!) and the shadows look neutral.*

Applying a Hue/Saturation adjustment

Via a Hue/Saturation adjustment, you can apply very targeted hue, saturation, and lightness corrections without having to create a selection. In the example shown below, we use it to correct a color cast and to recolor a garment. This is a very useful command.

To apply a Hue/Saturation adjustment:

1. Click a layer. **A**

2. On the Adjustments panel, ⬤ click the **Hue/Saturation** button. 🔲 The Hue/Saturation settings display on the Properties panel.

3. Do any of the following:

   To correct all the colors in the image, keep **Master** as the choice on the second menu; **B** to adjust a specific color range, choose that color on the

menu. Move the **Hue** slider to adjust the hue(s), **C** the **Saturation** slider to adjust the color intensity, or the **Lightness** slider to lighten or darken. If you adjust the Lightness, you may need to increase the Saturation to revive any colors that were lightened or darkened.

To change a hue, click the **Targeted Adjustment** tool 🖑 on the panel, then Ctrl-drag/Cmd-drag horizontally over the color area in the image that you want to adjust. The color range you dragged over is now listed on the menu, and the **Hue** slider shifts on the panel. Or to change the **Saturation** of a color range, drag horizontally with the same tool over a color area in the image without holding down Ctrl/Cmd.

A *The original image has a reddish color cast.*

B *To fix the overall color cast, we chose Master from the menu, then moved the Hue slider slightly toward the right.*

C *To recolor her top, we chose Magentas from the menu, then moved the Hue slider to –73 (blue).*

SPREADING A HUE/SATURATION RANGE

When a color range (e.g., Yellows or Greens) is chosen on the second menu on the Properties panel for a Hue/Saturation layer, you can spread an adjustment of a color range more gradually into an adjacent one by dragging one of the little squares outward.

For instance, to spread an adjustment of the Greens range into the Yellows range, you would drag the little square to the left, into the yellow-orange area. Try it and see how it affects the image. (To change which hue is adjusted, use the Targeted Adjustment tool, as described in step 3 on the preceding page.)

Applying a Vibrance adjustment

Here you will use the Vibrance controls to adjust the saturation of a color layer. On the next two pages, Vibrance is used as a desaturation method.

To guard against oversaturation and clipping, the Vibrance slider boosts the intensity of less saturated colors more than that of highly saturated colors, making this slider particularly useful for adjusting skin tones. The Saturation slider, by comparison, applies the same change to all colors regardless of their original saturation levels.

To adjust the vibrance of skin tones:

1. Click a layer or the Background.**A**
2. On the Adjustments panel, click the **Vibrance** button. The Vibrance settings display on the Properties panel.
3. Increase the **Vibrance** value.
4. If necessary, reduce the **Saturation** value slightly.**B**

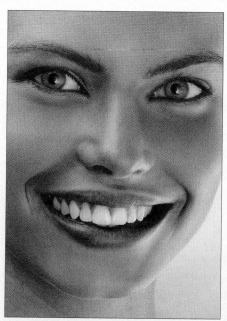

A *The color in this portrait is oversaturated.*

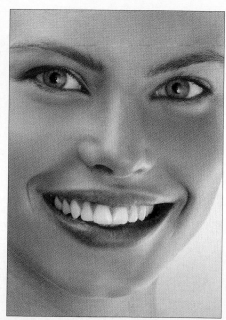

B *For the Vibrance adjustment layer, we set the Vibrance value to +42 and the Saturation value to −15. Now the skin tones look more natural.*

In this task, you will use a Vibrance adjustment layer to either strip the color completely from a layer or desaturate a layer partially, and then use the Vibrance slider to adjust the intensity of the remaining color.

To desaturate a layer using a Vibrance adjustment:

1. Click a layer or the Background.**A**

2. On the Adjustments panel,⬤ click the **Vibrance** button.▽ The Vibrance settings display on the Properties panel.

3. Do either of the following:

   For a simple, full desaturation, reduce the **Saturation** to its lowest value of −100.

   To adjust the color vibrance as you desaturate the layer, reduce the **Saturation** to between −60 and −80, then to control the color intensity in the now desaturated layer, increase or reduce the **Vibrance** value.**B–D** Remember, the Vibrance option boosts the intensity of the least saturated colors the most.

A *This is the original image.*

B *To desaturate the color partially, we lowered the Saturation value on a Vibrance adjustment layer to −60 and set the Vibrance value to −50.*

C *This is the image after we applied the Vibrance adjustment layer settings shown in the preceding figure.*

D *For this version, we kept the Saturation value of −60 but raised the Vibrance to the maximum value of +100.*

To desaturate a color layer using Vibrance, then restore color selectively:

1. Click a layer or the Background.**A**

2. On the Adjustments panel,◔ click the **Vibrance** button.▽ The Vibrance settings display on the Properties panel.

3. Reduce the **Saturation** to the lowest value of −100.

4. Choose the **Brush** tool,✐ and on the Options bar, choose a Soft Round brush, Normal mode, and an Opacity of 50% or less. Choose black as the Foreground color.

5. Adjust the brush diameter, make sure the mask thumbnail is still selected on the adjustment layer, then apply strokes where you want to restore the original colors.**B–C** You can change the brush opacity and diameter between strokes. To restore desaturated areas, set the brush Opacity to 100%, and paint with white (press X to swap the colors).

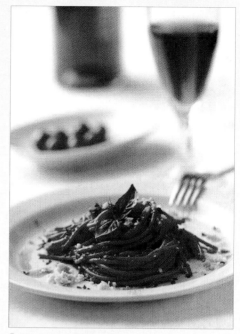

A *This is the original image.*

B *To strip the color from the image, we created a Vibrance adjustment layer, then lowered the Saturation value to −100. To reveal some color, we applied brush strokes to the adjustment layer mask.*

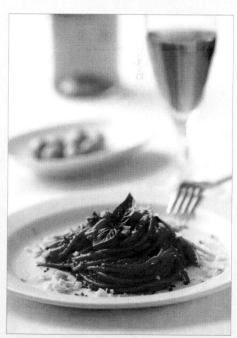

C *The pasta commands most of the attention now, because it is the only area in color.*

Applying a Curves adjustment

By using a Curves adjustment layer, you can limit tonal and color adjustments to a narrow range (such as to the highlights, quarter tones, midtones, three-quarter tones, or shadows). The corrections can be applied to the composite image (all the channels) or to individual color channels. In these steps, you will apply tonal corrections first, then apply color corrections.

Note: The information in the steps below pertains to RGB images. For a CMYK image, the controls work in the opposite way.

To apply tonal and color corrections using a Curves adjustment layer:

Part 1: Apply tonal adjustments

1. Open an image that needs color and/or tonal adjustments. **A**

2. On the Adjustments panel, ⬤ click the **Curves** button. 📈

3. On the Properties panel menu, choose Curves Display Options. In the dialog, **B** keep the Show Amount Of value on the default setting of Light, check all four of the Show options, then click OK.

4. If you need to increase the contrast in the image, do either of the following:

   The input sliders set the white and black tonal values in the image. To darken the shadows and brighten the highlights, drag the black shadow input slider and white highlight input slider inward so they align with the ends of the

gray areas in the histogram (**A**, next page) — or until you see that the contrast in the image is improved. The steeper the curve (which is, for the moment, still a straight line), the stronger the contrast.

To establish the white and black values via a high-contrast display of clipping (called Threshold mode), Alt-drag/Option-drag the black slider until a few areas of color or black appear; do the same for the white slider until a mere smidgen of white appears.

5. For more targeted adjustments, do either of the following:

   Drag part of the curve; a (selected) point appears on it. For example, to lighten the midtones, drag the middle of the curve upward, or to darken the midtones, drag the middle of the curve downward.

   ➤ When a tonal value is lightened, its Output value is increased above its Input value (the original brightness value). When a tonal value is darkened, its Output value is reduced below its Input value.

   Click the **Targeted Adjustment** tool 📷 in the panel, then move the pointer over an area of the image that contains the tonal level you want to darken or lighten; a small circle appears on the curve. Drag upward to lighten that level

Curves display for each adjusted color channel

A straight diagonal line that represents no adjustments (for comparison)

Axis guides that appear as you move a point on the curve

B For this task, check all the Show options in the Curves Display Options dialog. (The grid buttons control the size of the grid squares.)

A *This image is underexposed (too dark) and has a bluish cast.*

or downward to darken it. A point corresponding to that level appears on the curve.**B**

6. Keep the Curves controls showing on the panel. If the color also needs correcting, see the next page.

➤ If the "Calculate More Accurate Histogram" alert button appears on the Properties panel as you're applying a Curves adjustment, click the button to refresh the histogram in the panel.

➤ To cycle through and select each point on the curve, press the + (plus) key. To nudge a selected point, press an arrow key. To remove a selected point, press Backspace/Delete.

➤ To enlarge the graph and curve, drag an edge of the Properties panel.

Continued on the following page

A *To lighten the highlights, we created a Curves adjustment layer, then moved the white slider to the left.*

B *To lighten the midtones, we clicked the Targeted Adjustment tool, dragged upward slightly on the left side of the basket, then did the same on the right side of the basket (points appeared on the curve). Although our Curves adjustments improved the tonal balance, the colors look a bit washed out. We'll correct that next.*

Part 2: Correct the color

1. With the Curves adjustment layer still selected, from the second menu, choose **Red** to adjust that channel separately, then do any of the following:

   Add or subtract red in the shadows by dragging the lower part of the curve or the black slider, or in the highlights by dragging the upper part of the curve or the white slider.**A**

   Drag the middle of the curve upward to add red to the midtones or downward to subtract red **B** (to a lesser extent, this adjustment will also affect the reds in the shadows and highlights). Often, this midtone adjustment is all that's required.

   Click the Targeted Adjustment tool in the panel, then drag upward in the image to add red to that tonal level or downward to subtract red (the part of the curve that corresponds to that level adjusts accordingly).

2. Choose the **Green** channel, then the **Blue** channel, adding or subtracting that color from the image, as in the preceding step. You can switch back and forth between the color channels and readjust them if needed (**A–D**, next page).

3. *Optional:* To lessen the overall impact of the Curves adjustment layer, lower the layer opacity. Or to hide the effect from specific areas of the image, click the adjustment layer mask, then with the Brush tool and the Foreground color set to black, apply brush strokes in the image.

➤ To save your adjustment settings as a preset for future use, see page 232.

➤ As an alternative to adjusting the curves individually for each color channel, you could, theoretically, correct the overall color by selecting the gray point (middle) eyedropper on the Properties panel for Curves, then click a neutral gray area in the image. However, this method is less reliable than the method described in the task above, because locating a neutral gray is harder than it sounds (in fact, the image may not even contain a neutral gray).

A To add red to the highlights (such as on the basket), with the Red channel selected, we moved the white slider slightly inward (to the left).

B We dragged slightly downward on the lower part of the curve (where most of the red pixels are clustered on the histogram). This produced a point on the curve (shown at right) and removed some red from the midtones.

A *To add green to (and remove red and blue from) the highlights, with the Green channel selected, we dragged the white slider slightly inward.*

B *To reduce the amount of green in the midtones, we clicked the Targeted Adjustment tool, then dragged downward slightly in the image, starting from the center of the basket. A point appeared on the curve for the Green channel.*

C *Finally, to add blue to (and remove green from) the highlights, with the Blue channel selected, we dragged the white slider slightly inward.*

D *To reduce the amount of blue in the midtones, we dragged downward slightly on the lower part of the curve on the panel (where most of blue pixels are clustered); a point appeared on the curve. Although we made only minor adjustments to the curve for each channel, in the final image, you can see that overall, the colors are now better balanced.*

Applying a Black & White adjustment

Our preferred way to strip color from a layer is via a Black & White adjustment. With this awesome command, you can control how the individual R, G, B and C, M, Y color channels are converted to grayscale values. As an added option, you can apply a tint. Note that this feature has no effect on the document color mode.

To convert a layer to grayscale via a Black & White adjustment:

1. In an RGB image, click a layer or the Background. **A**

2. On the Adjustments panel, click the **Black & White** button. The Black & White controls appear on the Properties panel.

3. Do any of the following:

   Click **Auto** to let Photoshop choose the settings (**A–B**, next page), or choose a preset from the **Preset** menu. You can also customize the settings, as described below.

   Adjust any of the sliders. A lower value produces a darker gray equivalent for a color; a higher value produces a lighter gray equivalent (**C–D**, next page). For example, you could use the Yellows slider to lighten or darken the skin tones in a portrait or move the Cyans and Blues sliders to adjust the sky in a landscape.

   Click the **Targeted Adjustment** tool in the panel, then drag to the right in an area of the image to lighten that shade, or to the left to darken it. The slider corresponding to the predominant color in that area will shift accordingly.

4. *Optional:* To apply a tint to the image, check Tint, click the color swatch, choose a color in the Color Picker, then click OK (**A**, page 252).

5. *Optional:* To restore some of the original color to the whole layer uniformly, lower the opacity of the adjustment layer. To restore color to specific areas, click the adjustment layer mask thumbnail, choose black as the Foreground color, then with the Brush tool, apply strokes to the image (for a more subtle effect, lower the opacity for the tool first).

AUTO-SELECTING THE TARGETED ADJUSTMENT TOOL

To have Photoshop select the Targeted Adjustment tool (or) automatically on the Properties panel when you create a Curves, Hue/Saturation, or Black & White adjustment layer, display the controls for one of those three adjustment types, then choose Auto-Select Targeted Adjustment Tool from the panel menu.

ORCHESTRATING A SCENE

In our environment, as in fine art and photography, colors help to define shapes and spatial relationships and draw our attention to some elements in a scene more than others. When converting an image to grayscale, you will need to reinterpret the composition and orchestrate visual movement using lights and darks instead of color. For example, say there's a bright red shape in the center of the original color layer. When the layer is reduced to grayscale, you could lighten or darken that shape via the Black & White controls, to distinguish it from surrounding grays.

A *This image layer is a good candidate for a conversion to grayscale, because it has clearly defined shapes.*

A *This is the image after we created a Black & White adjustment layer and clicked Auto on the Properties panel.*

B *These are the slider values that Photoshop chose when we clicked the Auto button.*

C *To darken the cabin on the boat, we reduced the Reds value; to lighten the upper midtones on the boat deck, we increased the Yellows value; to darken the water in the foreground, we reduced the Greens value; and to darken the sky slightly, we reduced the Cyans value.*

D *This final version of the image has better contrast than the Auto version shown above.*

A *For this Black & White adjustment, we checked Tint on the Properties panel, clicked the Tint swatch, chose a color in the Color Picker, then used the sliders to intensify the color in some areas, such as on the boat cabin and upper sky. The settings we chose are shown at left.*

Tinting an image via a Gradient Map adjustment

A Gradient Map adjustment matches luminosity values of colors in a gradient to luminosity values in an image, replacing one with the other. It produces beautiful effects with little effort (you can look like a Photoshop pro even if you're not one — yet!). This is a fun feature to experiment with.

Note: A recommended prerequisite for this task is familiarity with the Gradient Editor, which is covered on pages 219–220.

To tint an image via a Gradient Map adjustment:

1. Click a layer or the Background. **B**

2. On the Adjustments panel, ⬤ click the **Gradient Map** button. ▭

3. On the Properties panel, click the Gradient picker arrowhead, then via the picker menu, ✿▾ load a preset library (or two), including the Photographic Toning library. Click a preset on the picker (**A**, next page). To minimize visible banding on print output, check Dither.

4. *Optional:* Click the Gradient thumbnail to open the Gradient Editor, then edit the gradient (e.g., add or change some color stops, or reposition some stops or midpoint diamonds) (**B**, next page).

5. *Optional:* Check Reverse to apply the lightest colors in the gradient to the darkest values in the image, and the darkest colors to the lightest values in the image (the opposite of the default behavior). If the gradient contains dark colors, this option may produce a "film negative" effect.

6. *Optional:* Change the blending mode of the Gradient Map layer (**C**, next page). Try Darken, Soft Light, Pin Light, Hue, or Luminosity.

B *This is the original image.*

A *Via a Gradient Map adjustment, we applied the Sepia 2 gradient (Photographic Toning library); we kept the default settings for the gradient.*

B *In a copy of the original image, we applied a Gradient Map adjustment using the Sepia-Selenium 2 gradient (Photographic Toning library). In the Gradient Editor, we deleted the second color stop, lightened the third color stop, and dragged the third stop slightly to the left.*

C *A different Gradient Map adjustment we made to the original image: Light Cyan gradient (Simple library), Reverse checked on the Properties panel, and Pin Light chosen as the blending mode for the adjustment layer.*

Applying the Merge to HDR commands

To produce an HDR (High Dynamic Range) image, multiple exposures of the same scene are combined into one image. The composite image contains a wider range of tonalities than could be captured in a single shot.

To shoot photos for an HDR composite:

➤ Use a tripod to ensure that the shots align uniformly, and a cable release to minimize camera shake.

➤ Use a low ISO setting to minimize noise.

➤ Capture the photos as raw files.

➤ To keep the aperture constant, set the camera to Aperture Priority mode (A mode for a Nikon; AV mode for a Canon).

➤ Set the auto bracket feature to capture either three or five shots using different exposures (shutter speeds) automatically. For a Nikon, use the Auto Bracketing Set > AE Only option; for a Canon, use the Exposure Comp/AEB Setting option. For three-shot bracketing, set exposures of two stops underexposed, one normal exposure, and two stops overexposed. For five-shot bracketing, set exposure differences of one and two stops underexposed, one normal exposure, and one and two stops overexposed.

To apply the Merge to HDR Pro command:

1. In Bridge, select the three or five bracketed photos you captured for the HDR image, **A** then choose Tools > Photoshop > **Merge to HDR Pro**.

2. Sit tight while Photoshop merges your photos. When the Merge to HDR Pro dialog opens, choose Mode: 16 Bit or 8 Bit and choose Local Adaptation from the menu as the conversion method (for 32 Bit mode, see the tip on page 256).

3. Under Tone and Detail, increase the **Detail** value to boost the image sharpness and contrast, and to provide more tonal variation for the other sliders to work with.

4. Under Edge Glow, increase the **Strength** value to increase edge contrast and create a white edge glow. Increase or reduce the **Radius** value to adjust the width of the glow (**A**, next page).

   Optional: To suppress the sharpness of the edges and allow for higher Detail values, check Edge Smoothness.

5. Under Tone and Detail, choose a low **Gamma** value to emphasize the midtones, or a high value to emphasize the highlights and shadows.

   Use the **Exposure** slider to adjust the overall lighting (**B**, next page).

Continued on page 256

A *This scene was shot using three different exposures: One setting for the exterior light, one setting for the interior light, and one normal exposure setting (in between the other two).*

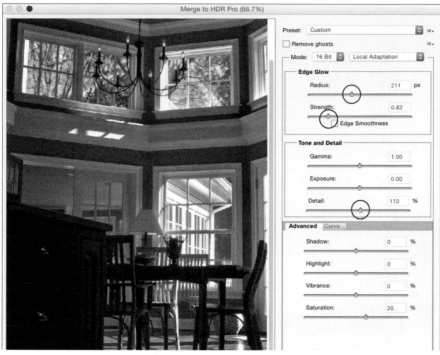

A *In the Merge to HDR Pro dialog, we increased the Detail, Strength, and Radius values to heighten the details and edges in the image.*

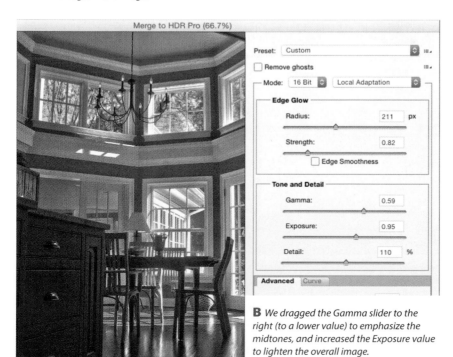

B *We dragged the Gamma slider to the right (to a lower value) to emphasize the midtones, and increased the Exposure value to lighten the overall image.*

6. In the Advanced tab, use the **Shadow** slider to adjust the lightness of the shadow areas. Lower the **Highlight** value if you need to recover details in the highlights.**A** If you plan to refine the HDR image in Camera Raw, as we recommend, use these sliders to apply only minor adjustments.

Readjust the Detail value to tweak the sharpness.

7. To remove any discrepancies between shots that resulted from the movement of the subject, check **Remove Ghosts** near the top of the dialog, then click one of the exposure thumbnails at the bottom of the dialog to designate it as the source for aligning the shots.**B–C** The normal (EV 0.0) or dark (EV -1.x) exposure thumbnail may work best.

8. To tweak the shadows, midtones, or highlights, click the Curve tab and gently drag the part of the curve for that tonal range, just as you would for a Curves adjustment (**A**, next page).

9. Click OK. The HDR file will open as a new document in Photoshop. Save the document in the Photoshop PSD format, then follow the steps on page 258 to refine it in Camera Raw.

➤ If you choose 32 Bit as the mode in the Merge to HDR Pro dialog, you can check Complete Toning in Adobe Camera Raw, then click the Tone in ACR button to access — and adjust the document in — the Camera Raw dialog. Be aware that 32-bit files are very large and must be converted to 8- or 16-bit for output.

A In the Advanced tab, we raised the Shadow value to recover shadow details, lowered the Highlight value to recover highlight details, reduced the Saturation value, and increased the Vibrance value to boost the color saturation.

B The leaves outside the window moved when we shot our three exposures, producing what are called "ghosts" — like a double exposure — in the composite image.

C We checked Remove Ghosts, then clicked the dark thumbnail to designate that image as the source for aligning the exposures.

A *Finally, in the Curve tab, we raised the lower part of the curve slightly to lighten the shadows and lowered the upper part of the curve slightly to darken the highlights and upper midtones. As you can see in the preview, these HDR Pro settings improved the image considerably.*

MAKING AN IMAGE LOOK SURREAL

In the Merge to HDR Pro dialog, choosing high values for the Radius, Strength, and Detail sliders (and checking Edge Smoothness) will produce a surrealistic image like the one shown at right, whereas lower values will produce a more naturalistic image. Some people like to apply a stylized sense of lighting to their HDR photos, while others prefer to apply a more natural sense lighting. It's your choice.

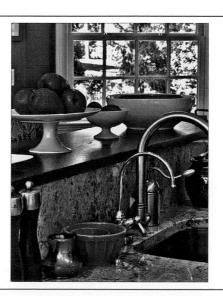

After using the Merge to HDR Pro command, we like to tweak the exposure, color, and tonal values in the new composite file by using the Camera Raw Filter.

To process an HDR file via Camera Raw:

1. After following the steps on pages 254–257, duplicate the Background, then right-click the duplicate layer and choose **Convert to Smart Object**.

2. Choose Filter > **Camera Raw Filter** (Ctrl-Shift-A/Cmd-Shift-A).

3. In the Camera Raw dialog, use sliders in the Basic or any other tab to further enhance or improve the image (see Chapter 4).

4. Click OK.**A**

A This is the final HDR image after we applied adjustments via the Basic and Tone Curve tabs in Camera Raw. While the exposure is well corrected, the lighting and exterior colors seem a bit harsh.

Camera Raw provides a one-step merge to HDR command of its own. Merging photos via Camera Raw uses the raw, unprocessed data from those photos, which results in an image that can better reproduce the tonal range from the original scene. (In contrast, the Photoshop Merge to HDR Pro command must work with photos whose data has been converted.)

Performing the merge operation right in Camera Raw will produce an image in a format that can be edited in Camera Raw at any time — using all the correction options found in Camera Raw. Any edits will be applied as instructions to the merged image and will not alter original data in the merged image.

To apply the Merge to HDR command: ★

1. In Bridge, select two or more thumbnails that will be used for the HDR image. Double-click one of the thumbnails to open them all in Camera Raw.

2. In the filmstrip panel in Camera Raw, right-click a thumbnail, then choose **Select All** (Ctrl-A/Cmd-A) from the context menu. Right-click again, then choose **Merge to HDR** (Alt-M/Option-M).

3. In the **HDR Merge Preview** dialog (**A**, next page), do any of the following:

   Drag a corner to enlarge the dialog.

   Check **Align Images** to align the photos.

   Check **Auto Tone** to preview automatically applied tonal corrections. You can uncheck Auto Tone if you plan on correcting the merged image yourself.

   Choose a **Deghost** option from the menu to remove any movement in the scene during image capture.

4. Click **Merge**. In the **Merge Result** dialog, enter a name and choose a folder location for the HDR image. Click **Save**. (Hold down Alt/Option and click to bypass this dialog and save the image in the same folder as the source photos.) Camera Raw will apply tonal, color, and distortion correction automatically to the merged image, then display the results in its preview.

5. Make any further enhancements to the resulting HDR image (**B**, next page) in Camera Raw (see Chapter 4). Click **Done**. A .dng file will be saved to the folder you chose in the previous step.

A *After selecting the three thumbnails and choosing Merge to HDR from the context menu, the HDR Merge Preview dialog opened. We chose the settings shown at left, then clicked Merge.*

B *We corrected the merged image in Camera Raw using the Basic and Tone Curve tabs. The Camera Raw merge to HDR did a good job of correcting the perspective and preserving the colors from the source photos.*

To output the Camera Raw HDR image to screen or print: ★

1. In Bridge, double-click the .dng file to open it into Camera Raw. Make any further edits, if desired.

2. Click **Open Image** to open a converted image into Photoshop.

3. Make any edits to prepare the file for its output medium, then save it in the appropriate output format (the original .dng file will not be altered).

Screening back a layer using Levels

When printing dark text or a logo on top of a photo, you need to make sure the picture is light enough for the text or logo to be readable, but not so light that the image content isn't discernible. To achieve both objectives, you can screen back (lighten) an image layer—or a selected area of an image layer—via Levels.

To screen back a layer using Levels:

1. Open an image. **A**

2. *Optional:* To limit the adjustment to a specific area of the image, create a selection.

3. On the Adjustments panel, ⬤ click the **Levels** button. ⬛ Levels controls display on the Properties panel.

4. To reduce contrast in the image, move the output levels shadows (bottom black) slider to the right.

5. To lighten the midtone values in the image, move the input levels midtones (gray) slider to the left. **B**

6. To feather the edge of the mask nondestructively, click the adjustment layer mask thumbnail, then set the Feather value on the Properties panel.

7. To compare the original layer and the adjusted version, press and hold \, then release. **C**

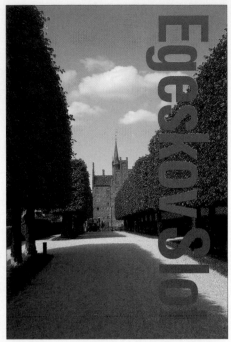

A *This document contains an editable type layer above an image layer.*

B *To lighten the selected image layer, we created a Levels adjustment layer and chose these settings.*

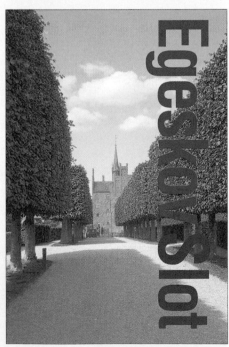

C *With the image screened back, the type is more eye-catching and easier to read.*

If we had to pick one topic that represents the heart and soul of Photoshop, it would be the art of combining images. In this chapter, you will learn various ways to copy selections and layers within the same document and between documents, use CC Library assets and Smart Objects, combine multiple exposures, and fade the edge of a layer with a layer mask. You will also learn how to use the Clone Stamp tool to clone imagery, the Merge to Panorama and Auto-Align Layers commands to merge multiple images, and Smart Guides and other Photoshop features to precisely position and align layers. You'll be amazed at how easy it is to create composite images!

Using the Clipboard

One way to transfer a selection of imagery from one layer or document to another is by using the Clipboard commands on the Edit menu. You choose the Cut, Copy, or Copy Merged command first to put the current selection into a temporary storage area in memory, called the Clipboard. Then you choose a paste command, such as Paste or Paste in Place, to paste the Clipboard contents as a new layer into the same document or another document. If there is an active selection in the target document, another option is to use the Paste Into or Paste Outside command to paste the Clipboard contents inside or outside of the selection.

If you cut (remove) a selection from the Background via the Cut command, the exposed area fills automatically with the current Background color.**A** If you cut a selection from a layer, the area left behind is replaced with transparent pixels (the same results that you get when you move pixels on a layer).**B**

The same Clipboard contents can be pasted as many times as needed. Only one selection can be stored on the Clipboard at a time, however, and it is replaced by new contents each time you use the Cut, Copy, or Copy Merged command. If Export Clipboard is checked

Continued on the following page

A *This selection was cut from the Background.*

B *This selection was cut from a layer.*

COMBINING IMAGES

in Edit/Photoshop CC > Preferences > General, the Clipboard contents will stay in temporary system memory when you exit/quit Photoshop — but only until you shut down your computer.

➤ To empty the Clipboard at any time in order to reclaim system memory, choose Edit > Purge > Clipboard, then click OK if an alert appears. (To prevent the alert from reappearing, check Don't Show Again.)

When you use a paste command, the contents of the Clipboard appear automatically on a new layer.

To copy and paste a selection:

1. Read the sidebar on this page, and change the resolution of a copy of the source file, if needed.

2. Click a layer in the source document, then create a selection. *Optional:* Refine the selection edge via the Refine Edge dialog (see pages 184–185).

3. Choose one of the following commands:

   Edit > **Copy A** (Ctrl-C/Cmd-C) to copy pixels from the current layer within the selection area.

   Edit > **Copy Merged** (Ctrl-Shift-C/Cmd-Shift-C) to copy all pixels from all visible layers within the selection area.

   Edit > **Cut** (Ctrl-X/Cmd-X) to cut the selection out of the current layer.

4. Click in the same document or in another document.

5. Do either of the following:

   To have the Clipboard contents land in the center of the document window (or if the dimensions of the copied content are larger than those of the target document, to the top and left edges of the canvas area), choose Edit > **Paste** (Ctrl-V/Cmd-V).

   To have the Clipboard contents land in the same *x/y* location as in the source layer or document, choose Edit > Paste Special > **Paste in Place** (Ctrl-Shift-V/Cmd-Shift-V).

6. If the source file has a different color profile than the target file, the Paste Profile Mismatch alert dialog will appear. We recommend that you click Convert (Preserve Color Appearance) to preserve the appearance of colors in the source image, then click OK.

7. The pasted pixels will appear on a new layer.**B** You can restack the layer, and you can reposition it in the image with the Move tool.

A *We created a selection, then pressed Ctrl-C/Cmd-C to copy its contents.*

B *In another document, we pressed Ctrl-V/Cmd-V to paste the Clipboard contents; they arrived on a new layer.*

HEY! MY PICTURE SHRANK!

When you paste or drag and drop a selection between documents, the copied imagery adopts the resolution of the target document. If the resolution of the target file is higher than that of the source one, the copy will look smaller than imagery on other layers; if the resolution of the target file is lower than that of the source document, the copy will look larger. If you want to prevent a size discrepancy when copying imagery between files, before creating the copy, change the resolution of a copy of the source file via Image > Image Size to match that of the target document (resharpen the image, too).

➤ To compare the relative sizes of the source and target documents, use the Window > Arrange submenu to arrange them side by side, and choose the same zoom level for both.

Working with pixels outside the canvas area

If the dimensions of the Clipboard contents that you paste are larger than those of the target document, some of the pasted pixels will be hidden from view outside the canvas area (they will save with the document). This will also occur if you use the Crop tool with the Delete Cropped Pixels option off. When you apply an image-editing command (such as a filter), it alters the entire layer, including any pixels outside the canvas area. Here are some ways to work with those pixels:

➤ To move hidden pixels into view, click the layer, then hold down V (Move tool) and drag in the image. **A**

➤ To select all the nontransparent pixels on a layer, including any pixels outside the live canvas area (and pixels that may be hidden by a layer mask), Ctrl-click/Cmd-click the layer thumbnail on the Layers panel. Select > All, in comparison, selects only the rectangular boundary of the canvas area.

➤ To enlarge the canvas area to include all hidden pixels on all layers, choose Image > Reveal All.

➤ To remove pixels that are outside the canvas area from all layers, choose Select > All, then choose Image > Crop. This can help reduce the file size.

➤ If a layer contains pixels outside the canvas area and you merge it with the Background (not with another layer), the hidden pixels will be discarded.

➤ To shrink the contents of the current layer, choose the Move tool, ⤧ check Show Transform Controls on the Options bar, Shift-drag a corner handle on the bounding box inward, then press Enter/Return.

ADJUSTING THE SELECTION EDGE

To shrink the edges of a selection, before you move, copy, or drag-copy it, click **Refine Edge** on the Options bar, then reduce the **Shift Edge** value. To soften the edges of the selection, use the **Feather** slider (see the sidebar on page 265). Or even better, if you store a selection as a layer mask, you can use the nondestructive controls on the **Properties** panel at any time to change the **Density** and **Feather** values of the mask (see page 194).

COPYING LAYER SETTINGS, TOO

To copy **layer settings** (e.g., blending mode, opacity, and layer effects) along with imagery when creating composite documents, instead of using the Clipboard, copy the whole layer, as described on page 266 or 268.

COPYING IMAGERY TO A NEW LAYER

To copy imagery to a new layer within the same document without using the Clipboard, click a layer or the Background, create a selection, then press Ctrl-J/Cmd-J, or right-click in the image and choose **Layer via Copy.** Or if you want to remove the selected pixels from the original layer and put them on a new layer, press Ctrl-Shift-J/Cmd-Shift-J, or right-click in the image and choose **Layer via Cut.**

A *We're dragging a layer from left to right to reveal hidden pixels.*

When you use the Paste Into command to paste the contents of the Clipboard into a selection, Photoshop creates a new layer and converts the selection to a layer mask. You can reposition the pasted imagery within the mask, edit the mask to reveal more or less of the imagery that it is hiding, or adjust the mask density or feather value via the Properties panel.

To paste into a selection:

1. Select an area of a layer or the Background in a source image from which you want to copy pixels. **A**

2. Choose Edit > **Copy** (Ctrl-C/Cmd-C) to copy pixels from only the currently selected layer, or choose Edit > **Copy Merged** (Ctrl-Shift-C/Cmd-Shift-C) to copy pixels within the selection area from all visible layers.

3. Click a layer in the same document or in another document.

4. Select the area (or areas) into which you want to paste the Clipboard contents. **B** *Optional:* Click Refine Edge on the Options bar and use the dialog controls to refine the selection edge.

5. Choose Edit > Paste Special > **Paste Into** or press Ctrl-Alt-Shift-V/Cmd-Option-Shift-V. **C** A new layer and layer mask appear.

6. *Optional:* Although the entire contents of the Clipboard were pasted, the layer mask may be hiding some of the imagery. To move the layer contents within the mask, hold down V (Move tool), click the layer thumbnail, then drag in the document. Or to move the layer mask, click the mask thumbnail before dragging. To move the layer and layer mask as a unit, click between the layer and mask thumbnails to produce a Link icon, 🔗 then hold down V and drag in the image.

7. *Optional:* To reshape the mask, click the mask thumbnail. With the Brush tool 🖌 (B or Shift-B), a Soft Round brush, and white chosen as the Foreground color, paint in the document to expose more of the pasted image. To hide more of the pasted image, press X to paint with black.

➤ When you open the File > New dialog, it lists the dimensions of the smallest rectangle that can surround the current contents of the Clipboard, if any.

➤ Unlike the Cut and Copy commands, the Edit > Clear command empties a selection area without putting the selection contents onto the Clipboard.

A *We used the Rectangular Marquee tool to select an area of this image layer, then chose the Copy command.*

B *Next, we used the Quick Selection tool to select the sky area in this document.*

C *Finally, we pasted the Clipboard contents into the selection via the Paste Into command, for a more Baroque sky.*

Drag-copying a selection on a layer

In this task, you will drag-copy a selection on a layer within the same document. On the next four pages, you will drag-copy layers and selections between files.

To drag-copy a selection on a layer:

1. Select an area of a layer or the Background.

2. Do either of the following:

   Choose the **Move** tool ▸⊹ (V), then hold down Alt/Option and drag the selection.**A** The duplicate pixels will remain selected.**B**

   Choose a tool other than the Move tool, then hold down Ctrl-Alt/Cmd-Option and drag the selection.

3. Deselect (Ctrl-D/Cmd-D).

➤ Include Shift with either shortcut listed above to constrain the movement to increments of 45°.

A *With the Rectangular Marquee tool, we selected the window area in this image, then we held down Ctrl-Alt/Cmd-Option (and Shift) and dragged the selection to the right …*

B *… to create a copy of the selection.*

FEATHERING THE EDGES OF A SELECTION

With a selection active and a selection tool chosen, click Refine Edge on the Options bar (Ctrl-Alt-R/Cmd-Option-R). Choose View: On White (W), increase the Feather value, choose Output To: Selection, then click OK. The feathering will become evident visually when you move, drag-copy, copy and paste, or edit (e.g., apply brush strokes or filters to) the selection.

We created a selection.

We applied a Feather value via the Refine Edge dialog.

We drag-copied the selection.

Drag-copying a selection or layer between files with the Move tool

When you drag and drop (drag-copy, for short) a selection of pixels from one document to another, presto, a duplicate of those pixels appears on a new layer in the target document. Pixels that land outside the canvas area can be moved into view at any time. An advantage of this method, as opposed to using the Clipboard, is that layer style settings (blending mode, opacity, and effects) in the layer that you drag and drop, along with any masks, are also copied. You can also drag-copy a shape, type, or Smart Object layer.

To drag-copy a selection or layer between documents with the Move tool:

1. Open the source and target documents. Change the resolution in a copy of the source file, if needed. Suggested contents for the target file are a white or solid-color Background, a photo of a texture, or a screened-back image.

2. Click in the source document, then on the Layers panel, click a layer or the Background. *Optional:* Select part of the layer or Background.

3. Choose the **Move** tool ⊕ (or hold down V).

4. Drag from inside the selection or layer in the source document window to the tab of the target document,**A** pause until the target document displays, then release the mouse where you want the selection or layer to appear.**B**

   ➤ To drop the copied selection or layer in the center of the source document, hold down Shift as you release the mouse.

5. If the source file has a different color profile than the target file, the Paste Profile Mismatch alert dialog will appear. We recommend that you click Convert (Preserve Color Appearance) to preserve the colors of the source image, then click OK.

   An alert will also appear if the source and target files have a different bits-per-channel setting. Click Yes to accept the change in image quality (or click No to cancel).

6. The duplicate content will appear on a new layer.**C** You can reposition or scale it with the Move tool.

   ➤ You can also drag and drop multiple selected layers. To copy a layer group, after step 3, above, check Auto-Select on the Options bar and choose Group on the menu, then continue with steps 4–6.

A *Drag a selection from inside a tabbed window to the tab of another document.*

B *When the target image displays, drag the selection into the image, then release.*

C *The selection appears as a new layer in the target image.*

REFINING THE EDGES OF A LAYER AFTER USING DRAG-COPY OR PASTE

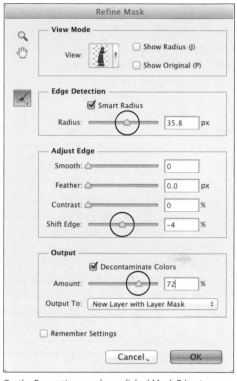

We drag-copied a layer containing a photo of a ukulele player from a source file into a beach image. We didn't like the white fringe around the edges of the figure, especially on the skirt (wrong kind of fringe!). To eliminate the fringe, our first step was to choose Layer > Layer Mask > From Transparency. The command converted the transparent areas of the layer into black areas in a layer mask.

On the Properties panel, we clicked Mask Edge to open this dialog, chose View: On Layers, used the settings shown above to mask the fringe, chose Output To: New Layer with Layer Mask, then clicked OK.

The refined mask appeared on a copy of the image layer.

Drag-copying layers between files via the Layers panel

Here you will drag-copy one or more layers from the Layers panel of a source document into a target document. An advantage of this method is that you can control specifically which layers are copied. As with the Move tool method (the previous task), any pixels that lie outside the live canvas area are also included.

To drag-copy a layer between files via the Layers panel:

1. Open the source and target documents. Change the resolution in a copy of the source file, if needed (see the sidebar on page 262).

2. From the Window > Arrange submenu, choose **2-Up Horizontal** or **2-Up Vertical**.

3. Click in the source document window, then on the Layers panel, 🔖 click a layer, a layer group, or the Background, or Ctrl-click/Cmd-click multiple layers.

4. Drag from the Layers panel of the source document into the target document; hold down Shift while dragging to make the new imagery appear in the center of the target document (**A**, next page). The new layer (or layers) will be stacked above the previously selected one (**B**, next page).

5. If the source document has a different color profile than the target document, the Paste Profile Mismatch alert dialog will appear. We recommend that you click Convert (Preserve Color Appearance) to preserve the appearance of colors in the source image, then click OK.

   An alert will also appear if the source and target documents have different bits-per-channel settings. Click Yes to accept the change in image quality (or click No to cancel).

6. Either close the source document or right-click the tab for the target document and choose Consolidate All to Here from the context menu.

7. *Optional:* With the Move tool ▶⊹ (V), reposition the new layer or layers.

8. *Optional:* To scale a new layer, choose the Move tool and check Show Transform Controls on the Options bar. If you don't see all the handles on the bounding box, press Ctrl-0/Cmd-0 for Fit on Screen view. Shift-drag a corner handle on the bounding box, then press Enter/Return to accept the new size.

SELECTING A LAYER OR GROUP IN THE DOCUMENT WINDOW

To select a layer or group in the document window without using the Layers panel, hold down V (temporary Move tool), check Auto-Select on the Options bar, choose Group or Layer from the menu, then click a pixel area, type, or a shape in the document.

CREATING A NEW DOCUMENT FROM A LAYER

To quickly create a new document from a layer, click the layer, then from the Layers panel menu, choose Duplicate Layer. The Duplicate Layer dialog opens. From the Document menu, choose New, enter a name for the new document in the Name field, then click OK. Save the new file.

CREATING A LAYERED DOCUMENT FROM FILE THUMBNAILS

To import multiple files as standard image layers (not Smart Objects) into a new Photoshop document, use the Load Files into Photoshop Layers command. Photoshop does all the work for you.

In Bridge, select one or more image thumbnails, then choose Tools > Photoshop > Load Files into Photoshop Layers.

A *After tiling two documents vertically, we clicked in the document on the left (our source document). In this shot, we're Shift-dragging a layer group from the Layers panel of the source document into our target document window.*

B *When we released the mouse, a duplicate of the layer group appeared in the center of the target document.*

Moving elements between files via Creative Cloud Libraries

Creative Cloud Libraries enable you to gather and organize common design assets into one panel, then use them across various projects and applications to promote design consistency.

Create library assets simply by copying layer content, colors, character styles, and layer styles into the Libraries panel. You can then use those assets to place a linked graphic, or apply a color or style to layer content, in any open Photoshop CC, Illustrator CC, or InDesign CC file (when running the latest versions of these programs). All CC Library assets are stored in the Creative Cloud (and synced to a storage cache on your local machine). Changes made to a library in one program will be updated in all Adobe Libraries panels.

To create a new library: ★

1. Choose Window > **Libraries** to display the Libraries panel.

2. From the menu at the top of the panel, choose **Create New Library.A** Enter a name, then click Create.

➤ To rename the currently active library, choose Rename "[library name]" from the panel menu, enter a new name, then click Rename.

➤ To delete the currently active library, choose Delete "[library name]" from the panel menu, then click Delete.

To copy layer content, styles, or color into a library: ★

1. Open a Photoshop document that contains design elements (image, shape, or text layers, and layer styles) you want to put into a library.

2. Display the **Libraries** panel. From the menu at top, choose a library.

3. Choose the **Move** tool (V or Shift-V). On the Options bar, check **Auto Select**, then choose **Layer** from the menu.

4. Do any of the following:

   To create a library-linked **graphics** asset, drag an image, shape, or type block into the Libraries panel,**B** or with a layer selected, click the **Add Graphic** button at the bottom of the panel.**C** Note: If the image in your document was a Smart Object, it will automatically be converted to a

A *On the Libraries panel, we chose Create New Library from the menu at the top.*

B *Separately, we dragged a type block, then a shape into the Libraries panel to add them as assets.*

Add buttons

Graphic	Character Style	Layer Style	Fill Color	Stroke Color	Foreground Color

C *We could also have selected a layer, then clicked one of the Add buttons at the bottom of the panel to add layer content, style, or color to one of the four asset categories.*

library-linked Smart Object. If you don't want this conversion, choose Undo immediately.

To create a **character style** asset, click a text layer, then click the **Add Character Style** button A at the bottom of the panel.

To create a **layer style** asset, click a layer containing layer styles (effects), then click the **Add Layer Style** button *fx* at the bottom of the panel.

To create a process **color** asset, click a shape layer containing a fill and/or stroke color, then click the **Add Fill Color** and/or **Add Stroke Color** button ■ at the bottom of the panel. You can also choose a Foreground color, then click the **Add Foreground Color** button at the bottom of the panel.

5. An asset thumbnail will be placed in the proper asset category in the panel automatically. **A** The actual asset is stored in your Creative Cloud Assets.

To use a library asset in your document: ★

1. Display the **Libraries** panel.

2. Do any of the following:

Click a layer on the Layers panel. Drag a **graphic** asset from the library into the document window (or right-click the asset and choose **Place Linked** from the context menu). **B** A library-linked Smart Object will be listed on the Layers panel (with a cloud badge ☁ on its layer thumbnail). (To learn about Smart Objects, see the next 12 pages.)

➤ To place the graphic as image layer(s) or a shape layer, hold down Alt/Option when dragging, or choose **Place Layers** from the context menu.

Click a type layer, then click a **character style** asset (or right-click and choose **Apply Character Style** from the context menu) to apply it to the text.

Click a layer, then click a **layer style** asset (or right-click and choose **Apply Layer Style** from the context menu) to apply it to the layer.

Click a type layer, then click a **color** asset to apply it to the type. Click any layer, then right-click a **color** asset and choose **Apply Color Overlay** from the context menu to apply the color as a layer effect.

Right-click a **color** asset and choose **Set Color** (context menu) to make it the Foreground color.

Click a shape layer, then right-click a **color** asset and choose **Apply Fill Color** or **Apply Stroke Color** from the context menu.

A *The resulting assets from adding layer content, styles, and color into the Libraries panel.*

Roll over an asset to display information about it in a Tool Tip.

B *Right-click an asset to display its context menu of available commands.*

VIEWING A LIBRARY ON CREATIVE CLOUD

From the Libraries panel menu, choose View on Website. Your default browser will launch and your Creative Cloud Assets page will display the assets in the current library. Click the back arrow to the left of the library name to display your Assets page **Libraries** view.

SHARING LIBRARIES WITH COLLABORATORS

From the Libraries panel menu, choose Collaborate. Your Creative Cloud Assets page will open in your browser and the Invite Collaborators widget will display.

To share a link to an asset, right-click the asset, then choose Share Link from the context menu. To share a link to a library, choose Share Link from the panel menu. Your Creative Cloud Assets page will open in your browser and the Send Link widget will display. See page 491.

To manage library assets: ★

Right-click any asset, then choose Duplicate, Copy To or Move To (another library), Rename, or Delete from the context menu to perform that task.

By placing a library graphic as a library-linked Smart Object multiple times in one or more Photoshop documents, you can edit the content of the library asset on your system and have all Adobe Libraries panels and all placed linked Smart Objects update automatically in all open documents.

To edit the content of a library asset: ★

1. Display the **Libraries** panel.⊜

2. Double-click a **color** asset, or right-click and choose **Edit** from the context menu. The Color Picker dialog opens. Edit the color. See page 206.

3. Do either of the following:

   Double-click a **graphic** asset, or right-click and choose **Edit** from the context menu.

   On the Layers panel, double-click a library-linked Smart Object thumbnail.

4. A temporary file opens. Edit, save, and close the temporary file to update the library asset and all linked Smart Objects. See page 281.

If a Photoshop document was closed when the content of a library asset was edited, renamed, or deleted, any linked Smart Objects in the file may not auto-update. If the library asset was modified remotely (on the network), no auto-update will occur, regardless of whether the document was open or closed.

To manually update a modified or missing library graphic asset: ★

Display the Properties panel.▦ Do either of the following:

On the Layers panel,◆ click the layer listing for any library-linked Smart Object displaying the out-of-date link alert.▨ On the Properties panel, click the path listing for the outdated link, and from the menu that opens, choose **Update Modified Content**.

On the Layers panel, click the layer listing for any library-linked Smart Object displaying the missing link alert.▨ On the Properties panel, click the path listing for the missing link, and from the menu that opens, choose **Relink to Library Graphic**. On the Libraries panel, pause while the panel redraws, then click an asset. Click **Relink** on the bottom of the panel.

ADOBE STOCK IMAGES ★

On the Libraries panel, click the Search Adobe Stock button ⓈⓉ to access the Adobe Stock website. Enter an image category in the Search field, then click Go. Roll over an image, roll over the white down arrow, then open the Save Preview widget menu (click the white arrowhead) and choose a Library name. A linked, watermarked image will be added as an asset to the Libraries panel. Drag the stock asset into your document to place the watermarked image as a comp. To acquire a license for the stock asset, in the Libraries panel, right-click the asset and choose License Image. All occurrences of the placed asset will automatically update to a high-resolution, watermark-free image.

Creating embedded Smart Objects

A Smart Object is pixel or vector art that is either embedded into or linked to a Photoshop file, and is edited differently from a layer. For example, if you create a Smart Object from an Illustrator file, you can edit the object content without altering the original file (Photoshop takes you to Illustrator temporarily). If you apply Photoshop filters to a Smart Object, the filter settings remain available and can be edited at any time.

To create an embedded Smart Object, you can convert one or more existing layers in a Photoshop document, or open or place an AI (Adobe Illustrator), PDF, PSD, TIFF, or Camera Raw file into Photoshop. On

this and the next three pages, we describe various methods for creating embedded Smart Objects; then on pages 276–279, we describe how to edit, duplicate, and replace them. To create and work with linked Smart Objects, see pages 280–283.

To convert one or more layers in a file to an embedded Smart Object:

1. Open a Photoshop document, then select one or more layers on the Layers panel.◆

2. Right-click one of the selected layers and choose **Convert to Smart Object** from the context menu (**A–B**, next page).

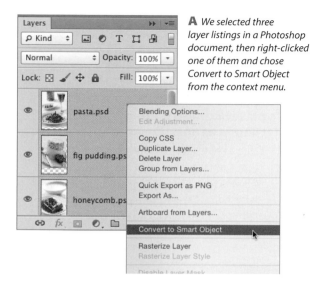

A *We selected three layer listings in a Photoshop document, then right-clicked one of them and chose Convert to Smart Object from the context menu.*

B *The command combined the layers into one Smart Object. Note the icon in the corner of the layer thumbnail.*

To open a file as an embedded Smart Object in a new Photoshop document:

1. In Photoshop, choose File > **Open as Smart Object.** In the dialog, locate and click a PSD, AI, PDF, JPEG, or TIFF file, then click Open.

2. For an AI or PDF file, the Open as Smart Object dialog opens.**C** For a multipage or multi-image PDF file, or an AI file that contains multiple artboards, choose a Thumbnail Size of Small, Large, or Fit Page for the preview in the dialog, and click the desired thumbnail. Also choose a Crop To option (if you want to exclude blank areas from outside the artwork, choose Bounding Box). Click OK.

3. The file opens as a Smart Object in a new Photoshop document.**D** Save the new file.

To open a file from Camera Raw into Photoshop as an embedded Smart Object in a new document:

1. From Bridge, open a photo into Camera Raw.

2. Apply any needed corrections.

3. Hold down Shift and click **Open Object** (Open Image becomes Open Object). Or if the button Is labeled Open Object (because Open in Photoshop as Smart Objects is checked in the Workflow Options dialog in Camera Raw), click the button without holding down Shift.

4. The photo appears as a Smart Object in a new Photoshop document. Save the new file.

C *We used the Open as Smart Object command to open an Adobe Illustrator (AI) file into Photoshop.*

D *The Illustrator file arrived as a Smart Object in a new Photoshop document.*

To paste Adobe Illustrator art into a Photoshop document as an embedded Smart Object:

1. In Adobe Illustrator, go to Edit/Illustrator CC > Preferences > File Handling & Clipboard. Under Clipboard, check On Quit: **PDF** and **AICB**, and click **Preserve Appearance and Overprints.** Click OK.

2. Continuing in Illustrator, open a file, then copy some artwork or type (Ctrl-C/Cmd-C).

3. Click in a Photoshop document, then paste (Ctrl-V/Cmd-V). The Paste dialog opens.**A**

4. Click Paste As: **Smart Object**, then click OK.

5. To accept the new Smart Object, double-click inside it, or click the Commit Transform button ✔ on the Options bar, or press Enter/Return.

➤ You can also drag artwork into the Libraries panel in Illustrator, then place it as a library-linked Smart Object in Photoshop. ★ See pages 270–272.

A *This little dialog opens if you paste a file into Photoshop.*

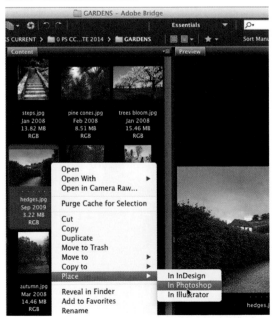

B *In Bridge, we right-clicked an image thumbnail and chose Place > In Photoshop.*

You can also drag or place a file into an existing Photoshop document as a Smart Object. The file can be in any format that is supported by Photoshop, such as an AI, JPEG, PDF, PSD, TIFF, or Camera Raw file. Note: For an Illustrator file, put the art that you want to import on its own artboard.

To place or drag a file into a Photoshop document as an embedded Smart Object:

1. Open a Photoshop document.

2. Go to Edit/Photoshop CC > Preferences > General, check **Resize Image During Place** (to let Photoshop scale placed images automatically), and, more important, check **Always Create Smart Objects When Placing.** Click OK.

3. Click the layer above which you want the Smart Object to appear, then do one of the following:

   Choose File > **Place Embedded.** In the dialog, locate the desired file, then click Place.

   In Bridge, right-click an image thumbnail and choose Place > **In Photoshop** from the context menu.**B**

   From Bridge or the Desktop, drag a file thumbnail into the Photoshop document window.

4. For an Illustrator AI or PDF file, the Open as Smart Object dialog opens. Choose a Thumbnail Size for the preview. If there are multiple thumbnails, click one. And choose a Crop To option (to exclude blank areas outside the artwork, choose Bounding Box).

   For a raw file or a file that was previously edited in Camera Raw, the Camera Raw dialog opens. Make any adjustments to the photo, if desired.

5. Click OK to exit any open dialog. The image will appear within a transform box in the Photoshop document (**A**, next page).

6. *Optional:* To scale the object proportionally, Shift-drag a handle on the transform box. To rotate it, position the pointer outside the transform box (two-headed arrow), then drag.

7. To accept the new Smart Object, double-click inside it (**B**, next page) or click the Commit Transform button ✔ on the Options bar, or press Enter/Return. (Or to cancel it, press Esc.)

➤ When you place vector art into a Photoshop document as a Smart Object, it stays as vector content (and when output, it is rendered at the resolution of the printer).

A *The placed image appeared in our target document. After we double-clicked the transform box …*

B *… the handles and the X disappeared from the object, and the icon for an embedded Smart Object appeared in the layer thumbnail.*

SMART OBJECTS SCALE BETTER

We opened a photo from Camera Raw into Photoshop, scaled it down via a transform handle, then accepted it.

Later, we enlarged the Smart Object: The image quality remained high (the details are still crisp) because Photoshop read pixel data from the original file, not from the image layer.

To compare, we opened the same Camera Raw photo as an ordinary pixel layer, shrank the layer, then later enlarged it: The image quality was diminished.

Editing embedded Smart Objects

To apply some kinds of edits to a Smart Object, such as Smart Filters (see pages 374–378), layer effects, transformations (e.g., scaling), and blending mode and opacity changes, you simply click the layer first.

Edits that change pixel data, however, such as those made with a painting, healing, sharpening, or cloning tool, can't be made directly to a Smart Object (try it, and you'll get an alert regarding rasterizing the layer; click Cancel). To make those types of edits, you double-click the Smart Object thumbnail; the embedded file opens in a separate (temporary) Photoshop window. After you edit, save, and close that window, your changes appear in the Photoshop file. Round-trip editing is similar for a Smart Object made from an Adobe Illustrator file, except the file opens in Illustrator, and for a Camera Raw file, which opens in Camera Raw.

To edit an embedded Smart Object:

1. Double-click a Smart Object thumbnail. If an alert regarding saving your changes appears, click OK.

2. If you created the Smart Object from one or more Photoshop layers, the embedded content will open in a separate, temporary document.**A–C** Edit the document, save it (Ctrl-S/Cmd-S), then close it (Ctrl-W/Cmd-W).

If the Smart Object contains imported content, that content will open in a temporary document in the creator application. For an Adobe Illustrator file, if a PDF Modification Detected alert dialog appears, click "Discard Changes, Preserving Illustrator Editing Capabilities." Edit the document, save it (Ctrl-S/Cmd-S), and close it (Ctrl-W/Cmd-W), then click back in your Photoshop document.

If you created the Smart Object by opening a photo from Camera Raw into Photoshop, it will reopen in Camera Raw. Adjust the settings, then click OK. (To open a photo from Camera Raw into Photoshop as a Smart Object, see page 273 or page 274.)

Note: You have just altered the embedded file. The file from which the original Smart Object was created wasn't altered.

➤ To use the Adobe Camera Raw filter, which gives you access to the Camera Raw features that can be applied from within Photoshop, see page 52.

A *We double-clicked a Smart Object thumbnail on our Layers panel.*

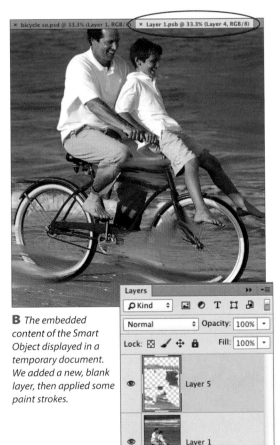

B *The embedded content of the Smart Object displayed in a temporary document. We added a new, blank layer, then applied some paint strokes.*

C *While the temporary document was open, only the layers for the embedded content displayed on the Layers panel.*

When you duplicate an embedded Smart Object via the Duplicate layer command, edits that you apply to the content of the Smart Object (e.g., painting, cloning, or healing strokes) will also appear in the duplicate object, and vice versa. Edits that don't change the content of an embedded file, on the other hand (such as transformations and filters), will appear only in the currently selected Smart Object.

To create duplicates of an embedded Smart Object:

On the Layers panel, click a Smart Object, **A** then press Ctrl-J/Cmd-J (**Duplicate Layer** command). A new Smart Object appears, bearing the same name as the original, with the word "copy" added.

To edit duplicates of an embedded Smart Object:

1. Click the thumbnail in the original or duplicate Smart Object listing, then apply a transformation (see pages 358–359), **B** a Smart Filter (see pages 374–378) (**A**, next page), or a layer effect (see pages 403–405). The edit will appear only in the Smart Object you clicked.

2. Double-click the original or duplicate Smart Object thumbnail, then apply a pixel edit, such as some brush strokes, or create an adjustment layer. Save and close the temporary document. Your edit will appear in the original and duplicate Smart Objects (**B–C**, next page).

COPYING A SMART OBJECT

To create a copy of a Smart Object that isn't linked to the original, right-click the Smart Object listing and choose New Smart Object via Copy. Edits made to either object won't affect the other one. This technique is used in the task on pages 284–285.

A *To create an image that showcases some duplicate Smart Objects, our first step was to convert an image layer ("pasta") to a Smart Object. (Note that in this document, the Background is solid white.)*

B *We duplicated the Smart Object via Ctrl-J/Cmd-J, scaled down and repositioned the duplicate, then copied and repositioned the duplicate twice more. Although our added Smart Objects were created as duplicates, each transformation affected only the currently active layer.*

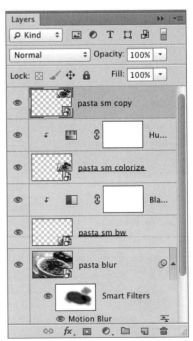

A *We clicked the original Smart Object ("pasta"), applied Filter > Blur > Motion Blur as a Smart Filter, and reduced the layer opacity. The filter didn't alter pixels in the embedded file, so the edit didn't appear in the duplicates of the Smart Object.*

B *Next, we double-clicked the thumbnail for the original Smart Object. The content opened in a temporary document, and the Layers panel listed only the embedded layer. We applied a Levels adjustment, then saved and closed the temporary document; the edit also appeared automatically in all the duplicates.*

C *Finally, we created a Hue/Saturation adjustment layer for the middle duplicate Smart Object and a Black & White adjustment layer for the layer below it. To restrict each adjustment effect to just the underlying Smart Object, we clicked the Clip to Layer button ⬇☐ on the Properties panel.*

Replacing an embedded or linked Smart Object

The Replace Contents command can be used, when desired, to swap existing embedded Smart Object content with a different file. You must use this command if you edit the original file (from which the Smart Object was created) directly in the creator application — not by double-clicking the Smart Object thumbnail — and you want the file to update in Photoshop. For example, say you place Illustrator art into a Photoshop document as an embedded Smart Object. Later, you open the original file directly into Illustrator, then edit, save, and close it. To update the artwork in Photoshop, you must replace the old file with the newly edited one. Note that any transformations, filters, or layer style settings that were applied to the original Smart Object will appear automatically in the replacement content.

The Replace Contents command can also be used to replace a linked Smart Object file with a different file (a file of a different name). To learn about linked Smart Objects, see pages 280–283.

To replace an embedded or linked Smart Object with a new or edited file:

1. On the Layers panel, ◆ right-click a Smart Object listing (not the thumbnail) and choose **Replace Contents** from the context menu.

   For a linked Smart Object, you have the option to access the Replace Contents command another way. Click the Smart Object listing on the Layers panel. Next, on the Properties panel, ▦ click the path listing, and from the menu that opens, choose **Replace Contents**.

2. In the dialog that opens, locate either a replacement file or, for an embedded object, it can be the original (newly edited) file, then click Place.

3. Respond to any dialogs that open (e.g., the Camera Raw dialog or the Open as Smart Object dialog). The replacement image will appear in the original Smart Object and in any duplicates that were made of that object. **A**

A *After completing the sequence shown on the preceding two pages, we right-clicked one of the Smart Object listings and chose Replace Contents, then chose a new food photo to replace the original one. Although we used the command just once, the new image appeared in the Smart Object that we right-clicked, and in all its duplicates. That's an efficient way to work!*

Creating linked Smart Objects

An alternative to creating an embedded Smart Object is to create a Smart Object from an external file that remains separate from—but linked to—your Photoshop file. If an external linked file is edited while the Photoshop files are open, the Smart Object updates automatically in all the documents in which it is being used. Among the advantages to linking Smart Objects are that a single Smart Object can be used in multiple Photoshop documents, the external files remain accessible for editing by multiple designers in a team, and linked Smart Objects produce a smaller Photoshop file size than embedded ones.

To create a linked Smart Object:

1. Open or create a Photoshop document. Go to Edit/Photoshop CC > Preferences > General, check **Resize Image During Place** (to let Photoshop scale placed images automatically), then click OK.

2. Do either of the following:

   Choose File > **Place Linked**. In the dialog, locate the desired file, then click Place.

   Go to Adobe Bridge. With Alt/Option held down, drag an image thumbnail from Bridge into your Photoshop document window.

3. The image appears in a box with an X through it.**A** Press Enter/Return to accept the placed art.

   On the Layers panel, the thumbnail of a linked Smart Object will have this icon: , whereas an embedded Smart Object will have this icon: .

4. If the file that you placed contains layer comps, from the **Layer Comps** menu on the Properties panel, choose a comp to be displayed in the Smart Object: Don't Apply Layer Comp to display the comp that was in effect when the linked file was last saved, or the Last Document State of the linked file, or a specific comp name.**B** To learn about layer comps, see the bonus chapter (Presentation).

   Note: The Properties panel lists the dimensions of the Smart Object, its *x/y* location in the document, and the path to the external file. Roll over the path listing to display the entire path in a Tool Tip.**C**

➤ If you transform a linked Smart Object, your edits will affect only the appearance of the content in Photoshop, not the content of the original file.

➤ Placing a graphic from the Libraries panel into your file will create a library-linked Smart Object.★ (See page 271.)

A *Via the Place Linked command, we placed an image as a linked Smart Object into a Photoshop document.*

B *Via the Layer Comps menu on the Properties panel, we're choosing a comp to be displayed in the Smart Object.*

C *The Properties panel displays info about the currently selected linked Smart Object. Here we're displaying the full path to the external file.*

Working with linked Smart Objects

When editing a linked Smart Object, you can follow the same general rules as when editing an embedded Smart Object. That is, some types of edits (such as Smart Filters, transformations, and changes to layer effect or opacity settings) will alter the appearance of the Smart Object, but not its pixel content. To apply edits that change pixel data (such as painting, healing, cloning, and sharpening), you must edit the contents of the linked file, as described in the task below. In other words, you can't apply pixel edits directly to a linked Smart Object.

To edit the contents of a linked Smart Object:

1. Do one of the following:

   On the Layers panel, ◆ double-click the thumbnail of a linked Smart Object.

   On the Layers panel, right-click next to the name of a linked Smart Object, then choose **Edit Contents** from the context menu.

   On the Layers panel, click the listing for a linked Smart Object, then on the Properties panel, ▦ click **Edit Contents.A**

2. If an alert dialog appears regarding missing or embedded profiles, click OK. Also respond to any alerts that appear regarding nonmatching profiles.

   If the Smart Object was created in a program other than Photoshop, that program will launch.

3. Edit the art as desired.

4. Choose File > Save (Ctrl-S/Cmd-S), then close the temporary document. The Smart Object will update automatically in your Photoshop document.

A *To edit the contents of our selected Smart Object, we're clicking Edit Contents on the Properties panel.*

RASTERIZING A SMART OBJECT

To rasterize a Smart Object (convert it to a standard image layer), right-click it and choose **Rasterize Layer**. If the Smart Object contained any Smart Filters, they will be applied permanently to the rasterized layer, whereas any layer style settings (blending mode, effects, and opacity) will remain editable. If you want to preserve the original Smart Object, duplicate it (Ctrl-J/Cmd-J) before applying the Rasterize Layer command.

If you link an external file to a Photoshop document as a Smart Object, then edit the external file while the Photoshop document is still open, your edits will display automatically in the linked Smart Object.

If you close a Photoshop document that contains a linked Smart Object, then subsequently edit the external file, the content of the Smart Object won't update. After reopening the Photoshop document, in order to display the recent edits to the external file, you must update the Smart Object content, as in the steps below.

To update a linked Smart Object that was edited outside of Photoshop:

On the Layers panel, look for a linked Smart Object that has an out-of-date link alert in its thumbnail, and do either of the following:

Right-click next to the name of the outdated Smart Object, then choose **Update Modified Content** from the context menu.**A**

Click the listing for the linked Smart Object. Display the Properties panel. Click the path listing for the outdated link, and from the menu that opens, choose **Update Modified Content**.

➤ To update the content for *all* linked Smart Objects in the current document, right-click any linked Smart Object listing and choose Update All Modified Content from the context menu.

➤ To update a library-linked Smart Object, ★ see page 272.

A *On the Layers panel, we clicked the listing for a linked Smart Object and are choosing Update Modified Content from the context menu.*

If you close a Photoshop document that contains a linked Smart Object, then move or rename the folder in which the external file is located, the link to the external file will be preserved, and it should update automatically when you reopen the Photoshop document. If Photoshop can't find the external file, however, a dialog will open, offering you a chance to locate and relink the missing file. See page 35.

If, while a Photoshop document is open, you move or rename the folder in which an external Smart Object file is located, the link to the external file will be broken, and you will need to follow the steps below to locate and relink the external file. Resolving the link is necessary because the external file must be accessed when the Photoshop document is output to a printer or packaged for export.

Note: A missing link icon may not appear next to a Smart Object listing until you try to edit the Smart Object content.

To relink a missing Smart Object: ★

1. On the Layers panel, look for a Smart Object that has a missing link alert in its thumbnail, and do either of the following:

   Right-click next to the name of the Smart Object, then choose **Relink to File** from the context menu.

   Click the listing for the linked Smart Object. Display the Properties panel. Click the path listing, then from the menu that opens, choose **Relink to File**.

2. The Locate Missing File dialog opens. Locate and click the missing file name, then click Place. The alert icon should disappear from the Smart Object listing on the Layers and Properties panels.

➤ To replace a linked Smart Object with a different external file, see page 279.

GETTING DATA ON MISSING LINKED OBJECTS

To learn the total number of missing and modified Smart Objects (including library assets) in your current document, from the Status bar menu at the bottom of the document window, choose Smart Objects; Missing and Changed totals will display on the Status bar. Similarly, to display this data on the Info panel, ❶ choose Panel Options from the Info panel menu, check Smart Objects, then click OK.

If desired, at any time, you can convert a linked Smart Object to an embedded one. The link to the external file will be broken, and a copy of the Smart Object content will be embedded into your Photoshop document. The appearance of the object in the document remains the same. Note that embedding a file will increase the storage size of your document; the new size will be apparent after you use the Save command.

To convert a linked Smart Object to an embedded one:

Do either of the following:

On the Layers panel, right-click next to the name of a linked Smart Object, then choose **Embed Linked** from the context menu.

On the Layers panel,◥ click the listing for a linked Smart Object,**A** then on the Properties panel,◳ click **Embed**.

Note that the icon within the Smart Object thumbnail has changed.**B**

➤ If you embed a linked Smart Object that contains "nested" imagery from another linked external file, that imagery will also be embedded, and the link between that file and your Photoshop document will also be broken.

The Convert to Linked command does the reverse of the above, which is that it converts an embedded Smart Object to a linked one. This is useful, say, if you want to organize the contents of multiple Smart Objects into one folder so they're more readily accessible for external editing; or if you created a Smart Object from multiple layers and you want to make those layers available for use in other Photoshop documents; or if you open a legacy Photoshop document and you want to convert some embedded Smart Objects in that document to linked objects.

To convert an embedded Smart Object to a linked one:

1. Do either of the following:

   On the Layers panel,◥ right-click the listing for an embedded Smart Object and choose **Convert to Linked**.

   On the Layers panel, click the listing for a linked Smart Object, then on the Properties panel,◳ click **Convert to Linked**.

2. The Save dialog opens. Choose a location in which to save the external linked file, then click Save.

A On the Layers panel, the thumbnail of a linked Smart Object has a link icon.

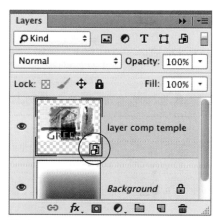

B After we applied the Embed Linked command, the icon in the thumbnail changed to an embedded Smart Object icon.

FILTERING SMART OBJECT LISTINGS ON THE LAYERS PANEL

From the Filter Type menu on the Layers panel, choose Smart Object, then click one or more of these buttons: Up-to-Date Library Linked Smart Objects, ▣★ Up-to-Date Locally Linked Smart Objects, ▣ Out-of-Date Linked Smart Objects, ▲ Missing Linked Smart Objects, ❓ or Embedded Smart Objects. ▣ (To turn filtering off, click the **Layer Filtering On/Off** button. ▮) To learn more about filtering layer listings, see pages 162–163.

Combining multiple "exposures"

You may have encountered this common dilemma when photographing a subject against a bright sky or in front of a window: If you set the exposure properly for the figure or object in the foreground, the brighter background areas are overexposed. One way to produce an image that captures the "best of both worlds" is to shoot dual exposures — one set for the foreground and one set for the background — and then combine them into one image in Photoshop. If you didn't bracket your photos during the shoot, an alternative method (described here) is to produce two exposure variations of a single raw photo via Camera Raw, then reveal the best areas of the two files in Photoshop by editing a layer mask.

To combine two "exposures" into one photo:

1. Open a raw photo into Camera Raw.**A** (Note: Avoid using a JPEG photo, which is unlikely to contain enough pixel data for this technique to work successfully.)

2. *Optional:* Use sliders in the **Basic** tab 🔘 to adjust the exposure properly for the shadows and lower midtones.

3. Hold down Shift (Open Image becomes Open Object) and click **Open Object**. Note: If Open in Photoshop as Smart Objects is checked in the Workflow Options dialog, the button will be labeled Open Object, in which case you should click it without holding down Shift.

COMBINING EXPOSURES VIA THE CAMERA RAW FILTER

When creating two different exposures of the same photo, an alternative method would be to apply the Camera Raw filter two times. Open a photo from Camera Raw into Photoshop as a **Smart Object** (hold down Shift and click Open Object). **Duplicate** the Smart Object layer.

Click the original Smart Object, then apply the **Camera Raw filter** using the Basic tab to adjust the exposure for the shadows and lower midtones. Next, click the duplicate of the Smart Object, then apply the **Camera Raw filter** using the Basic tab to adjust the exposure for the upper midtones and highlights. (When applied to Smart Objects, the Camera Raw filter will become an editable Smart Filter; see pages 374–378.)

Finally, follow the task for blending two exposure versions via a layer mask (see page 286).

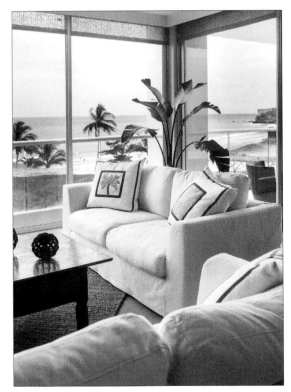

A *Because the wide range of light conditions in this scene couldn't be captured in one shot, the interior was correctly exposed but the exterior was overexposed.*

4. The photo opens as a Smart Object in a new Photoshop document. Save the file.

5. Right-click near the layer name and choose **New Smart Object via Copy** from the context menu (don't use Ctrl-J/Cmd-J, the Duplicate Layer command).**A**

6. Double-click the thumbnail on the copy of the Smart Object to open the photo into Camera Raw. Use sliders in the **Basic** tab to set the proper exposure for the upper midtones and highlights,**B** then click OK. Because you followed our directive to copy the Smart Object via the New Smart Object via Copy command (it isn't a duplicate of the original one), your newest Camera Raw edits affected just the copy.

7. Save the file again. To blend the best areas of the two layers, follow the steps on the next page.

A *The New Smart Object via Copy command created a copy of the Smart Object.*

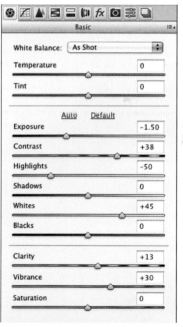

B *We opened the copy of the Smart Object into Camera Raw, used sliders in the Basic tab to recover highlight details (particularly in the exterior areas), then clicked OK to return to our Photoshop file.*

To blend two exposure versions via a layer mask:

1. Continuing in Photoshop, on the Layers panel, ⬗ click the upper of the two Smart Objects. If more of the properly exposed areas are on the upper layer, click the Add Layer Mask button ⬚ to create a white mask; if more of the properly exposed areas are in the lower layer, Alt-click/Option-click the button to create a black mask. (To compare the two exposures, hide the upper layer, then show it.)

2. Choose the Brush tool ✎ (B or Shift-B), a Soft Round tip, Normal mode, and Opacity of 80–100%.

3. If you created a white mask, make the Foreground color black; if you created a black mask, make the Foreground color white.

4. Press [or] to set the brush diameter, then apply strokes to hide areas of the current layer and expose the underlying layer, or to reveal areas of the current layer and hide the underlying layer. **A–C** If you need to remask any areas, press X and paint with the reverse color.

A *We added a black mask to a copy of the Smart Object, then with the Brush tool (100% Opacity) and white as the Foreground color, we applied brush strokes in the window areas to reveal the corrected background and sky on that layer.*

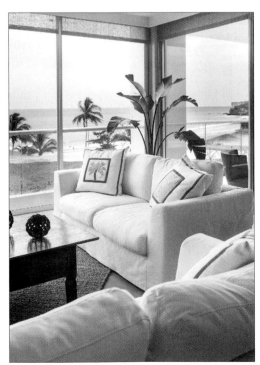

B *In the original image (shown for comparison), only the interior of the room has the correct exposure.*

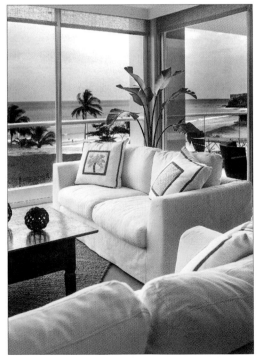

C *In the final image, the exposure data from the two Smart Objects is combined. The sky colors are stronger and you can see more details in the landscape.*

Fading the edge of a layer via a gradient in a layer mask

Once you have gathered multiple layers into one document (regardless of the method used), you can soften the edges of any layer to make it look as if it's blending into the underlying layers. Here this is done by applying a gradient to a layer mask. This technique works equally well for image, type, and shape layers.

To fade the edge of a layer via a gradient in a layer mask:

1. Gather several layers into a target document by following the steps on page 262, 266, or 268. Position and scale the layers with the Move tool as necessary.**A**

2. On the Layers panel, ▼ click one of the layers, then click the **Add Layer Mask** button.▢ Keep the mask thumbnail selected.

3. Choose the **Gradient** tool ▇ (G or Shift-G).

4. On the Options bar, do the following;

   Click the Gradient picker arrowhead on the Options bar, then click the "Black, White" gradient. Note: If you don't see this preset, choose Reset Gradients from the picker menu, then click OK In the alert dialog. "Black, White" is the third gradient in the default library.

   Click the Linear Gradient button.▇

   Choose Mode: Normal and an Opacity of 100%.

5. In the image, start dragging horizontally or diagonally from where you want the complete fadeout to be located, and stop dragging where you want the layer to be fully visible.**B** Hold down Shift while dragging to constrain the angle to an increment of 45°.

   The gradient will appear in the layer mask, and the content of that layer will be partially hidden **C** (see also **A–B**, next page).

➤ To redo the mask effect, click the layer mask thumbnail, then with the Gradient tool at 100% Opacity, drag in the document again in a new direction or from a different starting point.

A *We dragged layers from other documents onto our target image (a photo of burlap), scaled and repositioned the new layers, and rotated a couple of them.*

B *We added a mask to the "BLUE" layer, chose the Gradient tool and the "Black, White" preset, then dragged to the left, as shown by the arrow.*

C *The gradient in the mask is hiding the right side of the "BLUE" layer.*

A *Next, we added a layer mask to the "WALL" layer, and dragged diagonally with the Gradient tool (note the gradient in each mask).*

B *This is the final image.*

HIDING A SEAM WITH A BRUSH

You can also edit a layer mask with the Brush tool, a basic Photoshop technique that is described fully on page 193.

The edge of a layer in this image is partially hidden by a gradient that we applied to the layer mask. To hide the seam, we chose the Brush tool, a Soft Round brush, an Opacity value of 100%, black as the Foreground color, and a large brush diameter. We clicked the layer mask thumbnail, then dragged downward.

With a couple of quick swipes of the brush, the seam is masked.

Aligning and distributing layers

Using buttons on the Options bar, you can align the nontransparent content of two or more selected layers by their edges or centers, or equalize the spacing among three or more selected layers. The buttons work for image, type, and shape layers.

To align and/or distribute layers:

1. Do either of the following:

    On the Layers panel, ❖ Ctrl-click/Cmd-click two or more layers, then choose the **Move** tool ⊕ (V).

    Choose the **Move** tool ⊕ (V), then check **Auto-Select** and choose **Layer** on the Options bar. In the document window, click a layer, then Shift-click one or more additional layers. **A**

2. Do either or both of the following:

    Click one of the "Align" buttons on the Options bar. **B**

    If three or more layers are selected, you can click one of the "Distribute" buttons on the Options bar. **C**

➤ Oops! Clicked the wrong button? Choose the Undo command, then try a different button.

➤ To align layers to the edge of a selection, create a selection before following the steps above.

A *We chose the Move tool, then selected four layers.*

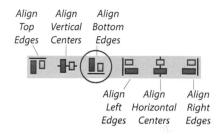

Align Top Edges · Align Vertical Centers · Align Bottom Edges

Align Left Edges · Align Horizontal Centers · Align Right Edges

B *We clicked the Align Bottom Edges button …*

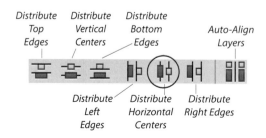

Distribute Top Edges · Distribute Vertical Centers · Distribute Bottom Edges · Auto-Align Layers

Distribute Left Edges · Distribute Horizontal Centers · Distribute Right Edges

C *… then clicked the Distribute Horizontal Centers button.*

Using the Clone Stamp tool and the Clone Source panel

By applying strokes with the Clone Stamp tool, you can clone all or part of an image from one layer to another in the same document or between documents. This tool is useful for creative montaging, commercial retouching, and video editing. Using the Clone Source panel, you can assign and keep track of up to five different source documents (represented by a row of buttons at the top of the panel), as well as transform the source pixels before or as you clone them.

To use the Clone Stamp tool and the Clone Source panel:

1. Open one or more RGB documents to be used as source imagery, and create or open a target document.

2. Choose the **Clone Stamp** tool ▲ (S or Shift-S). On the Options bar, choose a Soft Round brush, a Mode, an Opacity percentage, and a Flow percentage, and check Aligned.

   Optional: If you have a stylus and tablet, you can activate the Pressure for Opacity button ☒ and/or the Pressure for Size button ☒ on the Options bar.

   Optional: If the source file contains any adjustment layers and you want the Clone Stamp tool to ignore their effects when sampling, activate the Ignore Adjustment Layers When Cloning button.☒

3. Show the Clone Source panel.☒ **A** By default, the first source button is selected. Check **Show Overlay** and **Auto Hide**, then set the **Opacity** to around 35–50% so you'll be able to preview the source image as an overlay (a faint version of the source layer). If you want the overlay to display only within the brush cursor instead of across the whole document, check **Clipped**.

4. In the target document, create a new, blank layer.

5. Click the source document tab. From the **Sample** menu on the Options bar, choose the part of the document from which you want to clone: **Current Layer**, **Current & Below**, or **All Layers**. For either of the first two options, also click a layer.

6. Alt-click/Option-click an area in the image to set the source point.**B** The source file and layer will be assigned to, and will be listed below, the first source button on the Clone Source panel.

7. Click the target document tab.

8. To position the clone, move the pointer over the image without clicking. Adjust the tool diameter by pressing [or], then start dragging to make the cloned pixels appear (**A**, next page). The overlay will disappear temporarily (because you checked Auto Hide), then will reappear when you release the mouse. (For other ways to transform the overlay, see the next page.)

9. To clone from another open document, click the second source button at the top of the Clone Source panel, then repeat steps 4–8. At any time, you can switch between clone sources by clicking a different button.

   Beware! The Clone Source panel keeps the links active only while the source documents are open. If you close a source document, its link to the Clone Source panel is broken. We warned ya.

➤ To use the Clone Stamp tool to retouch imagery within the same document, see pages 326–327.

A *Using the Clone Source panel, you can switch between multiple sources, transform the clone overlay, and choose display options.*

B *With the Clone Stamp tool, we held down Alt/ Option and clicked in a source document.*

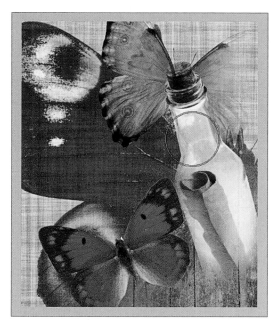

A *We're dragging with the Clone Stamp tool on a new, blank layer in our target document to "brush in" part of a bottle image layer from a source document.*

B *Before we began cloning the bottle, we clicked the Flip Horizontal button on the Clone Source panel and changed the Offset values (as shown in the panel at right).*

When using the Clone Stamp tool, the position and orientation values of the source overlay stick unless you change them. Between strokes with the tool, you can reposition, scale, flip, or rotate the overlay via the Clone Source panel or via keyboard shortcuts. New settings will apply only to the currently selected clone source.

To reposition, scale, flip, or rotate the clone source overlay:

With the **Clone Stamp** tool ▣ selected and an overlay displaying in your document, do any of the following (on the Clone Source panel, you can use the scrubby sliders):

To reposition the source overlay, uncheck Clipped, then change the **Offset X** and/or **Y** values on the panel or Alt-Shift-drag/Option-Shift-drag in the image.

To scale the source overlay, hold down Alt-Shift/Option-Shift and press (and keep pressing) [or]. Or to scale the overlay via the panel, activate the **Maintain Aspect Ratio** button ▣ to preserve the aspect ratio of the source imagery, then change the **W** or **H** value. To preserve the image quality, avoid scaling the source more than 120% or –120%.

To flip the source, click the **Flip Horizontal** ▣ and/or **Flip Vertical** ▣ button.**B**

To rotate the overlay, change the **Rotate** value, ▣ or hold down Alt-Shift/Option-Shift and press (and keep pressing) < or >.

➤ To restore the default flip, scale, and rotation values to the current clone source, click the Reset Transform button. ▣

➤ To show the Clone Source panel when the Clone Stamp tool is selected, you can click the Toggle Clone Source panel button ▣ on the Options bar.

Creating a panorama

The Camera Raw Merge to Panorama command combines two or more photos of the same scene into a single panoramic image. Merging via Camera Raw has become our preferred choice because it enables us to correct one of the source photos, then have those settings applied automatically to the other source photos used in the panorama. Better results are achieved because you are working with raw data from the original scene and can correct the resulting panorama right in Camera Raw at any time.

To merge photos into a panorama via Camera Raw: ★

1. In Bridge, select the thumbnails that will be used for the panorama. Double-click one of the thumbnails to open them all in Camera Raw.

2. On the filmstrip panel in Camera Raw, click a thumbnail, then apply corrections to it using any of the Camera Raw features.

3. Right-click a thumbnail and choose **Select All** (Ctrl-A/Cmd-A) from the context menu. Right-click again and choose **Merge to Panorama** (Ctrl-M/Cmd-M). **A**

4. In the **Panorama Merge Preview** dialog, drag a corner to enlarge the dialog. Uncheck **Auto Crop** to better evaluate how the different options merge the photos. Click a Projection option:

Spherical, **Cylindrical**, or **Perspective**. After evaluating, recheck **Auto Crop**.

5. Click **Merge**. In the **Merge Results** dialog, enter a name and choose a folder location for the panorama. Click **Save**. (Hold down Alt/Option and click to bypass this dialog and save the image in the same folder as the source photos.) Camera Raw will apply color matching and distortion correction automatically to the merged panorama, then display the results in its preview.

6. Make any further corrections to the resulting panorama (**A–C**, next page). Click **Done**. A .dng file will be saved to the folder you chose in the previous step.

7. In Bridge, double-click the .dng file to open it into Camera Raw. Make any further edits, if desired. Click **Open Image** to open a converted image into Photoshop. Make any edits to the image (the .dng file will not be altered), then save it in the Photoshop (PSD) format. Done!

COMBINING SHOTS VIA AUTO-ALIGN LAYERS

It can be a challenge to get a group of people to smile simultaneously for a portrait, or to have them refrain from blinking. If you take multiple shots of the same scene, you can blend the choice areas of two shots in Photoshop via Auto-Align Layers.

Open two RGB photos from the same shoot, then choose a 2-Up option (Window > Arrange submenu). Shift-drag the Background from the Layers panel of one photo into the window of the other. Redisplay just the target document; save your file.

On the Layers panel, Shift-click the two layers, then choose Edit > **Auto-Align Layers**. In the dialog, click a Projection option: **Reposition** if you used a tripod, or **Auto** for other shooting situations. Click OK.

Click the upper layer, Alt-click/Option-click the **Add Layer Mask** button, and keep the mask thumbnail selected. Choose the **Brush** tool, a Soft Round tip, Normal mode, and 100% Opacity. Zoom in, then paint strokes with white as the Foreground color to reveal the desirable parts of the top layer. To touch up the mask, decrease the brush diameter and zoom in more. Apply brush strokes along the edges of shapes to reveal more of the top layer, or press X and apply strokes with black to reveal more of the underlying layer.

A *In Camera Raw, select all the source thumbnails in the filmstrip panel, then choose Merge to Panorama.*

A *We opened these three source photos for our panorama into Camera Raw. We used the Basic and HSL/Grayscale tabs to correct the exposure and improve the color in the source photo on the left, then chose the Merge to Panorama command.*

B *The Spherical option in the Panorama Merge Preview dialog produced this seamless image. Notice that the corrections applied to the leftmost source photo were automatically applied to the entire merged image.*

C *After clicking Merge, we applied further corrections to the resulting panorama thumbnail while still in Camera Raw.*

SHOOTING PHOTOS FOR A PANORAMA

To get good results from the Merge to Panorama command, follow these guidelines from Adobe:

► For better alignment, and to help prevent distortion, use a **tripod** and shoot all the photos from the exact same spot, in the sequence needed for the panorama.

► Choose the same **focal length** (zoom) setting for all the photos.

► **Overlap** the viewing area from one shot to the next by approximately 40%.

► Choose the same **exposure** or **aperture** setting for all the shots for better color matching and more seamless blending across the merged image.

Using Smart Guides, ruler guides, and column guide layout

Sometimes a great composite image comes together in a serendipitous way without much forethought or careful alignment. At other times — say, if your Photoshop image must fit perfectly within the confines of a specific Web or print page layout — you need to plan ahead or position objects more precisely. To accomplish this, you can use any of the Photoshop layout features, such as grids, rulers, or guides.

Our favorite alignment feature is Smart Guides. If this feature is on in a multilayer document, and you drag a layer, temporary, magnetic (default color magenta) guide lines will appear where that layer nears the top, middle, or bottom edge of content on another layer. You can also use this feature to align multiple layers, or to create and align a copy of a layer. Note: To use Smart Guides while moving a path, use the Path Selection tool instead of the Move tool.

To use Smart Guides while moving or copying a layer:

1. Verify that both View > **Extras** and View > Show > **Smart Guides** have a check mark.

2. Choose the **Move** tool ⊕ (V)

3. On the Layers panel, select one or more layers.

4. To **move** the layer(s), drag it near the top, middle, or bottom of content on another layer.**A** Or to **copy** the layer(s), press and hold down Alt/Option, then start dragging. The black label shows the distance you have moved the layer. Let the layer snap to a horizontal or vertical guide, or to the intersection of two guides. If you create a copy, a colored label shows the distance between the bounding box of the original layer and the copy.**B–C**

➤ To show the distance (in a label) between the currently active layer and the edges of the canvas, hold down Ctrl/Cmd and position the pointer outside the bounding box. With Ctr/Cmd pressed, roll over an object on another layer; the distance between those layers shows in a colored label.

SHOWING EXTRAS

The View > **Extras** command (Ctrl-H/Cmd-H) shows or hides whichever features are currently enabled on the View > **Show** submenu (e.g., the Grid, [ruler] Guides, Smart Guides). These choices affect the current document and any documents that you subsequently open.

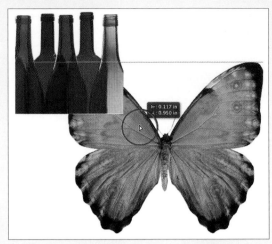

A As we drag the butterfly layer, we're aligning its upper edge with the vertical center of the bottles layer via a Smart Guide.

B To copy a shape layer, we're dragging it to the right with Alt/Option held down. The magenta label indicates the distance between the original layer and copies; the black label indicates the distance the layer has been moved.

C We selected the original and duplicate shape layers, then dragged downward to copy those layers and align the copies.

When you enable the Rulers command in Photoshop, rulers display along the top and left sides of the document window. From the rulers, you can create magnetic, movable horizontal and vertical guides.

To show or hide the rulers:

Choose View > **Rulers** or press Ctrl-R/Cmd-R.

Move the pointer in the image (mouse button up), and you'll notice that its current location is indicated by a dotted marker on each ruler.**A**

➤ To change the units for both rulers quickly, right-click in either ruler and choose a unit from the context menu. Or to get to the Units & Rulers panel in the Preferences dialog quickly, where you can change the units and other settings, double-click either ruler. Changing the unit in one location also changes it in the other.

➤ To change the ruler origin (so you can measure distances from a specific location in the image), starting from the upper-left corner where the two rulers meet, drag diagonally into the image. To restore the default origin, double-click the upper-left corner.

Guides that you create from the horizontal or vertical ruler can be repositioned or removed at any time. Like Smart Guides, they are magnetic, but unlike Smart Guides, they linger onscreen and save with your document.

To create ruler guides:

Show the rulers, then drag from the horizontal or vertical ruler into the image, releasing the mouse where you want the guide to appear.

If View > Snap is checked as you create a guide, you can snap it to a selection, to the edge of content on the currently selected layer,**B–C** or to a grid line, if the grid is displayed.

➤ To show the guides if they are hidden, choose View > Show > Guides.

➤ You can relocate an existing guide with the Move tool (double-arrow pointer), provided guides aren't locked (see the next page). As you move a guide, its current *x* or *y* position displays in a readout.

➤ Hold down Alt/Option as you create a guide to swap its orientation from vertical to horizontal, or vice versa.

➤ To change the color and other attributes of guides, Smart Guides, and the grid, see page 468.

A As we move a layer, the current location of the pointer is indicated by a dotted line on each ruler.

B To create a guide, we are dragging downward into the image from the horizontal ruler.

C We snapped the new guide to the top edge of the butterfly layer (which was selected).

When the View > Snap command is on, as you move a selection or layer it will snap to a guide or the edge of content in the document with a little magnetic tug.

To turn on the Snap To feature:

1. Choose View > Snap To > **Guides**, **Grid**, **Layers**, **Slices**, **Document Bounds**, or **All** (of the above). Note: For the Snap To > Guides, Grid, or Slices option to be available, that option must have a check mark on the View > Show submenu.

2. Make sure View > **Snap** has a check mark (Ctrl-Shift-;/Cmd-Shift-;).

3. With the **Move** tool (V), drag a selection or layer near a guide, the edge of layer content, or the edge of the canvas. It will "snap" to your target.

To reposition any of your ruler guides (Move tool), you must unlock them first. Conversely, to prevent guides from being moved, lock 'em up.

To lock or unlock all ruler guides:

Choose View > **Lock Guides** or press Ctrl-Alt-;/Cmd-Option-;.

To remove one or all ruler guides:

Do either of the following:

To remove an unlocked guide, hold down V (Move tool), then drag the guide off the edge of the document window. (Don't press Backspace/Delete, which would delete the current layer!)

To remove all guides from the document, choose View > **Clear Guides**.

Print and Web designs are often built on a multi-column guide layout to facilitate easy alignment of elements and create uniformity between designs. You can use the New Guide Layout command to quickly create multiple column guides.

To create a multicolumn guide layout: ★

1. With a Photoshop file open, choose View > **New Guide Layout**.

2. In the New Guide Layout dialog, **A** check Preview, then do any of the following:

Choose a preset layout from the **Preset** menu.

Check **Columns**, then enter a value in the **Number** field to create multiple columns. Enter a **Width**

value for a specific width (in any measurement unit used in Photoshop) and check Preview again, or leave the field blank to evenly distribute columns across the canvas width.

Check **Rows**, then enter a value in the **Number** field to create multiple rows. Enter a **Height** value for a specific height and check Preview again, or leave the field blank to evenly distribute rows along the canvas height.

Change either **Gutter** value to modify the space between columns or rows. Check Preview again.

Check **Margin**, then enter values in any of the Margin fields to create guides that are indented in from the top, left, bottom, or right edge of the canvas.

3. Click OK.

➤ Check Center Columns, if you have entered a value in the Width field, to center the custom-width columns on the canvas.

➤ Check Clear Existing Guides to delete any previously created guides, including ruler guides.

➤ Use the scrubby slider over any of the field names to increase or reduce the current value. Hold down Alt/Option when using the scrubby slider to change the value in smaller increments.

➤ From the Preset menu, choose Save Preset to save the existing layout as a preset (and list it in this menu), or Load Preset to load in a saved preset, or Delete Preset to open a dialog for deleting a preset.

A *The New Guide Layout dialog can be used to create a multi-column guide layout.*

In this chapter, you will paint with the Brush tool, customize your brush using a wide assortment of controls, and manage brush presets. You will also create bristle, erodible, and airbrush tips for the Mixer Brush tool, use the Mixer Brush to transform a photo into a painting, and use the History Brush tool to restore areas of an image.

Note: Although we recommend using a stylus and tablet for the instructions in this chapter, it's not a requirement.

Using the Brush tool

Before delving into the complexities of the Brush panel, take a few minutes to familiarize yourself with the Brush tool. To do this, you will choose a brush preset for the tool and choose Options bar settings to control its behavior.

To use the Brush tool:

1. Click an image layer or create a new, blank layer.
   Optional: To confine your brush strokes to a specific area of the layer, create a selection.

2. Choose the **Brush** tool ✏ (B or Shift-B).

3. Choose a Foreground color.

4. Right-click in the image to display the Brush Preset picker, then either click a brush in the scrolling window, **A** or click a recently used brush in the horizontal tray.

Continued on the following page

A *On the Brush Preset picker, click a brush and, if desired, change any of the brush settings temporarily.*

PAINTING

14

USE YOUR GRAPHICS PROCESSOR

In order to access on-image hardness and opacity controls for brushes (see page 131), and to enhance painting performance (particularly for large brushes), go to Preferences > Performance and make sure Use Graphics Processor is checked (if it's not, check it, click OK, then close and reopen your document).

Optional: Change the brush Size or Hardness setting, drag the arrowhead on the circle to change the brush angle, or drag one of the little circles to change the roundness.

Note: You can also open the Brush Preset picker by clicking the arrowhead or thumbnail on the Options bar.

5. On the Options bar, do the following:

    Choose a blending **Mode**.

    Choose an **Opacity** percentage. At 100%, the stroke will completely cover the underlying pixels.

    Choose a **Flow** percentage for the rate at which "pigment" is applied (for thick or thin coverage).

6. *Optional:* If you're using a stylus and tablet, you can activate the Pressure for Opacity button and/or the Pressure for Size button on the Options bar.

7. *Optional:* If you want to edit only nontransparent pixels on the current layer, activate the Lock Transparent Pixels button on the Layers panel.

8. Draw brush strokes in the image. Feel free to change the Options bar settings between strokes.

➤ To choose custom settings for the Brush tool — beyond the basics that are covered in this task — see the next section.

➤ To draw a straight stroke with a painting tool (e.g., the Brush tool), hold down Shift while dragging.

➤ To sample a color with a temporary Eyedropper, Alt-click/Option-click in the document.

➤ Via the Brush Presets panel menu, you can change the panel view.

Customizing a brush

On pages 130–131, you learned how to set basic size, hardness, and opacity settings for a brush preset. Here you will use a wide array of features on the Brush panel to further customize the characteristics of a brush. Brushes are used with the Brush, Mixer Brush, Eraser, and History Brush tools (all of which are featured in this chapter), as well as with the Pencil, Clone Stamp, Pattern Stamp, Art History Brush, Blur, Sharpen, Smudge, Dodge, and Burn tools.

   On the Brush panel, most of the settings for customizing brushes are organized into option sets; a few lone options are simply switched on or off. Many of the options add randomness or variation to a stroke, such as to its shape, texture, or color.

   The availability of options varies depending on the currently chosen tool and tip, and some options apply only to a graphics tablet and stylus (when an option set is unavailable, the set name is dimmed). The choices are vast, so we'll just focus on a few of our favorites. With practice, you'll learn which options and settings suit your painting style.

To customize a brush via the Brush panel:

1. To see the greatest differences among the settings, choose the **Brush** tool or **Mixer Brush** tool (B or Shift-B). You could also choose one of the tools that we listed in the first paragraph of this section.

2. To show the Brush panel, click the panel tab or icon, or click the Toggle Brush Panel button on the Options bar or Brush Presets panel. Click **Brush Tip Shape** in the top-left corner of the panel, and for this task, click a round or static tip (see the sidebar on this page) (**A**, next page).

3. As you adjust settings for the tip, keep an eye on the stroke preview at the bottom of the panel:

    To change the brush **Size** (diameter), use the slider or scrubby slider.

    ➤ To restore the original size to a static tip, click the Restore Original Size button.

    To change the **Angle** (slant) of an elliptical tip, use the scrubby slider, or drag the arrowhead around the circle, or enter a specific angle.

SHOPPING FOR BRUSH TIPS

When you load a library of brush tips onto the Brush Presets panel (see page 133 or 135), the presets will also appear in the scrolling window on the Brush panel. Not seeing them on the Brush panel? Click Brush Tip Shape at the top of the panel. Below are the basic icons (or examples of them).

To change the **Roundness** of the tip (make it more oval or more circular), **B** use the scrubby slider or drag either of the two small dark circles on the ellipse inward or outward.

To change the **Hardness** of the tip (feather or sharpen its edge), **C** use the scrubby slider.

To control the distance between marks within the stroke, check **Spacing**, then move the slider, **D–E** or turn this option off to let the speed of your brush stroke control the spacing.

➤ If you're going to paint with a mouse and you want to produce variations in the stroke via the Jitter and Minimum sliders (found in other sections of this panel), set the Spacing value above 10.

4. Next you'll customize the behavior variations for the brush using five of the option sets on the panel. Checking the box for an option set activates the current settings for that set; clicking the set name both activates the current settings and displays the set options.

Continued on the following page

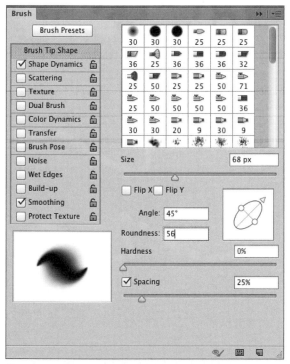

A *In the Brush panel, you can select a brush tip, customize it via an assortment of options, and save it as a preset. The preview updates dynamically as you change the settings.*

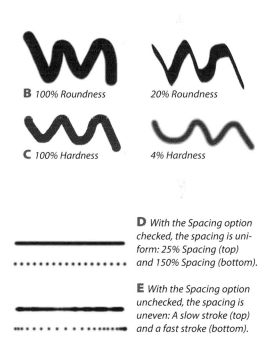

B *100% Roundness*   *20% Roundness*

C *100% Hardness*   *4% Hardness*

D *With the Spacing option checked, the spacing is uniform: 25% Spacing (top) and 150% Spacing (bottom).*

E *With the Spacing option unchecked, the spacing is uneven: A slow stroke (top) and a fast stroke (bottom).*

To control the amount of allowable variation in the brush tip shape, click **Shape Dynamics**, then do any of the following:

Choose **Size Jitter,A Angle Jitter**, and **Roundness Jitter** values to establish an allowable amount of random variation for those attributes. For more noticeable variation, increase the Spacing value in the Brush Tip Shape option set.

Check **Brush Projection** to enable round and static tips to respond to stylus movement, or to Tilt and Rotation settings in the Brush Pose option set. Note that enabling Brush Projection disables the Roundness Jitter option.

If you're using a stylus, from each of the **Control** menus, choose which stylus feature is to control the variation for that option. Note that variations will occur even when this setting is Off.

Choose **Minimum Diameter** and **Minimum Roundness** percentages.

5. To control the placement of pigment in the stroke, click **Scattering**, then do any of the following:

Check **Both Axes** to scatter pigment along and perpendicular to the stroke you draw, or uncheck this option to scatter pigment only perpendicular to the stroke.**B** For a stylus, choose a Control option.

Choose a **Scatter** percentage to control how far the pigment can stray from the stroke. The lower the Scatter percentage, the more solid the stroke.

Choose a **Count** value to control the number of marks in the stroke (you may need to increase the Spacing value to see any effect).

Choose a **Count Jitter** percentage to control the amount of variation in the Count.**C**

6. For the Brush tool, you can use the **Color Dynamics** option set to control the variation in hue, saturation, and brightness. Check **Apply per Tip** to allow jitter settings to display randomly in each tip mark in a stroke, for a multicolor effect.

7. To display a texture in the stroke, click **Texture**, then do all of the following:

Click the **Pattern** picker thumbnail, then click a pattern swatch. (Via the picker menu, you can load the Artist Surfaces or Artists Brushes Canvas library.)

Choose a **Scale** value for the pattern.

100% Size Jitter, 25% spacing

A *0% Size Jitter*

0% Scatter, 100% Spacing

500% Scatter, the Both Axes option checked

B *500% Scatter, the Both Axes option unchecked*

0% Count Jitter, 100% Spacing

C *100% Count Jitter: The Count varies randomly from 1% to 100% of the Count value.*

Choose values for **Brightness** and **Contrast**. For a more prominent texture, choose a low Brightness value and a high Contrast value.

Choose a **Depth** value to simulate the depth of a fibrous drawing surface. High values produce more ridges and therefore a more noticeable texture.**A**

A *Canvas pattern, 200% Scale, –90 Brightness, 80 Contrast*

8. To control how randomly the overall stroke opacity can vary as you use the tool, and to make the Texture option more pronounced,**B** click **Transfer**, then do either or both of the following:

    Choose an **Opacity Jitter** percentage for the amount the opacity can vary.**C–D** To control the fading, for a stylus, choose a Control option, or for a mouse, choose Off or Fade.

    Choose a **Flow Jitter** percentage to control the rate at which paint is applied. A high Flow Jitter will make the stroke dry and blotchy, but that may be the look you're after. For a stylus, choose a Control option; for a mouse, choose Off or Fade.

B *The same Texture settings as above with Transfer: 60% Opacity Jitter, 60% Flow Jitter*

9. *Beware!* The custom settings that you have chosen are only temporary. To save them as a preset for future use, click the **New Brush** button ⬚ at the bottom of the Brush panel. Enter a descriptive name in the Brush Name dialog, check Capture Brush Size in Preset (if desired), then click OK. Your saved preset will appear at the bottom of the Brush Presets panel and the Brush Preset picker.

C *10% Opacity Jitter, 10% Flow Jitter*

10. You're ready to paint with your customized brush!

➤ Click the open 🔓 or closed 🔒 lock icon for an option set to prevent or allow the settings in that set from being edited, regardless of the current preset.

D *80% Opacity Jitter, 80% Flow Jitter*

An Erodible Point tip behaves like a soft pencil: The beginning of the stroke is sharp and then it gradually wears down (widening and becoming more blunt) toward the end of the stroke.

To use an Erodible Point tip:

1. Choose the **Brush** tool ✎ or **Mixer Brush** tool. ✎

2. On the left side of the Brush panel, click Brush Tip Shape, then click an Erodible Point tip ▰▰ in the scrolling window.

3. Activate the **Live Tip Brush Preview** button 👁 (see the sidebar at right).

4. Choose a **Size** value to set the width of the end of the stroke (where the tip is worn down), and

Continued on the following page

USING THE LIVE TIP BRUSH PREVIEW

To display a schematic of the current brush tip that updates dynamically as you change the settings, activate the Live Tip Brush Preview button 👁 on the Brush or Brush Presets panel. For this feature to work, Use Graphics Processor must be checked in Edit/Photoshop CC > Preferences > Performance. Note: The Live Tip Brush Preview doesn't display for round or static tips.

➤ To reposition the preview, move the pointer over the top-left corner, then drag the black bar.

➤ To view the current tip at various angles, keep clicking in the preview.

choose a **Softness** value to control how quickly the tip erodes. Lower values keep the tip more sharp.**A**

5. From the **Shape** menu, choose a preset shape.

6. *Optional:* To display some texture in the stroke, click the Texture option set and choose a burlap or canvas texture in the Pattern picker (see step 7 on pages 300–301).

➤ To change the tilt of a tip when drawing with a mouse, adjust the Tilt Y value in the Brush Pose option set.

➤ Once you start painting with an Erodible tip (Shape: Point or Round and an increased Softness setting), you can resharpen the tip by clicking Sharpen Tip.

Note: To produce long strokes when using an Erodible Point tip or Airbrush tip with the Mixer Brush tool, choose the Dry, Heavy Load preset from the Useful Mixer Brush Combinations menu on the Options bar.**B** To learn more about this tool, see pages 304–305.

The Airbrush tips simulate the look of paint that is sprayed from an airbrush device. Via panel options, you can control the degree of graininess and feathering.

To use an Airbrush tip:

1. Choose the **Brush** tool or **Mixer Brush** tool.

2. On the left side of the Brush panel, click **Brush Tip Shape**, then click one of the Airbrush tips in the scrolling window.

3. Activate the **Live Tip Brush Preview** button.

4. Change any of the following settings:

Choose a **Size** value to set the size of the stroke.

Choose a **Hardness** value to control the amount of feathering at the edges of the stroke.

Increase the **Granularity** value to make the stroke look more speckly, and set a **Spatter Size** and **Spatter Amount** to control the size and number of droplets in the stroke.**C**

(See the Note, above, regarding the Mixer Brush.)

➤ If you're going to paint with a mouse, display the Brush Pose option set. To spray a conical stroke from the point where you click, change one or both Tilt values; to widen the stroke, lower the Pressure value. To further elongate a conical shape, in the Brush Tip Shape option set, choose a high Distortion value. (See also the sidebar on page 304.)

A *We used the Pencil brush preset (an Erodible Point tip) to create the blue lines in this drawing. A high Softness value was used for the upper stroke; a very low Softness value was used for the lower one.*

B *We drew the green lines with the Charcoal Pencil preset and the brown strokes with the Triangle Pastel preset.*

C *We used the Watercolor Spatter Big Drops preset (which has a high Granularity value) to draw the dotted stroke on the left, the Airbrush Soft High Density Grainy preset to draw the blue line in the center, and the Watercolor Wash brush preset to draw the wide blue stroke on the right.*

➤ *All of the presets used here are in the default library. To identify them by name, choose either of the List views from the Brush Presets panel menu.*

Managing brush presets

The Brush Presets panel stores and displays presets, like the Brush Preset picker, plus it offers several additional features. You can use this panel to save and choose brush presets, resize the current preset, save and load brush preset libraries, and access the Preset Manager. **A** Unlike the Brush Preset picker, the Brush Presets panel can be kept open.

To use the Brush Presets panel:

1. Choose a tool that uses brushes, such as the Brush, Mixer Brush, or Pencil.

2. To show the Brush Presets panel, click the panel tab or icon ⛄ (Window > Brush Presets), or click Brush Presets in the upper-left corner of the Brush panel.

3. On the panel, do any of the following:

   Click a **brush** to use with the chosen tool: either a recently used preset in the tray at the top of the panel (the last-used brush is shown first), or a preset in the scrolling window. If the tray is hidden, check Show Recent Brushes on the panel menu.

   Change the brush **Size** (diameter). Note: You can restore the original size to a static tip by clicking the Restore Original Size button. ↻

   Activate the **Live Tip Brush Preview** button 🖌 (if available) to display a schematic of the brush tip.

   To **load** different presets onto the panel, choose a library name from the panel menu, then click Append or OK (see also page 133). (Via the panel menu, you can also choose a different thumbnail or list option for the panel display.)

   To save the current brush and settings as a preset, click the **New Brush** button, 🗒 add to or change

the name in the Brush Name dialog (use a descriptive name), then click OK.

To save all the presets that are currently on the panel as a library, choose **Save Brushes** from the panel menu, type a name for the library, keep the default location, then click Save.

To access the Preset Manager dialog, from which you can append, replace, and reset the items that load onto the Brush and Brush Presets panels and the Brush Preset picker upon launch, click the **Open Preset Manager** button, 🖾 then see "Using the Preset Manager" on page 135. (This button is also available on the Brush panel.)

To delete the currently selected preset from the panel (but not from its library), click the **Delete Brush** button, then click OK in the alert dialog. 🗑

➤ If you click a preset and then customize its settings via the Brush panel, its listing on the Brush Presets panel will have an orange highlight, indicating that it was modified. If you click a recently used brush in the tray, then modify and use it, a new icon will display in the tray, with "(modified)" in its name. If you modify just the Size value for a preset, the preset must include a size value (a numeral in its panel listing) for it to be designated as "modified."

A Use the Brush Presets panel to select a preset from the current library, change the brush size, load a different library, create a new library, or access Preset Manager.

QUICK ACCESS TO THE BRUSH PANELS

➤ From the Brush panel, you can open the Brush Presets panel by clicking this button: [Brush Presets]

➤ From the Brush Presets panel, you can open the Brush panel by clicking the Toggle Brush panel button: 🖾

RESETTING THE PRESETS

To restore the original settings to an individual brush preset (including settings in the option sets, and including the size, if the preset includes a size value), simply click the preset again. To restore the whole library of default presets to the Brush Presets panel, see page 134.

TOOL PRESETS STORE MORE SETTINGS

The brush presets contain only settings from the Brush panel, not settings from the Options bar. When you save settings as a tool preset via the Tool Presets panel or picker (e.g., for the Brush or Mixer Brush tool), on the other hand, it will contain the Brush and Options bar settings and, optionally for some tools, the current Foreground color (see page 136).

Using the Mixer Brush tool

By choosing brush characteristics for the Mixer Brush tool, you can mimic different types of natural bristle brushes, such as oil paint or gouache. You can also control the wetness of the paint, the paint flow, and the degree to which existing colors mix with new strokes. Photoshop "paint" lacks the viscosity of traditional oils, but you can achieve some nice effects with it nevertheless.

To build a bristle brush:

1. Choose the **Mixer Brush** tool (B or Shift-B).

2. Display the Brush panel. If you don't see any bristle tips on the panel, click Brush Presets. From the Brush Presets panel menu, choose Reset Brushes. Click OK in the alert dialog, then click the Toggle Brush Panel button to return to the Brush panel.

3. Click **Brush Tip Shape**, then click a bristle tip in the scrolling window. **A** The shape name is listed on the Shape menu.

4. Activate the **Live Tip Brush Preview** button.

5. To pare down the number of options that will affect your brush, either uncheck all the options on the left side of the panel except Smoothing or choose **Clear Brush Controls** from the panel menu.

6. Use the **Bristle Qualities** sliders to choose these physical characteristics for the tip, while noting the changes in the preview:

   Bristles controls the number (density) of bristles.

   Length controls the length of the bristles.

   Thickness controls the width of the bristles (and therefore affects the overall density of the stroke).

   Stiffness controls how easily the bristles bend. Choose a low value for smooth, fluid strokes or a high value for scratchy, dry bristle marks.

   Angle controls the brush angle if you're using a mouse. Angle variations are most noticeable when a "Flat" shape is chosen for the tip.

7. Before using the Mixer Brush tool, choose Options bar settings, as in the steps on the next page.

➤ You can record the creation of a painting or drawing via an action, and then replay the process again at any time. The artwork will reappear onscreen, stroke by stroke. See Chapter 22.

A When the Mixer Brush tool and a bristle tip are selected, Bristle Qualities options display on the Brush panel.

USING THE BRUSH POSE OPTION SET FOR A MOUSE

When painting with a mouse, click the Brush Pose option set (Brush panel) to access brush handling options, such as the following:

➤ Use Tilt X or Tilt Y to tilt the entire brush as you apply brush strokes, and thereby mix colors with only part of the tip.

➤ Use a high Pressure value to bend the brush bristles more, mimicking the way a brush presses into the surface of the paper or canvas, for a darker stroke (akin to decreasing the Stiffness), or lower the Pressure value for a lighter stroke.

➤ Uncheck the Override boxes, which are for use with a stylus.

Before using the bristle brush that you have just chosen qualities for, you also need to choose settings to control how the brush applies pigment.

To choose paint options for a bristle brush:

1. After following the instructions on the preceding page, and with the **Mixer Brush** tool still selected, on the Options bar, do both of the following:

   Activate the **Load Brush After Each Stroke** button to have the current Foreground color reload onto the brush after each stroke.

   Activate the **Clean Brush After Each Stroke** button to have a clean Foreground color reload after each stroke, or deactivate this option to allow the last colors in the brush to mix with the current Foreground color.

2. To choose a Foreground color, click the **Current Brush Load** thumbnail on the Options bar, then use the Color Picker; or click a color on the Swatches or Color panel.

3. From the **Useful Mixer Brush Combinations** menu, choose a preset combination of settings. The Dry presets are good for defining object details and edges (because they set the wet value to 0% and thereby disable the Mix option), the Moist presets allow for moderate paint mixing, and the Wet and Very Wet presets work well for blending new strokes with existing ones.

   If you prefer to choose custom options (or to refine the settings from a preset), do any of the following:

   Choose a **Wet** value to control the wetness of the existing paint and the extent to which your brush can pick it up in the stroke.**A–B**

   Choose a **Load** value to control how much paint is supplied to the brush (how quickly the brush runs out of paint), most noticeable with a low Mix value.

   Choose a **Mix** value to control the degree to which new strokes mix or smear with existing strokes (including any white from the Background).**C–D**

   Choose a **Flow** value to control the rate at which paint is applied (the amount of coverage).

   Check **Sample All Layers** to allow the brush to mix with and pick up paint from all layers. With this option checked, the current Foreground color may not appear in your brush strokes.

4. Create a new, blank layer (it can be above an image layer). It's time to paint!

Use this method if you want to wipe a brush clean or reload color to the brush manually, on a one-time basis — that is, override inactivated Load Brush After Each Stroke and Clean Brush After Each Stroke buttons.

To wipe a bristle brush clean:

With the Mixer Brush tool selected, click the **Current Brush Load** menu on the Options bar, click **Clean Brush**, then click **Load Brush**.

A *Options bar settings of Wet 10 and Mix 10: The stroke barely blended with the existing color.*

B *Wet 90 and Mix 10: The stroke blended somewhat with the existing color.*

C *Wet 10 and Mix 90: The stroke blended and smeared more with the existing color.*

D *Wet 90 and Mix 90: The stroke blended and smeared almost entirely with the existing color.*

PICKING UP COLORS FROM AN IMAGE

Check Sample All Layers for the Mixer Brush tool, then Alt-click/Option-click an area of an image layer. Imagery from the sampled area will appear in the Current Brush Load thumbnail on the Options bar.

In this exercise, you will reinterpret shapes in a photo with the Mixer Brush tool, to produce a digital painting. This is a fun exercise.

To turn a photo into a painting:

1. Open a photo **A** and duplicate the Background.

2. Hide the duplicate layer, click the original Background, then use Edit > **Fill** to fill it with White. To add a texture, use Edit > Fill again, except this time choose Use: Pattern, choose the Canvas pattern (Artist Surfaces library) from the Pattern picker menu, set the Opacity to 75%, uncheck Scripted Patterns, then click OK.

3. Click the Background copy, and make it visible again. Create several blank layers, and keep one of them selected.**B**

4. Choose the **Mixer Brush** tool (B or Shift-B).

5. On the Brush Presets panel, click a bristle preset, such as a flat, blunt preset to fill in broad areas or a flat, pointed preset to draw fine lines.

6. On the Options bar, do all of the following:

   From the **Useful Mixer Brush Combinations** menu, choose a preset to control the character of the paint. The Wet and Very Wet presets are good for painting broad areas, such as backgrounds, and for picking up colors from a photo; the Moist and Dry presets are better for defining details.

   Check **Sample All Layers** to allow the brush to pick up and mix colors from all the underlying layers (strokes will appear only on the selected layer).

   If you're using a stylus and tablet, activate the **Pressure Controls Size** button.

7. To transform your photo into a painting, do either of the following:

   To reinterpret the photo with a "clean" brush, deactivate the **Load Brush After Each Stroke** button on the Options bar and activate the **Clean Brush After Each Stroke** button (now the current Load value will have no effect and the Foreground color isn't applied). As you apply brush strokes in the image, start each new stroke over the desired color (**A**, next page).

   To sample a color from the photo, activate the **Load Brush After Each Stroke** and **Clean Brush After Each Stroke** buttons on the Options bar, then hold down I (temporary Eyedropper tool) and click in the photo. Click a paint layer, then paint with the sampled color (**B–C**, next page, and **A–B**, page 308). Repeat.

➤ Paint the picture in sections, each one on a separate blank layer. To erase any unwanted strokes, use the Eraser tool (see page 308). To view just your brush work, lower the opacity of the photo layer temporarily.

➤ As you apply brush strokes, mimic the direction of shapes in the photo. To add variety to your paint, switch bristle tips and change the brush size occasionally between strokes.

A This is the original photo — a quintessential New England landscape.

B This is how the Layers panel looked by the end of step 3 on this page.

A *For the Mixer Brush tool, we deacti-vated the Load Brush After Each Stroke option so we could pick up colors from the photo layer, chose "Wet, Heavy Mix" from the Useful Mixer Brush Combinations menu, then applied brush strokes on a few blank layers.*

B *We activated Load Brush After Each Stroke, sampled a color in the photo, clicked another blank layer, then painted with a couple of the Moist preset combi-nations and a couple of the Wet ones.*

➤ *To view just your brush strokes in the document (as shown here), lower the opacity of the photo layer. To resume sampling colors, reset the photo layer opacity to 90%–100%.*

C *Next, we painted the sky with the Round Fan Stiff Thin Bristles and Flat Point Medium Stiff presets, painted the water with the Round Blunt Medium Stiff and Round Point Stiff presets, and painted the siding on the building with the Round Point Stiff preset and the Dry, Heavy Load combination.*

➤ *All the presets mentioned above are in the default brush library. To view the preset names, choose Small or Large List from the Brush Presets panel menu.*

Continued on the following page

A *Finally, we applied brush strokes on the topmost layer using the Round Point Stiff preset, with the Dry combination chosen to prevent the final line work from blending with the other paint layers. Now the image looks like an artist's painting. Note that we didn't slavishly replicate every tiny detail in the photo — that's what artistic license is all about!*

B *We transformed this photo in a similar way to the one shown above, using the Mixer Brush tool, a bristle tip, and a few different Useful Combination presets.*

Using the Eraser tool

The Eraser tool removes image pixels permanently, so it should be used only to delete areas from a duplicate layer or from a layer that contains, say, just retouching or painting edits that were made via the Sample All Layers option. Don't use it on the original Background!

To use the Eraser tool:

1. Choose the **Eraser** tool ![eraser icon] (E or Shift-E).

2. On the Options bar, do the following:

   Click a Soft Round brush on the **Brush Preset** picker.

   Choose a Mode (shape) of **Brush**, **Pencil**, or **Block**.

   For Brush or Pencil mode, choose an **Opacity** percentage; for Brush mode, deactivate the **Airbrush** button ![airbrush icon] and keep the **Flow** setting at 100%.

3. Click a layer, make sure the Lock Transparent Pixels button ![lock icon] is deactivated, adjust the brush size by pressing [or], then drag to erase pixels.

➤ Instead of erasing image pixels permanently, an option that we prefer is to hide them via an editable layer mask (see pages 192–193).

Using the History Brush tool

When you apply strokes to a document with the History Brush tool, pixels below the pointer are restored from whichever state or snapshot you have designated as the history source.

Note: Photoshop prevents the use of the History Brush tool if you apply certain kinds of edits after opening your document, such as changing the document color mode or canvas size or cropping. Also, the tool can't be used to recover pixels from a layer that you have deleted.

To use the History Brush tool:

1. Click an image layer (or duplicate the Background), and apply some edits, such as a filter or brush strokes (but none of the edits listed in the Note above). **A–C**

2. Choose the **History Brush** tool 🖌 (Y or Shift-Y).

3. On the Options bar, do all of the following:

   Click the Brush Preset picker arrowhead, then click a brush on the picker.

Continued on the following page

A *This is the original image.*

B *We duplicated the image layer via Ctrl-J/ Cmd-J, then applied the Gaussian Blur filter to the duplicate layer.*

C *We used a Hue/Saturation adjustment layer (Colorize option) to apply a blue-green tint, then merged that layer into the duplicate image layer.*

Choose a blending Mode, Opacity percentage, and Flow percentage.

4. On the Layers panel, click the layer you edited, and make sure the Lock Transparent Pixels button ▦ is deactivated.

5. On the History panel, click in the leftmost column for a state, to designate it as the source for the History Brush tool. The history source icon ✎ appears in that slot. **A** Note: If you added a layer during the course of editing (step 1), set the history source to the New Layer or Layer via Copy state.

6. Apply strokes to the image. Pixel data from the source state will replace the current data where you apply strokes. **B–C**

➤ We recommend using the History Brush immediately after applying edits that you want to remove selectively. This way, it will be easier for you to identify which state you want to use as a source.

A To set the history source icon, we clicked in the leftmost column for the state in which we duplicated the image layer.

B We set the Opacity for the History Brush to 70% and chose the Round Blunt Medium Stiff bristle preset. We applied strokes to selectively restore the original, unedited image in scratchy strokes.

C Finally, with a Soft Round tip and the History Brush Opacity set to 50%, we partially restored some areas of the model's face and neck from the original Background image.

Photoshop provides tools for correcting many kinds of imperfections in a photo, from smoothing pores and wrinkles to removing blemishes, unsightly power lines, and other unwanted elements. Methods are also available for correcting colors, such as whitening teeth, and for replacing colors, such as on a garment in a fashion shot.

In this chapter, you will change colors by using the Replace Color command and the Color Replacement tool; whiten teeth or eyes; correct red-eye; smooth wrinkles with the Healing Brush and Patch tools; remove blemishes with the Spot Healing Brush tool; soften skin and other textures with the Surface Blur and Gaussian Blur filters; replace pixels with the Clone Stamp tool; eliminate unwanted elements from a picture with the Spot Healing Brush tool, Patch tool, and Fill command; and move or extend areas of an image with the Content-Aware Move tool.

Note: Performance improvements to the Mercury Graphics Engine inside Photoshop CC enable Content-Aware results to display faster.

The following are some guidelines we recommend following when applying retouching edits:

➤ Do the small stuff first. For instance, if you need to heal blemishes or other small imperfections In a facial shot as well as smooth the skin, start with the blemishes. Next, either merge the healing layer into the image layer or select both the healing and image layers, then copy and merge (stamp) them onto a new layer (see page 167). Finally, apply skin smoothing to the newly merged layer.

➤ Preserve the original pixels and keep your edits flexible. One way to accomplish this is by duplicating the image layer and editing the duplicate. For some tools, an even better option is to choose Sample: All Layers on the Options bar, then apply edits to a new, blank layer. The tool will sample pixels from all the visible layers and send the results to the new layer. You can easily add strokes to, or erase your editing strokes from, that layer at any time.

➤ Restore some realism. After applying edits to a duplicate or blank layer, you can lower the opacity of that healing or retouching layer slightly to reveal a bit of the original, imperfect (but more natural-looking) photo.

RETOUCHING

IN THIS CHAPTER

Using the Replace Color command

Using the Replace Color command, not only can you apply hue, saturation, and lightness adjustments, but via selection controls in the dialog, you can limit those edits to specific color areas of the image. This command works best for recoloring discrete areas that are easy to isolate.

To use the Replace Color command:

1. *Optional:* In an RGB document that you're going to send to a commercial printer, choose View > Proof Setup > Working CMYK to view a soft proof of the image in simulated CMYK color.

    Once you've made a choice from the Proof Setup submenu, you can toggle the proof on and off while the Replace Color dialog is open by pressing Ctrl-Y/Cmd-Y. Regardless of whether the Proof Colors command is on or off, the Color and Result swatches in the Replace Color dialog are going to display in RGB.

2. Click a layer (not a Smart Object) or the Background, press Ctrl-J/Cmd-J to duplicate it, and keep the duplicate layer selected.

3. *Optional:* To confine the color selection and replacement to an area of the image, create a selection.**A**

4. Choose Image > Adjustments > **Replace Color**. The Replace Color dialog opens.

5. In the document, click the color to be replaced. The color you click will appear in the Color swatch at the top of the dialog.

6. Do any of the following:

    To add more color areas to the selection, click the **Eyedropper** tool 🖋 in the dialog, then Shift-click or drag either in the preview or in the document.

    Increase the **Fuzziness** value to add similar colors to the selection, or reduce it to narrow the range of selected colors.**B**

    Check **Localized Color Clusters** to limit the selection to similar, contiguous colors. (We sometimes get similar or better results by lowering the Fuzziness value instead.)

7. If you need to subtract any areas from the selection, with the Eyedropper tool, 🖋 hold down Alt/Option and click or drag in the preview or document window (this is a temporary Subtract from Sample Eyedropper tool).

A *To recolor the purple eye shadow in this image, our first step was to select that area loosely.*

B *We opened the Replace Color dialog, then clicked the pot of eye shadow. Areas matching that color displayed as a selection in the preview window. We tried setting the Fuzziness slider to 86.*

8. To replace the colors you have selected, do either of the following:

In the **Replacement** area, choose replacement **Hue**, **Saturation**, and **Lightness** values (you can use the scrubby sliders).**A** The Result swatch will update as you do this. Note: A Saturation value greater than +25 may produce a nonprintable color.

Click the **Result** swatch, choose a replacement color in the Color Picker, then click OK. The sliders will shift to reflect the values of the new color.

Note: If you click a different area of the image or add to or subtract from the selection, the Color and Result swatches will change but the Replacement sliders will stay put.

> To toggle the selection and the image in the preview, press and release Ctrl/Cmd (or click Selection or Image below the preview).

9. *Optional:* To save your settings (e.g., to apply to a series of similar photos), click Save, enter a name for the data file, keep the default location, then click Save.

10. Click OK.**B**

> In a CMYK document, the Replacement sliders don't affect the value of the Black (K) component. That value is established by the CMYK Working Space, which you chose in Edit > Color Settings.

> You can restore the original dialog settings by holding down Alt/Option and clicking Reset (Cancel becomes Reset), but be aware that you will then need to create a new selection from scratch.

A *We settled on a Fuzziness value of 64, Shift-clicked more areas in the eye-shadow pot to add them to the selection, then changed the Hue.*

B *The eye shadow that was originally purple is now reddish brown.*

Using the Color Replacement tool

The Color Replacement tool lets you change color values in areas of an image, but instead of using a dialog, as you do with Replace Color, you apply changes manually with a brush. Unlike the Brush tool, the Color Replacement tool attempts to preserve the original texture (luminosity values) of an area as it replaces colors. This tool, like the Replace Color and Match Color commands, will be of particular interest to advertising and catalog designers.

To use the Color Replacement tool:

1. Duplicate the Background in an RGB image to preserve the original pixels, and keep the duplicate layer selected.

2. Choose the **Color Replacement** tool (B or Shift-B).

3. As the replacement color, choose a **Foreground** color via the Color or Swatches panel, or sample a color by Alt/Option clicking in the document.

4. If the color you chose isn't on the Swatches panel, add it to the panel by clicking the **New Swatch of Foreground Color** button.

5. On the Options bar, choose parameters for the tool: **A**

   On the Brush Preset picker, choose a high **Hardness** value and a low **Spacing** value.

   To control which color characteristics the tool applies to the image, choose a **Mode** of Hue, Saturation, Color, or Luminosity. (We've gotten good results with Color mode.)

   Click a **Sampling** button: **Continuous** to apply the current Foreground color to all pixels the brush touches (we prefer this option because it lets us replace both light and dark colors); or **Once** to sample the first pixel the brush clicks and apply the Foreground color only to pixels

that match that initial sampled color (because this option confines the sampling to just one color; if you need to replace, say, different shades of a particular color, you would have to sample each one separately); or **Background Swatch** to replace only colors that match or are similar to the current Background color (for this option, choose a Background color).

From the **Limits** menu, choose **Discontiguous** to recolor only the color that is sampled under the pointer; or **Contiguous** to recolor the sampled color plus adjacent pixels within the current Tolerance value; or **Find Edges** (our favorite option) to recolor pixels under the pointer plus adjacent pixels, while keeping the color replacement within discrete image shapes.

Choose a **Tolerance** value (1–100%) for the range of colors to be replaced. A high Tolerance value permits a wide range of colors to be recolored; a low value allows only pixels that closely match the sampled color to be recolored.

Optional: Check Anti-alias for smoother transitions between the original and replacement colors.

If you're using a stylus and tablet, click the **Pressure Controls Size** button, and from the Size menu on the Brush Preset picker, choose **Pen Pressure** or **Stylus Wheel**.

6. Adjust the brush diameter by pressing [or], then drag across the areas to be recolored (**A–D**, next page). Only pixels that fall within the chosen Sampling, Limits, and Tolerance parameters will be recolored.

➤ When using the Color Replacement tool, you can change Options bar settings or the brush diameter between strokes.

| | | Mode: | Color | | | | Limits: | Find Edges | | Tolerance: | 20% | | ☑ Anti-alias | |

A *Choose settings for the Color Replacement tool from the Options bar.*

A *We want to change the color of the light green stripes on this woman's sweater to aqua blue.*

B *With the Color Replacement tool and the settings shown in the figure on the preceding page, we're "painting" over the light green areas on the woman's sweater, to replace it with aqua blue, which is the current Foreground color.*

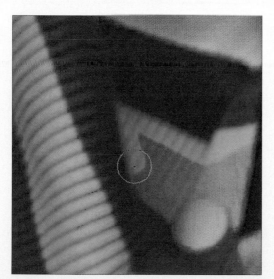

C *To recolor both highlights and shadows within a stripe in a small area, we zoomed in, then used the Color Replacement tool with a Tolerance setting of 40%. Here we're replacing colors along the edges of a stripe using a lower Tolerance setting of 15%.*

D *Although the Limits setting for the tool was Find Edges, it recolored some dark stripes, which was not our intention. To repair this error, we Alt/Option clicked to sample the original color in the darker stripe (as shown above). Our next step would be to apply strokes with the newly sampled color.*

Whitening teeth or eyes

Another use for a Hue/Saturation adjustment layer (a feature that you learned about in Chapter 12) is to whiten the teeth or the white areas of eyes in a portrait. The first step is to select the problem area(s).

To whiten teeth or eyes in a portrait photo:

1. Open a portrait photo, zoom in on the area to be corrected, then do either of the following:

   Choose the **Quick Selection** tool, then drag to create a tight selection of the teeth **A** or of the white areas of both eyes.

   Paint a **Quick Mask** on the teeth by following the steps on page 191.

2. On the Adjustments panel, click the **Hue/Saturation** button.

3. On the Properties panel, for teeth, choose **Yellows** from the second menu; for the whites of the eyes, choose either **Master** or **Reds**. Reduce the Saturation value and increase the Lightness value. **B**

   ➤ Try not to overdo the whitening, or the teeth or eyes will look unnatural. To view the layer without the correction, click the Layer Visibility button on the Properties panel; click it again to re-enable the correction.

4. Also on the Properties panel, click the Masks button, then increase the **Feather** value to soften the edge of the mask (the transition to the adjusted area). Try a value between 5 and 8 px). **C–D** You can also lower the Density value of the mask.

A *We used the Quick Selection tool to select the teeth in this photo.*

B *On the Properties panel for a Hue/Saturation layer, we lowered the Saturation and increased the Lightness.*

C *Then we adjusted the Feather value for the mask.*

D *Brighter, whiter teeth!*

Using the Red Eye tool

Red-eye (red in the pupil areas) in a portrait photo results when a person in a relatively dark room looks straight into the camera lens, and light emitted by an electronic flash reflects off his or her retinas. This is less likely to occur if you use a flash bracket and an off-camera flash — and if the subject looks away from the camera. To remove red-eye from a photo that was taken without such preventive measures, you can use the Red Eye tool in Photoshop.

To remove red-eye from a portrait:

1. Open a portrait photo, duplicate the Background, and zoom way in on the eye area.

2. Choose the **Red Eye** tool ⊕ (J or Shift-J).

3. On the Options bar, do both of the following:

   Choose a **Pupil Size** for the size of the correction. You can start with the default setting of 50%, and see if you like the results. You don't want the tool to enlarge (dilate) the pupil.

   Choose a **Darken Amount** to control how much the tool darkens the pupil in order to remove the red. Try a setting below 30% for light-colored eyes, or above that value for dark-colored eyes.

4. Click once on the red area in each pupil. The tool should remove all traces of red, replacing it with black. **A–B** If not, see the next task.

   Note: If the tool enlarged the pupil too much, undo the results, lower the Pupil Size value, then click again. Similarly, if the red removal was incomplete or the pupil became too dark, undo the results, then try again with a different Darken Amount value.

➤ You don't need to drag across the eye with the Red Eye tool; the tool is clever enough to find the pupil area automatically with a simple click.

➤ Some photographers prefer to keep the red-eye feature of their camera off, because it delays the shutter action and they can miss the "magic moment." Also, the subject can mistake the click of the red-eye feature for the shutter, which comes afterward.

If you notice traces of red in the irises of the eyes (the area around the pupils), you can eliminate them.

To remove redness from the irises of the eyes:

1. Zoom in on one eye.

2. Choose the **Color Replacement** tool ⊕ (B or Shift-B).

3. On the Options bar, choose Mode: Color, Sampling: Once, ⊕ Limits: Contiguous, and Tolerance: 30%.

4. Make the brush tip very small, Alt-click/Option-click a color in the iris of the eye, then apply short strokes over the remaining traces of red to recolor them with the sampled color.

5. Repeat with the other eye.

USING THE RED EYE REMOVAL TOOL IN CAMERA RAW

The **Red Eye Removal tool** in Camera Raw is similar to the Red Eye tool in Photoshop, except in Camera Raw, you drag before using the sliders. Choose the Red Eye Removal tool, choose a Type option of Red Eye (for humans) or Pet Eye; drag across one of the eyes, including some surrounding area; then adjust the sliders. Uncheck Show Overlay (V) to view the results. Repeat for the other eye.

A With the Red Eye tool, we clicked once on each eye.

B Click, click, the red-eye is gone.

Unlike the Clone Stamp tool, which merely copies a source color without blending it into the target area (see pages 326–327), the three tools discussed next will sample a texture, apply it to the target area, and blend the texture into the existing color and brightness values. With these tools, it's easy to fix imperfections, such as facial blemishes or paper creases in a vintage photo, and the results are usually seamless.

With the Healing Brush tool, you Alt-click/Option-click to sample from an unblemished or smooth area, then apply strokes in the area to be retouched. **A** The blemish pixels are replaced with sampled pixels.

With the Patch tool, you select the blemish area first, then drag the selection over an unblemished area for sampling. Here too, the blemish pixels are replaced with the sampled ones.

And with the Spot Healing Brush tool, you simply click a blemish without sampling. Pixels are replaced (almost magically!) based on data gathered from neighboring pixels.

Using the Healing Brush tool

To use the Healing Brush tool:

1. Choose the **Healing Brush** tool ✐ (J or Shift-J).

2. Create a new, blank layer in a portrait photo. (The healing strokes will be applied to this layer.)

3. On the Options bar, do all of the following: **B**

   Via the Brush Preset picker, choose a high **Hardness** value (you can also do this by right-clicking in the image, or by using the interactive cursor, as described on page 131). Also, in Edit/Photoshop CC > Preferences > Cursors, click Full Size Brush Tip, so you will be able to preview the diameter of the brush cursor.

   Choose Mode: **Normal** to preserve the grain, texture, and noise of the area surrounding the target; or if you don't need to preserve those characteristics, choose a different mode, such as Lighten (for subtle retouching or to correct wrinkles or creases that are very close together, to prevent them from cloning onto one another).

   Click Source: **Sampled**.

Check **Aligned** to maintain the same distance between the source point and the areas that you drag across, even if you release the mouse between strokes, or uncheck this option to resample from the original source point each time you release the mouse.

From the Sample menu, choose **All Layers**. This setting will permit the tool to sample pixels from all the layers below the pointer (the corrected pixels will appear on the selected, blank layer).

Optional: If the document contains adjustment layers, the effects of which you want the Healing Brush tool to ignore when sampling (so the effect of the adjustments isn't doubled), activate the Ignore Adjustment Layers When Healing button. 🚫

If you're using a stylus and tablet, click the **Pressure Controls Size** ◉ button.

Click the **Toggle Clone Source** panel button, 🔳 then check **Show Overlay** and **Clipped** on the Clone Source panel so you will be able to preview the cloned pixels within the brush cursor.

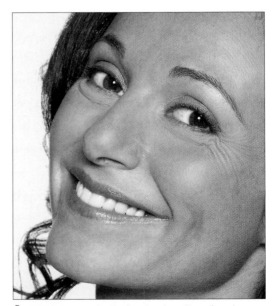

A *We're going use the Healing Brush tool to soften the wrinkles around the woman's eyes in this photo.*

| ✐ ▾ | ● 19 ▾ | 🔳 | Mode: Normal ⬍ | Source: Sampled Pattern: | ▾ | ☐ Aligned | Sample: All Layers ⬍ | 🚫 |

B *We chose these Options bar settings for the Healing Brush tool.*

4. Press [or] to scale the brush to suit the area to be healed.

5. Alt-click/Option-click a smooth or unblemished area to sample it as the source texture.**A** The sampled area displays within the brush cursor.

6. With the new, blank layer still selected, drag a short stroke across the area to be repaired.**B** As you drag, the source texture will be applied in real time to the target area ★ and will be blended into neighboring pixels.**C**

7. *Optional:* To establish a new source point for further repairs, Alt-click/Option-click a different area, then apply more strokes.

8. *Optional:* To soften the results, lower the opacity of the healing layer slightly to blend it with the original layer.**D**

➤ Because you applied the healing strokes to a separate layer, you can easily erase any mistakes. Hide the image layers below the healing layer temporarily, then with the Eraser tool, drag across any unwanted strokes.

A *With the Healing Brush tool, we held down Alt/Option and clicked the area to be used as replacement pixels…*

B *…then dragged across the area to be repaired. Note that the brush tip is separate from the sampling pointer.*

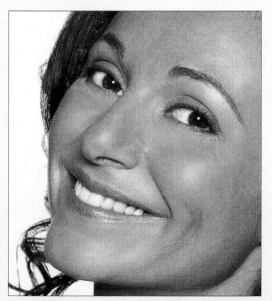

C *The wrinkles around her eyes are softened.*

D *Our retouching brush strokes are on a separate layer (labeled "healing brush"). To make the portrait look more natural, we lowered the Opacity of that layer to 90%.*

REMOVING FACIAL HOT SPOTS

The Healing Brush tool is also handy for removing shiny hot spots, caused by harsh, uneven lighting, from a portrait. You can remove them by doing the following: Choose Mode: Darken on the Options bar for the tool, then Alt-click/Option-click to sample a medium-tone area of skin.

Create a new, blank layer, size the brush, then drag once or twice over a hot spot, letting your stroke(s) follow the natural contours of the face.

With Darken mode chosen for the tool, it repaired only the lightest area. We repeated this process on the model's forehead and nose. (If you want to soften the results, lower the opacity of the healing layer.)

Using the Spot Healing Brush tool

The Spot Healing Brush tool heals imperfections without your having to sample a source area. With one click or a very short drag, you can zap blemishes or wrinkles, or repair a tear or crease in a vintage or damaged photo.

To use the Spot Healing Brush tool:

1. Create a new, blank layer to contain your healing strokes, and keep it selected.

2. Choose the **Spot Healing Brush** tool 🖌 (J or Shift-J), and zoom the document to 100%.

3. In Edit/Photoshop CC > Preferences > Cursors, under Painting Cursors, click Full Size Brush Tip (so you will be able to preview the diameter of the brush cursor) and check Show Crosshair in Brush Tip (to help you position the cursor).

4. On the Options bar, do all of the following:

   Choose a **Mode**. To preserve skin tones, try Normal or Lighten mode. (When used in Replace mode, the tool may pick up unwanted facial details in the stroke, such as hair or eyelashes.)

   To help preserve existing tonal values in the image, such as in skin tones, click Type: **Content-Aware** (for more about this option, see page 328).

   Check **Sample All Layers** to allow the brush to sample pixels from all the layers below the pointer.

5. Position the pointer above the area to be repaired, press [or] to make the brush just slightly wider than that area, then drag once across it in a short stroke. **A–B** Repeat to repair other problem areas.

6. *Optional:* For a more subtle result, lower the opacity of the healing layer slightly.

7. Because you applied Spot Healing strokes to a separate layer, you can show and hide those edits (or erase any unwanted strokes with the Eraser tool) at any time.

A *With the Spot Healing Brush tool, we clicked a blemish.*

B *The blemish disappeared.*

RETOUCHING WITH LIQUIFY

To reshape an area of an image (e.g., to slim down a chin or waistline in a portrait), try using the Liquify filter. See pages 366–369.

Healing areas with the Patch tool

The Patch tool is also a good choice for retouching bags or wrinkles below the eyes in a portrait and for repairing rips, stains, or dust marks in a scanned image (such as a vintage photo).

To retouch an area using the Patch tool:

1. Press Ctrl-J/Cmd-J to duplicate the Background, and keep the duplicate layer selected.

2. Choose the **Patch** tool 🔲 (J or Shift-J).

3. On the Options bar, click **Patch: Normal** and **Source**.

4. Drag a selection around the entire area to be repaired.**A** You can Shift-drag to add to the selection or Alt-drag/Option-drag to subtract from it.

   ➤ If you're retouching an under-eye area, avoid selecting any of the lower eyelid.

5. Drag from inside the selection to the area to be sampled.**B** When you release the mouse, imagery from the sampled area will appear within the original selection, and will be blended with the luminosity and texture of original pixels. Deselect (Ctrl-D/Cmd-D).**C**

6. *Optional:* If the results of the Patch repair look too smooth or slick, lower the opacity of the duplicate layer (try 70% or 80%) to reveal some of the original image.**D**

➤ See also the tip on page 332. (The Patch tool is also used on that page.)

A *With the Patch tool (Normal setting), we selected the area to be repaired.*

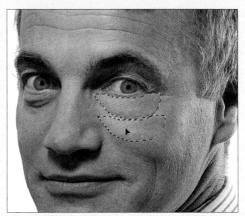

B *We dragged from the selected area to a nearby area for Photoshop to sample.*

C *Photoshop blended pixels from the sample area into the original selection area.*

D *We repeated the same steps for the left eye, then lowered the layer Opacity to 70% to soften the effect.*

Smoothing skin and other surfaces

Using the Surface Blur filter, you can easily smooth out unwanted textures, such as skin pores in a portrait or grainy paper in a scanned photo or drawing.

To smooth surfaces with the Surface Blur filter:

1. Press Ctrl-J/Cmd-J to duplicate the Background in an image that needs some surface smoothing. Right-click the duplicate layer and choose **Convert to Smart Object**.

2. Choose Filter > Blur > **Surface Blur**. The Surface Blur dialog opens. Check Preview.

3. Choose a low **Threshold** value (try 3–6) to blur only low-contrast areas, such as the cheeks and fore-head in a portrait, while preserving the contrast in key details, such as the eyes and mouth.

4. Adjust the **Radius** just to the point that the desired degree of smoothing is reached. To soften skin (e.g., cheeks, forehead), try a value of 6–12.

5. Readjust the **Threshold** to increase or decrease the amount of blurring in the low-contrast areas. Bear in mind that too much smoothing can make a sur-face look artificial—but then again, this whole task is a lesson in artifice!

6. Click OK. To edit the settings at any time, double-click the Surface Blur listing on the Layers panel (under Smart Filters); the filter dialog reopens.

7. *Optional:* To soften the overall filter effect, lower the opacity of the Smart Object.

8. *Optional:* To selectively reveal details from the unaltered layer, click the mask thumbnail for the Smart Filters listing. Choose the Brush tool ![brush] (B or Shift-B). On the Options bar, choose a Soft Round brush and an Opacity of 80–90%. Choose black as the Foreground color and size the brush cursor, then draw strokes on key details, such as the lips, eyes, eyebrows, or hair in a portrait. To reveal the surface blur effect in any areas that you masked unintentionally, paint with white.

➤ If you want to use the Spot Healing Brush or Healing Brush tool to retouch areas of the Smart Object, check Sample All Layers on the Options bar and work on a new, blank layer. If you want to use the Patch tool, double-click the Smart Object thumbnail to access the embedded image.

➤ To learn about Smart Filters, see pages 374–378.

A *The pores on this woman's skin look too prominent.*

B *The Surface Blur filter successfully smoothed the skin texture while keeping the facial features crisp (we chose a Radius setting of 9 pixels and a Threshold setting of 6 levels for our 300 ppi file). Compare the cheeks and under-eye areas in this image with those in the preceding one.*

C *Finally, we lowered the opacity of the Smart Object and painted with black on the Smart Filters mask to reveal some of the sharp facial details from the underlying layer.*

Here we show you how to soften a skin texture with an extra degree of control. You will apply the Gaussian Blur filter twice, in each case using a mask and a layer blending mode to control the visibility of the smoothing effect, first in the light areas, then in the dark areas.

To smooth skin with the Gaussian Blur filter:

1. Open an RGB photo of a face. **A** Press Ctrl-Alt-J/Cmd-Option-J to open the New Layer dialog. Rename the duplicate layer "blur darken," then click OK.

2. Choose Filter > Blur > **Gaussian Blur**. In the dialog, drag the cheek or forehead area into view, then move the Radius slider until the skin starts to look smooth and blurry. Press, then release, on the preview to judge the blur effect. **B** Click OK. Don't be concerned that the facial features now look too blurry.

3. Choose **Darken** as the blending mode for the "blur darken" layer (to smooth only lighter areas), then lower the layer opacity setting until a hint of texture marks reappear in the skin.

4. Alt-click/Option-click the **Add Layer Mask** button ◻ on the Layers panel to add a black mask, and keep the new mask thumbnail selected.

5. Choose the **Brush** tool ✎ (B or Shift-B), a Soft Round tip, Normal mode, and 100% Opacity, and press X to make the Foreground color white.

Apply strokes to areas where you want to reveal the smoothing effect, such as on the cheeks, forehead, chin, and nose (**A–B**, next page).

If you paint over any facial features unintentionally, such as the eyes or eyebrows, press X to make the Foreground color black, and paint over your strokes.

➤ Press [to reduce the brush diameter to paint over small areas, such as between the eyes and eyebrows or between the nose and lips, then press] to enlarge it again.

6. Press Ctrl-Alt-J/Cmd-Option-J to duplicate the "blur darken" layer. The New Layer dialog opens. Rename the duplicate layer "blur lighten," then click OK.

7. Change the blending mode of the "blur lighten" layer to **Lighten** (to smooth only darker areas), then increase or reduce the layer opacity until any dark texture marks on the skin look softer. The skin should now look smoother.

8. To put the top two layers in a group, Shift-click the "blur darken" layer, then press Ctrl-G/Cmd-G (**C–D**, next page).

9. *Optional:* To restore a bit of "reality" to the portrait, click the group listing, then lower the opacity of the group until the desired amount of skin texture is revealed.

A *In the original image, the pores of the woman's skin look too pronounced.*

B *In the Gaussian Blur dialog, we chose a Radius value of 20.5 pixels.*

B *The smoothing effect is visible only where we added white areas to the layer mask, and is hidden by the black areas that are masking the rest of the face.*

A *We chose Darken as the blending mode for the "blur darken" layer, lowered the layer Opacity to 70%, Alt/Option clicked the layer mask thumbnail, then applied brush strokes to reveal the smoothing effect on the cheeks, forehead, chin, and nose. Because the layer blending mode is Darken, the effect can be seen only in the lighter areas.*

C *We duplicated the "blur darken" layer, renamed the duplicate "blur lighten," chose Lighten as the blending mode, and changed the layer Opacity to 80%. Finally, we put the two blur layers in a group.*

D *Now the skin on the woman's forehead, cheeks, and nose looks smoother, while the eyes, eyebrows, lips, and hair still look sharp.*

Retouching by cloning

The Clone Stamp tool lets you clone pixels either within the same document or between documents. Use it to remove distracting elements from an image, such as the metal pipe shown in our example, or to duplicate an element, such as leaves or a texture.

To retouch a photo by cloning imagery:

1. Open an RGB document, and if desired, open a second RGB document from which to clone. If you open two documents, display them both by choosing a tiling option from the Window > Arrange submenu.

2. Choose the **Clone Stamp** tool ![clone stamp icon] (S or Shift-S).

3. On the Options bar, do the following: **A**

   On the **Brush Preset** picker, choose a Soft Round brush.

   Choose **Normal** as the blending Mode.

   Choose an **Opacity** percentage.

   Choose a **Flow** percentage to control the rate of application.

   Check **Aligned** to maintain the same sampling point even if you release the mouse between strokes (to clone a large area seamlessly); or

uncheck Aligned to resample from the original source point each time you release the mouse (to clone the same area numerous times, separately).

From the Sample menu, choose **All Layers** to allow the tool to sample pixels from all the visible layers that are directly below the pointer (the new pixels will appear on the blank layer that you create in step 5).

Optional: If the source document contains adjustment layers, the effects of which you want the Clone Stamp tool to ignore when sampling (so the effect of the adjustments isn't doubled), activate the Ignore Adjustment Layers When Cloning button. ![icon]

Optional: If you have a stylus and tablet, you can activate the Pressure for Opacity button ![icon] and/or the Pressure for Size button. ![icon]

4. Click in the source document (it can be the same document or a second one), then Alt-click/Option-click a point from which to clone. **B–C** For seamless cloning, pick an area that looks very similar to the area being repaired.

A *We chose these settings for the Clone Stamp tool from the Options bar.*

B *This is the original image. Our objective was to remove the metal pipes from the side of the building and add more leaves to fill in the front of the trellis.*

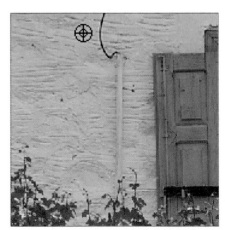

C *We Alt/Option clicked with the Clone Stamp tool to sample a blank area of the wall.*

5. Click in the target document (it can be the same document as the source or a different one). Create a new, blank layer, and keep it selected.

6. In Edit/Photoshop CC > Preferences > Cursors, under Painting Cursors, click Full Size Brush Tip (so you will be able to preview the brush diameter).

7. Press [or] to scale the brush, then click or drag in very short strokes to make the cloned pixels appear.**A–B** Imagery from the source point will display within the brush cursor. Note: If the whole layer displays in the overlay as you clone, show the Clone Source panel, 🖼 then check Clipped.

8. *Optional:* To establish a new source point for further cloning, Alt-click/Option-click a different area in the source document.**C–D** You can also change settings for the Clone Stamp tool between strokes.

➤ To create a "double-exposure" effect, with the original pixels partially remaining, lower the Opacity percentage for the Clone Stamp tool.

➤ To keep track of multiple source documents while using the Clone Stamp tool, use the Clone Source panel (see pages 290–291).

A *We're dragging with the Clone Stamp tool to replace the wire and pipe with pixels from the blank wall.*

B *We're continuing to sample the wall and clone away the pipe.*

➤ *To prevent noticeable (tacky!) seams from appearing in a cloned texture, either apply short strokes or just click, and sample multiple times.*

C *We're sampling the vine leaves because we want to add more leaves to the front of the trellis.*

D *Compare this new, improved image with the original one, on the preceding page.*

USING THE CONTENT-AWARE OPTION OF THE SPOT HEALING BRUSH TOOL

For a quick, easy, and powerful way to remove an "object" from a photo, try using the Spot Healing Brush tool, 🩹 with its Content-Aware option (Options bar). This tool works better if the object being removed is surrounded by many small, random shapes (such as foliage, water, or clouds in a landscape) **A–B** than if the surrounding area contains isolated, distinct objects. This tool and option also work well for repairing tears or scratches in a vintage photo.

A *To remove the fire hydrant from this image, for the Spot Healing Brush tool, we chose a brush Hardness of 100% (to let Content-Aware healing — not the brush — blend the edges), Normal mode, and Content-Aware. With a medium-sized brush and one continuous stroke, we covered the hydrant and its shadow.*

B *We sat back while the Spot Healing Brush tool analyzed and sampled pixels from neighboring areas to use as replacement pixels for the hydrant… Poof! That was as easy as retouching gets.*

SAME FEATURE, DIFFERENT RESULTS

*To zap the red barn from this photo, we followed the same steps as described in figure **A**, above.*

Unfortunately, in this case, the automatic healing process of the tool left behind a red tint.

We undid the prior results, then used the same tool, except this time with Replace mode chosen (on the Options bar) instead of Normal. Success!

Applying a Content-Aware fill

Sometimes the Content-Aware option of the Fill command does a seamless (or almost seamless) job of removing a distinct shape from a nondistinct background. You can tweak the results with the Clone Stamp, Healing Brush, or Patch tool (or if the Fill results are unsatisfactory, undo and use one of those tools instead).

To replace an image element with a Content-Aware fill:

1. Duplicate the Background in an image (Ctrl-J/Cmd-J), then hide the Background. Keep the duplicate layer selected.

2. *Optional:* Add a layer mask to the layer, and with the Brush tool and black as the Foreground color, stroke over any areas in the background that you want to prevent Photoshop from sampling as replacement pixels. Click the layer thumbnail.**A**

3. Loosely select the element in the image to be removed, then choose Edit > **Fill**.

4. Choose Contents: **Content-Aware**, check **Color Adaptation** for enhanced color blending, choose Mode: Normal and Opacity: 100%, then click OK.**B**

5. If you created a mask in step 2, deactivate it by Shift-clicking the mask thumbnail.**C**

A *Our goal was to eliminate the red shed from this image. To prevent Photoshop from sampling the bushes and rocks on the right side, we hid those areas via a layer mask. Next we selected the shed loosely with the Lasso tool.*

B *We chose these options in the Fill dialog, then clicked OK.*

C *We deactivated the layer mask. The Fill command removed the shed and a small section of the fence, and replaced that area with random grass and stone textures.*

NOT SURE WHICH AREAS TO MASK?

Do a practice run through the steps on this page, minus the mask (step 2), and note if there are any unwanted elements that Photoshop included in its calculations. Undo the Fill command, mask any areas that you want the program to ignore, then follow steps 3–4.

Using the Content-Aware Move tool

The Content-Aware Move tool can be used to reposition, or to extend, an element in an image. Photoshop will use Content-Aware calculations to fill any exposed areas and camouflage any seams, blending pixels into the texture and colors of the destination area.

To move or reshape an image element with the Content-Aware Move tool:

1. Create a new, blank layer and keep it selected.

2. Choose the **Content-Aware Move** tool ⚔ (J or Shift-J). On the Options bar, check **Sample All Layers**.

3. *Optional:* On the Options bar, check **Transform on Drop** to enable scaling of the moved pixels. ★

4. Drag loosely around the element to be moved or extended.**A** To add areas to the selection, hold down Shift while dragging; to subtract areas, hold down Alt/Option while dragging.

5. Do either of the following:

   To move the selected area, choose **Move** from the Mode menu on the Options bar, then drag the selection, preferably to an area that looks similar to the original background in the setting.

   To extend the object, choose **Extend** from the Mode menu, then drag the selection in the direction in which you want it to be enlarged.

   The tool will send the selected pixels and any filled-in areas to the new, blank layer.

6. If you checked **Transform on Drop**, the Transform box will display. Drag a corner of the Transform box to scale or rotate the selection.**B** Hold down Alt/Option to scale from the center of the selection. To accept the transformation, press Enter/Return or click the Commit Transform button ✓ (Options bar). ★

7. On the Options bar, choose a **Structure** value (1–7), via the pop-up slider or via the scrubby slider, to control how loosely (1) or strictly (7) the repositioned and replacement pixels blend into the image. Also choose a **Color** value (0–10); the higher the Color value, the more color blending will be applied. ★ A value of 0 disables color blending. (**A–B**, next page). Pause while the setting is applied. Settings can be changed only while the selection is active.

8. Deselect (Ctrl-D/Cmd-D). See also **C–D**, next page.

➤ To hide (then show) the Content-Aware Move selection border, press Ctrl-H/Cmd-H.

A *With the Content-Aware Move tool (Mode: Move), we dragged to loosely select the jogger and his shadow, …*

B *… then dragged the selected area to the right. The Transform box displayed. We dragged the upper-left corner outward to increase the scale of the jogger, then accepted the transformation.*

A *Next, we hid the selection border. With a Structure value of 3 (loose) and a Color value of 1, the jogger is misshapen and a color halo appears around his head and arms.*

B *With a Structure value of 7 (strict) and a Color value of 5, the replacement pixels look more seamless. The edges of the jogger are cleaner and the color halo has been removed.*

C *With the Content-Aware Move tool, we selected the pastry (more tightly than we selected the dude on the beach, who was on a more complex background).*

D *We set the tool Mode to Extend, dragged upward to create another tier of pastry, then chose a Structure value of 4 and a Color value of 4 to seamlessly blend the extended pixels.*

Removing an image element with the Patch tool

Another way to replace image content is by using the Patch tool with its Content-Aware option. You draw a selection, then drag it to a source area for Photoshop to analyze as replacement pixels. To vary the blending results, change the Structure and Color settings.

To eliminate an image element with the Patch tool:

1. Create a new, blank layer, and keep it selected.

2. Choose the **Patch** tool ▓ (J or Shift-J).

3. On the Options bar, choose **Patch: Content-Aware** and check **Sample All Layers**.

4. Drag a selection around the area to be removed.**A** You can Shift-drag to add to the selection or Alt-drag/Option-drag to subtract from it.

5. Drag the selection to an area that looks most like the original background behind the object.**B** When you release the mouse, Photoshop will fill in the exposed area based on those sampled pixels.

6. On the Options bar, choose a **Structure** value (1–7), via the pop-up slider or via the scrubby slider, to control how loosely (1) or strictly (7) the replacement pixels blend into the image.**C–D** ★ Also choose a **Color** value (0 –10); the higher the Color value, the more color blending will be applied. A value of 0 disables color blending. These parameters can be changed only while the selection is still active.

7. Deselect (Ctrl-D/Cmd-D).

➤ To hide the selection border temporarily, press Ctrl-H/Cmd-H (repeat to redisplay it).

A *With the Patch tool set to Content-Aware, we selected the elements to be removed.*

B *Next, we dragged the selection to an area that looked similar to the one around the elements being removed.*

C *At a Structure value of 1 and Color value of 0, the texture and color of the replacement pixels did not blend well.*

D *At a Structure value of 6 and a Color value of 3, the replacement pixels make a cleaner, more believable match.*

In Photoshop, just as in photography, you can use focusing techniques to enhance a scene, such as a shallow depth of field to differentiate a subject from its background or blurriness to convey a sense of motion. And you can use sharpening methods to counteract the effects of resampling, to remedy blurring from camera shake, or to prepare a file for output.

In this chapter, you'll blur areas of an image using the Field Blur, Iris Blur, Tilt-Shift, Path Blur, and Spin Blur filters (collectively called the Blur Gallery). And you will apply sharpening via the Smart Sharpen, Unsharp Mask, and Shake Reduction filters, and via the Sharpen tool.

Note: For lens corrections, we recommend using the Lens Correction tab in Camera Raw (instead of the Lens Correction filter in Photoshop), either before you open your photo into Photoshop, or by way of Filter > Camera Raw Filter in Photoshop. See pages 78–81.

Applying a filter in the Blur Gallery

The Field Blur, Iris Blur, Tilt-Shift, Path Blur, and Spin Blur filters provide powerful and flexible on-canvas and panel controls for blurring parts of an image.

Note: To apply filters in the Blur Gallery, Use Graphics Processor must be checked in Edit/Photoshop CC > Preferences > Performance. You will see a more accurate preview while making on-canvas adjustments if your system has a graphics card with 1 GB or more of VRAM or an embedded HD graphics processing unit.

To apply a filter in the Blur Gallery:

1. Open an image (preferably one that is all or mostly in focus). To keep the filter settings nondestructive and editable, convert a duplicate of an image layer or the Background to a Smart Object.

   Optional: To mask the filter effect partially, create a selection. The selection area will appear in the Smart Filters mask when you exit the gallery.

2. Choose Filter > Blur Gallery > **Field Blur** to produce multiple blur areas, **Iris Blur** to blur areas around a focus ellipse, **Tilt-Shift** to apply blurring in straight bands across portions of the image, or **Spin Blur** to create an effect of radial motion within a circular area. To apply the **Path Blur** filter, see pages 338–339.

3. A default pin with controls appears in the image, and panels with option settings appear in a dock on the

Continued on the following page

REFOCUSING

16

right. On the Options bar, make sure Preview is checked (P).

To control the degree of blurring for a Field, Iris, or Tilt-Shift blur, either adjust the **Blur** slider in the dock; or in the image, drag around the blur ring that surrounds the pin (add more black to the ring to reduce the blur, or reduce black to increase the blur). Note: If pins or controls do not display, check Edit Pins in the View > Show > submenu. ★

4. For a **Field Blur**, add another pin by clicking in the image. Set the Blur value for one pin to 0% (full focus), then click the other pin and give it a higher Blur value (blurring). To use the full potential of this filter, add more pins, some with a Blur value of 0 and some with a Blur value greater than 0 (**A–C**, next page).

   For an **Iris Blur**, do any of the following: To adjust the shape of the focus ellipse, drag one of the small outer round handles; to scale the ellipse uniformly, drag its edge; to rotate the ellipse, drag outside one of the small handles (double-arrow pointer); to reposition where the blurring begins, drag one of the feather handles (or to move one feather handle separately, drag it while holding down Alt/Option); to change the ellipse to a rounded rectangle, drag the square Roundness knob outward (**A–D**, page 336).

   For a **Tilt-Shift Blur**, do any of the following: To adjust where the blurring begins, drag either or both of the solid focus lines; to adjust the transition between the in-focus and blurred areas, drag either or both of the dashed feather lines; to rotate the focus area, drag a rotation handle slightly to the left or right (**A–C**, page 337).

   For a **Spin Blur**, do any of the following: To reshape the focus ellipse, drag one of the outer round handles; to scale the ellipse uniformly, drag its edge; to adjust the angle, drag around the blur ring or change the Blur Angle value in the panel; to move the blur, drag anywhere inside the ellipse; or to reposition the rotation point (say, to make it look as if subject was shot at an angle), drag the point with Alt/Option held down. See **A–C**, page 340.

5. You can also do any of the following optional steps:

   To **add** a pin, click in the image.

   To **reposition** a pin, drag its center point. You can move a pin outside the canvas area.

To **delete** a pin, click its center point, then press Backspace/Delete.

To **copy** a pin, drag its center point with Alt-Ctrl/ Option-Cmd held down.

To control the amount of focus within the currently selected ellipse for an Iris Blur, or between the two feather lines for a Tilt-Shift blur, adjust the **Focus** setting on the Options bar.

6. To hide the on-canvas controls to judge the blur-ring effect, press and hold down H (then release).

7. *Optional:* To brighten the blur highlights to the point that they become abstract, colored orbs, for a Field, Iris, or Tilt-Shift Blur, click a pin, check Bokeh in the Blur Effects panel, then adjust the settings (**A–C**, page 342).

8. *Optional:* To save the blur mask that Photoshop created for the filter to an alpha channel, check Save Mask to Channels on the Options bar (**A–D**, page 343). To preview the mask, press and hold down M (then release).

9. To accept your blur filter edits, press Enter/Return or click OK on the Options bar. To edit the blur settings or to mask the results, see pages 374–376.

➤ To remove all blur pins from an image, click the Remove All Pins button 🔁 on the Options bar.

➤ To switch to a different filter in the Blur Tools panel, uncheck the box for the current filter, then expand the category for the desired one.

➤ To the same Smart Object, you can also apply nonblur filters. We don't recommend applying multiple Blur Gallery filters to an image, as doing so is likely to blur the whole photo.

USING A SELECTION WITH A BLUR FILTER

➤ If you create a selection before applying a Blur Gallery filter to a Smart Object, the selection area will appear as the white area in the editable mask for the Smart Filter. If desired, you can click the mask thumbnail on the Layers panel, then feather the edge of the mask via the Properties panel (Mask options).

➤ If you create a selection before displaying the Blur Gallery controls for a standard layer (not a Smart Object), you can control how gradually the blurring bleeds to the edge of the selection via the Selection Bleed slider on the Options bar.

A *This is the original image.*

THE FIELD BLUR FILTER

Use the Field Blur filter when you need the most flexibility and control in blurring specific areas of an image (such as the hair, arms, and background in the photo on this page), while keeping other, more important, areas in sharp focus. Use as many pins as you like, but be sure to place a few pins with a Blur value of 0% in areas that you want to keep in focus, and place other pins with a Blur value between 5% and 100% in areas that you want to blur (the blurring occurs between the high and low values).**A–C** You can reposition any pin individually by dragging it in the image. This is one of our favorite features of Photoshop!

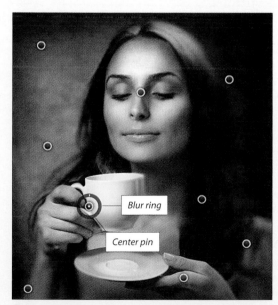

B *We applied the Field Blur filter using a Blur value of 0% for the pins on the woman's face and hands to keep those areas in focus, and Blur values above 10% for all the other pins.*

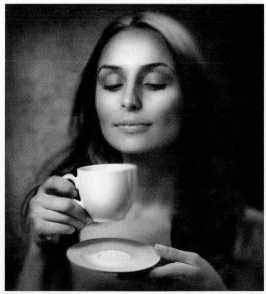

C *This is the result.*

THE IRIS BLUR FILTER

The Iris Blur filter applies blurring around a focus ellipse. You can use just a single pin or click in the image to create additional ones.**A–D**

A *This is the original image.*

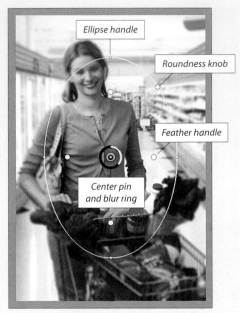

B *When we chose the Iris Blur filter, the default on-canvas controls displayed.*

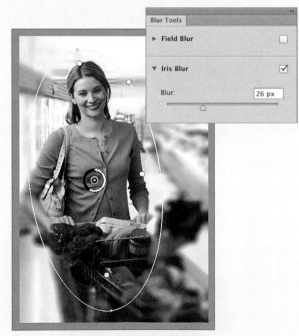

C *We moved the ellipse slightly to the left by dragging the pin, elongated the ellipse, rotated it slightly to match the angle of the figure, then held down Alt/Option and dragged just the top feather handle upward to keep the woman's face in full focus.*

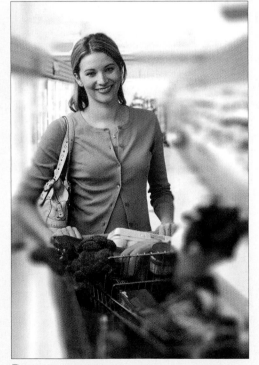

D *In the final image, the figure and part of the shopping cart are in focus, while the background is blurred.*

THE TILT-SHIFT FILTER

The Tilt-Shift filter applies blurring in two straight bands across the image, while keeping a band in the center in focus. You can control the width of the blurred area by dragging either or both of the focus lines, adjust the amount of feathering by dragging either or both of the feather lines, or shift the whole widget to a new angle by dragging a rotation handle slightly.**A–C** You can also choose a negative Distortion value to distort a blurred area along imaginary lines that curve around the pin, or a positive value to distort a blurred area along lines that radiate outward from the pin. Additionally, you can check Symmetric Distortion to apply the distortion in both sides.

A *This is the original image.*

B *We chose the Tilt-Shift filter settings shown at right, rotated the pin, and dragged the feather and focus lines.*

C *This is the result of our applying the Tilt-Shift filter.*

TILT-SHIFT IN PHOTOGRAPHY

When a small- or medium-format camera is outfitted with a special tilt-shift lens, that lens can be tilted slightly toward a landscape so as to capture the whole scene in focus. This tilt feature can also be used with selective focusing to make the foreground and background more blurry than the midground (an intentional change from what is expected), with the result that the landscape looks miniaturized.

The shift feature of a lens sets the image plane so it is parallel to the subject, thereby preventing buildings or other objects that have parallel planes from converging. This feature can also be used to heighten that convergence deliberately.

The Path Blur filter applies a motion blurring effect to a path. You can edit the path to control the shape of the blur, say, to mimic the result of camera movement.

To apply the Path Blur filter:

1. On the Layers panel, click a Smart Object. **A**

2. Choose Filter > Blur Gallery > **Path Blur.** A blue path appears on the image. The arrow on the path indicates the direction of motion.

3. After doing any of the following, you can press and hold down H to hide the on-canvas controls:

   To change the **length** or **angle** of the path, drag either endpoint.

   To produce a **curve**, drag the center point or a straight segment. **B**

   To **add** more curve points, drag a segment.

   To **convert** a curve point to a corner point, or to convert a corner point to a curve point, hold down Alt/Option and click it.

   To produce **another** (straight) **path**, drag in the image (**A**, next page). Or to produce a path that has multiple segments, hold down Alt/Option and click several times, then to end the path, press Enter/Return or Esc, or click the last point you created. To produce multiple curve segments, click without Alt/Option.

   To control the speed of the blur, adjust the **Speed** value in the panel. To control how gradually the blur fades, use the **Taper** slider. These settings affect all Path Blurs in the image (**B**, next page).

   Check **Centered Blur** for a more uniform, anchored blur; or uncheck this option for a more malleable blur, and to let imagery move more fluidly as you drag paths or blur shapes.

   To **move** a path, hold down Ctrl/Cmd and drag it.

   You can also move the **midpoint** along the length of a path (you can't delete the midpoint).

   To **delete** a point or path, click it, then press Backspace/Delete.

   To further manipulate a blur shape, click an endpoint, check **Edit Blur Shapes** in the panel, then drag the white dot at the end of the red guide to rotate just that guide.

A *This is the original image of a country road.*

B *To create an illusion of fast motion, we repositioned the two endpoints on the blue path for a Path Blur, then dragged to curve the path to match the road. To minimize blurring at the end of the road, we set the right endpoint to an End Point Speed of 0%.*

To change the blur speed, raise the **End Point Speed** value on the panel; or with Edit Blur Shapes checked in the panel, drag the end of the red guide to lengthen or shorten it.

To remove the blur from a blue endpoint, hold down Ctrl/Cmd and click the endpoint; or click the endpoint, then set the **End Point Speed**

value in the panel to 0 (zero).**C–D** The red guide disappears and the endpoint becomes gray.

4. Keep **High Quality** checked to help prevent the blur from looking jagged.

5. To accept your blur filter edits, press Enter/Return or click OK on the Options bar.

A To straighten the blurring on the left side of the road, we dragged to create a new, straight path.

B We chose these Speed and Taper settings for all of our Path Blur paths.

C To eliminate blurring from the background, we dragged to create another Path Blur, then set the End Point Speed for both endpoints on that path to 0 px.

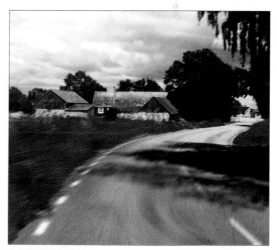

D The final image is shown above. The Path Blur effect draws your eye down the road.

THE SPIN BLUR FILTER

The Spin Blur filter applies blurring around a circular focus ring. The filter creates the effect of a spinning object. It can be used with other motion filters to create a more realistic sense of motion on a static or in-focus moving object. **A**

After choosing the Spin Blur filter, roll over the image to make the on-image controls appear. **B–C**

ADDING A STROBE-AND-FLASH EFFECT

To add a strobe effect to a Path or Spin Blur, use these options in the **Motion Blur Effects** tab:

➤ **Strobe Strength** controls how much blur is visible between flash exposures. The higher the strength, the stronger the strobe effect.

➤ **Strobe Flashes** controls the number of exposures in the image (positions where a blurred shape is captured).

➤ **Strobe Flash Duration** (for a Spin Blur only) controls the amount of rotation that is captured in each strobe flash. The shorter the duration, the more distinct the shapes in the blur.

A *This is the original image of the in-focus bicycle wheel.*

B *We chose the Spin Blur filter, set the Blur Angle to 15°, and enlarged the focus ring by dragging its edge.*

C *After exiting the Blur Gallery, we clicked the Smart Filters mask thumbnail, then applied brush strokes to the bike frame and foot to mask the Spin Blur filter effect from those areas.*

USING THE NOISE OPTIONS IN THE BLUR GALLERY ★

On an image that contains noise or grain,**A** you can use the Noise panel to reintroduce noise into blurred areas **B** to balance the amount of texture displayed in blurred and non-blurred areas.

➤ In the Blur Gallery on-canvas controls, from the menu on the Noise panel, choose a method for generating noise: Gaussian, Uniform, or Grain (the method used in Camera Raw).

➤ To increase the noise in blurred areas of the image to match the level of noise in non-blurred areas, move the Amount slider. Note: Moving any slider will automatically check the box to turn the option on.

➤ When Grain is chosen in the menu, do the following:

Move the Size slider to control the size of grain particles.

Reduce the Roughness value below 50% for a more uniform grain, or increase it above 50% for an uneven, coarse grain.

➤ To control the amount of color in the noise, move the Color slider. Low values produce monochrome noise; high values produce color noise.

➤ To reduce noise in highlight areas to better balance the amount of texture displayed in highlight and shadow areas, lower the Highlights value.**C–D**

A *The original image contains visible grains of texture throughout.*

B *We applied a Field blur using multiple pins to blur the background areas. No noise was added, so blurred areas appear smooth.*

C *We used the settings shown above to add monochrome noise to blurred areas.*

D *This the final image.*

A *This is the original image.*

B *We created multiple pins for the Field Blur filter, checked Bokeh, increased the Light Bokeh value to brighten the bokeh, increased the Bokeh Color to intensify the color saturation, and moved the Light Range sliders near each other at the right end of the bar to limit the effect to the image highlights.*

WHAT IS BOKEH?

The word bokeh (pronounced "BOH-kay") is derived from a Japanese word meaning blur or haze. In photography, the term is used to describe a pattern that is formed by highlights and shadows in blurred areas. Some camera lenses produce more pleasing bokeh than others (good bokeh, bad bokeh).

USING THE BOKEH OPTIONS IN THE BLUR GALLERY

To achieve good results from the Bokeh feature in the Blur Gallery, you may need to experiment with various images and settings (it took us a number of tries).

The bokeh will be more pronounced in some areas of an image than in others; you will see this if you drag a pin to a different part of the image. Also, if you change the Blur value for a pin, the size of the bokeh is also affected.

➤ To control the brightness of the bokeh, adjust the Light Bokeh value.**A–C**

➤ To control the amount of color variation in the bokeh, adjust the Bokeh Color value.

➤ To control the range of brightness values in which the bokeh can appear, drag the Light Range sliders. For smaller bokeh spots, position the sliders near each other at either end of the bar.

➤ For higher-quality bokeh (but slower rendering), check High Quality on the Options bar.

C *This is the final image.*

USING THE MASK FROM A BLUR GALLERY FILTER

As we stated in step 8 on page 334, while applying a filter in the Blur Gallery, you can save the blur mask to an alpha channel by clicking Save Mask to Channels on the Options bar. After accepting the filter, save your file.

To use the mask in your document, before applying an image edit (such as an adjustment layer, artistic filter, or brush strokes), hold down Ctrl/Cmd and click the alpha channel thumbnail on the Channels panel ● to load the mask as a selection. It will protect the nonblurred areas of the layer. **A–D**

B *We held down Ctrl/Cmd and clicked the alpha channel thumbnail to load the Blur Mask as a selection.*

A *When we applied the Iris Blur filter to this image, we checked Save Mask to Channel.*

C *We created a Color Balance adjustment layer, then moved the Yellow slider to the left to make the image slightly warmer.*

D *Finally, we reloaded the selection, then used a Levels adjustment to lighten the image. The mask on each adjustment layer is hiding the adjustment from the center of the image.*

Applying the Smart Sharpen filter

Most digital photos need to be sharpened, and the need increases if you change a file's dimensions or resolution with the Resample Image option checked, convert a file to CMYK Color mode, or apply a transformation command.

To sharpen an image, you can use either the Smart Sharpen filter or the Unsharp Mask filter (the latter, despite its name, has a sharpening effect; see pages 347–348). Be aware that these filters can introduce noise, and therefore should be applied as a final step before output, after all image editing is completed.

High-resolution commercial printing also causes some minor blurring due to dot gain. You can anticipate and compensate for this by sharpening the image again as you prepare it for output. With practice, you will learn how much sharpening is needed.

The Smart Sharpen filter has several unique features that you won't find in the Unsharp Mask dialog (see the sidebar below), but both are powerful commands. We typically use the Smart Sharpen filter for targeted sharpening, as it helps to minimize noise in soft, low-contrast areas, among other benefits, and use the Unsharp Mask filter for output sharpening. Regardless of which command you use, be sure to sharpen, period!

To apply the Smart Sharpen filter:

1. Open a photo that needs sharpening. **A** To protect the original layer, on the Layers panel, click an image layer or the Background, then press Ctrl-J/Cmd-J to duplicate it. Right-click the duplicate layer and choose **Convert to Smart Object**.

2. Choose Filter > Sharpen > **Smart Sharpen**. The Smart Sharpen dialog opens. The dialog is resizable.

   ➤ Set the zoom level for the preview to 100%. To bring a different area of the image into view, either drag in the preview or click in the document. On the menu in the dialog, ⚙ . make sure Use Legacy is unchecked.

3. From the Preset menu, choose **Default**.

4. Lower the **Reduce Noise** slider to around 5% to view the full sharpening effect.

5. Choose an **Amount** value for the strength of the sharpening (for a 300 ppi document, set this value to 250–350%). Increase the **Radius** value until halo effects display along sharp edges, then reduce it just enough to remove the halos. Don't worry if the image now looks too sharp (**A**, next page).

6. From the **Remove** menu, choose an algorithm for the correction: Gaussian Blur is a good

---

SMART FEATURES OF THE SMART SHARPEN FILTER

➤ It lets you sharpen (then fade the sharpening) separately in the shadow and highlight areas of an image.

➤ It detects edges, and therefore produces fewer color halos than Unsharp Mask.

➤ With its Reduce Noise option, the filter sharpens edges without sharpening noise.

➤ Smart Sharpen lets you choose from three algorithms (to correct Gaussian blur, lens blur, or motion blur), whereas Unsharp Mask corrects only Gaussian blur.

➤ Smart Sharpen lets you save and reuse your settings, for greater speed and consistency in your workflow.

A We'll use the Smart Sharpen filter to sharpen specific tonal areas in this blurry portrait (the resolution of this image is 300 ppi).

A *The settings we chose in the Smart Sharpen dialog successfully sharpened the key details, such as the eyes and lips, but in the process also oversharpened the skin (now the pores look too pronounced). Note that we chose Remove: Gaussian Blur because we used that filter to soften this photo originally.*

all-purpose choice; Lens Blur sharpens details with fewer resulting halos (we prefer this option); Motion Blur is useful for correcting blurring due to slight movement of the camera or subject, but to use this option effectively, you need to enter the correct angle of movement.

7. Increase the **Reduce Noise** value to lessen the amount of noise that is produced by the sharpening. Keep this value between 10% and 20% so image details aren't softened too much.

8. Expand the Shadows/Highlights category. To reduce the amount of sharpening in the shadow areas, drag in the preview to display an area of the image that contains both shadows and midtones, then under **Shadows**, make these adjustments: **B**

Choose a **Radius** value (between 10 and 25) to control how many neighboring pixels will be compared to each adjusted pixel. The higher the Radius, the larger the area that Photoshop uses for comparison.

Move the **Fade Amount** slider until you see the desired reduction of oversharpening in the shadows.

Choose a **Tonal Width** value to control the range of midtones that are affected by the Fade Amount.

Continued on the following page

B *Under Shadows, we chose a moderate Fade Amount to soften the sharpening and noise in the shadows (such as in the area between the woman's face and hands), and we chose a moderate Tonal Width value to sharpen the shadows fully and the midtones only partially (to keep the midtones looking smooth).*

The higher the Tonal Width, the wider the range of midtones that are affected, and the more gradually the sharpening fades into the shadows. At a low value (5–20%) only very dark shadow areas will be sharpened.

9. To reduce the amount of sharpening in the highlight areas, drag the image in the preview to display an area that contains both highlights and midtones, then under **Highlights, A** adjust the **Radius**, **Fade Amount**, and **Tonal Width** values (in that order), as you did in the preceding step.

10. To compare the unsharpened and sharpened versions of the image, press on the dialog preview, then release. Hopefully, the image details are sufficiently sharp. If the overall image looks too sharp, either reduce the uppermost **Radius** value slightly or raise the **Reduce Noise** value slightly.

11. *Optional:* To save the current settings as a preset, choose Save Preset from the Preset menu, enter a name, then click Save. Saved presets are available on the Preset menu for any image.

12. Click OK. **B–C**

➤ To modify the Smart Sharpen results, double-click the Smart Sharpen listing for the Smart Object.

Amount:	330	%
Radius:	2.8	px
Reduce Noise:	10	%
Remove:	Gaussian Blur ⬧	0	°

▼ **Shadows**

Fade Amount:	52	%
Tonal Width:	50	%
Radius:	16	px

Highlights

Fade Amount:	52	%
Tonal Width:	58	%
Radius:	20	px

A *Finally, under Highlights, we chose a moderate Fade Amount to soften the sharpening in the highlights, and a higher Tonal Width value to extend the softened sharpening into the midtones (the broad, flat areas, such as the forehead, cheeks, and chin).*

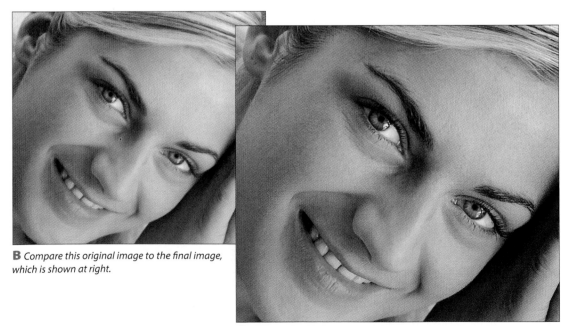

B *Compare this original image to the final image, which is shown at right.*

C *The Smart Sharpen filter improved the clarity of the facial features without applying unflattering sharpening to the cheeks and forehead.*

Applying the Unsharp Mask filter

In order to do its job of sharpening, the Unsharp Mask filter increases the contrast between adjacent pixels. To control the level of contrast, you will choose settings for three variables: Amount, Radius, and Threshold.

To apply the Unsharp Mask filter:

1. Choose a zoom level of 50–100% for your image.

2. Duplicate an image layer (Ctrl-J/Cmd-J),**A** then right-click the duplicate layer and choose **Convert to Smart Object**.

3. With the Smart Object layer selected, choose Filter > Sharpen > **Unsharp Mask**.

4. In the dialog, choose an **Amount** percentage to control how much the contrast will be increased.**B** For some recommended settings, see the sidebar on this page.

   ➤ Press P to toggle the Preview off, then on, to compare the original and sharpened images. To bring a different area of the image into view, drag in the preview or click in the document.

5. The **Radius** setting controls how many neighboring pixels around high-contrast edges the filter affects. When setting a value, consider the pixel count of the image and its subject matter. The higher the pixel count, the higher the Radius value needed.**C** For a low-contrast image that contains large, simple objects and smooth transitions, try a high Radius of 2; for an intricate, high-contrast image that contains many sharp transitions, try a lower Radius of around 1.

Continued on the following page

SUGGESTED SETTINGS FOR UNSHARP MASK

For an image that is 2000 x 3000 pixels or larger, try using these values:

Soft-edged subjects, such as landscapes	Amount 100–150%, Radius 1–1.5, Threshold 6–10
Portraits	Amount 100–120%, Radius 1–2, Threshold 4–6, or to the point that skin areas begin to look smoother
Buildings, objects, etc., for which contrast is a priority	Amount 150–200% or higher, Radius 1.5–3, Threshold 0–3

A *This original 300 ppi image is slightly blurry.*

B *A high Amount value and a low Radius value for the Unsharp Mask filter barely sharpened the image.*

C *A high Radius value of 4.0, on the other hand, produced ugly halos around the numerals on the ruler and on the blue lines of the graph paper.*

Note: The Amount and Radius settings are interdependent, meaning that if you raise the Radius, you'll need to lower the Amount, and vice versa.

6. Choose a **Threshold** value to establish how different in value an area of pixels must be from an adjacent area for it to be affected by the filter.**A** Start with a Threshold value of 0 (to sharpen the entire image), then increase it gradually. At a Threshold of 5–10, high-contrast areas will be sharpened and areas of lesser contrast will be sharpened much less. When increasing the Threshold, you can also increase the Amount and Radius to sharpen edges.

A proper Threshold setting will prevent the filter from oversharpening low-contrast areas.

7. Click OK.**B** To adjust the filter settings at any time, double-click the Unsharp Mask listing on the Layers panel.

➤ If the sharpening produced color halos along the edges of some of the objects, choose Luminosity as the blending mode for the Smart Object. This mode will limit the sharpening to just the luminosity (light and dark) values and remove it from the hue and saturation (color) values.

A *At a high Threshold value of 12, the Unsharp Mask filter sharpened only the high-contrast edges. The lower-contrast (light blue) lines on the graph paper remained blurry.*

B *A low Threshold value of 0–1 worked better for this image because it contains a lot of flat surfaces, hard edges, and fine lines.*

Applying the Shake Reduction filter

The Shake Reduction filter detects, then resharpens, edges in a photo that were blurred due to slight shaking of the camera. The filter produces better quality results on indoor shots of a static subject taken in good natural lighting with a slow shutter speed and no flash, or on indoor or outdoor photos taken with a long focal length. The photos should contain few bright highlights and minimal noise.

Improvements to the Shake Reduction filter include a new check box that disables or enables Artifact Suppression, as well as controls for adjusting the length or direction of a blur trace path. You can compare and adjust the Smoothing and Suppression settings for any pair of blur trace regions via sliders in a loupe. The dialog preview provides support for retina displays, and the preview on large monitors is also improved.

To apply the Shake Reduction filter:

Part 1 — Choose basic settings

1. Do either of the following:

   For the best results, open a raw photo into Camera Raw; correct for noise; apply minimal exposure adjustments, if necessary; then hold down Shift and click **Open Object.A**

   Open an RGB photo into Photoshop. Duplicate the photo layer (Ctrl-J/Cmd-J), then right-click the duplicate layer and choose **Convert to Smart Object** from the context menu.

2. Choose Filter > Sharpen > **Shake Reduction**. To let the filter evaluate the amount of noise in the image, keep the **Source Noise** menu set to Auto.

3. An area of the photo in which the filter detects blurred edges displays in a loupe (enlarged detail).**B** If the loupe is docked and you want to float it over the image, click the **Undock Detail** button 🔼 (Q) in the Detail area; or if the loupe is floating and you want to dock it in the panel, click its close (X) button. It works the same in both locations.

4. You can change the area that the filter evaluates for the correction. If the loupe is floating, drag it to a new location; if the loupe is docked, drag within it. Or choose the **Blur Estimation** tool 🔲 (E), then click another area of the image. To optimize the filter results based on the new area, click the **Enhance At Loupe Location** button 🔘 in the lower-left corner of the loupe. The blur and

ghosting correction will render first within the loupe, then in the overall preview.

5. To try out a few **Blur Trace Bounds** values, drag the slider to the lower portion of its range, then release to preview the results; next, drag the slider to the middle portion of its range, then release to preview; and finally, do the same for the upper portion of its range (**A**, next page). Set the slider to the value that produced the best results.

6. If you're satisfied with the filter results, click OK. If not, continue with Parts 2 through 7…

➤ To compare the sharpened and unsharpened versions of the image, press P, then press P again. You can also press and hold on the loupe, then release.

Continued on the following page

A *This original photo is blurred due to camera movement.*

B *The Shake Reduction filter chose a location for the loupe.*

Part 2 — Reduce edge noise

1. Check **Artifact Suppression**; the Artifact Suppression slider appears. To eliminate noise artifacts in low- and medium-contrast areas of the image, set the slider to a medium value (30–50%). (If you leave Artifact Suppression off, the image may look sharper, but will also contain more artifacts.)

2. The **Smoothing** option reduces noise in an image, but in so doing also makes the image look less sharp. With artifacts now remedied by Artifact Suppression, we suggest that you reduce the Smoothing value until noise begins to reappear. The lower Smoothing value will make the edges look sharper.

3. If you're satisfied with the results, click OK. If not, continue with Part 3, below.

In its standard mode, the Shake Reduction filter analyzes just one region. To enable it to analyze more than one region, follow these steps.

Part 3 — Create multiple blur trace regions

1. If the Advanced area isn't expanded, click the arrowhead. Click the **Add Suggested Blur Trace** button **+** to add a new blur estimation region.**B** Another thumbnail appears in the side panel.

2. If you need to reposition the estimation region, drag the pin in its center. If you need to resize the region, drag any handle.**C**

3. To designate the region the filter will use to optimize the sharpening, check the box under one or both thumbnails. If you check both boxes, the filter will optimize the sharpening for each region, then apply a combination of those settings to other areas of the image (**A**, next page).

   ➤ To remove a blur estimation region, click its thumbnail, then press Backspace/Delete; or right-click the thumbnail or its pin in the preview, and choose Delete Blur Trace from the context menu.

Part 4 — Create and adjust a blur trace path

1. Zoom to around 200–300% in an area that shows ghosting from camera shake. Choose the **Blur Direction** tool ⟍ (R), then drag a very short distance from the ghosted edge to the spot where you want it to be relocated. Another blur trace thumbnail appears in the side panel. Check Preview.

A We tried out low-, mid-, and high-range Blur Trace Bounds values before deciding on a high value of 132 px.

B When we clicked the Add Suggested Blur Trace button, the estimation region created by the filter straddled the edge of the picture frame and produced more ghosting.

C To prevent the high-contrast edges of the picture frame from being analyzed, we sized the blur estimation region to fit the oil painting. By manually designating the region to be analyzed, we obtained better results.

➤ If you want to select (and then adjust) an existing path that you drew with the Blur Direction tool, in the Advanced area, click a blur trace thumbnail (a thumbnail that has a padlock icon), then make sure the box below the thumbnail is checked.

2. Under Blur Trace Settings,**B** move the **Blur Trace Length** slider to adjust the length of the path (to match the distance that edges in the photo were moved, and therefore blurred, by the camera shake). If needed, also rotate the **Blur Trace Direction** dial to adjust the angle of the path.

➤ Remember, if you want to compare the sharpened and unsharpened versions of the image at any time, press P (then press P again).

3. Click OK to apply the filter settings and exit the dialog, or continue with another part of this task.

Part 5 — Compare and adjust blur trace settings in a loupe

1. If you haven't already done so, create two or more blur estimation regions in the preview either by clicking the **Add Suggested Blur Trace** button,✚ or by dragging twice in the preview with the **Blur Estimation** tool ▫ (E). Adjust the blur trace settings for each region.

2. In the Advanced area, hold down Ctrl/Cmd and click two blur trace thumbnails for which you want to compare and adjust settings. The results of the current settings for the selected thumbnails will display side by side in a large loupe.**C**

3. Adjust the **Smoothing** and [Artifact] **Suppression** sliders in either or both panels of the loupe.

4. *Optional:* To compare and adjust the tracing results while viewing a different part of the image, drag in either panel of the loupe.

5. To close the loupe, click the close box (X) in its upper-left corner or press Esc.

Continued on the following page

A *To produce a combined sharpening result, we checked both thumbnails in the Advanced area. The white shapes in the thumbnails indicate the shape and direction of a blur that was caused by camera shake.*

B *Using the controls under Blur Trace Settings, you can customize any user-created blur trace path.*

C *We held down Ctrl/Cmd and clicked two blur trace thumbnails: The adjustment results for the two regions displayed side by side in a large loupe.*

Part 6 — Save your Shake Reduction settings for future use

1. From the Advanced menu In the Shake Reduction dialog, choose **Save Workspace** to save the current estimation regions, blur trace thumbnails, and slider settings; or choose **Save Blur Trace** to save just the currently selected blur trace thumbnail and its settings.**A**

2. In the Save Workspace or Save Blur Trace dialog, enter a file name (keep the default extension), choose a location, then click Save.

   To access a saved Shake Reduction workspace or saved blur trace settings at any time, choose Load from the Advanced menu, locate the saved workspace or blur trace file, then click Open.

   ➤ To restore the default settings to the dialog at any time, hold down Alt/Option and click Reset (Cancel becomes Reset).

Part 7 — Exit the Shake Reduction dialog

When you're satisfied with the filter results, click OK.

Using the Sharpen tool

When used with the Protect Detail option checked on the Options bar, the Sharpen tool enhances details without introducing noticeable artifacts. With this tool, you can sharpen areas selectively without having to use a mask.

To use the Sharpen tool:

1. Create a new, blank layer to contain the sharpened pixels, and keep it selected.**B**

2. Choose the **Sharpen** tool △ (it's on the same fly-out menu as the Blur tool).

3. On the Options bar, choose a **Strength** value, and check **Sample All Layers** and **Protect Detail**.

4. Press [or] to adjust the brush diameter, then drag across the areas that need sharpening.**C** For stronger sharpening, drag again in the same area.

5. *Optional:* To reduce the overall effect of the sharpening, lower the opacity of the new layer.

A *Via the menu in the Advanced area of the Shake Reduction dialog, you can save and load your custom settings.*

B *The eyes in this photo look too soft.*

C *With the Sharpen tool, we quickly sharpened just the eyes.*

Now that you're familiar with many of the basic controls in Photoshop, it's time to learn some fun ways to manipulate the content of your layers. In this chapter, you will learn how to clip (hide the visibility of) multiple layers using a mask, blend pixels between layers using advanced controls, apply transformation commands to a layer (including normal and Content-Aware scaling), create artboards ★ for mobile screen layouts, apply the Liquify filter, and apply the Warp command.

Note: For faster previewing of your Liquify, Warp, and transform edits, make sure Use Graphics Processor is checked in Edit/Photoshop CC > Preferences > Performance before opening your file.

Using clipping masks

When layers are put into a clipping mask, the content of the bottommost layer, called the "base" layer, clips (limits which areas are visible on) the layers above it. The mode and opacity of the base layer are also applied to the clipped layers. Layers in a clipping mask remain fully editable and can be repositioned individually.

To create a clipping mask:

1. On the Layers panel, make sure the layers to be clipped are listed consecutively. The base layer can be a type, image, or shape layer or a Smart Object; stack it below the layers to be clipped.**A**

2. Do either of the following:

    Click a layer to be clipped, or Shift-click multiple layers to be clipped (not the base layer) (**A**, next page), then press Ctrl-Alt-G/Cmd-Option-G (**B–C**, next page).

Continued on the following page

A *This document contains five layers (including an editable type layer that is currently hidden behind the image layers).*

MORE LAYER ESSENTIALS

17

IN THIS CHAPTER

YUM YUM

To create the image shown above, we used a type layer to clip an image layer (see this page and the next page), warped the type (see page 370), and applied the Emboss, Stroke, and Outer Glow effects (see Chapter 20). We duplicated the type and image layers, moved the duplicate type layer downward, then added a Pattern Fill layer just above the Background.

To clip one layer at a time, Alt-click/Option-click the line between two layers (⌐□ pointer), or right-click one of the layers to be clipped (not the base layer) and choose Create Clipping Mask.

3. *Optional:* To include more layers in the mask, either restack them between existing layers in the mask or repeat the preceding step.

4. *Optional:* You can reposition one or more selected layers in the clipping mask with the Move tool (V).

To link two or more clipped layers so they can be moved more easily as a unit, select their listings, then click the Link Layers button.⚮ Click the listing for one of the linked layers, then with the Move tool, drag in the document.**D** To unlink the layers, select them, then click the Link Layers button.

➤ To use grouped layers in a clipping mask, all the layers (including the base layer) must be in the group.

When you release a layer from a clipping mask, any and all of the masked layers above it are also released.

To release one or more layers from a clipping mask:

Do either of the following:

Alt-click/Option-click the line below the layer to be released.

Click a layer to be released (not the base layer), then press Ctrl-Alt-G/Cmd-Option-G.

To release an entire clipping mask:

Alt-click/Option-click the line above the base layer.

Click the layer directly above the base layer, then press Ctrl-Alt-G/Cmd-Option-G.

➤ To merge clipped layers, see pages 166–167.

A *We held down Shift and clicked four layers …*

B *… then pressed Ctrl-Alt-G/ Cmd-Option-G to put them in a clipping group. The base layer name has an underline; the clipped layers are indented.*

C *The type (base) layer is clipping the four image layers (it's a "ski mask," ha-ha).*

D *We selected and moved the clipped image layers to the left with the Move tool, while the base layer stayed put.*

Blending layers

In these steps, you'll edit a duplicate image layer, then blend the original and duplicate layers via the opacity and blending mode controls on the Layers panel. You can use this method to soften the effect of a filter or other image edits or simply to see how various blending modes or opacity settings affect your document.

To blend a duplicate, edited layer with the original one:

1. On the Layers panel, click an image layer, then press Ctrl-J/Cmd-J to duplicate it.

2. Apply some creative edits to the duplicate layer, such as some brush strokes or a filter or two from the Filter menu (to learn about the Filter Gallery, see pages 372–373).

   Note: If you want to apply a filter as an editable Smart Filter (see page 374), right-click the duplicate image layer and choose Convert to Smart Object before going to the Filter menu.**A**

3. Keep the duplicate layer or Smart Object selected, then on the Layers panel, do either or both of the following:

   Choose a different **blending mode**. Or if you want to cycle through the blending modes, press Shift - – or Shift- +.

   Lower the layer **Opacity** percentage to make the layer semitransparent.**B–C**

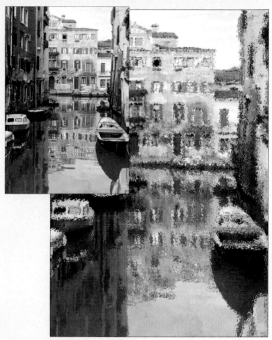

A *We duplicated the Background in this image, converted the duplicate layer to a Smart Object, then applied the Distort > Ocean Ripple filter (Filter Gallery).*

B *We chose Lighten mode for Layer 1 and lowered the layer Opacity to 84%.*

C *The final image combines characteristics of the original Background and the filtered Smart Object.*

The Advanced Blending options in the Layer Style dialog let you control how a layer blends with underlying layers. Here we focus on the Blend If sliders.

To choose blending options for a layer:

1. Double-click next to the name of a layer or layer group on the Layers panel. **A–B**

2. The Layer Style dialog opens (Blending Options should be selected in the upper left). Check Preview.

   The first three controls — Blend Mode, Opacity, and Fill Opacity — are the same as on the Layers panel. (The Fill Opacity changes the layer opacity without altering the opacity of any layer effects. To learn about layer effects, see Chapter 20.)

3. Use the **Blend If** sliders to control which pixels in the current layer stay visible and which pixels from the underlying layer show through the current layer:

   Move the black **This Layer** slider to the right to drop out shadow areas from the current layer.

A *We opened a photo of a surface texture, then created some editable type in a dark color.*

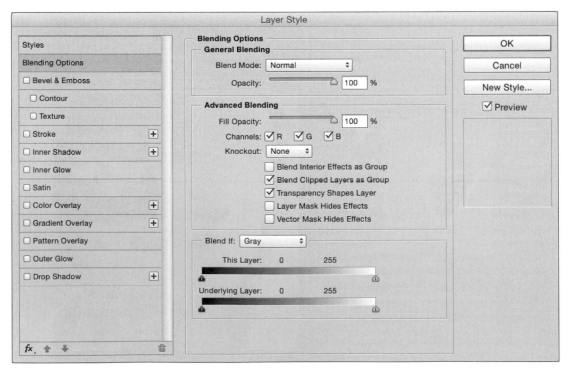

B *We double-clicked the type layer name to open the Layer Style dialog.*

Move the white **This Layer** slider to the left to drop out highlight areas from the current layer.

Move the black **Underlying Layer** slider to the right to reveal shadow areas from the underlying layer.**A**

Move the white **Underlying Layer** slider to the left to reveal highlight areas from the underlying layer.

To adjust midtone colors separately from the lightest and darkest colors, Alt-drag/Option-drag a slider (it will divide into two sections), then drag each half of the slider separately.**B**

4. Click OK. On the Layers panel, the layer will have this badge, indicating that the Advanced Blending options currently have nondefault settings.

➤ To display only layers that contain nondefault Advanced Blending settings, choose Attribute from the Filter Type menu on the Layers panel, and Advanced Blending from the second menu.

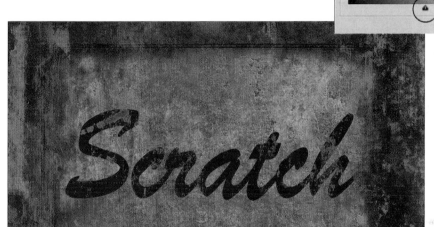

A *In the Blend If area of the Layer Style dialog, we dragged the black Underlying Layer slider to the right. Dark colors from the texture layer now show through the type layer.*

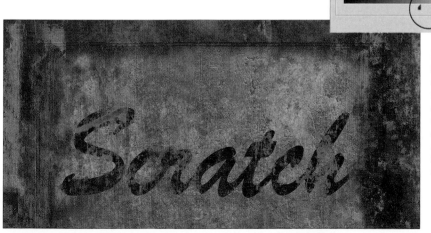

B *To enable midtone colors from the underlying texture layer to show through the type layer, we held down Alt/Option and dragged the Underlying Layer slider to divide it, then dragged each section separately. Now the type looks as if it's been worn away by the elements.*

Applying transformations

You can apply scale, rotate, skew, distort, and perspective transformations to a layer or layer group, among other things (see the sidebar at right). We'll show you how to apply multiple transformations via the Free Transform command and the Move tool — the methods that we find to be most intuitive.

Note: To help preserve the image quality, if you need to apply multiple transformations, do them consecutively and accept the edits only after the last one, so Photoshop resamples the image data just once.

To apply transformations using the Free Transform command or the Move tool:

1. On the Layers panel, click a layer, a layer group, or the Background, or Shift-select multiple layers.**A** Any layers that are linked to the selected one(s) will also be transformed. Or to transform a path, select it via the Paths panel.

   To transform the Background, you *must* create a selection, and you also should choose a Background color because Photoshop will fill any exposed areas with that color.

2. *Optional:* If you clicked a single image layer, you can create a selection to limit which area is transformed.

3. Do either of the following:

   Press Ctrl-T/Cmd-T (or choose Edit > Free Transform; or for a path, choose Edit > Free Transform Path).

   Choose the **Move tool** ⊹ (V), check **Show Transform Controls** on the Options bar, then click any handle on the transform box to display transform features on the Options bar.

4. For the Free Transform commands, you can select a resampling method from the **Interpolation** menu on the Options bar, if available (we pick Bicubic Automatic to let Photoshop use the best method).

5. A transform box with handles surrounds the selection, path, or opaque part of the layer. Do one or more of the following:

   To **scale** the item horizontally and vertically, drag a corner handle; to scale it just horizontally or vertically, drag a middle handle; to scale it proportionally, Shift-drag a corner handle; or to scale it from the current reference point (marked by a crosshair in the transform box), Alt-drag/Option-drag a handle (add Shift to scale it proportionally from the reference point).**B**

WHAT CAN I TRANSFORM?

► You can transform an image, type, or shape layer; a path; a layer group; a Smart Object; or a selection of pixels on an image layer or the Background.

► You can scale, rotate, or skew an editable type layer. To apply a distortion or perspective transformation to type, you must rasterize the layer first. Right-click the layer name and choose Rasterize Layer from the context menu.

► To transform a selection border (not its contents), choose Select > Transform Selection, then follow steps 5–6 in the main task on this page and the next.

► Read about the Snap Vector Tools and Transforms to Pixel Grid preference on page 421.

USING SMART GUIDES

Check View > Extras and View > Show > Smart Guides. As you apply a transformation, you can snap the edge of the transform box to a Smart Guide, which will display as your pointer nears the edge or middle of the contents of another layer.

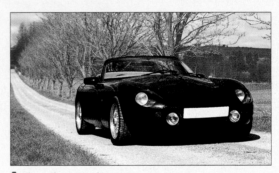

A *This is the original image.*

B *We selected the car, then copied it to a new layer. Here we're scaling the new layer.*

To **rotate** it, position the pointer outside the transform box (the pointer becomes a curved, two-headed arrow), then drag. Shift-drag to constrain the rotation to a multiple of 15°.

To **skew** it, Ctrl-drag/Cmd-drag a middle handle. Include Shift to constrain the movement.

To **distort** it, Ctrl-drag/Cmd-drag a corner handle.**A–B**

To apply **perspective**, Ctrl-Alt-Shift-drag/Cmd-Option-Shift-drag a corner handle vertically or horizontally; an adjacent corner moves symmetrically.**C**

➤ To undo the last handle edit, choose Edit > Undo.

➤ As you perform a transformation, a dynamic readout listing the dimensions or angle of your edits displays next to the pointer.

6. To resume normal editing, you must either accept or cancel the transformation:

To accept the edit(s), double-click inside the bounding box, press Enter/Return, or click the Commit Transform button ✔ on the Options bar.

To cancel the edit(s), press Esc or click the Cancel Transform button.🚫

➤ Before dragging a handle to scale or rotate, you can drag the reference point, from which the layer or selection is transformed, to a new location.

MORE TRANSFORM SHORTCUTS

EDIT	METHOD
Transform a duplicate of a selected layer*	Hold down Alt/Option and choose Edit > Free Transform (or Edit > Free Transform Path)
Repeat the last transformation (the repeat transformation is added to the last one)	Choose Edit > Transform (or Edit > Transform Path) > Again or press Ctrl-Shift-T/Cmd-Shift-T
Repeat the last transformation and duplicate the current layer*	Press Control-Alt-Shift-T/Cmd-Option-Shift-T

*When the edit is applied to a path, Photoshop adds the transformed duplicate to the same Path listing.

A This is the original shape layer.

B We're applying a distort transformation.

C We're applying a perspective transformation.

APPLYING TRANSFORMATIONS VIA THE OPTIONS BAR

When you choose the Edit > Free Transform or Free Transform Path command (Ctrl-T/Cmd-T), transform controls become available on the Options bar (you can enter specific values or use the scrubby sliders). If you want to change the reference point from which a transformation occurs, click a square on the reference point locator.

Horizontal Position of Reference Point   Use Relative Positioning for Reference Point (in its off state)   Maintain Aspect Ratio   Vertical Scale   Vertical Skew Angle   Switch Between Free Transform and Warp Modes   Cancel Transform

X: 782.50 px   Y: 636.50 px   W: 100.00%   H: 100.00%   0.00   H: 0.00   V: 0.00   Interpolation: Bicubic

Reference Point locator   Vertical Position of Reference Point   Horizontal Scale   Angle of Rotation   Horizontal Skew Angle   Interpolation method   Commit Transform

Applying Content-Aware scaling

The standard transform features in Photoshop scale an entire layer uniformly, regardless of the layer content. The Content-Aware Scale command is smarter in that it tries to scale background areas without distorting shapes that have clearly defined borders, such as figures or objects. You can help protect areas from distortion by creating and using an alpha channel.

To apply Content-Aware scaling:

1. Duplicate an image layer to be scaled (not a Smart Object), then hide the original layer (**A**, next page).

2. *Optional:* To minimize distortion in an area of the layer, select that area, then on the Channels panel, click the Save Selection as Channel button. Deselect.

3. Choose Edit > **Content-Aware Scale** (Ctrl-Alt-Shift-C/Cmd-Option-Shift-C).

4. On the Options bar, do either of the following:

   If you created an alpha channel (step 2, above), select the channel name from the **Protect** menu.

   If the image contains figures, check the **Protect Skin Tones** button 👤 to help prevent distortion. Note that this feature does a better job of recognizing skin than clothing.

5. Slowly drag a handle on the bounding box (**B**, next page), or Shift-drag a corner handle for more proportional scaling.

6. *Optional:* To permit some normal (non Content-Aware) scaling to occur, set the Amount percentage on the Options bar below 100%. The lower the Amount, the greater the distortion and the less protective the effect of the alpha channel.

7. To accept the transformation, press Enter/Return or click the Commit Transform button ✔ on the Options bar (**C–D**, next page). To cancel the edits, press Esc or click the Cancel Transform button. ⊘

► The Content-Aware Scale command can be applied only to a single image layer (not to multiple layers, a Smart Object, or other kinds of layers).

► To specify the stationary point from which the layer is scaled, click a square on the reference point locator ⊞ (Options bar) before dragging a handle.

► To scale a layer based on a percentage of its original size, set the W (width) or H (height) percentage on the Options bar. To scale it proportionally, activate the Maintain Aspect Ratio button. 🔗

PROTECTING AREAS FROM SCALING

We selected the buildings in this image, then saved the selection as an alpha channel.

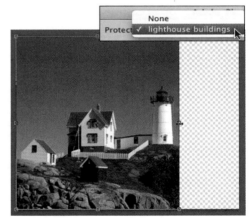

We chose the Content-Aware Scale command, selected the channel name from the Protect menu, then dragged the middle-right handle of the bounding box to the left.

The channel protected the buildings while allowing the rest of the image to be scaled.

A *This is the original image.*

B *We chose Edit > Content-Aware, then dragged a side handle to the left.*

C *The figures scaled less than the surrounding landscape.*

D *For comparison, we scaled the original image with the Move tool instead of the Content-Aware Scale command. The whole picture looks squashed, including the figures.*

Creating artboards

Photoshop CC contains a special layer type called an artboard. Like a layer group, an artboard can have layers grouped (nested) inside it. Any part of a layer that extends beyond the edge of the artboard boundary will be clipped automatically — no need to manually create clipping groups or masks.

Screen designers can create layer content, then use artboards to quickly mock up design layouts scaled to the different pixel dimensions of various device screens (desktop, laptop, iPad, smart phone, etc.). Multiple artboards can be created within one Photoshop file, allowing you to view the multiple screens in one place.

To create an artboard via the New command: ★

1. Choose File > **New** (Ctrl-N/Cmd-N).

2. In the New dialog, choose **Artboard** from the Preset Type menu, then choose a preset screen size from the Artboard Size menu and a profile from the Color Profile menu (for color management). Click OK.

3. An Artboard group containing a blank layer will be listed on the Layers panel.

To create an artboard in an existing document: ★

1. Create an RGB document with a resolution of 72 ppi.

2. Do either of the following:

   Choose the **Artboard** tool ⬚ (V or Shift-V), then drag in the document window.**A**

From the Layers panel menu, choose **New Artboard**. In the New Artboard dialog, enter a name and choose size options. Click OK.

3. An Artboard group listing (designated by a darker shade of gray) containing a white Solid Color fill layer will display on the Layers panel and the Background listing will be removed. The boundary of a selected artboard listing will display in the document window.

   Subsequent use of the tool or panel menu command will create an empty artboard group listing.

➤ To rename an artboard, double-click its name on the Layers panel, enter a descriptive name, then press Enter/Return.

To resize or reposition an artboard: ★

1. Choose the **Move** ⬚ tool (V or Shift-V), then click the artboard name label in the document window to select the artboard. The Artboard tool will be selected automatically.

2. To **resize** the artboard, drag any handle or side segment on the boundary,**B** or choose a screen size from the **Set Artboard to Preset** menu on either the Properties panel ▦ **C** or the **Size** menu on the Options bar.

3. To **reposition** the artboard, drag the artboard name label.

A Drag with the Artboard tool to create an artboard.

B To resize an artboard, drag a side segment (or handle) …

C … or choose a screen size from the Set Artboard to Preset menu on the Properties panel.

To add hand-drawn content to an artboard: ★

1. On the Layers panel, click the arrowhead to expand an **artboard** group listing. Click the **New Layer** button 🔲 to create a blank layer in the group.

2. Choose the **Brush** tool ✔ (B or Shift-B), then create strokes (see Chapter 14).

To add text or shapes to an artboard: ★

1. Turn on **Auto-Nest Layers** (see sidebar below).

2. Do any of the following:

   Choose the **Horizontal Type** tool T (T or Shift-T), then click within a selected or unselected artboard boundary and create type (see Chapter 19).

   Choose one of the shape tools, then drag within a selected or unselected artboard boundary.**A**

3. A text and/or shape layer will be placed into the artboard group listing automatically.**B–C**

To create an artboard over existing layer content: ★

1. Position layer content in the document window.

2. Do either of the following:

   Choose the **Artboard** tool 🔲 (V or Shift-V). Turn on **Auto-Nest Layers** (see sidebar below). Drag over the layer content.

   On the Layers panel, select the layer listings for the layers from the previous step. Choose **Artboard from Layers** on the Layers panel menu. Enter a name, then choose a size from the **Set Artboard to Preset** menu. Click OK.

3. The layers will be placed into the artboard group listing.

➤ For the first artboard created in the file, the group will also contain a Fill layer and the Background will be removed.

Artboard 1

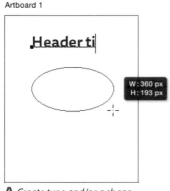

A Create type and/or a shape over an unselected artboard.

Artboard 1

B The type and shape are added to that artboard automatically …

C … and their layers are placed inside the artboard group listing.

THE ARTBOARD TOOL OPTIONS BAR ★

The Artboard tool Options bar provides several options for creating and modifying artboards:

➤ Choose a preset screen size from the Size menu, or enter custom values in the Width and Height fields.

➤ Click the Make Portrait 🔲 or Make Landscape 🔲 button to change the orientation of an artboard.

➤ Click the Add New Artboard 🔲 button, then click in the document to create an artboard using the current Options bar size and orientation settings.

➤ Click the gear ⚙ icon to display the Set Artboard Behaviors menu (for all artboards), then do the following: Check Auto-Nest Layers to nest an object into another

artboard group when using the Move tool to move or copy the object from one artboard boundary to another. Check Auto-Size Canvas to automatically enlarge the canvas when repositioning an artboard near the canvas edge. Note: To reduce the canvas size, use the Canvas Size command (see page 142).

Check Keep Relative Position During Layer Reordering to place an object in the same position relative to the upper-left corner of its artboard boundary when dragging its layer listing from one artboard group into another group.

The innovative design functionality of artboards can be seen when moving content between multiple artboards to quickly produce layout variations for different size screens.

For the two methods listed below, you will need to first create an artboard containing some layer content and then create another blank artboard. Also, turn on **Auto-Nest Layers** (see sidebar on previous page).

To copy content between artboards: ★

Method 1 — copy the whole artboard

1. Choose the **Move** tool ✛ (V or Shift-V). Click an artboard name label in the document window.

2. Hold down Alt/Option, then drag the name label.**A** The artboard copy and its contents will display in the document window and be listed as an artboard group "copy" on the Layers panel.

3. Resize the artboard copy via the menu on the Properties panel 🖳 or Options bar or by dragging a handle or side segment,**B** then reposition and scale the layer content.**C**

Method 2 — copy selected layers

1. Do either of the following:

   Choose the **Move** tool. ✛ On the Options bar, check **Auto Select** and choose **Layer** from the adjacent menu.

   Choose the **Move** tool. On the Layers panel, 🖘 select one or more layers in an artboard group.

2. In the document window, hold down Alt/Option, then drag copies of the selected layers over another artboard boundary. On the Layers panel, the destination artboard group will now contain copies of those layers.

3. Reposition and scale the copied layer content.

➤ To move layer content out of an artboard, use the Move tool to drag a layer from the artboard boundary onto an empty area of the canvas. The layer listing will be moved out of the artboard group on the Layers panel.

A *With the Move tool, we clicked an artboard name label, held down Alt/Option, then dragged the name label to create a copy.*

B *We resized the artboard copy to create a vertical screen.*

C *We modified layer content to fit the vertical layout and changed the artboard name.*

To copy existing assets into artboards: ★

1. Import or create all your design assets and place them on the side of the canvas.**A** Note: Image assets should be placed as Smart Objects to enable nondestructive scaling.

2. Create several artboards via the **Artboard** tool. Size each to a specific screen size via the **Set Artboard to Preset** menu on the Properties panel or the **Size** menu on the Options bar.

3. Turn on **Auto-Nest Layers** (see sidebar on page 363.) Choose the Move tool, hold down Alt/Option,

then drag a copy of an asset into one or more artboards. Repeat for the other assets

4. Rearrange and scale the assets in each individual artboard boundary.**B**

➤ To quickly zoom in on an artboard, hold down Alt/Option, then click an artboard group listing on the Layers panel.

➤ To display the canvas edge surrounding any artboards, choose Edit/Photoshop CC > Preferences > Interface, then, for Standard Screen Mode:, choose Line from the Border menu.

A *We created and placed our design assets on one side of the canvas.*

Artboard 5 horizontal

Artboard 5 vertical

Artboard banner

small vertical

B *We dragged a copy of each asset into our different artboards. We scaled and rearranged the assets in each artboard to fit that particular layout. We also created a banner text asset for one artboard, then copied it to another artboard. This ability to quickly add, copy, and rearrange assets among multiple screen-size boundaries illustrates the incredible design functionality of artboards.*

Using the Liquify filter

Using the tools in the Liquify dialog, you can reshape any part of an image: Slim a waistline, shrink an oddly shaped area of clothing, twirl part of a landscape — or if you're in the mood, apply bizarre distortion (as in Dr. Spock ears). Note: When using this feature, make sure Use Graphics Processor is checked in Edit/Photoshop CC > Preferences > Performance before opening your file. Also, in Preferences > Tools, ★ check Vary Round Brush Hardness Based on HUD Vertical Movement so you will be able to change the brush density interactively (see the tip in step 8; a graphics card with at least 512 MB of memory is required).

To use the distortion tools in Liquify:

1. Open an RGB image.**A** Duplicate the Background, and keep the duplicate layer selected.

   Note: If you want to keep the Liquify results non-destructive and editable, convert the duplicate layer to a Smart Object (Photoshop will save a compressed mesh into the Smart Object). This method increases the file size.

2. *Optional but recommended:* Select the area of the image you want to edit.**B** The rest of the image will be protected from Liquify edits. Other options are to create a layer mask or an alpha channel, to be chosen in the Liquify dialog.

3. Choose Filter > **Liquify** (Ctrl-Shift-X/Cmd-Shift-X). In the dialog, check **Advanced Mode**. If necessary, zoom in on the area to be reshaped.

4. If you want to protect areas of the image from Liquify edits, do either of the following:

   To apply a mask based on an active selection, or on layer transparency, a layer mask, or an alpha

channel in the document, choose that option from the **Replace Selection** (first) menu under **Mask Options**.

To paint a mask manually or to add to an existing mask, choose the **Freeze Mask** tool ☞ (F), choose settings under Tool Options (**A**, next page), then draw strokes in the preview (**B**, next page).

5. You can also use any of these masking controls:

   Hide or show the mask via the **Show Mask** check box.

   To remove areas of the mask, choose the **Thaw Mask** tool ☞ (D), then draw strokes in the preview (or hold down Alt/Option while using the Freeze Mask tool). (If you need to remove the whole mask, click None under Mask Options.)

   To reverse the masked and unmasked areas, click **Invert All**.

6. Choose the **Forward Warp,** ⩔ (W) **Twirl Clockwise** ⟳ (C), **Pucker** ▓ (S), **Bloat** ◈ (B), or **Push Left** ▓ (O) tool.

7. To size the brush cursor so that it covers the entire width of the area to be edited, press [or], or hold down Alt-right-click/Control-Option and drag horizontally in the image. You can also adjust the brush size via the improved Brush Size slider. The larger the brush, the less choppy the distortion.

8. Under **Tool Options**, do all of the following:

   To control the degree to which the distortion is feathered at the edges, set the **Brush Density** (the lower the density, the greater the feathering).

A *This is the original image.*

B *We selected the sky area before opening the Liquify dialog.*

Note: If you're using a stylus, check **Stylus Pressure** and lower the Brush Pressure value.

To control the overall strength of the distortion, set the **Brush Pressure**.

➤ To adjust the brush pressure interactively, hold down Alt-right-click/Control-Option and drag vertically in the preview.

To control the speed at which tools that are held down in one spot (e.g., Twirl Clockwise, Pucker, Bloat) produce distortion, choose a **Brush Rate**.

To prevent the edges of the layer from becoming transparent as you drag pixels, check **Pin Edges**.

9. Depending on the chosen tool, do the following:

With the **Twirl Clockwise**, **Pucker**, or **Bloat** tool, click and hold on an area. If you want to intensify the effect, repeat the click and hold.

Continued on the following page

Continued on the following page

CANCEL, DEFAULT, OR RESET

➤ Click Cancel to exit the Liquify dialog without applying any edits to your document.

➤ Hold down Ctrl/Cmd and click Default (Cancel becomes Default) to restore the default Photoshop settings to the dialog.

➤ Hold down Alt/Option and click Reset (Cancel becomes Reset) to restore the settings that were in place when you opened the dialog.

A *Check Advanced Mode to display and access the full array of Liquify options.*

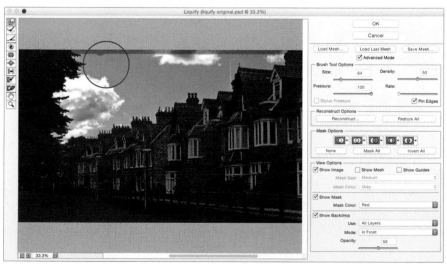

B *Our selection appeared as the nonmasked area in the Liquify dialog. With the Freeze Mask tool, we Shift-clicked the top edge of the image to add that area to the mask (in a straight line).*

With the **Forward Warp** tool, drag in the image preview.**A**

With the **Push Left** tool, drag downward to push areas to the right, or drag upward to push areas to the left (see the next page).

➤ If a tool doesn't seem to be having an effect, increase the brush size. To reverse the tool behavior, hold down Alt/Option while clicking or dragging.

➤ Each tool retains its own settings.

10. *Optional:* To compare the Liquify layer with any underlying layers, check Show Backdrop. From the Use menu, choose All Layers, and choose an Opacity value for the underlying layers.

11. *Optional:* If you applied Liquify to a Smart Object, the current mesh will save with the document. To save the current mesh (Liquify edits) as a preset for use in any image, click Save Mesh, enter a name, choose a location, keep the extension, then click Save. (To load a saved mesh at any time, click Load Mesh).

12. Click OK. If you applied the Liquify filter to a Smart Object and you want to edit the results, double-click the Liquify listing on the Layers panel. To reload the last-used mesh onto the current document, click Load Last Mesh in the dialog.

➤ If you applied the Liquify filter to a Smart Object, you can mask any part of the results by editing the filter mask (see page 376).

There are several ways to restore layer pixels to their pre-Liquify state.

To remove Liquify edits:

In the Liquify dialog, do any of the following:

To undo Liquify edits manually, choose the **Reconstruct** tool (R), set the brush size, then press and hold on an area you want to restore.

To apply subtle smoothing to ripples and other irregularities that were produced by multiple small distortion edits, choose the **Smooth** tool (E), then drag in the preview.

To restore all the Liquify edits to a specified amount, under Reconstruct Options, click **Reconstruct**. The Revert Reconstruction dialog opens. Set the Amount slider to the desired value, then click OK.

To undo all the Liquify edits completely, under Reconstruct Options, click **Restore All**.

QUICK ACCESS TO THE LIQUIFY TOOLS			
Forward Warp	W	Bloat	B
Reconstruct	R	Push Left	O
Smooth	E	Freeze Mask	F
Twirl Clockwise	C	Thaw Mask	D
Pucker	S	Hand H	Zoom Z

A *We're using the Forward Warp tool to elongate the top cloud.*

USING LIQUIFY FOR RETOUCHING

When used with restraint (e.g., low density and pressure settings), Liquify can be useful for retouching.**A–F**

A The shirt and pants on this fellow are billowing out in an unflattering way.

B With the Push Left tool, we dragged downward along the left side of the shirt a few times (here the Show Backdrop option is on).

C Next, we dragged upward with the same tool (smaller brush size) on the right side of the shirt…

D …and along the hip area (here the Show Backdrop option is off).

E With the Pucker tool, we clicked and held the mouse down on the billowy shirt to contract it inward.

F This image contains all of our Liquify edits.

Applying the Warp command

To apply warp edits to a layer:

1. Click a type, image, or shape layer, or a Smart Object.

2. Choose Edit > Transform > **Warp**.

3. Do either or both of the following:

   On the Options bar, choose a preset style from the **Warp** menu.**A–B** You can also click the **Warp Orientation** button 🔁 to toggle horizontal and vertical distortion (not available for all presets), or reshape the grid by using the scrubby sliders for **Bend: H** (horizontal distortion) or **V** (vertical distortion).

   Choose **Warp: Custom** on the Options bar (not available for editable type), then drag any of the interior squares, square corner points, grid lines, or direction line handles in the grid.**C** Note: If you don't see the grid, turn on View > Extras.

4. To accept the warp edits, press Enter/Return or click the Commit Transform button ✔ on the Options bar **D** (to cancel the edits, click the Cancel Transform button ⊘ or press Esc).

➤ To edit the warp settings for a type layer or a Smart Object, repeat steps 1–4, above. If you want to remove the warp, choose None from the Warp menu on the Options bar. The warp settings for a standard image layer can't be edited. To remove warp edits from an image layer, you would have to click the state prior to the "Warp" state on the History panel.

➤ While warp or transform controls are showing in your document, you can click the Switch Between Free Transform and Warp Modes button 🎭 on the Options bar to toggle one mode to the other. In fact, to minimize resampling and preserve the image quality when you need to apply multiple transform and/or warp edits, it's best to choose all your settings (by toggling the modes), then accept them all at once.

USING THE WARP TEXT DIALOG

To open the Warp Text dialog, which has the same controls as the Warp command, except that they apply only to a type layer, choose Type > Warp Text; or if a type tool is selected, you can click the Warp Text button 🔲 on the Options bar.

A In this image, the cups are on a Smart Object layer (separate from the yellow Background).

B We applied the Warp command to the cups layer (Twist preset).

C Finally, we chose the Custom warp option, then dragged a few of the control handles on the grid.

D This is the result (it reminds us of the Mad Hatter tea party in Alice in Wonderland).

You may already have used a filter or two in Photoshop (perhaps as a step in an earlier chapter). In this chapter, filters are the star players. Depending on which filters you apply and which settings you choose, the results can range from a subtle change to a total morph. **A–B** You can make an image look (almost) as if it's hand painted, silkscreened, or sketched; apply distortion; add a pattern, texture, or noise; create a mosaic or a patchwork of tiles — the creative possibilities are infinite. Once you start using the Filter Gallery, you'll see … time will fly by.

Using this chapter, you will learn techniques for applying filters, including using the Filter Gallery, Smart Filters, and the Smart Filters mask. We also suggest some ways to use filters creatively, to whet your appetite. (To locate tasks in other chapters in which individual filters are used, see "Filter menu" in the index.)

Applying filters

You can apply filters to a whole layer or just to a selection on a layer. Most of the Photoshop filters are applied either via the Filter Gallery or via an individual dialog. A small handful of them, such as Clouds and Blur, are applied in one step simply by choosing the filter name from a submenu on the Filter menu. If you apply a filter to a Smart Object, it becomes an edItable, removable Smart Filter (see pages 374–378).

If you try to select a filter and discover that it's not available, the likely cause is that it's incompatible with the current document color mode or bit depth. All the Photoshop filters are available for RGB files, most of the filters are available for Grayscale files, fewer are available for CMYK Color, Lab Color, and 16-bits-per-channel files, still fewer are available for 32-bits-per-channel files, and none are available for Bitmap and Indexed Color files.

FILTERS

18

A *This is the original image.*

B *We applied the Charcoal filter.*

Most of the Photoshop filters are housed conveniently under one roof in the Filter Gallery dialog. There you can preview dozens of filters and filter settings, show and hide each filter effect that you've previewed, and change the sequence in which Photoshop applies them to your document.

To use the Filter Gallery:

1. Open an 8-bit, RGB image. Click an image layer; or for more flexibility, work on a duplicate image layer or a Smart Object (see "To apply a Smart Filter," on page 374).

2. *Optional:* To limit the filter to a specific area of the image, create a selection.

3. The Foreground and/or Background colors are used by many filters (see the sidebar on this page), and you must choose those colors now, before opening the Filter Gallery.

4. Choose Filter > **Filter Gallery**. The resizable gallery opens (**A**, next page).

5. To change the zoom level for the preview, hold down Ctrl/Cmd and press – or +. (If the preview is magnified, you can drag it in the window.)

6. Do either of the following:

   In the middle pane of the dialog, click an arrowhead to expand any of the six filter categories, then click a filter thumbnail.

   Choose a filter name from the menu on the right.

7. On the right side of the dialog, choose settings for the filter. Note: Some effects and settings take longer to process than others (a progress bar may display below the preview).

8. To edit the list of effects (bottom-right portion of the dialog), do any of these optional steps:

   To apply an additional filter effect, click the **New Effect Layer** button, click a filter thumbnail in any category, then choose settings.

   To **replace** one filter effect with another, click a filter effect name on the scroll list (don't click the New Effect Layer button), then choose a replacement filter and settings.

   To **hide** (or show) a filter effect, click in the visibility 👁 column next to the effect name. To hide or show the previews for all but one filter effect, Alt-click/Option-click a visibility icon.

   To remove a filter effect from the list, click it, then click the **Delete Effect Layer** button. 🗑

To change the **stacking position** of a filter effect to produce a different result in the image, drag the effect name upward or downward on the list.

9. Click OK.

➤ To remove a non-Smart Filter edit from an image, use the History panel.

➤ In Edit/Photoshop CC > Preferences > Plug-Ins, uncheck Show All Filter Gallery Groups and Names to list, on the submenus on the Filter menu, only filters that are not in the Filter Gallery, or check this option to list all Photoshop filters on the submenus, including those that are in the Filter Gallery (the gallery opens when you choose a filter name).

➤ The filter effects in the Filter Gallery are sticky, meaning that the last-used settings will redisplay when you open the dialog.

FILTERS THAT USE THE FOREGROUND AND BACKGROUND COLORS

The filters listed below use the current Foreground and/or Background colors. We find that some filters, such as Charcoal, Graphic Pen, and Photocopy (in the Sketch category), look good in the default Photoshop colors of black and white, whereas others look better in color. But don't just take our word for it — experiment and see for yourself.

➤ Artistic > Colored Pencil (Background color), Neon Glow (Foreground and Background colors)

➤ Distort > Diffuse Glow (Background color)

➤ Pixelate > Pointillize (Background color)

➤ Render > Clouds, Difference Clouds, Fibers (Foreground and Background colors)

➤ Sketch > Bas Relief, Chalk & Charcoal, Charcoal, Conté Crayon, Graphic Pen, Halftone Pattern, Note Paper, Photocopy, Plaster, Reticulation, Stamp, Torn Edges (Foreground and Background colors)

➤ Stylize > Tiles (Foreground or Background color)

➤ Texture > Stained Glass (Foreground color)

REAPPLYING THE LAST FILTER QUICKLY

➤ To reapply the last-used filter(s) using the same settings, choose Filter > [last filter name or Filter Gallery] (Ctrl-F/Cmd-F).

➤ To reopen either the last-used filter dialog or the Filter Gallery showing the last-used settings, press Ctrl-Alt-F/Cmd-Option-F.

Click this button to hide (or show) the thumb-nails and expand (or shrink) the preview area.

To preview a filter effect, click a thumbnail or choose a filter name from this menu.

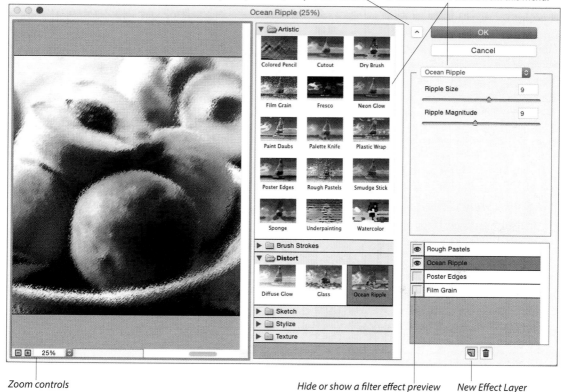

Zoom controls

Hide or show a filter effect preview

New Effect Layer

A *The Filter Gallery dialog includes a preview area, filter categories (with thumbnails), settings for the currently selected filter effect, and a listing of the currently applied effects.*

USING THE PREVIEW IN AN INDIVIDUAL FILTER DIALOG

Some Photoshop filters are applied via an individual dialog (not via the Filter Gallery). Of those individual dialogs, some have a preview window and some do not.

➤ For individual filter dialogs that have a preview window, you can click the + button to zoom in or the − button to zoom out (we usually do the latter). Most of the individual dialogs also have a Preview check box.

➤ In some filter dialogs (such as Blur > Gaussian Blur and Motion Blur), if you click in the document window (square pointer), that area of the image will appear in the Preview window. You can drag the image inside the Preview window.

➤ To compare the image with and without the current filter effect, click and hold on the preview, then release.

Preview window

Zoom Out and Zoom In buttons

Creating and editing Smart Filters

When you apply a filter or an adjustment ★ to a Smart Object, it becomes what is called a Smart Filter. You can edit or remove a Smart Filter at any time, apply multiple Smart Filters to the same Smart Object, hide individual Smart Filters while keeping others visible, and move or copy Smart Filters from one Smart Object to another. You can also edit the filter mask (which is created automatically), and change the stacking order of the Smart Filters. To learn about Smart Objects, see pages 272–283. To learn about our views on adjustments as Smart Filters, see page 231.

The file formats that support Photoshop layers — such as PSD, PDF, and TIFF — also support Smart Filters.

To apply a Smart Filter:

1. On the Layers panel,⬥ do either of the following:

   Click an existing Smart Object.

   Click an image layer, then choose Filter > **Convert for Smart Filters** (or right-click the layer and choose Convert to Smart Object). If an alert appears, click OK.

2. *Optional:* To limit the effect, create a selection. (The selection area will appear in the filter mask after you do the next step.)

3. Apply a filter via the Filter menu, or apply an adjustment command ★ via the Image > Adjustments submenu. A Smart Filters listing, mask thumbnail, and filter listing will appear on the Layers panel.**A**

➤ Be careful when applying adjustments and filters to a Smart Object. The effects don't always work well together.

The most significant advantage to using Smart Filters is that you can edit the filter settings at any time.

To edit the settings for a Smart Filter:

1. Do either of the following:

   Double-click on or next to the Smart Filter name on the Layers panel.

   Right-click the Smart Filter name and choose **Edit Smart Filter** from the context menu.

2. If any Smart Filters are listed above the one you're editing, an alert will appear, indicating that those effects will be hidden until you exit the filter or adjustment dialog.**B** Click OK.

3. Make the desired changes in the filter or adjustment ★ dialog, then click OK.

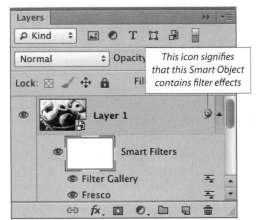

This icon signifies that this Smart Object contains filter effects

A *If you apply a Smart Filter by choosing Filter > Filter Gallery, the filter will be listed as "Filter Gallery," whereas if you apply a Smart Filter by choosing its individual name, it will be listed by its name (see also the second tip on page 372).*

B *If you edit a Smart Filter and other filters or adjustments are listed above it on the same layer, this alert dialog will appear.*

CHANGING THE COLOR MODE OR BIT DEPTH

When changing the document color mode or bit depth, if the image contains Smart Filters that aren't supported in the new mode or depth, an alert will appear (shown below). If you click Don't Rasterize and then click Don't Flatten or Don't Merge, this symbol **⚠** will display next to the names of filters on the Layers panel that have become inaccessible. If you then convert the file to a mode or depth that does support the filter — and respond to the alerts in the same way — the icon will disappear and the filter settings will be editable again.

Not only can you change the blending mode and opacity of a Smart Object, you can also change the blending mode and opacity setting of each Smart Filter that is applied to that object. Granted, this can be a lot to keep track of. And unfortunately, there is no indicator on the Layers panel to let you know if those settings have been changed from the defaults.

To edit the blending options for a Smart Filter:

1. Double-click the **Blending Options** icon ≛ next to a filter or adjustment ★ name on the Layers panel, **A–B** then click OK if an alert dialog appears.

2. The Blending Options dialog opens.**C** Check Preview and, if desired, lower the zoom level. Change the blending **Mode** and/or **Opacity** (use the latter to fade the filter effect), then click OK.**D**

Hiding, copying, and deleting Smart Filters

To hide (or show) Smart Filter effects:

On the Layers panel, do either of the following:

Click the visibility icon 👁 for the Smart Filters listing to hide all the Smart Filters on that layer.

Click the visibility icon 👁 for any individual Smart Filter. This change may take longer to process than clicking the visibility icon for all the Smart Filters.

Note: Click where the icon formerly was to redisplay the hidden effect(s).

To copy Smart Filters from one Smart Object to another:

1. Expand the list of Smart Filters for a Smart Object.

2. Alt-drag/Option-drag either the Smart Filters listing or an individual filter or adjustment ★ listing to another Smart Object.

➤ You can restack any Smart Filter within a Smart Object list (pause for the edit to process).

➤ If you drag an individual Smart Filter or the entire Smart Filters listing from one Smart Object to another without holding down Alt/Option, that listing will be removed from the source layer and added to the target layer. Any preexisting Smart Filters on the target layer will be preserved. Pause for the edit to process.

A *We applied the Fresco and Dry Brush filters to this image.*

B *We double-clicked the Blending Options icon for the Fresco filter on the Layers panel.*

C *Via the Blending Options dialog, we lowered the Opacity of the Fresco filter.*

D *Now more of the Dry Brush filter is showing through.*

If you delete a Smart Filter from a Smart Object that contains multiple filters, it may take a moment or two for Photoshop to update the display.

To delete a Smart Filter:

On the Layers panel, ☰ do either of the following:

Right-click a Smart Filter listing and choose **Delete Smart Filter**.

Drag a Smart Filter listing to the **Delete Layer** button. 🗑

Working with the Smart Filters mask

When you apply a filter or an adjustment ★ to a Smart Object, a filter mask appears on the layer automatically. If you create a selection before applying the first effect to a Smart Object, the selection will appear as the white area in the mask. A filter mask can also be edited using the same methods as for a layer mask. **A**

To edit a filter mask:

1. In a Smart Filters listing on the Layers panel, click the filter mask thumbnail.

2. Do either of the following:

   Click the **Brush** tool, 🖌 then apply strokes with black to hide the effect, or with white to reveal areas you've hidden. For a partial mask, use black and lower the tool opacity (**A–E**, next page).

   To hide the effect gradually from one side of the image to the other, click the **Gradient** tool, ▭ then drag across the image (**A–C**, page 378).

➤ To display the filter mask by itself in the document, Alt-click/Option-click the mask; repeat to redisplay the full Smart Object.

➤ To soften the transition between black and white areas in a filter mask, click the filter mask thumbnail, then on the Properties panel, ▤ adjust the Feather value. To control the overall opacity of the mask, use the Density slider.

If for some reason a filter mask is deleted and you want to restore it, do as follows.

To create a filter mask:

1. *Optional:* Create a selection.

2. Right-click the Smart Filters listing on the Layers panel and choose **Add Filter Mask**.

To deactivate a filter mask temporarily:

Shift-click the mask thumbnail (a red X appears over the thumbnail). Repeat to reactivate the mask.

To delete a filter mask:

Do either of the following:

Drag the filter mask thumbnail to the **Delete Layer** button 🗑 on the Layers panel.

Right-click a Smart Filter listing and choose **Delete Filter Mask**.

A *A gradient in the Smart Filters mask is hiding the filter effects fully on the left side of this image, and reveals gradually more of the effects on the right.*

SOLVING MEMORY PROBLEMS

If you encounter memory problems when applying filters (Photoshop memory, that is, not your own forgetfulness!), try choosing Edit > Purge > All to free up memory, or exit/quit other open applications. Also bear in mind that the processing time may vary for any given filter slider or option. For instance, a higher setting that produces many small shapes may take longer to process than a setting that produces just a few large shapes.

WORKING WITH SMART FILTERS: AN EXAMPLE

A *This is the original image.*

B *We duplicated the Background, converted the copy to a Smart Object, pressed D to reset the default Foreground and Background colors, then applied Filter Gallery > Sketch > Charcoal (values at left).*

C *We reduced the Opacity of the Smart Object to 62%.*

D *We clicked the filter mask, then with the Brush tool at 50% Opacity and black as the Foreground color, applied strokes to partially restore the tiger's face to its virgin state.*

E *This is the Layers panel for the image shown at left.*

Continued on the following page

A *Next, to wipe the filter mask clean so we could try a different approach, we clicked the filter mask thumbnail, pressed Ctrl-A/Cmd-A to select the whole mask, pressed Backspace/Delete, then pressed Ctrl-D/Cmd-D to deselect.*

B *With the Gradient tool (100% Opacity, "Black, White" preset, radial type), we dragged from the center of the image outward. The filter effect is at full strength where the mask is white, and it fades to nil where the mask is black.*

C *The gradient in the filter mask is diminishing the impact of the filter in the center of the image — the tiger's face — right where we want the focal point to be.*

USING THE MINIMUM OR MAXIMUM FILTER ON A MASK

If you want to expand or contract the dark area of a mask in a Smart Filters listing, click the mask thumbnail, then try using Filter > Other > **Minimum** (to expand) or **Maximum** (to contract).

FILTERS AND AN ADJUSTMENT LAYER

A *We duplicated the Background in this image, then converted the duplicate layer to a Smart Object.*

More filter techniques

If you apply filters to a Smart Object, you will be able to change the settings easily — and will feel more free to experiment. If you come up with a filter formula that you like, consider recording your steps in an action so you can apply it to other images. Here are a few more suggestions:

► Filters tend to make an image more abstract, reducing recognizable elements to line work, or to fewer or flatter areas of color. Start with an image that has a strong composition. Look for shapes that contrast in scale and have interesting contours, which will carry more weight once you apply filters.

► Fine-tune the resulting luminosity levels or colors via a Smart Filter adjustment ★ or an adjustment layer above the filtered layer.**A–D**

► Apply filters separately to a Smart Object one by one (not by creating multiple effects in the Filter Gallery), then via the Blending Options dialog, lower the opacity of the topmost filter and/or change its blending mode. You can also apply filters to separate layers, then change the layer opacity or blending mode of any layer (**A–E**, next page).

► For less predictable and "machine made" results, apply two or more filters that have contrasting or complementary effects. For instance, you could apply one filter that reduces shapes to line work (such as Poster Edges) and another filter that changes the color or applies an overall texture, such as Grain > Texturizer.

► For a personal touch, apply some paint strokes (**A–B**, page 381).

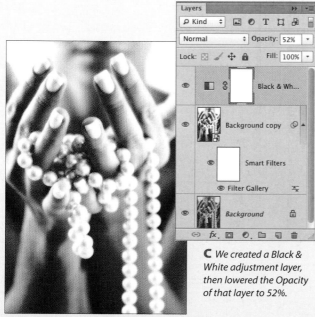

B *We applied Filter > Filter Gallery > Distort > Diffuse Glow.*

C *We created a Black & White adjustment layer, then lowered the Opacity of that layer to 52%.*

D *This is the final image.*

FILTERS, AN ADJUSTMENT LAYER, AND BLENDING MODES

A *We converted a duplicate of the Background to a Smart Object.*

B *We applied Filter > Other > Minimum (Radius 1), then Filter > Stylize > Find Edges.*

C *We changed the blending mode of the Smart Object to Linear Burn.*

D *We created a second duplicate of the Background, moved the duplicate to the top of the Layers panel, changed the blending mode of that layer to Divide, and lowered its Opacity to 50%. Finally, we used a Vibrance adjustment to boost the colors in both layers slightly.*

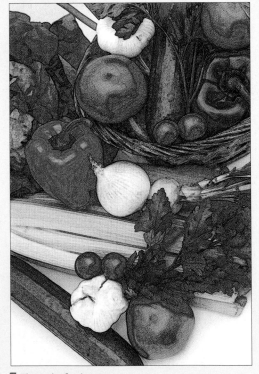

E *This is the final image.*

A TEXTURE FILTER AND PAINT STROKES

A *This is the original image.*

B *This is the image and the Layers panel after we converted a duplicate image layer to a Smart Object, applied the Texturizer filter (Burlap texture) via the Filter Gallery, and used the Mixer Brush tool (Sample All Layers checked) to apply paint strokes to six new layers. We also applied the Drop Shadow effect to a couple of the paint layers for added depth, and a Levels adjustment to heighten the contrast in the underlying image.*

In these steps, you'll turn a photo into a watercolor by applying a series of filters. Try devising some of your own formulas, too!

To turn a photo into a tinted drawing:

1. Duplicate an image layer in a high-resolution photo. **A**

2. Choose Filter > Stylize > **Find Edges**. **B**

3. Choose the **Brush** tool. On the Options bar, choose a Soft Round brush, Normal mode, and an Opacity below 40%.

4. Click the **Add Layer Mask** button on the Layers panel, and keep the layer mask thumbnail selected.

5. Make sure the Foreground color is black, size the brush cursor, then apply strokes to the image to reveal areas of the underlying layer.

6. Do any of the following optional steps:

   Lower the opacity of the duplicate layer.

   Change the blending mode of the duplicate layer (try Lighter Color, Hard Light, Pin Light, or Luminosity). **C–D**

   Intensify the contrast in both layers via a Levels adjustment layer.

A *We duplicated the Background in this original image.*

B *We applied the Find Edges filter to the duplicate layer.*

D *We applied brush strokes to the layer mask to reveal some of the underlying image, and chose Hard Light as the blending mode for the duplicate layer.*

C *This is the Layers panel for the final image, which is shown at right.*

We've never heard someone say "A word is worth a thousand pictures" (the reverse of the common adage), but so many artful things can be done with type in Photoshop, the line between pictures and words can be blurred — sometimes even literally! In this chapter, you will learn how to create editable type, then style and format it using a wide assortment of character and paragraph controls. You will also learn special techniques, such as how to transform type, screen it back (as in the image shown at right), rasterize it (convert it to pixels), and make it look like cut paper. Finally, you will learn how to put some type shapes into a spot color channel.

When you use the Horizontal Type tool or Vertical Type tool, editable type appears in your document and a new layer appears on the Layers panel. You can easily change the attributes of editable type, such as the font family, font style, and size; the kerning, tracking, leading, alignment, and baseline shift values; and the color. Moreover, you can transform, warp, or apply layer effects to editable type; change its blending mode; and change its opacity and fill values. To style type, you can use the Character panel **A** A, the Paragraph panel,¶ the Glyphs panel,𝓐 ★ the Paragraph Styles panel,▦ the Character Styles panel,▦ and the Options bar.

TYPE

19

Font Family — **Myriad Pro**

Font Style — **Bold**

Font Size — 12 pt

Leading — 14 pt

Kerning — Metrics

Tracking — 0

Vertical Scale — 100%

Horizontal Scale — 100%

Baseline Shift — 0 pt

Color:

Type Styles — T *T* TT Tᴛ Tⁱ T₁ T̲ T̶

OpenType options — fi ℴ st 𝒜 a⃗d T 1ˢᵗ ½

Language — English: USA

Anti-aliasing method — Sharp

A You can apply Character panel attributes to all the type on a layer or just to selected characters or words.

Creating editable type

You can be casual about where you position editable type initially and about which typographic attributes you choose for it, because you can easily edit those attributes or move, transform, or restack the layer.

To create an editable type layer:

1. On the Layers panel, ☰ click the layer above which you want the type layer to appear.

2. Choose the **Horizontal Type** tool T or **Vertical Type** tool ↓T (T or Shift-T).

3. On the Options bar, **A** do all of the following:

   Choose a **font family**, and from the adjacent menu, choose a **font style**. A sample of each font displays on the menu.

   Choose or enter a **font size** (you can use the scrubby slider).

   Choose an **anti-aliasing** method for the way in which Photoshop introduces partially transparent pixels along the edges of the characters, to make them look smoother. For print output, choose Sharp (sharpest), Crisp (somewhat sharp), Strong (heavier), or Smooth (smoothest). Or for Web output, choose an anti-aliasing option that allows your system to render the type, so it more closely matches the rendering by your browser. For Safari in the Mac OS, choose Mac LCD or Mac; or for Internet Explorer in Windows, choose Windows LCD or Windows. The LCD options render the type with sub-pixel anti-aliasing (shaded pixels that are added around the characters to make

them look more crisp). Note that in Photoshop, sub-pixels are grayscale, whereas in Safari and Internet Explorer, they display in RGB color. **B–C**

Click an **alignment** button to align point type relative to your original insertion point or to align paragraph type to the left edge, right edge, or center of the bounding box (see also page 394).

Click the **Text Color** swatch, then choose a color via the Color Picker or Swatches panel, or click a color in the document, then click OK.

4. Do either of the following:

   To create **point** type (suitable for a small amount of text), click away from any existing text in the document to establish an insertion point, then type the desired text. You can press Enter/Return to create line breaks where necessary, to prevent the type from disappearing off the edge of the canvas. (You can also move the type later with the Move tool.)

   To create **paragraph** type (suitable for a larger block of text), drag to define a bounding box for the type to fit into, then type the desired text. Let the words wrap naturally to the edges of the bounding box, pressing Enter/Return only when you need to start a new paragraph. Note: If you prefer to specify dimensions for the bounding box first, Alt/Option click in the document, then enter dimensions in the Paragraph Text Size dialog.

Tool Preset picker · Anti-aliasing method · Text Color

Text Orientation · Font Family · Font Style · Font Size · Alignment · Warp Text

Show or hide the Character and Paragraph panel group

A The Options bar offers many controls for the type tools.

B With anti-aliasing off, type edges look jagged.

C With anti-aliasing on, type edges look smoother.

5. To accept the new text, press Esc ★ or press Enter on the keypad (not on the main keyboard) or click the Commit button ✔ on the right end of the Options bar. (To cancel the type, click the Cancel button ⊘ on the Options bar.) Each time you create new type with the Horizontal or Vertical Type tool, it appears on a new layer.**A–B**

Note: To use Esc as a shortcut for the Commit command, Use ESC Key to Commit Text must be checked in the Type panel of the Edit/ Photoshop CC > Preferences dialog. ★

➤ Photoshop uses vector outlines for specific font families and styles when you resize editable type, save a file to the PDF format, or output a file to a PostScript printer. Like vector graphics, editable type outputs at the resolution of the printer, not at the resolution of the file.

➤ You can right-click an editable type listing on the Layers panel and choose an anti-aliasing method from the context menu. The new setting will display on the Anti-Aliasing menu on the Character panel.

➤ To display East Asian Features or Middle Eastern Features on the Character and Paragraph panels and panel menus, see "Choose Text Engine Options," on page 469.

➤ To fill a type bounding box with "dummy" text quickly, choose Type > Paste Lorem Ipsum. For overflow text, see page 398.

➤ If you place phrases, words, or characters on separate layers, you'll be able to move, align, and apply effects to them individually. To organize multiple type layers, gather them into layer groups. To display only type layers on the Layers panel, choose Kind from the Filter Type menu at the top of the panel, then click the Filter for Type Layers button. **T**

A *After typing "EcoStorage," we pressed Enter/Return so we could type the next word on a second line.*

B *Editable type layers have a* **T** *icon in the thumbnail and are given the name of the first word or few words of type in the layer.*

REMEMBER TO USE SMART QUOTES!

Typographer's quotation and apostrophe marks are shaped specially to fit around the beginning and end of quotations and abbreviations. To use them in Photoshop (as we highly recommend), go to Preferences > Type and check Use Smart Quotes. Straight (prime) marks should be used solely as abbreviations for foot and inch measurements.

IMPORTING ILLUSTRATOR TYPE AS A SMART OBJECT

For quick round-trip editing, import type from Illustrator into a Photoshop document as a Smart Object (see the methods on pages 271, 273, 274, and 280). To edit a Smart Object, see pages 276 and 281.

Selecting type

Before you can change the character or paragraph attributes or content of type, you have to select a type layer or a specific string of characters or phrases.

Note: To apply some kinds of edits to type, such as filters or brush strokes, you must rasterize it first (see page 400). Note that once type is rasterized, its character or paragraph attributes (such as the font and leading) can't be changed.

To select type for editing or style changes:

Do one of the following:

Click a type layer, choose the **Horizontal Type** tool T or **Vertical Type** tool ↓T (T or Shift-T), then drag across some characters or words to select them, A or double-, triple-, or quadruple-click, as described in the sidebar on this page.

With any tool selected, double-click the T icon on the Layers panel. All the type on the layer becomes selected. To reduce the selection, drag or double- or triple-click.

To change the attributes of all the type on a layer via the Character or Paragraph panel, such as the font size, leading, or alignment, simply click the layer (you don't need to select a type tool).

➤ To delete type characters that you have selected, press Backspace/Delete. Or to delete one character at a time in horizontal type, with a type tool, click to the right of the character to be deleted, then press Backspace/Delete (for vertical type, do the same except click below the character).

To exit type-editing mode:

When you're done editing your type, do one of the following:

Click the Commit button ✔ on the Options bar.

Press Esc ★ or press Enter on the keypad (not on the main keyboard).

Click a different tool.

Click a different layer.

(To cancel your edits before confirming them, click the Cancel button ⊘ on the Options bar.)

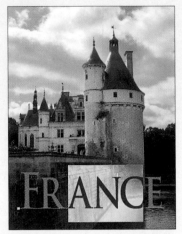

A To select type characters for editing, drag across them with a type tool.

SHOWING THE CHARACTER PANEL

➤ If the Character panel is open but collapsed to an icon, click the A icon.

➤ Select the Horizontal Type tool or Vertical Type tool, then click the Toggle Character and Paragraph Panels ▤ button on the Options bar.

➤ Choose Type > Panels > Character Panel or Window > Character.

SELECTING TYPE CHARACTERS

To select type for copyediting or restyling, choose the Horizontal Type or Vertical Type tool, then do any of the following:

Select consecutive characters or words	Drag across them. Or click at the beginning of a series of words, then Shift-click the end.
Select a word	Double-click a word.
Select consecutive words	Double-click a word, then drag without releasing the mouse.
Select a line	Triple-click a line.
Select a paragraph	Quadruple-click in the paragraph.
Select all the characters in a type object	Double-click the T icon on the Layers panel; or click in the text, then press Ctrl-A/Cmd-A.

Recoloring type

To recolor all the type in a type layer:

1. On the Layers panel, click a type layer.

2. Do either of the following:

   Choose the **Horizontal Type** tool T or **Vertical Type** tool, T then click the **Text Color** swatch on the Options bar.

   On the Character panel, A click the **Color** swatch.

3. Choose a color via the Color Picker or Swatches panel, or click a color in the image, then click OK to exit the Color Picker.

➤ You can also apply a color, gradient, or pattern to a type layer via an editable overlay layer effect (see pages 410–411).

To recolor select characters or words:

1. With the **Horizontal Type** tool T or **Vertical Type** tool, T select the characters or words to be recolored.

2. Do either of the following:

   On the Options bar, click the **Text Color** swatch.

   On the Character panel, A click the **Color** swatch.**A**

3. Follow step 3 above.**B**

Changing the font family and font style

To change the font family and font style:

Method 1 (choose from the full list)

1. Select the type to be restyled (use any method on the preceding page).

2. On the Character panel A or Options bar, click the **Font Family** menu arrow to display a scrolling list of available font families and styles.

   To scroll through the list, leave the mouse button up and press the up or down arrow on the keyboard; fonts will preview in your document.

   To jump to the next font family, press Shift-up arrow or Shift-down arrow.

3. To apply a font and exit the panel, click the font name; or to apply the currently highlighted font, press Enter/Return.

➤ If selected type already contains the desired font family and you want to change just the font style, you can use the Font Style area on the Character panel or Options bar.

➤ From the Type > Font Preview Size submenu, you can choose a size (e.g., Medium) for the samples of font families that display on the font menus in Photoshop. Note: If your samples preview too slowly, choose a smaller preview size or None.

Continued on the following page

A *With a type tool, drag across the characters to be recolored, then click the Text Color swatch on the Options bar.*

B *Choose a replacement color from the Color Picker.*

Method 2 (run a search)

1. Select the type to be restyled (use any method on page 386).

2. On the Character panel or Options bar, click in the Font Family field.

3. Do one of the following:

   Start typing a font name.

   Type a generic category, such as "semibold italic," "black condensed," or "ornaments".**A**

   Type an abbreviation for a specific font (e.g., "f g" for Franklin Gothic or "my p" for Myriad Pro). Note the inclusion of spaces.

   To display only Typekit fonts on the menu, click the **Toggle Typekit Fonts** button. [Tk] (To download fonts from Typekit.com, see the next task. See also the sidebar on this page.)

4. Unless you clicked either one of the Typekit buttons, a menu will display, listing the fonts that most closely match your search criteria. To scroll through the list, keep the mouse button up and press the up or down arrow on the keyboard. Fonts will preview in your document.

5. To apply a font and exit the panel, click the font name; or to apply the currently highlighted font, press Enter/Return.

➤ To exit the menu on the Character panel or Options bar during a font search without changing any fonts in your document, press Esc.

➤ To resolve a case of missing fonts upon opening a document, see page 34.

Using Adobe Typekit

Via the Creative Cloud, you can browse, preview, and download fonts from Typekit.com (an Adobe website), for use in Adobe programs. Before proceeding with this task, see the sidebar on this page.

To download fonts from Typekit.com: ★

1. To launch Typekit.com, do either of the following:

   Choose a type tool. On the font menu on the Character panel or Options bar, click the **Add Fonts from Typekit** button.[Tk]

   Deselect all type in your document. Choose Type > **Add Fonts from Typekit**.

2. On the Adobe Typekit web page, click **Fonts**. To narrow or customize the search for fonts, do any of the following (**A**, next page):

   From the Sort By menu, choose Featured or Newest, or for a full alphabetical list, choose Name.

   Narrow the search by clicking one or more of the categories on the right side, such as Classification.

   ➤ To change the text that is displayed in the thumbnails, in the field under the My Library tab, enter custom text, or from the Edit menu, choose an Alphabets or Pangrams option.

   ➤ To add any font to your list of Favorites, click the heart icon 💚 in the upper-right corner of its thumbnail.

3. Click a font you're interested in.

4. To change the way the font previews, click a tab category above the samples. If you want to enter custom text for the preview, click Type Tester.

TURNING ON TYPEKIT

Typekit will search for and sync fonts between the Creative Cloud and Photoshop only if the feature is turned on. You can verify this in either of two ways:

➤ Open the **Creative Cloud desktop app**, ☁ click Assets, then click Fonts. If Typekit is off, a **Turn Typekit On** button displays; click the button.

➤ Open the **Creative Cloud desktop app**, ☁ click the gear icon, ⚙ then click Preferences. In the Preferences panel, click Creative Cloud, click Fonts, then under Typekit On/Off, make sure the On button is clicked. Click the back arrow at the top. ★

A In the font search field on the Character panel, we entered "b cond," to display only bold condensed fonts on the Font menu.

A On Typekit.com, you can narrow the font search by clicking categories or via the Sort By menu, and you can preview any font via various methods.

5. When you find a font you want to use in an Adobe application, click **+ Use Fonts**.

6. For use in applications, click the **Sync** tab. Make sure all the fonts you want to download have a check mark. (For more info, click Learn More About Syncing.)

For Web use, click the **Web** tab. If you haven't already created a kit, click Create a New Kit. (For more info, click Learn More About Web Use.)

7. Click **Sync Selected Fonts.B** The selected fonts will be synced to your computer via Creative Cloud, and should now be available in Photoshop and other Adobe applications. Click Close.

➤ To search for a particular font on Typekit.com, enter the font name in the search field in the upper left, then press Enter/Return.

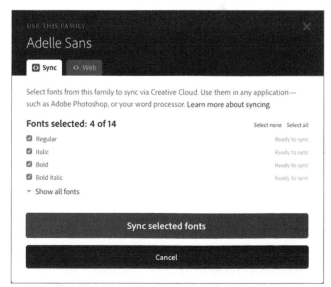

B Check all the fonts you want to download, then click Sync Selected Fonts.

Converting type

To convert paragraph type to point type:

On the Layers panel, right-click the name of a paragraph type layer and choose **Convert to Point Text**. A line break will be inserted at the end of every line of type except the last one. If the type object contains hidden (overflow) text, an alert dialog may appear, warning you that the hidden text will be deleted if you proceed; click OK.

To convert point type to paragraph type:

On the Layers panel, right-click the name of a point type layer and choose **Convert to Paragraph Text**. If you want to reshape the resulting bounding box, follow the steps on page 398. Be sure to delete any unwanted hyphens that Photoshop may have inserted.

Changing the font size

To assign a specific font (point) size to type, you can use either the Options bar or the Character panel.

To change the font size:

1. Choose the **Horizontal Type** or **Vertical Type** tool, then click a type layer or select the type characters to be resized.

2. Do either of the following:

   On the Options bar, use the **Font Size** icon as a scrubby slider (Alt-drag/Option-drag for smaller increments), or enter a value, or choose a preset size from the menu.**A**

   On the Character panel,**A** choose a **Font Size.B**

➤ To choose a measurement unit for the Character and Paragraph panels, see page 467.

You can also resize type interactively with the Move tool. This is especially useful if your type selection contains different point sizes and you want to preserve those relative differences while resizing.

To scale type with the Move tool:

1. On the Layers panel, click a type layer.

2. Click the **Move** tool and check **Show Transform Controls** on the Options bar. A bounding box with handles appears around the type.

3. Do either of the following:

   To scale both the height and the width of the type, click a corner handle, then drag it. To preserve the

original proportions of the characters while scaling them (better!), Shift-drag a corner handle.**C**

To scale just the height or width of the type, drag a middle handle.

4. To accept the scale transformation, click the Commit ✔ button on the Options bar or double-click in the text block. (To cancel the edit before accepting it, click the Cancel Transform ⊘ button on the Options bar or press Esc.)

➤ To typeset narrow or wide characters, we like to use a condensed or extended font, in which the characters have balanced proportions, instead of the Vertical Scale or Horizontal Scale control on the Character panel, which produces distortion.

A To change the font size of selected type via the Options bar, use the scrubby slider, enter a value, or choose a preset size from the menu.

B Another way to change the type size is via the Font Size scrubby slider, field, or menu on the Character panel.

C To scale type proportionally with the Move tool, Shift-drag a corner handle on the transform box.

Applying kerning and tracking

Kerning changes the spacing between a pair of text characters, whereas tracking changes the spacing between multiple characters.

To apply kerning:

1. On the Layers panel, double-click a **T** icon, then click to create an insertion point between two characters.

2. Do either of the following:

   On the Character panel, choose Metrics from the Kerning menu to apply the kerning value built into the current font, or choose Optical to let Photoshop control the kerning; or use the Kerning icon **VA** as a scrubby slider (for finer increments, hold down Alt/Option);**A** or enter or choose a positive or negative value.**B**

   Press Alt/Option plus the left or right arrow key on the keyboard (to kern in a larger increment, hold down Ctrl-Alt/Cmd-Option while pressing).

➤ To restore the spacing between two characters to the kerning setting of Optical, select both characters, then choose Optical from the Kerning menu.

To apply tracking:

1. Do either of the following:

   To apply tracking to a whole layer, click the layer.

   To apply tracking to part of a layer, double-click a **T** icon, then select some characters or words.

2. Do either of the following:

   On the Character panel, use the **Tracking** icon as a scrubby slider (hold down Alt/Option for finer increments) or enter or choose a positive or negative value.**C**

   If type characters are selected, you can press Alt/Option and the left or right arrow key (to track in a larger increment, hold down Ctrl-Alt/Cmd-Option).

➤ To reset the tracking value of selected characters to 0, press Ctrl-Shift-Q/Cmd-Control-Shift-Q.

➤ If Fractional Widths is checked on the Character panel menu, Photoshop uses fractions of pixels to control the spacing of type (on the entire layer), to optimize its appearance. Keep this option checked unless you're setting small type for Web output.

➤ To reset the Character panel and any selected type to the factory-default settings, choose Reset Character from the Character panel menu.

A *Kerning and tracking values can be set on the Character panel or via shortcuts (not on the Options bar).*

B *Use a negative kerning value to tighten the gap between a pair of characters (here we chose a value of –100).*

TRACKING IT OUT

Tracking can make type more or less readable, depending on the tracking value used. Try not to overdo it!

C *On occasion, we might spread out a few words, as in the header in this figure, but never a whole paragraph (that's a typesetting no-no!).*

Adjusting the leading

The Leading value controls the spacing between each line of paragraph type and the line above it. In a block of text that has a uniform font size, uniform leading looks best. Note: To reposition a whole layer, drag it with the Move tool.

To adjust leading in horizontal paragraph type:

1. On the Layers panel, do either of the following:

   Click a type layer.

   Double-click the T icon for a type layer, then select the lines of type for which you want to change the Leading value.

2. Show the Character panel. Use the **Leading** icon as a scrubby slider **A–C** (Alt-drag/Option-drag for finer increments), or enter a value, or choose a preset value from the menu. If you're not sure what value to use, start with a value that's a couple of points larger than the current font size.

   Note: The character that has the highest Leading value in a line controls the spacing of that line.

➤ The Auto setting for leading is calculated as a percentage of the current font size. To quickly restore the Auto setting to selected type, press Ctrl-Alt-Shift-A/Cmd-Option-Shift-A.

➤ To adjust the vertical spacing between characters in vertical type, click the type layer, then change the Tracking value (not the Leading value) on the Character panel.

➤ To change the orientation of type, right-click a type layer name on the Layers panel and choose Horizontal or Vertical. Or double-click a type layer thumbnail, then on the Options bar, click the Toggle Text Orientation button. To rotate characters in vertical type, uncheck Standard Vertical Roman Alignment on the Character panel menu.

Shifting type from the baseline

Use the Baseline Shift feature to raise or lower type characters from the normal baseline (1 point at a time).

To shift characters from the baseline:

1. On the Layers panel, double-click a T icon, then select the characters or words to be shifted.

2. On the Character panel, use the **Baseline Shift** icon as a scrubby slider (Alt-drag/Option-drag for finer increments), or enter a value. **D–E**

A *This 132-pt type has a Leading value of 154 pt.*

B *We're resetting the Leading value on the Character panel.*

C *A Leading value of 120 pt brought the bottom line of type closer to the top one.*

D *These characters have a Baseline Shift value of 0.*

E *Here the characters have an assortment of different Baseline Shift values, some positive (to raise characters) and some negative (to move characters downward).*

Inserting special characters

The OpenType buttons on the Character panel substitute alternate glyphs (stylistic variations) for standard characters, if available in the current OpenType font. Among the possible OpenType options are ligature glyphs for specific letter pairs (such as ff, ffl, and st), swash and titling characters, and fractions. The OpenType "Pro" fonts contain the most glyph options.

To insert or specify alternate glyphs for OpenType characters:

1. Do either of the following:

   To change all applicable occurrences in existing text, either click a type layer on the Layers panel or highlight characters with a type tool, and if you haven't already done so, choose an OpenType font family and font style.

   To specify alternate glyph options for text to be entered in a specific OpenType font, choose a type tool and that font family and style.

2. On the Character panel, **A** click the desired — and available (not dimmed) — OpenType button(s).**A**

You can also insert alternate glyphs manually by using the Glyphs panel. This panel can be used to locate and insert characters in OpenType and non-OpenType fonts.

To insert a glyph using the Glyphs panel: ★

1. Choose the **Horizontal Type** or **Vertical Type** tool, then select a character or click in a text block.

2. Display the Glyphs panel **A** (choose Glyphs from the Type> Panels submenu or Window menu).

3. From the menu at the top,**B** choose a category of glyphs to be displayed. Different options will be available depending on the current font.

4. *Optional:* You can choose a different font family and font style from the menus at the top of the panel.

5. Double-click a glyph to insert it into your text or to replace any selected character. If the square for a glyph has a mini black square in the lower-right corner, press and hold on the glyph, then choose a variation from the pop-up menu.**C** The glyph will appear in your text.

➤ To change the display size of the glyph squares on the Glyphs panel, click the Zoom Out or Zoom In button in the lower-left corner. Click the Scale Up **A⁺** or Scale Down **A⁺** button to scale the glyphs within their squares.

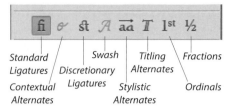

Standard Ligatures / Contextual Alternates | Discretionary Ligatures | Swash | Titling Alternates / Stylistic Alternates | Fractions / Ordinals

A These are the OpenType buttons on the Character panel.

B To control which category of glyphs displays on the Glyphs panel, choose an option from the menu on the panel.

C A glyph that has a mini black square in its lower-right corner contains variations. To display any variations, press and hold on that glyph, then choose a variation from the pop-up menu.

Applying paragraph settings

All the justification, alignment, indentation, and spacing options on the Paragraph panel apply to paragraph type. The first three alignment buttons also apply to point type.

To choose Paragraph panel settings:

1. Do either of the following:

   On the Layers panel, double-click a **T** icon, then click in a paragraph or select a series of paragraphs.

   To apply settings to all the type in a layer, click the layer, but don't select anything.

2. To show the Paragraph panel **¶ A**, choose Type > Panels > Paragraph Panel or Window > Paragraph. Or if a type tool is selected, you can click the Toggle Character and Paragraph Panels button 📋 on the Options bar, and then, if necessary, click the Paragraph tab.

3. Via one of the buttons at the top of the panel, apply an alignment option:

   For paragraph or point type, click a button in the first group — **Left Align Text**, **Center Text**, and **Right Align Text** — to align the type to the center or an edge of the bounding box that surrounds it.

   For paragraph type, click a button in the second group — **Justify Last Left**, **Justify Last Centered**, and **Justify Last Right** — to force all lines but the last one to span the full width of the bounding box.

   For paragraph type, click the last button, **Justify All**, to force all lines of type, including the last one, to span the full width of the bounding box.

4. If you want to enable automatic hyphenation, check Hyphenate at the bottom of the panel. We especially recommend that you turn on hyphenation for type that is justify-aligned, to help minimize gaps between words.

5. You can also change the Indent Left Margin, Indent First Line, or Indent Right Margin values and/or the Add Space Before Paragraph or Add Space After Paragraph values.

➤ To change the alignment of vertical type, the procedure is the same as described above, except the buttons have different labels.

➤ To reset all currently selected type and the Paragraph panel to the default paragraph settings, choose Reset Paragraph from the panel menu.

➤ To open a dialog in which you can specify parameters for hyphenation, choose Hyphenation from the Paragraph panel menu.

PICKING YOUR FAVORITE COMPOSER

The Single-Line Composer and Every-Line Composer algorithms on the Paragraph panel menu control the way in which type wraps within the bounding box. We prefer Every-Line Composer, because it automatically adjusts word breaks at the beginning of a paragraph, when necessary, to improve the line breaks near the end of the paragraph, and gives uneven lines a more aesthetically pleasing contour. Both composers abide by the current Word Spacing and Letter Spacing values in the Justification dialog (which opens from the Paragraph panel menu).

A These are the controls on the Paragraph panel.

Formatting type with paragraph and character styles

Using paragraph and character styles, you can format and style your type quickly, and ensure that it looks consistent throughout one document or among many related documents. When you edit a type style, all the type in which it is being used updates instantly. Open the Paragraph Style and Character Style panel group from the Type > Panels submenu or the Window menu.

To create a paragraph style:

Method 1 (based on sample text)

1. Apply the desired character and paragraph settings to some type, then click in the type with the **Horizontal Type** tool T or **Vertical Type** tool.↓T

2. On the Paragraph Styles panel,⬚ click the **New Paragraph Style** button.⬚ To rename the style, double-click the style name, enter a descriptive name in the dialog, then click OK.

Method 2 (based on an existing style)

1. Choose Select > **Deselect Layers**, or on the Layers panel, click a non-type layer or the Background.

2. On the Paragraph Styles panel,⬚ click a style, then choose **Duplicate Style** from the panel menu.

3. Double-click the duplicate style. In the Paragraph Style Options dialog, give the style a unique name, change the settings in any of the panels, then click OK.

To apply a paragraph style:

1. Click a type layer on the Layers panel; or with the **Horizontal Type** tool T or **Vertical Type** tool,↓T click in a paragraph or drag through some paragraphs.

2. On the Paragraph Styles panel, click a style.**A** Note: If the style doesn't apply correctly, click the Clear Override button ⬚ on the panel.

To create a character style:

1. Apply the desired character settings to a character or word, and keep the type selected.

2. On the Character Styles panel,⬚ click the **New Character Style** button.⬚ Double-click the style, rename it in the dialog, then click OK.

➤ You can also create a character style by duplicating it (follow the steps in Method 2, at left, except use the Character Styles panel instead).

To apply a character style:

1. Select the characters or words to be styled.

2. On the Character Styles panel, click a style.**B** Note: If the style doesn't apply correctly, click the Clear Override button ⬚ on the panel.

A *We applied a paragraph style to all the type in this document.*

B *Next, we applied a character style to just the numerals.*

When you edit a style that is currently assigned to type in your file, that type updates instantly.

To edit a type style:

Do one of the following:

Select and restyle a paragraph that contains the style to be edited, so it has the desired new attributes. Click the **Redefine Paragraph Style by Merging Override** button ✔ on the Paragraph Styles panel; or from the panel menu, choose **Redefine Style**.

Select and restyle one or more characters that contain the style to be edited, so they have the desired new attributes. Click the **Redefine Character Style by Merging Override** button ✔ on the Character Styles panel; or from the panel menu, choose **Redefine Style**.

Choose Select > Deselect Layers, then on the Paragraph Styles or Character Styles panel, double-click a style name. The Paragraph Style Options or Character Style Options dialog opens.**A** Change the settings in any of the panels (click a panel name on the left to switch panels), then click OK.**B**

A *For our Numerals character style, we changed the font family to Futura, the font style to Extra Bold Oblique, and the Color to an aqua blue.*

CLEARING OVERRIDES FROM TYPE

Overrides are attributes that are applied to text manually, in addition to any formatting already present in the text from a style. If you click in or select text that contains an override, a plus sign displays next to the style name on the panel.

To clear paragraph and character overrides from selected text — without removing any type style formatting — click the **Clear Override** button ⤺ on the Paragraph Styles panel. To clear just character overrides from selected text, click the Clear Override button ⤺ on the Character Styles panel.

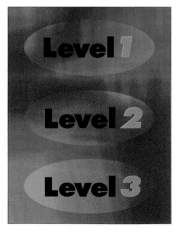

B *When we edited the color and font in the character style, the changes appeared instantly in all the styled type in our document.*

To load type styles from one document to another:

1. Open a Photoshop (.psd) document into which you want to load type styles.

2. Do either of the following:

   From the menu on the Paragraph Styles panel choose **Load Paragraph Styles**.

   From the menu on the Character Styles panel, choose **Load Character Styles**.

3. Locate and click a Photoshop (.psd) file that contains the desired styles, then click Open.

4. If a name conflict crops up, the Import Paragraph Styles or Import Character Styles dialog will open. **A** Click **Replace** to allow Photoshop to replace all existing styles bearing matching names with incoming styles, or click **Skip** to bar Photoshop from replacing existing styles that have matching names. (You can't pick and choose which individual style names Photoshop will replace or skip.) This is a good reason to give your styles unique names!

Paragraph and character styles can be saved as default styles, which will appear automatically in all future Photoshop documents and In any existing documents that you reopen.

To create default type styles:

1. Open a Photoshop (.psd) document. Create or load the paragraph and/or character styles that you want to save as defaults, and delete any styles that you don't want to save as defaults. All the styles in the document will be saved as defaults; you won't be able to pick and choose.

2. From the menu on the Paragraph Styles panel or the Character Styles panel, choose **Save Default Type Styles**.

➤ Each time you choose the Save Default Type Styles command, the new styles replace the existing ones and become the new defaults.

The Load Default Type Styles command loads all the current default paragraph and character styles into a document. You can't load individual styles or specify one kind of style over the other.

To load the current default type styles into a document:

1. With a Photoshop (.psd) document open, from the menu on the Paragraph Styles panel or the Character Styles panel, choose **Load Default Type Styles**. The command will load both paragraph and character styles, regardless of where you choose it.

2. If the current document contains styles bearing the same name as any incoming (default) styles, an alert dialog will appear. See step 4, at left.

➤ The Load Default Type Styles and Save Default Type Styles commands can also be chosen from the Type menu.

➤ To delete a selected style, deselect the type in your document (choose Select > Deselect Layers), and click the Delete Style button. If an alert dialog appears, click Yes. This can't be undone. To delete multiple styles, Ctrl-click/Cmd-click the style names first.

FADING PART OF A TYPE LAYER

To fade the editable type shown below, we added a layer mask to the type layer, then dragged with the Gradient tool from right to left.

Import Paragraph Styles

0 unique style(s) and 2 duplicate(s) were found in the document

Do you want to Skip the duplicate(s) or Replace the existing stylesheet(s) with them ?

Replace   Skip   Cancel

A If any incoming paragraph styles have the same names as styles in the existing document, the Import Paragraph Styles dialog will appear.

Transforming the bounding box for paragraph type

If you change the shape of the bounding box that surrounds paragraph type (e.g., make the box narrower or wider), the type will reflow to fit the new dimensions without the characters becoming distorted. Enlarging the bounding box is a necessity if you want to reveal overflow type (indicated by a tiny plus sign in the lower-right corner handle). Instructions are also given here for rotating the bounding box.

To transform paragraph type via its bounding box:

1. On the Layers panel, double-click the **T** icon for a paragraph type layer, then click anywhere in the text. A dashed bounding box with handles surrounds the type.

2. Do either or both of the following:

   To **reshape** the bounding box, drag a control handle.**A** To preserve the proportions of the bounding box while scaling it, start dragging a corner handle, then hold down Shift and continue to drag (release the mouse, then release Shift). The type will reflow into the new shape.**B**

   To **rotate** the bounding box, position the pointer just outside one of the corners (it will become a curved, double-arrow pointer), then drag in a circular direction.

3. To accept the transformation, press Esc ★ or press Enter on the keypad or click the Commit button ✔ on the Options bar. (To cancel the edits, click the Cancel button ⊘ on the Options bar.)

➤ To align or distribute multiple layers, including type layers, see page 289.

➤ To move a type object while a type tool is selected, drag the object with Ctrl/Cmd held down (temporary Move tool). Note: If you press V to access the Move tool instead, make sure your type cursor isn't inserted in type, or you will either replace selected type with that letter or insert the letter into your text.

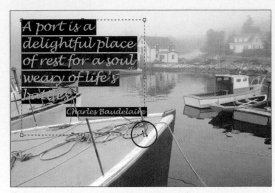

A *We're dragging a control handle to transform the bounding box that surrounds a type object.*

B *When we widened the bounding box, the type reflowed into the new shape.*

TRANSFORMING TYPE

➤ You can apply any transform command, such as Free Transform, to paragraph or point type (see pages 358–359). Both the bounding box and the characters within it will be affected by the transformation.

➤ You can move, scale, rotate, or skew editable or rasterized type; you can apply a distortion or perspective transformation command only to rasterized type.

➤ If you want to transform characters individually, create each one on a separate layer.

WAYS TO EMBELLISH TYPE

➤ Apply layer effects or styles to an editable or rasterized type layer (see the next chapter).

➤ "Fill" editable type with imagery by using it as the base layer in a clipping mask (see pages 353–354).

Screening back type

In these steps, you'll use a Levels adjustment layer to screen back type. A lightened version of the image will be visible only within the type shapes. This is a very "Photoshoppy" way to combine type with imagery.

To screen back type:

1. Create a document that contains a medium to dark image layer and an editable type layer (the type color doesn't matter), preferably in a large font size and a bold or black font style. **A**

2. On the Layers panel, Ctrl-click/Cmd-click the **T** icon to load the type as a selection. Hide the type layer, then click the underlying image layer or Background.

3. On the Adjustments panel, click the **Levels** button. The Levels controls display on the Properties panel, and the selection disappears from view.

4. Move the middle input slider to the left to lighten the midtones in the type (you can also move the highlights slider). Move the output shadows slider to the right to reduce the contrast in the type. **B–C**

➤ For added depth, apply layer effects to the adjustment layer. Try Inner Shadow, Bevel & Emboss, or Drop Shadow. See the next chapter.

➤ To reposition the type in the image, click the adjustment layer, then Ctrl/Cmd drag in the document.

➤ To screen back the imagery instead of the type, after following the steps above, click the adjustment layer mask thumbnail, then on the Properties panel, click Invert (or press Ctrl-I/Cmd-I).

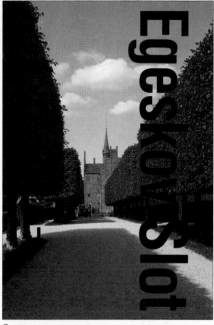

A The original document contains an image layer and an editable type layer.

B The mask on the Levels adjustment layer is hiding the adjustment everywhere but within the type shapes.

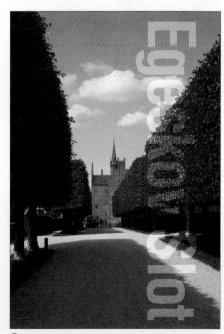

C In this screened-back version, the Levels adjustment is visible only within the type shapes.

Rasterizing a type layer

If you want to edit type by applying a filter or the Transform > Distort or Perspective command, or draw strokes on it directly with a tool such as the Brush, you have to convert it to pixels first via the Rasterize Type command. Although you can't change the typographic attributes of rasterized type, there are countless creative things you can do with it.

To rasterize type into pixels:

1. *Optional:* To preserve the editable type layer, duplicate it (Ctrl-J/Cmd-J), then hide the original. Keep the duplicate layer selected.

2. Right-click the editable type layer name and choose **Rasterize Type** (or choose Type > Rasterize Type Layer). In the layer thumbnail, you will see the type shapes surrounded by transparent pixels.

CREATING A CUT PAPER EFFECT

In this example, we'll "attack" the type characters with knives (well, actually, a lasso tool)!

1. Create an editable type layer, duplicate it, then right-click the duplicate layer and choose **Rasterize Type**. Hide the editable type layer.

2. To select a portion of a type "character," drag with the **Lasso** tool 🔾 (L or Shift-L) or click with the **Polygonal Lasso** tool. **A**

3. Choose the **Move** tool ⊕ or hold down Ctrl/Cmd, then drag the selection in the document window or press any of the arrow keys. **B**

4. Repeat steps 2–3 for other "characters" to create an aesthetically pleasing design (**A–C**, next page).

A *We created editable type in an extra bold font, duplicated and hid the type layer, and rasterized the duplicate. With the Polygonal Lasso tool, we created a straight-edged selection of the stem on the letter P.*

B *We repositioned the selection with the Move tool.*

A *With the Lasso tool, we created an irregular-shaped selection of the top of the letter A.*

B *We moved the selection.*

C *This is the final "cut paper" image after we moved more straight-edged and irregular selections of the rasterized type layer.*

PUTTING SECTIONS OF RASTERIZED TYPE ONTO SEPARATE LAYERS

With the Magic Wand tool (Tolerance 0, Contiguous checked), we clicked each piece of "cut paper" separately, then used the Layer > New > Layer via Cut command (Ctrl-Shift-J/Cmd-Shift-J) to put it on a new layer. Note: If you follow these steps, remember to reselect the original rasterized layer each time before clicking with the Magic Wand.

With the sections on different layers, we were able to apply the Color Overlay and Drop Shadow layer effects to each separate layer, and also to move the layers individually. Fun!

These are some of the Layers panel listings for the image shown at left.

Putting type in a spot color channel

To put type in a spot color channel:

1. Make sure your document has a suitable resolution for commercial printing (typically, 300 ppi).

2. Show both the Layers and Channels panels. If you haven't already done so, create some editable type, then choose the Move tool.

3. Display the Channels panel, then from the panel menu, choose **New Spot Channel**.

4. In the New Spot Channel dialog, click the **Color** swatch, and if necessary, click **Color Libraries** to get to the Color Libraries dialog.

5. From the **Book** menu, choose a spot color matching system, such as one of the PANTONE PLUS + systems (not Color Bridge); click the desired color or type a number that you have gotten from a printed swatch guide; then click OK to return to the New Spot Channel dialog. Optionally, change the Solidity (density) value just for the onscreen preview to simulate the transparency of the ink (this doesn't affect output). Click OK.

6. On the Layers panel, Ctrl-click/Cmd-click the **T** icon to select the type shapes,**A** then hide the type layer.

7. On the Channels panel, make sure the new spot color channel is still selected, then choose Edit > **Fill** (Shift-Backspace/Shift-Delete). In the dialog, choose Use: Black, Mode: Normal, and an Opacity value that matches the tint (density) value of the spot color ink to be used on press. Click OK. The selection will fill with the spot color.

8. Deselect (Ctrl-D/Cmd-D). On the Channels panel, the type shapes should display in only the spot channel thumbnail.**B** Click the RGB channel.

9. To preserve the spot color channel, save the file in the Photoshop or Photoshop PDF format.

➤ To reposition the type shapes, click the spot channel listing on the Channels panel, then drag in the document with the Move tool. When you're done, click the RGB channel listing.

➤ You can't edit the type characters in a spot color channel, since technically they're just areas of color, not type. If you don't like the results, you will need to redo it from scratch. Fill the channel with White, 100% Opacity, redisplay and edit the original type layer, then repeat steps 6–8, above.

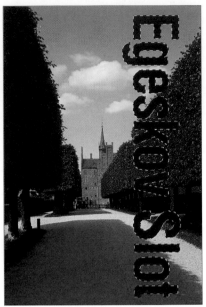

A The type is converted to a selection.

B With the type shapes in a spot color channel, a commercial printer will be able to print them from a separate plate.

As a Photoshop user, you're in the business of creating illusions. With layer effects, you can accomplish this in a few easy steps. The Photoshop effects that you can apply to a layer, either alone or in combination, include Bevel, Emboss, Stroke, Inner Shadow, Inner Glow, Satin, Color Overlay, Gradient Overlay, Pattern Overlay, Outer Glow, and Drop Shadow. Once applied, layer effects can be edited, hidden, or removed at any time. And best of all, when you modify type or pixels on a layer, any effects on that layer will update automatically (they should be called "Smart Effects"!). Once you develop a combination of effects that you like, you can save it collectively (along with other Layers panel settings) as a style to the Styles panel, for easy access and use in any document.

In this chapter, you will learn the generic steps for applying, copying, moving, and removing layer effects; change the layer fill percentage; learn specific steps for applying and duplicating ★ some individual effects; create, save, and apply layer styles; and finally, perform a couple of fun exercises that involve type and layer styles.

Layer effect essentials

Layer effects can be applied to any type, image, Smart Object, or shape layer (or group thereof), but not to the Background. They are applied and edited via the Layer Style dialog and are listed on the Layers panel below the layer they belong to. Layer effects appear either on or along the edges of layer pixels or vector shapes (including type), and will update instantly if you add, modify, or delete areas (or type characters) from the layer. You can edit the settings for a layer effect at any time, and turn the visibility of an effect on or off.

Before exploring any of the individual effects, familiarize yourself with these generic steps.

To apply layer effects (generic steps):

1. Do any of the following:

   Double-click to the right of or below a layer or layer group name; or for an image layer (not a type or shape layer or a Smart Object), you can double-click the layer thumbnail instead.

   Click a layer or layer group, then choose an effect from the **Add Layer Style** menu *fx* from the bottom of the Layers panel.

   The Layer Style dialog opens (**A**, next page). Check Preview.

Continued on the following page

LAYER STYLES

20

STYLES USED FOR THE ARROW

The arrow, above, was styled with the Bevel effect (under Bevel & Emboss, Style: Inner Bevel) and the Gradient Overlay effect.

2. Click an effect name on the left side of the dialog, then choose settings on the right side.

3. *Optional:* Click other effect names to apply additional effects to the same layer or group.

4. Click OK.

5. Edit the layer (e.g., transform or move a shape, edit the type in a type layer, add pixels to an image layer). Watch as the "smart" effect(s) update instantly.

   On the Layers panel, any layer that contains effects will have this icon: *fx*. Click the arrowhead next to the icon to collapse or expand that list of effects (**A**, next page).

6. To change the settings for an effect, or to add more effects to a layer, double-click the layer or the Effects listing or double-click an individual effect name (nested below the layer name).

7. To hide or show one layer effect, expand the effects list for the layer, then click the visibility icon 👁 for the effect.

   To hide or show all the effects on a layer, click the visibility icon for the Effects listing.

➤ Some effects have an Angle setting (e.g., Inner Shadow, Satin, and Drop Shadow). If you change the Angle for an individual effect while Use Global Light is checked, the angle will update on any other effects in which the Global Light option is being used. Use this feature to keep the lighting uniform among multiple effects.

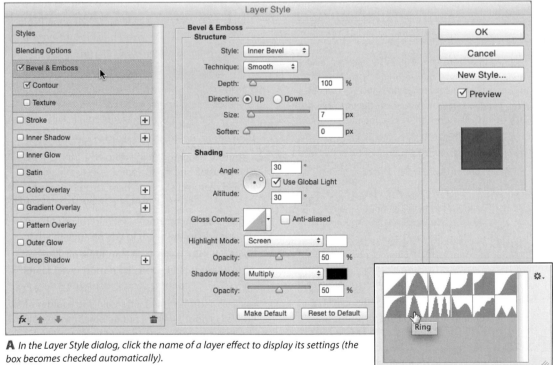

A *In the Layer Style dialog, click the name of a layer effect to display its settings (the box becomes checked automatically).*

The Contour presets define the effect profile. Gray areas in the thumbnail represent opaque pixels; white areas represent transparency. To close the preset picker, either double-click a contour or click anywhere outside the picker.

Choosing imagery for layer effects

➤ We usually apply layer effects that work inward or outward from edges — Bevel, Emboss, Stroke, Inner Shadow, Inner Glow, Outer Glow, and Drop Shadow — to a type or shape layer, or to an image layer that contains some transparent areas.**B** To produce a layer that contains transparency, click an existing image layer, create a selection, then press Ctrl-J/Cmd-J (for the Layer via Copy command).

➤ The Satin, Color Overlay, Gradient Overlay, and Pattern Overlay effects look fine on any kind of layer, whether the layer contains transparency or not.

➤ When applying effects that spread outward (e.g., Outer Glow, Drop Shadow) to type, allow some breathing room between the characters. You can use the Tracking and/or Kerning controls on the Character panel to adjust the horizontal spacing (see page 391).

DEFAULT LAYER STYLE SETTINGS

➤ To establish new default settings for a specific layer effect, choose the desired settings in the Layer Style dialog, then click **Make Default.**

➤ To apply the settings to a layer effect that you established by clicking Make Default (or to restore the factory default settings, if you didn't establish your own default settings), click **Reset to Default.**

➤ To restore all settings (in all panels) that were in place when you opened the Layer Style dialog, Alt-click/Option-click **Reset** (Cancel becomes Reset).

➤ To restore the factory default settings to all layer effects, you have to reset all the Photoshop settings files (do this only if it's a necessity): Hold down Ctrl-Alt-Shift/Cmd-Option-Shift as you relaunch Photoshop, and click Yes in the alert.

To hide or show all the effects on a layer, click the Effects visibility icon.

To hide or show one effect, click its individual visibility icon.

A *Click the arrowhead to expand or collapse a list of layer effects.*

The "fx" icon signifies that this layer contains layer effects.

To open the Layer Style dialog, choose an effect from the Add Layer Style menu (or double-click the layer). In the dialog, effects that are currently applied to the layer will have a check mark.

B *The Layers panel for this document is shown at left. Note that the image layer contains transparent areas.*

Applying a bevel or emboss effect

The Bevel and Emboss effects create an illusion of volume by adding a highlight and shading. The results can range from a chiseled bevel to a pillowy emboss that looks as if it's been stamped onto porous paper. For variety, experiment with the Contour options.

To apply the Bevel or Emboss effect:

1. On the Layers panel, double-click near a layer **A** or group name to open the Layer Style dialog.

2. Click **Bevel & Emboss.**

3. Under Structure, choose a **Size** for the depth of the bevel or emboss effect.**B**

4. Choose other **Structure** settings:

   Choose a **Style** option: **Outer Bevel, Inner Bevel, Emboss, Pillow Emboss,** or **Stroke Emboss C–D** (and **A–B,** next page). (Note: Before applying the Stroke Emboss style, we recommend applying the Stroke effect, at an increased Size setting.)

   From the **Technique** menu, choose **Smooth, Chisel Hard,** or **Chisel Soft.**

   Choose a **Depth** for the intensity of the highlight and the shadow.

   Click the **Up** or **Down** button to swap the positions of the highlight and shadow (try this on the Pillow Emboss style).

   Raise the **Soften** value if you want to blur the effect. The softening is most noticeable when a Chisel option is chosen as the Technique.

Steps 5–7 are optional.

5. Under **Shading,** do any of the following:

   Choose an **Angle** and an **Altitude** (height) to change the location of the light source, and therefore the position of the highlight and shadow. Check **Use Global Light** to apply the same Angle and Altitude settings to all effects in which the Global Light option is being used, for uniform lighting, or uncheck it to apply a unique setting for just this effect. Note: If you change the Angle or Altitude for an effect while Use Global Light is checked, all other effects that are using the Global Light option will adopt those values.

   Click the **Gloss Contour** arrowhead, then choose a profile in the Contour Preset picker.

   ► For a reverse bevel, try the Rolling Slope – Descending contour.

A *The original image contains two layers.*

B *We chose these Layer Style options to produce figure* **C.**

C *The Inner Bevel effect is applied (and also the Drop Shadow effect).*

D *Here we applied the Outer Bevel effect (plus a Drop Shadow).*

Choose a **Highlight Mode** and **Opacity** for the highlight and a **Shadow Mode** and **Opacity** for the shadow.

To change the highlight or shadow **color**, click the corresponding color swatch, then choose a color via the Color Picker (or, while the picker is open, click a color in the Swatches panel or the document). Click OK.

6. If you want to add a Contour to the edges of the bevel or emboss, do the following:

   On the left side of the dialog, under Bevel & Emboss, click **Contour**. Click the Contour arrowhead, then click a contour preset in the picker. This option can alter the appearance of the effect dramatically.

   Check **Anti-aliased** to soften the transition between the dark and light areas in the contour.

   For the Style option of Outer Bevel or Inner Bevel, adjust the **Range** (the position of the bevel on the chosen contour) to minimize or maximize the prominence of the bevel.

7. If you want to add a texture to the effect, click **Texture** on the left side of the dialog, click a pattern in the picker, then do any of the following: **C**

   Adjust the **Scale** of the pattern.

   Change the **Depth** to increase or reduce the contrast between the highlights and shadows in the pattern.

   Check **Invert** to swap the highlights and shadows. This has the same effect as changing the Depth percentage from negative to positive, and vice versa.

   Check **Link with Layer** to link the texture and layer so they will move as a unit when dragged in the document.

   Drag in the document to reposition the texture within the effect; click **Snap to Origin** if you want to realign the pattern to its default location.

8. Click OK.

➤ For another use of the Emboss effect, see page 420.

SAVE YOUR SETTINGS!

If you produce a layer effect or combination of effects and Layers panel settings that you want to preserve for future use, save that collection of settings as a **style** on the Styles panel, then save the styles on the panel as a library (see page 417).

A We imported these original Illustrator objects into Photoshop as a Smart Object.

B We applied the Pillow Emboss effect (Technique: Smooth).

C We added the Texture option of the Emboss effect.

Applying a shadow effect

You can create an inner shadow or drop shadow with just a few clicks of the mouse.

To apply the Inner Shadow or Drop Shadow effect:

1. On the Layers panel, double-click near a layer or group name to open the Layer Style dialog.**A**

2. Click **Inner Shadow** or **Drop Shadow**.**B–D**

3. Choose an overall **Size** for the shadow (in pixels).

   Choose a **Distance** value (in pixels) by which you want the shadow to be offset from the edge of the layer shapes.

   ➤ You can reposition a drop shadow by dragging in the document while the dialog is open, but be aware that this will also reposition any other effects that are using the Global Light option.

   Choose a **Choke** percentage for an Inner Shadow or a **Spread** percentage for a Drop Shadow to control where the shadow begins to fade.

4. Do any of the following (optional):

   Choose a **Blend Mode** from the menu. (For a drop shadow, we usually keep this on the default setting of Multiply.)

   To choose a different shadow **color**, click the color swatch, choose a color via the Color Picker or click a color in the document with the eyedropper (the color previews in the document), then click OK.

   Choose an **Opacity** percentage for the transparency level of the shadow. For a drop shadow, we usually lower the Opacity below the default value of 75%.

   Choose an **Angle** for the position of the shadow relative to the original layer shapes, and decide whether to check **Use Global Light**.

   In the Quality area, click the **Contour** arrowhead and choose a preset in the picker for the edge profile of the shadow (we're usually content with the shape of the default Contour).

   Check **Anti-aliased** to soften the edges between the shadow and the layer imagery.

   Adjust the **Noise** level. The addition of noise (speckling) can help prevent banding on print output, but a very low value is best.

   For the Drop Shadow effect, if the layer (not the effect) has a Fill value below 100% or has a

A *This original image consists of an image layer (hammer and nail and transparent pixels) above a solid-color Background.*

B *We applied the Drop Shadow effect to the image layer.*

C *This image consists of an image layer (popsicle and transparent pixels) above a solid white Background.*

D *We applied the Inner Shadow effect to the popsicle layer. Slurp.*

blending mode other than Normal, check **Layer Knocks Out Drop Shadow** to prevent the shadow from showing through the layer pixels.

5. Click OK. If you want to reshape the shadow, follow the steps below.

Depending on the time of day and the angle of the sun or other light source, cast shadows tend to be either short or elongated. You can reshape a drop shadow via the Distort command to mimic this natural effect.

To transform a Drop Shadow effect:

1. Apply the Drop Shadow effect to a layer (see the preceding instructions) and no other effects. Keep the layer selected.

2. To transfer the shadow effect to its own layer, right-click the Effects listing on the Layers panel, then choose **Create Layer** from the context menu. If an alert dialog appears, click OK.

3. Click the new Drop Shadow layer.**A**

4. Choose Edit > Transform > **Distort**, drag the handles of the transform box to slant the shape, or for a symmetrical perspective distortion, hold down Ctrl-Alt-Shift/Cmd-Option-Shift while dragging a corner handle. Press Enter/Return.**B** Note: If you don't see all the handles, press Ctrl-0/Cmd-0 (zero) to fit the image in the document window.

➤ To link the image and shadow layers so they will move and transform as a unit, Shift-click them, then click the Link Layers button 🔗 at the bottom of the panel.

➤ To limit any painting or fill edits that you apply to the Drop Shadow layer to just the existing pixels on that layer, activate the Lock Transparent Pixels button on the Layers panel first.

A *Starting with the image shown in figure* **B** *on the preceding page, we applied the Create Layer command to transfer the drop shadow to its own layer and then, as shown above, we applied a Distort transformation.*

B *This is the final image, the Layers panel for which is shown at left. Note: We lowered the Fill setting for the Drop Shadow to 68%.*

Applying the Stroke effect

The Stroke effect works particularly well on type.

To apply the Stroke effect:

1. Double-click near a layer or group name on the Layers panel to open the Layer Style dialog.

2. Click **Stroke**.

3. Do any of the following:

   Choose a **Size** (width) for the stroke.

   From the **Position** menu, choose a location for the stroke relative to the layer content: Outside, Inside, or Center.

   For the **Fill Type**, choose **Color**, **Gradient** (see steps 3–5 below), or **Pattern** (see steps 3–4 on the next page) and choose settings for the options that become available.

   You can also change the **Blend Mode** and **Opacity** percentage.

4. Click OK.**A**

Applying the Gradient and Pattern Overlay effects

You can apply the Gradient Overlay and Pattern Overlay effects to an image, shape, or type layer. On an image layer, the overlays work effectively whether the layer contains transparency or not. (Color Overlay, not covered here, works the same way.)

To apply the Gradient Overlay effect:

1. Double-click near a layer or group name on the Layers panel to open the Layer Style dialog.**B**

2. Click **Gradient Overlay**.**C–D**

3. Click the **Gradient** arrowhead, then click a gradient on the picker. (To load gradients from another library, choose a library name from the lower part of the picker menu; see page 133.) You could also click the gradient thumbnail and edit the gradient.

4. From the **Style** menu, choose Linear, Radial, Angle, Reflected, or Diamond.

5. Do any of the following (optional):

   Change the **Blend Mode**.

   Check **Dither** to help prevent noticeable color bands in the gradient on print output.

   Adjust the **Opacity** of the overlay.

   Check **Reverse** to swap the position of the colors in the gradient.

A *We applied the Stroke effect to a type layer, with Gradient selected as the Fill Type.*

B *We began by applying a Bevel effect (Inner Bevel style) to some type.*

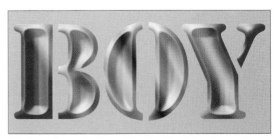

C *In the Layer Style dialog, we added the Gradient Overlay layer effect, choosing these settings.*

D *This is the Gradient Overlay effect (added to the Bevel effect).*

Change the **Angle** of the gradient.

Choose a **Scale** percentage to control how gradually the gradient colors transition across the layer.

Drag in the document to reposition the gradient within the layer shapes. To reset the gradient to its default position at any time, click **Reset Alignment**.

6. Check **Align with Layer** to fit the gradient within just the nontransparent pixels, type, or shape on the layer, or uncheck this option to center the gradient on the full layer.

7. Click OK.

➤ If you apply two overlay effects to the same layer (e.g., Gradient Overlay and Pattern Overlay), lower the opacity of the one that's listed first in the dialog; otherwise the bottom one won't be visible.

A *To produce these metallic letters, we created a pattern from a photograph of rusted metal, then applied it as a Pattern Overlay layer effect. (We also applied the Drop Shadow and Emboss effects.)*

Patterns that you apply via the Pattern Overlay effect can range from those that have an obvious repeat, such as polka dots or stripes, to overall textures resembling "real" surfaces, such as gritty sandpaper, handmade paper, woven fabric, or variegated stone.

To apply the Pattern Overlay effect:

1. Double-click near a layer or group name on the Layers panel to open the Layer Style dialog.

2. Click **Pattern Overlay**.

3. Click the **Pattern** arrowhead, then click a pattern preset in the picker. To load patterns from another library, choose a library name from the lower part of the picker menu (see page 133). To create a custom pattern, see page 222.

4. Do any of the following (optional):

    Change the **Blend Mode**.

    Adjust the **Opacity** of the overlay.

    Drag in the document to reposition the pattern; click **Snap to Origin** to realign the pattern with the upper-left corner of the document.

    Choose a **Scale** percentage for the pattern size.

    Check **Link with Layer** to link the pattern to the layer so they'll move as a unit if you drag the layer.

5. Click OK.**A**

SCALING LAYER EFFECTS

To scale just the effects on a layer without scaling other layer content, right-click the Effects listing and choose Scale Effects from the context menu, then specify the desired Scale percentage in the dialog.

APPLYING THE SATIN EFFECT

To make the surfaces of objects, type, or brush strokes look reflective or metallic, use the Satin effect.

➤ If the Satin effect doesn't look noticeable, try increasing the Distance and/or Size values.

➤ Before adding the Satin effect to type, or to intensify its effect, give the type a medium or light color and apply a strong Inner Glow or Bevel effect.

*To the type shown in figure **B** on the preceding page (which has an Inner Bevel), we added the Satin effect.*

Applying multiple effect settings

The Layer Style dialog now enables five specific effects (Stroke, Inner Shadow, Color and Gradient Overlay, or Drop Shadow) to have two or more settings applied to a layer. By choosing unique settings for these multiple effects, you can apply more complex styling to layer imagery.

To apply multiple settings to an effect: ★

1. Double-click near a layer or group name on the Layers panel to open the Layer Style dialog.

2. Apply one or more effects, including some that display a ⊞ icon next to their name, by following the tasks on previous pages in this chapter.**A**

3. Click a ⊞ icon to create a **duplicate** of any of the five multiple effects. Enter different values for some or all of its settings to create a visual difference between the duplicate and the original effect (**A**, next page).

4. Click OK.

▶ To apply a unique angle to a duplicate of an Inner Shadow or Drop Shadow effect, make sure Use Global Light is unchecked in the settings for the duplicate.

▶ When applying multiple stroke effects, the topmost stroke listing should have the smallest Size value and the bottommost stroke listing should have the largest Size value.

To work with the menu and buttons at the bottom of the effects list: ★

1. In the Layer Style dialog, apply effects and multiple settings for specific effects.

2. Click the *fx* button to display its menu (**B**, next page), then do any of the following:

   Click one of the five available **effect names** to either initially apply it using its default settings or apply a duplicate.

   Click **Delete Effect** to unapply (uncheck) the current effect and remove it from the list.

   Click **Delete Hidden Effects** to remove all unapplied (unchecked) effects from the list.

A *We opened an image (shown in inset), then applied four effects (shown in the Layer Style dialog effects list at left) to add some punch to the skateboard.*

Click **Show Hidden Effects** to redisplay all unapplied effects on the list.

Click **Reset to Default List** to restore the default list of effects (each with its default settings) and remove any duplicate effects.

3. Click the **Move Up** or **Move Down** button to move a **duplicate** effect above or below its original.

4. Click the **Delete** button to unapply (uncheck) and remove the current effect from the list.

Delete Hidden Effects was chosen from the fx menu for this view.

A *We duplicated the Drop Shadow effect to add a blue shadow, duplicated the Gradient Overlay effect to add a more colorful gradient over the original gray gradient, and duplicated the Stroke effect two times to stack a low-opacity stroke and a narrow blue stroke above the wide yellow stroke.*

B *In the Layer Style dialog, click the fx button, at the bottom of the effects list, to display its menu of options.*

Copying, moving, and removing layer effects

If you like how an individual effect looks on one layer or group, you can copy or move it to another layer or group; no existing effects are deleted from the target layer. However, if an existing effect has the same name as an incoming effect, the new settings will override the existing ones. If you move *all* the effects from one layer to another, the incoming effects will replace any and all existing effects on the target layer, and will be removed from the source layer.

To copy an individual effect from one layer to another:

Alt-drag/Option-drag an individual effect name from one layer or group to another. The original effect stays where it is, and a copy of the effect appears in the target layer or group.

➤ Layer effects applied to a layer group will be applied to any layers within, or added to, the group.

To move an effect to another layer:

Drag an individual effect name from one layer to another. The effect is removed from the source layer and appears in the target layer.

To move all the effects from one layer to another:

Drag the Effects listing from one layer or group to another. All effects on the target layer will be replaced with the effects from the source layer.

Clicking to remove the visibility icon for a layer effect or unchecking the box for an effect in the Layer Style dialog doesn't remove the effect — it merely hides it from view. If you want to permanently delete one or all effects from a layer, do as follows.

To remove layer effects:

Do any of the following:

Click an effect listing in the Layer Style dialog, then click the Delete button 🗑 in the same dialog. ★

Drag a single effect name to the Delete Layer button 🗑 at the bottom of the Layers panel.

To remove all the effects from a layer, drag the Effects listing over the Delete Layer button. 🗑

➤ If you turn off an effect via the check box in the Layer Style dialog and then check it to turn it back on again, its last-used options will be reapplied.

LAYER EFFECTS ARE LIVE

Layer effects reshape automatically when you edit the object(s) they're applied to, as illustrated below.

We applied the Emboss, Gradient Overlay, Outer Glow, and Drop Shadow effects to the type layer, and the Inner Glow and Drop Shadow effects to the image layer.

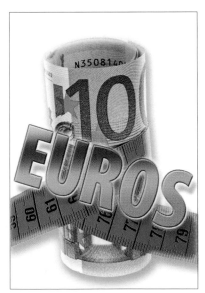

When we shrank the image layer and added a type character, the effects updated automatically.

Changing the layer fill percentage

The Fill feature on the Layers panel affects the opacity of a layer, excluding any layer effects (as shown below), whereas the Opacity feature controls the opacity of a layer, including any layer effects (see page 160).

To change the layer fill percentage:

1. Click any kind of layer (not the Background) or select multiple layers.**A**

2. On the Layers panel, set the **Fill** percentage (you can use the scrubby slider).**B** The lower the Fill value, the more content from the underlying layer(s) is revealed.

➤ To change the layer fill percentage via the Layer Style dialog, click Blending Options on the left side, then adjust the Fill Opacity setting.

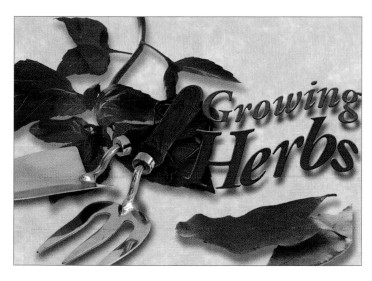

A *This image contains three image layers and an editable type layer. The Drop Shadow effect is applied to all the layers.*

B *When we lowered the Fill percentage of the type layer to 60%, the layer opacity changed but the Drop Shadow effect remained at full opacity. When we lowered the Opacity of the basil and bay leaf image layers to 70%, the drop shadows on those layers also became lighter.*

Applying layer styles

You can conveniently store multiple layer settings collectively as a style on the Styles panel. The style will include layer effects (e.g., Drop Shadow, Outer Glow) and/or blending options (blending mode and layer opacity and fill settings). Once stored, styles can be quickly applied to a type, image, or shape layer. To acquaint yourself with this panel, apply one of the predefined styles to a type layer or to a layer that contains some transparency.

To apply a style to a layer:

1. Show the Styles panel. 🔳 You can load additional style libraries onto the panel via the panel menu.

2. Do either of the following:

   Click a layer (not the Background) on the Layers panel, then click a style on the Styles panel. **A–D**

   Double-click a layer to open the Layer Style dialog, click Styles at the top left, click a style thumbnail, then click OK. **E**

➤ Normally, when you apply a style, it replaces any and all existing effects on the current layer. If you want to add the effects from a style to the existing effects on a layer, hold down Shift as you click the desired style. Note: Whether or not you hold down Shift, if two effects have the same name, the settings in the incoming style will replace the old.

➤ You can also apply a style via the Libraries panel. ⭐ (See pages 270–272.)

To remove styling from a layer:

Click a (hidden or visible) layer that contains layer style edits, then click the **Clear Style** button 🚫 on the Styles panel (or right-click the layer listing and choose Clear Layer Style from the context menu). All layer effects are removed, the layer Opacity is reset to 100%, and the blending mode is reset to Normal.

A *Click a layer, then click a style thumbnail on the Styles panel.*

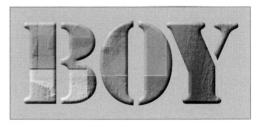

B *Web Styles library > Blue Paper Clip*

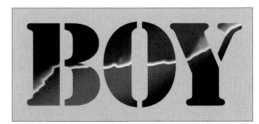

C *Abstract Styles library > Rose Impressions*

D *KS Styles library > Lightning*

E *Styles can also be applied to a layer via the Layer Style dialog. Click Styles at the top-left side of the dialog, then click a thumbnail.*

Creating layer styles

In addition to using the layer style presets, you can create and save custom layer styles. You can use an applied preset as a starting point or begin from scratch with your own settings. An option is provided via a dialog for the style to include the layer effects and/or the blending option settings that are applied to the currently selected layer.

To save a style to the Styles panel:

1. To any layer, apply the effects settings and/or blending option settings that you want to save collectively as a style.

2. Do either of the following:

   On the Layers panel, click the layer that contains the desired settings, **A** then on the Styles panel, click either the blank area or the **New Style** button. **B**

   On the Layers panel, double-click the layer that contains the desired settings, then on the right side of the Layer Style dialog, click **New Style**.

3. In the New Style dialog, enter a name for the new style, check whether you want to **Include Layer Effects** and/or **Include Layer Blending Options** (e.g., blending mode, opacity, and fill opacity settings) in the style. Check **Add to My Current Library** to add the style as a layer styles asset to the Libraries panel. ★ (See pages 270–272.) Click OK.

   The new style appears as the last listing or thumbnail on the Styles panel, and can be used in any document. **C–D**

4. Your custom styles will be deleted from the Styles panel if you allow them to be replaced by another library or if the Adobe Photoshop CC 2015 Prefs. psp file is deleted or damaged. To save the styles on the panel as a permanent library, choose Save Styles from the Styles panel menu, enter a name, keep the default location, then click Save again. (See also page 133 or 135.)

➤ To copy a style between layers, right-click the layer that contains the desired effects and settings and choose Copy Layer Style. Click the target layer, then right-click it and choose Paste Layer Style. The incoming style will replace any existing style settings on the target layer.

➤ You can't edit an existing style on the Styles panel, but you can apply a style, edit the settings, and save the new settings as a new custom style.

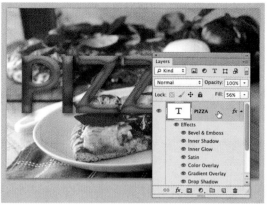

A *On the Layers panel, we clicked a layer that contains the effects and/or other settings to be saved as a style.*

B *On the Styles panel, we clicked the New Style button.*

C *Our new custom style appeared at the bottom of the panel.*

D *We applied the new style to a shape layer in another document.*

Applying multiple layer effects

With the exception of Drop Shadow and Overlay, layer effects tend to produce a more convincing visual illusion when applied in combination, as in the example shown here **A–B** (and **A–C**, next page) and on page 420. After applying a series of effects, remember to preserve your settings as a layer style — and in a custom library!

MAKING TYPE LOOK LIKE RUSTED METAL

A *We created editable type (Bauhaus 93 Regular font, 223 pt.) above a photo of rusted metal.*

B *We applied the Inner Shadow, Inner Glow, Outer Glow, and Drop Shadow effects, using the settings shown above.*

A *To reveal some of the underlying layer within the type, we lowered the Fill percentage of the type layer.*

B *To further "corrode" the edges of the letters, we Ctrl/Cmd clicked the type layer thumbnail to create a selection from the characters, clicked the Add Layer Mask button, then applied Filter > Filter Gallery > Brush Strokes > Spatter. The filter roughed up the edges of the mask. This is the Layers panel for the final image, which is shown below.*

C *The Spatter filter added just the finishing touch we were after. (You can try the Distort > Glass filter instead of Spatter.)*

EMBOSSING LEATHER

Note: For the Outer Glow effect, we clicked the color swatch, then clicked to sample a color in the image.

To create these embossed letters, we opened a photo of leather and created some type (Trajan Pro font, Bold, 112 pt.). We chose the Move tool, clicked the Color swatch on the Character panel, chose a color for the type by clicking in the image (eyedropper pointer), then exited the Color Picker. In the Layer Style dialog, we chose the Emboss and Outer Glow settings shown above, and in the Blending Options option set of the same dialog, chose the layer settings of Multiply mode, Opacity 52%, and Fill Opacity 69%.

We saved the settings shown above as a layer style, then applied it to a type layer above a Background photo of a leather-covered book. We changed the color of the Outer Glow effect by sampling a light area in the image, and also lowered the layer Fill Opacity value to 10%.

The shape and path tools in Photoshop produce vector objects, which have crisp and precise edges, like objects in a vector drawing program. You can use these tools to add a precisely drawn element to a photo (such as a filled rectangle or ellipse), to produce a precisely-shaped selection, or to create a sharp-edged mask that hides areas of a layer.

Unlike pixel layers, vector objects are resolution independent, meaning they print at the resolution of the output device (not at the resolution of the file) and keep their original crispness when transformed or exported.

Before you create a vector object, you must decide whether it will be stored as a colored shape on its own layer on the Layers panel (with a built-in Shape Path that is listed on the Paths panel when the shape layer is selected), or as a path on the Paths panel (a wireframe object not associated with any layer, from which you can produce a vector mask, a selection, or a filled pixel area). You can create a vector object by using one of the shape or pen tools or by converting an existing selection. An existing vector object can be reshaped via the usual transform controls or by manipulating its segments or anchor points.

Aligning vector objects for Web output

➤ To minimize anti-aliasing along horizontal and vertical edges of objects for sharper rendering onscreen, before you create, transform, or edit any vector objects, go to Edit/Photoshop CC > Preferences > Tools ★ and verify that **Snap Vector Tools and Transforms to Pixel Grid** is checked. Photoshop will snap the bounding box of a shape, or anchor points that are created with the Pen tool, to the pixel grid. (To view the grid, choose View > Show > Pixel Grid and zoom in to 600% or greater.)

➤ To have Photoshop minimize or remove anti-aliasing from the edges of a selected shape that was created with the "Snap Vector Tools" preference off, check **Align Edges** on the Options bar. Horizontal and vertical edges of the shape that touch the edges of its bounding box will be aligned to the pixel grid. Note: This feature may offset the stroke on an object from its path.

VECTOR DRAWING

21

IN THIS CHAPTER

Creating shape layers with a shape tool

The easiest way to create a shape layer is by using one of the ready-made presets, as in the steps here. Later in this chapter, you'll learn how to draw custom shapes.

Note: If you want to use a shape tool to produce a path instead of a shape, follow steps 1–3 in the task on page 431.

To create a vector shape:

1. On the Layers panel, click the layer (not a shape layer) above which you want a new shape layer to appear.

2. On the Tools panel, choose one of the shape tools (U or Shift-U).**A**

3. On the Options bar, do the following:

   From the **Tool Mode** menu, choose **Shape**.

   You can choose **fill** and **stroke** settings from the Options bar now, or change the shape properties after finishing this task (see the next two pages).

   Open the tool options menu. If it lists an **Unconstrained** option, make sure it's selected.

   If you're using the Custom Shape tool, click a shape on the **Custom Shape** picker (or right-click in the image and choose from the preset picker on the context menu).**B**

4. To produce the shape, do either of the following:

   Drag in the document. To constrain the proportions of the shape, hold down Shift while dragging.**C–D**

   Click in the document. A dialog opens. Enter values and choose settings, then click OK.

   A new vector shape layer appears on the Layers panel. All the Layers panel settings are available for it (e.g., blending mode, opacity, layer effects).

➤ To load more libraries onto the Custom Shape picker, see page 133 or 135.

➤ To reposition a shape layer, drag in the document with the Move tool.

➤ To draw a straight, solid line, we use the Pen tool: One click to start the line, a second click to finish it, then Ctrl-click/Cmd-click to deselect it. We prefer this method to using the Line (shape) tool, which produces a very thin, hollow rectangle.

A We chose the Custom Shape tool on the Tools panel.

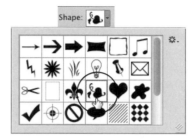

B On the Options bar, we chose the Shape option from the Tool Mode menu and a preset from the Custom Shape picker.

C Next, we Shift-dragged to produce this shape.

D The last-used fill and stroke attributes appeared in the shape layer. (To reveal the underlying wood texture within it, we chose Color Burn as the layer blending mode.)

Changing the attributes of a shape layer

You can change many attributes of a shape layer. For example, you can change the interior (fill) color or the edge (stroke) color, or for either component, you can apply a color of None. You can change the details of a stroke, such as the width, style (solid, dotted, or dashed), alignment, cap style, and corner style. And you can change unique properties for specific kinds of shapes, such as the radius of one or more corners of a Rounded Rectangle.

To change the properties of a shape layer:

1. To access the properties controls, do as follows:

   If you just created a new Rectangle, Rounded Rectangle, or Ellipse shape layer, and if Show on Shape Creation is checked on the Properties panel menu, that panel will open automatically.

   On the Layers panel, ❤ click one or more existing Rectangle, Rounded Rectangle, or Ellipse shape layers. Choose the **Path Selection** tool ▶ (A or Shift-A), click the shape(s) in the document, show the Properties panel, 🖳 then click the **Live Shape Properties** button.⬚

   For other kinds of shapes, click one or more layers, then use the Options bar.

2. To recolor the shape(s), click the Fill Color or Stroke Color swatch to open the picker, then do any of the following (when you're done using a picker, click outside it to close it):

   Click the **No Color** button ⬚ to apply a fill or stroke color of None.

   Click the **Solid Color** button, then click a color swatch;**A** or click the Color Picker button,⬛ choose a color, then click OK. Colors that you try out are added as temporary swatches below Recently Used Colors.

   Click the **Gradient** button to display a gradient editor, then click a gradient swatch.**B** To add another color stop, click below the bar. To recolor a stop, double-click the stop to open the Color Picker, choose a color, then click OK. To use the other controls on the picker (e.g., add opacity stops, change the gradient style or angle), see pages 219–220.

   Click the **Pattern** button, click a pattern swatch, and adjust the Scale percentage, if desired.**C**

   ➤ To load other libraries onto the Solid Color, Gradient, or Pattern preset picker, see page 133.

Continued on the following page

A *We clicked the Fill Color swatch to open the picker, clicked the Solid Color button, clicked a few colors, then clicked our favorite swatch under Recently Used Colors.*

B *We clicked the Gradient button, then clicked a gradient swatch.*

C *We clicked the Pattern button, then clicked a pattern swatch (we also applied a color to the object's stroke).*

3. To change the stroke details of a Rectangle, Rounded Rectangle, or Ellipse, you can use the Properties panel or Options bar; for other kinds of shapes, you must use the Options bar or the Stroke Options picker on the Options bar:

Change the **Stroke Width** value.**A**

Click the **Stroke Options** picker, then click a stroke preset in the scrolling window.**B**

From the **Align** menu, choose an option for the position of the stroke on the path.**C**

From the **Caps** menu, choose an option for the shape of the stroke at the endpoints — if the path is open — or for the shape of dots or dashes.

From the **Corners** menu (Stroke Options picker) or **Join** menu (Properties panel), choose an option to make angles in the path (if any) mitered, round, or beveled.

To create and save a custom dashed or dotted stroke, see Photoshop Help.

4. *Optional:* To save customized stroke details as a preset, choose Save Stroke from the picker menu.

5. To change other properties of the shape, do any of the following, if available:

To resize the shape, change the **W** and/or **H** values.

To move the shape to an exact location, change the **X** and/or **Y** values.

To adjust the **radius** of any individual corner in a Rectangle or Rounded Rectangle, make sure the Link icon is deactivated, and use a corner icon as a scrubby slider or enter a value in the field. Or to adjust the value of all four corners simultaneously, activate the Link icon, then change any one value (**A–C**, next page).

A *This is the original shape layer.*

B *We chose a dotted preset from the Stroke Options picker on the Properties panel.*

C *We changed the Align setting to Outside. The screen capture at right shows the selected path.*

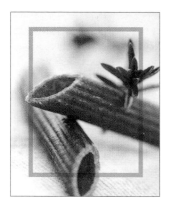

A *This document contains a Rectangle shape layer above an image layer. (The blending mode of the shape layer is set to Multiply, and the Opacity of the layer is 50%.)*

B *Via the Properties panel, we changed the stroke width and color and chose a different radius value for two of the corners.*

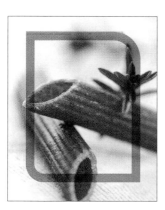

C *The results of our Properties panel edits are shown here.*

To copy properties from one shape layer to another:

Do one of the following:

To copy a fill or stroke color, gradient, or pattern between shapes, click a shape layer, and choose the Path Selection tool ▶ (A or Shift-A). From the menu on the Fill Color or Stroke Color picker on the Options bar or Properties panel, choose **Copy** [Fill or Stroke]. Click another shape layer, then choose **Paste** [Fill or Stroke] from the same menu.

To copy stroke details (not colors) between shapes, click a shape layer. From the menu on the Stroke Options picker on the Options bar or Properties panel, choose **Copy Stroke Details**. Click another shape layer, then choose **Paste Stroke Details** from the same menu. Note: If the new details don't appear, make sure the target shape has a Stroke color (not a setting of None).

To copy all the stroke and fill settings from one shape to another, including the colors and stroke details, right-click a shape layer and choose **Copy Shape Attributes** from the context menu. Click another shape layer, then choose **Paste Shape Attributes** from the context menu.

➤ Only one set of fill and stroke settings (e.g., one fill color, stroke color, and stroke option preset) can be applied to a given shape layer. You can't apply unique settings to a subshape within a multishape layer.

To load a shape layer as a selection:

Hold down Ctrl/Cmd and click the shape layer thumbnail on the Layers panel.

➤ To convert a shape layer to a standard pixel layer, right-click the shape layer and choose Rasterize Layer from the context menu. If you want to restrict future image edits to the newly rasterized shape areas, activate the Lock Transparent Pixels button ⊞ on the Layers panel.

CREATING BUTTONS FOR A WEB PAGE

To create buttons for a Web page, draw some vector shapes, then apply a layer style to them via the Styles panel (see page 416). To align and redistribute the shape layers, see page 289.

Selecting shape layer paths

To select whole shape layer paths:

1. Choose the **Path Selection** tool ▶ (A or Shift-A).

2. Do either of the following:

   From the Select menu on the Options bar, choose **All Layers** to allow the tool to select any shapes that you drag across, regardless of which listings are selected on the Layers panel.**A**

   On the Layers panel, hold down Ctrl/Cmd and click all the layers that you want to potentially include in a selection. From the Select menu on the Options bar, choose **Active Layers**.

3. Drag across the shapes that you want to select. Note that if you drag across part of a shape, the entire shape will become selected.**B–E** (and **A–D**, next page).

A *We chose the Path Selection tool, then chose All Layers from the Select menu on the Options bar.*

B *Although only one layer happens to be selected on our Layers panel …*

C *… when we dragged across an area in our document, we were able to select shapes from multiple layers.*

D *Anchor points on the shape paths became selected and visible …*

E *… and the respective layer listings for the three shapes we dragged across became selected.*

A *We chose the Path Selection tool, then chose Active Layers from the Select menu on the Options bar.*

B *Next, we held down Ctrl/Cmd and clicked two shape layer listings on the Layers panel.*

C *We dragged across three shapes.*

D *Because the tool was set to Select: Active Layers, of the shape layers that we dragged across, only those that we had activated on the Layers panel became selected.*

SELECTING ANCHOR POINTS ON A SHAPE

To select a single anchor point on a shape layer path, with the Direct Selection tool and Select: All Layers chosen on the Options bar, click inside a shape (you don't have to click the edge of the path). The anchor points will become hollow.

Next, click the anchor point that you want to edit. The point will become filled. (To select multiple points, drag across them.)

With the Direct Selection tool, if you drag across a selected or unselected shape ...

... only the anchor points within your marquee will become selected.

Isolating a shape layer

When you isolate a shape layer, editing is temporarily limited to just that shape, and no other layers can be edited (note that the entire document remains visible).

To isolate a shape layer:

Method 1

1. Choose the **Path Selection** ▶ or **Direct Selection** ▷ tool (A or Shift-A selects whichever of the two tools was used last).

2. On the Option bar, choose Select: **All Layers**.

3. In the document, double-click a shape.**A**

Method 2

1. Choose the **Path Selection** or **Direct Selection** tool.

2. On the Option bar, choose Select: **Active Layers**.

3. On the Layers panel, click the listing for the shape layer that you want to edit.**B**

To de-isolate a shape layer and redisplay all layer listings on the Layers panel:

1. On the Options bar, make sure Select: **All Layers** is chosen.

2. Choose the **Path Selection** or **Direct Selection** tool.

3. Double-click on or outside the isolated shape.

➤ To filter layer listings on the Layers panel of a specific category, such as all shape or type layers, see pages 162–163.

➤ To clear all filtering from the Layers panel (even if the Layer Filtering On/Off button is activated), choose the Move, Path Selection, Direct Selection tool, or a pen tool, then right-click in the document and uncheck Isolate Layers on the context menu. You can also clear filtering by unchecking Select > Isolate Layers.

A *If you isolate a shape layer by double-clicking it in the document, that layer (temporarily) becomes the solo listing on the Layers panel.*

B *If you isolate a shape by choosing Select: Active Layers, then click its layer listing, all the layer listings will remain visible on the panel.*

Working with multiple shapes

To reposition or copy a shape:

1. On the Layers panel, click a shape layer.

2. Choose the **Path Selection tool** (A or Shift-A).

3. Drag a shape to a new location; or to copy the shape, hold down Alt/Option before and while dragging (the copy will appear in the same layer).

➤ To delete one shape in a multishape layer, with the Path Selection tool, click the shape you want to discard, then press Backspace/Delete.

To combine multiple shape layers into one layer:

1. On the Layers panel, select two or more shape layers.**A** The layers don't have to be consecutive.

2. Choose the **Path Selection tool** (A or Shift-A).

3. Right-click in the document and choose **Unite Shapes.B** Or to unite only the intersection of two overlapping shapes, choose **Unite Shapes at Overlap.C–D** All the shapes will adopt the fill and stroke settings of the uppermost of the selected layers; the other selected layers will be discarded. (For a different result, you could choose Subtract Front Shape or Subtract Shapes at Overlap.)

To align shapes within the same layer:

1. Choose the **Path Selection tool** (A or Shift-A).

2. In the document, Shift-click two or more shapes that reside on the same layer.

3. From the **Path Alignment** menu on the Options bar, choose one or more options (e.g., Top Edges).

➤ To align multiple shape layers, see page 289.

To unite, subtract, intersect, or exclude shapes within the same layer:

1. On the Layers panel, click a layer that contains multiple shapes.

2. Choose the **Path Selection tool** (A or Shift-A).

3. To see the effect of the button you will click in the next step, make sure that at least some area of two or more shapes overlap one another.

4. If you selected Rectangle, Rounded Rectangle, or Ellipse shapes, on the Properties panel, make sure the **Live Shape Properties** are displaying; for other kinds of shapes, use the Path Operations menu on the Options bar. Click the **Combine, Subtract, Intersect,** or **Exclude** button.

A *This document contains three shape layers.*

B *The Unite Shapes command combined all the shapes into one.*

C *We started with these two shape layers.*

D *We chose the Unite Shapes at Overlap command.*

ADDING A SHAPE TO A LAYER USING PATH OPERATIONS

To control how shapes interact as you add a shape to an existing layer, before drawing the shape with a shape tool, click a shape layer, choose an option from the Path Operations menu on the Options bar (the current Path Operations choice displays as the icon for the menu). Or to add a shape to an existing layer without having to use the Path Operations menu, drag with Shift held down; to subtract from an existing shape, drag with Alt/Option held down.

Creating vector masks

Like a pixel mask, the function of a vector mask is to hide areas of a layer. We'll show you how to create a vector mask from a shape layer or path, from a new path that you draw, and from a type layer.

To create a vector mask from a shape layer:

1. Arrange a shape layer so it overlaps the content of the layer to be masked (if needed, restack it via the Layers panel and/or reposition it).**A**

2. Hold down Ctrl-Alt/Cmd-Option and drag the shape layer listing over an image, type, adjustment layer, or layer group listing (not the Background). Release when a rectangular border appears around the target layer.

3. Hide the shape layer.**B–C**

To create a vector mask from an existing path:

1. On the Layers panel, 📑 click the image, type, or adjustment layer or layer group to which you want to add a vector mask (not the Background).

2. On the Paths panel, 📐 click a path listing.

3. Choose the **Path Selection** tool ▸ (A or Shift-A), then position the path over the layer content to be masked.

4. Right-click inside the document and choose **Create Vector Mask** from the context menu (**A–B**, next page).

A We created a shape layer with the Custom Shape tool (Flower 1 preset, Shapes library).

B We dragged from the shape layer to the image layer; the shape appeared within a new vector mask. Finally, we hid the shape layer.

C The mask is hiding parts of the image layer.

A *We created a path with the Custom Shape tool (Talk 4 preset, Talk Bubbles library), clicked an image layer, selected the path, then chose the Create Vector Mask command.*

B *The vector mask appeared on the image layer.*

To create a vector mask by drawing a path:

1. Choose a shape tool (U or Shift-U), the Pen tool, or the Freeform Pen tool (P or Shift-P).

2. From the Tool Mode menu on the Options bar, choose **Path**. If you're using the Custom Shape tool, also click a shape on the Custom Shape picker.

3. If you chose a shape tool, drag in the document, or Shift-drag to constrain the proportions of the object.**C** (If you want to reposition the path while it's being drawn, also hold down the Spacebar.) *Optional:* After drawing a path with the Rectangle, Rounded Rectangle, or Ellipse tool, you can change some of its properties via the Properties panel.

   If you chose the Pen or Freeform Pen tool, draw a path. To learn how to use the Pen tool, see pages 436–437, or for the Freeform Pen tool, see page 434.

4. On the Layers panel, click the image, type, adjustment layer, or layer group to which you want to add a vector mask (not the Background).

5. On the Options bar, click the **Mask** button.**D**

C *We dragged to produce a path with the Custom Shape tool (Diamond Card preset, Shapes library).*

D *We clicked the violin layer, then clicked the Mask button on the Options bar, which converted the path to a vector mask on the current image layer. The mask is hiding parts of the violin layer.*

To create a vector mask from type:

1. Create an editable type layer. **A**

2. Right-click the type layer listing and choose **Create Work Path**. Hide the type layer.

3. On the Layers panel, click an image layer or adjustment layer or a layer group, then Ctrl-click/Cmd-click the **Add Vector Mask** button. **B** (If the layer has a layer mask, you can click the button without holding down Ctrl/Cmd.)

MORE ESSENTIAL VECTOR MASK TOPICS

➤ To move or copy a vector mask to another layer, see page 196.

➤ To disable or delete a vector mask, see page 196.

➤ To lower the density of a vector mask, or to feather its edges, see page 194.

➤ To reshape a vector mask, click the mask thumbnail on the Layers panel, then either use Edit > Free Transform Path (see pages 358–359) or manipulate the points or direction lines on its path (see page 440).

A This is an editable type layer.

B We created a work path from the type layer, then used the path to create a vector mask on an image layer.

Working with vector masks

By moving a vector mask separately from the layer content, you can hide a different area of the layer.

To reposition a vector mask:

1. On the Layers panel, ☙ click a vector mask thumbnail.

2. Choose the **Path Selection** tool ▶ (A or Shift-A).

3. If the mask contains multiple subpaths (such as type shapes), Shift-click the ones you want to reposition.

4. Drag in the document.**A–B**

➤ To move the layer content instead of the mask, on the Layers panel, click the Link icon 🔗 between the layer and vector mask thumbnails (the icon disappears). Click the layer thumbnail, drag in the document with the Move tool, ▶⊕ then click between the thumbnails to restore the Link icon.

You can switch the hide and reveal functions of a vector mask.

To switch the function of a vector mask:

1. Choose the **Path Selection** tool ▶ (A or Shift-A).

2. On the Layers panel, ☙ click a vector mask thumbnail.**C**

3. If the path segments and anchor points aren't selected, click the path or drag a marquee around it.

4. From the Path Operations menu on the Options bar, choose **Subtract Front Shape**, ⬜ or press – (minus key).**D**

➤ To restore the default reveal and hide functions to a vector mask, choose Combine Shapes ⬜ from the Path Operations menu on the Options bar, or press + (plus key).

If a layer contains both a layer (pixel) mask and a vector mask, the layer mask thumbnail will be adjacent to the layer thumbnail (on the left), followed by the vector mask thumbnail (on the right).

To convert a vector mask to a layer mask:

1. *Optional:* To preserve a copy of the vector mask, on the Layers panel, duplicate its whole layer.

2. Right-click the vector mask thumbnail and choose **Rasterize Vector Mask** from the context menu.

A *We're repositioning a mask…*

B *… to reveal a different part of the image within the mask shape.*

C *We selected the leaf-shaped vector mask…*

D *… then switched the function of the mask by pressing – (minus key).*

Drawing with the Freeform Pen tool

The simplest way to draw a custom object is with the Freeform Pen tool. It produces bumpier and less precise curves than the Pen tool, but if you're new to vector drawing, it's a good tool to start with. If you have a stylus and tablet, use them.

To use the Freeform Pen tool:

1. Choose the **Freeform Pen** tool (P or Shift-P).

2. From the Tool Mode menu on the Options bar, choose **Path** or **Shape**.

3. If you're going to draw a path, display the Paths panel, then click the **New Path** button.

4. Drag to draw a shape or path, then release the mouse. If you want to close the shape, drag the pointer over the starting point (a little circle displays in the pointer); otherwise, just release.**A–C**

    Note: When you use the Freeform Pen tool, Photoshop creates the anchor points needed for the path. The higher the Curve Fit value you chose for the tool (options menu ⚙. on the Options bar), the smoother the path and the fewer anchor points are created, but the less precisely the path follows the movement of your mouse.

Saving, displaying, selecting, and repositioning paths

Note: The features discussed in this section apply only to path listings on the Paths panel (not to shape layers or their respective mask listings on the Paths panel).

If you draw a path without clicking the New Path button (or an existing path listing) on the Paths panel first, the path will be listed on the panel as a temporary Work Path. If you deselect the Work Path listing and then proceed to draw another path, the current Work Path will be replaced by a new Work Path. Due to the fleeting nature of the Work Path listing, we recommend always clicking the New Path button before drawing a path (we'll remind you to do this in our instructions). If you forget to create a new path listing before you start to draw, don't worry—you can still save the current Work Path as a permanent path, as described in the first task on the next page.

Note: If you click a Work Path or other listing on the Paths panel and then draw a new path, the new path will appear as a subpath within the same listing. To learn about combining paths, see page 441.

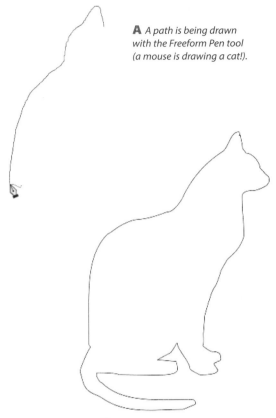

A *A path is being drawn with the Freeform Pen tool (a mouse is drawing a cat!).*

B *The path is completed.*

C *The new path displays in the thumbnail on the Paths panel.*

DRAWING STRAIGHT SIDES WHILE USING THE FREEFORM PEN TOOL

Start dragging with the Freeform Pen tool, keep the mouse button down, hold down Alt/Option and click to create points (straight sides), press the mouse button, release Alt/Option, then continue drawing.

To save a Work Path as a permanent path:

On the Paths panel, do either of the following:

Double-click the **Work Path** listing. The Save Path dialog opens. Change the name, if desired, then click OK.

To save the path under a default name, drag the Work Path listing to the **New Path** button.

➤ To rename a saved path, double-click the existing name, type a new name, then press Enter/Return.

➤ If you want to name a permanent path as you create it, Alt/Option click the New Path button, enter a name in the New Path dialog, then click OK.

To display one or more paths:

1. On the Paths panel, click a path listing. The path displays in the document window (or multiple paths display, if the listing contains subpaths).**A–B**

2. *Optional:* Hold down Ctrl/Cmd and click one or more additional path listings.

To hide one or more paths:

Do either of the following:

To hide all currently displayed paths, either hold down the A key and press Esc, or on the Paths panel, click the blank area below all the listings.

To hide just one of several visible paths, hold down Ctrl/Cmd and click a path listing on the Paths panel.

➤ To open a dialog in which you can change the size of the thumbnails on the Paths panel, choose Panel Options from the panel menu.

When you select a path, its anchor points become visible and accessible, ready for editing.

To select one or more paths:

1. Show one or more paths, as described in "To display one or more paths," above.

2. Choose the **Path Selection** tool (A or Shift-A).

3. Do either of the following:

Click the edge of a path.**C** If desired, Shift-click additional paths or subpaths.

Drag a marquee across multiple paths. (Note that if you use this method, any shape layers that you drag across will also become selected.)

When you deselect a path, its anchor points become hidden, but its listing on the Paths panel stays selected.

To deselect one or more paths:

Do either of the following:

To deselect all paths, choose a path selection or pen tool, then hold down Ctrl/Cmd and click a blank area of the canvas.

To deselect one path in a multiple selection, choose the **Path Selection** tool, then Shift-click one of the selected paths.

To reposition one or more paths:

1. Follow steps 1–3 in "To select one or more paths," on this page.

2. Drag the edge of one of the paths.

A *We held down Ctrl/Cmd and clicked two path listings.*

B *The paths displayed in the document.*

C *With the Path Selection tool, we clicked one of the paths.*

Drawing with the Pen tool

With the Pen tool, you can create shapes or paths. Shapes are listed on the Layers panel (and when a shape layer is selected, its path is also listed on the Paths panel); paths are listed only on the Paths panel. Depending on how you use the Pen, you can draw straight sides, smooth curves, nonsmooth curves — or a combination thereof.

To draw a straight-sided path or shape with the Pen tool:

1. Choose the **Pen** tool 🖋 (P or Shift-P).

2. On the Options bar, do the following:

   From the **Tool Mode** menu, choose **Path** or **Shape**.

   On the tool options menu, ✦ check **Rubber Band**.

3. If you chose the Path option, on the Paths panel, 🕋 click the **New Path** button. 🔲

   If you chose the Shape option, choose Select > Deselect Layers, then choose fill and stroke attributes via the Options bar. These attributes can easily be changed later.

4. Click to create the first anchor point, then click to create a second one; a straight segment will connect them automatically.**A** The last-created point will be solid (selected), then will become deselected (hollow) when you create the next point.

5. Click to create additional anchor points.**B** To constrain a straight segment to an increment of 45°, hold down Shift while clicking.

6. To complete the object, do one of the following:

   To close the object and keep it selected, position the pointer over the starting point (a tiny circle appears next to the pointer),**C** then click.

   To keep the object open and deselect it, Ctrl-click/Cmd-click anywhere on the canvas.

   To keep the object open and selected, press A or Shift-A for the Path Selection tool.

7. *Optional:* To change the fill color, stroke color, or stroke details of a shape, see pages 423–424.

➤ To draw paths that are aligned to the pixel grid, for better Web output, see page 421.

➤ To help you align the points that you produce while drawing a path (as shown in **A–C**), on the View menu, check Show > Guides, Rulers, Snap, and Snap To > Guides. Drag guides into the document from the rulers. See also pages 295–296.

A *We created a few ruler guides in our document, then with the Pen tool, we clicked to create two points. Photoshop connected them with a straight segment. Here we're about to click to produce another segment; the segment previews because the Rubber Band option is on.*

B *We clicked to create more points.*

C *The tool is positioned over the starting point (note the circle next to the pointer). When we click that point, Photoshop will close and complete the shape.*

To draw a curved path or shape with the Pen tool:

1. Choose the **Pen** tool ✏️ (P or Shift-P).

2. On the Options bar, do the following:

   From the **Tool Mode** menu, choose **Path** or **Shape**.

   On the tool options menu, ⚙️ check **Rubber Band**.

3. If you chose the Path option, on the Paths panel, click the **New Path** button. 🔲

   If you chose the Shape option, choose a nonshape layer, then choose fill and stroke attributes via the Options bar (see page 423).

4. Drag (don't click) to create the first anchor point. The direction you drag will determine the angle of the direction handles that appear on the point; the distance you drag will control the length of the handles. The handles, in turn, control the shape of the curve. Release the mouse.

5. Position the mouse where you want the first curve to change direction, then drag to define the next curve. A curved segment will connect the two anchor points, and the next pair of direction handles will appear. **A**

6. Drag to create more anchor points with direction handles. **B–C**

7. To complete the object, do one of the following:

   To close the object and keep it selected, position the pointer over the starting point (a little circle appears next to the pointer), then drag to produce the last pair of direction handles.

   To keep the object open and deselect it, Ctrl-click/ Cmd-click anywhere on the canvas.

   To keep the object open and selected, press A or Shift-A for the Path Selection tool.

8. *Optional:* To change the fill color, stroke color, or stroke details of a shape, see pages 423–424.

➤ For smoother curves, draw the minimum number of points needed to define the object. Remember, you can always reshape the curves later by adjusting the length and angle of the handles (see page 440).

A *To draw a curved shape with the Pen tool, we dragged to create the first anchor point, moved the mouse, then dragged to create the second point (note the direction handles). Photoshop connected the two points with a curved segment.*

B *We dragged to create a third point. (Note: The stroke on this path has the Align setting of Center; see page 424.)*

C *We dragged to create the final point and third curve (we'll end this shape as an open object).*

The anchor point on a nonsmooth curve can have either just one direction handle or two handles that can be rotated in different directions. In contrast, the pair of handles on a smooth curve always remain in a straight line.

To draw a nonsmooth curve:

1. While using the **Pen** tool ![pen] to draw a path or shape (see the preceding page), hold down Alt/Option, position the pointer over the last point you created, then do either of the following: **A**

   Drag the end of one of the direction handles (the handles will form a "V" shape).**B–C**

   Click the point to remove one of the handles.

2. Continue to draw nonsmooth curves, or click to create straight sides, or drag to create smooth curves.**D**

A *After dragging to produce a smooth curve, we're holding down Alt/Option and positioning the Pen tool over the last point.*

B *We're dragging the end of one of the direction handles. Now the handles are in a "V" shape.*

C *We released, then repositioned the mouse, and will proceed to create more points.*

D *For all of the paths in this image, from the menus on the Stroke Options picker, we chose the settings of Align: Center, Caps: Round, and Corners: Round (see page 424).*

More ways to create paths and shapes

You can create a path from a selection, such as an area of an image layer that you have selected with the Quick Selection tool. (If you prefer to create a path directly with a shape or pen tool, follow steps 1–3 in the task on page 431 instead of doing the task below.)

To produce a path from a selection or an existing shape layer:

1. Do either of the following:

   Create a selection with any selection tool (e.g., Quick Selection or a lasso tool).

   Hold down Cmd/Ctrl and click a shape layer thumbnail.

2. Display the Paths panel. If the panel contains a Work Path and you don't want it to be discarded, double-click it to save it as a permanent path.

3. Click the **Make Work Path from Selection** button, then double-click the resulting Work Path to save it as a permanent path.

You can paste a path from Illustrator into a Photoshop document, and have it appear as either a path or a shape layer.

To create a path or shape from Illustrator artwork:

1. In an Illustrator document, select one or more vector objects, then copy the artwork via Edit > **Copy**.

2. Open a Photoshop document. If you're going to create a path, make sure no paths are selected on the Paths panel and no layers are selected on the Layers panel.

3. Choose Edit > **Paste**.

4. In the Paste dialog, do either of the following:

   Click Paste As: **Path**, then click OK. A Work Path will appear on the Paths panel; double-click it to save it as a permanent path.

   Click Paste As: **Shape Layer.** The shape(s) will be given the current fill color and a stroke color of None.

To produce a shape from a path:

1. On the Paths panel, click a path listing.

2. Choose the **Pen** tool (P or Shift-P).

3. On the Options bar, make sure **Path** is chosen on the Tool Mode menu, then click the **Shape** button.

You can save any shape or path to the Custom Shape picker, for use in any document.

To save a vector object as a custom shape:

1. Do either of the following:

   On the Layers panel, click a shape layer; also choose the Path Selection tool (A or Shift-A).

   On the Paths panel, click a path listing.

2. Choose Edit > **Define Custom Shape.**

3. In the Shape Name dialog, enter a name, then click OK. The new shape appears as the last thumbnail on the Custom Shape picker. The picker displays on the Options bar when you use the Custom Shape tool (see page 422).

   Note: To save all the shapes currently on the Custom Shape picker as a permanent library, so they're not replaced if you load a new library, see page 133.

COMBINING YOUR PEN SKILLS IN ONE OBJECT

Once you become acquainted with the Pen tool, practice drawing an object that contains different kinds of segments. A few suggestions are shown below. Click to create a straight side (the point will have no direction handles), drag to create a smooth curve (the point will have a pair of direction handles that stay in a straight line; see page 437), or follow step 1 on the preceding page to create a nonsmooth curve (the point will have just one direction handle or a pair of handles that can be moved in different directions).

Reshaping vector objects

There are several ways to reshape a vector object: You can convert a corner to a smooth curve, or vice versa; rotate one handle independently of the other; drag an anchor point or segment; or add or delete points.

To convert points on a vector object:

1. Do either of the following:

   On the Paths panel, 🔲 click a path listing.

   On the Layers panel, 🔳 click a shape layer listing or a vector mask thumbnail.

2. Choose the **Direct Selection** tool ▶ (A or Shift-A).

3. Click the edge of a path, then click a point on the path; or click inside a shape.

4. To use a temporary Convert Point tool, hold down Ctrl-Alt/Cmd-Option and do any of the following:

   To convert a corner point to a smooth point (add direction handles), drag away from the point. **A–B**

   To convert a smooth point to a corner point (remove both direction handles), click the point.

   To rotate one direction handle on a point independently of the other handle, drag the handle. **C**

➤ In step 4 above, you can choose the Convert Point tool ▶ directly from the Pen tool menu; or if you're using the Pen tool, hold down Alt/Option.

To reshape a segment on a vector object:

1. Choose the **Direct Selection** tool ▶ (A or Shift-A).

2. Do either of the following:

   On the Layers panel, click a shape layer listing, then in the document, click inside the shape.

   Click a path listing on the Paths panel or a vector mask thumbnail on the Layers panel, then click the edge of the path in the document.

3. Do any of the following:

   Drag an anchor point.

   Drag a segment. (If you want to prevent adjacent segments from reshaping, check Constrain Path Dragging on the Options bar.)

   Click a point on a curve segment, then drag the end of a direction handle toward or away from the anchor point, or rotate it around the point. **D**

➤ If you click a selected anchor point on a path, all other selected anchor points become deselected automatically.

To add or delete anchor points from a vector object:

1. Follow step 1 in the first task on this page.

2. Choose the **Pen** tool 🖊 (P or Shift-P).

3. Choose Path from the Tool Mode menu on the Options bar, then check **Auto Add/Delete**.

4. Hold down Ctrl/Cmd (for a temporary Path Selection tool) and click the path in the document.

5. Do any of the following:

   To **add** a **point**, click a segment (note the plus sign in the tool pointer). **E–F** *Optional:* If you want

A *We're using the Convert Point tool to convert a corner …*

B *… to a curve.*

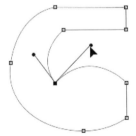

C *We rotated one of the new handles independently.*

D *We're dragging a direction handle on a smooth curve.*

E *We're adding point to a segment.*

F *With Ctrl/Cmd held down, we're dragging the new point downward.*

to remove both direction handles from the new point (convert it to a corner point), hold down Alt/Option and click the point; or to rotate one handle separately, drag it with Alt/Option held down.

To **delete** a **point**, click it (note the minus sign in the tool pointer).

To **add** a **segment** to an open path, click to select the endpoint, reposition the mouse, then click or drag to create one or more points.

Working with paths

To copy a path listing:

On the Paths panel, ⟆ Alt-drag/Option-drag a path listing upward or downward.

➤ To restack a path listing on the Paths panel (not a Work Path or Shape Path), drag it upward or downward; release when the double line appears in the desired position.

To transform one or more paths:

1. On the Paths panel, select one or more path listings.
2. Do either of the following:

   Choose Edit > **Free Transform Path** (Ctrl-T/Cmd-T).

   Choose an option from the Edit > **Transform Path** submenu (if you choose a rotate or flip option, skip the next step).
3. A transform box displays around the paths. Follow steps 5–6 on pages 358–359.

To delete one or more saved paths:

1. On the Paths panel, click the listing for the path to be deleted, or Ctrl/Cmd click multiple listings.
2. Click the **Delete Path** button, 🗑 then click Yes in the alert dialog (or to bypass the alert, hold down Alt/Option as you click the button).

FILE FORMATS THAT PRESERVE PATHS

To keep paths editable in your Photoshop document, save it in the Photoshop (PSD), Large Document Format (PSB), JPEG, JPEG 2000, Photoshop PDF, or TIFF format. Avoid the Photoshop EPS and Photoshop DCS formats, which will rasterize the paths (and remove their listings from the Paths panel) when you reopen the file in Photoshop.

Subpaths within a path listing can be edited individually or as a bloc.

To combine multiple paths into one listing:

Method 1 (Clipboard)

1. On the Paths panel, select one or more path listings, then press Ctrl-C/Cmd-C to copy them.**A**
2. Click the listing in which you want the copied paths to appear, then press Ctrl-V/Cmd-V.**B**

Method 2 (loading a path as a selection)

1. On the Paths panel, Ctrl-click/Cmd-click to select two or more path listings.
2. Click the **Load Path as Selection** button ⬚ at the bottom of the panel, then click the **Make Work Path from Selection** button. ⬡
3. A new Work Path appears on the panel. Double-click it to save it as a permanent path.

Method 3 (drawing)

1. On the Paths panel, click a path listing.
2. With the **Pen,** ✐ or **Freeform Pen,** ✐ or a shape tool, draw a path.

➤ To add a Shape Path as a subpath, click the shape layer on the Layers panel, then follow one of the methods above.

A On the Paths panel, we clicked our "LOGO1" listing, then used the Copy command.

B We clicked the "LOGO 2" listing, then used the Paste command. Now two subpaths display in the same thumbnail.

When you recolor a path, the color appears as an area of pixels on the current image layer.

To apply a fill and/or stroke color to one or more paths:

1. On the Layers panel, click an image layer or create a new blank layer.

2. Choose a Foreground color.

3. If you're going to apply a brush to the path stroke (next step), choose a tool that uses brushes, then right-click in the image and choose from the preset picker on the context menu.

4. On the Paths panel, select one or more path listings, then click the **Fill Path with Foreground Color** or **Stroke Path with Brush** button.**A–B**

5. Deselect the path listing(s).

➤ Instead of applying a fill or stroke color, after clicking a path listing in step 4, apply a style via the Styles panel.**C**

➤ You can also apply a stroke to a path using any painting or editing tool. Choose a tool and Options bar settings, then Alt-click/Option-click the Stroke Path button on the Paths panel. From the tools menu in the dialog, choose the tool for which you just chose settings, then click OK.

To load a path as a selection:

On the Paths panel, do either of the following:

Hold down Ctrl/Cmd and click a path thumbnail.**D**

Click a path listing, then click the **Load Path as Selection** button.

A *We created a blank layer on the Layers panel. Next, on the Paths panel, we clicked a path listing, then clicked the Fill Path with Foreground Color button.*

B *The area defined by the path filled with pixels.*

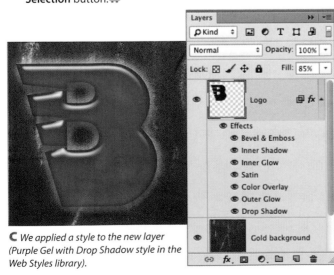

C *We applied a style to the new layer (Purple Gel with Drop Shadow style in the Web Styles library).*

D *We loaded a path as a selection.*

To automate repetitive (and boring) editing tasks, you can record a sequence of commands in an action and, at any time, replay the action on one image or on a batch of images. Actions can be used to execute anything from a simple edit, such as converting files to a different format or color mode, to a complex sequence of commands, such as applying a series of adjustments or filters, or a sequence of preflight steps to prepare your files for output. With actions, you can boost your productivity, relieve your life of (some) drudgery, and standardize your editing steps. You can use any of the ready-made actions that are included with Photoshop, or create your own custom actions for various tasks. In this chapter, you'll learn how to record, play, and edit custom actions, and how to save and load action sets (collections of actions).

Recording an action

Using the Actions panel, you can record, store, edit, play, delete, save, and load actions. The panel has two modes: List (edit) **A** and Button (**A**, page 445). When the panel is in List mode, you can expand or collapse the list of commands in an action; toggle a dialog control on or off; add, exclude, delete, rerecord, or change the order of commands; or save actions and action sets to an actions file. To put the panel into List mode, uncheck Button Mode on the panel menu.

An action set

An action

Toggle action or command on or off

A recorded command within an action

A dialog control (allows input from the user during playback)

Stop Playing/ Recording

Begin Recording

Play

New Set

New Action

Delete current action, step, or set

A *This Actions panel is in List mode.*

Each command that is recorded in an action is nested below the action name on the Actions panel. Actions, in turn, are stored in sets. Note: To include edits in an action that aren't directly recordable, see pages 449–450.

To record an action:

1. The action you're about to record has to be stored in a set. To create a set, click the New Set button ▢ at the bottom of the Actions panel,▶ type a descriptive Name, then click OK.

2. Open a document or create a new one. We recommend copying the document using File > Save As.

3. Click the **New Action** button ▣ at the bottom of the Actions panel.

4. In the New Action dialog, enter a **Name** for the action, and from the **Set** menu, choose a set (either the one you created in step 1 or a different one).**A**

5. *Optional:* Choose a shortcut for the action from the Function Key menu, and check Shift and/ or Command to prevent conflicts with the function keys that are assigned to system commands. Choose a color to display behind the action name when the panel is in Button mode.

6. Click **Record**.

7. We recommend as a first edit that you create a snapshot of the current state of the document on the History panel. Next, execute the commands that you want to record, as you would normally apply them to any image. Any time you enter values in a dialog and click OK, your settings will be recorded (unless you click Cancel).

8. When you're done recording edits for the action, click the **Stop Playing/Recording** button.▪

9. The new action listing appears on the panel. Note: To save your action sets to a file (recommended), see page 454.

➤ If you create layers or alpha channels while recording an action, assign them descriptive, nongeneric names to prevent the wrong layer or channel from being edited when the action is played.

➤ When recording the Save As command in an action, don't change the file name. To preserve the original file, either choose a different folder location or add a modal control to the action to make it pause at the Save As command to allow for user input (see page 451).

➤ To open the Action Options dialog for an action (e.g., to change the shortcut), double-click its listing.

RULER UNITS MATTER IN ACTIONS

The current ruler units affect how Photoshop records tool edits that are made in a specific x/y location in the image (e.g., by the Brush tool or by a selection or shape tool). An action that is recorded when the ruler units are actual (e.g., inches or picas) will play correctly only on a file that has the same dimensions as the file in which it was recorded. An action that is recorded when the default unit is **Percent** will work correctly on a file of any dimensions, because the tool edits will be positioned and scaled relative to each document. To establish the units setting, go to Edit/ Photoshop CC > Preferences > Units & Rulers, and from the Units: Rulers menu, choose an actual unit or Percent.

RECORDING BRUSH STROKES

To record the strokes for painting tools (e.g., Brush, Pencil, Mixer Brush), set the desired ruler units (see "Ruler Units Matter In Actions," above), and check **Allow Tool Recording** on the Actions panel menu. While recording an action, select the desired tool. If you're using the Brush tool, choose a Foreground color and Brush panel settings. Apply strokes in the image. You can change colors and settings between strokes. Note that if a desired setting is already chosen, you will need to choose a different one, then the desired one.

For the Brush or Mixer Brush tool, before you begin recording, you need to create a tool preset (via the Tool Presets panel) that contains the desired color and Options bar settings. Choose your preset while recording the action. For added variety, you can create multiple tool presets, then switch among them while recording.

New Action		
Name:	Rough black frame	Record
Set:	Frames	Cancel
Function Key:	None ☐ Shift ☐ Command	
Color:	▪ Violet	

A *Use the New Action dialog to assign a name and set to your action, as well as an optional shortcut and/or color, then begin recording.*

Playing an action

An action can be triggered in various ways: via the Play button on the Actions panel; via a keyboard shortcut that was assigned to it; by dragging a file or folder full of files onto a droplet icon that was made from the action; or by using the Batch feature. We'll begin with the Play button and shortcuts.

To play a whole action on one image:

1. Open an image and create or click an image layer.

2. *Optional:* If the action to be played doesn't include creation of a snapshot as an initial step, use the History panel to create one now, to preserve the option to restore the image to its pre-action state.

3. Do one of the following:

   If the Actions panel is in List mode, click an action name, then click the **Play** button.▶

   If the panel is in **Button** mode, click the button for the action to be played.**A**

   Execute the keyboard **shortcut**, if one has been assigned to the desired action.

➤ To load more action set libraries onto the panel, see page 454.

Actions	▶▶
Vignette (selection)	Frame Channel – 50 p...
Wood Frame – 50 pixel	Cast Shadow (type)
Water Reflection (type)	Custom RGB to Graysc...
Molten Lead	Make Clip Path (select...
Sepia Toning (layer)	Quadrant Colors
Save as Photoshop PDF	Gradient Map
Mixer Brush Cloning P...	Water Reflection F7
Gradient Map	brush shape

A *When the Actions panel is in Button mode, each action is listed as a colored button. Assigned shortcuts, if any, are also listed.*

B *To exclude a color change in our "brush shape" action from playback temporarily, we unchecked that step.*

To exclude a command from playback:

1. Put the Actions panel in List mode (actions can't be edited in Button mode).

2. Expand the list for the action to be edited.

3. Click in the leftmost column for the command that you want to exclude from playback, to remove the check mark.**B** The check mark for the main action listing turns red. (To reinclude the command, click in the same column again.)

   Note: If you click the check mark for an action, as an alert may inform you, Photoshop will uncheck or recheck all the commands in the action.

To play a partial action:

1. Put the Actions panel in **List** mode.

2. If necessary, click the arrowhead next to an action name to expand its list of commands.

3. Do either of the following:

   To play the action from a command onward, click the command name, then click the **Play** button.▶

   To play just one command in an action, click the command name, then Ctrl-click/Cmd-click the **Play** button (or simply Ctrl-double-click/Cmd-double-click the command).

CHOOSING PLAYBACK OPTIONS

Put the Actions panel in List mode, choose **Playback Options** from the panel menu, then click one of these options in the dialog:

➤ **Accelerated**: The fastest playback option.

➤ **Step by Step**: The list for the action expands on the panel, and the name of each command or edit becomes highlighted as it's executed. Slower than Accelerated.

➤ **Pause for [ ] seconds**: This option works like Step by Step, except that a pause for the duration you designate occurs after each step.

The ability to play an action on multiple files is a great timesaver. This can be done quickly by dragging a folder of files onto a droplet (see "To create a droplet for an action," on page 448). Or if you need to choose a destination, a file-naming scheme, and other options for the files to be processed by the action, use the Batch command instead, as described on this page.

To play an action on a batch of images:

1. In Bridge, put all the files to be processed into one folder and display the folder contents (or to limit which images are processed, select those thumbnails), then choose Tools > Photoshop > **Batch**.

2. The Batch dialog opens (**A**, next page). Under Play, choose an action set from the **Set** menu and an action from the **Action** menu.

3. For the **Source**, choose **Bridge**.

4. *Optional:* If the action contains an Open command, check Override Action "Open" Commands to have the batch command ignore the specific file name that was chosen when the Open step was recorded.

5. Check **Suppress File Open Options Dialogs** and/ or **Suppress Color Profile Warnings** to prevent those dialogs or alerts from appearing onscreen (and pausing the playback) as source files are opened.

6. *Optional:* By default, Photoshop will stop the Batch process if it encounters an error. To have it play the whole action and keep track of error messages in a text file instead, from the Errors menu, choose Log Errors to File, then click Save As. In the Save dialog, type a name for the text file (keep the extension), choose a location for it, then click Save. If errors are encountered, after the batch processing is finished, you will be alerted via a prompt that errors were logged into the designated error log file.

7. From the **Destination** menu, choose one of the following options:

    None to keep all the files open after processing.

    Save and Close to have the files save after processing and then close.

    Folder to have the files save to a new folder and to make the File Naming options for naming the resulting files accessible (the naming options prevent the new files from replacing the original ones). Click Browse/Choose, choose a destination folder, then click OK/Choose.

    Optional: If you check the Override Action "Save As" Commands option, the Batch command will ignore any Save As command that was recorded into the action and execute the Destination option that you have chosen instead.

8. If you chose Folder as the Destination, under **File Naming,** you can do the following:

    Type text to be included in the name in one or more fields on the left, or choose a file-naming option from one or more menus on the right. Look at the Example to verify your naming convention choice.

    If you chose a naming option that uses sequential (serial) numbers, enter a one- to four-digit starting number in the **Starting Serial #** field.

    Check any or all of the file-name **Compatibility** options for the platforms in which you need the files to be compatible.

9. Click OK to start the batch processing.

➤ When you play an action on an image, provided the last step in the action doesn't close the document, the action steps are listed as states on the History panel.

➤ To stop the batch command while it's processing, press Esc, then click Stop in the alert dialog.

A *In the Batch dialog, choose an Action to be played, choose Bridge as the source, specify a Destination for the processed files, and choose optional File Naming settings.*

PUTTING IDEAS INTO ACTIONS

Can't think of a good use for actions? Observe your typical Photoshop edits over the course of a week or two. Are there repetitive commands or tasks that you execute frequently? Did you devise a great image-editing effect that requires many time-consuming steps?

Here are a few suggestions:

➤ Record the use of the Crop tool set to a specific size and resolution.

➤ Use the Image Size dialog to size a document to a specific resolution or dimensions.

➤ Create a new document from the currently selected layer (Duplicate Layer command, choose New in the dialog).

➤ Record the steps needed to prepare a file for commercial printing: Flatten the file, convert the document color mode to CMYK Color, apply sharpening, and save a copy of the file.

➤ Create a few adjustment layers that you typically use for tonal or color correction. (The adjustment settings can be changed after the action is played.)

➤ Copy a layer, convert the copy to a Smart Object, then apply one or more of your favorite filters.

➤ Record an action that applies a frame or a vignette around the edge of an image. Add an Insert Stop command (see page 449) to let the user redraw or reposition the selection for the frame or vignette.

An action can be turned into its own little mini-app, called a droplet, that sits on the Desktop or in a folder, waiting to be triggered. **A** If you drag a file or a folder full of files onto a droplet icon, Photoshop will launch (if it's not yet running), and the action that the droplet represents will be played on those files. Droplets can be shared among Photoshop users.

To create a droplet for an action:

1. Choose File > Automate > **Create Droplet**. The Create Droplet dialog opens. **B**

2. Click **Choose**. The Save dialog opens. Enter a name in the Save As field (keep the extension), choose a convenient location for the droplet, then click Save to return to the Create Droplet dialog.

3. Choose an action set from the **Set** menu, then an **Action** to be saved as a droplet.

4. Check any **Play** options to be included in the droplet, and choose **Destination** and **Errors** options for the processed files (see steps 4–8 on page 446).

5. Click OK. The droplet will appear in the designated location.

6. To use the droplet, drag a file or a folder full of files onto it in Explorer/Finder. Photoshop will launch, if it's not already running, and the action will play on the files.

MAKING A DROPLET PLATFORM-COMPATIBLE

► To make a droplet that was created in Windows usable in Macintosh, drag it onto the Macintosh Photoshop application icon.

► To create a droplet in Macintosh for use in Windows, save it with an ".exe" extension.

A *This is a droplet icon for an action.*

gradient map

B *Use the Create Droplet dialog to choose a location and other options for your action droplet.*

Editing an action

If you want to experiment with an action or add to it without messing around with the original, duplicate it, then edit the duplicate.

To duplicate an action:

Do either of the following:

Click an action, then choose **Duplicate** from the Actions panel menu.

Drag an action over the **New Action** button on the Actions panel.

➤ To rename an action, double-click the name.

When you insert a Stop in an action, the playback will pause at that point so the user can perform a manual or nonrecordable edit (e.g., choose a source point for a cloning tool or create a selection at a specific size and location). You can also include an instructional message for the user, which will appear in an alert dialog when the pause occurs, such as a directive to use a tool in a specific way or to choose specific panel settings. After completing the manual edit, the user resumes the playback by clicking the Play button.

To insert a Stop in an action:

1. Do either of the following:

   While recording an action, pause at the point at which you want the Stop to appear.

   To add a Stop to an existing action, on the Actions panel, click the command name after which you want it to appear.

2. Choose **Insert Stop** from the Actions panel menu.

3. In the Record Stop dialog, type an instructional or alert message.**A** We recommend also spelling out in the message that after clicking Stop and performing the desired edit, the user should click the Play button to continue the playback.

4. *Optional:* Check Allow Continue to include a Continue button in the alert dialog (in addition to a Stop button). If the user opts not to perform the requested manual edits, he or she can click Continue to resume the playback (instead of having to click Stop, then click the Play button on the panel). Don't check Allow Continue if the requested manual edit is essential to the user's

execution of the remaining steps in the action (e.g., the creation and positioning of a selection).

5. Click OK. The Stop listing will appear below the command you paused after or clicked in step 1.**B–C** If you expand the Stop listing, you will see your instructional message.

6. If you're creating a new action, record the remaining edits that you want it to contain, then hit the **Stop Playing/Recording** button.■

A *In the Record Stop dialog, we typed an instructional message for the user. We also checked Allow Continue to add a Continue button to the alert dialog, which will appear when the action is played.*

B *The Stop command appeared as a step within the action.*

C *When we played the action on an image, our instructional message and a Continue button appeared in this alert.*

Perhaps you neglected to include a particular menu command when you initially recorded an action. The Insert Menu Item command gives you a second chance. Also, some menu commands (e.g., on the View or Window menu) can't be included when an action is initially recorded. Using this feature, you can insert those commands afterward.

To insert a menu item into an action:

1. Expand the listing for an existing action, then click the command after which you want the new menu command to be inserted.

2. From the Actions panel menu, choose **Insert Menu Item**. The Insert Menu Item dialog opens.

3. From the Photoshop menu bar, choose the command to be added to the action. The command name appears in the Insert Menu Item dialog. **A**

4. Click OK. **B**

5. If the menu command that you inserted requires user input in a dialog, you will need to add a modal control to the action for that command. See the first task on the next page.

If you forgot to include a particular command or editing step in an action, or you want to improve an action by adding a command, here's your second opportunity.

To add a command or edit to an action:

1. On the Actions panel, expand the listing for the action to which you want to add an edit, then click the command name after which you want the new edit to appear.

2. Click the **Begin Recording** button. ⬤

3. Execute the desired command(s). Note: You can't add a command that's available only under certain conditions (e.g., the Feather command, which requires an active selection) unless those conditions are present and the creation of those conditions is also recorded as steps in the action.

   ➤ To record an action that produces different results depending on whether a specified condition is detected in the document, see pages 452–453.

4. Click the **Stop Playing/Recording** button. ◼

➤ To expand or collapse all the steps that are nested within an action, Alt-click/Option-click the arrowhead next to the action name.

A *When we chose the Fill command from the Edit menu, the command name appeared automatically in the Insert Menu Item dialog.*

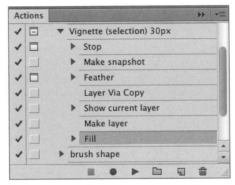

B *The menu item that we inserted appeared as a listing within the action on the Actions panel.*

DUPLICATING COMMANDS WITHIN OR BETWEEN ACTIONS

➤ To copy a command from one action to another, expand the listings for both actions, then hold down Alt/Option and drag the command to be copied from one list to the other (if you don't hold down Alt/Option, you'll move the command out of the original action). Note: Use caution when copying a Save command, as it may contain information that pertains only to the original action.

➤ To duplicate a command within an action, hold down Alt/Option and drag it upward or downward to the desired stacking position.

You can enable a pause, called a modal control, for any step in an action that enables user input, such as a dialog in which the user chooses custom settings or an edit that requires Enter/Return to be pressed (such as a transform command).

To add a modal control to a command in an action:

1. Put the Actions panel in List mode, and expand the list for an action.

2. For any individual listing within the action, click in the second column; the **Dialog** icon ☐ appears.**A**

   When the action is played, it will pause when it encounters the command that has that modal control, and the dialog or on-canvas controls will appear onscreen. In the case of a dialog, the user can enter new values, or accept the original recorded settings just by clicking OK, or click Cancel. When the user exits the dialog or commits to the edit, the playback continues automatically.

➤ To toggle a modal control off, click the Dialog icon.

To enable or disable all modal controls for an action:

Click in the Dialog column for an action name. Depending on their current state, all the modal controls in the action will be turned on or off. If an alert prompt appears, click OK.

Note: A short horizontal line in the Dialog icon ☐ for an action listing indicates that the modal controls in the action are in a mixed state (some off and some on). To reset the modal controls to their original state, click the Dialog icon; if an alert prompt appears, click OK.

To re-record an action using different dialog settings:

1. Click the name of the action that contains the settings to be edited.

2. From the Actions panel menu, choose **Record Again**.

3. The action will play back, stopping at each command that uses a dialog. Enter new settings where needed, then click OK. Each time you close a dialog, the re-recording continues.

4. The action will stop automatically after the last command. If you want to halt the re-recording midstream, click Cancel in a dialog.

A *Via the Dialog icon, you give the user an opportunity to enter custom settings in a dialog when it opens during playback.*

When you insert a conditional step into an action, it will test for a specified condition in the documents in which it is played, then will play one of two other additional specified actions (or none) based on whether or not that condition is detected.

To add a conditional step to an action:

1. Create two actions that accomplish an editing task in different ways: one that performs specific edits when a specific condition is found **A** and another that performs alternative edits (or no other edits) when that condition is not found.**B** Save both actions in the same set.

2. To create a third action that is designed to test for the specific condition, click the **New Action** button 🔲 on the Actions panel. In the New Action dialog, enter a Name, and from the Set menu, choose the same set as in step 1. Click **Record**.

3. *Optional:* On the History panel, create a snapshot of the current state of the document.

4. From the Actions panel menu, choose **Insert Conditional**. The Conditional Action dialog opens. From the **If Current** menu, choose the condition for which you want documents to be tested.**C**

5. Choose from the other two menus in the dialog, (the menus will list only actions in the current set):

   From the **Then Play Action** menu, choose the action to be played when the specified condition

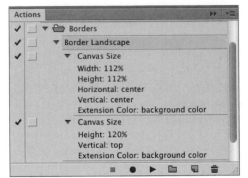

A *In the sequence of steps shown on these two pages, we created an action that adds a white border with extra white space on the bottom if played on a horizontal image, or adds extra white space on the right if played on a vertical image. To begin, we created an action called "Border Landscape," used Image > Canvas Size to add a uniform white border around the image, then used the command once more to add extra canvas area to the bottom of the image.*

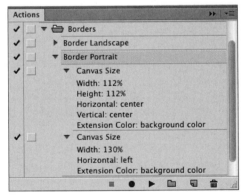

B *We created a second action called "Border Portrait" in which we used Canvas Size first to add a uniform white border, then a second time to add extra canvas area to the right side of the image.*

C *Next, we created a third action called "Add Border." To enable this action to detect the orientation of documents on which it is played, we chose the Insert Conditional command, then from the If Current menu in the Conditional Action dialog (shown at left), we chose Document Is Landscape.*

is detected in documents on which it is played (see step 1 on the preceding page).

From the **Else Play Action** menu, choose the alternative action to be performed when the specified condition is not found, **A** or to prevent any alternative action from being played, choose None.

6. *Optional:* Perform any additional editing steps to be played by the original action after the conditional action step is completed.

7. Click the **Stop Playing/Recording** button. ■ **B**

8. To test the three actions that you created in this task, open an image that contains the condition you chose in step 4 and another image that doesn't contain that condition.

9. On the Actions panel, click the action that tests for the specified condition, then click the **Play** button. ▶ **C–D** Click in the second document, then play the action again.

10. When you're ready to play the action containing the conditional step on multiple files, use the **Batch** command (see pages 446–447).

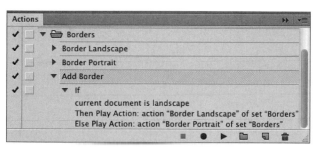

A *From the Then Play Action menu, we chose our Border Landscape action, and from the Else Play Action menu, we chose our Border Portrait action.*

B *Our last step was to click the Stop Playing/Recording button on the Actions panel. The "Add Border" action now contains the conditional "If" command.*

C *When we played our Add Border action on this photo, because the conditional step in the action detected the "Document is Landscape" condition, it played the Border Landscape action. Now there's room for some type.*

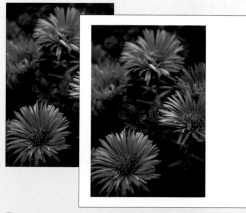

D *In this photo, the same action detected that the Document is Landscape condition was not present, so it played the alternative action that we specified for this scenario, which was Border Portrait.*

To change the settings for a command in an action:

1. On the Actions panel, ▶ expand the listing for an action, then double-click a command that uses a dialog for which you want to change the settings.

2. Enter new settings.

3. Click OK.

This may seem obvious, but remember that if you change the order of edits in an action, the new sequence may produce different results than the original.

To change the order of edits in an action:

1. On the Actions panel, expand the list for an action, if it's not already expanded.

2. Drag a command upward or downward on the list.

Deleting commands and actions

You can delete a whole action, or just delete individual commands from an action.

To delete an action or delete a command from an action:

1. If you created (or edited) any custom action sets that you want to preserve for future use, follow the steps in "To save an action set to a file," at right.

2. On the Actions panel, click the individual command or action to be deleted, then, if desired, Ctrl-click/Cmd-click to highlight additional commands or actions.

3. Click the **Delete** button, 🗑 then click OK (or to bypass the prompt, Alt-click/Option-click the Delete button).

Saving and loading action sets

Be sure to save any custom or edited action sets that you want to preserve for future use. Saved action sets can be shared among Photoshop users.

To save an action set to a file:

1. On the Actions panel, click the action set to be saved.

2. Choose **Save Actions** from the panel menu.

3. In the **Save** dialog, type a name for the action set file, keep the extension and default location, then click Save. Each file is regarded as one set, regardless of how many actions it contains.

4. When you relaunch Photoshop, your newly saved set will appear on the Actions panel menu. Note: If you edit any actions in the set, you will need to resave the set by following the steps above.

Photoshop includes many useful actions beyond those in the default set. To load them on the panel, or to load any user-created set, follow the instructions below.

To load a set onto the Actions panel:

1. On the Actions panel, click the set name that you want the loaded set to appear below.

2. From the Actions panel menu, choose a predefined action set (Commands, Frames, Image Effects, LAB–Black & White Technique, Production, Stars Trails, Text Effects, Textures, or Video Actions), or a user-saved set.

To reload the default action set:

From the Actions panel menu, choose **Reset Actions**. In the alert dialog, click Append to add the default set to the existing sets on the panel, or click OK to replace the existing sets with the default one.

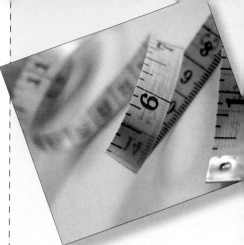

Preferences are settings that you specify for various Photoshop application features, such as the gray shades for the Photoshop interface and measurement units for the rulers. Most preference changes take effect immediately (and are saved to the Photoshop Preferences file when you exit/quit Photoshop), but a handful of preference changes don't take effect until you relaunch Photoshop or Bridge; we note such exceptions.

Opening the Preferences dialogs

To open the Preferences dialog for **Photoshop CC**, press Ctrl-K/Cmd-K, or choose Edit/Photoshop CC > Preferences > General or another option from the submenu. In the dialog, click one of the 18 ★ panel names on the left side, **A** or click Prev or Next, or press a shortcut between Ctrl-1/Cmd-1 and Ctrl-0/Cmd-0 (zero).

To open the Preferences dialog for **Adobe Bridge CC**, in Bridge, press Ctrl-K/Cmd-K or choose Edit/Adobe Bridge CC > Preferences.

A The Preferences dialog in Photoshop contains 18 panels.

RESETTING ALL THE PREFERENCES

► To reset all the **Photoshop** preferences to their default settings, hold down Ctrl-Alt-Shift/Cmd-Option-Shift as you launch the program. When the alert dialog appears, release the modifier keys, then click **Yes** to delete (and reset) the Adobe Photoshop Settings file.

► To reset the **Bridge** preferences, hold down Ctrl/Option as you launch Bridge. When the Reset Settings dialog appears, check **Reset Preferences**, then click OK.

General Preferences A ★

For the default **Color Picker**, choose either Adobe (the default setting) or your system color picker.

For the onscreen **HUD** (Heads-Up Display) **Color Picker**, choose a strip or wheel style and size. See page 206.

Choose a default **Image Interpolation** option for Photoshop edits that involve resampling or transforming, such as a use of the Crop tool; we recommend choosing one of these four higher quality options: Bicubic (Best for Smooth Gradients); Bicubic Smoother (Best for Enlargement); Bicubic Sharper (Best for Reduction); or the default setting of Bicubic Automatic (Photoshop determines the best method).

Options

Check **Auto-Update Open Documents** to have open Photoshop documents that you edit in other applications update automatically when you return to Photoshop, such as when you assign metadata to a file in Bridge.

Check **Do Not Show Welcome Screen on Launc**h to hide the Welcome window that displays when Photoshop is launched. The window contains links to videos and help files that cover new features, tips, and techniques for using Photoshop. Note: When this option is unchecked, you can choose Help > Welcome to display the window at any time.

Check **Beep When Done** to have a beep sound when a command is done processing. This can be handy for commands that take a while to process (so you can take a break).

Check **Export Clipboard** to retain the current Clipboard contents on the system Clipboard when you switch between Photoshop and other programs.

Check **Resize Image During Place** to have images or graphics scale to fit the current canvas area automatically when they are imported via the File > Place Embedded or File > Place Linked command.

Check **Always Create Smart Objects When Placing** to have raster images that you bring into Photoshop via the Place Embedded command arrive automatically as Smart Objects (see page 274).

Reset Warning Dialogs

Click **Reset All Warning Dialogs** to reactivate all alert dialogs in which you have clicked Don't Show Again.

A *General Preferences*

Interface Preferences A ★

Appearance

Click a **Color Theme** for the Photoshop interface, including the background and text color in the panels, Options bar, and Application frame, and the blank background behind the canvas area.

Via the Color menus next to **Standard Screen Mode**, **Full Screen with Menus**, and **Full Screen**, choose a shade or color for the area around the canvas for each screen mode: Default (the shade associated with the current Color Theme); Black or a Gray option; or Select Custom Color. For the latter option, choose a color from the Color Picker; thereafter, that color will appear if you choose the Custom option. For the Border around the canvas area, choose Line, Drop Shadow, or None. Note: For the Line and Drop Shadow options, you must also check Use Graphics Processor in the Performance panel. For the screen modes, see page 104.

Text

As noted in the dialog, to implement these Text options, you must relaunch Photoshop.

If you are using a multilingual version of Photoshop, from the **UI Language** menu, choose a language for the interface.

From the **UI Font Size** menu, choose Tiny, Small, Medium, or Large as the font size for features in the Photoshop user interface (panels, Options bar, etc.).

In Windows, from the **UI Scaling** menu, choose a scale option for displaying interface features on a HiDPI display. ★ We recommend choosing Auto.

Options

Check **Show Channels in Color** to display RGB or CMYK channels in color thumbnails on the Channels panel and in the document window when clicked individually. Uncheck this option (as we do) to display the channels in grayscale, which is useful for judging luminosity values.

Check **Show Menu Colors** to activate the display of background colors that have been assigned to menu commands via Edit > Menus and to workspaces in which they were saved (e.g., the "What's New" workspace).

Check **Dynamic Color Sliders** to have the colors above the sliders on the Color panel update as you move the sliders.

Check **Enable Text Drop Shadows** to display a very subtle drop shadow behind text labels in panels.

A *Interface Preferences*

Workspace Preferences A ★

Options

If **Auto-Collapse Iconic Panels** is checked and you open a collapsed panel, then click anywhere outside it, the panel will collapse back to an icon. With this option unchecked, the panel will remain expanded. See page 106.

Check **Auto-Show Hidden Panels** to allow panel docks that you have hidden to redisplay temporarily. In Standard Screen mode, you can hide the docks by pressing Tab or Shift-Tab, then redisplay them temporarily at any time by letting the pointer pause on the dark gray vertical bar at the right edge of the Application frame (or the left edge of the frame, for the Tools panel). Move the pointer away from the docks, and they will disappear again. In either of the Full Screen modes, let the pointer pause at the edge of your display to make the dark bar appear, followed by the docks.

Check **Open Documents as Tabs** to have documents dock automatically as tabs when opened instead of

as floating windows (we recommend checking this option). Note: In the Mac OS, if you check this option but hide the Application frame, images will dock as tabs within one document window automatically.

Check **Enable Floating Document Window Docking** to allow a floating document window to be docked as a tab when you drag its title bar just below the Options bar in the Application frame or next to an existing document tab in a floating window. (We recommend keeping this option checked.)

Condensed

If you're using Photoshop on a laptop, check **Enable Narrow Options Bar** for a compact Options bar.

Click **Restore Default Workspaces** to restore, to the Workspace menu, any predefined Adobe workspaces that were deleted via the Window > Workspaces > Delete Workspace dialog.

A *Workspace Preferences*

Tools Preferences (A, next page) ★

Options

If **Show Tool Tips** is checked and the pointer is currently hovering over a Photoshop feature (mouse button up), a label pertaining to that feature appears briefly onscreen. This is a good way to identify panel and dialog options, as well as tools and tool shortcuts.

Check **Enable Gestures** if you have a touch device, such as a laptop, a Microsoft Surface Pro running Windows 8.1, ★ or a desktop computer with a Magic Mouse or Magic Trackpad, and you want to enable the capability of the touch device to zoom, rotate, or flick images. Uncheck this option if you find that the gestures are causing unwanted highlighting or pointer movements.

With **Use Shift Key for Tool Switch** checked, in order to access tools from a fly-out menu, you must press Shift plus the assigned letter (e.g., press Shift-B to cycle through the Brush, Pencil, Color Replacement, and Mixer Brush tools). If you uncheck this option (as we do), you can cycle through related tools simply by pressing their assigned letter. To learn the tool shortcuts, see pages 113–116 or use Tool Tips.

Check **Overscroll** to enable scrolling via the scroll bars or Hand tool beyond the normal window bounds regardless of the size of the image within the document window. ★

Check **Enable Flick Panning** to enable a magnified image to quickly float across the screen when you drag it with the Hand tool a short distance, then release the mouse (Use Graphics Processor must be checked in the Performance panel of this dialog; see page 464).

If your mouse has a scroll wheel and you check **Zoom with Scroll Wheel**, you can change the zoom level by scrolling the wheel horizontally or vertically.

Check **Animated Zoom** for smooth, continuous zooming as you click and hold with the Zoom tool to zoom in, or hold down Alt/Option and click

and hold to zoom out. Note: To use this feature, Use Graphics Processor must be checked in the Performance panel of this dialog; see page 464.

With **Zoom Resizes Windows** checked, a floating document window will resize when you change the zoom level via the Ctrl/Cmd- + (plus) or Ctrl/Cmd- – (minus) shortcut or the Zoom tool. You can also control this behavior for the Zoom tool via the Resize Windows to Fit check box on the Options bar. Note: With this option checked, as you change the zoom level, the document is also positioned over — but not docked into — the document window area of the Application frame.

Check **Zoom Clicked Point to Center** to have Photoshop center the image at the location you click when zooming.

With **Vary Round Brush Hardness Based on HUD Vertical Movement** checked, you can hold down Alt-right-click/Control-Option and drag vertically to change the brush hardness; with this option unchecked, the shortcut changes the brush opacity instead. This option affects the Brush, Pencil, Color Replacement, Clone Stamp, History Brush, Sharpen, and other tools (see page 131). HUD stands for "Heads Up Display," and it refers to the ability of the user to choose settings via on-canvas controls. Note: To display the hardness or opacity value as a tint within the cursor, check Use Graphics Processor in the Performance panel of this dialog.

Check **Snap Vector Tools and Transforms to Pixel Grid** to have future vector paths that you create, and existing shapes that you transform, snap to the pixel grid for sharper rendering in onscreen output (see page 421).

From the **Show Transformation Values** menu, choose a location (e.g., Top Left or Bottom Right) for the label that appears and updates dynamically as you transform objects, indicating the current rotation, scaling, or other values. Choose Never from the menu if you prefer to turn this feature off.

A *Tools Preferences*

History Log Preferences B ★

Check **History Log** to have Photoshop generate a log of your editing activity from each work session. The log can be useful if you need to preserve an exact record of your editing steps or need to tally your billable hours for clients.

For **Save Log Items To**, choose where the log is to be saved: to the Metadata of a file, to a separate Text File, or to Both of the above. For either of the latter two options, choose a location for the text file in the dialog that opens automatically, then click Save.

From the **Edit Log Items** menu, choose what data is to be saved in the log: Sessions Only to log just the date and time when you launch or exit/quit Photoshop and which files were opened; Concise to log Sessions information plus a list of edits (states on the History panel); or Detailed to include all of the above data plus any actions used and the options and parameters used in each editing step.

B *History Log Preferences*

Sync Settings Preferences A ★

You can sync Photoshop settings, including your preferences, between your Creative Cloud account and any computer on which you've signed in to Photoshop using your Adobe ID. Via the Sync Settings panel in Preferences (or via commands on the Edit/Photoshop CC > [your Adobe ID] submenu), you can upload the current Photoshop settings on your computer to your Creative Cloud Assets, then download the settings from the Creative Cloud to another computer on which you've signed in to Photoshop. See pages 495–496.

Creative Cloud

The **Signed In As** info is your current Creative Cloud membership ID. Also listed are the date and time of the **Last Upload** and **Last Download**.

Advanced Settings

From the **What to Sync** menu, choose Everything (to check all the boxes); or choose Custom, then check the kinds of settings that you want to upload or download (Preferences, Workspaces, and presets for Photoshop panels and pickers).

Next, click **Upload** to upload the specified Photoshop settings from your computer to the Creative Cloud, or click **Download** to download the current settings in the Creative Cloud to your computer.

Log

The **Log** lists settings that were uploaded and downloaded, and the times they were uploaded or downloaded. The Log window clears when you exit/quit Photoshop.

A *Sync Settings Preferences*

File Handling Preferences (A, next page)

File Saving Options

Choose **Image Previews**: Never Save to save files without a thumbnail preview for the Desktop, or Always Save (our preference) to have an updated preview save with files each time they're saved, or Ask When Saving to decide which previews to include via Image Previews check boxes when saving files via the Save or Save As dialog. See pages 18–20.

In the Mac OS, check **Icon** to have the thumbnails of files display as their icons on the Desktop and in the File > Open dialog. Check **Windows Thumbnail** to have the thumbnail for a file display when the file is selected in File > Open.

In the Mac OS, choose **Append File Extension**: Always (our preference) to have Photoshop include a three-letter abbreviation of the file format (e.g., .tif, .psd) automatically when you save a file via the Save As command; or Ask When Saving to be given the option to decide in each case via File Extension check boxes in the Save As dialog. Extensions are helpful when converting files for Windows, and are necessary when saving files for the Web.

In Windows, choose **File Extension**: Use Lower Case or Use Upper Case.

Check **Save As to Original Folder** (as we do) to have the location in the Save As dialog always default to the existing location of the current file.

Check **Save in Background** to permit image editing to occur while Photoshop is saving a file.

Check **Automatically Save Recovery Information Every**, and choose a time interval from the menu, to let Photoshop save a temporary copy of the current document to your hard disk. If Photoshop exits/quits unexpectedly, the temp file will open by default upon relaunch.

File Compatibility

Click **Camera Raw Preferences** to open that dialog.

Check **Prefer Adobe Camera Raw for Supported Raw Files** to have raw files that you open via File > Open open into Camera Raw, as opposed to other conversion software. We keep this option checked.

Files that are 32-bit (e.g., the files that are produced by the Merge to HDR Pro command from multiple exposures) must be converted to 8- or 16-bit for export or printing. With **Use Adobe Camera Raw to Convert Documents from 32 bit to 16/8 bit** checked,

32-bit files will open into Camera Raw automatically when you convert them to a lower bit depth via the Image > Mode > 16 Bits/Channel or 8 Bits/Channel command, so you can apply color and tonal adjustments.

Ignore EXIF Profile Tag enables Photoshop to read a camera's EXIF metadata color space data when opening files. This option is necessary only for files from early digital cameras, so we keep it unchecked.

Check **Ignore Rotation Metadata** to have Photoshop ignore any rotation settings that are applied to image thumbnails in Bridge.

Check **Ask Before Saving Layered TIFF Files** to have an "Including layers will increase file size" alert dialog appear when saving a layered file in the TIFF format. This alert is a good reminder to uncheck the Layers option in the Save As dialog.

Check **Disable Compression of PSD and PSB Files** to prevent Photoshop from compressing files when saving them in the PSD or PSB format. When this option is checked, documents save more quickly but have a larger file size.

To save your files so they can be opened in applications that don't support layers, choose an option from the **Maximize PSD and PSB File Compatibility** menu. Photoshop will save a composite preview with your layered files, along with a rasterized copy of any vector art. Although this option produces larger files, it's necessary for compatibility. Choose Ask to have Photoshop offer this as an option via an alert dialog when files are saved, or choose Always to have Photoshop produce compatible files automatically without an alert appearing. See pages 18–20.

Note: Upon saving a layered file, if Ask is the current Maximize PSD and PSB File Compatibility preference and you check Maximize Compatibility and Don't Show Again in the Photoshop Format Options dialog, Photoshop will switch the preference setting to Always. If you uncheck Maximize Compatibility but do check Don't Show Again in the alert, the preference setting will switch to Never.

File list

In the **Recent File List Contains [ ] files** field, enter the maximum number of files (up to 100) that can be listed at a time on the File > Open Recent submenu in Photoshop.

A *File Handling Preferences*

Export Preferences B ★

Quick Export Format

From the menu, choose the file format that will be applied to any file exported via the Quick Export as [format] command. For PNG, check Transparency. For JPG, choose a quality setting. The format chosen in this panel will be displayed at the end of the "Quick Export as" command name.

Quick Export Location

Click **Ask Where to Export Each Time** to have the Save As dialog display each time you use the Quick Export command. Click **Export Files to an Assets Folder Next to the Current Document** (our preference) to have Photoshop generate a "[Photoshop file name] – assets" folder that will display next to your Photoshop file in Bridge or in Explorer/Finder.

B *Export Preferences*

Performance Preferences A ★

Note: To implement changes made in this panel (except for Use Graphics Processor) you must relaunch Photoshop. For Use Graphics Processor, you must close and then reopen any open documents.

Memory Usage

The **Let Photoshop Use** field and slider control the maximum percentage of your computer's RAM that can be used by Photoshop. We recommend keeping this value on the default setting.

Graphics Processor Settings

The **Detected Graphics Processor** area lists the graphics card that is currently installed in your system.

Check **Use Graphics Processor** if your system has OpenGL capability and you want to use the OpenGL features of Photoshop, such as the Rotate View tool, Animated Zoom, Scrubby Zoom, Flick Panning, Pixel Grid, HUD Color Picker, the Sampling Ring for the Eyedropper tool, a tint in the brush cursor for hardness and/or opacity, the Live Tip Brush Preview, and better performance when using some commands or filters, such as the Blur Gallery. (For a complete list, rest your pointer in the Graphics Processor Settings option, and look in the Description area.)

History & Cache

Low-resolution versions of the current file are saved in cache buffers to help the image and histograms redraw more quickly onscreen. To optimize the cache levels and tile size for Photoshop, click a generic document type (not your body type!): **Tall and Thin** (for smaller documents that contain many layers), **Default** (best for general use), or **Big and Flat** (best for larger documents that contain few layers).

Enter the maximum number of **History States** the History panel can list at a time. When this number is reached, older states are deleted.

Choose a higher **Cache Levels** value for large files that contain few layers and a lower Cache Levels value for smaller files that contain many layers.

The **Cache Tile Size** value controls how much data Photoshop processes at a given time. If you need faster processing of large images, you can choose a higher value.

Description

In the **Description** window at the bottom of the dialog, you can read about whichever feature your pointer is currently hovering over.

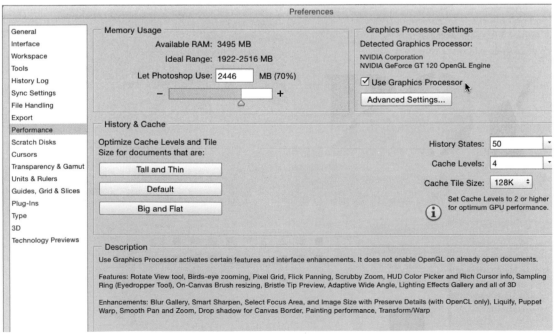

A *Performance Preferences*

Scratch Disks Preferences A ★

Scratch Disks

Check which hard drives Photoshop may use as **Scratch Disks** when available RAM is insufficient for processing or storing image data. To change the sequence of drives that have a check mark, click a drive, then click the up or down arrow on the right side.

➤ Hold down Ctrl-Alt/Cmd-Option while launching Photoshop to open the Scratch Disk Preferences dialog.

➤ From the Info panel ⓘ menu in Photoshop, choose Panel Options, then check Efficiency under Status Information. When Photoshop is using the scratch disk, the Efficiency readout value on the panel is below 100%.

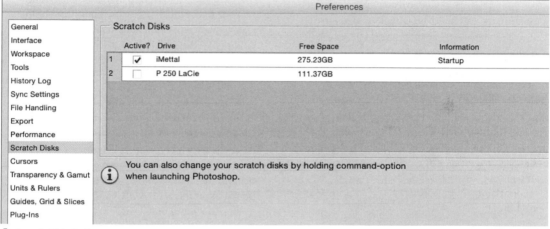

A *Scratch Disks Preferences*

Cursors Preferences A

Painting Cursors

For the **Painting Cursors** (used with such editing tools as the Blur, Brush, Burn, Clone Stamp, Color Replacement, Dodge, Eraser, Healing Brush, History Brush, Mixer Brush, Pattern Stamp, Pencil, Quick Selection, Sharpen, Smudge, and Spot Healing Brush tools), click the preferred cursor to be displayed onscreen: **Standard** for the tool icon; **Precise** for a crosshair; **Normal Brush Tip** for a circle that is half the size of the current brush; or **Full Size Brush Tip** for a circle that is the full size of the current brush. For either of the latter two options, you can also check **Show Crosshair in Brush Tip** to have a crosshair appear in the center of the circle and/or **Show Only Crosshair While Painting** to have only a crosshair display when the mouse is dragged, for faster performance when using large brushes.

Other Cursors

For the **Other Cursors** (such as the Eyedropper and Crop tools), click **Standard** to have the tool icon display onscreen as you use the tool, or click **Precise** to display a crosshair instead.

➤ Press Caps Lock to turn a Standard cursor into a Precise cursor (crosshair) or, if Precise is the current Painting Cursors setting, to turn any Painting cursor into a Full Size Brush Tip (circle).

Brush Preview

Click the **Color** swatch and choose a color via the Color Picker to represent the current brush hardness or opacity as a tint in the brush cursor as you Alt-right-click/Control-Option drag vertically (Use Graphics Processor must be checked in the Performance panel).

Transparency & Gamut Preferences B

Transparency Settings

Choose a **Grid Size** for the checkerboard that Photoshop uses to represent layer transparency on the Layers panel and in the document window.

For the transparency checkerboard, choose one of the **Grid Colors** options from the menu, or click each color swatch and choose a color via the Color Picker.

Gamut Warning

To change the color that Photoshop uses to mark out-of-gamut colors when the View > Gamut Warning feature is on, click the **Color** swatch. You can also change the **Opacity** of the Gamut Warning color.

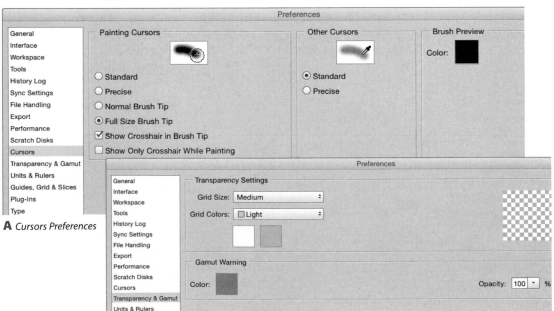

A Cursors Preferences

B Transparency & Gamut Preferences

Units & Rulers Preferences A

➤ To get directly to the Units & Rulers panel of the Preferences dialog, double-click either ruler in the document window.

Units

From the **Rulers** menu, choose a unit of measure to display on the horizontal and vertical rulers; in dialogs, such as Image > Canvas Size; and on panels, such as the Info panel. To learn about the rulers in Photoshop, see page 295.

➤ To change the ruler units without opening the Preferences dialog, right-click either one of the rulers in the document window and choose a unit from the context menu. When changed this way, via the Info Panel Options dialog, or via the Preferences dialog, the units change in all locations.

From the **Type** menu, choose Pixels, Points, or Millimeters as the unit of measure for the Character panel and Paragraph panels, and for the Font Size field on the Options bar when a type tool is selected.

New Document Preset Resolutions

Enter a **Print Resolution** value in either one of the available units to display as the Resolution setting when you choose one of the three print presets (such as U.S. Paper) in the New dialog; the default value is 300 ppi. For the **Screen Resolution,** enter a value to display as the Resolution when you choose the Web, Mobile & Devices, or Film & Video preset (the default value is 72 ppi). See pages 15–16.

Column Size

If you need to fit your Photoshop images into a specific column width in a page layout program, enter values in the **Width** and **Gutter** fields here. Thereafter, when you open the New, Image Size, or Canvas Size dialog and then choose Columns from the units menu next to the Width field, Photoshop will use your Width and Gutter preference values to calculate the Width.

Point/Pica Size

Click **PostScript** (the default, and recommended, setting) to have Photoshop use the standard PostScript value as the points-to-inch ratio.

A *Units & Rulers Preferences*

Guides, Grid & Slices Preferences A

Note: Changes made in this dialog will preview immediately in your document.

Guides

For ruler guides, choose a **Color** from the menu (or click the swatch and use the Color Picker), and choose a **Style**. See pages 295–296.

Smart Guides

For Smart Guides, temporary lines that display as you move a layer or selection, choose a **Color** from the menu (or click the swatch and use the Color Picker). See page 294.

Grid

For the nonprinting grid, choose a **Color** and a **Style**. (To show or hide the grid in your document, press Ctrl-'/Cmd-'.)

To display grid lines onscreen at specific intervals, choose a unit from the menu, then enter a **Gridline Every** value. If you choose Percent from the menu and enter a value, grid lines will appear at those percentage intervals of the document width, starting from the left edge of the canvas. To control the spacing between the thinner grid lines that fall within the main grid lines, enter a **Subdivisions** value.

Slices

Choose a **Line Color** for the slice boundaries. Check **Show Slice Numbers** to have Photoshop display a slice number in the upper-left corner of each slice. (To learn about the slice tools, see Photoshop Help.)

Plug-ins Preferences (A, next page)

Note: To implement changes made in this panel, you must relaunch Photoshop.

Generator

With **Enable Generator** checked, you can generate GIF, JPEG, PNG, or SVG image assets from Photoshop layers for output to the Web or mobile devices.

Check **Enable Remote Connections** to let Photoshop set up a wireless connection with companion apps that run on tablets and iPads. To learn more about this feature, see "Companion Apps" in Photoshop Help.

Filters & Extension Panels

Check **Show All Filter Gallery Groups and Names** to list all Photoshop filters in the submenus on the Filter menu, including those that are accessible in the Filter Gallery. With this option off, the submenus list only the filters that are not in the Filter Gallery, and the menu is more streamlined.

Panels from Adobe and third-party suppliers are accessed in Photoshop via Window > Extensions. Check **Allow Extensions to Connect to the Internet** here to enable those extension panels to connect to the Internet in order to access updated content.

Check **Load Extension Panels** to have the extension panels that are currently residing in the Plug-ins folder (within the Photoshop application folder) load automatically when you launch Photoshop.

A Guides, Grid & Slices Preferences

Preferences

General	**Generator**
Interface	☑ Enable Generator
Workspace	☐ Enable Remote Connections
Tools	Service Name: Photoshop Server
History Log	
Sync Settings	Password: ••••
File Handling	Password must be six characters or longer.
Export	Hostname:
Performance	IPv4 Address:
Scratch Disks	
Cursors	**Filters & Extension Panels**
Transparency & Gamut	☐ Show all Filter Gallery groups and names
Units & Rulers	☑ Allow Extensions to Connect to the Internet
Guides, Grid & Slices	☑ Load Extension Panels
Plug-Ins	ⓘ Changes will take effect the next time you start Photoshop.
Type	
3D	

A *Plug-ins Preferences*

Type Preferences B ★

Type Options

Check **Use Smart Quotes** to have Photoshop insert typographically correct (curly) apostrophes and quotation marks automatically as you input type, instead of the incorrect (straight) foot and inch marks.

Check **Enable Missing Glyph Protection** to permit Photoshop to substitute Roman characters for missing glyphs, such as Japanese or Chinese characters.

Check **Show Font Names in English** to have non-Roman font names display in English on the Font menus (e.g., "Adobe Ming Std" instead of in the equivalent Chinese characters).

Check **Use ESC Key to Commit Text** to enable pressing the Esc key to accept entered or edited text while the Type tool is selected.

Choose Text Engine Options

To display special language features on the Character and Paragraph panels and panel menus, click **East Asian** or **Middle Eastern and South Asian** here, then on the Type > Language Options submenu in Photoshop, check East Asian Features or Middle Eastern Features. (One of those two options will be listed in addition to the Default Features listing.)

Note: A change in the Text Engine Options setting won't affect existing documents, but will apply to new documents without relaunching Photoshop.

Preferences

General	**Type Options**	**Choose Text Engine Options**
Interface	☑ Use Smart Quotes	⦿ East Asian
Workspace	☑ Enable Missing Glyph Protection	◯ Middle Eastern and South Asian
Tools	☑ Show Font Names in English	ⓘ Changes will take effect the next time
History Log	☑ Use ESC key to commit text	you create a document.
Sync Settings		
File Handling		

B *Type Preferences*

Technology Previews Preferences ★

Technology Previews

Here you can enable features that Adobe is currently working on (that are not yet part of Photoshop) to try them. Roll over a feature to display its description.

Click **Learn More** to get info about the features in Adobe Help.

Preferences for Adobe Bridge CC

General Preferences A

Appearance

Click a **Color Theme** for the Bridge interface.

Choose a gray value as the overall **User Interface Brightness**, which appears in the side panes.

Choose a gray value for the **Image Backdrop**, the area behind the Content and Preview panels. This value also displays as the background behind images when displayed in Full Preview View or in Slideshow or Review mode.

Choose an **Accent Color** for the highlight border around selected folders, thumbnails, and stacks, and for text that is selected in the panels.

Behavior

Check **When a Camera Is Connected, Launch Adobe Photo Downloader** to make the Downloader the default system utility for acquiring photos (this option is for Mac OS users only).

Check **Double-Click Edits Camera Raw Settings in Bridge** to have raw files open into Camera Raw, hosted by Bridge, when double-clicked. See page 50.

If **Ctrl-Click/Cmd-Click Opens the Loupe When Previewing or Reviewing** is checked, you have to hold down Ctrl/Cmd while clicking an image preview to make the loupe display. With this option unchecked, you can make the loupe appear simply by clicking the preview (see page 31).

For **Number of Recent Items to Display**, enter the maximum number of files (0–30) that can be listed at a time on the Open Recent File menu 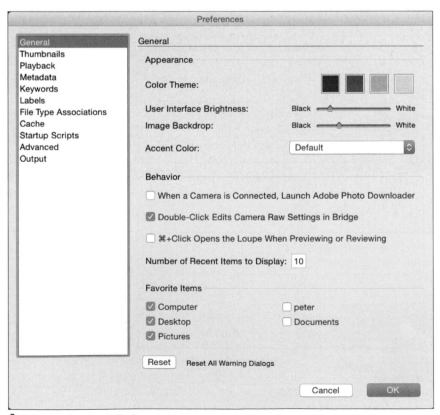 and on the Reveal Recent File or Go to Recent Folder menu 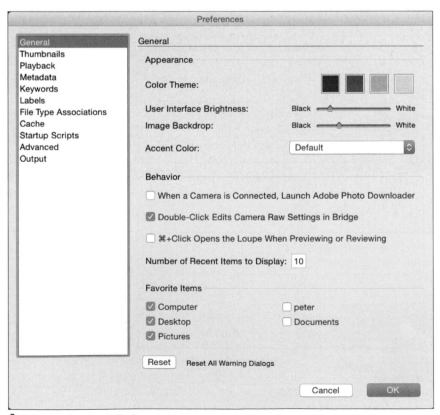 on the Path bar.

Favorite Items

Check the items and system-generated folders you want Bridge to list in the **Favorites** panel.

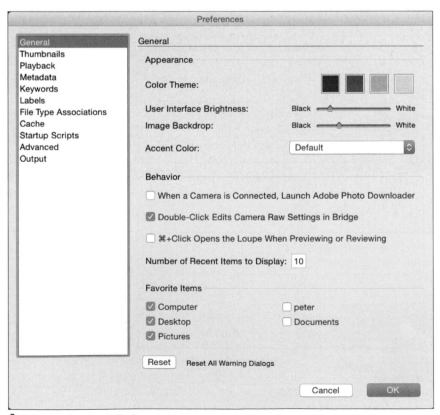

A *General Preferences, in Bridge*

Thumbnails Preferences A

Performance and File Handling

Note: To implement a change to the Performance and File Handling setting, you must purge the folder cache by choosing Tools > Cache > Purge Cache for Folder [folder name].

For **Do Not Process Files Larger Than**, enter the maximum file size for which you will permit Bridge to display a thumbnail (the default value is 1000 MB). Bear in mind that large files preview slowly.

Details

For **Additional Lines of Thumbnail Metadata**, check Show for each line of metadata that you want Bridge to display, and choose the category of file information you want listed next to or below the image thumbnails in the Content panel (see page 37).

Check **Show Tooltips** to allow Tool Tips to display in Bridge, such as when you rest the pointer on an image thumbnail.

Playback Preferences

Stacks

Choose a **Stack Playback Frame Rate** to control the speed at which a stack of thumbnails plays back via the Play button.

Audio and Video

Choose options to control whether audio and video files will play automatically when previewed and/or loop automatically when viewed in the Preview panel.

Metadata Preferences

Check the categories of metadata you want Bridge to display in the **Metadata** panel.

Check **Hide Empty Fields** to hide any fields on the Metadata panel that are empty.

Check **Show Metadata Placard** to display camera data in a separate section at the top of the Metadata panel (see page 29).

A *Thumbnails Preferences, in Bridge*

Keywords Preferences

Check **Automatically Apply Parent Keywords** to have the parent keyword also apply automatically when a subkeyword box is checked in the Keywords panel. If this option is on and you want to apply just a subkeyword, Shift-click the check box in the Keywords panel. See pages 38–39.

For **Write Hierarchical Keywords,** click an Output Delimiter character to be used to separate keywords in files that are exported from Bridge; and for **Read Hierarchical Keywords,** click an Input Delimiter character to be used to separate keywords in files that are imported into Bridge.

Labels Preferences

Check whether to **Require the Control/Command Key** [to be pressed in the shortcut] **to Apply Labels and Ratings** to selected file thumbnails (see page 40). You can also change the label names here, but not the colors.

File Type Associations Preferences

These settings tell Bridge the applications into which it may open files of different types. Don't monkey around with these settings unless you know what you're doing!

Cache Preferences

Options

Check **Keep 100% Previews in Cache** to save large JPEG previews of image thumbnails to disk for faster previewing when using the loupe and when previewing images in Slideshow mode at 100% or in Full Screen Preview view. We keep this option unchecked, because it uses a lot of disk space.

Check **Automatically Export Caches to Folders When Possible** to have Bridge export all cache files (in which metadata and thumbnail information is stored) to the same folders in which the images are located or to which they are copied. See page 42.

Location

If you need to specify a different location for the Bridge cache, click **Choose**, choose a folder, click

Open, then relaunch Bridge. We recommend leaving this setting alone.

Manage

If you have a very large hard disk, you can use the **Cache Size** slider to increase the maximum number of items that Bridge can store in its cache.

Click **Compact Cache** to allow previously cached items that are no longer available to be removed from the cache, for improved performance.

Click **Purge Cache** to purge all cached thumbnails and previews from the central database, in order to free up space on your hard disk or as a remedy if Bridge is having trouble displaying your image thumbnails. Do this only when absolutely necessary.

Startup Scripts Preferences

All **Startup Scripts** that are checked in this dialog will be activated at startup. We recommend keeping all of them checked, unless you have a specific reason to uncheck any. Changes to these settings take effect when you relaunch Bridge.

Advanced Preferences

Miscellaneous

If (and only if) you encounter display problems in Bridge, check **Use Software Rendering**, then relaunch Bridge. This option turns off hardware acceleration for the Preview panel and Slideshow mode.

Check **Generate Monitor-Size Previews** to have Bridge generate previews based on the resolution of your display. In a dual-monitor setup, the previews are sized according to the resolution of the larger of the two monitors.

Check **Start Bridge at Login** if you want Bridge to launch automatically upon startup.

International

To implement a change in **Language** that you choose for the Bridge interface and/or for the **Keyboard**, you must exit/quit and relaunch Bridge.

When you're done editing your Photoshop image, you can gather all the linked files used in the image, output the image to a desktop inkjet printer, prepare it for commercial printing, export it to another application (such as Adobe InDesign), or generate assets from any of its individual layers for display on the Web and mobile devices.

In the first task in this chapter, you will learn how to package all linked files used in an image. In the second task, you will view your document as a simulation of three different kinds of output: an inkjet print, a commercial press print, and display on the Web. This simulation, called a soft proof, will give you useful feedback so you can apply final tweaks and adjustments to your image.

Once your document is finalized, you will learn how to output it from Photoshop to an inkjet device, and how to convert it to CMYK Color mode for commercial printing. We offer guidelines for exporting files to Adobe InDesign and Adobe Illustrator, give instructions for saving files in the versatile TIFF and PDF formats, and finally, show you how to create image assets from Photoshop layers via export or extract options for output to the Web and mobile devices.

Important note: If you're planning to output your document to a desktop inkjet printer, keep it in RGB Color mode. Although desktop printers print using six or more process ink colors, their drivers are designed to receive RGB data.

Using the Package command

The Package command gathers a copy of every linked Smart Object file (located on your hard disk or on a connected network server) that is being used in your document, and puts the copies in a destination folder.

To gather copies of linked Smart Objects:

1. Choose File > **Package**. The **Choose Package Destination** dialog opens.

2. Choose a location for the package folder or create a new folder, then click Choose. A copy of the Photoshop file will appear in a new folder (labeled with the Photoshop file name) inside the folder you designated. Within this new folder you will also find a subfolder labeled "Links," containing a copy of all the files that you linked to the Photoshop document, as well as copies of any files that were linked into those linked files.

PRINT & EXPORT

24

Proofing document colors onscreen

In this phase of color management, you'll create a custom proof setting for your specific inkjet printer and paper, and use it to view a soft proof (onscreen simulation) of the document as if it were output to print. Although this proof won't be perfectly accurate, it will give you a rough idea of how your colors will look, without costing you a cent.

To proof a document as an inkjet print onscreen:

1. Open an RGB image. From the View > **Proof Setup** submenu, choose **Custom**. The Customize Proof Condition dialog opens. In the following steps, you will choose proofing settings for your specific output device.

2. Check Preview, then from the **Device to Simulate** menu, choose the correct color profile for your inkjet printer and paper — the profile that you either downloaded from the manufacturer's website or installed with your printer driver file (see page 11).**A**

3. Uncheck **Preserve RGB Numbers**, if available, to allow Photoshop to simulate how the colors will look when converted to the output profile.

4. Choose a **Rendering Intent** to control how colors will change as the image is shifted to the output profile (see the sidebar on the next page). We recommend choosing either Perceptual or Relative Colorimetric. To compare these options, choose them one by one and look at your document onscreen — or even better, output a test print for each one and compare the results.

Check **Black Point Compensation** to allow adjustments to be made for differences in the black point among different color spaces. With this option chosen, the full dynamic range of the image color space is mapped to the full dynamic range of the color space of your output device. With this option off, black areas in the image may display or print as grays. For an inkjet proof, we recommend checking this option.

5. *Optional:* For Display Options (On-Screen), check Simulate Paper Color to preview the white of the printing paper, as defined in the chosen printer profile, or if you're going to print the file on uncoated paper, check Simulate Black Ink to preview the full range of black values that the printer profile can produce.

6. To save your custom proof setup, click **Save**, enter a name, keep the .psf extension, keep the default location (the Proofing folder), then click Save.

7. Your newly saved proof setup appears on the Custom Proof Condition menu. Click OK. The setup is now also available on the View > Proof Setup submenu for use at any time, and View > **Proof Colors** is checked automatically so you can study the soft proof onscreen. (While Proof Colors is checked, the color profile that is currently chosen on the Proof Setup submenu is also listed in the document tab.)

Remember, the Proof Setup options control only how Photoshop simulates colors onscreen. Colors in the file won't actually be converted to the chosen profile until you physically output the document to an inkjet printer or convert it to a different color mode (such as from RGB to CMYK).

A *To generate a soft proof of our document, from the Device to Simulate menu in the Customize Proof Condition dialog, we chose the profile for our Canon Pixma inkjet printer.*

CHOOSING A RENDERING INTENT

➤ Perceptual changes colors in a way that seems natural to the human eye, while attempting to preserve the appearance of the overall image. It's a good choice for continuous-tone images.

➤ Saturation changes colors with the intent of preserving vivid colors. It is a good choice for charts and graphics, which typically contain a limited number of colors, but it can compromise the color fidelity of continuous-tone images.

➤ Absolute Colorimetric maintains the color accuracy only of colors that fall within the destination color gamut (i.e., the color range of your printer), but in so doing it sacrifices the accuracy of colors that are outside that gamut.

➤ Relative Colorimetric, the default intent for all the Adobe predefined settings in the Color Settings dialog, compares the white, or highlight, of your document's color space to the white of the destination color space (the white of the paper, in the case of print output), shifting colors where needed. This is the best rendering intent choice for documents in which most of the colors fall within the color range of the destination gamut, because it preserves most of the original colors.

Note: Consult the manual for your inkjet printer before choosing a rendering intent (e.g., for some models, Perceptual may be recommended over Relative Colorimetric).

DO THE RESEARCH

➤ When preparing files for commercial printing, ask your output service provider which settings and formats you should select in Photoshop.

➤ For more specialized technical information that is beyond the scope of this chapter, refer to the documentation for your specific printer model, and to Photoshop Help.

➤ Regardless of the output medium, you can learn from trial and error. Output a file, study the print, make adjustments to the file, then output it again. The experts become so by learning from both their successes and their failures.

In this task, you will choose a Proof Setup preset, then turn on the soft-proof feature so you can preview onscreen how the colors in your file will look if printed using CMYK inks or viewed online on a Windows or older Macintosh display.

To proof colors onscreen for commercial printing or online output:

1. From the View > **Proof Setup** submenu, choose the preset for the output display type that you want Photoshop to simulate:

   Working CMYK to simulate colors for the type of commercial press that is currently selected on the CMYK menu under Working Spaces in the Edit > Color Settings dialog in Photoshop.

   ➤ If your file will be sent to a commercial print shop, ask them for a .csf or .icc profile. After you install the profile, it will be available on, and should be chosen from, the Settings menu in the Color Settings dialog (see page 11). If you're not given a profile, ask your print shop to suggest which predefined CMYK profile you should choose instead (see page 8).

   Legacy Macintosh RGB (Gamma 1.8) to simulate colors for online output using the legacy Mac gamma setting of 1.8 as the proofing space, or **Internet Standard RGB (sRGB)** to simulate online output using the more common Windows gamma of 2.2.

   Monitor RGB to simulate colors using the current display profile that is assigned to your monitor.

2. View > **Proof Colors** will be checked automatically, so you can examine your document for any color changes.

   When you're ready to turn off soft proofing, uncheck it on the menu or press Ctrl-Y/Cmd-Y.

Outputting a file to an inkjet printer

In this section, you'll learn how to output your file to an inkjet printer so the results match, as closely as possible, the document you have been editing and viewing onscreen. We have divided the steps for using this dialog into three parts: Choose settings for your printer driver, choose settings for printing (including color management), and finally, verify that color management has been turned off for the printer and print the file from Windows or the Mac OS.

Phase 1

In this phase, you will tell Photoshop what type of printer you're going to use via the Print Settings dialog, then use the print dialog for your operating system to specify the paper size, paper type, and other options for your printer.

To choose settings for your printer driver:

1. Open the RGB file to be printed, then choose File > **Print** (Ctrl-P/Cmd-P). The Photoshop Print Settings dialog opens. **A** (You can enlarge the dialog to increase the preview size.)

2. From the **Printer** menu, choose your target inkjet printer.

3. Click **Print Settings** to open the [**Printer Name**] **Properties/Print** dialog for your operating system.

4. The menu names will vary depending on the chosen printer model and your operating system, so we refer to them here generically:

   In Windows, in the Main (or Paper/Quality) tab, choose the best-quality option for photo printing. For the paper options, choose the source for your paper, the specific type of paper to be used, and the paper size (**A**, next page).

   In the Mac OS, if necessary, click Show Details to display the full dialog. The inkjet printer you chose in step 2 will be listed on the Printer menu. Choose the desired paper size for the print (for a borderless print, pick a size that includes the word "borderless"). From the fourth menu, choose the category (e.g., Quality & Media or Print Settings) that lets you choose media type and print quality

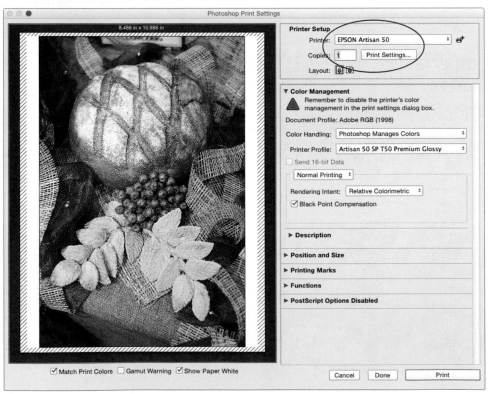

A In the Photoshop Print Settings dialog, choose your inkjet device from the Printer menu, then click Print Settings.

settings). From the media or paper type menu, choose the type of paper you will be using, **B** and from another menu, choose a print quality option. **C**

➤ In Windows and the Mac OS, the printer and paper type should match the printer profile you have downloaded and installed (see page 11).

5. Click OK/Save to close the print dialog for your operating system and return to the Photoshop Print Settings dialog. Keep the latter dialog open and follow the steps on the next page to choose print settings for Photoshop.

➤ The gray background in the preview matches the current background in the Photoshop document window. If you want to change that shade, right-click the gray area in the preview and choose a shade from the context menu.

A This is the Print Settings > [Print Name] Properties dialog for an Epson printer in Windows 8. We chose a Quality Option and Paper Options.

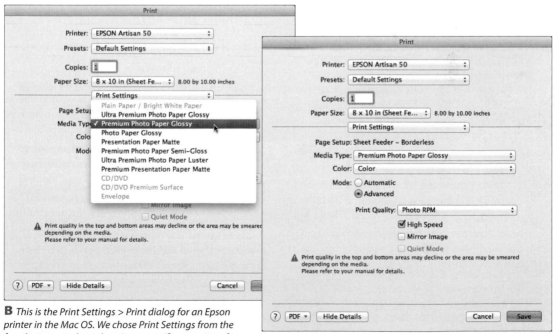

B This is the Print Settings > Print dialog for an Epson printer in the Mac OS. We chose Print Settings from the fourth menu, and are choosing a specific paper type from the Media Type menu.

C Next, in the same dialog, we clicked Mode: Advanced and chose a Print Quality option.

Phase 2

After choosing print settings as described on the preceding two pages, the next step is to choose color management, position, scale, and other output options in the Photoshop Print Settings dialog.

To choose Photoshop print settings:

1. In the Photoshop Print Settings dialog (**A**, next page), click the portrait 🖼 or landscape 🖼 **Layout** button.

2. Expand the **Color Management** category. The current document profile is listed at the top.

   From the **Color Handling** menu, choose **Photoshop Manages Colors** to let Photoshop handle the color conversion, for optimal color management (see the sidebar on the next page).

3. From the **Printer Profile** menu, choose the custom printer/ink/paper profile that you downloaded from the printer or paper manufacturer's website and installed in your system (see page 11). This is the last phase of the color management workflow that you began in Chapter 1. Note: All installed profiles for the currently selected printer are listed on the top part of the menu.

4. If the chosen device has the capacity to output a 16-bit file (and your document is 16-bit), you can check **Send 16-Bit Data** to produce a print with finer details and smoother color gradations.

5. From the next menu, choose **Normal Printing**.

   From the **Rendering Intent** menu, choose the same intent that you used when you created the soft-proof setting for your inkjet printer, which most likely was either Perceptual or Relative Colorimetric (see the sidebar on page 475).

   ➤ You can run one test print for the Perceptual intent and one for the Relative Colorimetric intent, and see which one yields better results.

6. Check **Black Point Compensation**. This option maps the full color range of the document profile to the full range of the printer profile, to preserve shadow details and the darkest blacks.

7. Scroll down and expand the **Position and Size** category.

   Under Position, check **Center** to print the image in the center of the paper. Or to reposition the image on the paper, uncheck Center and choose new Top and Left values (note the change in the preview) or drag the image in the preview.

8. *Optional:* To scale the print output slightly, under Scaled Print Size, do either of the following:

   Check **Scale to Fit Media** to fit the image automatically on the paper size you chose in step 4 on pages 476–477.

   Uncheck Scale to Fit Media, then change the **Scale** percentage or enter specific **Height** and **Width** values (you can change the unit via the Units menu). These three values are interdependent; changing one causes the other two to change.

   Note: Use these features to scale the print by only a small amount (i.e., a fraction of an inch or 5–10 percentage points). If a greater scale change is needed, cancel out of the dialog, use Image > Image Size to scale a copy of the file (see pages 139–141), then resharpen it.

9. Uncheck **Print Selected Area** to reset the margins to the chosen paper size, or check it to adjust the margins for the current printout. If you check this option, drag a margin control ▼ to adjust the top, bottom, left, or right margin for the printout; or Alt/Option-drag a margin control to move the top and bottom, or left and right, margins in unison; or Ctrl/Cmd-drag a margin control to move all four margins simultaneously.

10. Below the preview, do the following:

    Check **Match Print Colors** to display a color-managed soft proof of the image in the preview, based on the current printing device and profile settings.

    Uncheck **Gamut Warning**. Monitoring out-of-gamut colors (shown as gray in the preview) is beneficial only when printing to a commercial CMYK printer.

    Check **Show Paper White** to have Photoshop simulate the paper color in any white areas in the preview, based on the current printer profile.

11. To print the image, do either of the following:

    In the Mac OS, click **Print**.

    In Windows, verify that **color management** has been turned off for your printer (see page 481).

    ➤ To save all of your settings for the current file and close the dialog without printing, click Done in the Photoshop Print Settings dialog, then save your file.

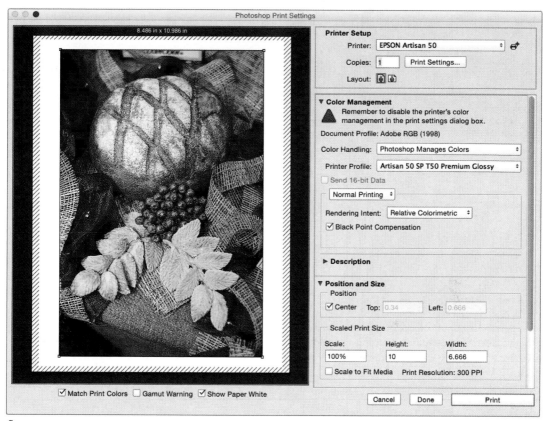

A *Choose settings in the various expandable categories in the Photoshop Print Settings dialog.*

BENEFITS TO LETTING PHOTOSHOP MANAGE YOUR DOCUMENT COLORS

Via the Color Handling menu of the Photoshop Print Settings dialog, you can opt to have Photoshop or your printing device manage the document colors. What's the difference?

➤ If you choose Photoshop Manages Colors (the option we recommend), you will be able to select a profile that matches the paper type you selected in the Print Settings dialog. Choose either the printer and paper profile that you downloaded from your paper or print manufacturer's website or a profile that was installed for your printing device. Photoshop will adjust your document colors to fit that profile, then send the data to the printer. Using the profile preserves your color-managed workflow and allows Photoshop to produce the best possible color.

➤ If you choose Printer Manages Colors, the printer driver will handle the color conversion instead of Photoshop. This may limit the print quality, for two reasons. First, the printer won't be aware of your custom paper choice and custom printer profile. And second, the color conversion will be subject to the printer's ability to convert colors rather than the color management settings you have established. If you're still not convinced that it's a good idea to avoid this setting, at least resist the temptation to adjust the amount of individual ink colors used by the printer (in the Print Settings dialog), which would override the printer settings.

CHOOSING OUTPUT OPTIONS

Options for commercial printing on a PostScript printer are found in the Printing Marks and PostScript Options categories in the Photoshop Print Settings dialog. Some of the Printing Marks options are listed (and illustrated) below; for other options, see Photoshop Help.

In the Printing Marks category, check any of these options:

➤ **Corner Crop Marks** and **Center Crop Marks** print short little lines that a print shop uses as guide lines when trimming the final print.

➤ **Registration Marks** prints marks that a print shop uses to align color separations.

➤ **Description** prints user data below the image. Click Edit in this category to enter or edit a description (you can also enter data in the Description field of the Description tab in the File > File Info dialog).

➤ **Labels** prints the file name on each page (outside the image area).

These three options in the PostScript Options category pertain only to PostScript printing:

➤ **Calibration Bars** prints a grayscale and/or color calibration strip outside the image area.

➤ **Include Vector Data** prints vector objects (such as type, shapes, or imported vector art) at the printer resolution, not at the document resolution. This option is checked automatically (and should be kept checked) if the file contains type or vector art.

➤ Keep **Interpolation** unchecked.

To specify a bleed width for your document:

Click Bleed in the Functions category, then specify a distance (0–3 inches). Crop marks will be placed within the image area at that specified distance from the outer edge of the image.

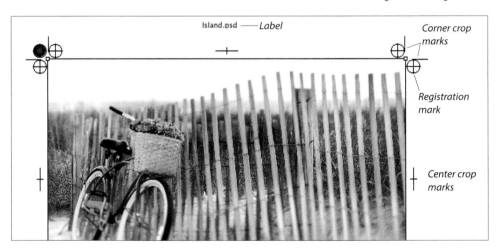

Island.psd —— *Label*

Corner crop marks

Registration mark

Center crop marks

OUTPUTTING A QUASI HARD PROOF

To output a simulation of output (a quasi "hard" proof) to a desktop printer, expand the Color Management category in the Photoshop Print Settings dialog and choose Hard Proofing from the menu. From the Proof Setup menu, choose the soft-proof setup that you created by following the steps on page 475. Check Simulate Paper Color to preview the white of the paper as defined in the chosen printer profile, or uncheck this option and check Simulate Black Ink to preview the full range of black values as defined by the printer profile.

Color Handling: Photoshop Manages Colors
Printer Profile: Canon iP6600D PR1
☐ Send 16-bit Data
Hard Proofing
Proof Setup: Web coated Swop
Proofing Profile: U.S. Web Coated (SWOP) v2
☑ Simulate Paper Color ☑ Simulate Black Ink

Phase 3

The final step before outputting a file to an inkjet printer is to verify that color management is turned off for that device, to enable Photoshop to manage the color conversion from RGB color to actual inks. (Remember, you chose Photoshop Manages Colors in step 2 on page 478.) Note: Mac OS users, choosing Photoshop Manages Colors turns off the color management settings for the printer driver automatically.

Color management options in any print dialog vary depending on the printer driver for the chosen output device, and on the operating system. In the following tasks, we describe how to verify that color management is turned off for an Epson printer. If your printer is a different brand, or you see different options in a dialog, use these steps as general guidelines.

Windows: To verify that color management is turned off for your printer, then print the file:

1. In the Photoshop Print Settings dialog, click **Print Settings** to get to the [Printer Name] Properties dialog for your Windows system.

2. Click the **Advanced** tab.**A** These options include controls for color management. (Your dialog may have a Paper/Quality tab with an Advanced button.)

3. In the Color Management area, click **ICM**, if it's not already selected, to switch control of color management from the Epson driver to the color management system that's built into Windows.

4. Below the ICM button, make sure **Off** (**No Color Adjustment**) is checked.**B**

5. Click OK to close the Properties dialog and return to the Photoshop Print Settings dialog.

6. Click **Print**. Phew! You made it.

Mac OS: To verify that color management is turned off:

1. In the Photoshop Print Settings dialog, click **Print Settings** to open the Print dialog for the Mac OS.

2. From the fourth menu, choose **Color Management**. (Your printer driver may list Color Options or another menu option name that involves color).

3. Verify that **Off** (**No Color Adjustment**) is selected. With color management turned off for the printer, depending on the printer model, the color controls and the Advanced Settings sliders either won't display at all or will be dimmed.

A *In the Print Settings > Properties dialog for an Epson printer in Windows, we clicked the Advanced tab to display these Color Management options.*

B *We verified that ICM was selected, and that Off (No Color Adjustment) was checked.*

Preparing a file for commercial printing

Computer monitors display additive colors by projecting red, green, and blue (RGB) light, whereas commercial presses print subtractive colors using CMYK (cyan, magenta, yellow, and black) and/or spot color (mixed) inks. Obtaining high-quality CMYK color reproduction from a commercial press is an art that takes experience and know-how.

When preparing a file to be sent to a print shop for output to a commercial press, you need to establish the correct CMYK working space in Photoshop. Ask your print shop to give you the necessary color settings file, then be sure to save it in the correct folder (see page 11) so it's available in the Color Settings dialog for the CMYK conversion.

To convert your file from RGB to CMYK Color mode:

1. Use the File > Save As dialog to save a flattened copy of your file (uncheck the Layers option).

2. Choose Edit > **Color Settings** (Ctrl-Shift-K/ Cmd-Shift-K).

3. To specify which profile will be used to control the conversion of your image to CMYK Color mode, do one of the following:

    From the **Settings** menu, choose the .csf profile that you received from your commercial printer and installed in your system.

    Click **Load**, locate the .csf profile that you received from your commercial printer and copied to your hard drive, then click Open.

    In the Working Spaces area, from the **CMYK** menu, choose either the .icc prepress profile that you received from your print shop, or the predefined profile your print shop says is the closest match to their press and paper.**A**

4. Click OK.

5. Choose Image > Mode > **CMYK Color**. If an alert appears, click OK.

6. Save the file.

A WORKFLOW FOR COMMERCIAL, FOUR-COLOR PRINTING

The steps needed to prepare a file for commercial printing are too complex to be covered fully in this *QuickStart Guide*, but we offer this summary:

1. Make sure your display is properly calibrated, and that you have established all the necessary color settings (see Chapter 1).

2. Ask your commercial print shop what type of press and lines-per-inch setting will be used to print your document and what settings they recommend you choose in Photoshop, such as the resolution, file format, and color mode. Save the file according to their specs.

3. Ask your commercial printer to supply you with a printer profile for their press, ink, and paper, then load it into the Color Settings dialog (see page 11).

4. Use the printer profile to create a custom proof condition, and view a soft (onscreen) proof of the image for that specific press (see page 475).

5. Save a copy of the file in the requested format.

6. Convert your RGB files to CMYK, using the printer profile from your print shop.

7. Make any final tonal adjustments (e.g., to the midtones or contrast) and any final color adjustments.

8. Sharpen the image (see pages 344–348).

9. Have your print shop output a CMYK color proof for you to analyze. If it looks good, the document is good to go. If not, tweak it based on the problems you noted in the proof, then print and analyze another proof.

A *In the Color Settings dialog, from the CMYK menu in the Workspace Spaces area, choose the correct CMYK profile.*

Saving a file in the PDF format

PDF (Portable Document Format) files can be opened in many Windows and Macintosh applications and in all of the Acrobat programs (Adobe Reader, Acrobat Standard, and Acrobat Pro). This format saves 8-bit and 16-bit files (but not 32-bit files) in any color mode except Multichannel.

If you want to preserve image, font, layer, and vector data in the PDF file, and have it include just one image, you should check Preserve Photoshop Editing Capabilities in the Save Adobe PDF dialog. If you need to save multiple images in one PDF file, see "Creating a PDF presentation of images" in the bonus chapter (Presentation).

If you want Photoshop to produce a generic PDF file, similar to a PDF that is produced by a drawing or page layout application, uncheck the Preserve Photoshop Editing Capabilities option. The image will be flattened and rasterized, so your ability to re-edit it in Photoshop will be very limited.

To save a file in the PDF format:

1. Choose File > **Save As**, enter a file name or keep the current name in the File Name/Save As field, choose a location for the file, choose Save As Type/ Format: **Photoshop PDF**, then click Save. If an alert dialog appears, click OK.

2. From the **Adobe PDF Preset** menu in the Save Adobe PDF dialog, **A** choose a preset that's best suited to your target output medium.

   Note: The High Quality Print and Press Quality presets produce a large Photoshop PDF file, compress the file using JPEG compression and an Image Quality setting of Maximum, embed all fonts automatically, and preserve transparency. The Preserve Photoshop Editing Capabilities option is checked. For commercial printing, ask your shop for advice regarding these settings.

   High Quality Print (the default preset) creates PDF files that are suitable for desktop printers and color proofing devices. The color conversion is handled by the printer driver. The file won't be PDF/X-compliant (see the PDF/X presets below).

   Press Quality is designed for high-quality prepress output. Colors are converted to CMYK.

   Note: Preserve Photoshop Editing Capabilities isn't available for the PDF/X presets and is unchecked for the Smallest File Size preset, so these presets produce generic PDF files:

   PDF/X-1a:2001, **PDF/X-3:2002**, and **PDF/X-4: 2008** create PDF files that will be checked for compliance with specific printing standards, to help prevent printing errors.

   Smallest File Size uses high levels of JPEG compression to produce very compact PDF files for output to the Web and mobile devices. All colors are converted to sRGB.

3. Click Save PDF, then click Yes if an alert dialog appears.

➤ To learn more about the PDF format, see Photoshop Help.

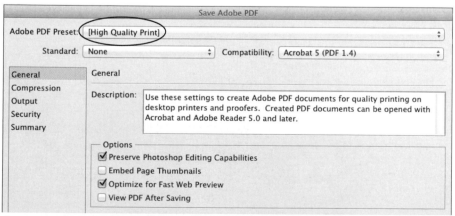

A *In the Save Adobe PDF dialog, choose a preset from the Adobe PDF Preset menu.*

Getting Photoshop files into Adobe InDesign and Illustrator

Photoshop to Adobe InDesign

Files in the Photoshop PSD and Photoshop PDF formats can be imported directly into Adobe InDesign using the File > **Place** command.

InDesign can color-separate RGB and CMYK files, it can read embedded ICC color profiles, and it works with Bridge, for file and color management. Photoshop layers (and layer comps) are preserved, and you can turn their visibility on or off in InDesign; alpha channels, layer masks, and transparency are also preserved. If you want to import just an area of a Photoshop image into InDesign, see our easy steps on the next page.

Photoshop to Adobe Illustrator

Here are some ways to get Photoshop content into Illustrator:

Method 1 ★

In Photoshop, use the Move tool ▶⊕ to drag a layer or layer group into the **Libraries panel**, then in Illustrator, drag the graphics asset from the Libraries panel into the document. Opacity settings are reset to 100% (but are preserved visually). Nondefault blending modes are ignored and any masks are applied. Type or shape assets containing layer effects are rasterized. Hold down Alt/Option, then drag a type or shape asset (containing no layer effects) to place it as type or a vector shape (whose opacity is preserved). Library Character Styles assets can be applied to Illustrator type.

Method 2

Arrange your Photoshop and Illustrator windows so they're both visible. Select one or more layers on the Layers panel. With the Move tool, ▶⊕ **drag and drop** the layer(s) from the Photoshop document window (not the layer listing) into the Illustrator document. Opacity settings are reset to 100% (but are preserved visually), nondefault blending modes are ignored, and any masks are applied. Type and vector shapes are rasterized.

Method 3

Select all or part of an image layer in Photoshop, **copy** it, then **paste** it into Illustrator. The effects of any layer or vector masks, nondefault blending modes, and opacity settings are ignored.

Method 4

In Illustrator, use File > **Place** to import either a whole Photoshop image or one layer comp. If you place a Photoshop image with the Link option checked, the image will appear on the Layers panel on a single image layer, and any masks will be applied. If you embed the Photoshop image as you place it (uncheck the Link option), then Shift-click in the document with the loaded graphics pointer, you will be given the option via the Photoshop Import Options dialog to **Convert Layers to Objects (Make Text Editable Where Possible)** or **Flatten Layers to a Single Image (Preserves Text Appearance)**.

If you click Convert Layers to Objects, each Photoshop layer will appear on a separate nested layer within a group. Opacity values are preserved, whereas only the blending modes that have matching names on the Transparency panel in Illustrator will remain editable in Illustrator. Both transparency and modes are listed as editable appearances. Layer masks become opacity masks. Layer effects are applied to the layer, and their visual appearance is preserved.

If you click Flatten Layers to a Single Image, the effect of all opacity settings, blending modes, and layer masks will be preserved visually, but won't be editable in Illustrator.

Check **Import Hidden Layers** if you want to place any hidden image layers from the Photoshop file.

Notes

➤ If a Photoshop file contains visible adjustment layers, or a layer that contains layer effects, those layers won't arrive as individual layers when opened or placed into Illustrator. Before importing the file, hide or merge down any adjustment layers, and reset the blending mode to Normal.

➤ Any type or shape layer that contains layer effects will be rasterized. Delete those layer effects before placing the file.

➤ Via the Effect menu in Illustrator, Photoshop (raster) effects and Illustrator (vector) effects can be applied to an imported Photoshop image.

➤ A layer mask in the Photoshop document won't convert to an opacity mask in Illustrator if the layer containing the mask also contains layer effects.

➤ When you open or place a TIFF or PSD file into Illustrator, it adopts the color mode of the Illustrator file automatically.

To place just a portion of a Photoshop PSD image into InDesign or Illustrator, you need to either isolate that area onto a separate layer or use a layer mask.

To isolate part of an image layer in Photoshop:

1. Do either of the following:

   Select an area of a layer, then click the **Add Layer Mask** button (Layers panel) to create a layer mask.**A**

   Select the area to be isolated, and put it on its own layer by pressing Ctrl-J/Cmd-J.**B**

2. Using File > Save As, save a copy of the file in the Photoshop format. In the dialog, check As a Copy and keep Layers checked.

3. Follow the steps on this page for InDesign or Illustrator.

To place a Photoshop layer into InDesign:

1. In InDesign, open or create a document, then choose File > **Place**. In the Place dialog, click the

Photoshop file, uncheck Show Import Options, then click Open. Drag with the loaded graphics pointer.

2. Choose Object > **Object Layer Options**.

3. In the dialog, check Preview, show the layer that contains transparency or a mask, hide all other layers (click their visibility icons), then click OK.

To open or place Photoshop layers into Illustrator:

1. In Illustrator, do either of the following:

   Use File > **Open** to open the Photoshop file.

   Open a file, then use File > **Place** to import the Photoshop file (Link option unchecked). In the document, Shift-click with the loaded graphics pointer.

2. The Photoshop Import Options dialog opens. Click **Convert Layers to Objects**, then click OK. The Open command converts each Photoshop layer to a separate layer in Illustrator, whereas the Place command nests the layers within a group.**C–D**

A *In Photoshop, we hid part of an image layer via a layer mask.*

B *Alternatively, we could have copied a selected area to a new layer.*

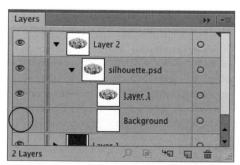

C *In Illustrator, we used the Place command to import the Photoshop file, then clicked the visibility icon on the Layers panel to hide the Background.*

D *This is how the imported Photoshop file looks in Illustrator (you have to take our word for it!).*

Saving a file in the TIFF format

TIFF files can be imported into most applications and are usable in many color management scenarios. If your target application can't read a Photoshop PSD or Photoshop PDF file, this is the next best option. InDesign can color-separate a CMYK color TIFF.

Note: Most other applications can't read a TIFF file that is larger than 2 GB.

To save a file in the TIFF format:

1. If your document will be printed on a four-color press and your commercial printer requests that you convert it to CMYK Color mode, choose Image > Mode > CMYK Color (see page 482).

2. Choose File > **Save As**, enter a name or keep the current one, choose Save as Type/Format: **TIFF**, and choose a location for the file.

3. In the Save area:

   Check **As a Copy** to keep the existing file open onscreen and save a copy of it to disk.

   Uncheck **Layers** to flatten the file. Note that most other image or layout programs can't work with layered TIFFs and will either flatten the layers or ignore the layer data.

   If you need to save **Alpha Channels**, **Notes**, or **Spot Colors** in the file, check any of those options.

4. Check ICC Profile/Embed Color Profile to include any embedded color profile with the file.

5. Click Save. The TIFF Options dialog opens.**A**

6. If the file is going to be color-separated (e.g., from InDesign), under **Image Compression**, click None (output service providers prefer to receive uncompressed files). If you need to reduce the storage size of the file, click LZW or ZIP; these methods are non-lossy, meaning that they don't discard image data. Note that some programs can't read a ZIP-compressed TIFF, so that's something to investigate. Avoid the JPEG compression option, which causes data loss.

   Leave **Save Image Pyramid** unchecked.

   Under **Pixel Order**, keep the default setting of Interleaved (RGBRGB).

   Under **Byte Order**, click IBM PC or Macintosh, for the platform on which the file will be used.

   If the bottommost layer in the file is a layer (not a Background), and has an Opacity setting below 100% and/or contains some transparent pixels, you can preserve that transparency by checking **Save Transparency**. In the alert dialog, click Yes.

7. Click OK.

A *This is the TIFF Options dialog in the Mac OS.*

IMAGE PROCESSOR COMMAND

Use the Image Processor command to quickly save copies of multiple files in a different format.

► In Bridge, open a folder of images, then choose Tools > Photoshop > Image Processor.

► In the dialog, choose a location to save for the processed files (same location or another folder), check a file type format, and choose settings.

► Click Run. Processed files will display in the folder location chosen above.

Exporting image assets from Photoshop layers

Comparing formats used for exporting files to the Web and mobile devices

Using the Export As or Quick Export commands, ★ you can create a file in the GIF, JPEG, PNG, or SVG* file format from a Photoshop layer or document, for output to the Web or mobile devices.

Below is a comparison of these file formats.

GIF

➤ GIF preserves flat colors and sharp edges of a layer (such as a type or shape layer) better than JPEG, although not as well as SVG.

➤ GIF is an 8-bit format, meaning it's limited to no more than 256 colors in a file. It's a good choice for a layer that contains a small number of solid colors.

➤ GIF preserves existing transparency in an image or gradient layer, but transitions between opaque and transparent areas won't be smooth.

JPEG

➤ The JPEG format preserves the full 24-bit color depth — and therefore the color fidelity — of photos, gradients, and other continuous-tone image layers.

➤ The JPEG format can shrink an image significantly. Specifying a lower quality setting increases the compression and also the data loss; higher quality settings result in less compression but larger file sizes. The ultimate goal is to produce a file that downloads quickly while keeping its quality as high as possible.

➤ The JPEG format doesn't preserve transparency.

PNG

➤ PNG doesn't cause data loss (it's "lossless").

➤ The PNG format supports bit-depth values of 8, 24, and 32. If you generate a file from a continuous-tone layer and assign it an 8-bit depth, no more than 256 colors will be preserved, whereas if you assign the file a bit depth of 24 or 32, the original color fidelity will be preserved.

➤ The PNG format preserves existing transparency in an image by using an alpha channel. A PNG

file that you assign an 8-bit depth will have non-smooth transitions between opaque and transparent areas. A PNG file that you assign a 24- or 32-bit depth will have smooth transitions between those areas, making this file format the best choice for a layer that contains a transparent background.

SVG

➤ Unlike the three bitmap formats described above, SVG is vector based, making it the best choice for generating files from shape layers.

➤ SVG files are not only compact, but also resolution independent, meaning that they output at the resolution of the current output medium — whether that medium is the Web, a mobile device, or a printing device.

Exporting layers or an entire document ★

The Export As command provides a visual interface that enables you to quickly export a PNG, JPEG, GIF, or SVG file from the content of one or more selected layers, layer groups, artboards, or an entire document.

The Export As dialog provides a preview of each selected layer (or the entire document), a menu for easily choosing file formats and settings, and options for applying custom Image Size and Canvas Size settings to each exported file. Settings applied in the dialog do not affect the original Photoshop file.

The Quick Export As [format] command (page 489) provides a quick, one-step way to export selected layers or an entire document using the current image size and canvas size of the file. No dialog will display.

These methods for exporting layer content (or a document) to separate files are faster than manually copying layer content into separate files. You can place the exported files into programs that generate output for Web or mobile devices.

Note: Options for including color profiles and metadata via the export commands will be added in a future release of Photoshop CC.

Continued on the following page

In case you're wondering, GIF stands for Graphics Interchange Format, JPEG stands for Joint Photographic Experts Group (the group that created the format), PNG stands for Portable Network Graphics, and SVG stands for Scalable Vector Graphics.

To export selected layers or a document via Export As: ★

1. Open your PSD design file. Place multiple layers that make up a design element into a layer group. Clip any adjustment layer to the layer below. Rasterize any Fill layers.

2. Do either of the following:

   To export layers, on the Layers panel, ▰ Ctrl-click/Cmd-click each layer, layer group, and/or artboard you want to export. Right-click a selected layer, then choose Export As from the context menu.

   To export the entire document, or only the artboards in a file, choose File > Export > **Export As.**

3. In the Export As dialog, **A** click a layer listing in the column on the left to preview it. In the column on the right, do any of the following:

   Under File Settings, from the **Format** menu, choose a file format. For PNG (actually PNG-24), check Transparency; for JPG, choose a quality setting (the higher the setting, the larger the file size).

   Under Image Size, enter a value in the **Width** or **Height** field for the size of the exported asset.

Enter a value in one field, then press Tab to have the proportional value entered into the other field. Or choose a value below or above 100% from the **Scale** menu. Choose an option from the **Resample** menu to help preserve image quality when resizing (we recommend choosing Bicubic Automatic, which lets Photoshop determine the best bicubic method).

Under Canvas Size, enter values in the **Width** and/or **Height** fields to increase or reduce the amount of canvas or transparency around the image (helpful when assets, such as icons or buttons, need to be a specific overall size). To "crop" the exported image, reduce the Width and/or Height values (**A**, next page). Click **Reset** to restore the original canvas size for that asset.

4. Click **Export.** In the Export To Folder dialog, keep the current location, then click Export. A flattened file for each selected layer or group, or for the entire document, will be placed in a generated folder named "[Photoshop file name] – assets" that displays next to your Photoshop file in Bridge or in Explorer/Finder.

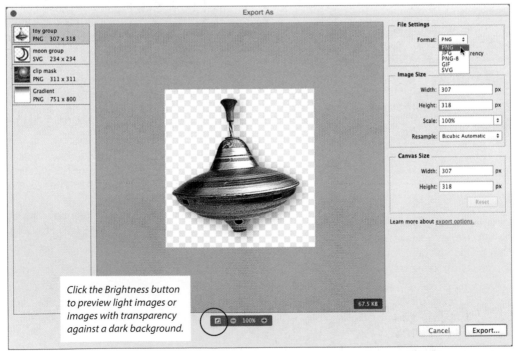

Click the Brightness button to preview light images or images with transparency against a dark background.

A *In the Export As dialog, the selected layers from the PSD document are displayed as a list in the column on the left. The selected layer in the list displays in the preview.*

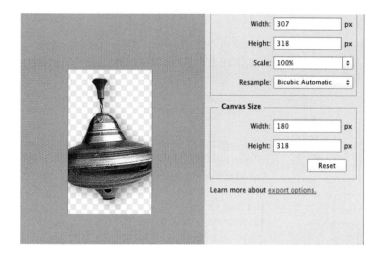

A *Under Canvas Size, we lowered the Width value to crop the image in the exported file.*

To export selected layers or a document via Quick Export: ★

1. Choose File > Export > **Export Preferences**. In the Export panel (Preferences dialog), do the following:

   Under Quick Export Format, choose a file **format** from the menu. (The chosen format will be listed in the command name.)

   Under Quick Export Location, choose **Export Files to an Assets Folder Next to the Current Document**. (We prefer this option because it places all quick exports from the current file in one folder and bypasses the Save As dialog both when initially exporting content and then when re-exporting the same content after editing it. The other location option causes the Save As dialog to open every time.)

2. In your PSD design file, do either of the following:

   To export layers, on the Layers panel, ⬛ Ctrl-click/Cmd-click each layer, layer group, and/or artboard you want to export. Right-click a selected layer, then choose **Quick Export As [format]** from the context menu.

   To export the entire document, or only the artboards in a file, choose File > Export > **Quick Export As [format]**.

3. The exported file(s) will be placed in a generated folder named "[Photoshop file name] – assets" that displays next to your Photoshop file in Bridge or in Explorer/Finder.**B**

B *We used Quick Export, with the Export preference set to Export Files to an Assets Folder Next to the Current Document, to export selected layers. The newly generated assets folder and its contents are shown at left in a Mac OS Finder window.*

Extracting image assets from Photoshop layers

To prepare a PSD file for the Creative Cloud Extract feature: ★

1. Open your PSD web design file. Use the File > **Save As** dialog to save a copy of the file.

2. In the **copy** of your file, do the following:

   In Preferences > Units & Rulers, set both the Rulers and Type fields to pixels.

   If you plan to scale an image layer for viewing on a HiDPI or Retina display, convert the layer to an embedded Smart Object to prevent a loss of quality when scaling. Next, double-click the Smart Object thumbnail, then use Image Size to set the resolution to 72 ppi and enter width and height values that are twice the amount needed for the standard web layout (see pages 139–140). Save and close the embedded file. Remember, the pixel dimensions (not resolution) determine how large an image will look in a browser or mobile device.

   Set the resolution of the PSD file to 72 ppi and the width and height to the size of your web page (see the second task on page 141).

   Clip any adjustment layer to the layer below. Place multiple layers (including adjustment layers) that make up a design element into a layer group.**A**

   Make sure the name of each layer and layer group is unique and descriptive.

   Use the Free Transform tool and the transformation readouts by the pointer to scale each image and shape layer to the proper pixel dimensions for the web layout. Select any type and remove any fractional pixel values that display in the Font Size field on the Options bar.

   If you want to extract a type layer in the SVG format, apply Convert to Shape to a **copy** of the type layer. In the Creative Cloud Extract feature, you will be able to save the shape layer in the SVG format (see pages 492–493).

3. Save the file, then proceed with the next task.

A *When creating a web page design (shown at left), we put layers that make up a design element into a layer group and assigned a descriptive name to each layer and group.*

You can sync your PSD file to your Creative Cloud Assets page to share it with Web developers who can view, copy data, and extract downloadable assets. People who share your PSD file and assets don't need to sign in to a Creative Cloud account. People who collaborate on a folder of assets will need to sign in, however.

To sync a PSD file or folder to Creative Cloud and enable collaboration: ★

1. Copy your PSD file to your User/[username]/ **Creative Cloud Files** folder.

2. Click the Creative Cloud icon on your taskbar/ menu bar, then under Assets, click **Files**.

Click **View on Web.A** (Sign in, if necessary.)

3. On your **Assets** page (My Assets section), do either of the following:

Click the arrowhead below a file thumbnail, then choose **Send Link.B** In the widget that opens, click Create Public Link. Click Advanced Options and confirm that Allow Use of Extract is checked. Enter the email address for your Web developer, then click **Send Link**.

Click the arrowhead below a folder thumbnail, then choose **Collaborate.C** In the widget that opens, enter the email address for your Web developer, then click **Invite** to invite them to work with assets in the folder.

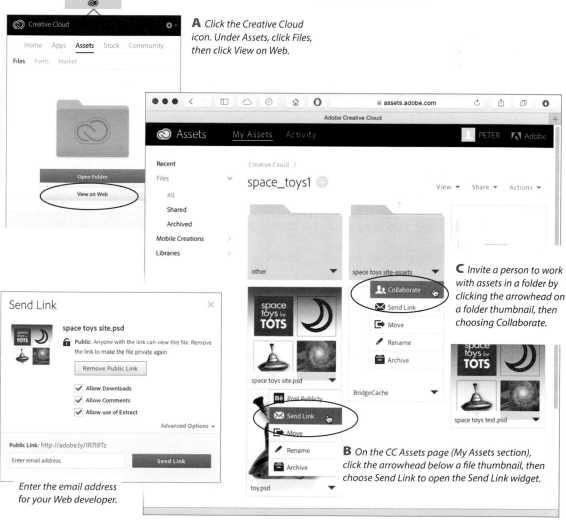

A *Click the Creative Cloud icon. Under Assets, click Files, then click View on Web.*

C *Invite a person to work with assets in a folder by clicking the arrowhead on a folder thumbnail, then choosing Collaborate.*

Enter the email address for your Web developer.

B *On the CC Assets page (My Assets section), click the arrowhead below a file thumbnail, then choose Send Link to open the Send Link widget.*

To work with the Creative Cloud Extract feature: ★

1. Display your **Creative Cloud Assets** page (My Assets section) (see step 2 on the previous page).

2. Click the PSD thumbnail of your design to display it in **Extract** view.**A**

3. Click an object in the preview, then do any of the following:

   In the blue **Info panel** for that object, click a **field** to copy that data (including text or CSS) to the Clipboard. You or your Web developer can click the down arrow ⬇ to display the **Save as Image** widget for choosing a file format and a scale

setting. Click Save to save an asset. Click away from the widget to cancel.

Shift-click another object to display a small black readout of the distances between the objects or to the edge of the canvas. Click a field in the readout to copy that value. Shift-click to deselect the other object.

On the right side of the page, click **Styles**. Scroll down the panel to view CSS, font, and color data. You or your Web developer can click Copy All to copy data — particularly type data — in the CSS Inspector to the Clipboard. Click either a font size, or a color swatch to display its data. Click Copy (press Ctrl-C/Cmd-C for color data) to copy the data to the Clipboard.

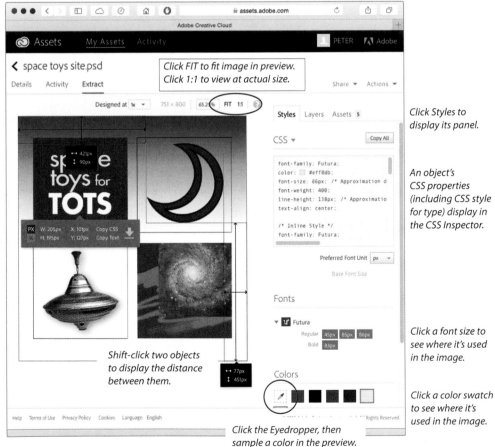

Click an object to view its blue info panel.

Click a field on the blue panel to copy the data to the Clipboard.

Shift-click two objects to display the distance between them.

Click FIT to fit image in preview.
Click 1:1 to view at actual size.

Click Styles to display its panel.

An object's CSS properties (including CSS style for type) display in the CSS Inspector.

Click a font size to see where it's used in the image.

Click a color swatch to see where it's used in the image.

Click the Eyedropper, then sample a color in the preview.

A The Styles panel in Extract view for a selected Creative Cloud file.

4. Click **Layers.A** Click a visibility icon to hide/show a layer in the preview. Click a folder icon to expand/contract a layer group. Click the down arrow ⬇ to display the same **Save as Image** widget (described in the previous step) for saving an asset. Click away from the widget to cancel.

   If you converted a copy of a type layer into shapes (see step 2 on page 490), save the type layer as a PNG asset and the shape layer as an SVG asset.

5. Click **Assets** to display a list of saved assets from steps 3 and 4 above. Click an asset thumbnail or the blue down arrow to download the asset to your computer. Click ⚙ to open the Edit Image Properties widget (containing the same options

as in the Save as Image widget). Click ❌ to delete that asset.

Click **Show Files** to open a new browser page as either a tab or a window. The page will display the auto-generated "[PSD file name]-assets" folder that contains a file for each extracted asset listed on the Assets panel. Close the browser tab or window when done.

6. Click the **back arrow** to the left of the file name (below the menu bar) to return to your Creative Cloud Assets page and the All Files view of thumbnails. The auto-generated "assets" folder will display next to the Photoshop file thumbnail.

➤ The CC Extract feature doesn't alter the PSD file.

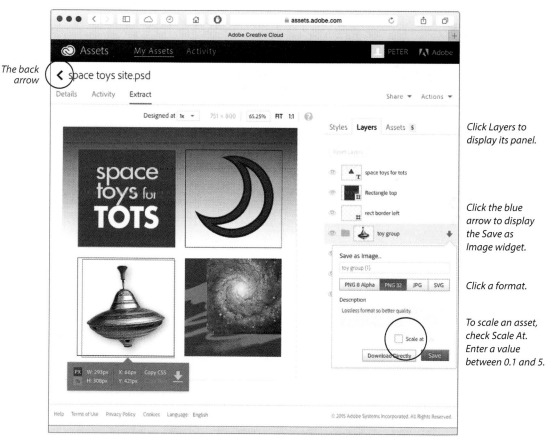

The back arrow

Click Layers to display its panel.

Click the blue arrow to display the Save as Image widget.

Click a format.

To scale an asset, check Scale At. Enter a value between 0.1 and 5.

A The Layers panel in Extract view for a selected Creative Cloud file.

You can easily generate scaled copies of **all** the assets listed in the Assets panel. Use this method to scale assets for viewing on a HiDPI or Retina display.

To specify multiple scales for all assets: ★

1. After creating assets in the CC Assets page Extract view, click the Assets tab, then click **Extract for Devices.A**

2. In the Extract for Devices widget, under the **Extract As** column, check one or more resolution-specific **scale** listings to enable/disable them.

3. *Optional:* Change the **suffix** that will be added to each scaled asset file name to designate its extract as scale setting.

   Change the **name** of the **folder** that will contain the scaled asset files for an enabled scale setting.**B**

4. Click Apply. Creative Cloud will generate a separate folder for each scale setting you checked. The name of each folder will be either the default name or a custom name you entered in the previous step. The folder(s) will be in the "assets" folder automatically created by the Extract feature.

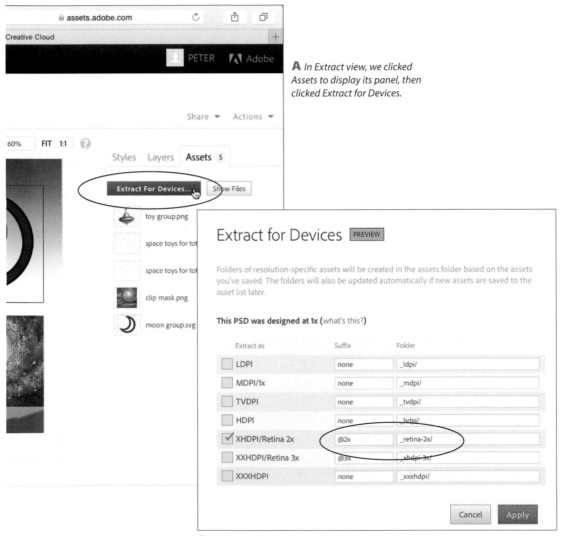

A *In Extract view, we clicked Assets to display its panel, then clicked Extract for Devices.*

B *In the Extract for Devices widget, we checked the scale setting for Retina 2x, kept the default suffix (that will display in the scaled asset name), and changed the name of the folder that will contain the Retina-scaled assets to "_retina-2x/."*

Syncing Photoshop settings via the Creative Cloud

Via the Adobe Creative Cloud, you can sync Photoshop presets and application preferences between two computers (e.g., a desktop computer and a laptop); manage your files (e.g., post them publicly); and view uploaded files on your CC Assets page.

Adobe permits each user to activate his or her licensed copy of Photoshop on two computers. For a more consistent workflow, you can sync your Photoshop presets, workspaces, preferences, and other settings to the Creative Cloud. You can then sync your settings from the Creative Cloud to any other computer on which you have signed in to your Creative Cloud account.

To upload settings from your current computer to the Creative Cloud:

1. Choose settings in the Preferences dialog and/or in any Photoshop panels or pickers. For example, you could add swatches to the Swatches panel or gradients to the Gradient preset picker, define custom shapes, create brushes or actions, or load Adobe default or user-created libraries onto any panels. You can also create and save custom workspaces.

2. To verify that you are signed in to your Creative Cloud account, click the Edit/Photoshop CC menu; your account name should be listed.

3. To choose or change which categories of settings are synced, choose Edit/Photoshop CC > Preferences > **Sync Settings.A** From the What to

Sync menu, choose **Everything** or **Custom**. If you chose Custom, check boxes for the categories of settings that you want to sync. Click **Upload**.

4. While the settings are being uploaded, a progress bar displays in the dialog. A list of the settings, and their individual time of upload, will appear in the **Log** window (the latest one is at the top of the list). The first time you upload settings to the Creative Cloud, all checked settings will be uploaded. On subsequent uploads, only checked settings that have been changed will be uploaded. Any existing presets and workspaces in the Creative Cloud that have the same names as those that are being uploaded will be overwritten with the settings from your current computer. Note: When you exit/ quit Photoshop, the Log window will be cleared.

5. Click OK.

➤ To upload Photoshop settings from your computer to the Creative Cloud at any time using the current What to Sync settings (bypassing the Preferences dialog), choose Edit/Photoshop CC > [your Adobe ID] > Upload Settings.

➤ To stop an upload (or download) while it's in progress, click Stop.

➤ Workspace settings that you create on one operating system can't be downloaded to a computer that is running a different operating system.

Continued on the following page

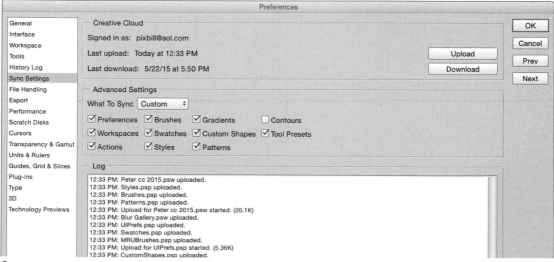

A *To upload our Photoshop settings to the Creative Cloud, we clicked Upload in the Sync Settings panel of the Preferences dialog.*

➤ If you need to deactivate the Sync Settings feature, from the What to Sync menu in the Sync Settings panel of the Preferences dialog, choose Nothing (all categories will be unchecked).

Once you have uploaded your settings from your first computer to the Creative Cloud, you can sync (download) those settings to another computer at any time.

Note: If any of your panels or pickers contain unsaved presets that you want to preserve, save them as a library before following the steps below (see page 133); otherwise, when you follow those steps, your unsaved presets will be overwritten with settings from the Creative Cloud. If you have made edits to any user-created preset library, save it under a new name. Also, if you have reconfigured any default or user-created workspace, save it under a new name (see page 108).

To download settings from the Creative Cloud to another computer:

1. On another computer, launch Photoshop, and verify that you're signed in to your Creative Cloud account.

2. Choose Edit/Photoshop CC > Preferences > **Sync Settings**. From the What to Sync menu, choose **Everything** or **Custom**. If you chose Custom, check the boxes for the categories of settings that you want to download.

3. Click **Download**. While the settings are being downloaded, a list of those settings, and their individual time of download, will appear in the **Log** window. Any existing presets and workspaces on your current computer that have the same names as those that are being downloaded will be replaced by the settings in the Creative Cloud.

4. Click OK.

➤ To download Photoshop settings from the Creative Cloud to your current computer at any time using the current What to Sync settings (bypassing the Preferences dialog), choose Edit/Photoshop CC > [your Adobe ID] > Download Settings.

VIEW CREATIVE CLOUD INFORMATION VIA THESE RESOURCE LINKS ★

➤ To display your Creative Profile widget and access links to Creative Cloud **Apps, Assets, Adobe Stock,** and **Community**, on your CC Assets page, click your name on the menu bar. In the widget, you can also click the **Manage Account** link to manage your account. Click one of the five category tabs, then choose account options to view and edit them.

➤ To display support resources, on any Creative Cloud web page, click **Adobe** on the menu bar. On the new web page, click **Menu**, then click the **Learn & Support** tab.

Managing files via the Creative Cloud

With a Creative Cloud account, you are allotted storage space to store your files (as of this writing, up to 20 GB). Once stored in the Creative Cloud, you can access the files from any computer, post them publicly, or share links to them via email. Note: The Assets > Files panel in the Creative Cloud desktop app lists how much of your Creative Cloud Storage is occupied.

To upload files to the Creative Cloud: ★

1. Click the Creative Cloud icon 🌀 on the taskbar/menu bar.

2. Click **Assets**, click **Files**, then click **View on Web**.

3. Your personal Creative Cloud **Assets** page (My Assets section) displays in your browser. Do any of the following:

From the Actions menu on the right side of the page, choose **Upload**. In the dialog, locate and click one or more file names, then click Choose. An uploading progress bar will display at the top of the page.

Drag a file thumbnail (or multiple selected thumbnails) from Bridge into the Creative Cloud Assets page window. An uploading progress bar will display at the top of the page.

Move your files into the **Creative Cloud Files** folder in your Users/[username] folder (see page 491).

4. A thumbnail for each uploaded file will display on your CC Assets page (My Assets section).

To share, rename, move, or archive files via the Creative Cloud: ★

1. Follow steps 1–2 in the preceding task.

2. From the View menu at the top right of your Assets page (My Assets section), choose **Mosaic**.

3. From the menu in the lower-right corner of any file thumbnail, choose one of these options: **A**

   To share the file via Behance, choose **Post Publicly** (if available for the current file format).

   To email a link to the file, choose **Send Link**. In the Send Link widget, click Create Public Link to unlock the file; expand Advanced Options, then check Allow Downloads, if desired; enter the email address of the recipient; then click Send Link.

   To put the file into a folder on your Assets page, choose **Move**, click a folder name in the widget,

then click Move [number of] Items. (If you need to create a new folder first, from the Actions menu on the right side of the page, choose Create Folder, enter a name, then click Create Folder.)

To rename the file, choose **Rename**, enter the desired name, then click Rename.

To archive the file (move it from your All Files view to the Archived view, for potential deletion from the Creative Cloud), click **Archive**, then click Archive again. To filter your Assets page to display the Archived view, click **Archived** on the categories list in the left column. Check the boxes next to the files that you want to delete or restore, click Permanently Delete or Restore (at the top of the list), then click the button of the same name. To filter your Assets page to display the All Files view again, click **All** on the categories list in the left column.**B**

A *You can post, send a link, move, rename, or archive any individual file on your Creative Cloud Assets page via commands on the menu in the lower-right corner of the file thumbnail.*

B *Click All on the categories list to filter the Creative Cloud Assets page to display the All Files view (as shown here).*

To manage an individual file via other commands on the Creative Cloud: ★

1. On your Creative Cloud Assets page (My Assets section), click a file thumbnail.

2. The file displays in an enlarged view. Click **Details** to display information about the file.**A** Do any of the following:

   Use the **Share** menu to access the Post Publicly and Send Link commands. Use the **Actions** menu to access the Download, Rename, Archive, and Replace commands.

   To load swatches of colors that are found in the current image into Adobe Color CC (color.adobe.com) — an Adobe web service used for browsing and creating color themes — click the swatches bar under **Made With**. The swatches will display on the Create page of the Adobe Color CC web site. See pages 210–212 to learn about working with color themes and Adobe Color CC.

3. Click **Activity** to display the Activity section, which lists any comments and/or prior revisions to the file. Do any of the following:

   To add a comment, click **Add Comment**, type your remarks, then click **Add Comment**. To delete a comment, roll over the comment and click the X, then click Delete Comment.

   To display prior revisions to the file, click a **Revised at [time]** listing below a specific date. If multiple revisions were done on a specific date, click **Multiple Revisions**, then click one of the revised listings. Click ⟳ to restore an older version, then in the widget, click Restore. To display the current version of the file, click **Current Version**.

4. To return to your CC Assets page All Files view, click the back arrow to the left of the file name.

To sign out of your Creative Cloud account:

Click your name on the menu bar, then in the widget click **Sign Out**. We recommend keeping yourself signed in when working on your own personal computer.

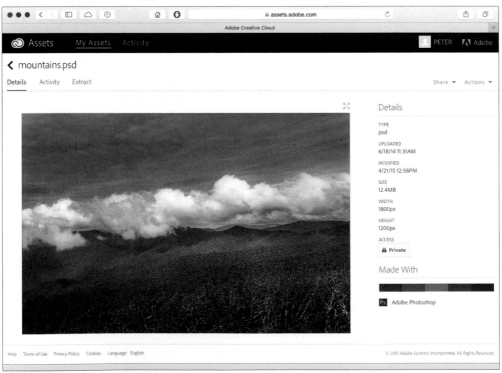

A *After clicking a file thumbnail on our Creative Cloud Assets page, an enlarged view of the image displayed. We clicked Details (at the top) to display information about the file.*

Previewing the Design Space interface

Adobe is previewing an alternate interface for Photoshop called Design Space.★ In Adobe's words, "It's a new, modern, and streamlined experience for Web and Mobile App Designers." Currently, a limited number of features are available in the four or five minimalist panels and in the menus. Being that this is a work in progress, the interface may grow over time.

Use the four screenshots (with callouts) below to become familiar with some of the panels in the interface. To turn on the Design Space preview, choose Edit/ Photoshop CC > Preferences > **Technology Previews**, and check **Enable Design Space (Preview)**. Click the **Switch to Design Space** button ▢ at the bottom of the Tools panel to display the alternate interface.

Design Space Preview

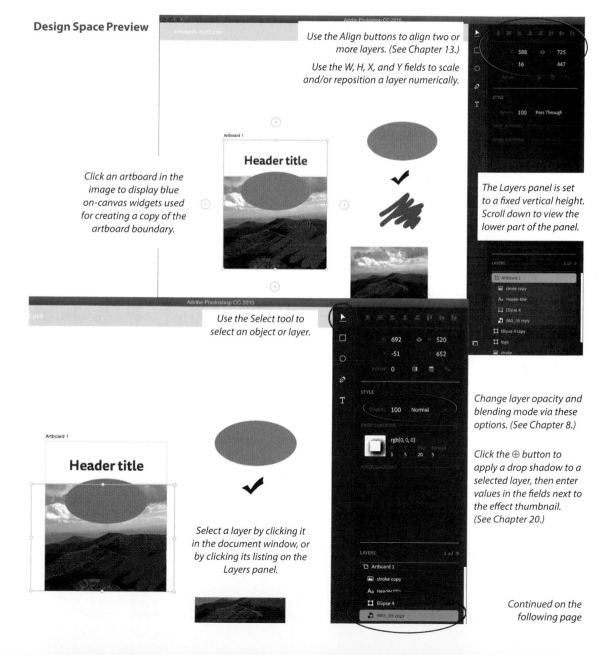

Use the Align buttons to align two or more layers. (See Chapter 13.)

Use the W, H, X, and Y fields to scale and/or reposition a layer numerically.

Click an artboard in the image to display blue on-canvas widgets used for creating a copy of the artboard boundary.

The Layers panel is set to a fixed vertical height. Scroll down to view the lower part of the panel.

Use the Select tool to select an object or layer.

Change layer opacity and blending mode via these options. (See Chapter 8.)

Click the ⊕ button to apply a drop shadow to a selected layer, then enter values in the fields next to the effect thumbnail. (See Chapter 20.)

Select a layer by clicking it in the document window, or by clicking its listing on the Layers panel.

Continued on the following page

Design Space Preview (continued)

Click the Select Previous or Select Next arrowhead to display another open Photoshop document.

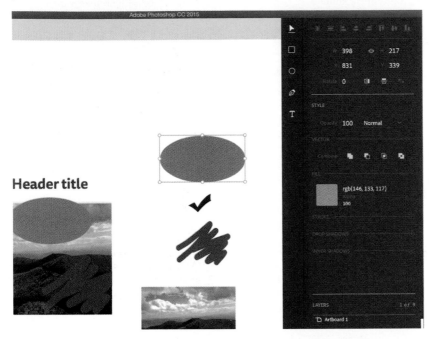

When a shape layer is selected, the Vector options of Combine, Fill, and Stroke display on the Style panel. (See Chapter 21.)

Click a thumbnail to set the fill color or stroke color.

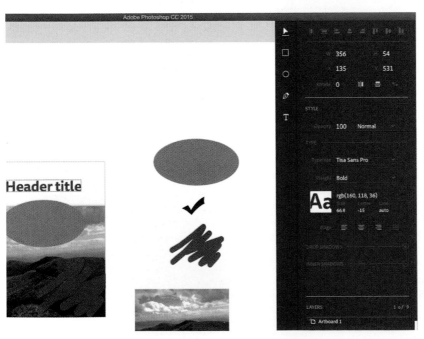

Choose the Type tool, then enter text. When a type layer is selected, the Type options display in the Style panel. (See Chapter 19.)

Click the thumbnail to set the text color.

Click this button (bottom of Tools panel) to return to Standard Photoshop.

Unless noted otherwise, the listings in this index pertain to Photoshop.

Photography credits

Shutterstock.com
Photographs on the following pages are © ShutterStock.com: 1, 2, 21, 22, 40, 44, 54, 55, 61, 66, 72, 75, 79, 82, 83, 88, 90, 97, 100, 103, 104, 137, 138, 140, 142, 143, 144, 145, 150, 152, 153, 160, 169, 170, 171, 172, 173, 174, 176, 177, 178, 180, 181, 182, 185, 186, 190, 191, 192, 202, 203, 204, 206, 213, 214, 216, 217, 228, 233, 236, 238, 239, 240, 242, 243, 244, 245, 246, 250, 252, 262, 264, 265, 267, 275, 276, 277, 284, 288, 306, 309, 312, 318, 320, 321, 322, 323, 324, 326, 329, 330, 331, 332, 335, 336, 337, 338, 341, 344, 348, 352, 353, 361, 366, 369, 370, 375, 379, 380, 405, 407, 408, 412, 414, 415, 417, 420, 421, 422, 430, 431, 433, 453, 476

Gettyimages.com
Pages 14, 315, 358, 371, 398

Other photographs
Page 25 Rob Knight © Rob Knight Photography

All other photographs © Elaine Weinmann and Peter Lourekas